Encyclopedia of Classic Rock

DAVID LUHRSSEN WITH MICHAEL LARSON

BLOOMSBURY ACADEMIC
NEW YORK • LONDON • OXFORD • NEW DELHI • SYDNEY

BLOOMSBURY ACADEMIC
Bloomsbury Publishing Inc
1385 Broadway, New York, NY 10018, USA
50 Bedford Square, London, WC1B 3DP, UK
29 Earlsfort Terrace, Dublin 2, Ireland

BLOOMSBURY, BLOOMSBURY ACADEMIC and the Diana logo
are trademarks of Bloomsbury Publishing Plc

First published in the United States of America by ABC-CLIO 2017
Paperback edition published by Bloomsbury Academic 2024

Copyright © Bloomsbury Publishing Inc, 2024

For legal purposes the Acknowledgments on p. xix constitute
an extension of this copyright page.

Cover photo: Vintage rock poster t-shirt design. (tairygreene/Adobe Stock)
Cover design by Silverander Communications

All rights reserved. No part of this publication may be reproduced or
transmitted in any form or by any means, electronic or mechanical,
including photocopying, recording, or any information storage or retrieval
system, without prior permission in writing from the publishers.

Bloomsbury Publishing Inc does not have any control over, or responsibility for,
any third-party websites referred to or in this book. All internet addresses given
in this book were correct at the time of going to press. The author and publisher
regret any inconvenience caused if addresses have changed or sites have
ceased to exist, but can accept no responsibility for any such changes.

Library of Congress Cataloging-in-Publication Data
Names: Luhrssen, David. | Larson, Michael.
Title: Encyclopedia of classic rock / David Luhrssen with Michael Larson.
Description: Santa Barbara, California: Greenwood, [2017] |
Includes bibliographical references and index.
Identifiers: LCCN 2016038277 (print) | LCCN 2016038768 (ebook) |
ISBN 9781440835131 (alk. paper) | ISBN 9781440835148 (ebook)
Subjects: LCSH: Rock music—Bio-bibliography—Dictionaries.
Classification: LCC ML102.R6 L84 2017 (print) | LCC ML102.R6 (ebook) |
DDC 781.66092/2 [B] —dc23
LC record available at https://lccn.loc.gov/2016038277

ISBN: HB: 978-1-4408-3513-1
PB: 979-8-7651-2086-6
ePDF: 978-1-4408-3514-8
eBook: 979-8-2160-6170-0

To find out more about our authors and books visit www.bloomsbury.com
and sign up for our newsletters.

Encyclopedia of
Classic Rock

Contents

Preface	xvii
Acknowledgments	xix
Introduction	xxi
Chronology	xxv
A–Z Entries	
Ackles, David	1
Aerosmith	1
Allman Brothers Band	2
America	4
Amon Duul II	5
Ange	5
Animals	6
Aphrodite's Child	7
Argent	8
Ash Ra Tempel	8
Auger, Brian	9
Ayers, Kevin	10
Babe Ruth	11
Bachman-Turner Overdrive	11
Bad Company	11
Badfinger	12
Baez, Joan	14
Baker, Ginger	15
Band	16

CONTENTS

Barrett, Syd	19
Beach Boys	20
Beatles	23
Beau Brummels	28
Be-Bop Deluxe	28
Beck, Jeff	28
Bee Gees	30
Big Brother and the Holding Company	31
Big Star	32
Black Rock	32
Black Sabbath	33
Blackmore, Ritchie	35
Blind Faith	35
Blodwyn Pig	36
Blood, Sweat & Tears	36
Bloomfield, Mike	37
Blue Cheer	37
Blue Oyster Cult	38
Blues	39
Blues Magoos	40
Blues Project	40
Bond, Graham	41
Bowie, David	42
Brewer and Shipley	46
British Invasion	46
Brown, Arthur	47
Browne, Jackson	48
Bruce, Jack	48
Bubblegum	49

Buchanan, Roy	50
Buckley, Tim	50
Budgie	51
Buffalo Springfield	52
Butterfield, Paul	53
Byrds	54
Cale, J. J.	57
Cale, John	57
Cambodian Rock	59
Can	60
Canned Heat	61
Captain Beefheart	61
Caravan	63
Chambers Brothers	64
Charlatans	64
Chicago	65
Chrysalis	67
Clapton, Eric	67
Cluster	70
Cocker, Joe	70
Cohen, Leonard	71
Collins, Judy	73
Colosseum	74
Concept Album	74
Cooder, Ry	75
Cooper, Alice	76
Country Joe & the Fish	78
Country Rock	79
Cream	80

viii CONTENTS

Creation	81
Creedence Clearwater Revival	82
Crosby, Stills, Nash & Young	85
Curved Air	87
Davis, Spencer	89
Deep Purple	90
Delaney & Bonnie	90
Denny, Sandy	91
Derek and the Dominos	92
Donovan	93
Doobie Brothers	94
Doors	95
Doo-wop	98
Drake, Nick	98
Driscoll, Julie	99
Dylan, Bob	99
Eagles	107
Eastern Bloc Rock	110
Eire Apparent	111
Electric Flag	112
Electric Light Orchestra	113
Embryo	115
Emerson, Lake & Palmer	115
Eno, Brian	117
Entwistle, John	119
Faces	121
Fairport Convention	122
Family	123
Faust	123

CONTENTS ix

Fischer, Wild Man	124
Flamin' Groovies	124
Fleetwood Mac	125
Flock	128
Flying Burrito Brothers	128
FM Radio	130
Focus	131
Fogerty, John	131
Folk-Blues Revival	133
Folk-Rock	136
Fool	137
Frampton, Peter	137
Free	138
Funk	139
Gallagher, Rory	141
Genesis	142
Gentle Giant	144
Glitter Rock	145
Golden Earring	145
Gong	146
Grateful Dead	147
Groundhogs	150
Guess Who	150
Guru Guru	151
Guthrie, Arlo	152
Harper, Roy	155
Harris, Emmylou	156
Harrison, George	157
Hawkwind	159

CONTENTS

Heavy Metal	160
Hendrix, Jimi	162
Hollies	165
Hot Tuna	167
H.P. Lovecraft	167
Humble Pie	168
Hunter, Ian	169
Ides of March	171
Incredible String Band	171
It's a Beautiful Day	172
Jade Warrior	173
James Gang	173
Jazz-Rock	174
Jefferson Airplane/Jefferson Starship	175
Jethro Tull	178
Joel, Billy	180
John, Elton	183
Joplin, Janis	186
Kaleidoscope	189
Kansas	190
King, Carole	191
King Crimson	192
Kinks	195
Kooper, Al	198
Korner, Alexis	199
Kraftwerk	200
Le Orme	203
Led Zeppelin	204
Left Banke	207

Lennon, John	208
Les Variations	211
Little Feat	211
Love	212
Love Sculpture	214
Lovin' Spoonful	215
Lynyrd Skynyrd	216
Magma	219
Mahavishnu Orchestra	219
Mahogany Rush	221
Mamas and the Papas	221
Man	222
Mann, Manfred	223
Manzarek, Ray	224
Mark-Almond	224
Marshall Tucker Band	225
Martyn, John	225
Mason, Dave	226
Masters Apprentices	227
Mayall, John	227
McCartney, Paul	229
MC5	231
McLean, Don	233
Miles, Buddy	234
Miller, Steve	235
Mitchell, Joni	236
Moby Grape	238
Mods	239
Monkees	239

CONTENTS

Moody Blues	241
Morrison, Van	242
Mott the Hoople	244
Mountain	246
Move	247
Murphy, Elliott	248
Nazz	249
Nektar	250
Neu!	250
New Riders of the Purple Sage	251
New York Dolls	251
Newman, Randy	252
Nice	254
Nico	254
Nilsson, Harry	255
NRBQ	257
Nuggets	257
Nyro, Laura	258
Oldfield, Mike	261
Os Mutantes	261
Otis, Shuggie	262
Parks, Van Dyke	265
Parsons, Gram	266
Pentangle	267
Pink Fairies	268
Pink Floyd	268
Poco	271
Pop, Iggy	272
Popol Vuh	274

Power Pop	274
Pretty Things	275
Price, Alan	276
Prine, John	277
Procol Harum	278
Producers	278
Progressive Rock	281
Psychedelia	283
Pub Rock	284
Pulsar	285
Punk Rock	285
Pure Prairie League	286
Quatermass	289
Quatro, Suzi	289
Queen	290
Quicksilver Messenger Service	292
Rascals	293
Reed, Lou	294
Reggae	296
Renaissance	297
REO Speedwagon	297
Rock and Roll	298
Rock Criticism	299
Rock Festivals	300
Rock Opera	301
Rockabilly	302
Rolling Stones	303
Ronson, Mick	307
Ronstadt, Linda	308

xiv CONTENTS

Rotary Connection	310
Roxy Music	310
Rundgren, Todd	312
Rush	314
Russell, Leon	317
Ryder, Mitch	317
Sadistic Mika Band	319
Sainte-Marie, Buffy	319
Santana	320
Savoy Brown	322
Scaggs, Boz	322
Schulze, Klaus	323
Searchers	324
Seeds	325
Seger, Bob	326
Simon, Carly	328
Simon, Paul	328
Simon & Garfunkel	330
Sir Douglas Quintet	333
Skiffle	334
Slade	334
Sly and the Family Stone	335
Small Faces	336
Smith, Patti	338
Soft Machine	338
Soul Music	339
Souther-Hillman-Furay Band	340
Southern Rock	340
Space Rock	342

Sparks	342
Spirit	343
Spooky Tooth	344
Springsteen, Bruce	345
Starr, Ringo	349
Status Quo	351
Steeleye Span	351
Steely Dan	352
Steppenwolf	354
Stevens, Cat	355
Stewart, Al	355
Stewart, Rod	356
Stills, Stephen	358
Stories	359
Strawbs	360
String Driven Thing	360
Surf Music	361
Tangerine Dream	363
Taste	363
Taylor, James	364
10cc	365
Ten Years After	366
Them	367
Thin Lizzy	368
13th Floor Elevators	370
Thompson, Richard	371
Tomorrow	373
Traffic	373
T. Rex	374

xvi **CONTENTS**

Troggs	376
Trower, Robin	377
Turkish Psychedelia	378
Turtles	378
Uriah Heep	381
Van der Graaf Generator	383
Vangelis	384
Velvet Underground	385
Walsh, Joe	387
War	388
Who	389
Winter, Johnny	394
Wood, Roy	394
Yamash'ta, Stomu	397
Yardbirds	397
Yes	399
Young, Neil	400
Youngbloods	403
Zappa, Frank	405
Zevon, Warren	407
Zombies	408
ZZ Top	409
Recommended Reading	411
Index	415

Preface

The *Encyclopedia of Classic Rock* offers a historically grounded definition of new and aesthetically daring forms of rock music that became culturally dominant from 1965 through 1975 in the wake of the creative breakthroughs of the Beatles and Bob Dylan. With the example of those artists before the ears of the world, rock music coalesced as a self-conscious art form by 1965, stretching the boundary of popular music and elevating the long-playing album into a primary canvas for artistic expression. Many aspiring writers who in an earlier epoch might have penned short fiction or poetry turned instead to rock songs. Rock also absorbed much of the musical creativity directed in earlier times toward jazz and blues. By 1975 much of that energy had begun to dissipate.

The *Encyclopedia of Classic Rock* does not explore the sociology behind the music but takes for granted that the post–World War II baby boom, the music's primary audience from 1965 through 1975, represented a historically large cohort of young people conscious of being distinct from previous generations, and with unprecedented affluence in ideas as well as consumer goods. Classic rock's depth of influence was made possible by the rise of middle-class youth in North America and Western Europe but spread across the globe.

The first book of this kind, Lillian Roxon's *Rock Encyclopedia* (1969), was published as events were still unfolding and therefore lacked historical perspective. *The Rolling Stone Encyclopedia of Rock & Roll* (1983) included many artists who had nothing to do with rock, much less classic rock, and its compilers were sometimes misinformed on exact titles and release dates of albums and on biographical details. The *All Music Guide to Rock: The Definitive Guide to Rock, Pop, and Soul* (2002) encompassed all popular music from the rock era and, as the work of many hands, lacked a consistent perspective. The *Encyclopedia of Classic Rock* is the only encyclopedia with its particular focus and fills in gaps in the existing literature by stressing the musical and cultural importance of rock groups from outside the United States and United Kingdom, especially bands from West Germany in the 1970s. It reminds readers of the fact, often overlooked in recent accounts of the 1960s, that Dylan's primary importance was not as a protest singer, a label he soon rejected, but for affirming the possibility of rock lyrics as the poetry for a new age and raising the prospect, alongside the Beatles, of rock as an art form that transcended its roots. In tone and manner, the encyclopedia is written to accommodate a broad audience ranging from secondary school students to scholars in postgraduate settings.

The introduction proposes a precise definition of classic rock in art history terms and aims to establish "classic rock" as a distinct artistic movement comparable to

xviii PREFACE

Dadaism or German Expressionism, modernist movements that flourished briefly in the 20th century and left behind a residue of enduring influence. The text entries are arranged alphabetically, permitting the reader to easily browse the roster of artists from the classic rock era. The authors have endeavored to balance the twofold goal of understanding the meaning of those artists in historical hindsight while at the same time remembering the often startling impression they made within the context of their time. Appended to each artist entry is a list of suggested albums chosen for aesthetic merit or historical importance and dated according to the year of their original release. Alphabetized along with artist entries are short essays on particular topics germane to the encyclopedia's themes, including definitions of genres from blues to space rock, related topics including rock criticism and rock festivals, and entries focused on rock music in such unexpected locations as Eastern Europe, Cambodia, and Turkey. A Recommended Reading list at the end of the *Encyclopedia of Classic Rock* lists the works that most profoundly influenced our thinking about rock music and attempts to sift the wheat of meaningful rock scholarship and criticism from the mountains of chaff produced by pseudo-intellectuals, starstruck fans, and scandal-seeking gossipmongers. The *Encyclopedia of Classic Rock* examines the personal lives of its subjects only to the extent that the personal became public through their music.

Acknowledgments

The authors were fortunate to come of age during the final half of the period covered in this book in a city where the music from the classic rock era was easily accessible. Milwaukee had no less than two free-form FM rock stations in the early 1970s, WZMF and WQFM, as well as occasional "underground rock" programs on college station WUWM. The names of most of the DJs escape our memory, but one was outstanding for influencing the imagination of his listeners, Bob Reitman. We were also fortunate to have a local rock critic, Pierre Rene Noth, whose ideas and search for lesser-known artists provided weekly stimulation through his column in the city's evening paper, the *Milwaukee Journal*. Additionally, we were exposed to album releases and concert reviews in the local "underground newspaper," the *Bugle American*, and a music publication, *Fallout*.

Many of our perceptions were formed from lively conversations with musicians and music buffs throughout our lives. We especially thank Glen Rehse for his insights into psychedelia, classical rock, and the German scene of the 1960s and 1970s; Martin Jack Rosenblum for his understanding of the roots of rock and the role of Bob Dylan in the 1960s; Mark Krueger for his knowledge about Van der Graaf Generator and continental European bands; and Jamie Lee Rake for African American music and his contributions to the entry on the band War. Our research benefited from the eager assistance of Bruce Cole at Marquette University's Raynor Memorial Library, Kevin Coxworth for lending us some rare recordings, and Mary Manion for her tireless searches on a medium whose future existence we never suspected while growing up, Amazon.

Introduction

Classic rock is a contested term. When used casually in conversation, journalism, or the business plans of media conglomerates, it might mean almost any rock song or artist that emerged before the 21st century. *Rock* itself presents another problem of definition, since it has been used at one time or another to describe any music since the late 1950s that was not demonstrably something else.

One of the purposes of the *Encyclopedia of Classic Rock* is to define terms and rescue classic rock from careless usage. In art history, *classic* usually describes a period when primitive, archaic, or inchoate cultural elements rise to unprecedented heights of expression and mastery, often falling afterward into decadence or decline but leaving a heritage that calls for periodic neoclassical revivals.

The *Encyclopedia of Classic Rock* proposes that rock and roll reached a new level of ambition by 1965 and entered a period of remarkable innovation and expressiveness that lasted through 1975. The most significant players in this evolutionary leap were Bob Dylan and the Beatles, with a host of usually British bands (including the Rolling Stones and the Who) but occasionally American groups (the Beach Boys) trooping behind and sometimes overtaking their leaders. Unlike rock and roll, which despite its folk roots was understood as entertainment, rock by 1965 aspired to become art; its characteristic medium was not the single but the wider canvas of the long-playing album. AM radio continued to play popular classic rock songs, but FM radio became the music's primary broadcast medium.

Many factors helped shape the aspirations of the artists who rose to prominence in the classic rock era. Dylan emerged from an American subculture that honored both the hoary traditions of folk and blues music along with the avant-garde literature of Beat Generation writers such as Allen Ginsberg and Jack Kerouac. Dylan's first insight was to combine folk music with modernist poetry; his second was to marry that combination with the rock and roll music he had experienced as a teenager. In the United Kingdom, a system of art schools provided a generation of rock and roll performers with an education in aesthetics that enabled them to transform rock into pop art. With the benefit of distance, British bands such as the Rolling Stones had a clearer perspective on the direction of American roots idioms such as the blues than most of their U.S. generational peers, emphasizing electric guitars and harder urban textures. Across much of the world, young people responded to rock music that echoed as well as proclaimed the dawn of a new sensibility, a counterculture opposed to many existing social norms and arrangements.

In some cases ambition outstripped ability. Not all art is good art. By 1975, the burst of innovation that began in the 1960s had largely run its course, and elements of classic rock were being repurposed into rigid commercial radio formats and formulaic music. Classic rock became a hollow shell, the object of rebellion by a new generation often determined to return the music to its primitive origins, whether through pub rock, punk rock, rockabilly revival, or any number of "roots" movements. When examined closely, this same push and pull between origins and innovation occurred within the classic rock era, 1965–1975, as when psychedelia hardened into metal or found its way into country rock.

One aspect of classic rock involved enlarging the scope of rock as music, embracing influences and formal possibilities considered outside the range of early rock and roll. The other involved the depth of lyrical expression. Lyrics in popular song always had the possibility of being poetic, but rock lyricists were suddenly expected to be poets. Many failed, yet the effort broadened the range of meaning in popular music.

African American rock musicians were so unusual during the 1965–1975 period that the scarcity of "black rock" has often been bemoaned. Aside from Jimi Hendrix and Arthur Lee (fronting the band Love), black faces were hard to spot in the rock album bins of record stores and their voices were seldom heard on rock radio. Segregation of music by the entertainment industry according to race and other categories had been prevalent since at least the 1920s, and yet during the 1950s and early 1960s those barriers seemed to dissolve. Elvis Presley enjoyed high positions on *Billboard*'s pop, R&B, and country charts; Alan Freed, an important impresario of the early rock and roll era, presented the music as multiracial; and black-owned Motown Records marketed itself as "The Sound of Young America." From November 1963 through January 1965, *Billboard* abolished its R&B chart on the assumption that white and black pop audiences were no longer distinct, but this proved to be an anomaly. Music and audiences pulled apart as the sixties progressed, with African American artists and listeners drawn to soul music and whites to classic rock.

The close of the classic rock era did not spell the end to the ambitions that prevailed from 1965 through 1975. Some post mid-seventies acts, from Elvis Costello and XTC through Prince, Metallica, and Radiohead, continued to conceive their music in terms of albums as well as individual songs. Songwriters such as REM's Michael Stipe wrote allusive lyrics that would have been inconceivable to Doc Pomus or Chuck Berry. The breakthroughs of the classic rock era continue to reverberate, albeit in an age that has increasingly turned its back on albums in favor of single songs purchased from online menus.

The *Encyclopedia of Classic Rock* can be read as a roster of recording artists emblematic of the classic rock era, with global hitmakers sharing space with obscure but fascinating acts. Some of those artists began recording prior to 1965 or continued past the end dates of this book; their careers will be summarized in full. However, performers influenced by classic rock whose debut albums were released after 1975, such as Tom Petty or Alan Parsons, are excluded. Setting chronological bookends is easy. Maintaining a meaningful definition of classic rock is more challenging. Most pop music performers to emerge during the decade under consideration cannot be defined as classic rock, and many others are problematic. Rock and roll is generally understood as a popular music that emerged as an identifiable genre from blues, rhythm and blues, country, and gospel during the 1950s. Classic rock describes what happened next as a generation of artists led by the example of Dylan, the Beatles, and the Stones worked from those influences to build new, ambitious genres of music.

A slender handful of artists included in this account did not play rock by any meaningful musicological definition, but were associated sociologically and had a pronounced influence on rock acts. Chief among them is Leonard Cohen, whose classic albums fall somewhere between art song and folk music but were staples on free-form FM radio and were inseparable from 1960s popular culture.

Although the classic rock era was born in the United States and United Kingdom, it spread to other regions and influenced music outside the Anglophone world. While the majority of artists described in the *Encyclopedia of Classic Rock* are American and British, significant artists from continental Europe, Africa, Asia, and Latin America are also included. Many of these performers incorporated local influences into their music. A few non-Anglo-American artists, notably Germany's Kraftwerk, who became a source for much electronica and an unlikely inspiration for hip-hop, would have an enormous influence on the shape of music to come.

Chronology

1965

Malcolm X assassinated, Feb. 21

Rolling Stones release "The Last Time," Feb. 26

Operation Rolling Thunder, the sustained U.S. air assault on North Vietnam, begins March 2

On "Bloody Sunday," Selma, Alabama, civil rights march broken up by police, March 7

Bob Dylan releases *Bringing It All Back Home*, March 22

"Teach-ins" at U.S. campuses to protest Vietnam War, March 24

Yardbirds release "For Your Love," Eric Clapton leaves the band in protest, March 25

Rolling Stones release "(I Can't Get No) Satisfaction," June 6

The Byrds release *Mr. Tambourine Man*, June 21

Bob Dylan faces skeptical crowd for playing rock at Newport Folk Festival, July 25

Voting Rights Act of 1965, guaranteeing the right to vote for African Americans, takes effect Aug. 6

Watts Riot begins in Los Angeles, Aug. 11

Beatles release *Help!*, Aug. 13

Dylan releases *Highway 61 Revisited*, Aug. 30

Rolling Stones release "Get Off of My Cloud," Sept. 25

The Who releases "My Generation," Oct. 29

Rhodesia's white-minority regime declares independence from United Kingdom, Nov. 11

Beatles release *Rubber Soul*, Dec. 3

1966

Rolling Stones release "19th Nervous Breakdown," Feb. 4

xxvi **CHRONOLOGY**

Rolling Stones release *Aftermath*, April 15

Dylan releases *Blonde on Blonde*, May 16

The Kinks release "Sunny Afternoon," June 3

U.S. Supreme Court issues *Miranda* ruling to ensure suspects are informed of their rights, June 13

Beatles release *Yesterday and Today*, June 20

Dylan seriously injured in motorcycle accident and disappears from view, July 29

Beatles release *Revolver*, Aug. 5

Beatles' final concert, San Francisco's Candlestick Park, Aug. 29

Black Panther Party founded, Oct. 15

John Lennon meets Yoko Ono, Nov. 9

1967

The Doors release their eponymous debut album, Jan. 4

Rolling Stones release *Between the Buttons*, Jan. 20

Jefferson Airplane releases *Surrealistic Pillow*, Feb. 1

Velvet Underground & Nico released, March 12

Grateful Dead releases its eponymous debut album, March 17

Martin Luther King Jr. condemns Vietnam War, April 15

The Kinks release "Waterloo Sunset," May 5

Mick Jagger and Keith Richards arraigned on marijuana charges, May 10

Jimi Hendrix releases *Are You Experienced*, May 12

Beatles release *Sgt. Pepper's Lonely Hearts Club Band*, June 1

Six-Day War between Israel and Arab neighbors begins June 5

Monterey Pop Festival, June 16–18

Jagger's and Richards's convictions for drug charges overturned on appeal, July 31

Director Arthur Penn's film *Bonnie and Clyde* opens, Aug. 13

Beatles manager Brian Epstein dies, Aug. 27

The Doors release *Strange Days*, Sept. 25

Thurgood Marshall, first African American Supreme Court justice, takes his seat, Oct. 2

CHRONOLOGY xxvii

Rolling Stone magazine publishes its first issue, Nov. 9

Cream releases *Disraeli Gears*, Nov. 10

Beatles release *Magical Mystery Tour*, Nov. 27

Jimi Hendrix releases *Axis: Bold as Love*, Dec. 1

Dylan releases *John Wesley Harding*, Dec. 27

1968

Tet Offensive, North Vietnam attack against U.S. forces in South Vietnam, begins Jan. 30

Lyndon B. Johnson announces he will not seek reelection as U.S. president, March 31

Stanley Kubrick's *2001: A Space Odyssey* opens, April 2

Martin Luther King Jr. assassinated, April 4

Sly and the Family Stone release *Dance to the Music*, April 27

Student and worker riots in Paris shake the regime of President Charles de Gaulle, May 3 through July

Presidential candidate Robert F. Kennedy assassinated, June 6

Roman Polanski's film *Rosemary's Baby* released, June 12

Immigration and Nationality Act of 1965, removing ethnic quota–based restrictions to immigration, becomes law, June 30

Big Brother and the Holding Company (featuring Janis Joplin) release *Cheap Thrills*, Aug. 12

Democratic National Convention in Chicago, marred by violence between police and protesters, begins Aug. 26

The Byrds release *Sweetheart of the Rodeo*, Aug. 30

Jimi Hendrix releases *Electric Ladyland*, Oct. 16

Richard Nixon elected U.S. president, Nov. 6

Beatles release *White Album*, Nov. 22

Rolling Stones release *Beggars Banquet*, Dec. 6

1969

Led Zeppelin releases its debut album, Jan. 12

Paris peace talks begin between United States and North Vietnam, Jan. 25

xxviii CHRONOLOGY

Paul McCartney marries Linda Eastman, March 12

John Lennon marries Yoko Ono, March 20

Dylan releases *Nashville Skyline*, April 9

Creem magazine publishes its first issue, May

Sly and the Family Stone release *Stand!*, May 3

The Who releases *Tommy*, May 23

Rolling Stones guitarist Brian Jones found dead, July 3

Apollo 11 lands on the Moon, July 20

Sharon Tate and friends murdered by Manson Family, Aug. 8

Woodstock Music & Art Fair, Aug. 15–17

Beatles release *Abbey Road*, Sept. 26

Led Zeppelin II released, Oct. 22

Antiwar rally in Washington, D.C. draws 600,000 protesters, Nov. 15

Rolling Stones release *Let It Bleed*, Dec. 5

Altamont rock festival ends in violence, Dec. 6

1970

Black Sabbath releases its eponymous debut album, Feb. 13

Miles Davis releases *Bitches Brew*, March 30

Beatles breakup announced, April 10

Flight of the aborted Apollo 13 moon launch, April 11–17

U.S. invades Cambodia, April 30

Protest against the Cambodian invasion at Kent State University ends in death of four students, May 4

Beatles release *Let It Be*, May 8

The Kinks release "Lola," June 12

Grateful Dead releases *Workingman's Dead*, June 14

Trial begins for Charles Manson, accused of masterminding the Sharon Tate murders, June 15

Edward Heath becomes Great Britain's prime minister, June 19

Jimi Hendrix dies, Sept. 18

CHRONOLOGY   xxix

Janis Joplin dies, Oct. 4

Led Zeppelin III released, Oct. 5

Grateful Dead releases *American Beauty*, Nov. 1

Derek and the Dominos release *Layla and Other Assorted Love Songs*, Nov. 9

George Harrison releases *All Things Must Pass*, Nov. 27

John Lennon/Plastic Ono Band released, Dec. 11

1971

First episode of CBS-TV show *All in the Family* airs Jan. 12

Charles Manson convicted in Tate murder case, Jan. 25

The Doors release *L.A. Woman*, April 19

Rolling Stones release *Sticky Fingers*, April 23

Voting age for U.S. citizens lowered from 21 to 18, July 1

Jim Morrison dies, July 3

George Harrison hosts Concert for Bangladesh, Aug. 1

The Who releases *Who's Next*, Aug. 14

John Lennon releases *Imagine*, Sept. 8

Elton John releases *Madman Across the Water*, Nov. 5

Led Zeppelin IV released, Nov. 8

David Bowie releases *Hunky Dory*, Dec. 17

1972

Nixon visits Communist China, Feb. 21–28

Francis Ford Coppola's *The Godfather* released, March 15

Rolling Stones release *Exile on Main Street*, May 12

Gunman attempts to assassinate presidential candidate George Wallace, May 15

Elton John releases *Honky Chateau*, May 19

David Bowie releases *The Rise and Fall of Ziggy Stardust and the Spiders from Mars*, June 16

Roxy Music releases its eponymous debut album, June 16

xxx   CHRONOLOGY

Burglars arrested at Democratic Party headquarters at Watergate Hotel, June 17

Nixon denies any involvement in Watergate break-in, Aug. 29

Nixon reelected president, defeating Democratic candidate George McGovern in a landslide, Nov. 7

Lou Reed releases *Transformer*, Nov. 8

1973

Elton John releases *Don't Shoot Me I'm Only the Piano Player*, Jan. 26

Paris Peace Accord signed by U.S. and North Vietnam, Jan. 27

U.S. Senate established committee to investigate Watergate break-in, Feb. 7

Pink Floyd releases *Dark Side of the Moon*, March 1

Led Zeppelin releases *Houses of the Holy*, March 28

New York's World Trade Center opens, April 4

David Bowie releases *Aladdin Sane*, April 13

Chile's president, Salvador Allende, killed in U.S.-backed coup, Sept. 11

Elton John releases *Goodbye Yellow Brick Road*, Oct. 5

Yom Kippur War, Oct. 6–25

OPEC oil embargo against the United States begins, Oct. 16

In "Saturday Night Massacre," Nixon orders firing of officials responsible for investigating Watergate, Oct. 20

The Who releases *Quadrophenia*, Oct. 26

John Lennon releases *Mind Games*, Oct. 29

1974

Dylan releases *Planet Waves*, Jan. 17

U.S. House of Representatives empanels committee to investigate Watergate, Feb. 6.

Harold Wilson becomes Great Britain's prime minister, March 4

OPEC ends oil embargo against the United States, March 17

David Bowie releases *Diamond Dogs*, May 24

Dylan and the Band release *Before the Flood*, June 20

CHRONOLOGY **xxxi**

Roman Polanski's film *Chinatown* released, June 20

Elton John releases *Caribou*, June 28

Facing impeachment, Nixon resigns as president, Aug. 9

President Gerald Ford pardons Nixon, Sept. 8

John Lennon releases *Walls and Bridges*, Sept. 26

Rolling Stones release *It's Only Rock 'n' Roll*, Oct. 16

Kraftwerk releases *Autobahn*, Nov. 1

1975

Dylan releases *Blood on the Tracks*, Jan. 20

John Lennon releases *Rock'n'Roll*, Feb. 17

Led Zeppelin releases *Physical Graffiti*, Feb. 24

David Bowie releases *Young Americans*, March 7

South Vietnam falls to North Vietnamese forces, April 30

Patti Smith releases *Horses*, Dec. 13

A

ACKLES, DAVID (1937–1999)

Cited as an inspiration by Elton John and Elvis Costello, David Ackles was a pianist and storytelling songwriter with a small but avid following. The Hollywood child actor pursued scholarly endeavors as well as musical theater as a young man before signing with Elektra Records. On his self-titled debut (1968), Ackles was accompanied by a combo of accomplished session players who placed his songs in an art-rock context; the music's usual exuberance was supplanted by a sense of the cost of being alive. On *Subway to the Country* (1969), Ackles came into his own as a writer in the Bertolt Brecht–Kurt Weill tradition with lyrics about outcasts performed in cabaret style. Frederic Myrow, formerly composer in residence under Leonard Bernstein at the New York Philharmonic, orchestrated the album.

Elton John's lyricist Bernie Taupin, also a fan, produced Ackles's *American Gothic* (1972), culling musicians from the London Symphony and employing a Salvation Army chorus. In keeping with the album's title, Ackles drew from Americana influences, appropriating themes from Aaron Copland's *Appalachian Spring*. Dropped by Elektra, he released one more album, taught college, and tried his hand at freelance songwriting and screenwriting. He died in 1999.

Suggested Albums: David Ackles (1968); *Subway to the Country* (1969); *American Gothic* (1972)

AEROSMITH

Aerosmith's brief encounter with progressive rock on their first album, "Dream On" (1973), introduced them to a wide audience through FM airplay. The lyrically world-weary, musically dramatic track had little to do with the rock they honed in Boston clubs before spreading their touring net across the world. As late as 1983, *Rolling Stone* called them "heavy metal," but early Aerosmith is better described by another critic's catchphrase from the 1970s, "the American Rolling Stones." In younger years, vocalist Steve Tyler was a Mick Jagger lookalike physically and in performance, while guitarist Joe Perry played Keith Richards's role.

Not unlike the Stones, Aerosmith drew from blues and rhythm and blues, but they represented the next generation of blues-based rock and took on heavier attributes. Their rendition of the rockabilly classic "The Train Kept a-Rollin'" (1974) begins in the blues-boogie mode of their Boston bar years before becoming a cover of the Yardbirds' version in a tip of the hat to the influence of 1960s British rock. By the

One of the leaders among the younger wave of 1970s hard rock acts, Aerosmith went on to enjoy a durable career. Vocalist Steven Tyler and guitarist Joe Perry are seen here at a 1989 concert at the Boston Garden. (Eautographhunter/Dreamstime.com)

time of *Toys in the Attic* (1975), their energized boogie had mutated into cadences that foresaw the rise of rap on tracks such as "Walk This Way" and "Sweet Emotion." FM hits from *Rocks* (1976), including "Last Child" and "Back in the Saddle," continued in this vein. A young crew of rappers from Queens, Run-D.M.C., later sampled "Walk This Way" and scored a crossover hit with their recording, featuring Tyler and Perry as guest stars (1986).

Exuding more streetwise swagger and playing more aggressively than many 1970s bands with similar roots, Aerosmith were considered punky but were too closely associated with the hard rock circuit to be classed with punk rock. They traveled the same thorny path as many rock bands with exhausting tours and increasing antipathy among members. The lineup changed by the end of the 1970s, including the departure of Perry, who formed the Joe Perry Project. Perry rejoined Aerosmith in 1984, but the band's career sputtered until the success of Run-D.M.C.'s "Walk This Way." Afterward, they became a consistent presence on MTV with hits such as "Dude (Looks Like a Lady)," "Love in an Elevator," and "What It Takes," and reached platinum status with the albums *Permanent Vacation* (1987), *Pump* (1989), and *Get a Grip* (1993).

Aerosmith became deeply embedded in pop culture through their appearance on *The Simpsons* and in video games as well as successful concert tours. Tyler assumed a grizzled celebrity role as a judge on the popular TV music show *American Idol* (2011–2012) and is the father of actress Liv Tyler, who appeared in the Aerosmith video for "Crazy" (1993). Aerosmith has been inducted into the Rock and Roll Hall of Fame.

Suggested Albums: Aerosmith (1973); *Get Your Wings* (1974); *Toys in the Attic* (1975); *Rocks* (1976)

ALLMAN BROTHERS BAND

The Allman Brothers Band tasted enough success and acclaim, and endured enough tragedy and drama, to fill a hefty novel or a premium cable show for several seasons. Before they played under their own name, vocalist Gregg Allman and guitarist

Duane Allman had already logged many years together in bands such as the bluesy Allman Joys, the psychedelic Hour Glass, and finally the 31st of February with drummer Butch Trucks. Gregg also played in the Second Coming with guitarist Dickey Betts and Berry Oakley. The aforementioned musicians formed the Allman Brothers Band in 1969 in Jacksonville, Florida, adding a second drummer, session player Jai Johnny Johanson. At that time, the Allman Brothers were unusual as a racially integrated rock band and were in the vanguard of longhaired Southern rock. Their first two albums attracted slight attention when released, but *Idlewild South* (1970) included the outlaw ballad "Midnight Rider," which became a hit on the rock and country charts in renditions by Joe Cocker (1972) and Willie Nelson (1980), and was later covered by reggae, jazz, and alternative rock artists.

The brothers were terrifically talented musicians. Gregg was a gritty-voiced, emotionally convincing blues singer. Duane's guitar playing (especially on slide guitar) was outstanding, recognizably based in blues and rhythm and blues, but played with a more aggressive rock attitude. While many blues-based guitarists either sought a purist approach to faithfully recreating the playing of the masters (Eric Clapton), or sought to transform blues guitar into purely rock and roll by creating something totally distinct (Jimmy Page and Jeff Beck), Duane managed to remain faithful to the blues while infusing the form with the passion of rock. He was not the only guitar player to do this, of course, as Clapton proved in Cream, but he did it better than most. He incorporated a soulful style honed during his sessions work at FAME Studio in Muscle Shoals, Alabama, backing Wilson Pickett, Aretha Franklin, and Percy Sledge along with rock acts such as Boz Scaggs, Laura Nyro, and Delaney and Bonnie. Admiring his work, Clapton convinced Duane to join Derek and the Dominos.

Meanwhile, the Allman Brothers Band earned a reputation as one of the era's greatest live rock bands. Their studio albums were always patchy but their soul was on stage. Fiery, intense performances were a given. Their greatest album, *At Fillmore East* (1971), was cut in concert and broke them nationally on FM radio with such signature blues numbers as "Statesboro Blues" and "One Way Out" along with Betts's elegiac instrumental "In Memory of Elizabeth Reed." In October 1971, three months after the release of *At Fillmore East*, Duane died in a motorcycle accident. The band's next album, *Eat a Peach* (1972), included tracks recorded before his death and reached number four on the charts. Later that year, Oakley died in a motorcycle crash three blocks from the site of Duane's death. Heroin addiction began to dog some of the band members.

In the aftermath of Duane's death, the creative center of gravity shifted to Betts, who wrote the band's first hit song, "Ramblin' Man" (1973). Blues influences receded in favor of country, songwriting became more the focus on records than live jams, and the Allmans became a prototype for the genre of "Southern rock," centered around their label, Capricorn Records, and their home base, Macon, Georgia. Hairline cracks in the band's façade could be discerned as early as 1974 when Allman and Betts began pursuing solo recording and touring careers. In 1975, Allman's short-lived marriage and musical partnership with Cher brought him into the sights of paparazzi and *People* magazine. His personal life triggered dismay

One of the era's greatest live bands, the Allman Brothers Band brought the idea of blues-based "Southern rock" to audiences across the world. While their albums were always patchy, their heart and soul was best expressed in concert. (Larry Hulst/Michael Ochs Archives/Getty Images)

from fans for whom Cher was a slick pop singer inimical to Allman's rooted authenticity. The Allman Brothers Band broke up in 1976 amidst recriminations after Allman testified against their manager in a narcotics trial.

The breakup proved short lived but the future would be spotty. In 1978, Allman, Betts, Trucks, and Johanson reformed just as Capricorn Records collapsed into bankruptcy. Their name recognition made them a desirable catch for major labels, with the caveat that the Allmans must "modernize" their sound. The albums they released in the late 1970s and early 1980s are generally considered the nadir of their career. Realizing that their legacy was being tarnished, the Allman Brothers disbanded in 1982, but beginning in 1989, various lineups of the band featuring Allman and Betts have toured and recorded. Their live shows remain credible. The Allman Brothers Band has been inducted into the Rock and Roll Hall of Fame.

Suggested Albums: Idlewild South (1970); *At Fillmore East* (1971); *Eat a Peach* (1972); *Brothers and Sisters* (1973)

AMERICA

In an interesting twist, the trio named America began in England, the creation of three sons of U.S. servicemen stationed in the United Kingdom. Formed in 1970, they burst upon the music scene in 1972 with a hit single, the melancholy Neil Young–influenced ballad "A Horse with No Name." America became a regular presence on AM radio, thanks to a string of Top 40 hits that extended into the early

1980s. Their acoustic-oriented sound was more folk than rock, and at times more pop than either, but some of their songs, like the ominous "Sandman," found their way onto FM rock airwaves, thanks to the free-form ethic prevalent in the early days of album rock radio.

America never sounded better than when teamed with ex-Beatles producer George Martin, who guided them to perhaps their finest recording, the 1975 hit "Sister Golden Hair," an up-tempo acoustic rocker with a nod to George Harrison's "My Sweet Lord" in the guitars, as well as touches of the Beach Boys in the vocal harmonies. Despite the death of a founding member, the group continues to record and tour to this day.

Suggested Album: Hearts (1975)

AMON DUUL II

In 1968, a dozen Munich University students flocked together in an urban commune called Amon Duul. They were active in the radical upheavals of the day, playing at sit-ins and protests regardless of their musical skills and handing instruments to audience members to dissolve the wall between spectacle and spectator. A division within the commune led one faction to record an abrasive set of jams, eventually released on LP under the Amon Duul name. The more proficient communards, tempted by a recording contract, split and became one of the flagship bands of Germany's nascent "Krautrock" scene, Amon Duul II.

The band's early albums documented the morphing of psychedelia into space rock. Most of their lyrics were sung in the international language of rock, English, albeit often heavily accented. Vocals were shared, though Renate Knaup, one of the only women fronting a German band, stood out for her Wagnerian chorister voice. With the release of their greatest album, *Vive La Trance* (1973), Amon Duul II found a golden mean between wild jams and focused songwriting. The brief flutter of U.S. record industry interest in Krautrock after the Top 40 success of Kraftwerk's "Autobahn" led to FM airplay for Amon Duul II's *Hijack* (1974). Later years were marked by hiatuses and personnel changes; however, versions of Amon Duul II remained active into the 21st century.

Suggested Albums: Phallus Dei (1969); *Yeti* (1970); *Tanz der Lemminge* (1971); *Carnival in Babylon* (1972); *Wolf City* (1972); *Vive La Trance* (1973)

ANGE

The keyboard-powered pomp and circumstance of Ange's debut, *Caricatures* (1972), is roughly comparable to King Crimson's *In the Court of the Crimson King*. The French progressive rock ensemble, formed in 1969, drew from sources favored by like-minded groups from across the world, placing classically influenced keyboards, acoustic balladry, busy jazz rhythms, and scathing guitar in a post-psychedelic rock context. Singing in French and scoring a hit with a Jacques Brel cover from their second album (1974), Ange became popular in their homeland

and attracted notice from the international progressive rock cognoscenti. Their effort to break worldwide with an English-language album, *By the Sons of Mandrin* (1976), failed to sell and was poorly regarded. Original guitarist Christian Decamps continues to lead versions of Ange in the 21st century.

Suggested Albums: Caricatures (1972); *Le Cimetiere des arlequins* (1973); *Au-dela du delire* (1974)

ANIMALS

As a singles band performing covers of other people's songs, the Animals ran contrary to the direction of classic rock. And yet, during their best years (1964–1965), they made records as powerful as anything produced during the British Invasion and influenced future rock stars such as Bruce Springsteen and Tom Petty.

The original Animals never painted across the broad canvas of albums but were miniaturists, etching vivid and unforgettable impressions of factory towns, soot-covered and gritty. They sounded like their northern English city, Newcastle upon Tyne, epitomized working-class consciousness, and transliterated their blues influences into something fully authentic and lived out. The desperation that clung to the Animals had few precedents in rock.

They grew out of various combos led by jazz and rhythm and blues–immersed keyboard player Alan Price. By the time vocalist Eric Burdon joined in 1962, jazz had receded except for their live version of Duke Ellington's "C-Jam Blues" and their penchant for following singer Nina Simone in choosing material. Burdon brought pain and turmoil to his greatest performances and should be ranked with the best rock singers of the 1960s.

The Animals gained international attention with "House of the Rising Sun." A song with roots in late medieval British balladry, "House of the Rising Sun" was collected in the 1930s by Library of Congress folklorist Alan Lomax; by the 1950s it had already been recorded by country singer Roy Acuff, bluesmen Josh White and Lead Belly, and folksinger Woody Guthrie. A somber standard in the folk-blues revival, it received an emotionally turbulent rendition by Nina Simone (1962). Price's churning organ was key to the Animals' "House of the Rising Sun," along with Hilton Valentine's arpeggiated guitar and the forlorn anguish of Burdon's vocal. The single reached number one in the United States and United Kingdom.

The Animals followed with another number from Simone's repertoire, a song that had been written for her, "Don't Let Me Be Misunderstood." In an unusually mature take on relationships for rock of that era, Burdon cast himself as a hard man on his knees, full of regret and recrimination, desperate for understanding and a final chance.

A string of hits followed, sounding as if they should have been written by the Animals even though they were products of New York's Brill Building, where professional songwriters toiled in little rooms to fabricate hits. "We Got to Get Out of This Place" (1965) and "It's My Life" (1965) were defiant assertions of upward mobility in the face of social barriers.

The Animals began to unravel with the departure of Price at the end of 1965, followed by bassist Chas Chandler, who became Jimi Hendrix's manager. Billed as Eric Burdon and the Animals, the new lineup reached the charts with an original song echoing the lyrical themes of previous hits, but built on a raga riff and with a heavier sound, "When I Was Young" (1967). Transplanted to California, Burdon led the band through a pair of uninspired hits that tapped the wave of West Coast counterculture, "Warm San Francisco Nights" (1967) and "Monterey" (1967). He followed with an antiwar psychedelic production number, "Sky Pilot" (1968).

Afterward, Burdon fronted a variety of lineups sometimes billed as the New Animals, as well as solo projects. Recording with Los Angeles soul group War, he scored one last number one hit, an inane lyric recited over a Latin riff, "Spill the Wine" (1970). The original Animals lineup reunited on two occasions, notably for their new wave–inspired album *Ark* (1983), which resulted in a modest hit single, "The Night." Ownership of the name has been the subject of much litigation in recent decades. The original Animals have been inducted into the Rock and Roll Hall of Fame.

Suggested Albums: The Animals (1964); *The Animals on Tour* (1965); *Animal Tracks* (1965); *Ark* (1983)

APHRODITE'S CHILD

As it did in many countries, the British Invasion inspired young musicians in Greece to form bands. By 1967, keyboardist Vangelis Papathanassiou, vocalist-bassist Demis Roussos, drummer Loukas Sideras, and guitarist Anargyros "Silver" Koulouris emerged from this wave of Greek bands to form Aphrodite's Child. Their intention was to become a "Byzantine folk group" with a contemporary rock edge.

The 1967 coup in their homeland by a military junta may have inspired thoughts of exile, but their decision to move to London was also spurred by the British capital's role as Europe's music mecca. Travel problems left them stranded in Paris in 1968, where they recorded a brace of heartbreakingly romantic psychedelic singles along with their debut album. *End of the World* (1968) was drenched in *Sgt. Pepper* Beatles and Procol Harum and lifted by Roussos's distinctive high tenor. Most of the lyrics were in English, but they also recorded in Italian. "Rain and Tears," a baroque rock adaptation of Pachelbel's Canon in D Major, was a hit in France and other European countries. The band's Byzantine aspirations found expression in the Oriental modes of psychedelia.

Aphrodite's Child followed with a non-LP single. "I Want to Live" (1969) was based, like Elvis Presley's hit "Can't Help Falling in Love with You" (1961), on the 18th-century French ballad "Plaisir D'Amour." The Greek band's rendition went to number one in many European countries. Their next album, *It's 5 O'Clock* (1970), continued in the Procol Harum vein but was considerably more eclectic than its predecessor and included Mediterranean-accented pop songs that presaged Roussos's solo career.

Aphrodite's Child reached a high water mark for progressive rock with their final album, *666* (1972). Housed in a two-LP set, *666* was a song cycle based on the book of Revelations. The opening tracks bore the stamp of the Pretty Things' *S.F. Sorrow* and the Who's *Tommy*, but most of the music drew from less obvious sources. Roussos had been schooled in Greek Orthodox choirs and continued throughout his career to sing in liturgical settings. The influence of Greek sacred music on his vocals is discernible. Koulouris's guitar playing was often blues-rock in origin, but jazz and Eastern Mediterranean rhythms also factored into Papathanassiou's compositions. The choice of subject matter is perhaps unsurprising. According to tradition, St. John wrote Revelation on the Greek island of Patmos. Later interpreters have suggested that the psychedelic mushrooms that grow wild on the island might have triggered his world-shattering visions.

By the time *666* was released, Roussos and Papathanassiou, the latter recording as Vangelis, had already begun solo careers and were ready to pursue their own directions. Koulouris often played with both artists and Sideras also recorded after Aphrodite's Child disbanded. During the 1970s, Roussos became an international pop star in Western Europe. Before his death in 2015 he had expanded his circuit to include the former Soviet bloc and the Middle East. Vangelis enjoyed a prolific career in electronic music and gained his greatest success recording soundtracks for films and television, notably *Blade Runner*, *Chariots of Fire,* and Carl Sagan's *Cosmos*.

Suggested Albums: End of the World (1968); *It's Five O'Clock* (1970); *666* (1972)

See also: Vangelis

ARGENT

In 1969, former Zombies keyboardist Rod Argent formed Argent with bassist Jim Rodford, drummer Robert Henrit, and guitarist Russ Ballard. Their self-titled debut (1970) continued along the Zombies' path with keyboards tuned to minor keys, but with a heavier sound. Argent enjoyed one AM and FM hit, "Hold Your Head High" (1972), the best track from their third album, *All Together Now*. For their fourth album, *In Deep* (1973), Ballard wrote a deliberate attempt at a glam rock hit, "God Gave Rock and Roll to You." The song failed to sell, but became familiar through Kiss's cover version (1991). As Argent's take on progressive rock lost inspiration, the band dissolved to pursue solo careers and, for Rodford, membership in the Kinks. Reunited in the 21st century with Zombies vocalist Colin Bluntstone, Rod Argent has toured at the head of a proficient version of the Zombies.

Suggested Album: Argent (1970)

See also: Zombies

ASH RA TEMPEL

Germany's Ash Ra Tempel was formed in 1971 by Tangerine Dream keyboardist Klaus Schulze along with guitarist Manuel Gottsching and bassist Hartmut Enke.

Schulze left after their self-titled debut (1971) but occasionally rejoined the group. Ash Ra Tempel attracted a cult following for early albums featuring free-form space rock jams that filled entire LP sides. For a short period, Ash Ra Tempel sought outside collaborators, including Timothy Leary during his fugitive years following his escape from a U.S. prison. The raving prophet of psychedelia recorded *Seven Up* (1972) with Ash Ra Tempel, providing lyrics and vocals. On *Starring Rosi* (1973), German pop singer Rosi Mueller Ash fronted Ash Ra Tempel. After 1975, the band called itself Ashra and veered toward more conventionally melodic rock.

Suggested Albums: Ash Ra Tempel (1971); *Schwingungen* (1972)

See also: Tangerine Dream

AUGER, BRIAN (1939–)

While few rock fans know the name Brian Auger, his harpsichord riff that forms the hook on the Yardbirds' 1965 hit "For Your Love" has been heard by millions over the years. Auger, a sessions player, was brought into the session to play his main instrument, the Hammond B3 organ, but the band had to settle for harpsichord when it turned out to be the only available keyboard. However, organ would be the instrument with which Auger would fashion a lengthy and often interesting musical career.

Auger's first band, Steampacket, is notable for including a young Rod Stewart, as well as British blues singer and Elton John mentor Long John Baldry. Formed in 1965, contractual difficulties prevented the band from releasing any material, but demo tapes from the time showcase Auger's jazz-influenced, soulful organ playing, similar in style to the Animals' Alan Price and the Zombies' Rod Argent. And, while Steampacket never got off the ground, Auger's next band, Brian Auger and the Trinity, fared better. Featuring the vocals of British singer Julie Driscoll, the band produced several fine albums of spirited rhythm and blues–based songs, and enjoyed U.K. hits with smoky, psychedelic-tinged covers of Bob Dylan's "This Wheel's on Fire" and David Ackles's "Road to Cairo."

Auger's jazz influences became more prominent as the Trinity's career progressed, and following the group's breakup in 1969, he formed a more jazz-driven band, Brian Auger's Oblivion Express. While the band's sound is sometimes categorized as jazz-fusion, the label is at times more convenient than accurate. From their debut album, *Oblivion Express* (1969), the band's rock and rhythm and blues elements were as prominent as the jazz influences, and over time Oblivion Express added funk and soul touches, even as jazz became more dominant in their sound.

Oblivion Express disbanded in the mid-1970s after having contributed a couple members to the popular Scottish blue-eyed soul group the Average White Band. Auger released a number of solo albums in the 1980s, toured and jointly released a live album with Eric Burdon in the early 1990s, and eventually reformed Oblivion Express in 2005. The group has continued to record and tour. In 2012, Auger released a solo album, *Language of the Heart.*

Suggested Albums: Brian Auger & the Trinity: *Open* (1967); *Definitely What* (1968); *Streetnoise* (1969); Brian Auger's Oblivion Express: *Oblivion Express* (1970); *Closer to It* (1973)

AYERS, KEVIN (1944–2013)

In his beguiling English eccentricity, guitarist Kevin Ayers could have been Syd Barrett's better-grounded songwriting partner. By the time Ayers attempted to form a band with Pink Floyd's founding genius, he discovered that Barrett's mind was no longer tuned to any discernable wavelength. They played together on one song, "Religious Experience," released years later as a bonus track on the CD version of Ayers's *Joy of a Toy* album.

Ayers provided the whimsical leaven to Soft Machine, a combo driving toward jazz-fusion along an avenue of psychedelically tinged rock. Leaving the band after a grueling U.S. tour, Ayers began his solo career with *Joy of a Toy* (1969). The album often suggested the orchestrated playfulness of Gilbert and Sullivan transposed to 1960s Britain. Storybook images flashed by in kaleidoscopic colors, and the music was grounded in those aspects of the Beatles for which producer George Martin was most responsible. *Joy of a Toy* was recorded at Abbey Road Studio with members of Soft Machine and arrangements by avant-garde composer David Bedford.

Bedford played keyboards and saxophone on Ayers's follow-up, *Shooting at the Moon* (1970), and provided orchestral arrangements for what many consider Ayers's finest hour, *Whatevershebringswesing* (1971), featuring progressive rock guitarist Mike Oldfield and Soft Machine drummer Robert Wyatt along with the freewheeling Franco-British-Australian band Gong. By the time of *Bananamour* (1973), Ayers's songwriting was becoming spottier and the sunny psychedelic optimism that provided the context for his early work had evaporated. He remained a respected figure on the margins, recording a live album with John Cale, Nico, and Brian Eno, *June 1, 1974,* but was left behind by a succession of new cultural and musical trends from disco and punk rock through heavy metal. Ayers continued to record and perform sporadically until his death in 2013.

Suggested Albums: Joy of a Toy (1969); *Shooting at the Moon* (1970); *Whatevershebringswesing* (1971)

See also: Soft Machine

B

BABE RUTH

Fascination with the American West runs deep in British culture with manifestations that include the Texas gentleman in Bram Stoker's *Dracula* and the dime novel–reading subaltern in Carol Reed's *The Third Man*. Formed in 1970 in Hatfield, Hertfordshire, and fronted by vocalist Jenny Haan, Babe Ruth scored FM airplay with their evocation of the cowboy era, "Wells Fargo." The hard rock tune from the band's first album, *First Base* (1972), was not a paean to the global financial giant but to the cash-ferrying stagecoach line of Western lore. Afterward, Babe Ruth splintered, underwent personnel changes, but reemerged in the 21st century with a credible lineup of original members. Their song "The Mexican" became a dance club hit in a remix by DJ-producer Jellybean Benitez (1984).

Suggested Album: First Base (1982)

BACHMAN-TURNER OVERDRIVE

After leaving the Guess Who in 1970, Canadian guitarist Randy Bachman formed a recording act, Brave Belt, which evolved into Bachman-Turner Overdrive. Their self-titled debut album (1973) attracted attention in their homeland and the United States on the strength of relentless touring. *Bachman-Turner Overdrive II* (1973) brought the band into the higher echelons of the U.S. charts with a pair of radio hits, the boogie-based "Takin' Care of Business," a leftover song from the Guess Who, and the more melodic "Let It Ride," whose sound harkened back to the Guess Who. Bachman-Turner Overdrive focused on basic hard rock; their later albums were of little distinction, but the band maintained an audience and continued to tour in the 21st century.

Suggested Album: Bachman-Turner Overdrive II (1973)

See also: Guess Who

BAD COMPANY

The late 1960s saw the advent of what became known as "supergroups," formed from the remains of dissolved bands or with members that had become creatively restless and were looking for fresh inspiration from working with other musicians. Bad Company was one such supergroup, but differed from predecessors that were largely short-lived projects whose members took time off from their primary band or solo careers. Bad Company was designed to function as a full-fledged band with a lengthy career and commercial success.

Bad Company was a joint venture formed in 1973 by former members of Free, Mott the Hoople, and King Crimson, and it became one of the first bands signed to Led Zeppelin's Swan Song label. Free vocalist Paul Rodgers and Hoople guitarist Mick Ralphs provided the core of the group's meat and potatoes hard rock style, which owed more than a bit to Free's blues-based approach, but lacked the inspiration provided by Free's legendary guitarist Paul Kossoff. Bad Company's self-titled debut album (1974) found a receptive audience in the United States when "Can't Get Enough of Your Love" and "Movin' On" climbed the singles charts.

Subsequent albums and singles sold well until the 1980s. The band's popularity dwindled in the face of changing musical tastes, although they reformed after a short breakup and continue to tour to this day. Bad Company's musicianship was solid, but their music was too often predictable and rarely strayed from a well-worn formula of no-frills, mid-tempo rock. It can be argued that Bad Company served as a model for the rise of "corporate rock" acts such as Foreigner and Toto, bands formed by seasoned veteran musicians that hewed to a commercially successful sound driven by heavy radio airplay.

Suggested Album: Bad Company (1974)

BADFINGER

Badfinger's story contains enough drama and tragedy for a Hollywood biographical picture. Perhaps the reason no film based on Badfinger has been produced is that there was no happy ending. After the suicide of two members and lawsuits rivaling the case at the heart of Charles Dickens's *Bleak House*, the third act concluded in a series of whimpers rather than a victory lap. It was a poor finish for a Beatles-associated band whose hit records inspired the inception of a new genre, power pop.

The group's leading figure, vocalist-guitarist Peter Ham, was active in rock bands from the early 1960s in his hometown, Swansea, Wales. By 1966 he brought his group, the Iveys, to London, where his songs eventually caught the interest of the Beatles' new label, Apple Records. Although the Iveys were signed to Apple in 1968, they were frustrated by the label's labyrinthine politics. Their first single, the morosely hopeful "Maybe Tomorrow" (1968), was a hit in some European countries but not the United States or United Kingdom. An album by that name was released the following year, but only in Japan, Italy, and Germany.

Complaints by the band reached Paul McCartney and action came swiftly. The Iveys were given a more modern-sounding name, Badfinger, and a McCartney song, "Come and Get It." With little confidence in Badfinger's judgment, McCartney forced them to copy his song demo note for note. "Come and Get It" reached number one worldwide and was included in Peter Sellers's film comedy *The Magic Christian* (1969) and on Badfinger's first album. *Magic Christian Music* (1970) included other Badfinger songs from the film and seven tracks from the little-heard *Maybe Tomorrow*.

By the time of their first purpose-recorded album, *No Dice* (1970), Badfinger's sound had gelled. Indebted to the Beatles' melodicism and vocal harmonies, their guitars were pushed higher in the mix in punchier, more contemporary productions. No one called it power pop at that time, but by the end of the decade Badfinger would be recognized as a progenitor. Ham penned a series of heartbroken love songs primed for a younger record-buying audience. Melancholy even hovered near the ostensibly upbeat lyric of their hit from *No Dice*, "No Matter What." Also from that album, "Without You" became a number one hit in Harry Nilsson's more melodramatic rendition (1972). Ham's lovelorn suicide note has been seen as foreshadowing his fate.

Badfinger became musical sidekicks for the former Beatles, performing on George Harrison's *All Things Must Pass* (1970) and *Concert for Bangladesh* (1971) and backing John Lennon on *Imagine* (1971) and Ringo Starr on his hit, "It Don't Come Easy" (1971). Despite ties to the label's owners, Apple repeatedly rejected Badfinger's demos and quashed their recording sessions. Their third album, *Straighten Up* (1971), was produced by Todd Rundgren and included the downhearted hit singles "Day After Day" and "Baby Blue." *Straighten Up* marked the band's zenith.

Although their music was all over AM and FM radio in the United States in 1972, Badfinger's success rapidly unraveled. A series of ill-conceived management deals left them with little money, and financial troubles at Apple resulted in slender advances. Their final album for Apple, the unfortunately titled *Ass* (1973), contained a swipe at the label, "Apple of My Eye," and sold poorly. Badfinger moved to Warner Brothers and quickly recorded *Badfinger* (1973) while dashing off songs in the studio. Their eponymous LP was released almost simultaneously with *Ass* and failed to garner attention. As management and legal problems mounted, Warner Brothers pulled Badfinger's *Wish You Were Here* (1974) from distribution seven weeks after release. A year later, with the existence of Badfinger's LP barely noticed, Pink Floyd faced no difficulties titling their next album *Wish You Were Here*.

Told he had no money and unable to contact his management, Ham hanged himself in his recording studio in April 1975. He left behind a note blaming the band's American manager, Stan Polley. Badfinger dissolved as members joined bands of little note, played on sessions, or performed manual labor to survive in light of their missing royalties. Economic necessity drew vocalist-bassist Tom Evans and vocalist-guitarist Joey Molland to call their new band Badfinger. "Love Is Gonna Come at Last" from their album *Airwaves* (1979) received modest airplay, as did "Hold On" from *Say No More* (1981). Afterward, Evans and Molland led rival bands under the Badfinger name. Lawsuits pursued their endeavors. In 1983, Evans followed Ham's lead by hanging himself at his home. Despite his death, Molland reunited with other bandmates and toured as Badfinger.

Bright notes in recent decades include Mariah Carey's hit with "Without You" (1994), the resolution of the legal imbroglio surrounding royalties (2013), and the release of previously unissued tracks by the Iveys and Badfinger on CD. The lugubrious "Baby Blue" returned to the hit parade after factoring in the climactic scene of the popular TV drama *Breaking Bad* (2013).

Suggested Albums: Maybe Tomorrow (1969) (as The Iveys); *Magic Christian Music* (1970); *No Dice* (1970); *Straighten Up* (1971)

BAEZ, JOAN (1941–)

Joan Baez embraced rock belatedly, but her importance in the music's development as it transitioned from entertainment to self-conscious art form by the mid-1960s is incalculable. She was primarily responsible for introducing Bob Dylan to the burgeoning folk music scene by performing his songs and adding him to her concerts. Baez had already become an iconic figure in the folk-blues revival, setting the image for female troubadours with her long hair, casual yet never grungy clothes, acoustic guitar, and earnest vocals. Many female singer-songwriters of recent decades owe her an enormous debt, whether they know it or not.

Baez was drawn to the coffeehouses of the folk-blues revival while at Boston University in the late 1950s. She was thrust into the spotlight with her performance at the first Newport Folk Festival (1959). An offshoot of the Newport Jazz Festival, the event's inception signaled the shift among hip youth from jazz to folk music. The concert brought together Earl Scruggs, the Reverend Gary Davis, and other authentic rural performers with revivalists such as the New Lost City Ramblers and the Kingston Trio and gained media attention for the rising folk revival.

Baez became the movement's most respected younger star. Unlike the Kingston Trio or Peter, Paul and Mary, who tailored their music for pop audiences, Baez was a resolute purist. Turning down the opportunity to record for Columbia, she signed instead with Vanguard Records, a small New York label that had released recordings by performers blacklisted during the McCarthy era such as the Weavers and Paul Robeson.

The publicity she received at Newport carried her early albums to a wider public. Haloed with a countercultural chic, the pure tone of her fervid soprano voice balanced nicely with her uncompromising embrace of folk tradition and its association with leftist politics. She was slightly eclectic on her self-titled debut album (1960), favoring Anglo-American balladry but including a Mexican folk song and a number from the Yiddish musical theater. Her first recordings spurred a young generation of college-educated women to adopt her look and take up folk singing. She inspired the rise of Joni Mitchell, Emmylou Harris, Judy Collins, Bonnie Raitt, and Baez's sister, Mimi Farina.

Dylan had no greater champion than Baez, and she had trouble at first winning her audience to his side. They were an odd match on stage, her crystal tone and tight vibrato against his barbaric yawp and insistence on using the folk tradition as a foundation for a new kind of songwriting rather than an end in itself. Dylan was sometimes a cruel friend, but they were close and remained in touch through the years. It often seemed as if Baez kept a torch burning for the musician she befriended as a young unknown. She kept returning to the well of Dylan's songs at recording sessions, joined him on his freewheeling Rolling Thunder Revue tour (1975), and wrote candidly about her feelings for him on one of her few hit songs, "Diamonds and Rust" (1975), the title track of her last and perhaps only album to achieve significant FM rock radio airplay. *Diamonds and Rust* was her bestselling album ever.

Baez previously enjoyed a hit single with a cover of the Band's "The Night They Drove Old Dixie Down" (1971), an unusual choice for a civil rights activist given the song's Confederate sympathies. Raised as a Quaker and faithful to its tenets of nonviolence, Baez didn't separate her musical career from her vocation in social advocacy. Unlike some of her mentors, she was not blind to problems on the left. Although she visited Hanoi during Richard Nixon's "Christmas bombing campaign" (1972), she later criticized the Vietnamese Communist regime for human rights abuses and took part in a provocative concert in Czechoslovakia that was one of the triggers for the Velvet Revolution toppling the Soviet bloc government (1989).

Baez came late to writing, first recording her own songs in 1970. Her catalog of albums includes spoken word, collaborations with classical composer Peter Schickele (aka P.D.Q. Bach), recordings made in Nashville, and the eventual embrace of rock-era songwriters other than Dylan. Her participation in George Harrison's *Concert for Bangladesh* (1971) was characteristic of her spirit. Her presence at Harrison's Madison Square Garden event to raise money for typhoon victims connected rock's first major benefit concert with folk music's long tradition of fundraising for causes.

In the late 20th and early 21st centuries, Baez received many honors and recorded with younger players such as John Mellencamp, the Indigo Girls, Mary Chapin Carpenter, and Dar Williams. Rebel country singer Steve Earle produced her album *Day After Tomorrow* (2008), retaining her basic folk approach but modernizing it with a stripped-down Americana rock sound and the inclusion of songs by Earle, Elvis Costello, T Bone Burnett, and Tom Waits.

Suggested Albums: Joan Baez (1960); *Joan Baez, Vol. 2* (1961); *Joan Baez in Concert, Part 1* (1962); *Joan Baez in Concert, Part 2* (1963); *Farewell, Angelina* (1965); *Diamonds and Rust* (1975); *Day After Tomorrow* (2008)

See also: Folk-Blues Revival

BAKER, GINGER (1939–)

Ginger Baker drummed in the seminal British band Blues Incorporated before joining the Graham Bond Organisation and co-founding two of the most important "supergroups" of classic rock, Cream and Blind Faith. Rooted in jazz, he had adventurous tastes, drawing from African and other sources decades before "world music" became fashionable. He was one of the most talented and distinctive drummers of 1960s rock before setting course for less well-known sonic territory. He also enjoyed a quarrelsome reputation.

16   BAND

When Blind Faith disbanded in 1969, he launched a project called Ginger Baker's Air Force. The debut recording under that name (1970), a live album, featured members of Blind Faith, including guitarist Eric Clapton, bassist Ric Grech, and keyboardist Stevie Winwood. Baker showcased drums as a lead instrument, not simply a timekeeper. Playing across the lower end of his kit, Baker emphasized floor toms and bass drums, generating polyrhythms and some of the most musically dynamic drum solos in rock. *Ginger Baker's Air Force 2* (1970), a studio effort, was superbly uncategorizable, drawing oddly angled jazz solos into rock music with Afro-Cuban roots. An almost baroque arrangement for the Drifters' "I Don't Want to Go On Without You" shared the album with Graham Bond's "Gates of the City," which sounded like gospel music if the genre had originated in the Near East instead of the Old South.

Baker's interest in African music led him to the continent during the 1970s where he worked with Nigerian Afro-beat bandleader Fela Kuti. Kuti appeared on Baker's *Stratavarious* (1972), and Baker guest-starred on recordings by Kuti's band Africa '70. He also recorded three undistinguished hard rock albums with British guitarist Adrian Gurvitz under the Baker Gurvitz Army moniker.

After the 1970s, Baker's musical journey brought him through many unexpected stops, including the space rock band Hawkwind for their album *Levitation* (1980). More surprising was his collaboration with John Lydon's post–Sex Pistols, postpunk project Public Image Ltd. The puckish Lydon suggested Baker to his producer, Bill Laswell, as a joke, but warmed to the idea of working with a percussionist who was the antithesis of punk drumming. Baker recorded several tracks on Public Image's *Album* (1986), but jazz musician Tony Williams played drums on the album's hit, "Rise." During the 1990s Baker continued working at the interstices of jazz, rock, and experimental music with estimable musicians such as bassist Charlie Haden and guitarist Bill Frisell. He reunited briefly with Cream bassist Jack Bruce in the power trio BBM and grudgingly participated in a brief Cream reunion (2005).

In the 21st century, the drummer focused on the Ginger Baker Jazz Confusion with former James Brown saxophonist Pee Wee Ellis (heard on the 1960s soul hit "Cold Sweat") and bassist Alec Dankworth, a British jazzman whose resume includes pop and rock sessions as well as Mose Allison and Dave Brubeck. Baker's volatile personality came to the fore in director Jay Bulger's documentary *Beware of Mr. Baker* (2012) when the drummer, outraged at the filmmaker's ignorance of his career, assaulted Bulger on camera.

Suggested Albums: Ginger Baker's Air Force (1970); *Ginger Baker's Air Force 2* (1970); *Stratavarious* (1972); *Horses and Trees* (1986); *Middle Passage* (1990); *African Force* (2013)

See also: Blind Faith; Bond, Graham; Cream

BAND

If rock music had existed during the Civil War, it might have sounded like the Band, and if the Band had emerged in the 1860s rather than the 1960s, one imagines them favoring the Confederate cause. Their debut album, *Music from Big Pink* (1968), was a rebuke of contemporary rock culture. Rather than extoll the kicks derived from new drugs, the Band looked as if their drug of choice was aged Kentucky bourbon, and maybe Tennessee white lightning if they knew the moonshiner well. Sartorially, they could have stepped out of a traveling show from the 19th century. While many rock bands were seen as avatars of the future, the Band were rooted in history, specifically of the white American South. In "The Night They Drove Old Dixie Down" from their self-titled second album (1969), they regretted Robert E. Lee's surrender. Perhaps even more unconventional in an era of youth rebellion, the Band stood on the opposite side of the generation gap, siding with parents on "Tears of Rage" from *Big Pink*.

Remarkably, only one member of the Band, drummer Levon Helm, who grew up on a cotton farm near Turkey Scratch, Arkansas, was Southern. His bandmates were Canadians who fashioned a Romantic vision of an older America with the benefit of distance and exposure to the country, blues, and rhythm and blues from cross-border U.S. radio. They hooked up with Helm when they signed on as backing musicians for Ronnie Hawkins, an Arkansas singer. Recreating himself as the "King of Rockabilly," Hawkins based himself in Toronto. During the early 1960s as Ronnie Hawkins' Hawks, the future Band spent many nights on the road, playing the roadhouses of the bandleader's homeland for audiences that were drunk, dangerous, and demanding. They learned to play as well as anyone in rock and roll. The records they made with Hawkins, including a lacerating rendition of Bo Diddley's "Who Do You Love" (1963), reveal that they were traveling in a time warp, several years behind the trajectory of popular music. For the most part, the Band would always be a bit out of time.

Breaking with Hawkins by 1964, they played under several names. As Levon and the Hawks, they released a single written by their guitarist, Robbie Robertson, which sounded uncharacteristically like contemporary rhythm and blues. They caught the ear of Bob Dylan, who was looking for backing musicians as he turned from folk to rock. According to legend, Dylan wanted only Robertson and Helm, but they refused to go on the road without bassist Rick Danko, drummer Richard Manuel, and keyboardist Garth Hudson. The Band went on tour with Dylan from 1965 through 1966, minus Helm, who left because, as he later said, "I wasn't made to be booed" by folk fans disgruntled by Dylan's change of direction.

As Dylan recuperated from a motorcycle accident, the Band moved nearby to a loudly painted house dubbed "Big Pink." They began to work out their distinctive sound in the basement, often with Dylan in attendance, listening closely to each other and writing songs in a process described by them as intuitive verging on telepathic. By then they were as familiar as family, and shared inspiration with Dylan, who determined to once again break his own mold. The music Dylan recorded with the Band at Big Pink began leaking out in the form of bootleg albums, which by the 1970s became a cottage industry flourishing in the shadow of the music business and supported by fans seeking to collect missing pieces from their favorite artists. Some of the Big Pink tracks finally surfaced on an official album, *The Basement Tapes* (1975).

Those basement sessions also gave rise to *Music from Big Pink*. Trading instruments and lead vocals, the Band depicted a world with affinities closer to the Southern gothic stories of Flannery O'Connor than anything rock music had previously produced. There was solemnity and joy, the wheezing organ of church and circus. Some critics called the Band country rock but despite the rustic references, their country influences had been thoroughly sublimated. They sounded like nothing heard before them and gave rock new musical and lyrical signposts.

The Band sustained its collaborative creativity through *Stage Fright* (1970), but began to falter with *Cahoots* (1971). Robertson, now the primary songwriter, was left to conjure ghosts from his own past. The Band's momentum was sustained for a time by sidestepping the prospect of new music. They made a fine live album, *Rock of Ages* (1972), followed by a robust tribute to their roots in early rock and roll, *Moondog Matinee* (1973). The Band regrouped with Dylan on a tour that resulted in the acclaimed live album *Before the Flood* (1974). Robertson composed all the songs on the Band's belated next album of new material, *Northern Lights–Southern Cross* (1975).

Deciding to retire on a high note, the Band held a farewell concert whose distinguished roster of guests included Dylan, Neil Young, Emmylou Harris, Eric Clapton, Muddy Waters, and their old mentor, Ronnie Hawkins. The concert was released as an album, *The Last Waltz* (1978), and a concert film of the same name directed by Martin Scorsese.

Rick Danko, Levon Helm, and Robbie Robertson perform at the Band's 1976 farewell concert, documented in the film *The Last Waltz*. The Band, minus Robertson, regrouped in 1983 and its members continued to influence rock music with deep roots in southern American culture. (Michael Ochs Archives/Getty Images)

After retiring from the Band, Robertson became the musical director for Scorsese films such as *Raging Bull* (1980) and *The Color of Money* (1986), released solo albums to little acclaim, and produced recordings by Neil Diamond, the BoDeans, and others. Manuel performed on Robertson-produced soundtracks; Danko and Hudson released solo projects. Helm is ranked as truest to the Band's spirit, fronting the RCO All Stars and hosting a series of "Midnight Ramble" concerts in his studio at Woodstock, New York. He earned Grammy awards for Best Traditional Folk Album for *Dirt Farmer* (2007) and Best Americana Album for *Electric Dirt* (2009) and *Ramble at the Ryman* (2011). Helm also enjoyed an acting career, appearing in *Coal Miner's Daughter* (1980) and *The Right Stuff* (1983). He died in 2012.

The Band minus Robertson reformed in 1983, touring and recording even after Manuel's postconcert suicide in 1986. When Danko died in 1999, the Band ended for good. They were inducted into the Rock and Roll Hall of Fame in 1994.

Suggested Albums: Music from Big Pink (1968); *The Band* (1969); *Stage Fright* (1970); *Rock of Ages* (1972); *Moondog Matinee* (1973); *Northern Lights–Southern Cross* (1975); *The Last Waltz* (1978)

See also: Dylan, Bob

BARRETT, SYD (1946–2006)

The fate of Syd Barrett wasn't immediately clear after his 1968 dismissal for irregular behavior from the band he had led, Pink Floyd. Despite his discomfort with stardom and the decentering effects of LSD and other drugs, Barrett wasted no time entering Abbey Road studio as a solo artist. Dispelling the notion that he was artistically spent and psychologically disabled, he forged forward on sessions that resulted in *The Madcap Laughs* (1970). Backed by former bandmates Roger Waters and David Gilmour along with Soft Machine, he drew inspiration from Henry Wadsworth Longfellow for "Swan Lee" and James Joyce for "Golden Hair," along with Mother Goose rhymes and modernist allusions and ellipses intended to short-circuit linear meaning.

However, by the time he recorded *Barrett* (1970), his focus had grown fuzzy. Gilmour, who returned to produce the album, was forced to construct musical accompaniment for the lyrics from the sketchiest ideas. The mood is mostly despondent. Barrett retreated from public life following the album's release, performing occasionally in small venues before disappearing altogether in 1972. He became a legendary figure after returning to Cambridge, the university town where Pink Floyd began. Spotting the reclusive artist became a pastime for fans. Barrett's cult status was enhanced by his inaccessibility and, given his refusal to perform, his inability to disappoint fans.

Barrett's legacy haunted Pink Floyd even before his former band recorded *Wish You Were Here* (1975) in his honor. His apparent unwillingness to conform to the music industry made him a hero to the punk rock movement, while his songwriting influenced Robyn Hitchcock and the second wave of psychedelia that emerged in the

BEACH BOYS

1980s. A good deal of unreleased studio material surfaced in the 21st century before Barrett's death from cancer.

Suggested Albums: The Madcap Laughs (1970); *Barrett* (1970)

See also: Pink Floyd

BEACH BOYS

Famously, only one of the original Beach Boys, Dennis Wilson, surfed. And yet they sang often about a sport associated with the baby boom, America's fun-loving consumer culture, and the dream of California as a middle-class paradise on the Pacific. Surfers or not, the Beach Boys depicted the freewheeling spirit with an exuberant series of hit singles about surfing, hot rods, and girls that kept them in the charts from 1962 through 1965. Dick Dale, the Ventures, and other bands captured the physical and emotional exhilaration of surfing through guitar-powered instrumentals, but the Beach Boys bottled the dream of sunny beaches and sold it to a wide audience. With the arrival of the Beatles and the British Invasion, and the growing influence of Bob Dylan, the Beach Boys lost their tight grip on the Top 40, although they continued to score hits with "Help Me, Rhonda" and "California Girls" (1965).

Hints of greater sophistication could already be heard with "In My Room" (1963), which in hindsight foreshadowed the agoraphobia of the group's musical genius, Brian Wilson, as well as "Don't Worry Baby" (1964). "I Get Around" (1964) boasted unusual chords and "modular songwriting" with four distinct parts melded into one song. The Beach Boys' sound was based on carefully manicured vocals indebted to doo-wop and the jazz-influenced pop group the Four Freshmen. The Wrecking Crew, the informal house band for Los Angeles recording studios whose members included Glen Campbell and Leon Russell, often played the instrumental parts on their recordings. When backing Sonny and Cher or Jan and Dean, the Wrecking Crew shaped the recordings through their own arrangements. For the Beach Boys, however, they were more like an orchestra with Brian Wilson conducting. Wilson wrote the charts and sometimes sang them to the musicians until they understood his concepts.

Wilson was stung when the Beatles displaced the Beach Boys as Capitol Records' top-selling act. After hearing the Beatles' *Rubber Soul* (1965), he was determined to go toe-to-toe with the British usurpers in forging new roads for rock. His ambitions became evident on "Good Vibrations," released as a hit single in 1966 (and on *Smiley Smile* the following year). "Good Vibrations" was a symphony in three minutes, composed from splicing and editing 90 minutes of recorded music, featuring the Theremin, an electronic instrument previously heard in movie soundtracks to suggest weird emotional states or situations. "Good Vibrations" was recorded within the same timeframe as *Pet Sounds* (1966), often called the greatest rock album ever. A song cycle united sonically rather than lyrically, its layered production recalled Phil Spector but with more sophisticated melodies and arrangements, harmonies and intervals unheard of in rock, and unusual instrumentation. *Pet*

In the early 1960s the Beach Boys embodied the fun-loving teenage spirit of southern California with a series of carefully manicured hits. Under Brian Wilson's leadership they would become one of the decade's most sophisticated recording acts. (Photofest)

Sounds pushed recording technology forward with its lavish multitracking. Although the album produced hits, including a cheery rendition of the folk tune "Sloop John B" (inspired by a Kingston Trio recording) and the hopeful "Wouldn't It Be Nice," *Pet Sounds* fell short of sales expectations in the United States. However, it was received enthusiastically in Britain, where it inspired the Beatles to record *Sgt. Pepper's Lonely Hearts Club Band* (1967).

The creative momentum continued with the sessions for rock's greatest unfinished album, *Smile*, described by Wilson as "a teenage symphony to God." Working from the impressionist lyrics of Van Dyke Parks and with found sounds as well as conventional instrumentation, *Smile* was a work in continuous flux, a concept album whose concept remained in motion. The Beach Boys' Mike Love hated the project, hoping to continue the group's hitmaking formula of the early 1960s. Love's resistance helped scuttle *Smile*, along with the druggy atmosphere suffusing the sessions. For a song about the Great Chicago Fire, "Mrs. O'Leary's Cow," the Wrecking Crew donned fireman's helmets. When a blaze erupted in a neighboring building, Wilson blamed the song's psychic energy. Portions of *Smile* surfaced on succeeding Beach Boys' albums, including "Heroes and Villains" on *Smiley Smile* (1967) and the title track from *Surf's Up* (1971).

In the aftermath of *Smile*, Wilson suffered a crisis of confidence and increasingly withdrew from the group as he underwent a breakdown in slow motion. During this time, brother Dennis Wilson introduced aspiring rock star Charles Manson to the Los Angeles music scene and stole one of his songs, released on *20/20* (1969) as "Never Learn Not to Love." The Beach Boys entered a period of uncertainty. Inextricably linked to songs about wholesome teenage fun, they grappled with their role in the counterculture, their influence on progressive rock, and the prospect of bankruptcy from profligate spending. They often went without the guidance of Brian Wilson, who came and went like a specter. Capitol Records dropped them for poor sales. During his short tenure as a music industry executive, Van Dyke Parks signed the Beach Boys to Reprise with the stipulation that Brian Wilson play a role on each album.

The Beach Boys enjoyed occasional hit singles after the 1960s, including "Sail on Sailor" (1973), "Rock and Roll Music" (1976) and "Kokomo" (1988). Wilson was a sporadic participant, heard in the studio but seldom seen in public, as the group solidified its image as an oldies act steeped in nostalgia for the early 1960s. *Surf's Up* was intended to announce the end of an era, but in the end, the Beach Boys never escaped the image of surfboards and tanning lotion and even garnered fans in high places in the form of Ronald and Nancy Reagan. Their old songs sold well when repackaged on greatest hits albums.

By the end of the 1970s Wilson was paranoid, bedridden, and drug addicted. His story became tabloid material, especially after the intervention of controversial psychotherapist Eugene Landy, whose celebrity client list included Rod Steiger and Alice Cooper. Landy probably saved Wilson's life, but exploited him by becoming his business manager, songwriting collaborator, and even co-producer. Landy lost his license to practice in California for ethical misconduct and was barred from contact with Wilson in 1992. Wilson regained direction in the 1990s, collaborating with Parks on *Orange Crate Art* (1995) and revisiting tapes from the *Smile* sessions. He began performing material from the lost album and released a newly recorded reconception of the project called *Brian Wilson Presents Smile* (2004), which earned him his first Grammy Award. Many of the original 1967-era recordings for the aborted album were finally released in a box set, *The Smile Sessions* (2011).

Versions of the Beach Boys continued to tour in the 21st century despite the death of Dennis Wilson (1983) and Carl Wilson (1998). Inducted into the Rock and Roll Hall of Fame (1988), the Beach Boys have left behind a curious legacy. Occasionally their repertoire is tapped by newer acts; David Lee Roth scored a hit with a salacious video of "California Girls" (1985). The teenage exuberance of the early Beach Boys was echoed in the Ramones, while musically ambitious postpunk groups such as XTC and the High Llamas are indebted to the Beach Boys' vocal arrangements and Brian Wilson's groundbreaking productions. Wilson's story was the subject of a popular film, *Love & Mercy* (2014).

Suggested Albums: Shut Down Volume 2 (1964); *All Summer Long* (1964); *The Beach Boys Today!* (1965); *Summer Days (And Summer Nights!)* (1965); *Pet Sounds* (1966); *Smiley Smile* (1967); *Wild Honey* (1967); *20/20* (1967); *Surf's Up* (1971); *The Smile Sessions* (2011)

BEATLES

No band had a more fundamental, transformative effect on rock music and world culture than the Beatles. They played a vital role in the ascent of rock and roll from entertainment into self-conscious art, a medium of expression that became a sounding board for the changes that overtook society in the 1960s. Although the Beatles launched the British Invasion, they initially made a greater impression on bands in the United States and elsewhere than at home where they emerged from an already extant music scene. The impression the Beatles made worldwide was unprecedented not in intensity—mobs of screaming women greeted Rudolph Valentino and Frank Sinatra—but in scale and enduring importance. Elvis Presley's reach fell short in comparison. They left no genre of rock music untouched except jazz-rock, yet the Beatles opened the door to it by demonstrating that rock could go in any direction and absorb influences from anywhere.

By 1958 George Harrison, John Lennon, and Paul McCartney had joined a Liverpool skiffle band, the Quarrymen. The do-it-yourself music of British teenagers in the 1950s, skiffle made a virtue of the country's postwar scarcity by employing cheap or homemade instruments. While lively, it was not quite rock and roll. After graduating from high school in 1959, the three guitarists transitioned into a rock band under various names, including the Silver Beetles (inspired by Buddy Holly and the Crickets), before settling on the Beatles. Stuart Sutcliffe joined on bass guitar, an instrument that supplanted the upright bass of early rock and roll with a powerful undertow that drove 1960s rock. As a five-piece with Pete Best on drums, they played clubs in Hamburg. Clad in dangerous black leather and playing loud and lean, their Hamburg phase would be dramatized in the film *Backbeat* (1994) and embraced by punk rock fans. However, their repertoire puzzled later generations for mixing Tin Pan Alley with rock and roll and rhythm and blues. The Beatles loved many kinds of music and entertained a tough crowd with eclectic tastes. Their lack of single-mindedness was an asset.

When Sutcliffe left to study art, McCartney switched to bass and the Beatles assumed what became the classic rock band lineup of two guitars, bass, and drums. They backed British singer Tony Sheridan on tour and recordings in Germany before returning to Liverpool where a thriving music scene coalesced around a sound dubbed Merseybeat. Skiffle's lighthearted enthusiasm carried over into Merseybeat; unlike contemporary London bands such as the Rolling Stones, blues was only an echo in Liverpool, where Buddy Holly and Chuck Berry were the primary inspirations. Merseybeat rhythms were flexible, not metronomic, and focused on driving backbeats.

In 1962, while playing Liverpool's tiny Cavern Club, they met their manager, record-store owner and music columnist Brian Epstein. Epstein obtained an audition with George Martin, a producer at London's Abbey Road studio, who signed the band to Polyphone Records. After Martin complained about Best's musicianship, Ringo Starr replaced him. In the fall of 1962, the Beatles began recording under Martin's supervision, albeit on their first session, the haunting "Love Me Do," Starr was relegated to tambourine on the producer's orders. Martin's role was

The Beatles seized the imagination of young people across the world in 1964 with their reinvention of rock and roll and unique personal style. They retained their importance through the end of the 1960s and helped transform rock from entertainment into self-conscious art music. (AP Photo)

crucial, encouraging their songwriting and helping them articulate their vision for the sound of the music.

The Beatles began their ascent in 1963, rising to the top of the British charts and triggering the riotous outbursts by screaming girls depicted in Richard Lester's film *A Hard Day's Night* (1964). Meanwhile, plans were laid for conquering the United States. Reports in the British press led to a booking at Carnegie Hall, and Ed Sullivan, host of America's most-watched network entertainment program, saw the Beatles while vacationing in England and signed them. Word of their phenomenal British popularity led to a U.S. contract with Capitol Records, which released "I Want to Hold Your Hand" in January 1964. Quickly shooting to number one, it was followed by "She Loves You" and "Please Please Me." Capitol promoted the band vigorously to AM disc jockeys. The mainstream media took notice. When the Beatles landed in New York in February, the press succumbed to their contagious wit.

They reached superstardom with their February 9 appearance on *The Ed Sullivan Show*. Sullivan is credited with introducing Presley to a national audience, but it is often forgotten that the singer ascended to that top-ranked program on the steps of Milton Berle and other shows. The Beatles came into American living rooms with less warning and turned the nation upside down. The rest of the world soon followed. Many reasons have been offered for the Beatles' astonishing success, starting with their music, which sounded unlike anything their teenage audience was likely to have heard, and the irresistible hooks of their hits. Their sartorial style, from boots to haircuts, was not unknown in Europe but was striking in America. Unlike most pop groups, featuring a leader with largely faceless backup, the Beatles included four distinct personalities, giving teenage girls a range to choose from for fantasy boyfriends. They were playful and unthreatening, but their boisterous lunacy hinted at significance to astute adult observers. Finally, they were British, which licensed their eccentricity and endowed them with cultural cachet in America.

The Beatles increased the vocabulary of rock music from early on. Lennon and McCartney's songwriting was inventive and prolific, more melodically and harmonically unpredictable than that of their peers. Their sound struck many ears as outrageous, especially the falsetto leaps in songs such as "She Loves You," which might have been inspired by Little Richard but sounded unprecedented. Lennon's stint at art school opened his imagination, as it did for Pete Townshend, Ray Davies, and other British rock stars of the 1960s. Neither Lennon nor McCartney were purists, but were comfortable drawing from show tunes or whatever sources they fancied. They followed no rulebook but invented their own. In early years their best songs, such as "Please Please Me" and "She Loves You," were often oddly bittersweet compounds of Lennon's pessimism and McCartney's optimism, along with a competitive spirit that pushed their songs in surprising directions.

At first their lyrics adhered to timeworn themes of romance. Less concerned with words than the spirit of their recordings, Lennon and McCartney focused on sound more than sense. Although they seldom aspired to poetry, they became fascinated with Bob Dylan after Harrison purchased Dylan's second album in Paris just before they launched their epochal first American tour. His influence was heard directly on occasion, as in the proto–folk-rock "I'm a Loser" (1964) and the oblique "Norwegian Wood" (1965), but was felt throughout their succeeding releases as the ambition to lift popular music to new heights. Much has been made of the Beatles' mood-altering first encounter with Dylan in the summer of 1964, when they imbibed marijuana for the first time. Cannabis encouraged their willingness to try anything, nudging them farther down the road of experimentation.

Signposts for the Beatles' growth came quickly along the fast lane of mid-1960s British rock culture. Influenced by the Who's rumbling, weighty rhythms, "Ticket to Ride" (1965) was a step toward heavy metal. Scored by Martin for a string quartet, "Yesterday" (1965), cited by the *Guinness Book of Records* as the most recorded song ever, bridged the gap between rock and classical.

With *Rubber Soul* (1965), the Beatles reached a new milestone musically as well as lyrically. By then rock's development became reminiscent of modern painting's rapid advances in the early 20th century, albeit accelerated by the pace of mass communication. The emotional insights of their songs became more sophisticated. "Norwegian Wood," which introduced sitar to rock, was Dylanesque for telling a story bearing multiple interpretations. The Beatles looked beyond Anglo-American rock and pop, drawing "Girl" from the Oriental modes of Greek folk music. Harrison, whose occasional songwriting contributions had been relatively unremarkable, emerged as a powerful writer with the Byrds-influenced "If I Needed Someone." The calm fatalism of "In My Life" was spiced by Martin's brief solo on electric piano, recorded at half-speed to simulate a harpsichord. *Rubber Soul's* sonic depth was achieved by multitracking. Four continuous weeks were devoted to recording sessions at Abbey Road, a generous allotment of time for a rock album in those years.

With Martin's know-how, the Beatles continued to explore the recording studio as a musical instrument on their pinnacle album, *Revolver* (1966). Echoing the band's use of LSD under the reckless psychedelic advocacy of Timothy Leary, the music often tries to catch the aural dimension of an acid trip. The result was incredibly inventive yet always coherent as the band erased boundaries of time and culture. Ancient met modern on "Tomorrow Never Knows" as sitars encountered tape loops. "Tomorrow Never Knows" reintroduced the sustained repetition of the drone, absent in Western music since the Middle Ages and only recently rediscovered by avant-garde composer La Monte Young.

Every song on *Revolver* was remarkable, starting with the opening number, "Tax Man," Harrison's protest against high taxes on the rich. With its downbeat images of loneliness and alienation, "Eleanor Rigby" continued the Beatles' conversation with the classics through Martin's string octet arrangement. *Revolver* was a quantum leap for the Beatles and for rock music; much of it would have been unimaginable only two years earlier. The album's serious mood is lightened by the Motown exuberance of "Got to Get You into My Life" and a novelty number, "Yellow Submarine," whose nonsense lyrics and merry sound effects recalled Martin's earlier work as a producer of comedy records.

Released only weeks after *Revolver* was completed, the Beach Boys' *Pet Sounds* impressed McCartney, who determined to surpass it. His response, *Sgt. Pepper's Lonely Hearts Club Band* (1967), was a loose concept album by a fictitious group, costumed in the Edwardian finery in vogue in London and California and referencing music of an earlier era. The songs seldom reached the heights of *Revolver*, but *Sgt. Pepper* was appreciated more for its totality than for its parts. Appearing at the onset of the Summer of Love, the album was a major cultural event as fans lined up outside record stores on the day of its release. *Sgt. Pepper* broadened the oracular aura that had already developed around the Beatles, leaving many listeners scrutinizing the lyrics for messages and the dense production for hidden revelations. Charles Manson would eventually misread the Beatles and find support in their songs for his attempt to trigger Armageddon.

The Beatles' breakup occurred in slow motion. The foursome drifted apart after returning from India, where they sought the fashionable wisdom of Maharishi Mahesh Yogi, the founder of Transcendental Meditation. Lennon soon denounced him as a humbug. Harrison continued to pursue Hindu spirituality while chafing under his limited options as a songwriter with the Beatles. Lennon's relations with avant-garde artist Yoko Ono played a role in the breakup. Ono replaced McCartney as his creative partner, especially in light of *Magical Mystery Tour* (1967), McCartney's failed attempt to rekindle the high spirits of the band's earlier years in the form of a television movie. The other Beatles resented Ono for inserting herself into their artistic process. The death of manager Brian Epstein (1967) added to the sense that the glue holding them together was dissolving. Despite this, the Beatles launched an ambitious enterprise, Apple, a boutique that grew into a record label and music management company with plans to enter the fields of film and electronics. Largely innocent about business, the Beatles wanted an outlet for their music and the recordings of favored artists, but the company soon sank into rancor and mismanagement.

By the time of their two-LP set, *The Beatles* (1968), known as the White Album for its blank covers, they were tired of one another. The album was less a band effort than the work of four solo artists in one package. Bountiful in variety, the White Album included the sensitive acoustic ballad "Julia," the harsh proto-metal of "Helter Skelter," the puzzling musique concrète of "Revolution No. 9," the homespun country of "Don't Pass Me By" and the hard rock of "Revolution." Eric Clapton guest-starred with a searing solo on Harrison's "While My Guitar Gently Weeps." While musically diverse, the tracks flowed well together.

During their last year together, the Beatles managed to record a pair of albums under trying circumstances. *Abbey Road* (1969), a collection of songs and a medley of fragments, was followed by *Let it Be* (1970). Producer Phil Spector finished the latter album, adding lush orchestral arrangements. At McCartney's behest, the music was re-released stripped of Spector's influence as *Let It Be . . . Naked* (2003).

All four ex-Beatles enjoyed initial success as solo artists. Unlike most rock bands, their breakup was final. During the 1970s they resolutely refused high-priced offers to reunite. The murder of John Lennon (1980) ended all realistic hopes of a reunion, and Harrison's death (2001) put to rest fantasies of a concert featuring the sons of Lennon standing in for their father with the remaining Beatles. Unreleased material continued to surface on anthologies. During the 1960s the U.S. releases of Beatles albums usually differed significantly from the U.K. versions. The British albums, considered canonical, have become the standard editions. With the exception of *Let it Be* and *Abbey Road*, the Beatles released monophonic and stereophonic versions of albums, with mono prized by aficionados, given the primitive state of early stereo recordings. A box set, *The Beatles in Mono* (2009), collects their recordings in that format.

The Beatles raised standards, making it mandatory that serious rock bands aspire to be artists, not merely entertainers. They encouraged album cover design as an art form, not merely a packaging decision. They set unfulfilled expectations for a second coming, a "new Beatles." Coming closest was Nirvana, which briefly became flag bearers for their generation before Kurt Cobain's death (1994) cut them short. Although screaming teenage girls continue to turn up for One Direction and other "boy bands," none of those acts moved pop culture forward or achieved the breadth and depth of the Beatles' fandom. In the socially fragmented 21st century, the Super Bowl is the only experience simultaneously shared by millions of Americans. If a musical group appeared with the potential of the Beatles, it might well go unnoticed, at best receiving a viral flurry before receding into obscurity.

Suggested Albums: Please Please Me (1963); *With the Beatles* (1963); *A Hard Day's Night* (1964); *Beatles for Sale* (1964); *Help!* (1965); *Rubber Soul* (1965); *Revolver* (1966); *Sgt. Pepper's Lonely Hearts Club Band* (1967); *Magical Mystery Tour* (1967); *The Beatles* (1968); *Abbey Road* (1969); *Let It Be* (1970); *Hey Jude* (1970)

BEAU BRUMMELS

With the hit single "Laugh, Laugh" (1965), the Beau Brummels became the first successful San Francisco rock band of the 1960s. Produced by Sylvester Stewart (aka Sly Stone) and released on the independent Autumn Records, "Laugh, Laugh" was a Beatles imitation with echoes of early 1960s pop folk. Led by jangly strummed electric guitar, the Beau Brummels became masters of melancholy folk-rock with a string of hits in 1965 including "Just a Little," "You Tell Me Why" and "Don't Talk to Strangers." After Autumn Records was sold to Warner Brothers, the Beau Brummels were forced to record an album of ill-conceived cover songs, *The Beau Brummels '66* (1966).

The band began losing original members, including one to the military draft. They continued to evolve in the wake of a rapidly changing music scene. The Beau Brummels collaborated with Van Dyke Parks on the psychedelic *Triangle* (1967) and went to Nashville to cut a country rock album, *Bradley's Barn* (1968), recording original songs as well as tunes by the still little-known Randy Newman. By the end of 1968, the band members split to pursue other projects but regrouped in the 1970s and continued to record and tour in various incarnations into the 21st century.

Suggested Albums: Introducing the Beau Brummels (1965); *Volume 2* (1965); *Triangle* (1967); *Bradley's Barn* (1968)

BE-BOP DELUXE

Opting for a guitar over a paintbrush, art student Bill Nelson formed Be-Bop Deluxe in 1972. His band was championed by influential BBC announcer John Peel, achieving success in Great Britain but stirring only slight notice in the United States. Drawing from influences similar to the sources of David Bowie's early 1970s albums, Be-Bop Deluxe's first recordings were clever, suffused with references to science fiction and early 20th-century modern art, and led by Nelson's orchestral guitar playing. After disbanding Be-Bop Deluxe in 1979, Nelson went on to a prolific career as a solo artist and producer.

Suggested Albums: Axe Victim (1974); *Futurama* (1975); *Sunburst Finish* (1976)

BECK, JEFF (1944–)

Jeff Beck came to prominence in the mid to late 1960s as rock music evolved toward a heavier, more guitar-dominated sound. This development gave rise to a new type of rock star, the "guitar hero." A guitar hero was almost always the leader of the band, a virtuoso proficient in prominent lead riffs and lengthy, demanding guitar solos. While Beck has never achieved the commercial success of such peers as Eric Clapton, Jimi Hendrix, or Jimmy Page, he has gone on to carve a singular creative path and deserves his place in the guitar hero pantheon.

The British-born Beck became interested in guitar after hearing a Les Paul record in the early 1950s and took up the instrument as a teenager. His skills developed quickly and by 1964 he was getting gigs as a sessions player. When Clapton left the Yardbirds in 1965, Beck was chosen as his replacement. With the Yardbirds, Beck demonstrated his interest in expanding the sonic potential of his instrument, using distortion to make the guitar sound like a sitar on "Heart Full of Soul," and creating inventive, at times explosive solos that expanded the expressive boundaries of guitar. Personality conflicts led to Beck's dismissal from the band in 1967, and the mercurial guitarist set out on his own, forming the Jeff Beck Group that same year.

The Jeff Beck Group began as a prototypical supergroup, which included Jimmy Page, John Paul Jones, Keith Moon, and session keyboardist Nicky Hopkins. The lineup's most famous recording was the searing "Beck's Bolero," a classically infused instrumental rave-up. Since the original members of the group were on loan from other bands, Beck reconfigured the band's lineup and recruited Rod Stewart as lead vocalist and Ron Wood on rhythm guitar. The Jeff Beck Group's first two albums, *Truth* (1968) and *Beck-Ola* (1969), were seminal works of heavy blues-based guitar rock. Stewart's frenetic vocals and Beck's stinging vibrato influenced the developing genre of heavy metal. The group broke up in 1969, with Stewart and Wood heading off to the Faces, and Beck's career going on hiatus following a serious automobile accident that same year.

Recovering from his injuries, Beck reformed the Jeff Beck Group with a less star-studded lineup. Beck's work with that iteration never achieved the prominence of his earlier recordings, but did see the band experiment with jazz and rhythm and blues along with heavy blues-rock. Beck spread his wings further, forming a power trio with Vanilla Fudge members Tim Bogert and Carmen Appice. *Beck, Bogert & Appice* (1973) was notable for a memorable cover of Stevie Wonder's "Superstition."

By the mid-1970s, Beck began to experiment with jazz-fusion, and his efforts paid off with *Blow by Blow* (1975), an entirely instrumental album produced by George Martin. The genius of *Blow by Blow* lay in Beck's bringing jazz styles into a rock format without surrendering any of the fire and drive of rock music. The album included a cover of Stevie Wonder's "'Cause We've Ended as Lovers," a tour de force tastefully merging blues runs and soulful bends to create an impassioned masterpiece. *Blow by Blow* was followed by *Wired* (1976), another well-regarded jazz-fusion effort.

By the 1980s Beck's recording career became more sporadic, largely focusing on instrumental releases. A notable exception was *Flash* (1985), which made use of a variety of vocalists and brought Beck and Rod Stewart a minor hit with a gospel-touched cover of the Impressions' "People Get Ready." Beck continued to record and tour throughout the 1990s and into the new millennium, continuing to focus on instrumental music, adopting a finger style method of guitar playing, and consistently displaying fine form and guitar virtuosity.

While Beck is surely as respected and influential as Page and Clapton, he never came close to consistently achieving their level of popularity. One likely reason is that while Beck was a great guitar player, he was never as strong a songwriter as Clapton or as proficient in the studio as was Page. Beck also displayed a quirkier, less radio friendly sensibility, exploring less commercially viable forms such as jazz and often eschewing vocals. Nevertheless, Beck's guitar playing is equal to that of his fellow members in the trio of surviving 1960s guitar heroes, memorable for its intense vibrato, dramatic melodicism, and tasteful use of the vibrato bar.

Suggested Albums: Truth (1968); *Beck-Ola* (1969); *Beck, Bogert & Appice* (1973); *Blow by Blow* (1975); *Wired* (1976); *Jeff Beck's Guitar Shop* (1989); *Emotion & Commotion* (2010)

See also: Yardbirds

BEE GEES

The Bee Gees truly lived a life in music. Brothers Barry, Maurice, and Robin Gibb were sons of a British bandleader, began performing as children, and signed their first record deal while still in their mid-teens. From there, they launched a career that spanned the better part of three decades and was halted only by the death of two of the Gibb brothers. Their career at times resembled a roller-coaster ride, with more than a few commercial ups and downs, most notably throughout the 1970s, which saw them rise from near oblivion to become a legitimate worldwide phenomenon.

The Gibb brothers were born in England, but emigrated to Australia with their family in the late 1950s. They had already begun performing as a group prior to the move, and their career quickly took off. A stint hosting a television show was followed by a recording contract with an Australian label. Christened the Bee Gees after Barry Gibb's initials, the group released two poor-selling albums and returned to England, where they formed a musical partnership with producer Robert Stigwood that would prove commercially and at times artistically fruitful for years to come. Under Stigwood's guidance the group found an audience, releasing a string of hits in the United States and United Kingdom. The Gibb brothers wrote their own pop-oriented material, and from the start they displayed a strong sense of melody, lyrical intelligence, and ambitious orchestrated arrangements. The Bee Gees' strong three-part harmonies bore more than a passing resemblance to those of the Beatles, leading radio listeners to occasionally confuse them with the Fab Four. Their melodic pop ballad sense was shown to best effect in singles such as "To Love Somebody" (1966) and "Words" (1967), but too often their hits were marred by lachrymose vocals. However, the group was at times musically adventurous, as demonstrated by their fine 1969 double album, *Odessa*.

The Bee Gees' string of hits ran out in the early 1970s, and by 1974 they were all but consigned to has-been status. However, Stigwood came to the rescue by relocating the group to Miami, where they changed direction and recorded the bouncy, infectious, funk-influenced song "Jive Talkin'" (1975), which immediately revitalized their sagging career. The next two years saw more rhythm and blues–influenced hit singles, but that success was nothing compared with what came with the release of the 1977 soundtrack to *Saturday Night Fever*. The film (which also catapulted John Travolta to stardom) chronicled the rising New York City disco movement's impact on young people's lives, and the Bee Gees provided several hit singles to the soundtrack, including "Stayin' Alive." From that point, the Bee Gees became synonymous with disco and the group was ubiquitous on the radio for the remainder of the decade. The sound was highlighted by Maurice Gibb's trademark falsetto and syncopated disco rhythms; the group found itself loved by disco fans and loathed by those for whom the style of music was anathema.

However, much of the Bee Gees' disco-era work has stood the test of time, and songs such as "How Deep Is Your Love" show the band retained their ability to write stirring, memorable melodies, coupled with excellent vocal arrangements. The Gibbs also wrote hit singles during this time for younger brother Andy Gibb, Yvonne Ellimen, Frankie Valli, and Samantha Sang.

As the 1970s came to a close, the Bee Gees fell from the top of the musical world after starring in the ill-considered cinematic disaster, *Sgt. Pepper's Lonely Hearts Club Band* (1978), based on the classic Beatles album. This artistic and commercial debacle, coupled with shifting musical winds, led to a decline in the group's popularity by the start of the 1980s. The coming years saw the Bee Gees all but disappear from the airwaves, although they did write hits for Kenny Rogers and Dolly Parton, Diana Ross, and Dionne Warwick. Andy Gibb's death from drug-influenced heart problems led to the group's exodus from the public eye for a time, although they returned a few years later, releasing albums and occasionally touring. Maurice Gibb's death from a heart attack in 2003 effectively ended the group. Robin Gibb died from cancer in 2012. The Bee Gees were inducted into the Rock and Roll Hall of Fame in 1997.

Suggested Albums: The Bee Gees Sing and Play 14 Barry Gibb Songs (1965); *Bee Gees 1st* (1967); *Odessa* (1969); *Main Course* (1975); *Children of the World* (1976); *Saturday Night Fever: The Original Movie Sound Track* (1977); *Spirits Having Flown* (1979)

BIG BROTHER AND THE HOLDING COMPANY

Although Big Brother and the Holding Company are remembered for their lead vocalist, Janis Joplin, they existed before her arrival and continued after her departure. Formed in 1965, Big Brother was the house band at San Francisco's Avalon Ballroom, site of many early psychedelic "happenings." Joplin joined in 1966 and recorded two albums with them.

On *Big Brother and the Holding Company* (1967), the band often sounded hard-pressed to keep up with their singer. Joplin brought a uniquely passionate voice to their hard blues-rock on such self-penned songs as "Down on Me." They followed their modestly successful debut with one of rock's greatest albums, *Cheap Thrills* (1968), featuring cover art by underground cartoonist Robert Crumb.

Although concert applause was added to simulate a concert album, the only track actually recorded live was the agonizingly intense cover of Big Mama Thornton's "Ball and Chain." *Cheap Thrills* included a rendition of George Gershwin's "Summertime" outstanding for dynamic range and the Bach-like solo by classically trained guitarist Sam Andrews as well as Joplin's vocal, sizzling like a heat mirage on an asphalt highway. Their cover of a soul number by Erma Franklin, "Piece of My Heart," became a major hit.

Joplin left Big Brother at the end of 1968, taking Andrews with her, and achieved stardom in her own right. Big Brother continued to record and perform with ex-Electric Flag vocalist Nick Gravenites before disbanding in 1972.

Suggested Albums: Big Brother and the Holding Company (1967); *Cheap Thrills* (1968)

See also: Joplin, Janis

BIG STAR

Aside from a coterie of rock critics, few people actually heard Big Star during their existence due to poor promotion and worse distribution of their albums. But in the aftermath, they became exemplary in the emerging power pop genre; the rarity of their albums made them more admirable to cult audiences than such better-selling contemporaries as the Raspberries.

Big Star began in Memphis in 1974. Emulating the Beatles' songwriting team of John Lennon and Paul McCartney, most of the band's songs were penned by Alex Chilton and Chris Bell. Having touched stardom as the preternaturally soulful voice of the Box Tops' hit, "The Letter" (1967), Chilton believed Big Star could live up to its name. Along with the Beatles, Big Star echoed the Byrds, and the guitars sometimes spoke with a country rock accent. Their hard rock songs could have been played on FM and their ballads would have been comfortable on AM, but they received airplay on neither frequency. Big Star became that not uncommon paradox of an unpopular pop group. They broke up in 1974.

By the end of the 1970s, and with the posthumous release of their third album, Big Star's melodious rock became an inspiration for a wave of power pop acts as well as nascent alternative bands such as REM and the Replacements, who honored them with a song, "Alex Chilton," from their album *Pleased to Meet Me* (1987). Bell died in a car accident in 1978 just as the Big Star cult began to grow. Chilton enjoyed an eclectic career as a solo artist and producer before reorganizing Big Star in 1993 with original drummer Jody Stephens and members of the alternative rock band the Posies. He died of heart problems in 2010.

Suggested Albums: #1 Record (1972); *Radio City* (1974); *Third* (aka *Sister Lovers*) (1978)

BLACK ROCK

Rock and roll's roots are solidly in the African American tradition, even if the music that developed in the wake of Elvis Presley had a strong admixture of country. While some of the music's early promoters, notably disc jockey–impresario Alan

Freed, kept African Americans in the forefront, there was a strong push in the entertainment industry from early on to disguise the music's roots by promoting white cover versions of songs by African American performers and by marketing rock and roll to a white teenage audience. Despite the prevailing segregation of American society, *Billboard* magazine abolished its rhythm and blues chart from November 1963 through January 1965 on the assumption that record buyers were becoming colorblind. The experiment was short lived. While the black-owned Motown Records, billing itself as "The Sound of Young America," sold hit records across racial lines, the arrival of the Beatles and the British Invasion seemed to mark a musical resegregation.

While British groups such as the Rolling Stones awakened interest among white American teenagers in black American music, they pointed fans toward an older genre, the blues, already being rejected by young blacks in favor of soul music. As the major labels eagerly promoted the new white bands to young white audiences, black nationalism rose on the other side of the racial divide. Rock and soul were running on separate tracks. Jimi Hendrix was exceptional as an African American musician performing in a "white" if obviously black-rooted medium; almost universally embraced by white rock fans, Hendrix was criticized by some Black Power advocates for keeping company with the oppressors.

Anomalies occurred. Sly Stone tried to reunite increasingly disparate forms of music and, like Prince 15 years later, created a genre unto himself. Also coming out of the late 1960s is another unusual case, Funkadelic. The group's leader, rhythm and blues veteran George Clinton, infused soul and funk with hard-driving Hendrix-derived guitar on a series of albums that sold poorly but would later be admired, including *Funkadelic* (1970), *Free Your Mind . . . and Your Ass Will Follow* (1970) and *Maggot Brain* (1971). Through much of the 1970s Funkadelic was ignored by soul and FM rock radio alike. They gained attention from a coterie of rock critics, especially *Creem* magazine, headquartered in Funkadelic's home base, Detroit, but few rock fans heard the music until the end of the decade. In the 1980s, Clinton became widely recognized as a forerunner, cited by alternative rock and hip-hop acts alike.

By some accounts, Detroit's Black Merda was the first band to call its music "black rock." Emerging from their hometown's thriving rhythm and blues scene, the guitar-based band backed Edwin Starr on "War" and other tracks, and released a pair of albums under their own name in 1970 and 1972. They received little attention.

Bands identifying themselves as black rock had virtually no influence during the classic rock era but set a precedent for such African American groups as the jazz-infused punk band Bad Brains and the funky alternative act Fishbone.

BLACK SABBATH

Black Sabbath was unique among the first wave of heavy metal bands. Gloomier than Deep Purple or Led Zeppelin, their gritty music seemed to amplify their hometown, the gray industrial city of Birmingham, England. Although their eponymous debut album (1970) betrayed blues-rock roots, they were already moving beyond

Gloomier and heavier than their generational peers, Black Sabbath became one of the most influential heavy metal bands after their 1970 debut album. Original members Ozzy Osbourne (left) and Tony Iommi (right) are seen here performing at the 1985 Live Aid concert in Philadelphia. (AP Photo/Rusty Kennedy)

conventions, making liberal use of the tritone, the "devil's interval," little known in the blues tradition or in rock before Black Sabbath but heard in Beethoven and Wagner. Great devourers of horror movies, Black Sabbath may have derived the menacing tritone from the scary music of film scores. They took their name from the 1963 movie by pioneering Italian horror director Mario Bava.

The essential elements of Black Sabbath's image and sound were already in place by 1970, including the spooky autumnal churchyard on their debut album cover. Ozzy Osbourne's high-pitched vocals lacked the machismo or the blues influences of Robert Plant or Rod Stewart; he wailed like a tormented soul in Gustave Dore's engravings of hell. Bassist Geezer Butler, principal lyricist, drew inspiration from nightmares. The music's primary author, guitarist Tony Iommi, had lost two fingertips in an industrial accident. Iommi's characteristically heavy low-end sound may have resulted from playing with prosthetic tips, along with his testing the limits of amplification and disdain for treble.

Their popularity grew when "Paranoid," from their second album (1971), became an unlikely hit single. "Paranoid's" double-time guitar and rhythm forecast punk rock, and the lyric was in keeping with the band's preoccupation with darkness. The menacing "Iron Man" from that same album was a far cry from the cartoon character's wisecracking Robert Downey Jr. iteration, despite an unusual melody oddly suggestive of Gilbert and Sullivan.

Black Sabbath was far from the only band of their era with occult preoccupations, but as much as anyone, they imparted a gothic sensibility to the nascent heavy metal genre. After a few years, however, Black Sabbath fell into making albums that conformed to expectations. By 1979, bickering and drugs led to Osbourne's replacement by American vocalist Ronnie James Dio, formerly of Ritchie Blackmore's Rainbow. Despite other personnel changes, Black Sabbath continued to sell albums and fill American arenas while Osbourne achieved stardom as a solo recording artist and became the material of urban legend. He denied biting off the head of a bat on stage. His notoriety led to an Emmy-winning reality TV show featuring his family, *The Osbournes* (2002–2005).

Osbourne reunited with Black Sabbath to co-headline Ozzfest with his own solo band. The core original lineup regrouped again for a short tour and a Rick Rubin–produced album, *13* (2013), featuring Rage Against the Machine's Brad Wilk on drums. Black Sabbath has been inducted into the Rock and Roll Hall of Fame.

Suggested Albums: Black Sabbath (1970); *Paranoid* (aka *War Pigs*) (1971); *Masters of Reality* (1972); *Sabbath Bloody Sabbath* (1973)

BLACKMORE, RITCHIE (1945–)

Britain's Ritchie Blackmore brought classical virtuosity to rock guitar. As a member of an early 1960s instrumental band, the Outlaws, he played behind many English pop singers. Co-founding Deep Purple in 1968, Blackmore led the band onto the singles chart as well as the international hard rock circuit. As dissension grew, he left Deep Purple in 1975 to form Ritchie Blackmore's Rainbow (later shortened to Rainbow).

One track from the band's 1975 debut album received consistent FM rock airplay, "Man on the Silver Mountain," co-written with Rainbow vocalist Ronnie James Dio. Despite frequent personnel changes, Rainbow built a large audience for its baroque-inspired metallic rock. After Dio departed in 1979 to join Black Sabbath, Rainbow alienated some of their fans by moving toward a more homogenized album rock sound. Blackmore rejoined Deep Purple from 1984 through 1993, regrouped Rainbow in 1994, and formed a medieval folk-rock duo with Candice Night, Blackmore's Night, in 1997. For those who heard medieval modes in Blackmore's most famous riff, for Deep Purple's "Smoke on the Water," his embrace of early music was no surprise. Blackmore's guitar style influenced a generation of diverse guitarists who emerged in the 1980s, including Steve Vai, Joe Satriani, Lars Ulrich, and Yngwie Malmsteen.

Suggested Albums: Ritchie Blackmore's Rainbow (1975)

See also: Deep Purple

BLIND FAITH

Blind Faith was the classic "supergroup" of British musicians who had already attained stardom. Formed in 1969, the group would be short lived. Guitarist Eric Clapton and drummer Ginger Baker came from the just-disbanded Cream. Keyboardist Stevie Winwood was on hiatus from Traffic. Bassist Rick Grech had been in Family, little known in the United States but popular in the United Kingdom. Blind Faith recorded one superb and bestselling album, yielding a pair of FM hits, Winwood's enigmatic ballad "Can't Find My Way Home" and Clapton's blues-rock testament "Presence of the Lord." The supergroup embarked on a sold-out tour of American amphitheaters and broke up after returning home.

Suggested Album: Blind Faith (1969)

See also: Baker, Ginger; Clapton, Eric; Traffic

BLODWYN PIG

Blodwyn Pig was the creation of original Jethro Tull guitarist Mick Abraham, who formed the band in 1968 after leaving Tull due to creative differences with co-leader Ian Anderson. Abraham favored a more blues-based approach than Anderson, and Blodwyn Pig reflected that philosophy.

While many guitar-based blues-rock bands of the late 1960s centered around one form of the genre, such as boogie or heavy rock, Blodwyn Pig trod a more eclectic path. Beginning with their debut album *Ahead Rings Out* (1969), they demonstrated a willingness to sample a variety of blues styles, including country and delta blues, driving boogie, rhythm and blues–based horn arrangements, and even some jazz-colored numbers. The band's two albums sold well in the United Kingdom, but never found the same acceptance in the United States. The group disbanded in 1970, but reformed in the 1990s for a couple of albums. Abraham continues to work as a solo artist and has occasionally appeared live with Tull as a guest guitarist in recent years.

Suggested Album: Ahead Rings Out (1969)

See also: Jethro Tull

BLOOD, SWEAT & TEARS

Blood, Sweat & Tears' creative years are divisible into two parts. They debuted with *Child Is Father to the Man* (1968) under vocalist Al Kooper and with trumpeter Randy Brecker, who went on to a career in pop jazz. They enjoyed their greatest commercial success afterward with vocalist David Clayton-Thomas.

Kooper had been a member of the Blues Project and gained notoriety as a sideman for Bob Dylan. His organ on "Like a Rolling Stone" (1965) was one of the era's sonic touchstones. Inspired by the horn-driven pop productions of James William Guercio, who had worked with the Buckinghams and would graduate to Chicago, and the arrangements of the Maynard Ferguson Orchestra, BS&T was part of the brass-heavy jazz-rock trend that emerged by the end of the 1960s. *Child Is Father to the Man* included the psychedelically tinged "I Can't Quit Her" and the blues-drenched "I Love You More Than You'll Ever Know," staples on FM rock radio.

After Kooper was forced out, the bellowing Clayton-Thomas took the helm and led BS&T through a string of hits, including "You've Made Me So Very Happy" (1969), "Spinning Wheel" (1969), "And When I Die" (1969), "Hi-De-Ho" (1970), "Lucretia MacEvil" (1970), and "Go Down Gamblin'" (1971). Their appeal rested in part on the familiarity of American school bands whose arrangements they sometimes recalled in an updated fashion; in turn, BS&T's songs entered the repertoire of many marching bands. Clayton-Thomas left BS&T, returned, and exited again. The following years saw few hits but many personnel changes. A version of BS&T is still on the road performing concerts.

Suggested Album: Child Is Father to the Man (1968)

See also: Kooper, Al

BLOOMFIELD, MIKE (1944–1981)

Guitarist Mike Bloomfield was a teenager from Chicago's affluent North Side when he began to venture regularly to the city's South Side, where he learned the blues at the feet of the masters. By 1964 he formed a band with harmonica player Charlie Musselwhite, cutting demos for Columbia Records that reveal a firmer command of the idiom than the Rolling Stones possessed at that time. The following year, Bloomfield joined the Paul Butterfield Blues Band and played guitar behind Bob Dylan at the Newport Folk Festival as the former protest singer broke with folk music purists. Bloomfield was prominent on Dylan's *Highway 61 Revisited* (1965).

In 1967 Bloomfield co-founded the Electric Flag, the first important jazz-rock horn band. He left the following year to pursue his own career. Bloomfield collaborated with Stephen Stills and Al Kooper on *Super Session* (1968) and followed with *Live Adventures of Mike Bloomfield and Al Kooper* (1968). He recorded a notable album of expressive blues guitar under his own name, *It's Not Killing Me* (1969), with Electric Flag's Nick Gravenites as producer and vocalist.

Although considered one of American rock's great blues guitarists, he made limited inroads with the general public. Bloomfield continued to record prolifically during the 1970s, including an album with John Hammond Jr. and Dr. John, *Triumvirate* (1973). He also contributed to soundtracks for *Medium Cool* (1969), *Steelyard Blues* (1973), and *Andy Warhol's Bad* (1977). His death in 1981 was probably an accidental overdose. Bloomfield was inducted into the Rock and Roll Hall of Fame.

Suggested Albums: Super Session (1968); *Live Adventures of Mike Bloomfield and Al Kooper* (1968); *It's Not Killing Me* (1969); *Triumvirate* (1973)

See also: Electric Flag; Kooper, Al

BLUE CHEER

Blue Cheer was among the earliest bands to forge blues-rock into heavy metal. Aspiring to become the next Jimi Hendrix Experience, the California power trio fell short except for shearing, ear-splitting volume. Blue Cheer crashed the sonic barrier, testing the mettle of the newly introduced Marshall amplifiers that became the standard for loud and heavy rock acts. Their creative limitations were evident on their debut album, *Vincebus Eruptum* (1968). Half the songs were covers and half were undistinguished originals. However, two of the covers were interesting. Blue Cheer's rendition of Eddie Cochran's "Summertime Blues" cleverly reconceived the rockabilly tune for the youth of a less innocent time. Their take on "Parchman Farm," written by droll white Southern jazzman Mose Allison, set a precedent for the Who's heavy cover of Allison's "Young Man Blues." The original Blue Cheer broke up in 1972, but various lineups continued to use the name.

Suggested Album: Vincebus Eruptum (1968)

BLUE OYSTER CULT

Evolving out of several psychedelic groups in the late 1960s and working their way out of Long Island biker bars, Blue Oyster Cult was cut from the leathery tough sound and image of Steppenwolf. By the time of their eponymous debut LP (1972), they developed a mysterious image, complete with a cryptic hooked-cross symbol suggesting a forgotten fascist movement from a secondary nation. Their use of umlauts introduced a Teutonic touch to heavy metal that would be magnified by Motorhead and other bands.

Guitarist Donald "Buck Dharma" Roeser, whose playing was fluid and expressive yet pyrotechnic, drove BOC's music. Rock critic Richard Meltzer, a philosophy major who authored *The Aesthetics of Rock* (1970), was one of the band's lyricists. Their songs combined intelligence, power, and intimations of darkness. They were also capable of transforming apocalyptic anxiety into the entertainingly cartoonish "Cities on Flame with Rock and Roll," a hyperbolic number from their first album that dominated live shows for many years.

By *Tyranny and Mutation* (1973), BOC had sharpened its approach to a hard edge through incessant touring. By this time keyboardist Allen Lanier had acquired a poet for a girlfriend, the aspiring rock star Patti Smith, who contributed lyrics. With song titles such as "Career of Evil," "Subhuman," and "Harvester of Eyes," *Secret Treaties* (1974) was a loose concept album of horrific themes. Meltzer and Smith returned as lyricists. BOC finally rose from cult status on the FM airplay garnered by their sardonically titled live album, *On Your Feet or On Your Knees* (1975).

BOC achieved a commercial breakout with an unlikely hit from *Agents of Fortune* (1976), "(Don't Fear) the Reaper." With spine-tingling timbres suggesting the Byrds more than the band's usual hard rock, "Reaper's" evocation of the calm inevitability of death suggested Ingmar Bergman's *Seventh Seal* retold in four minutes. Smith was heard on *Agents of Fortune*, lending whispery vampiric vocals to the enigmatic "The Revenge of Vera Gemini." *Agents* was a sonic triumph for BOC's producer-manager and sometime lyricist, Sandy Pearlman.

Succeeding BOC albums saw their sales fall, rise, and fall again like Wall Street in uncertain times. They continued to work with Meltzer and Smith and added another notable lyricist, British science fiction–fantasy writer Michael Moorcock. The band scored a Top 40 hit with the new wave–like "Burnin' for You" from *Fire of Unknown Origin* (1981), but underwent personnel changes and intraband acrimony. BOC was eclipsed in the 1980s by new generations of heavy metal acts. However, they set the tone for bands such as Metallica, whose "Enter Sandman" and "Master of Puppets" were indebted to BOC's subtle malice. Their influence can also be measured in the large number of BOC cover versions by punk, metal, and alternative rock bands.

Suggested Albums: Blue Oyster Cult (1972); *Tyranny and Mutation* (1973); *Secret Treaties* (1974); *On Your Feet or On Your Knees* (1975); *Agents of Fortune* (1976); *Fire of Unknown Origin* (1981)

BLUES

The blues began as an African American vernacular music that emerged in the rural poverty of the American South by the start of the 20th century. It had roots in the work songs of slaves and sharecroppers. Although memories of Africa were audible, blues was born from encounters with European American songwriting. Largely the product of a preliterate society, blues songs belonged to a folk culture, a common well from which performers freely drew.

The blues flourished in Mississippi, whose black population lived precariously in the face of floods, famine, and virulent racism. Blues singers transmuted calamity into cathartic entertainment at Saturday night dances. The most enduring figure that rose from Mississippi Delta blues, Robert Johnson, played guitar with such uncanny acumen that Faustian legends grew. According to a popular account, he sold his soul to Satan in exchange for his talent. Although death claimed him soon enough, Johnson recorded a batch of songs in 1936 and 1937 whose reissue on the LP *King of the Delta Blues Singers* (1961) turned the heads of a generation of British rock guitarists. Upon hearing the album, Keith Richards is said to have thought he was listening to a guitar duo and was astonished to learn that it was the work of a lone player. The Rolling Stones and Cream covered Johnson's "Love in Vain" and "Crossroads Blues."

With the large northward migration of African Americans came the founding of a thriving black community and blues scene on Chicago's South Side. Chief among the musical migrants was Muddy Waters, who embraced electric guitar in response to the louder urban environment and played with a full band whose lineup, including a jazz drum kit and a bass, set the precedent for rock bands. The Rolling Stones took their name from his song "Rollin' Stone." During the 1940s, urban African American music split onto two tracks, blues played with electric guitars but rooted in the Southern experience and the more urbane jazz-inspired rhythm and blues, which continued to evolve over the decades into soul music and funk. Chess Records became the prominent purveyor of electric blues, and its South Side Chicago studio became a pilgrimage point for rock musicians in the 1960s.

Blues had long been an undercurrent in jazz and was one of the foundational elements of rock and roll. Elvis Presley's debut recording, "That's All Right" (1954), was a cover of Chicago bluesman Arthur Crudup. However, the first generation of white American rock fans, at least outside of the South, had little if any awareness of the blues. The situation was different in the United Kingdom where connoisseurship of American music had been cultivated since the Jazz Age. Most of the musicians associated with the 1960s British Invasion had been exposed to blues recordings. Extolling their roots, the Rolling Stones and like-minded bands exposed many white Americans to music that was still flourishing within a few miles of their homes. Blues-rock, which described bands that transposed Chicago electric blues into more aggressive rhythms and amplification, fed the birth of heavy metal. Jimi Hendrix was unique as an African American blues guitarist who achieved stardom fronting a British band; his music was recognizably blues based

BLUES MAGOOS

but was indebted to funkier contemporary sources and the quest for psychedelic experience.

Blues became the common source for many rock bands by the end of the 1960s and was considered a touchstone of authenticity for rock musicians at a time when young African American audiences had largely rejected blues in favor of the ostensibly more liberated, certainly more contemporary sound of soul music. As blacks sought to leave behind the culture undergirding the blues, many whites raced to embrace elements of that culture as an exotic, emotionally alive world of experience.

BLUES MAGOOS

The Blues Magoos began in 1964 as folk-rockers in the Lovin' Spoonful manner, but the New York band's sound darkened under the organ-powered spell of the Animals. Their debut, *Psychedelic Lollipop* (1966), reached the Top 20 and included a hit single, "We Ain't Got Nothin' Yet." The album's title was one of rock's earliest explicit references to psychedelia. The doomy sadness of the music was a bridge between blues, garage punk, and the edgy excursions of acid rock. The Blues Magoos' more calculatedly psychedelic follow-up, *Electric Comic Book* (1967), also sold well, but the band was soon torn by internal disputes and fell under the leadership of their singer, Peppy Castro. After the final lineup disbanded in 1969, Castro joined the cast of the rock musical *Hair*. During the 1970s he recorded with Barnaby Bye and Wiggy Bits and scored a pair of hits in the 1980s with Balance.

Suggested Album: Psychedelic Lollipop (1966)

BLUES PROJECT

Despite a name suggesting fieldwork by musicology students, the Blues Project was anything but dry or academic. They were a great American blues-rock band, musically talented and with a dangerously cool image, forecasting the droogs from Stanley Kubrick's *A Clockwork Orange*. Co-founder Danny Kalb had been a Greenwich Village denizen during the early 1960s folk-blues revival. He contributed to a compilation album called *The Blues Project* (1964). Kalb borrowed the name a year later when he launched his band, which jelled around the lineup of guitarist Steve Katz from the Even Dozen Jug Band, drummer Roy Blumenfeld, English-sounding vocalist Tommy Flanders, session keyboardist Al Kooper, and bassist Andy Kulberg, who doubled on flute.

Their debut, a collection of furiously performed blues covers, *Live at the Café Au Go Go* (1966), captured the raw excitement of young musicians bursting out of the folk scene and into rock. Katz had never played electric guitar before joining the band, and the thrill of accelerating toward new horizons is palpable. Flanders's departure from the group spoiled MGM's plans to market them as America's Rolling Stones, yet they progressed musically without him.

Projections (1967) featured original songs by Kooper and Katz that pushed toward psychedelia within supple soulful grooves. Never blues purists, the Blues Project could slip into Renaissance folk music and cool jazz before bounding back into supercharged blues. They continued to fill their sets with covers, including a long noir rendition of Muddy Waters's "Two Trains Running."

Never attaining a large audience beyond the East Coast, the Blues Project disbanded by the end of 1967 with Kooper moving on to Blood, Sweat & Tears and Kulberg and Blumenfeld forming Seatrain. The Blues Project reunited several times with various lineups during the 1970s.

Suggested Albums: Live at the Café Au Go Go (1966); *Projections* (1967); *Live at Town Hall* (1967)

See also: Kooper, Al

BOND, GRAHAM (1937–1974)

Graham Bond was a singular talent who worked with exemplary musicians from the classic rock era. Surfacing from Britain's New Orleans–oriented "trad jazz" scene of the 1950s, the multi-instrumentalist, accomplished on alto saxophone and piano, veered toward bebop by 1960. In 1962 he switched to Hammond organ as his principal instrument and joined Alexis Korner's influential Blues Incorporated, the band that was the seedbed for British blues-rock. Within a year he left Korner and took Blues Incorporated's rhythm section, drummer Ginger Baker and bassist Jack Bruce, forming the Graham Bond Organisation. Guitarist John McLaughlin, a leading figure in jazz-rock fusion during the 1970s, was briefly a member.

The Organisation's two albums, *The Sound of '65* (1965) and *There's a Bond Between Us* (1965), represented a distinct convergence of blues, rhythm and blues, and jazz with Near Eastern modes and exotic rhythms. Baker's exceptional drumming propelled the gritty music led by Bond's full-throated vocals. On his second album, Bond became the first rock musician to employ the mellotron, an orchestral-emulating instrument popularized before the end of the 1960s by the Moody Blues and King Crimson.

After Baker and Bruce departed to form Cream with Eric Clapton, Bond played with the Dutch psychedelic art collective–musical group the Fool. He founded Graham Bond's Initiation, a band whose name gave indication of his growing fascination with occultist Aleister Crowley. While performing with the freewheeling lineup of Ginger Baker's Air Force, he made a remarkable album, *Holy Magick* (1970). Recorded with the musicians arranged in set order on a pentagram painted on the studio floor, Holy Magick was a unique marriage of late John Coltrane with rock. It was also a Crowleyan ritual invocation of archangels and other entities.

Bond's final years were erratic and included arrests for illegal drugs and other charges, and a short court-imposed stint at a mental institution, as well as several short-lived musical collaborations. He was found dead in 1974, crushed under the wheels of a London subway train. Deep Purple's organist Jon Lord cited Bond's Hammond organ playing as an influence.

Suggested Albums: The Sound of '65 (1965); *There's a Bond Between Us* (1965); *Holy Magick* (1970)

See also: Baker, Ginger; Bruce, Jack

BOWIE, DAVID (1947–2016)

David Bowie began a lifetime of transformation when he shed his given name, David Jones. But unlike such Golden Age Hollywood figures as Hedy Lamarr or Cary Grant, whose name changes were tailored to a particular persona, Bowie adopted a series of personae. He resembled a multitalented actor switching from role to role, while his music passed through distinct periods much like the work of the early 20th-century modern artists he admired. One of his best-known songs, "Changes," became a summation of his career. Unlike most recording artists who came of age in the 1970s, Bowie was seldom content to repeat himself; he was a star more interested in surprising fans than fulfilling their expectations. From 1970 through 1983, Bowie showed an intuitive grasp of emerging trends and a willingness to seize them.

Bowie first surfaced as part of the mod movement, a British youth subculture of the mid-1960s that stressed sharp style and the importance of appearance. For Bowie, style became inseparable from content. Theater was integral to his act; he lived out his rock star roles and sought acceptance as a legitimate actor. Bowie starred as an alien not unlike himself in Nicolas Roeg's film *The Man Who Fell to Earth* (1976) and won over skeptical critics playing John Merrick in the American National Theatre production of *The Elephant Man* (1980). He went on to star in other films during the 1980s. As with many of the era's most creative British rock musicians, he attended art school, but unlike most, he became a credible visual artist. Unique among rock singers of his era, Bowie's vocals were seldom indebted to blues or rhythm and blues but echoed the era of the crooners. He was a comfortable guest on Bing Crosby's Christmas television special (1977).

Bowie released a number of inconsequential recordings before touching stardom in 1969 with "Space Oddity," a downbeat narrative of space flight released as NASA prepared for its triumphant moon landing. Wrapped in Gustav Holst–style orchestration, contrasting the immensity of the cosmos with the insignificance of a lone astronaut, "Space Oddity" came from his self-titled album. The songs were poetic, emotionally vulnerable folk-rock redolent of the 1960s counterculture.

The shrill blast of feedback opening *The Man Who Sold the World* (1970) dispelled the mood of its predecessor. For Bowie, the hippie dream was already over. In "All the Madmen," insanity is a rational alternative to contemporary reality; in "Running Gun Blues," a soldier continues fighting after peace is declared. The foreboding present was bracketed by the dystopian future of "The Savior Machine" (à la Ray Bradbury) and the dystopian past of "The Supermen" (H. P. Lovecraft). Bowie was backed by a power trio led by guitarist Mick Ronson, an acolyte of Jeff

Beck who pushed blues-rock into the red zone even as the music suggested Béla Bartók, Dave Brubeck, and Richard Wagner. Although producing no hit single, *The Man Who Sold the World* continued to stir imaginations years afterward. Nirvana included the title number in its repertoire.

Hunky Dory (1971) veered into the eclectic. The hit "Changes" meditated on time's passage in a nightclub arrangement Tony Bennett might have appreciated. Much of *Hunky Dory* was devoted to acknowledging Bowie's influences, including the self-explanatory "Andy Warhol," the country rock "Song for Bob Dylan," and "Queen Bitch's" evocation of the Velvet Underground. Other songs, sounding like show tunes for an unwritten musical, were preoccupied with Aleister Crowley and theories of a coming race that soon would supplant *Homo sapiens*.

Afterward, Bowie became the brightest figure in glitter rock. With *The Rise and Fall of Ziggy Stardust and The Spiders from Mars* (1972), he reinvented himself as a fictitious rock star with androgynous hair, wardrobe, and makeup. His emergence as Ziggy coincided with his public pronouncement of bisexuality. Acting as arranger, Ronson played guitar and keyboards throughout, anchoring the album's commentary on stardom (suffused as usual with science fiction) in solid music.

The Spiders from Mars continued to back Bowie on *Aladdin Sane* (1973), bringing surprise to every track. The album includes some of Bowie's most familiar songs. "Panic in Detroit," a remarkable impression of anxiety from a time of leftist terrorism, builds from a Bo Diddley beat accompanied by salsa percussion, Ronson's razor-sharp guitar, and a pair of soulful background singers wailing in terror. The blues-rock of "The Jean Genie" supports slithering images of decadence. On his cover of the Rolling Stones' "Let's Spend the Night Together," Bowie burns away the feigned innocence of the original. The album draws from sources as varied as doo-wop ("The Prettiest Star"), Kurt Weill ("Time"), and McCoy Tyner ("Aladdin Sane").

Announcing the breakup of the Spiders from Mars, Bowie bought time before recording new music by releasing an album that was both a stopgap and a labor of love. *Pinups* (1973) featured songs by bands Bowie admired in his youth, including a melodramatic reading of Them's "Here Comes the Night" and a deliciously fey version of the Merseys' "Sorrow."

Diamond Dogs (1974) was a dystopian concept album, a vision of glitter rock amidst the postapocalyptic rubble of New York City with more than a few nods to George Orwell. The orchestrated paranoia of "1984" was a holdover from Bowie's aborted plans to stage a musical based on Orwell's novel. The album's hit, the celebratory androgyny of "Rebel Rebel," became Bowie's farewell to glam. Once again, he would turn dramatically in a new direction.

Moving to the United States, Bowie was enamored of the slick Philadelphia soul music produced by hitmakers Kenny Gamble and Leon Huff. This was the moment when Hall & Oates and the Bee Gees also embraced contemporary pop soul, and even Elton John responded with "Philadelphia Freedom." Bowie recorded *Young Americans* (1975) at Gamble and Huff's Sigma Sound studio, enveloping his crooner's voice in a soulful chorale led by Luther Vandross. John Lennon stopped by the session and co-wrote the funky "Fame" based on a James Brown riff. Bowie attracted enough attention to be invited onto television's *Soul Train*, a rare gift for a white entertainer. "Fame" would later be sampled by acts ranging from Vanilla Ice to Lady Gaga.

Bowie emerged the following year as the Thin White Duke, a fastidiously dressed embodiment of lonesome power and cocaine addiction. He portrayed the new character on his next album, *Station to Station* (1976). Aside from the playful "TVC 15" and the future nostalgia of "Golden Years" (culminating in a whistle à la Bing Crosby), the mood of *Station to Station* was saturated in dark romance and unease. The music was a distinctly European style of soul bleached of African American influences.

Aware that he was slipping into an abyss, Bowie retreated from the American limelight and the rock star high life. He rented a flat above an auto repair garage in an unfashionable neighborhood of West Berlin, still a precarious enclave hemmed by the Iron Curtain and the Berlin Wall. Collaborating with Brian Eno, Bowie recorded a trilogy of albums, *Low* (1977), *Heroes* (1977), and *Lodger* (1979), which stunned the mainstream audience for their lack of reliance on the familiar tropes of rock, pop, or soul. However, listeners to Kraftwerk, Neu, and other German electronic bands recognized many sources for the Berlin Trilogy. Eno's songwriting strategies, which harkened to the I Ching rather than the Brill Building or the Beatles, also opened new doors in Bowie's imagination. Iggy Pop sang on *Low*; his presence led to a pair of Bowie-produced albums in the Berlin style, *The Idiot* (1977) and *Lust for Life* (1977).

As Bowie caught his breath on Scary *Monsters . . . And Super Creeps* (1980), the rock world caught up with him. Gary Numan, Joy Division, Human League, and a host of British techno-pop or synth-driven rock bands had emerged over the previous two years from the whirlwind of punk rock, but took their music from the Berlin Trilogy rather than the Sex Pistols. Bowie put his cinematic interests to work, staging "Fashion," "Ashes to Ashes" and other *Scary Monsters* songs as music videos. A year later, MTV debuted, pushing the medium to the center of the music industry.

Sensing a new mood in the wider culture, Bowie changed again, returning as the suit-and-tie singer of *Let's Dance* (1983). Co-produced by Nile Rodgers, the creative mind behind one of the disco era's most imaginative groups, Chic, *Let's Dance* was an irresistibly romantic and pointedly conservative album drawn from elements of Motown and the nascent sounds emerging postdisco from dance clubs in the world's great cities. *Let's Dance* repositioned Bowie in the pop mainstream.

It would be his final triumph for several years. Suddenly devoid of inspiration, Bowie dismissed his later 1980s albums as his "Phil Collins period." Realizing his creativity had ebbed, Bowie withdrew from the spotlight once again, this time by becoming a member of Tin Machine, a credible hard rock band that released two albums (1989, 1991). Reuniting with Rodgers, Bowie returned as a solo act with *Black Tie White Noise* (1993) and with Eno for *Outside* (1995) and experimented with electronic and industrial sounds. *Earthling* (1997) yielded "I'm Afraid of Americans," mixed by Nine Inch Nails' Trent Reznor. He continued to record and

David Bowie continually reinvented his music and persona over a career that stretched from the late 1960s through his death in 2016. Like the modern artists he admired, Bowie equated stasis with stagnation and sought new ways to express himself sonically and visually. (Photofest)

tour into the early 21st century, with his pace slowing in 2004 from health problems. He enjoyed a creative resurgence with *The Next Day* (2013), an album that conjured ghosts from his Berlin period, and melded his past with the present on *Black Star* (2016), an album recorded with young jazz–hip-hop fusion musicians. He died of cancer two days after its release.

Along with popularizing or embodying several trends and setting a high bar for artistic and commercial achievement, Bowie was an influential force in culture during the 1970s. Although he later proclaimed his heterosexuality in a *Rolling Stone* interview, Bowie's Ziggy Stardust character was widely embraced by LGBT youth at a time when "gay rights" remained precarious. Bowie also exposed a young generation of fans to cultural currents beyond the usual references of rock musicians through his interest in Weimar Berlin, Surrealism, and the possibility that new art could still shock the public into awareness.

Suggested Albums: David Bowie (aka *Space Oddity*) (1969); *The Man Who Sold the World* (1970); *Hunky Dory* (1971); *The Rise and Fall of Ziggy Stardust and the Spiders from Mars* (1972); *Aladdin Sane* (1973); *Pinups* (1973); *Diamond Dogs* (1974); *Young Americans* (1975); *Station to Station* (1976); *Low* (1977); *Heroes* (1977);

Lodger (1979); *Scary Monsters . . . And Super Creeps* (1980); *Let's Dance* (1983); *Earthling* (1997); *The Next Day* (2013); *Black Star* (2016)

BREWER AND SHIPLEY

Coming from a folk background, Mike Brewer and Tom Shipley met as songwriters in Los Angeles during the late 1960s. A&M Records released an album of their demos without their consent, *Down in L.A.* (1968). Their best songs were included on a pair of albums produced by the Electric Flag's Nick Gravenites, *Weeds* (1969) and *Tarkio* (1970). Their métier was mid-tempo country rock with thoughtful lyrics steeped in countercultural ethos and sung in close harmony. "One Toke over the Line" from *Tarkio* was a Top 10 hit despite its marijuana reference. The duo continued to record but with waning inspiration and diminished sales.

Suggested Albums: Weeds (1969); *Tarkio* (1970)

BRITISH INVASION

The Beatles' triumphant entry into the United States in 1964 led to an avalanche of young British acts releasing records in America in the mid-1960s, as the music industry sought to capitalize on the Fab Four's runaway success. The Dave Clark Five, Peter and Gordon, Gerry and the Pacemakers, and Petula Clark were in the vanguard of the British Invasion of young British performers that dominated the U.S. charts by 1965. Some simply emulated the Beatles' look and sound, while more distinct acts such as the Rolling Stones, the Kinks, and the Who brought breadth and depth to the movement. The phenomenon was not confined to North America. The Beatles' tours took them as far away as the Philippines, and even in Franco's Spain, British rock recordings were issued by their labels' Spanish subsidiaries. Rock bands sporting two guitars, bass, drums, and Beatles haircuts sprang up in Japan, Indochina, South Korea, Australia, Latin America, and Western Europe.

Many factors coalesced to create the stunning phenomenon that was the British Invasion. The post–World War II baby boom hit the United Kingdom as well as the United States, creating a large generational cohort of British youths bored with the big bands and tame pop favored by their parents. Unencumbered by much of the racial bigotry pervasive in the United States, many young British musicians embraced American blues, providing a significant influence on the direction of the British Invasion. Some musicians swept up by the British Invasion emerged from the United Kingdom's "traditional jazz" scene, which emulated American jazz from before the swing era, or learned their instruments playing skiffle, a British movement based on American folk music. The vitality of American vernacular music was striking to young people growing up after a harsh war that had ruined Britain's economy and diminished its imperial ambition.

The United Kingdom's geographical confinement led to a proximity of similarly minded musicians, creating a musically creative cross-pollination that blossomed into a crop of energetic bands. Musicians such as John Lennon, Pete Townshend, and Ray Davies attended the new art schools founded by British educational reformers and applied aesthetic concepts to their music. Some bands became an aural analogue to pop art.

For the British Invasion's American fans, the Englishness of the musicians was pleasantly exotic, a contrast to the crew-cut preppiness of much American pop music but not formidably alien. Within weeks of the Beatles' apparition on Ed Sullivan, U.S. rock bands began growing their hair and emulating the sounds of Britain. In the wake of the British Invasion, young Americans formed garage bands emulating the new music, and a generation of white musicians discovered black blues through the Rolling Stones and other U.K. bands, even though they often lived within a few miles of the great living musicians that influenced the Stones.

The British Invasion is usually thought to have died down by the end of 1966 but the reverberations continued for many years. Throughout the classic rock era, British rock stars possessed a cool factor lacked by their peers in the United States and elsewhere. Even America's rebels struck an Anglophile pose. Through most of the first Ramones album (1976), vocalist Joey Ramone maintained a British accent despite his Queens, New York, origins.

BROWN, ARTHUR (1942–)

Although Arthur Brown had only one hit, "Fire" (1968), his stage show became the basis for Alice Cooper and every shock rock act that followed. He was seldom heavy or metallic, but his quasi-operatic singing was the precursor for many heavy metal vocalists.

Brown came out of the 1960s London blues and rhythm and blues scene and had a background in theater. Those influences were evident on his debut album, *The Crazy World of Arthur Brown* (1968), transmogrified by the spirit of the era and infused with hints of the progressive rock path his music would soon follow. Aside from "Fire," the album's key track was his cover of Screamin' Jay Hawkins's maniacal voodoo rhythm and blues number "I Put a Spell on You." In concert, Brown braved injury by being lowered onto the stage wearing a flame-throwing helmet. He wore outrageous makeup and pushed rock in a theatrical direction.

Brown's inclination toward grandiosity, already audible on his debut, was given free rein on a trio of progressive rock albums released under the name Arthur Brown's Kingdom Come (1971–1973). His most notable accomplishments in the 1970s were his contributions to other people's projects. He played the Priest in a memorable scene from director Ken Russell's film adaptation of *Tommy* (1975) and added a needed dose of insanity to the Alan Parsons Project's Edgar Allan Poe album, *Tales of Mystery and Imagination* (1976).

In the 1980s Brown moved to Austin, Texas, and earned a degree in counseling. In 1992 he co-founded Healing Songs Therapy, in which Brown wrote songs as part of the treatment program for his clients. After returning to the United Kingdom in 1996, Brown continued to record solo albums and appeared as guest vocalist on Hawkwind's *Take Me to Your Leader* (2005).

Suggested Album: The Crazy World of Arthur Brown (1968)

BROWNE, JACKSON (1948-)

Although he became linked to the Los Angeles music scene of the 1970s, Jackson Browne emerged during the 1960s in New York, where he worked as a songwriter for Elektra Records, played guitar with Tim Buckley, and frequented Andy Warhol's Factory. He backed his girlfriend, Velvet Underground chanteuse Nico, on her first solo album (1968). Afterward, he returned to Southern California, where Tom Rush and other artists recorded his songs. The Eagles' version of a song he co-wrote with Glenn Frey, "Take It Easy" (1972), became Browne's first hit. During that time he established himself touring as an opening act for such Los Angeles friends as Joni Mitchell and the Eagles, setting the stage for a solo career. His eponymous debut album (1972) netted a hit single, "Doctor My Eyes."

Browne's lyrics and music often suggested disappointment following the idealism of the 1960s. The title song from *Running on Empty* (1977), an album of new material recorded in concert, summed up Browne's anxiety that the best years had already passed. Confessional and occasionally self-absorbed, Browne was among the most successful of the 1970s singer-songwriters ensconced in Los Angeles. He reached platinum with *The Pretender* (1976). *Running on Empty* yielded a hit with a cover of Maurice Williams and the Zodiacs' doo-wop number "Stay."

Although inextricably associated with the pre-punk 1970s, he enjoyed some hits afterward, including the laconically delivered pop song "Somebody's Baby" (1982) and a misguided effort at emulating Bruce Springsteen, "You're a Friend of Mine" (1985), sung with Springsteen's saxophonist Clarence Clemons. Browne became prominent in the antinuclear movement and other activist causes and produced Warren Zevon. A talented writer but a bland performer, Browne's songs were often more remarkable when covered by others. Nico transmuted his despondent "These Days" into winsome chamber pop and the Eagles elevated the laconic "Take It Easy" into an anthem. Had he chosen to, Jerry Lee Lewis could have turned "Redneck Friend" from Browne's first album into a killer. Browne has been inducted into the Rock and Roll Hall of Fame.

Suggested Albums: Jackson Browne (1972); *For Everyman* (1973); *Running on Empty* (1977)

BRUCE, JACK (1943-2014)

One of rock music's most formidable bassists, Jack Bruce earned a scholarship to the Royal Scottish Academy of Music and Drama. Forced to leave when the school disapproved of him playing in jazz combos, he joined the Murray Campbell Big Band before moving to London in 1962 where he enlisted in Alexis Korner's seminal Blues Incorporated. He departed a year later with organist Graham Bond and drummer Ginger Baker to form the Graham Bond Organisation with guitarist John McLaughlin. In 1965 he joined John Mayall's Bluesbreakers whose lineup included guitarist Eric Clapton. He moved on again, playing on Manfred Mann's hit "Pretty Flamingo" (1966). Later that year, Bruce co-founded one of the late 1960s' most influential bands, Cream, with Baker and Clapton. The original rock power trio lasted into 1969.

Bruce began his solo career with *Songs for a Tailor* (1969). Following the trajectory of his contributions to Cream, Baker continued to write harmonically ambitious, jazz-influenced rock with lyricist Peter Brown, singing the surreal words in an urgent tenor and playing bass as a lead instrument. One of the album's songs, "Theme for an Imaginary Western," became a staple in the repertoire of American hard rock band Mountain.

Bruce carried on in the same direction with *Harmony Row* (1971) and *Out of the Storm* (1974), but his restless ambition could not be contained within that format. Bruce regrouped with McLaughlin in the pioneering jazz-rock fusion band Tony Williams Lifetime for one album, *Turn It Over* (1970), and collaborated with McLaughlin on a jazz jam released as *Things We Like* (1970). Bruce never achieved great commercial success as a soloist, but was always in demand as a bassist. He played on a remarkable array of albums, including *Escalator over the Hill* (1972) by free jazz composer Carla Bley, Lou Reed's *Berlin* (1973), and Frank Zappa's *Apostrophe* (1974). He released three albums with the power trio West, Bruce and Laing (1972–1973) and toured with ex–Rolling Stone guitarist Mick Taylor as the Jack Bruce Band (1975).

In the early 1980s Bruce performed as Jack Bruce & Friends with jazz drummer Billy Cobham, ex–Humble Pie guitarist Clem Clempson, and a former member of Bruce Springsteen's band, pianist David Sancious. Afterward, he joined Rolling Stones pianist Ian Stewart in the roots rhythm and blues band Rocket 88 and formed a power trio with guitarist Robin Trower, releasing *BLT* (1981) and *Truce* (1982). The prolific Bruce also recorded with Soft Machine and Anton Fier's Golden Palominos and released a half dozen albums with Afro-Cuban jazz producer Kip Hanrahan. In 1989 he reunited with Baker for a tour and an album, *A Question of Time*. While busy with projects that genuinely interested him, Bruce also spent much of the 1980s chasing trends, flirting with disco, synth pop, and pop soul.

Although slowing down from declining health, Bruce performed in jazz and power trio settings during the 1990s and toured as a member of Ringo Starr's All-Starr Band. He participated in Cream's brief reunion (2005), recorded with jazz saxophonist Courtney Pine. Bruce died of liver disease in 2014 shortly after the release of *Silver Rails*, which featured Trower and Roxy Music's Phil Manzanera on guitar.

Suggested Albums: Songs for a Tailor (1969); *Things We Like* (1970); *Harmony Row* (1971); *Out of the Storm* (1974); *How's Tricks* (1977); *More Jack Than God* (2003); *Silver Rails* (2014)

See also: Baker, Ginger; Bond, Graham; Clapton, Eric; Cream

BUBBLEGUM

A prevailing trend in the history of rock has been the industry's efforts to tame the music's more rebellious instincts with artists who are easier to market and control. The bubblegum music that emerged in the late 1960s was one of the industry's most successful attempts to clean up rock. Just as 10 years earlier the industry looked to replace the reckless abandon of Little Richard and the menacing sexuality of Elvis Presley with the more polite Pat Boone and better behaved Frankie Avalon, the record labels used bubblegum to kick back against late 1960s rock with a more "acceptable" sound.

Producer Don Kirshner is crucial to bubblegum's development. In 1966, he attempted to manufacture a more acceptable version of the Beatles for network television, the Monkees, but the group mutinied and took charge of their creative destiny. In 1968, frustrated with live musicians, Kirshner debuted the Archies, a fictional recording act featured in an animated television cartoon whose records cracked the hit parade soon enough. Bubblegum featured bright, simple pop melodies, upbeat tempos, sugary arrangements, and inoffensive lyrics. The songs were hook laden, and manufactured acts such as the 1910 Fruitgum Company, the Partridge Family, and the Ohio Express dominated the charts. While bubblegum's music lacked even the pretense of substance and was intentionally disposable, there is no denying that songs such as the Archies' "Sugar, Sugar" (1969) and Tommy James's "I Think We're Alone Now" (1967) were well-written, catchy pop tunes.

Bubblegum waned by the mid-1970s. However, as more recent performers such as Justin Bieber and Miley Cyrus have demonstrated, the spirit if not the sound of bubblegum has never truly disappeared from the airwaves.

BUCHANAN, ROY (1939–1988)

Roy Buchanan is rarely mentioned with rock's legendary guitar heroes. However, his powerful, melodically inventive, roots-oriented playing demonstrates the truth in the title of one of his posthumous albums, *The World's Greatest Unknown Guitarist*. The Arkansas-born Buchanan's recording career began in the early 1960s and picked up steam in 1971 with a much-praised PBS television documentary, *Introducing Roy Buchanan*, which brought his guitar mastery to a wide audience and led to two gold records.

While Buchanan is often labeled as a blues guitarist, he was equally adept at country guitar and rhythm and blues. Regardless of the style, Buchanan demonstrated a mastery of harmonics and stinging string bends that brought emotional depth and power to his playing. A possibly apocryphal story of Jimi Hendrix shying away from a guitar showdown with Buchanan is testimony to the legend surrounding his guitar genius. Buchanan died in 1988, but his career has been extended thanks to a string of posthumous albums, affording a new generation of listeners the opportunity to appreciate a great unsung talent of the classic rock era.

Suggested Albums: Roy Buchanan (1972); *Second Album* (1973); *In the Beginning* (1974)

BUCKLEY, TIM (1947–1975)

Tim Buckley sprang from the same mid-1960s Southern California folk scene as Jackson Browne, and despite the fact that both were singer-songwriters with a penchant for intensely emotional, introspective songs, the two artists could have scarcely followed more divergent career paths. While Browne never veered far from the soft rock mainstream prevalent in the 1970s, the enigmatic Buckley never showed much interest in commercial success, as was demonstrated by a musical vision that took wild turns and unexpected shifts. Browne's path led to international superstardom, while Buckley's earned him status as a cult figure for his unique vocal style and restless creativity.

Born in Washington, D.C., Buckley grew up in Southern California where he was weaned on country music and jazz while learning to emulate the musical range of saxophone and banjo with his voice. Buckley was able to create a distinctly personal vocal style, featuring a muscular yet tremulous voice with incredible range and dynamics, capable of shifting from a gentle quaver to a powerful roar with seemingly little effort. Buckley fell in with a group of folk musicians, landing a recording contract in 1966. His first two albums, *Tim Buckley* (1966) and *Goodbye and Hello* (1967), had the familiar jangle and chime of folk-rock, yet with more complex songwriting and the somber tone common to the emerging singer-songwriter movement. The albums sold modestly, but attracted notice.

Few could have imagined the abrupt change in direction to come. Beginning with *Happy Sad* (1969) and *Blue Afternoon* (1969), Buckley experimented with jazz forms, eventually abandoning folk-rock entirely. The musical experimentation went into full overdrive with *Lorca* (1970), in which Buckley deconstructed traditional songwriting structure and melody in meandering, at times incoherent avant-garde, jazz-derived music that defied categorization. *Starsailor* (1970) continued in the same vein, albeit in a slightly more listenable manner.

As sales plummeted, Buckley again shifted gears, moving to a more accessible blend of soul and funk, with suggestive lyrics he described as "sex funk." The change of direction did little to enhance Buckley's commercial standing. His career ended with his death from a drug overdose in 1975.

While Buckley was not widely known during his life, he has come to be appreciated by a new generation of primarily folk musicians drawn to his poignant songwriting and musical individuality. Perhaps his greatest legacy lay in his son Jeff Buckley, whose well-regarded album *Grace* (1994) was a critical smash and achieved a level of commercial success far beyond that of his father. The album's best-known song, a cover of Leonard Cohen's "Hallelujah," helped make that song a modern standard. Like his father, Jeff Buckley suffered an untimely passing, drowning while swimming in the Mississippi River in 1997.

Suggested Albums: Tim Buckley (1966); *Goodbye and Hello* (1967); *Blue Afternoon* (1969); *Starsailor* (1970); *Greetings from L.A.* (1972)

BUDGIE

Budgie's story is a classic tale of a hard-rocking band whose influence penetrated far more deeply than its lack of commercial success or fame would have indicated. The group was little known, despite releasing a slew of albums in the 1970s, but those who heard them apparently listened carefully, as Budgie's influence was sufficiently strong to mark them as unsung heroes in the development of heavy metal.

Formed in Wales in 1967, Budgie released its self-titled debut album in 1971 under the direction of Black Sabbath's producer Roger Bain. The dark, ponderous riffing and distorted guitars was clearly reminiscent of Black Sabbath, although subsequent albums featured more melodic acoustic songs and complex song structures that hinted at progressive rock influences. However, the group's heavy, riff-based guitar onslaught remained the primary feature of Budgie's sound.

Budgie's albums had little commercial impact in the United Kingdom, and even less in the United States, but by the early 1980s a new wave of heavy metal bands began citing Budgie. Bands such as Iron Maiden, Van Halen, and (especially) Metallica have either listed Budgie as a significant influence, or covered the band live or on record. Budgie's primary sound is clearly a prototype for heavy metal, and while perhaps derivative at times of Black Sabbath and Led Zeppelin, was sufficiently influential for the Welsh rockers to earn at least a footnote in heavy metal history.

Suggested Albums: Budgie (1971); *Never Turn Your Back on a Friend* (1973); *In for the Kill* (1974)

BUFFALO SPRINGFIELD

Buffalo Springfield was a supergroup in retrospect. Unknowns in 1966 when the band began, two of its vocalists and guitarists, Neil Young and Stephen Stills, became stars, and a third, Richie Furay, enjoyed a long musical career afterward. Buffalo Springfield was predicated on the rise of Los Angeles as the new center of the music industry, ending the century-long dominance of New York. Its members were migrants drawn by the city's promise. Young and bassist Bruce Palmer came from Toronto; drummer Dewey Martin originated in Ottawa; and the peripatetic Stills came from a Southern military family. The band's existence and name resulted from synchronicities, especially an apparently chance encounter in a Los Angeles traffic jam. Stills and Furay, in a white van, met Young and Palmer, driving a black hearse, and, recognizing kindred spirits, began waving and gesturing to each other across the congested street. Repairing to a supermarket parking lot, they decided to become a band. Later, passing a steamroller belonging to a company called Buffalo Springfield, they decided on their vaguely old-time Americana moniker.

Although Furay contributed several songs, Young and Stills were Buffalo Springfield's yin and yang visually and creatively. Young was rigged up like a hippie while Stills, often clad in suit, tie, and Stetson hat, could pass for a Southern gentleman of the old school. They were excellent guitarists with complementary songwriting talents.

Catching the ear of Chris Hillman from the Byrds, Buffalo Springfield became regulars at LA's prominent rock club, the Whiskey a Go Go, and was signed to a major label within months. Their self-titled debut album (1966) was thin and tentative. The band's producers, dismayed by Young's warbled singing, gave Furay the lead vocals on several Young songs. Some numbers, including Young's lovely "Do I Have to Come Right Out and Say It," betrayed the Merseybeat influence of the early Beatles. Several of Stills's contributions represented an early stirring of country rock. The album's hit, Stills's "For What It's Worth," became one of the signature songs of the 1960s and continues to find its way into soundtracks for documentaries on the era. Usually considered a protest song, the lyric is oddly ambivalent and articulates, more than anything, uncertainty and unease, the simmering paranoia conveyed by Stills's remarkable lead guitar line.

Buffalo Springfield Again (1967) was their finest and most coherent album despite bickering and Young's protracted absences from the studio. Stills's songs were ambitious with sophisticated time changes and poetic lyrics. Psychedelia mingled easily with jazz on his "Everydays"; "Bluebird" was a pocket-size suite built on raga rock and concluding quietly on banjo. Young's "Mr. Soul" was like the Rolling Stones overheard through a blast of fuzz tone. His "Expecting to Fly" and "Broken Arrow" were orchestrated works arranged by Jack Nitzsche, a Phil Spector acolyte.

The eyes of Buffalo Springfield's members were focused down the road to the next stages on their individual journeys. Palmer was the first to leave, replaced by Jim Messina, who became half of the popular 1970s duo Loggins and Messina. By the release of their swansong album, *Last Time Around* (1968), the band had already broken up. Young and Stills quickly established solo careers and grouped together with David Crosby and Graham Nash. Furay founded one of country rock's early acts, Poco. Martin attempted to keep Buffalo Springfield alive with other musicians but was roundly ignored.

Suggested Albums: Buffalo Springfield (1966); *Buffalo Springfield Again* (1967); *Last Time Around* (1968)

See also: Crosby, Stills, Nash & Young; Stills, Stephen; Young, Neil

BUTTERFIELD, PAUL (1942–1987)

The Paul Butterfield Blues Band was one of the first racially integrated blues combos, formed in 1963 by Butterfield with bassist Jerome Arnold and drummer Sam Lay from Howlin' Wolf's band. Butterfield, a harmonica player of formidable ability, was among the white American pioneers who discovered electric Chicago blues and brought the music into the rock era. Joining the band early on were keyboardist Mark Naftalin and a pair of exceptional guitarists, Mike Bloomfield and Elvin Bishop. Their reputation was such that Bob Dylan used them as his backing band when he performed to a hostile crowd at the Newport Folk Festival (1965).

On their self-titled debut album (1965), the Butterfield Blues Band performed a mix of traditional numbers and originals, adding a hard rocking drive to the essence of the blues. Butterfield was a convincing blues singer; Bloomfield and Bishop's dueling guitars pulled the music into overdrive. By *East-West* (1966), the band had pushed through blues-rock into jazz and rock-accented ragas, setting a precedent for Miles Davis with their version of Cannonball Adderley's "Work Song" and the title cut, an original by Bloomfield and Nick Gravenites.

After *East-West*, Bloomfield left to co-found, with Gravenites, one of the first jazz-rock horn bands, the Electric Flag. Butterfield moved in a musically similar direction, adding a horn section for *The Resurrection of Pigboy Crabshaw* (1967) and *In My Own Dream* (1968). Among the new members was saxophonist David Sanborn, who went on to a successful crossover career in jazz-pop during the 1980s. Bishop left after *In My Own Dream*, becoming an important figure in Southern rock during the mid-1970s.

The Butterfield Blues Band played Woodstock and their memorable song from the festival, "Love March," appeared on their next album, *Keep on Movin'* (1969). The songwriting became inconsistent even before Butterfield disbanded the final lineup of his blues band in 1971. He continued to record under his own name into the 1980s and, admired for his harmonica playing, was a welcome guest on projects by artists as diverse as Muddy Waters and Levon Helms. Butterfield died of a heroin overdose in 1987.

Suggested Albums: The Paul Butterfield Blues Band (1965); *East-West* (1966); *The Resurrection of Pigboy Crabshaw* (1967); *In My Own Dream* (1968)

BYRDS

Jim McGuinn, a banjo player for the Chad Mitchell Trio, and Gene Clark, guitarist with the New Christy Minstrels, met in 1964 while performing in Los Angeles folk clubs. Impressed with the Beatles' sound and dissatisfied with their respective folk groups' commercial approach, the two musicians began exploring a merger of the lyrical intelligence of folk and the musical excitement of rock and roll. The duo joined forces with David Crosby, bassist Chris Hillman, and drummer Michael Clarke, and under the name the Jet Set, began preparing material to record.

At the urging of their manager (and after their initial misgivings), the band (now renamed the Byrds) agreed to record their version of Bob Dylan's "Mr. Tambourine Man." Producer Terry Melcher insisted on hiring studio musicians to play on the record (although the band sang all the vocals); McGuinn was the only Byrd to play on the released single version of the song. But it was McGuinn's gloriously chiming 12-string electric guitar (inspired by George Harrison in *A Hard Day's Night*) that defined the record, a smash hit that forever changed popular music. McGuinn's jangling guitar, coupled with the bright melodies of folk and the band's folk revival–inspired harmonies, laid claim to an entirely fresh sound, a true merging of folk and rock music. Later that year, Bob Dylan plugged in his guitar and went electric at the Newport Folk festival to a decidedly cool reception from the folk purists but to commercial acclaim. Folk-rock had entered the popular lexicon.

The subsequent album, *Mr. Tambourine Man* (1965), contained several other Dylan covers, leading to the unfair charge that the Byrds were mere Dylan ciphers, a claim belied by such originals as the soaring Clark-penned "I'll Feel a Whole Lot

Better," one of the album's highlights. The Ecclesiastes via Pete Seeger title cut of their second LP, *Turn, Turn, Turn* (1965), continued the band's commercial success and furthered folk-rock's social awareness. While the Byrds' sound owed much to folk, both records echo a true rock ethos. Merseybeat influences and 4/4 beats abound, blending seamlessly with the simple, unpretentious (amplified) instrumentation and melodies of folk, as well as various folk covers. Many artists followed the Byrds' path, and acts such as the Beau Brummels, Barry McGuire, Love, and Buffalo Springfield were direct descendants that enjoyed commercial success.

However, the Byrds did not stay long strictly in the realm of folk-rock. The growing counterculture with its emphasis on mind-expanding drugs influenced the group. *Fifth Dimension* (1966) reflected those changes. More musically experimental, the album reflected the band's diverse tastes with hints of jazz, psychedelia, and more ambiguous musical and lyrical themes. The most prominent track, the single "Eight Miles High," was written about the band's first tour of the United Kingdom. Infused with elements of John Coltrane, raga music, folk, and likely references to drug use, "Eight Miles High" proved to be one of the most groundbreaking songs of the 1960s, a watershed in the development of what became known as psychedelic rock.

The Byrds' musical development continued on subsequent albums. By 1967 major changes were on the horizon after two of the Byrds' songwriters, Clark and Crosby, left the band. The Byrds needed new creative blood, and it was supplied by Gram Parsons. Formerly of the International Submarine Band, Parsons had a deep, genuine love of country music. At the suggestion of fellow country enthusiast Hillman, he joined the Byrds. Parsons's influence was evident on *Sweethearts of the Rodeo* (1968), which represented one of the most unexpected changes of musical direction in rock history. Recorded in Nashville, *Sweethearts* was an attempt at full-blown country music replete with steel guitar, fiddles, and mandolin. The band did not shed all rock influences, and yet another term, "country rock," was born.

Sweethearts of the Rodeo had a profound influence on the course of rock music, representing a turn away from the drug haze and rebellion of psychedelia and toward more traditional musical forms, if not always the cultural values associated with them. And, while the Nashville country establishment sneered, many rock and roll musicians took up the mantle, adding a heavy dose of country to their rocking 4/4 beat and more roots-oriented approach to music.

Parsons did not stay long in the band, taking Hillman with him to form the seminal country rock group the Flying Burrito Brothers. Now the lone remaining original Byrd, McGuinn (who had since changed his name to Roger), soldiered on, leading the Byrds through various different lineups with increasingly diminished artistic and commercial success. The band's soundtrack to the countercultural hit film *Easy Rider* offered a few highlights, and the addition of country-influenced lead guitarist Clarence White offered some hope of revival of fortunes.

However, White left the band in 1973, and the five original Byrds agreed (apparently for financial reasons) to re-form and record together. The reunion album, titled *The Byrds*, was released later that year. It enjoyed moderate commercial success, but was a critical flop. By the start of 1974 the Byrds had ceased to exist as a band.

Following the breakup, each Byrd pursued various solo projects, and occasionally worked in various combinations with one another. Crosby was the most successful, forming the supergroup Crosby, Stills, Nash & Young. McGuinn developed a following as a solo artist, while Hillman enjoyed substantial musical and artistic success on the country charts in the late 1980s with the Desert Rose Band. Clark, while arguably the band's finest songwriter, never achieved success on his own, and died in 1991 of heart failure. Clark died two years later.

While other surviving original members seem receptive to the idea, McGuinn has resisted any attempt to re-form the band, and other than a one-off reunion at the band's 1991 induction into the Rock and Roll Hall of Fame, the Byrds have yet to fully reunite.

Few bands can rival the Byrds' artistic legacy, which is both deeply and widely felt throughout rock music. A flood of folk-rock acts swept through the charts following the release of "Mr. Tambourine Man." The Byrds were pivotal in the development of psychedelic rock in the late 1960s, even as the band quickly moved away from that style of music. In the wake of *Sweethearts of the Rodeo*, country rock became a commercial and artistic mainstay of the 1970s. Today's more rock-flavored version of country music has its roots in *Sweethearts*, as does much of the Americana movement in popular music.

But the jangly, 12-string guitar–driven sound of the Byrds' first two albums is perhaps the band's greatest gift to rock and where their influence is most deeply felt. Acts such as Tom Petty, the Pretenders, R.E.M, Bruce Springsteen, the Flamin' Groovies, Dream Syndicate, and Richard Thompson are indebted to the Byrds' original sound. From commercial jingles to musical soundtracks, wherever one hears the bright jangle of electric guitar, McGuinn and the Byrds' influence is present.

Suggested Albums: Mr. Tambourine Man (1965); *Turn, Turn, Turn* (1965); *Fifth Dimension* (1966); *Younger Than Yesterday* (1967); *The Notorious Byrd Brothers* (1968); *Sweethearts of the Rodeo* (1968); *Farther Along* (1971)

CALE, J. J. (1938–2013)

Eric Clapton emulated J. J. Cale's distinctive sound in the 1970s, and Cale's carefully considered guitar playing influenced Mark Knopfler of Dire Straits. Although he had been a professional musician and recording engineer with a few singles to his credit, he first became known through Clapton's 1970 hit version of his song "After Midnight." While establishing professional ties with Los Angeles and Nashville, Cale preferred the familiar comforts of his hometown, Tulsa, Oklahoma.

A Midwest regionalist, Cale crafted a conversationally sung, laconic oeuvre that drew from country, blues, and rockabilly. Performing at a relaxed tempo, Cale conveyed the impression that he was entertaining himself and his friends and was unmoved by the urge to sell records or put on a show. Nonetheless, he managed a Top 40 hit, "Crazy Mama," from his debut album, *Naturally* (1972). Among the diverse performers who covered his songs were Kansas ("Bringing It Back"), Lynyrd Skynyrd ("Call Me the Breeze"), Waylon Jennings ("Clyde"), and Jose Feliciano ("Magnolia"). Clapton's rendition of Cale's "Cocaine" became a rock standard.

Rooted to a particular place in America's heartland., Cale's music was notable for its genuineness and utter lack of pretense. He recorded sporadically into the 21st century and died in 2013 after suffering a heart attack.

Suggested Albums: Naturally (1972); *Really* (1972); *Okie* (1974); *Troubadour* (1976); *Number 5* (1979)

CALE, JOHN (1942–)

A coal miner's son, John Cale rose from a gritty life in Wales through classical music, but made his mark on the world through a seminal rock band, the Velvet Underground. He played viola in the National Youth Orchestra of Wales and studied music at London's Goldsmith College, where he pursued an interest in the avant-garde. In 1963 Aaron Copland recommended him for Tanglewood, the summer home of the Boston Symphony Orchestra. From there Cale went to New York, where he performed Erik Satie's 18-hour *Vexations* on piano with John Cage. He was drawn to the early minimalism of La Monte Young and Tony Conrad, joining their group, the Theatre of Eternal Music (later called the Dream Syndicate). Young and Conrad inspired many classically trained composers who emerged in the 1960s with their emphasis on drone and the influence of non-Western traditions.

Cale busked on the New York streets with Lou Reed before they co-founded the Velvet Underground in early 1965. Although Reed was the principal songwriter, Cale was instrumental in giving the band its daring musical edge by applying the lessons of minimalism to rock. He played viola, organ, and piano on their first two albums, *The Velvet Underground and Nico* (1967) and *White Light/White Heat* (1968). Cale played as well as contributed songs to Nico's debut solo album, *Chelsea Girl* (1967). He would continue collaborating with Nico, producing her albums *The Marble Index* (1969), *Desertshore* (1970), *The End* (1974), and *Camera Obscura* (1985).

After creative disagreements with Reed, who wanted a less unconventional approach, Cale left the Velvet Underground to pursue a dual career as a solo artist and producer.

Illustrating his scope as a composer-performer were his first, considerably different albums, *Vintage Violence* (1970) and *Church of Anthrax* (1971). The former was an eclectic collection of enigmatic balladry, piano-powered rock, and pop songs with gorgeous melodies derived from Brian Wilson's ambitious post-1964 work with the Beach Boys. The latter was a full-blown sortie into the avant-garde in collaboration with minimalist composer Terry Riley.

Cale followed with another album of minimalist experimentation, *The Academy in Peril* (1972), featuring fractured piano variations recorded with the Royal Philharmonic Orchestra. The Andy Warhol cover, a photographic sequence of Cale's face and eyes, represented the album's placement as a bridge between serious art and pop culture. By contrast, *Paris 1919* (1973) was a melodic, lovely song cycle with literary references ("Graham Greene," "Child's Christmas in Wales") in arrangements suggesting George Martin and Procol Harum.

Afterward, Cale moved back to Great Britain and released a trio of albums that became a link between the Velvet Underground and the nascent punk rock movement. The mood was anxious on *Fear* (1974), whose titular song dissolved from calm acceptance into emotional hysteria and musical chaos. Cale worked with musicians influenced by the Velvet Underground, Roxy Music's Brian Eno and Phil Manzanera, who embraced *Fear* as a sonic experiment. Manzanera's detuned guitar was played through Eno's analog synthesizer, generating unusual textures in a rock context. As in the Velvet Underground, beauty intruded on dissonance.

Slow Dazzle (1975) includes "Mr. Wilson," Cale's tribute to the Beach Boys' mastermind. By radically reimagining Elvis Presley's "Heartbreak Hotel" as dramatic horror, Cale pointing the way to postpunk recording artist Nick Cave. *Helen of Troy* (1975) was comprised of brittle, despondent rock along with a song Cale wrote for Frank Sinatra, the lushly melodic "I Keep a Close Watch." Sinatra's response is unrecorded.

Cale had no trouble adjusting to the primal frenzy of punk rock. Returning to New York, where he was embraced as a forerunner, Cale recorded a pair of albums at punk's epicenter, CBGB, *Sabotage/Live* (1979) and *Even Cowgirls Get the Blues* (unreleased until 1991). His studio albums from the period were confrontational in tone, addressing the world situation with rancor on *Honi Soit* (1980) and *Music for a New Society* (1981). Even in his edgiest phases, Cale never entirely disavowed pop music or the prospect of reaching wider audiences. *Artificial Intelligence* (1985) nodded to the synthesizer-driven production values of 1980s rock. It failed to climb the charts but included several songs admired by fans.

Focusing on fatherhood, Cale withdrew from music for the rest of that decade. He reemerged in collaboration with Eno for *Wrong Way Up* (1990) and *Words for the Dying* (1992) and was involved in many projects, including recording "Hallelujah" for the Leonard Cohen tribute album *I'm Your Fan* (1991). He reunited with Reed for *Songs for Drella* (1990), which reflected on their experiences with Warhol. Despite the unresolved ambivalence of their relationship, they agreed to re-form the Velvet Underground for an album and tour (1993). Cale became more prolific in the 21st century, touring and releasing albums indebted to contemporary rock.

Impressive as is his varied body of work, Cale's greatest legacy may be as the producer of other artists. His most significant productions helped steer the direction of punk rock, especially the debut album by the Stooges (1969), Jonathan Richman's *The Modern Lovers* (recorded in 1972 but released in 1976), and Patti Smith's epochal *Horses* (1975).

Suggested Albums: Vintage Violence (1970); *Church of Anthrax* (1971); *The Academy in Peril* (1972); *Paris 1919* (1973); *Fear* (1974); *Slow Dazzle* (1975); *Helen of Troy* (1975); *Sabotage/Live* (1979); *Honi Soit* (1980); *Music for a New Society* (1981); *Even Cowgirls Get the Blues* (1991). With Lou Reed: *Songs for Drella* (1990)

See also: Reed, Lou; Velvet Underground

CAMBODIAN ROCK

While South Vietnam's rock bands often catered to GIs by copying Anglo-American hits, in neighboring Cambodia, where American troops were never stationed, indigenous rock bands playing to local audiences incorporated ancient principles into Western forms. Whatever awareness the country's musicians may have had of psychedelia, Cambodian rock from the 1960s fits that label with Asian influences woven into rock band settings.

Cambodia was home to several record labels, and star performers received airtime on the national radio station during the tolerant regime of Prince Norodom Sihanouk. As early as 1960, Chum Kem set the stage with the "Kampuchea Twist"; before long the identically suited Baksey Cham Krong performed surf-like instrumentals. The Beatles and Rolling Stones were influential after 1964, but the vocal melodies of Cambodian performers often shimmered like a mirage of Angkor Wat. Female vocalist Pen Ran achieved a fusion of East with West in harmonically dynamic rock songs about the plight of women. In 1974 Drakkar released an album of heavy rock with distorted guitars and echoes of Cambodian melody.

Rock music, along with religion, private property, and personal freedom were swept aside when the Khmer Rouge emerged from the jungle and seized the country in 1975. Most musicians were forced into the countryside when the radical

Communist regime emptied Cambodia's cities. Their death dates are usually given as 1975–1979, since the Khmer Rouge kept few records. The slaughter ended when the 1979 invasion by Communist Vietnam ended Khmer Rouge rule.

Interest in Cambodian rock, which had never been known outside its homeland, has grown in recent years. The album *Cambodian Rocks* (1996) was compiled by American tourist Paul Wheeler from tapes of pre–Khmer Rouge bands discovered at outdoor markets. Fronted by Cambodian expatriate singer Chhom Nimol, the 21st-century American band Dengue Fever includes songs by 1960s-era Cambodian recording artists in its repertoire. Director John Pirozzi's film *Don't Think I've Forgotten* (2015) documents the country's music during the 1960s and 1970s and was accompanied by a soundtrack album.

CAN

The lure of "primitivism" was irresistible to early 20th-century modern artists seeking inspiration beyond the refinements of Western civilization. Pablo Picasso's painted faces mirrored the contours of African masks and Igor Stravinsky's ballets pulled from the rhythms of rural Russia. The impulse underlined the origins of Can, formed in Cologne, Germany, during the tumultuous year of 1968. Two of Can's founders, keyboardist Irwin Schmidt and bassist Holger Czukay, were students of German composer Karlheinz Stockhausen, a pioneer in electronic music and musique concrète, and sought primitivism in rock and roll. Unlike many of the era's venturesome rock artists who pursued classical music or jazz, Can reduced rock to its skeletal repetitious essence, building their sonic experiments on a primal foundation. Can cited the Velvet Underground for inspiration, but their early recordings bore affinity with psychedelic garage rock bands such as the 13th Floor Elevators.

Can recruited its vocalists among expatriates in Germany, starting with the American sculptor Malcolm Mooney. In 1970 Japanese street musician Damo Suzuki replaced Mooney. Drawing from Stockhausen, Can constructed much of their music from tape edits, essentially sampling themselves from their studio jam sessions. On *Future Days* (1973), Suzuki's final album with the band, Can moved toward the nascent genre of ambient music. Although the band had several German hits, *Flow Motion* (1976) included their only song to climb the British charts, the disco single "I Want More." Afterward, Can headed down more conventional paths, adding Traffic's bassist Rosko Gee and percussionist Rebop Kwaku Baah to their lineup.

By the end of the 1970s Can became inactive, albeit sporadic reunions have occurred, including a contribution to the soundtrack of director Wim Wenders's film *Until the End of the World* (1991). Can influenced many postpunk bands of the early 1980s. For his debut album under the name Public Image Ltd., John Lydon (formerly Johnny Rotten of the Sex Pistols) chose a metal film can for packaging in tribute to the German band. Members of Can enjoyed active solo careers, often performing with younger British musicians influenced by their 1970s recordings.

Suggested Albums: Monster Movie (1970); *Tago Mago* (1971); *Ege Bamyasi* (1972); *Soundtracks* (1973); *Future Days* (1973); *Soon Over Babaluma* (1975); *Unlimited Edition* (1976); *Flow Motion* (1976)

CANNED HEAT

Canned Heat began in 1965 as a jug band founded by two blues aficionados, Bob "Bear" Hite and Alan "Blind Owl" Wilson. Unlike many white blues researchers–record collectors of their generation who became musicians, they were not purists. While preserving the integrity of the blues and drawing from pre–World War II blues songs for material, they were soon determined to set their influences in a rock context. Taking their name from a 1920s blues lyric, Canned Heat drew from African American boogie rhythms for much of their repertoire.

However, their biggest hits departed from that format. "On the Road Again" (1968) made common cause between blues and raga in an intriguing alliance between Mississippi and India. Tapping into the back-to-the-land ethos of the 1960s counterculture, their rewrite of a 1920s blues number, "Going Up the Country" (1969), featured a joyous flute solo. Wilson's falsetto voice, largely unprecedented among blues singers, added to the band's distinction.

Although Canned Heat played major rock festivals at Monterey (1967), Woodstock (1969), and elsewhere and were widely recognized, they were plagued by ill fortune, including drug arrests and Wilson's death from a drug overdose (1970). The band continued through numerous lineups even after Hite's death (1981). Recent versions of Canned Heat have involved no original members but include such players from the band's best years as bassist Larry Taylor, drummer Adolpho de la Parra, and guitarist Harvey Mandel.

Suggested Albums: Canned Heat (1967); *Boogie with Canned Heat* (1968); *Living the Blues* (1968); *Vintage Heat* (1970); *Hooker 'n Heat* (1971)

CAPTAIN BEEFHEART (1941–2010)

Don Van Vliet was a child prodigy featured with his clay animal sculptures on a weekly Los Angeles television program at age four. Van Vliet achieved recognition in adulthood as an abstract expressionist painter. However, he was better known for making challenging, often perplexing albums at the fringe of rock under his musical pseudonym, Captain Beefheart. His most recognized paintings appeared on the covers of several of his albums.

Beefheart and Frank Zappa became friends while attending high school and enjoyed a sporadic creative relationship with Zappa in the role of presenting Beefheart to a wider public. They were both autodidacts who shared a love for avant-garde music and rhythm and blues, but traveled decidedly different paths. Zappa embraced shock value while Beefheart was shocking only to those with limited ideas of what rock could be. Zappa delivered his music with prurient humor while Beefheart seemed to chuckle at a joke only he could understand. When the group

CAPTAIN BEEFHEART

they intended to form failed to materialize, Beefheart formed the first version of his backing group, the Magic Band, in 1964.

Like many modern artists, Beefheart firmly believed that art should march bravely from the past into an uncertain future. The singles he released in 1966 were blues-rock à la the Yardbirds, fronted by his gruff vocals and wailing harmonica, grounded in distortion and ornamented by the harpsichord of producer David Gates, who later formed the "soft rock" band Bread. Beefheart moved forward on his first album, *Safe as Milk* (1967), whose sophisticated psychedelia was painted across a palimpsest of Mississippi Delta blues and Indian raga. The Magic Band's guitarist Ry Cooder, dismayed by Beefheart's eccentricity, departed afterward to begin his own extensive solo career.

Recorded in 1967 but released in 1971, *Mirror Man* was essentially a blues jam session topped by stream-of-consciousness poetry. By *Strictly Personal* (1968), Beefheart had developed the approach that characterized most of his succeeding albums. His lyrics introduced rock to genuine surrealism (as opposed to the pretentious weirdness of some of the era's lyricists), and his music orchestrated the solo style of pre–World War II Delta blues guitarists for rock band, complete with the irregular rhythms and odd meters of those self-schooled musicians. There was something spooky at times about his vocalizations; drawing from Rev. Gary Davis, Blind Willie McTell, and certain other 1930s blues musicians, he had absorbed the resonance of music that seemed projected into the void for no one. Beefheart announced his distance from current trends in rock with "Beatle Bones 'N Smokin' Stones," opaquely spoofing the most popular bands of the day.

Zappa produced *Trout Mask Replica* (1969), Beefheart's most difficult album, which was greeted with incomprehension by the 1960s counterculture but embraced by a fervent cult following led by rock critic Lester Bangs. By this time the Magic Band lived together and spent entire days in rehearsal under Beefheart's tutelage. The chaos was strictly disciplined in a regimen not unlike the rule Zappa imposed on his bands. Many songs were composed from fragments originating in melodies Beefheart whistled to his colleagues. Band members adopted colorful pseudonyms, including guitarists Winged Eel Fingerling (aka Eliot Ingber) and Zoot Horn Rollo (Bill Hackleroad), and wore bizarre garb for theatrical effect.

Beefheart's post–*Trout Mask Replica* music pulled back from the dizzying brink. *Lick My Decals Off, Baby* (1970) may not have been much less weird than its predecessor, but sounded more refined and distilled. With *Clear Spot* (1972) and *The Spotlight Kid* (1972), Beefheart continued his tour of the Mississippi delta with oddly orchestrated blues, swamp boogie, and abstract versions of New Orleans brass bands delivered with strange time signatures and hairpin rhythmic turns. Beefheart's lyrics remained remarkable for their invention and startlingly right images.

By 1974 the Magic Band's classic lineup ended, with several members forming a new recording act called Mallard. Although Beefheart had trouble in recruiting musicians who understood his ideas, he recorded two albums of conventional rock, *Unconditionally Guaranteed* (1974) and *Bluejeans & Moonbeams* (1974), before collaborating with Zappa on *Bongo Fury* (1975). While his career went on hold because of contractual lawsuits, he guest-starred on an album by the Tubes and recorded with Zappa in a session released years later as *Bat Chain Puller* (2012).

Beefheart rerecorded some of the material from the aborted Zappa project for *Shiny Beast (Bat Chain Puller)* (1978), a stubbornly idiosyncratic yet strangely accessible album. By this time Beefheart had inspired at least one important new American band that sounded nothing like him, Devo, and another where his influence was more pronounced, Pere Ubu. Admired by John Lydon, Mark E. Smith, and others in Britain's postpunk scene, Beefheart found a new and slightly larger audience for *Doc at the Radar Station* (1980) and *Ice Cream for Crow* (1982), supporting their release with American and European tours and an appearance on *Saturday Night Live*.

Although Beefheart retired from music by the mid-1980s, became reclusive, and devoted his creativity to painting, his influence grew. The hardcore punk band the Minutemen drew from his irregular rhythms, and Tom Waits's abrupt shift from jazz vaudeville into the avant-garde resulted from exposure to Beefheart's music. Recent bands such as the White Stripes and the Black Keys have covered his songs. Beefheart's final recording, a 34-second rewrite of "Happy Birthday" called "Happy Earthday," was phoned in for a 2003 benefit album for Earth Justice. Beefheart died in 2010 after years of declining health, apparently from muscular sclerosis.

Suggested Albums: Safe as Milk (1967); *Strictly Personal* (1968); *Trout Mask Replica* (1969); *Lick My Decals Off, Baby* (1970); *Clear Spot* (1972); *The Spotlight Kid* (1972); *Unconditionally Guaranteed* (1974); *Bluejeans & Moonbeams* (1974); *Shiny Beast (Bat Chain Puller)* (1978); *Doc at the Radar Station* (1980); *Ice Cream for Crow* (1982); *Bat Chain Puller* (2012)

CARAVAN

The ancient cathedral town of Canterbury, a mecca for medieval pilgrims and the destination for the protagonists of Geoffrey Chaucer's *Canterbury Tales*, sheltered a gaggle of unique bands in the late 1960s. Caravan was emblematic of that scene's eccentric ethos.

Formed in 1967 from the remnants of the Wilde Flowers, a Canterbury group that included Robert Wyatt and Kevin Ayers before they formed Soft Machine, Caravan's original lineup was responsible for three albums of psychedelia in transit to progressive rock. The influence of English folk music converged with the then-futurism of mellotron and distorted electric guitar and organ. Caravan had a tendency toward long jams yet were capable of lively, concise pop rock. The jazz digressions were reminiscent of their better-known contemporaries, Traffic. Caravan's eclectic music was the setting for whimsical lyrics, with much sipping of tea, smoking of "punk weed," and allusions to knights, dragons, and dreamland. Although they performed at major European rock festivals in the late 1960s and early 1970s, Caravan acquired only a cult following.

After keyboardist David Sinclair left in 1971 to join Wyatt's new band, Matching Mole, Caravan drifted toward jazz fusion and many lineup changes. Despite breaking up in 1978, Caravan continued into the 21st century, periodically regrouping with some original members.

Suggested Albums: Caravan (1968); *If I Could Do It All Over Again, I'd Go It All Over You* (1970); *In the Land of Grey and Pink* (1971)

CHAMBERS BROTHERS

As an African American group marketed as rock and with a psychedelic Top 40 hit, "Time Has Come Today," the Chambers Brothers were an anomaly in many respects. The core members were siblings and older than most rock acts that emerged in the 1960s. They began in a Mississippi Baptist church choir before moving to Los Angeles where they performed on the gospel music circuit. Gravitating toward the folk-blues revival, they were booked by Pete Seeger at the 1965 Newport Folk Festival. Inspired by Bob Dylan's full electric band performance at the festival, the brothers shifted toward rock.

Written by Joe and Willie Chambers, the original version of "Time Has Come Today" from their album *The Time Has Come* (1967) was 11 minutes long. Trimmed for AM airplay, the fuzz-toned, echo-drenched celebration of changing times and the uplifting effects of psychedelics became a hit the following year. The Chambers Brothers, unable to capitalize on the song's success due to problems with management, broke up and re-formed sporadically. George Chambers returned to gospel music and became a deacon. "Time Has Come Today" has often been used in movie and television soundtracks. The Ramones recorded it in 1983 and many punk and alternative rock bands have followed suit.

Suggested Albums: People Get Ready (1965); *The Time Has Come* (1967)

See also: Black Rock

CHARLATANS

The Charlatans led San Francisco's youthful musicians from the folk-blues revival into the psychedelia that characterized the Bay Area in the 1960s. Formed in 1964, the Charlatans attracted attention for their jangly folk-rock rendition of Buffy Sainte-Marie's "Cod'ine." The cautionary tale on the dangers of drug addiction (as opposed to psychedelic consciousness bending) entered the repertoire of other San Francisco bands following their example. Embodying the antiquarian current that stirred psychedelia on both sides of the Atlantic, the Charlatans were longhaired and dressed in starched high collars, Edwardian waistcoats, and vintage suits. They cut the sartorial image of riverboat gamblers in the early years of the 20th century. Some of the earliest examples of Art Nouveau–style psychedelic poster art were created to promote their shows.

Misdirected by their record labels, the Charlatans released singles but only one album during their time together. Demos and other material have since found their way onto posthumous compilations. The Charlatans broke up following their 1969 LP. Drummer Dan Hicks became the leader of the country–gypsy swing band Dan Hicks and His Hot Licks while guitarist Mike Wilhelm joined the Flamin' Groovies.

Suggested Album: The Charlatans (1969)

CHICAGO

Chicago was the most popular of the horn-driven jazz-rock bands that emerged in the late 1960s and were a ubiquitous pop group through the 1970s and 1980s. They became the first rock act to assume the characteristics of a corporate brand, complete with a recognizable logo displayed prominently on album covers. Anticipating the methods of Hollywood movie franchises, they titled their succeeding albums with Roman numerals as if each were somehow a sequel in an ongoing story. The astute marketing seems paradoxical from a band whose early lyrics often placed them on the barricades of political and social upheaval.

Windy City guitarist Terry Kath and saxophonist-clarinetist Walter Parazaider formed the Big Thing in 1967, the name signaling their ambitions for a rock group scaled larger than the quartets common in the wake of the Beatles. They took the name Chicago Transit Authority in time for their debut album and shortened it afterward to Chicago.

Chicago Transit Authority (1969) was an album Stan Kenton might have recorded had he been a young man in the 1960s. The horn section was not ornamental as in many pop recordings but integral to the music; instrumentalists were allowed their own voicings in arrangements so precise that even the sternest conservatory instructor could find no fault. Cool jazz digressions were launch pads for Kath's extraordinary solos, which melded the fluid touch of Wes Montgomery with rock's harsh, amplified distortion. A staple on FM, their reinvention of the Spencer Davis Group's "I'm a Man" was a postpsychedelic guitar tour de force riding on tribal rhythms. The album's AM hit, "Does Anybody Really Know What Time It Is?," had a jazzy bounce suitable for Frank Sinatra's repertoire.

In an extraordinary move for an unknown band's debut, *Chicago Transit Authority* was a two-LP set. The voluminous album included scathing blues-rock and Brazilian rhythms, free improvisation and carefully composed horn charts, enigmatic lyrics and demonstrative love songs along with the chanting of protesters recorded on Chicago's streets during the 1968 Democratic National Convention. Like the great albums of the era, it contained multitudes.

The band followed with another double LP, *Chicago* (1970), whose inner cover proclaimed: "With this album, we dedicate ourselves, our futures and our energies to the people of the revolution. And the revolution in all its forms." Chicago managed to infiltrate the hit parade with three Top 10 singles from the album, "25 or 6 to 4," "Make Me Smile," and "Color My World," the latter becoming a wedding band standard through the 1970s. *Chicago III* (1971), also a two-LP set, contained only one hit, the funky "Free." The band reached the pinnacle of monumentalism

The most popular horn-driven jazz-rock band to emerge in the late 1960s, Chicago mellowed into a ubiquitous pop act by the late 1970s. Even in their more rabble-rousing early years, Chicago's arrangements were as precise and well executed as any top big band from the swing era. (Lewton Cole/Alamy Stock Photo)

with the four-LP box set *Chicago at Carnegie Hall* (1971), which documented a week-long concert series at the venue.

Chicago V (1972) was a more modest affair, a single LP with a pair of hit singles. "Dialogue (Part 1 & 2)" recounted a conversation between a political activist and an uncommitted student. "Saturday in the Park," whose political sensibility was woven subtly into a vivid depiction of everyday life, was more in tune with the political cool-down occurring in America.

If never a bellwether, Chicago was a musical echo of the public mood. By the time of *Chicago VIII* (1975), the band traded revolution for nostalgia in "Harry Truman" and "Old Days." That summer, they embarked on a joint U.S. tour with an act epitomizing nostalgia for the era before the unrest of the 1960s, the Beach Boys.

Afterward, Chicago continued to release albums annually. Even Kath's 1978 death from a shooting accident failed to slow their momentum of a lengthening track record of Top 40 love ballads starting with the Grammy-winning "If You Leave Me Now" (1976) and continuing through "Baby, What a Big Surprise" (1977), "Alive Again" (1978), "Hard to Say I'm Sorry" (1981), "You're the Inspiration" (1984), "Hard Habit to Break" (1984), "What Kind of Man Would I Be?" (1988), and "You're Not Alone" (1989). Most were carefully crafted earwigs that reduced the horn section to a decorative trademark and expunged any jazz influence. The personnel changed from album to album as the musicians calling themselves Chicago continued touring and recording into the 21st century, releasing *Chicago XXXVI* in 2014.

Suggested Albums: Chicago Transit Authority (1969); *Chicago* (1970); *Chicago III* (1971); *Chicago at Carnegie Hall* (aka *Chicago IV*) (1971)

See also: Jazz-Rock

CHRYSALIS
Formed by graduate students in Ithaca, New York, in 1966, Chrysalis gravitated to Greenwich Village clubs and released one LP, a lost masterpiece. Built from J. Spider Barbour's songwriting and producer Jim Friedman's lush woodwind, brass, and string arrangements, *Definition* was a song cycle of orchestral sweep and drama. In the studio, Chrysalis wove rock timbres together with classical and baroque textures, Middle Eastern tonalities, and jazz rhythms. Barbour shared vocals with Nancy Nairn in often poetic songs that painted gossamer moods and sketched character studies. Madcap humor and airy pop harmonies provided contrast to more somber songs. *Definition* is a superb example of the album as work of art as well as rock music's spongelike ability to absorb a world of influences. Chrysalis disbanded in 1970.

Suggested Album: Definition (1968)

CLAPTON, ERIC (1945–)
Eric Clapton was rock's first guitar hero. Although working from the example of the blues like many guitarists of his generation, he internalized that music on a deeper level, achieving greater clarity and power. While Chuck Berry established the importance of electric guitar in rock and roll, primitive amplification limited the instrument's potential, and the focus on singers in popular music left many of the best early rock and roll guitarists, such as Elvis Presley's sideman Scotty Moore, in the shadow of stardom. Even with the ascent of the Beatles, the electric guitar carried the music but seldom pushed it forward.

A self-taught guitarist, working in isolation to master the strange sounds from the American South and Chicago's South Side that he heard on LP, Clapton gravitated toward the blues while attending art school. He was especially captivated by the anguish heard on *King of the Delta Blues Singers*, the 1961 album collection of Robert Johnson songs from 1936 and 1937. He related the deep emotional experience of those songs to his own loneliness. Rather than simply copy Johnson, he eventually transmuted the existential fear of "Crossroads" and "Hell Hound on My Trail" through the newfound power of distortion and amplification.

By the end of 1962 Clapton, lacking confidence in his voice but already an accomplished guitarist, had made a name in London's nascent blues scene. A year later he joined the Yardbirds, putting his signature on the band's de rigueur repertoire of Howlin' Wolf, John Lee Hooker, and Bo Diddley. Still something of a blues purist, he objected to the Yardbirds' ascent into the pop charts with "For Your Love" (1965). Quitting the band before the end of 1965, he joined John Mayall's Bluesbreakers, where he cemented his reputation as Britain's most extraordinary guitarist for the dramatic flair of his solos and his cutting, knife-like tone. "Clapton is God" read a famous graffito on London streets, echoing similar sentiments from the previous decade on Charlie Parker. A mythology long familiar to jazz fans gathered around Clapton, fueled by his membership in the cult of virtuosity and his look-sharp style inspired by Miles Davis and other jazz artists.

In 1966, Clapton was ready to step into the new vistas offered by rapid advances in rock music and formed the archetypal rock power trio, Cream, with bassist Jack Bruce and drummer Ginger Baker. The chemistry was combustible, but Cream's music was a touchstone of the era with top-selling albums such as *Disraeli Gears* (1967), *Wheels of Fire* (1968), and the aptly named *Goodbye* (1969). Clapton then joined Blind Faith for one album (1969), but became more interested in playing with that band's world tour opening act, Delaney & Bonnie and Friends.

The husband and wife team of Delaney and Bonnie Bramlett produced and co-wrote most of Clapton's eponymous first solo album (1970). Clapton emerged as a confident vocalist on the LP, which included a minor hit, "After Midnight," written by a recording artist who emerged as a profound influence on his music, J. J. Cale. As if still uncertain of his ability to lead, Clapton formed another group, Derek and the Dominos. With their hit, "Layla" (1970), Robert Johnson's inspiration reached its apotheosis in Clapton's music as he magnified the sound of terror on an electric guitar.

After disbanding Derek and the Dominos, Clapton withdrew from performing and broke the heroin addiction that threatened his life but seemed to fuel his music. He emerged as a new artist, less a guitar hero than a guitarist-accompanist. Although many Clapton fans were dismayed by *461 Ocean Boulevard* (1974), the album solidified his presence on Top 40 radio with a number one hit, "I Shot the Sheriff." Although Clapton's version of the Bob Marley song pales before the original, his recording was a milestone in reggae's ascent from Jamaica and the diaspora to the world stage.

Starting with *461 Ocean Boulevard*, Clapton seemed determined to avoid the emotional places he had visited with Derek and the Dominos. Clapton recorded *No Reason to Cry* (1976) with the Band; Bob Dylan visited the session and contributed a previously unrecorded song, "Sign Language." For several years Clapton side-stepped the blues in favor of an easygoing, backcountry American shuffle indebted to J. J. Cale. His cover of Cale's "Cocaine" from *Slowhand* (1977) became a standard in the rock repertoire. By the end of the 1970s Clapton had become that which he once despised, a dependable hitmaker delivering gold with "Lay Down Sally" (1978) and "Promises" (1979), before moving deeper into nondescript pop with "I Can't Stand It" (1981) and a set of hits produced by Phil Collins, "Forever Man" (1985), "She's Waiting" (1985), and a song from the soundtrack of Paul Newman's movie *The Color of Money*, "It's in the Way You Use It" (1986).

Rock's first guitar hero, Eric Clapton, began as a blues musician but brought his roots to new places in the late 1960s. In the 1970s he began to enjoy a successful solo career and remains a respected elder statesman of rock in the twenty-first century. (Jerry Coli/Dreamstime.com)

Tragedy seemed to awaken Clapton from the artistic slumber of the 1980s after his four-year-old son Conor fell from the window of a New York apartment (1991). The death inspired a heartfelt ballad, "Tears in Heaven," from the album that marked his creative resurgence, *Unplugged* (1992). Recorded for the cable series *MTV Unplugged*, the album placed Clapton in a relaxed acoustic setting where he revisited Robert Johnson and other blues influences and transformed "Layla" into a calm ramble through his past. *Unplugged* marked a return to Clapton's vitality as an artist without compromising his commercial appeal. It earned three Grammy Awards and climbed to number one on *Billboard's* chart. *From the Cradle* (1994), an album of Willie Dixon, Muddy Waters, and other blues covers, solidified Clapton's return to the blues.

Since then, Clapton has busied himself touring, performing at benefit concerts, and collaborating with musicians as varied as Sheryl Crow, Carlos Santana, B. B. King, Tom Petty, Mark Knopfler, and his bandmate from Blind Faith, Steve Winwood. He won Grammy awards for "Change the World" (1996) and "My Father's Eyes" (1999), was musical director for the star-studded Concert for George (2002) in honor of George Harrison, and finally recorded an album with J. J. Cale, *The Road to Escondido* (2006). He has been inducted into the Rock and Roll Hall of Fame.

70 CLUSTER

Suggested Albums: Eric Clapton (1970); *461 Ocean Boulevard* (1974); *No Reason to Cry* (1976); *Slowhand* (1977); *Backless* (1978); *Unplugged* (1992); *From the Cradle* (1994); *Slowhand at 70: Live at the Royal Albert Hall* (2015)

See also: Blind Faith; Cream; Derek and the Dominos

CLUSTER

The front cover of Cluster's 1977 album with Brian Eno visualizes their music perfectly with a microphone on a stand tilted upward as if to amplify the evening sky. Formed in 1969 as Kluster, the German electronic group anglicized its name when it signed with a major label in 1971. The core members, Dieter Moebius and Hans-Joachim Roedelius, were often joined by producer-composer Conny Plank and guest appearances by musicians from Germany's flourishing rock scene, including Can's Holger Czukay. Much of their music was parallel to the minimalism of Philip Glass and Steve Reich, with analogue synthesizers and piano producing celestial melodies that unfolded into trance-inducing soundscapes. For *Zuckerzeit* (1974), Cluster deviated into minimalist rock whose roots can be traced to the Velvet Underground.

Moebius and Roedelius also recorded several albums with members of Germany's Neu under the name Harmonium. Cluster had a crucial influence on Eno's concept of ambient music. The group disbanded in 1981 but has reunited several times.

Suggested Albums: Cluster (1971); *Cluster II* (1972); *Zuckerzeit* (1974); *Sowiesoso* (1976); *Cluster & Eno* (1977); *After the Heat* (1978)

See also: Eno, Brian; Neu!

COCKER, JOE (1944–2014)

Joe Cocker's origins were like those of many British rock performers of his generation. Reared in gritty working-class Sheffield, Cocker began as a teenager in a 1950s skiffle band but was soon caught up in northern England's enduring fascination with the exotic sounds of R&B and soul.

Cocker became a popular singer in local pubs for strenuously copying the recorded voices of Otis Redding and other great African American singers. For years he juggled a day job at the East Midlands Gas Board with local gigs, releasing singles that attracted regional interest and opening for the Rolling Stones and the Hollies. After moving to London in 1967 with his group, the Grease Band, he had a minor U.K. hit written with his keyboardist Chris Stainton, "Marjorine" (1968). Although the song and arrangement was uncharacteristically baroque for Cocker, his distinctive vocal style was already apparent.

The exposure led to his first album with the Grease Band, with guest performances by Led Zeppelin guitarist Jimmy Page and Procol Harum drummer B. J. Wilson. *With a Little Help from My Friends* (1969) established him as a remarkable interpreter of other people's songs by melding the fervent testifying of soul with the dynamics of rock. The Beatles' "A Little Help from My Friends," a charming interlude on *Sgt. Pepper's Lonely Hearts Club Band*, was performed as if it were the climactic hymn at a gospel church service. Cocker electrified "Feelin' Alright" with a funkiness only suggested by Traffic's original recording.

While on tour in the United States, he met pianist Leon Russell. Russell coproduced his next album, *Joe Cocker!* (1969), with covers of Leonard Cohen, Bob Dylan, and the Beatles and a song by Russell, "Delta Lady," a pop tune that foreshadowed the musical direction Cocker would eventually take.

Its name adopted from a Noel Coward song, *Mad Dogs and Englishmen* (1970) was a boisterous live album and concert film featuring a large retinue of talented rock musicians including Russell, drummer Jim Gordon and bassist Carl Radle from Derek and the Dominos, and singer Rita Coolidge. The album netted two hits, a soul revue revamping of the jazz standard "Cry Me a River" and an expansively soulful rendition of the Box Tops' hit "The Letter."

Although he had performed at Woodstock and other prominent rock festivals in the late 1960s and early 1970s, Cocker's career was hampered by alcoholism. He sometimes appeared too drunk to recall the lyrics; sometimes he vomited on stage; tours were cancelled. For many who came of age in the 1970s, Cocker was epitomized by John Belushi's parody on *Saturday Night Live*, complete with gravelly vocals and spastic attempts at emulating the sharp movements of African American soul singers.

Despite setbacks, Cocker regained his stamina. He recorded popular albums with reggae and fusion influences, and maintained an enduring career with a string of innocuous adult contemporary hits. Among them were the Billy Preston–penned love song "You Are So Beautiful" (1974); his Grammy-nominated collaboration with the Crusaders, "So Glad I'm Standing Here Today" (1982); his duet with Jennifer Warnes from the film *An Officer and a Gentleman*, "Up Where We Belong" (1982); "When the Night Comes" (1990); and "Feels Like Forever" (1992). Cocker's "A Little Help from My Friends" was used as the theme for a television series set in the 1960s, *The Wonder Years* (1988–1993). He continued touring and recording into the 21st century until his death from lung cancer in 2014.

Suggested Albums: With a Little Help from My Friends (1969); *Joe Cocker!* (1969); *Mad Dogs and Englishmen* (1970); *Joe Cocker* (a.k.a. *Something to Say*) (1972)

COHEN, LEONARD (1934–2016)

Although Leonard Cohen emerged as a recording artist in the 1960s, he seemed to be in but not of those times. The memorable songs he authored in those years, including "Suzanne," "Bird on a Wire," and "Sisters of Mercy," make few discernible references to anything that could later be sold as nostalgia. More than any songs of the 1960s, they deserve to be called timeless. Unlike many songwriters who debuted in that decade, Cohen remained a viable presence in the 21st century rather than a ghost from the past.

Cohen was the only important singer-songwriter already acclaimed as a significant poet and novelist before becoming a recording artist. He grew up in Montreal and gained recognition in Canada. By the early 1960s Cohen had drawn positive notice for poetry collections such as *The Spice-Box of Earth* and *Flowers for Hitler*, and a pair of novels, *The Favorite Game* and *Beautiful Loser*. Steeped in W. B. Yeats and Walt Whitman as well as Henry Miller, Cohen was fed by the cultural lions of an earlier generation; unlike Bob Dylan, he bypassed Allen Ginsberg, Jack Kerouac, and the Beats and leaped from literature to the concert stage.

Cohen can scarcely be considered a rock musician, but from his debut, *Songs of Leonard Cohen* (1967), he appealed to a highbrow segment of the rock audience with his often mordant, biblically leavened poetry of the spirit entwined with the body. Gravely, Cohen sang-spoke lyrics written on the road of experience but with eyes fixed in the rearview mirror on his rabbinical forebears. Strumming his guitar, he was accompanied on his debut by gentle female chorales and strings that evaded kitsch only by juxtaposition with the somber themes they accompanied. The arrangements for *Songs from a Room* (1969) and *Songs of Love and Hate* (1971) were more austere as Cohen continued his exploration of the duplicity of expectations and the complexity of the human experience.

While Cohen's albums suggested a poet more comfortable in coffeehouses than traveling the rock circuit, Cohen appeared at Britain's anarchic Isle of Wight Festival (1970) as rampaging crowds broke fences, set fires, and disrupted performances. Stepping onstage at 4 a.m. wearing 5 o'clock shadow and a safari suit, Cohen calmed the mob with a childhood recollection and held them captive through a set of grave yet hopeful songs intoned with ragged authenticity.

New Skin for the Old Ceremony (1974) was Cohen's first album featuring percussion and Ashkenazi musical influences. For *Death of a Ladies Man* (1977), Cohen chose an unlikely collaborator in producer Phil Spector, who shrink-wrapped the songs in elaborate but schmaltzy arrangements that jarred against Cohen's monochromatic voice and rendered his lyrics ridiculous. Realizing his error, Cohen returned to form with *Recent Songs* (1979).

"Hallelujah" from *Various Positions* (1985) was overlooked upon release but was already on its way to becoming a standard when Jeff Buckley's cover reached number one on the charts (2008). A meditation on the ecstasy of sexuality and spirituality, "Hallelujah" has seen hundreds of recordings, including Rufus Wainwright's notable cover. However, during the 1980s, Cohen's career was at a low ebb as he was passed over by punk rock, new wave, heavy metal, dance music, and other trends. And yet, even as the music press focused on younger stars and flashes-in-the-pan, a new generation of artists as diverse as Bono, Kurt Cobain, and Michael Stipe grew up admiring Cohen's early work. A tribute album, *I'm Your Fan* (1991), featured performances of Cohen songs by the Pixies, REM, Nick Cave, and other popular alternative rock bands.

Heartened by the renewed attention, Cohen regained critical acclaim and a measure of sales with *I'm Your Man* (1988) and *The Future* (1992), which packaged his uncompromised vision in a more contemporary rock format. He went into seclusion for much of the 1990s at a Zen Buddhist monastery; although ordained as a Buddhist monk in 1996, he never abandoned his Jewish identity. Cohen returned to music with *Ten New Songs* (2001), recorded with soul singer Sharon Robinson in a home studio with low-fidelity production and Cascio synthesizers generating backing tracks. With the worried gravity of his performances set in a new light, he followed with *Dear Heather* (2004).

In 2004 Cohen was shocked to discover that his manager had stolen much of his money. Afterward he embarked on a series of lengthy international tours, filling a stadium in Israel and the Royal Albert Hall in London and drawing some of the largest audiences of his career. Circumstances might have forced him on the road, but Cohen took to the challenge with aplomb. Clad in dark suit and fedora, he performed before tall, moodily lit curtains and a large ensemble of musicians and singers. The sonic palette of Cohen's live shows drew from the tonal hues of the Near East and the Deep South, invoking prayer as well as evoking the funk, performed in a craggy voice with a stony face. The hard edges of his performance were softened by the sweet accompaniment. With a dozen studio albums behind him, from *Songs of Leonard Cohen* (1967) through *Old Ideas* (2012) and *Popular Problems* (2014), he had plenty of songs to choose from for his three-hour concerts. The early stages of his late life tour were captured on *Live in London* (2009), the most recent among a batch of concert albums released across his career.

Cohen's poetic search for wholeness in a broken world and exploration of the shoals between desire and fulfillment continues to move young songwriters such as Conor Oberst and others in the 21st century. Cohen died shortly after the release of his album *You Want It Darker* (2016).

Suggested Albums: Songs of Leonard Cohen (1967); *Songs from a Room* (1969); *Songs of Love and Hate* (1971); *Live Songs* (1973); *New Skin for the Old Ceremony* (1974); *Cohen Live: Leonard Cohen in Concert* (1974); *Recent Songs* (1979); *Various Positions* (1985); *I'm Your Man* (1988); *The Future* (1992); *Field Commander Cohen: Tour of 1979* (2001); *Ten New Songs* (2001); *Dear Heather* (2004); *Live in London* (2009); *Old Ideas* (2012); *Popular Problems* (2014)

COLLINS, JUDY (1939–)

Classically trained, Judy Collins could have pursued a life in art songs but the gravitational pull of the folk-blues revival was too strong. Her earliest albums, *A Maid of Constant Sorrow* (1961) and *Golden Apples of the Sun* (1962), featured traditional ballads. With *Judy Collins #3* (1964) and *The Judy Collins Concert* (1964), she began performing protest songs by Bob Dylan and Phil Ochs. With *In My Life* (1966), Collins began to embrace rock with the help of the album's producer, conductor and music scholar Joshua Rifkin, whose album *The Baroque Beatles Book* (1965) was an early meeting of classical music and rock.

Unlike many performers who emerged from the folk-blues revival, Collins never affected a bluesy or homespun folksiness but maintained a bel canto voice. She became adept at choosing up-and-coming songwriters, sometimes before the writers had a chance to record their own songs. Collins scored her first hit with Joni

Mitchell's "Both Sides Now" from *Wildflowers* (1967) and covered Leonard Cohen, Gordon Lightfoot, and Randy Newman. She had a minor country rock hit with Ian & Sylvia's "Someday Soon" from *Who Knows Where the Time Goes* (1968). Testifying to her ability to span audiences, Collins's version of Mitchell's "Chelsea Morning" was a hit a year later on easy listening radio.

Although in some circles Collins is best known as the inspiration for Stephen Stills's "Suite: Judy Blue Eyes," she has enjoyed an eclectic career since the 1960s, including hit singles with an a cappella "Amazing Grace" (1974) and a melancholy rendition of Stephen Sondheim's "Send in the Clowns" (1975). She was nominated for an Oscar as co-director of the classical music documentary *Antonia: A Portrait of the Woman* (1974); performed symphony pops concerts; has been active promoting children's and health issues; has written a novel and a memoir; and continues to record and give concerts. At the 1993 inauguration of President Bill Clinton, she sang "Amazing Grace" and "Chelsea Morning." The Clintons' daughter Chelsea was named for Collins's rendition of the song.

Suggested Albums: A Maid of Constant Sorrow (1961); *Golden Apples of the Sun* (1962); *Judy Collins #3* (1964); *The Judy Collins Concert* (1964); *In My Life* (1966); *Wildflowers* (1967); *Who Knows Where the Time Goes* (1968)

COLOSSEUM

Colosseum was an adventurous British band exploring the potential of electric jazz to give new shape to rock without losing rock's hard punch. Some of their music sounded much like Jack Bruce's contributions to Cream. Bassist Tony Reeves followed Bruce's example in treating electric bass as a frontline instrument. As if acknowledging the debt, Colosseum covered Bruce's "Rope Ladder to the Moon" on *The Grass Is Greener* (1970). Bandleader-drummer Jon Hiseman played in a polyrhythmic style similar to that of Cream's drummer Ginger Baker. Hiseman and saxophonist Dick Heckstall-Smith had previously served with Bruce and Baker's mentor, Graham Bond. Some Colosseum tracks, especially those featuring organist Dave Greenslade, recalled the Graham Bond Organisation.

After the original Colosseum disbanded in 1971, Hiseman formed Tempest and later organized Colosseum II, a more conventional jazz-fusion band than its predecessor, with Thin Lizzy guitarist Gary Moore. Hiseman released three albums under that name before breaking up the band in 1978. In 1994 Hiseman, Greenslade, and other original members revived Colosseum as a touring and recording act.

Suggested Albums: Those Who Are About to Die Salute You (1969); *Valentyne Suite* (1969); *The Grass Is Greener* (1970); *Daughter of Time* (1970)

CONCEPT ALBUM

Some have called Woody Guthrie's *Dustbowl Ballads* (1940) the first concept album. Released as a collection of recordings at 78 revolutions per minute, *Dustbowl Ballads* was comprised of a batch of songs about the environmental crisis that turned thousands of Midwest farmers into refugees during the 1930s. New technology made the concept album more viable. Frank Sinatra was perhaps the first recording artist in popular music to fully understand the potential of the newly introduced long-playing album. Spinning slowly at $33\frac{1}{3}$ revolutions per minute, the LP could accommodate 20 uninterrupted minutes of music per side and offered higher fidelity than pre-1948 recordings. With albums such as *In the Wee Small Hours* (1955) and *Come Fly with Me* (1958), Sinatra conceived LPs holistically with songs that flowed in an emotionally significant sequence. The template was set for rock bands to follow suit.

Concept album is a term without clear boundaries. Early Beach Boys' albums might have been accidental concept albums, given the preponderance of songs about Southern California's teenage culture. But on the level of conscious artistry, the Beach Boys' *Pet Sounds* (1966) might be rock's first significant concept album. Not unlike Sinatra's LPs from a decade earlier, *Pet Sounds* was sequenced to achieve a particular emotional resonance. It inspired *Sgt. Pepper's Lonely Hearts Club Band* (1967), whose concept is hard to identify but might simply be the Beatles role-playing as a fictional band, or be discerned in songs presenting Britain's psychedelic scene from various perspectives.

The idea of an album whose songs explicitly narrate a story gathered momentum with the Pretty Things' *S.F. Sorrow* (1968), credited as the first rock opera and as inspiration for the Who's *Tommy* (1969) and *Quadrophenia* (1973). Not all story albums were called rock operas. Genesis avoided the term for their elaborate tale, *The Lamb Lies Down on Broadway* (1974). However, the Kinks embraced rock opera for albums such as *Preservation Act 1* (1973) and *Preservation Act 2* (1974).

Despite their differences, Pink Floyd's *The Dark Side of the Moon* (1973) and *Wish You Were Here* (1975), and Bruce Springsteen's *Darkness at the Edge of Town* (1978) and *Nebraska* (1984), can be considered concept albums for the recurring ideas embedded in the lyrics. Concept albums were considered unfashionable in light of punk rock's insistence on returning to basics, but recent years have seen their return. Neil Young's "audio novel" about a California town, *Greendale* (2003), and Green Day's story of disillusioned youth, *American Idiot* (2004), have both been called rock operas.

COODER, RY (1947–)

Guitarist Ry Cooder surfaced in Southern California's folk-blues revival of the early 1960s. While possessing an archivist's love for learning from historic blues and folk performers and committed to sounding authentic, he was eager from early on to pull together diverse influences, notably from Bahamian guitarist Joseph Spence. In 1966 Cooder cofounded the Rising Sons with the similarly inclined Taj Mahal and played on his eponymous debut album (1967). He then joined Captain Beefheart's Magic Band but left after their first album, *Safe as Milk* (1967). Cooder has always been in demand as a session player. He recorded with the Rolling Stones on *Let It Bleed* (1969) and *Sticky Fingers* (1971). Cooder claimed the riff of "Honky Tonk Women" was his; his slide guitar is prominent on "Sister Morphine." Cooder was considered for membership in the Rolling Stones but was rejected for not possessing the proper Stones image.

His first solo albums, *Ry Cooder* (1970), *Into the Purple* (1972), and *Boomer's Story* (1972), showcased his phenomenal abilities on electric slide guitar, which remained a hallmark throughout his career. They were idiosyncratic folk and blues recordings, occasionally reminiscent of Captain Beefheart for orchestrating the irregular rhythms of antique blues for a rock band. Although he wrote songs, Cooder drew much of his material from his knowledge of old music.

Paradise and Lunch (1974) included a duet with jazz pianist Earl "Fatha" Hines. Not unlike the Band, *Chicken Skin Music* (1976) conjured memories of an earlier America. *Jazz* (1978) explored the roots of jazz in ragtime and vaudeville. On *Bop Till You Drop* (1979), Cooder infused rock with gospel harmonies.

Starting in the 1980s Cooder became a prolific contributor to motion picture soundtracks. He continued his session work and production. Among his most prominent projects was producing an album in Cuba in defiance of the U.S. embargo. The much-acclaimed *Buena Vista Social Club* (1997) revived the career of bandleader Juan de Marcos Gonzalez and other pre-Castro musicians. Cooder's campaign to revive interest in this music was documented in director Wim Wenders's Oscar-nominated film *Buena Vista Social Club* (1999).

Less remarked at the time but of enduring influence was Cooder's contribution to the soundtrack for *Crossroads* (1986). The movie incorporated elements of the Robert Johnson legend into the story of an aspiring young blues guitarist (played a bit improbably by Ralph Macchio). In the climactic scene, Macchio's aspirant duels with a wild-eyed, Paganini-like guitar virtuoso (played more plausibly, and performed by guitar hero Steve Vai) for the contract to Macchio's mentor's soul. Cooder supplied the slide parts used by Macchio to combat Vai's pyrotechnics. The thrilling battle provided an edge the film otherwise lacked, inspiring a generation of young guitarists to aspire to heights of instrumental mastery. Vai's playing was probably the more influential of the two, but Cooder's efforts provided a dramatic contrast between old school and new in a memorable scene that helped inspire a generation of would-be guitar legends.

In the 21st century Cooder continues to record, perform, and explore connections between ethnic and traditional music from around the world.

Suggested Albums: Ry Cooder (1970); *Into the Purple* (1972); *Boomer's Story* (1972); *Paradise and Lunch* (1974); *Chicken Skin Music* (1976); *Jazz* (1978); *Bop Till You Drop* (1979); *Borderline* (1980); *Chavez Ravine* (2005); *I, Flatland* (2008)

COOPER, ALICE (1948–)

Alice Cooper began as a band fronted by a singer who also called himself Alice Cooper. The singer was born Vincent Furnier; the band formed in Phoenix and was called the Nazz until Todd Rundgren's group of the same name was signed to a major label. Alice Cooper moved to Los Angeles in 1968 where they caught the ear of Frank Zappa, who signed them to his Straight Records. The albums they recorded for Straight, *Pretties for You* (1969) and *Easy Action* (1970), sold poorly and scarcely suggested what was to come. With furious rock jams, musique concrète, and high-flying psychedelic lyrics, *Pretties* sounded closer to London's Carnaby Street than the band's seedy Los Angeles base. *Easy Action* focused on hard rock with progressive rock aspirations. The lyrical allusions to *West Side Story* spoke to their frontman's growing fascination with rock as theater.

By *Love It to Death* (1971), Alice Cooper had paired their sound to its essentials. Their first hit, "I'm Eighteen," boasted an empathetic lyric that caught the emotional confusion of a teenager on the cusp of manhood. The formula was set: Alice Cooper married hard rock, powered by guitarist Glen Buxton, to a pop sensibility, delivered with their eponymous singer's flair for teenage anthems.

Alice Cooper shocked audiences in the early 1970s when he unveiled his Grand Guignol rock horror show. Nowadays he's a universally recognized entertainer, seen here at a 2011 performance in Berlin. (Yakub88/Dreamstime.com)

By this time, the band's singer devised increasingly elaborate stage shows starring himself. His androgynous image linked Alice Cooper to the rising tide of glitter rock, but his presentation was more Grand Guignol than glamorous. Some critics labeled Alice Cooper as "Dada rock." However, the horror show sensibility had less to do with Cabaret Voltaire than the cheeky films of B-director Roger Corman. "Shock rock" was the term that stuck to theatrics involving mock executions and live boa constrictors. Magician James Randi designed the illusion of the singer's execution by guillotine. It was shocking, especially to high school students who became the primary audience, most of them never realizing that Alice Cooper was a band and not simply the showman in the spotlight. Perhaps more shocking was the singer's endorsement of the Republican Party and love of golf.

Rumors circulated that their name derived from a Ouija board message about a 17th-century witch called Alice Cooper. The band and their show tapped into a morbid strain of violence and the occult rooted in Robert Johnson that continued as an undercurrent in rock and roll. It manifested in Elvis Presley's oeuvre with the spectral allusions of "Mystery Train" and the murderous implications of "Baby Let's Play House." The dark voodoo of Screamin' Jay Hawkins's "I Put a Spell on You" and his penchant for rising from coffins on stage also set a precedent, along with the more recent hellfire pyrotechnics of Britain's Arthur Brown.

The Alice Cooper show was part of the transgressive climate as the political radicalism of the 1960s migrated into the cultural sphere of the 1970s. If authority could no longer be confronted on the streets, it could be defied on stage. Taboos were being broken everywhere, even in that formerly most conservative media, American network television, where *All in the Family* broached topics once unmentionable.

The band set box office records for touring rock bands and enjoyed a string of hits from "School's Out" (1972) through "Elected" (1972), "Hello, Hooray" (1973), "Billion Dollar Babies" (1973), and "No More Mr. Nice Guy" (1973). By 1974 the former Vincent Furnier discharged his band but kept its name for himself. From then on, Cooper was a solo act.

Without the backing of a strong rock band, Cooper tended toward schlock. *Welcome to My Nightmare* (1975) established him as a mainstream entertainer complete with a hit pop ballad, "Only Women Bleed," and a guest appearance by Corman horror movie star Vincent Price. Coupled with the album's release was a prime-time television special, *Alice Cooper: The Nightmare*. Before long he took his act to Las Vegas and became a regular on *The Hollywood Squares*. He helped raise money to repair the Hollywood sign in the hills overlooking Los Angeles and was befriended by stars from the movie industry's Golden Age.

Although he had been shocking when the 1970s began, by decade's end Cooper was overtaken by changing times. Cooper responded shrewdly with *Flush the Fashion* (1980), which included a cover of a 1960s garage punk song, the Music Machine's "Talk Talk," familiar to him from his formative years. The synthesizer-driven originals were influenced by Devo and other rising new wave acts.

Afflicted by drug and alcohol problems, Cooper claims he can scarcely remember his albums from the early 1980s, a time when his 1970s persona influenced a host of new bands such as Twisted Sister and White Zombie. As the decade drew to a close he had sporadic success on tour and a hit single, "Poison" (1988). During the 1990s and 2000s he juggled an ongoing career of recording and touring with guest vocals on albums by Guns N' Roses and Insane Clown Posse and cameos in *Wayne's World*, *Nightmare on Elm Street,* and many other films and television shows. He was inducted into the Rock and Roll Hall of Fame, but was probably more gratified by being honored with a star on the Hollywood Walk of Fame.

Suggested Albums: Pretties for You (1969); *Easy Action* (1970); *Love It to Death* (1971); *Killer* (1971); *School's Out* (1972); *Billion Dollar Babies* (1973); *Flush the Fashion* (1980); *Constrictor* (1986); *Trash* (1989); *Brutal Planet* (2000); *Dragontown* (2001); *Along Came a Spider* (2008)

COUNTRY JOE & THE FISH

Joe McDonald emerged from the far left wing of the folk-blues revival. After busking on Berkeley streets and playing in jug bands, he formed Country Joe & the Fish in 1965 as a duo with Barry "The Fish" Melton. Recording political broadsides associated with the Berkeley Free Speech Movement, McDonald and Melton expanded into a larger folk band before belatedly embracing rock in 1966. Their debut album, *Electric Music for the Mind and Body* (1967), included their one Top 40 single, the psychedelic "(Not So) Sweet Martha Lorraine." The almost vaudevillian title number from *I-Feel-Like-I'm-Fixin'-to-Die* (1967) became one of the era's earliest and most familiar anti–Vietnam War songs.

Country Joe & the Fish played before large audiences at the Monterey Pop Festival (1967) and Woodstock (1969), and their concerts became infamous for the "Fish cheer," a letter-by-letter countdown of a four-letter profanity at a time when public profanity was still shocking. After several personnel changes, the Fish disbanded in 1970.

By then, McDonald had already begun his solo career with an album of folk covers, *Thinking of Woody Guthrie* (1969), and has continued recording into the 21st century. Country Joe & the Fish have regrouped occasionally to record and perform.

Suggested Albums: Electric Music for the Mind and Body (1967); *I-Feel-Like-I'm-Fixin'-to-Die* (1967)

COUNTRY ROCK

Country rock emerged as a definable genre in the late 1960s, rising from the social, political, and philosophical unrest of the era to provide a reassuring landscape of familiar sounds and bucolic themes that offered a troubled America a retreat from more turbulent times. One of its anthems, the Eagles' "Take It Easy," symbolized the soothing promise of country blended with rock music. The combination represented a family reunion of sorts, in which rock's rebellious prodigal son returned to its country ancestor.

Of course, rock music could never fully escape its country heritage. At Elvis Presley's legendary Sun Sessions, rockabilly was as influenced by country music as much as blues or rhythm and blues. Early rock and roll artists such as Jerry Lee Lewis, Roy Orbison, and Buddy Holly clearly owed a debt to country music, although the Nashville-based country music industry soon recoiled from the upstart genre, creating a wall of separation. And, as rock music came to be a more ambitious art form in the mid-1960s, many of its fans viewed country as hopelessly unsophisticated cornpone, the music of stock car racing, beer drinking, and the Bible-thumping segregationist South.

However, not all rock musicians shared these attitudes, as the Beatles, Rolling Stones, Beau Brummels, and Byrds either covered country songs or recorded songs with a distinctly country feel, demonstrating that the wall between the two musical forms rested on a somewhat shaky foundation.

The wall fell completely in 1968 with the Byrds' landmark LP *Sweethearts of the Rodeo*, a heavily country-influenced album recorded in Nashville. Newest member Gram Parsons drove the Byrds' foray. The Florida-born musician had discovered country in college and was especially enamored of the Bakersfield sound epitomized by Merle Haggard, and especially Buck Owens. Owens and his band the Buckaroos played traditional country fueled by more loudly amplified guitars and a more prominent drumbeat, giving the recordings more of a rock feeling than previously heard on country records. After leaving the Byrds, Parsons formed the Flying Burrito Brothers, a heavily country-influenced band that paid homage at times to the Bakersfield sound. The rise of country rock was given the imprimatur of respectability with the release of Bob Dylan's *Nashville Skyline* (1969), and it suddenly became fashionable for rock bands to record country-influenced music.

The rising country rock scene quickly became centered in Southern California. Far from the increasingly hidebound Nashville establishment and closer to Bakersfield, country rock seemed perfectly suited to the laid-back atmosphere associated with Southern California in the early 1970s. Bands such as Poco, New Riders of the Purple Sage, Pure Prairie League, and Rick Nelson's Stone Canyon Band began to record songs with country instrumentation, themes, melodies, and vocals. By far, the most successful country rock band was the Los Angeles–based Eagles, whose radio-friendly sound achieved almost instant chart success.

Country rock shared a similar back to basics ethos with groups such as the Band and Creedence Clearwater Revival. However, those bands demonstrated a moralizing tone, delving into the deeper issues of sin, betrayal, judgment, and redemption that lay beneath the rebellion and discontent of the late 1960s. In contrast, country rock's sweet melodies and often mellow lyrics were largely innocent of social criticism and moral evaluation, inviting listeners to step back and enjoy the simple pleasures of free love, recreational drugs, and the California sun. The Eagles' most thematically complex album, *Hotel California* (1976), was also their least country-influenced.

Over time, country rock began to splinter, with acts either moving deeper into roots-oriented Americana or else leaving rock completely and becoming true country artists. In fact, today much of what would have been called country rock in 1973 dominates the country charts. No longer is it considered remarkable for a rock artist to perform country music, and perhaps that is country rock's truest legacy.

CREAM

Cream was rock's original power trio and an influence on the development of heavy metal. Formed in 1966, the band's name alluded to the status of its members as the cream of London's blues and rock scene. Eric Clapton had already achieved adulation among guitar aficionados for his work with John Mayall's Bluesbreakers, while drummer Ginger Baker and bassist Jack Bruce were admired from their role in the Graham Bond Organisation. Not unlike a jazz combo, Cream focused on the musicianship of all its members. It had no designated frontman.

The idea of a rock trio was audacious at the time. Without the cover of lead and rhythm guitars or other instruments, the trio format demanded maximum proficiency from its members. Cream did not disappoint. *Fresh Cream* (1966) was a

CREATION 81

tentative first effort, yielding a U.K. hit, "I Feel Free," and "Toad," one of the first extended drum solos heard in rock. The band's distinctive sound emerged on *Disraeli Gears* (1967). One of the greatest rock albums, *Disraeli Gears* was a response to the emergence of Jimi Hendrix, whose playing filled Clapton with wonderment and fascination. Clapton laid Cream's blues foundation while Baker and Bruce added an inclination toward jazz. The sound was heavy, enabled by the signal breakups caused by high amplification and inspired by the spirit of an era that sought to push across boundaries sonic as well as social.

Although Baker and Clapton contributed to Cream's repertoire, Bruce, writing with poet-lyricist Pete Brown, was the primary source of original songs. However, the arrangements and textures of the recordings owed much to each member. For "Sunshine of Your Love," Clapton utilized what he called the "woman's tone"; by manipulating the volume knobs, he conjured a soft, slightly high-pitched, sensuous tone from his guitar. In his solo, Clapton quoted the Rodgers and Hart standard "Blue Moon" for subtle contrast with the "Sunshine" of the song's title.

Their follow-up, *Wheels of Fire* (1968), was a two-LP set composed of studio material and jams recorded in concert. For the album's hit, "White Room," Clapton made prominent use of the wah-wah pedal and deployed a descending riff echoed later on Derek and the Dominos' "Layla." For the instrumental bridge, Baker achieved Wagnerian thunder on drums. Bruce's playing was deep yet agile, positioning the bass as a lead instrument. Among the live material on *Wheels of Fire* was Clapton's version of Robert Johnson's "Crossroads," a staple of American FM rock radio.

Although Cream joined the ranks of rock's most acclaimed bands, their personalities were too combustible for the long haul. The final album, aptly titled *Goodbye* (1969), was cobbled together from live and studio tracks including the enigmatic "Badge," co-written by Clapton and George Harrison.

Following the breakup, Clapton joined the short-lived supergroup Blind Faith and commenced a long career that included Derek and the Dominos and many solo albums. Although they never achieved Clapton's stardom, Baker and Bruce enjoyed long and eclectic careers spanning rock, jazz, and ethnic music. Cream was inducted into the Rock and Roll Hall of Fame.

Suggested Albums: Fresh Cream (1966); *Disraeli Gears* (1967); *Wheels of Fire* (1968); *Goodbye* (1969)

See also: Baker, Ginger; Bruce, Jack; Clapton, Eric

CREATION

The Creation flourished briefly in Britain's Mod youth subculture, going through several lineup changes from inception in 1966 through dissolution in 1968. They released a handful of extraordinary singles comparable to the early Who. Sharing the Who's producer, Shel Talmy, the Creation reached the zenith of power pop as defined by Pete Townshend with loud guitars, power chords, and sharp melodies confined within three-minute songs bursting with creativity and imagination. The powerfully heavy "Making Time" (1966) was a minor British hit. "Painter Man" (1966) featured an electric guitar played with a violin two years before Jimmy Page introduced the idea to Led Zeppelin. With its humorous allusions to art school and commercial design, "Painter Man" was a Mod anthem and the band's biggest hit in their homeland.

Outside the Mod subculture, the Creation found its largest audiences in Germany and Scandinavia and made no impression on the U.S. charts. The group never had time to conceive a proper album and was overshadowed by the Who. However, memories of the Creation continued to circulate. "Painter Man" became a Top 10 British hit for the pop group Boney M (1979). The Creation was admired by the brief Mod revival in the wake of the Jam's emergence in the late 1970s and influenced Plasticland and other neo-psychedelic bands in the 1980s. "Making Time" factored in the soundtrack of director Wes Anderson's film *Rushmore* (1998).

Suggested Album: The Best of the Creation (1968)

CREEDENCE CLEARWATER REVIVAL

Although John Fogerty was raised in El Cerrito, on the east end of San Francisco Bay, his band, Creedence Clearwater Revival, turned its back on the mecca of the druggy counterculture and embraced the far country of backwater Louisiana. In the age before information was a click away, most listeners were easily persuaded that CCR was, as one of its songs was titled, "Born on the Bayou." CCR was a great singles band whose songs came together as superb albums. They were at home on both AM and FM radio with an audience that encompassed hippies and rednecks. The bikers in *Easy Rider* and the truckers who murdered them might have shared CCR's music, if little else.

John Fogerty was the band's guiding light, yet he initially took the backseat to his brother. Tommy Fogerty and the Blue Velvets, which released a pair of singles (1961, 1962), were a competent rock and roll combo featuring Tom as lead vocalist and primary songwriter. The future CCR lineup was otherwise entirely in place with John on guitar, Stu Cook on bass, and Doug Clifford on drums.

In 1964 the Blue Velvets mutated, as many American groups did, into a faux British Invasion act called the Golliwogs. By 1965 they often sounded more like Them than the early Beatles, their sound growing darker with foreshadows of the ominous mood of CCR's first album. In 1966 they released the single "Walking on the Water," which, as "Walk on the Water," was rerecorded for that debut LP. John and Tom shared the singing and songwriting in the Golliwogs.

By 1968 they abandoned the Golliwogs' moniker for a name in keeping with the era's undercurrent of 19th-century Americana, Creedence Clearwater Revival. After the band's long apprenticeship, they emerged on their eponymous debut album (1968) as masters of their own genre under John Fogerty's firm leadership.

The album vividly evoked a place Fogerty had visited often in his imagination, Louisiana's bayou. It was a vision of the mossy delta closer to the haunted spirit of Robert Johnson than the Crescent City jauntiness of Allen Toussaint. CCR's

Creedence Clearwater Revival spanned the AM and FM dials during the late 1960s by producing hit singles and albums. Their music's echoes of country and blues were transformed into signature songs by the band's songwriter, John Fogerty, seen here at the microphone during a 1970 concert. (Gijsbert Hanekroot/Redferns/Getty Images)

rendering of "I Put a Spell on You" set the tone. The 1956 original by Screamin' Jay Hawkins was already an anomaly, its staccato rhythm closer to Kurt Weill's Weimar jazz than rhythm and blues. Fogerty's guitar electrified the strange song as he sang with the bone-chilling assurance of a voodoo shaman. The other covers were also interesting. Elegantly arranged and forcefully sung, Wilson Pickett's "Ninety-Nine and a Half" acknowledged the rhythm and blues that had long filled the band's stage show. On "Susie Q," the album's tour de force and breakout hit, Dale Hawkins's 1957 Cajun rockabilly tune was endowed with a groove elastic enough to reach infinity. The hypnotic tom-toms suggested primeval rites in the dark swampland. Fogerty played with distortion and reverb to eerie effect.

Fogerty's original songs were also striking, including the sardonically defiant blue-collar ethos of "Working Man," the Southern gothic family trauma of "Porterville," and the terrifying nocturnal apparition of "Walk on the Water." A psychedelic residue clung to the proceedings as Fogerty mastered his baroque quasi-Southern enunciations, pronouncing turns as "toins" and man as "mayen."

Bayou Country (1969) sealed CCR's position on the top of the charts with its double-sided single, "Proud Mary" backed with "Born on the Bayou." Both songs gave additional evidence of Fogerty's love for Louisiana lore and rode on rhythms as unhurried and inevitable as the Mississippi on a muggy day. Fogerty's guitar

84   CREEDENCE CLEARWATER REVIVAL

rippled across them like stones skipping on the river's surface. "Proud Mary" was reassuringly even-tempered, a tonic in the troubled time of its release as utopian dreams of the 1960s faded against Charles Manson, Altamont, and mounting casualties in Vietnam. It rapidly became a standard for cover acts and wedding bands and received a wild-eyed rendition from Ike and Tina Turner. *Bayou Country* coincided with a resurgence in Cajun pride and the introduction of Cajun music to a wider public through fiddler Doug Kershaw.

Bayou Country also displayed Fogerty's blues roots on his Howlin' Wolf–inspired "Graveyard Train," and included a hard-rocking update of Little Richard's "Good Golly Miss Molly." Unlike many of his contemporaries, Fogerty had the humility to realize that it was better to do great versions of other people's songs than competent versions of mediocre originals.

Nineteen sixty-nine was an extraordinary year for CCR, which released two other best-selling albums during those 12 months, *Green River* and *Willie and the Poor Boys*. Fogerty continued to explore within the musical and lyrical borders he drew for himself. *Green River's* title track was echo-drenched rockabilly reinvented as swamp rock. Along with evoking bullfrogs calling across the bayou and barefoot Cajun girls in the moonlight, Fogerty expressed his everyman social-political perspective on "Wrote a Song for Everyone" and handed down an indictment of privilege on "Fortunate Son." A strong streak of pessimism ran through many of his songs. "Bad Moon Rising" promised apocalypse despite its deceptively upbeat rockabilly tempo. "Sinister Purpose" revisited the dark occult references of CCR's debut album.

Each of the two albums CCR released in 1970, *Cosmo's Factory* and *Pendulum*, added several outstanding songs to the band's repertoire. For "Travelin' Band," Fogerty finally shifted focus from the bayou to the big city, building its hard-rocking account of the rock touring circuit from the material of 1950s New Orleans rhythm and blues. On the whimsical "Lookin' Out My Back Door," Fogerty tipped his hat to the contemporary country sound of Buck Owens. CCR's rock jam of Marvin Gaye's "I Heard It Through the Grapevine" garnered FM airplay. A pair of chiming mid-tempo numbers, "Who'll Stop the Rain" and "Have You Ever Seen the Rain," rued the perennial failure of humanity's best intentions.

By *Pendulum*, the band was chafing under John Fogerty's direction, resenting their role as backing musicians. Tom left after *Pendulum* and John acceded to demands for more creative input from Clifford and Cook. On *Mardis Gras* (1972), all three members shared songwriting, lead vocals, and production, yet Fogerty contributed the only memorable numbers, "Someday Never Comes" and "Sweet Hitch-Hiker." CCR broke up before the end of 1972.

CCR's label, Fantasy Records, continued to mine the band's platinum-selling status by releasing live albums recorded in the early 1970s and greatest hits packages. Tom Fogerty released several solo albums and Clifford and Cook were in demand as a rhythm section. Enjoying the only significant post-CCR career, John Fogerty periodically recorded under his own name and as the Blue Ridge Rangers.

As one of the era's most commercially and artistically successful rock groups, CCR's music sounded integral to their era and yet has survived as a touchstone for

American music. In the 21st century, they continue to be admired by fans of country, Americana, hard rock, and roots rock and roll. CCR have been inducted into the Rock and Roll Hall of Fame.

Suggested Albums: Creedence Clearwater Revival (1968); *Bayou Country* (1969); *Green River* (1969); *Willie and the Poor Boys* (1969); *Cosmo's Factory* (1970); *Pendulum* (1970); *Pre-Creedence* (1975)

See also: Fogerty, John

CROSBY, STILLS, NASH & YOUNG

Most rock bands in the 1960s presented themselves as tight units. Crosby, Stills, Nash & Young adhered to a different model. They were a collection of individuals who pursued their own solo careers while grouping and regrouping in three configurations: Crosby & Nash; Crosby, Stills & Nash; and Crosby, Stills, Nash & Young. The seeds were already present in Buffalo Springfield, where Stephen Stills and Neil Young behaved as if they played in different bands. They found like-minded yet contentious fellow travelers in the farrago of late 1960s Los Angeles. After leaving the Byrds in a dispute with Roger McGuinn, David Crosby easily gravitated toward Stills, as did English expatriate Graham Nash, who had recently left the Hollies after arguing with his band mates. They sought maximum creative freedom within a loose collaborative structure.

Young was always the least comfortable in this setting and was not initially involved in the project. Atlantic Records mogul Ahmet Ertegun, a man whose ear for music was as keen as his business sense was shrewd, suggested and insisted that Young join the trio after the release of *Crosby, Stills & Nash* (1969), an album that helped launch the softer sounds of the 1970s. *Crosby, Stills & Nash* featured harmonies from three fairly high voices, blending while retaining individual integrity. Each singer shone through the collaborative performances with Nash's British accent adding a unique touch to this otherwise American ensemble. Each member contributed songs. The jubilant pop of Nash's "Marrakesh Express" was originally intended for the Hollies. Stills's "Suite: Judy Blue Eyes" was in the vein of his ambitious multifaceted compositions for Buffalo Springfield.

Young joined his colleagues in time to perform at Woodstock. He brought his unusual voice and a harder rock edge to the first CSN&Y release, *Déjà vu* (1970). Despite Young's potentially jarring presence, the album's most popular songs, Nash's "Teach Your Children" and "Our House," exemplified the emerging posthippie lifestyle in a Hegelian synthesis of family values and 1960s rebellion. The album's third hit, a cover of Joni Mitchell's "Woodstock," was an ode to the utopian vision the festival fostered in some minds.

Weeks after *Déjà vu*'s release, CSN&Y reacted to the Kent State shooting of student protesters by releasing a blistering song in keeping with Young's barbed-wire aesthetic, "Ohio." CSN&Y toured that year but soon disbanded, leaving the live album *4 Way Street* as a document.

Crosby, Stills, Nash & Young were an unstable supergroup whose lineup continually fractured and regrouped as its members pursued solo careers and diverse collaborations. Seen here, left to right, are Stephen Stills, David Crosby, Graham Nash, and Neil Young. (Armando Gallo/Zuma Press, Inc./Alamy Stock Photo)

While Stills and Young developed prolific solo careers in the early 1970s, Crosby managed to release only one solo album during that decade, *If I Could Only Remember My Name* (1971), which included contributions from Young, Joni Mitchell, and members of the Grateful Dead and Jefferson Airplane. Recorded with a similar cast of guest stars, Nash's *Songs for Beginners* (1971) sold well and included "Chicago," a Top 40 polemic on the trial of the Chicago Seven militants. His lone follow-up in the 1970s, *Wild Tales* (1974), found less attention. Crosby & Nash formed a durable partnership, releasing four albums together from 1972 through 1977.

Stills rejoined Crosby and Nash to record *CSN* (1977), which included a Top 10 hit, Nash's wistfully melodic "Just a Song Before I Go." The trio toured in 1978 in an acoustic format, and a year later became involved in antinuclear benefit concerts sponsored by Musicians United for Safe Energy (MUSE). CS&N returned to the Top 10 singles chart one last time with Nash's "Wasted on the Way" from *Daylight Again* (1982).

The aftermath was a complicated mess of drug and health problems, mutual acrimony, and Crosby's early 1980s prison sentence on drug and weapons charges. CSN&Y's *American Dream* (1988) was an overproduced effort so characterless that Young refused to tour in support of the album. CS&N received only slight attention for their two albums from the 1990s. CSN&Y were inducted into the Rock and Roll Hall of Fame and reunited for *Looking Forward* (1999), which was better received than its predecessor. A collection of previously unreleased material from their 1974 tour, *CSNY 1974* (2014), received good reviews.

Suggested Albums: David Crosby: *If I Could Only Remember My Name* (1971). Crosby, Stills & Nash: *Crosby, Stills & Nash* (1969); *CSN* (1977). Crosby, Stills, Nash & Young: *Déjà vu* (1970); *4 Way Street* (1971); *Looking Forward* (1999); *CSNY 1974* (2014)

See also: Buffalo Springfield; Byrds; Hollies; Stills, Stephen; Young, Neil

CURVED AIR

Named for minimalist composer Terry Riley's groundbreaking album *A Rainbow in Curved Air* (1969), the British group was formed in 1970 by classically trained musicians. The reference to Riley underscored the affinities between certain strains of progressive rock and avant-garde classical music. Both were built on repeating patterns, employed raga-like drones, and were constructed in the recording studio through overdubbing. Vocalist Sonja Kristina's background was in musical theater; her lyrics brought a female perspective unusual in the era's progressive rock. Darryl Way's electric violin filled the role normally reserved for electric guitar. Francis Monkman's synthesizers were integral to the sound.

"Vivaldi" from their debut album, *Air Conditioning* (1970), was the group's closes encounter with the classical rock characteristic of many British progressive rock bands. However, the song's digression into metallic abrasion was closer to the Velvet Underground than Emerson, Lake & Palmer. Curved Air broke into Britain's Top 10 singles chart with "Back Street Luv" from *Second Album* (1971), but personnel changes soon undercut the group's original vision. After *Phantasmagoria* (1972), the lineup became a shifting muddle that included Edie Jobson before he left to join Roxy Music and Stewart Copeland before the Police. Sporadic reunions have occurred into the 21st century.

Suggested Albums: Air Conditioning (1970); *Second Album* (1971); *Phantasmagoria* (1972)

DAVIS, SPENCER

At first, the Spencer Davis Group seemed to differ little from the host of rhythm and blues–influenced bands in the musical tidal wave known as the British Invasion. Their early output featured covers of the rhythm and blues and blues material that was standard fare for dozens of young British bands, but the Spencer Davis Group was set apart by a willingness to dabble in other musical forms, and most importantly by the dynamic singing and propulsive organ playing of their prodigy frontman, Steve Winwood.

Welsh guitarist Spencer Davis formed the group in 1963, enlisting the 15-year-old Winwood and his bassist brother Muff to join him and drummer Pete York in the Rhythm and Blues Quartet. The band quickly landed a recording contract and became the Spencer Davis Group. The appropriately titled *Their First LP* (1965) reflected the group's roots. Steve Winwood was already the standout performer, singing with a confidence and command that belied his age and playing organ with soulful authenticity. The album was a promising start, and the band built momentum with *The Second Album*, which displayed increasing originality. Winwood's keyboard playing became the focal point of the sound, and his powerful singing was placed up front in the mix. While the album stayed true to the group's rhythm and blues roots, Winwood's keyboard playing began to reflect his growing interest in jazz. Their first hit, "Keep On Running" by Jamaican songwriter Jackie Edwards, featured Davis's overdriven guitar and a beat that echoed the new ska sound that was gaining traction in Great Britain.

The unremarkable rhythm and blues covers of *Autumn 1966* (1966) were overshadowed by a song not included on the album, "Gimme Some Lovin'." The single, written by the Winwood brothers and Davis, was nothing less than a revelation, a surging stomper with a live feel fueled by Winwood's churning Hammond B3 Organ and passionately joyful soul vocals. "Gimme Some Lovin'" was a Top 10 hit and has become a rock standard, covered by numerous artists. It was followed by another classic single, the organ-driven rocker "I'm a Man" (1967).

Backed by consecutive hit singles, the band seemed headed for stardom, but that momentum halted when Winwood left to form the more musically adventurous Traffic. The Spencer Davis Group recorded several albums without Winwood (but with a Winwood sound-alike singer). They attracted little attention and broke up in 1974, albeit Davis occasionally tours under the Spencer Davis Group name. Winwood enjoyed great success in the 1970s with Traffic and Blind Faith. His career reached new heights in the 1980s, scoring a series of hit singles, culminating with the soul-influenced "Roll With It" (1988), which featured Hammond organ playing and could have easily followed "Gimme Some Lovin'" and "I'm a Man" in the Spencer Davis Group's catalogue.

Suggested Album: The Second Album (1966)

See also: Blind Faith; Traffic

DEEP PURPLE

The most familiar riff in rock music remains Ritchie Blackmore's elemental guitar line for "Smoke on the Water" from Deep Purple's chart-topping album, *Machine Head* (1972). Blackmore's father forced him to take classical music lessons and the instruction stuck. Blackmore formed the original Deep Purple lineup in 1968 with organist Jon Lord and drummer Ian Paice. They scored a hit from their first album, *Shades of Deep Purple* (1968), with a cover of American songwriter Joe South's "Hush." Traces of Blackmore's emerging style were audible, yet *Shades* and its follow-up, *The Book of Taliesyn* (1968), sounded directionless. Their third album, a recording of Lord's *Concerto for Group and Orchestra* (1970), was an interesting experiment in classical rock but barely hinted at things to come.

By this time Deep Purple's classic lineup was in place with Roger Glover on bass and singer Ian Gillan, who set the bar for heavy metal vocalists with a shriek derived from Arthur Brown. They became one of the world's leading hard rock bands with *Deep Purple in Rock* (1970), *Fireball* (1971), and *Machine Head* (1972). Their sound was led by Blackmore, who played guitar with thrilling intensity and forceful restraint, achieving breakneck speed while allowing for space between notes. His solos on "Black Night" and "Highway Star" owed more to classical music than blues, which had been the primary source for hard rock guitarists such as Eric Clapton and Jimmy Page.

Conflict between Blackmore and Gillan led the latter to depart in 1973 for a solo career. David Coverdale filled his spot. Glover soon left to pursue session work and production. The rancor continued. After Blackmore left in 1975, Deep Purple made one more album with Tommy Bolin on guitar before quitting in 1976. As has often been the case, the band continued to regroup with various lineups in later years. Blackmore achieved the greatest notoriety of Deep Purple's ex-members with two projects, the hard rock band Rainbow and the medieval folk-rock of Blackmore's Night.

Suggested Albums: Concerto for Group and Orchestra (1970); *Deep Purple in Rock* (1970); *Fireball* (1971); *Machine Head* (1972)

See also: Blackmore, Ritchie

DELANEY & BONNIE

Delaney and Bonnie Bramlett were united both as husband and wife and in a musical partnership that saw them become notable figures in late 1960s rock circles.

The couple recorded a series of albums that brought them into a circle of prominent musicians, affording them a level of influence beyond the rather modest commercial appeal of their music.

The duo met in Los Angeles, where Delaney had begun to establish a career as a sessions guitar player and Bonnie had migrated in hopes of finding success as a vocalist. The couple married in 1967 and began to form a band built around their vocal chemistry and a core of musician "friends" who had done sessions work with Delaney, most notably keyboard player Leon Russell. They landed a contract with Stax Records and flew to Memphis to record their debut, *Home* (1969), a fine rhythm and blues–based record replete with crack songwriting from Stax regulars Isaac Hayes, Steve Cropper, and Eddie Floyd. However, Stax's poor promotion led to the album tanking commercially. The duo switched to Elektra after a botched attempt by new fan George Harrison to sign them to Apple Records. Their follow-up album, *The Original Delaney & Bonnie (Accept No Substitute)* (1969), also sold poorly but attracted attention from Eric Clapton, who signed them as the opening act on his 1969 tour, where he frequently jammed onstage with the duo. The album also set the creative tone for much of their career, featuring up-tempo, piano-driven blues boogie with strong elements of gospel and hints of country thrown in the mix.

Despite garnering the admiration of significant artists, Delaney and Bonnie never really flourished commercially, although their version of Dave Mason's "Only You Know and I Know" did get them FM radio play. Despite the couple's soulful vocals, there was a generic quality to their music that failed to set them apart from scores of similar-sounding acts. Delaney and Bonnie did begin to depart from the boogie format with 1971's excellent *Motel Shot*, a relaxed album of gospel and blues standards played in a more traditional format, with a few solid Delaney originals thrown in for good measure. The couple's marriage began to deteriorate and they divorced in 1973, effectively ending their professional relationship.

Delaney and Bonnie are best remembered for their tour with Clapton, but it should be noted that Clapton cites Delaney as a primary influence in developing his vocal style, and George Harrison's slide guitar style was shaped by Delaney's work. Delaney Bramlett died in 2008 due to complications from gall bladder surgery, the same year Bonnie released her most recent album, *Beautiful*.

Suggested Albums: Home (1969); *To Bonnie from Delaney* (1970); *Motel Shot* (1971)

DENNY, SANDY (1941–1978)

American folk music is primarily rooted in the British Isles but Britain's folk traditions had largely been forgotten in its place of origin. It was the American folk-blues revival that reintroduced the islands' older musical traditions to a younger generation. The example of Bob Dylan was crucial for inseminating folk music in British cities during the early 1960s, and it might be interesting to measure the influence of Simon & Garfunkel's version of "Scarborough Fair" on the country where the song originated.

Sandy Denny attended the same art school as Jimmy Page, Eric Clapton, and another figure prominent in Britain's folk revival, John Renbourn. She sang in London coffeehouses while training as a nurse. In 1967 she recorded with the Strawbs during their country-folk period but departed to join Richard Thompson's seminal folk-rock band, Fairport Convention, in time for their second album, *What We Did on Our Holidays* (1969). Following the release of *Leige & Leif* (1969), she left Fairport to form a new band, Fotheringay.

On Fotheringay's self-titled album (1970), American country rock and the influence of bootlegged material from Dylan and the Band's *Basement Tapes* filled some tracks while others were devoted to Denny's vibratoless English vocals, which hovered like an incantation above her quasi-medieval melodies. Most memorable was Denny's haunting rendition of "Banks of the Nile," a ballad from the Napoleonic era testifying to the emotional toll of war.

Voted top female vocalist in Great Britain by the influential *Melody Maker* magazine in 1970 and 1971, Denny embarked on a solo career surrounded by a circle of musicians from Fairport Convention and Fotheringay. Her ensuing albums, *The North Star Grassman and the Ravens* (1971), *Sandy* (1972), *Like an Old Fashioned Waltz* (1973), and *Rendezvous* (1977), were rock transposed to the cadences of bygone ages. Her songwriting and piano playing became more prominent and the tone was often somber and fatalistic. Along with Thompson and her usual crew of British folk-rock collaborators she formed a side project called the Bunch, which released a low-key album of 1950s rock and roll, *Rock On* (1971).

Judy Collins covered one of Denny's most familiar songs, "Who Knows Where the Time Goes." Denny provides ghostly backing vocals on Led Zeppelin's "Battle of Evermore" from the band's fourth album (1971). Denny rejoined Fairport Convention for one album, *Rising for the Moon* (1975). She died after falling down a flight of stairs in 1978.

Suggested Albums: Fotheringay (1970); *The North Star Grassman and the Ravens* (1971); *Sandy* (1972); *Like an Old Fashioned Waltz* (1973); *Rendezvous* (1977)

See also: Fairport Convention; Thompson, Richard

DEREK AND THE DOMINOS

Although he had already begun a solo career with his self-titled 1970 album, Eric Clapton was still more comfortable subsumed into a band rather than standing center stage. Growing out of his collaboration with Delaney and Bonnie, Clapton recruited several members of their band for Derek and the Dominos, including bassist Carl Radle, drummer Jim Gordon, and keyboardist Bobby Whitlock. His admiration for fellow guitarist Duane Allman resulted in Allman's integral role on *Layla and Other Assorted Love Songs* (1970). Allman's crying slide guitar complemented Clapton's anguished playing.

Epitomized by "Layla," which became a hit single two years after the album's release, the music, fueled by desperation, was the sound of a man at the end of his rope. The inspiration was Clapton's unrequited love for Patti Boyd, the wife of his best friend, George Harrison (Clapton married Boyd in 1979). The album includes several of Clapton's most powerful performances on record, among them his version of the 1920s blues standard "Nobody Knows You When You're Down and Out" and his original "Bellbottom Blues," an expression of love as a prison. With *Layla and Other Assorted Love Songs*, Clapton transmuted the terror of 1930s Robert Johnson, one of his seminal influences, into melodic yet hard-driving rock.

During his interlude with Derek and the Dominos, Clapton was seen as rock music's next likely drug casualty as he struggled to hold himself together in the face of heroin addiction. Calling the band quits, Clapton withdrew from the public eye, broke his addiction, and reemerged with a softer, more relaxed sound that found great success throughout his solo career. The live album released in their aftermath, *In Concert* (1973), was superseded by *Live at the Fillmore* (1994), which includes the complete song list from one of the band's legendary performances.

Suggested Albums: Layla and Other Assorted Love Songs (1970); *Live at the Fillmore* (1994)

DONOVAN (1946-)

Donovan was under the spell of Bob Dylan when he began his recording career, but already on his first hit, "Catch the Wind" (1965), a Scottish lilt was in the air. Born Donovan Leitch in Glasgow, he always brought a distinct tone to his music. Donovan's best work was tightly packed into four prolific years (1965–1969), a time of almost incredible creativity. His albums framed a mirror image of an unusually fertile period in music and popular culture when revolution rather than evolution was the rule.

Literate and finding joy in the world, thoroughly modern yet familiar with things little known in the modern world, Donovan suggests what might have been if Yeats had come of age in the 1960s and set himself up in swinging London. His bejeweled words and gorgeous orchestrations adorned some of the era's most elegant popular recordings.

Donovan grew up in a milieu of literature and came to Robert Burns, one of Dylan's influences, with mother's milk; after a stint in art school he went on the road inspired by Jack Kerouac. As it did for many British musicians, the American folk-blues revival aroused an interest in taking up acoustic guitar and exploring folk music traditions. But having grown up with early rock and roll, Donovan would never be a purist. He had a keen sense throughout the 1960s for finding organic connections between folk, rock, jazz, and the music of faraway times and places.

His albums contained little if any filler; the craft of his songwriting was always at a high level in the 1960s. However, Donovan was known at the time and is remembered now for an extraordinary string of singles imbued with a striking lyrical sensibility. The offbeat melody and cadences of the trippy title track from *Sunshine Superman* (1966) recalled Beat coffeehouse jazz. "Season of the Witch" from that same album began with a folk melody but made advantage of the sinister potential

94 DOOBIE BROTHERS

of rock to convey a lyric that mixed foreboding with fascination. The playful title number from *Mellow Yellow* (1966) was a paean to a sex toy whose easygoing melody derived from British pop music of an earlier generation. Donovan was capable of beautifully idealized love songs such as "Wear Your Love Like Heaven" from *A Gift from a Flower to a Garden* (1967) and the jubilant, baroque-tinged "Jennifer Juniper" from *The Hurdy Gurdy Man* (1968).

Donovan's remarkable range was displayed on the latter album's title track. "Hurdy Gurdy Man" was proto-metal with a raga drone, and although memories conflict on who played on the session, the music was likely propelled by Jimmy Page's distorted guitar, John Bonham's thundering drums, and John Paul Jones's heavy bass in a foretaste of the band they would form in the following year, Led Zeppelin. On the title track from *Barabajagal* (1969), the Jeff Beck Group backed Donovan in a blazing hard rock assault. *Barabajagal* also included his final big hit single, "Atlantis," which recounted lore of the lost continent before erupting into a rousing endless chorus inspired by the Beatles' "Hey Jude."

Beneath the diverse musical influences and lyrical themes was a coherent worldview, a poetic rather than a prosaic reading of reality leavened by a Celtic sense of enchantment. Like the great rock posters of the era, Donovan's lyrics would have been at home amidst the luxuriant symbolism of Art Nouveau.

Although *Cosmic Wheels* (1973) sold moderately well, the world kept turning and left Donovan behind. His inspiration faded in the 1970s but he remained an endearing performer, especially on acoustic solo tours highlighted by a full version of "Hurdy Gurdy Man" complete with a verse written by George Harrison. After revitalizing Johnny Cash's career, producer Rick Rubin turned his attention to Donovan, producing *Sutras* (1996) in a stark acoustic format similar to his work with Cash. Although sales were sparse, the album helped introduce Donovan to post–Baby Boom music fans. He continues to perform in the 21st century and has been inducted into the Rock and Roll Hall of Fame.

Suggested Albums: What's Bin Did and What's Bin Hid (1965); *Fairytale* (1965); *Sunshine Superman* (1966); *Mellow Yellow* (1966); *A Gift from a Flower to a Garden* (1967); *The Hurdy Gurdy Man* (1968); *Barabajagal* (1969)

DOOBIE BROTHERS

The Doobie Brothers underwent changes so drastic that fans of their early rock albums had little to say to fans of their latter-day "white soul" records. During the early 1970s the Doobie Brothers were staples on FM rock stations but ended the decade on Top 40 and rhythm and blues radio. The California band began in 1970 playing at biker parties. Their note of distinction, high three-part vocal harmonies, caught the ear of the record industry and launched a string of familiar numbers from the era including "China Grove," "Long Train Running," "Listen to the Music," the countryish "South City Midnight Lady," and a cover of the Byrds' "Jesus Is Just Alright."

By 1975 lineup changes placed newly added members, including ex–Steely Dan guitarist Jeff "Skunk" Baxter and vocalist Michael McDonald, in charge of the band.

McDonald became the principal songwriter on *Takin' It to the Streets* (1976), an album of jazz-inflected, synthesized blue-eyed soul. The new direction proved commercially successful, placing the Doobie Brothers at the top of the charts in several industry formats through 1980 with "Keeps You Runnin'," "What a Fool Believes," "Minute by Minute," and other hit singles. Various versions of the band have reunited to tour and record in recent decades.

Suggested Album: Toulouse Street (1972)

DOORS

The Doors' reputation was so overshadowed by the image of their frontman, Jim Morrison, that it has been easy to forget that their music was a group effort. Morrison was only one of the band's four songwriters and although he fancied himself a poet, he was not even the sole lyricist. As for the Doors' sound, his chief contribution was the often sardonic howl of his vocals. Morrison's out-of-control stage antics ultimately attracted most of the media attention during the band's short life; his notorious death in a Paris bathtub from a heroin overdose cemented Morrison's image as a doomed rebel whose fast trip down the road of excess took him off the edge of a cliff.

According to legend, the Doors began in 1965 when Morrison recited his poem "Moonlight Drive," among his most beautiful lyrics, to fellow UCLA film student Ray Manzarek on a Los Angeles beach. They soon recruited a pair of local musicians, guitarist Robby Krieger and drummer John Densmore. The band's name came from Aldous Huxley's account of the psychedelic properties of mescaline, *The Doors of Perception* (1954). As Morrison and Manzarek knew, Huxley's title alluded to a line from William Blake: "If the doors of perception were open / Everything would appear as it is in reality / Infinite."

The Doors' mystic aspirations, encoded in their name, reflected the psychedelic aesthetic of tearing away the veil masking the essence of reality. Unlike many of their psychedelic cohorts, especially from the music scene that flourished contemporaneously in San Francisco, the Doors recognized darkness as well as light.

The Doors' discography can roughly be divided into three phases. In phase one, consisting of *The Doors* (1967) and *Strange Days* (1967), the band achieved a coherent and unique sound that harmonized the input of all its members. While Morrison brought poetic flights to life, complete with allusions to Blake and Louis-Ferdinand Celine, Manzarek sat bent over his keyboards like a conservatory professor giving a lesson. Despite his smoldering conclusion to their first single, "Break on Through (To the Other Side)," Krieger was underrated as a guitarist, perhaps because his playing was often buried in the mix. Densmore was a versatile drummer, whether undergirding "Break on Through" with a supercharged samba rhythm, laying down a Weimar Republic oompah on their carnival version of Kurt Weill's "Alabama Song (Whiskey Bar)" or keeping a straight rock beat on "Twentieth Century Fox."

The Doors and *Strange Days* maintained an ambience of carefully considered decadence, an aural as well as lyrical appreciation for the deep shadows cast by the

Although the stage antics of leather-clad singer Jim Morrison attracted much of the attention, the Doors were a group effort with each member contributing to their repertoire and unique sound. At this 1968 performance, Ray Manzarek plays keyboard, John Densmore plays drums, and Robby Krieger plays guitar. (Michael Ochs Archives/Getty Images)

bright California sun. The songs unfolded in a neon-streaked milieu whose roots are traceable to the film noir Los Angeles of Howard Hawks's *The Big Sleep* (1946) and continued through David Lynch's *Mulholland Drive* (2001). The Doors reached the top of the charts with an edited for AM version of "Light My Fire," which flowed with a jazz-like looseness and featured an outstanding solo by Krieger, building alongside Manzarek's organ toward the ecstasy of sexual climax. In the Doors' hands, sex could be the lucid dream of "The Crystal Ship" or fraught with danger in their ominous cover of Willie Dixon's "Back Door Man."

The Doors was marred only by the inclusion of Morrison's overheated essay in Freudian envy, "The End." The epic was put to better purposes outside the album, first in Nico's doomsday rendition (1974) and then in the tone-setting soundtrack from Francis Ford Coppola's *Apocalypse Now* (1979).

On *Strange Days*, producer Paul A. Rothchild used reverb and a Moog synthesizer to convey distortions of reality much as director Robert Wiene used unnaturally angled sets in the German Expressionist classic *The Cabinet of Dr. Caligari* (1920). The album had a more powerful bottom-end rock sound than its predecessor because Rothchild employed an electric bass player. On their debut Manzarek, like a church organist, maintained the bass notes with the pedals of his keyboards.

Phase two of the Doors' recording career began with *Waiting for the Sun* (1968), which lacked the consistency of mood and theme that prevailed on their earlier albums. It included a pair of the Doors' most beautiful songs, the melodically intriguing "Love Street" and the rueful "Summer's Almost Gone." Also on *Waiting* was the brisk rocker "Hello, I Love You," whose riff was stolen from the Kinks' "All Day and All of the Night," and a parcel of hastily written tunes. The album's inner jacket included Morrison's poem "The Celebration of the Lizard King," which introduced the dangerous persona he would adopt in the remaining years of his life.

Waiting for the Sun coincided with the beginning of Morrison's legal problems, especially allegations of lewd and lascivious behavior on stage. The Lizard King may have been informed by Antonin Artaud's Theater of Cruelty but often came across instead as an obnoxious drunk. Increasingly, alcohol in great quantity became his mood-altering drug of choice. Morrison's deliberately confrontational stage presence cost the band many cancelled shows, but inspired Iggy Pop and licensed a generation of aggressive rockers yet unborn.

The Doors reached nadir with *The Soft Parade* (1969), which included misguided attempts at "adult pop" sung by Morrison in an eager bellow. "Touch Me" was the hit, elevated with a solo by hard bop saxophonist Curtis Amy. The album was padded out with tired songs of dubious inspiration, occasionally salvaged by Krieger's inventive lead guitar. *Morrison Hotel* (1970) was patchy but stronger than its predecessor. The opening number, the superb blues-rock of "Roadhouse Blues," included a memorable forecast: "The future's uncertain, the end is always near." A few of the songs would not have been out of place on *The Doors* or *Strange Days*.

Phase three was the shortest, consisting of the Doors' final album released before Morrison's death, *L.A. Woman* (1971). The album maintained a tone that echoed the city of its title with grungy funk crisscrossed by dark shadows. The declaration of erotic and emotional devotion in "Love Her Madly" was more disconcerting than reassuring. The album's other hit, "Riders on the Storm," encapsulated the post-Manson murders, post-Altamont mood as the hopeful 1960s faded into the uncertain 1970s.

Morrison's death (1971) was the culmination in a cycle of major rock star deaths that began with Jimi Hendrix and continued through Janis Joplin. In Morrison's case, his demise attracted legends. Some said that the Lizard King slipped his skin much like his hero, the French Symbolist poet Arthur Rimbaud, who disappeared into a life of adventure in Asia and Africa. Manzarek promoted the legend even as he struggled to keep the Doors together.

Most Doors fans have no memory of the two albums the band released after Morrison's death, and despite impressive-looking sales figures for the first one, *Other Voices* (1971), few heard those recordings at the time. Before the advent of store scanners, chart rankings were malleable. After *Full Circle* (1972), the surviving Doors abandoned hope of keeping the band alive without Morrison.

Given the prominence of the band, the surviving Doors fell short of expectations. Manzarek released several albums that achieved limited notice; Krieger and Densmore formed the uneventful Butts Band before going separate ways. More fans made the pilgrimage to Morrison's grave in Paris's Lachaise Cemetery than purchased the recordings of his erstwhile bandmates.

The bestselling biography of Morrison, Danny Sugerman and Jerry Hopkins's *No One Here Gets Out Alive* (1980), revived interest in the Doors and introduced them to a generation too young to have been conscious of them in the 1960s. The Morrison legend filled a need for a safely dead rebel figure in the neo-conservative 1980s and became a romanticized touchstone of an era so close in time yet so far away. The revival led to Oliver Stone's film *The Doors* (1991) starring Val Kilmer as the Lizard King. At the band's induction into the Rock and Roll Hall of Fame (1993), Manzarek, Krieger, and Densmore performed together with Pearl Jam's Eddie Vedder standing in for Morrison. Since then, the trio has regrouped several times to record and perform, sometimes reworking leftover material by Morrison, sometimes with contemporary vocalists filling in. In 2002, Manzarek and Krieger toured as the Doors of the 21st Century until Densmore and the Morrison estate successfully sued over the name. Manzarek's death in 2013 brought Krieger and Densmore back together for a cancer benefit featuring performances by members of X, the Foo Fighters, and other recent bands.

Suggested Albums: The Doors (1967); *Strange Days* (1967); *Waiting for the Sun* (1968); *Morrison Hotel* (1970); *L.A. Woman* (1971); *Alive She Cried* (1983)

See also: Manzarek, Ray

DOO-WOP

A style of vocal music, doo-wop was born in African American urban settings in the late 1940s and became a pervasive style through the 1950s and early 1960s. Many doo-wop groups honed their a capella style on street corners with an echo chamber of asphalt and masonry. Vocal arrangements were often elaborate, featuring much onomatopoeia and vocal mimicry of the sound of other musical instruments. The 1950s saw the spread of doo-wop among Italian American and Puerto Rican youths, as well as many hits on the rhythm and blues and pop charts. Doo-wop set the stage for such "girl groups" of the early 1960s as the Ronettes and the Crystals; the most enduringly popular group to emerge from doo-wop, Frankie Valli and the Four Seasons, enjoyed their peak years of success in the early 1960s. Doo-wop was an occasional influence on classic rock–era artists as diverse as Frank Zappa and Billy Joel.

DRAKE, NICK (1948–1974)

The name of Nick Drake's first album, *Five Leaves Left* (1969), foreshadowed his future. The title refers to the inscription found in packs of British rolling paper, alerting the owner that the pack is almost exhausted with only five papers remaining. Drake died five years after the release of his debut from an overdose of antidepressants. The coroner suspected but could not confirm suicide.

Drake was discovered playing acoustic guitar in a London club by Ashley Hutchings of Fairport Convention, who introduced him to Fairport's producer, Joe Boyd. Boyd oversaw *Five Leaves Left*, setting Drake's somber ballads in austere arrangements. Although Britain's nascent folk-rock scene provided Drake with a milieu, his songs, intensely individual and inner directed, lent themselves uneasily to any genre.

Boyd produced *Bryter Layter* (1970) with guitarist Richard Thompson and other members of the Fairport circle providing accompaniment. The arrangements were often jauntier than on the debut, as if Boyd hoped to package Drake's melancholy in bright pop wrappers. Always reticent and with an awkward stage presence, Drake stopped performing in public in 1970 and became increasingly reclusive. His career continued fitfully. Drake recorded *Pink Moon* (1972) unaccompanied and, according to one version of the legend, sent the tapes to his label, Island Records, by post. Although he vowed to quit music, he began to write and record demos in the last months of his life.

In the years since his death, Drake has attracted a devoted cult following. The paucity of records sold during his lifetime along with the soft-spoken starkness of his vision have insulated him from comparisons to more popular confessional singer-songwriters such as James Taylor or Harry Chapin. Cast in the Romantic literary mode of the doomed young hero, he became an inspiration for the Cure and other mordant postpunk bands and has been the subject of several biographies and documentary films. The unlikely appearance of *Pink Moon*'s title number in a 2006 Volkswagen television ad testifies to the undercurrent of interest in his work.

Suggested Albums: Five Leaves Left (1969); *Bryter Layter* (1970); *Pink Moon* (1972)

DRISCOLL, JULIE (1947–)

Julie Driscoll emerged from the jazz-tinged, rhythm and blues end of 1960s British rock, singing alongside Rod Stewart in Steampacket from 1965 through 1966 before joining Brian Auger and the Trinity. The latter group had several hits in the United Kingdom and continental Europe, including covers of Donovan's "Season of the Witch" (1967) and Bob Dylan and the Band's "This Wheel's on Fire" (1968).

When the Trinity broke up in 1969, Driscoll began collaborating with the man who would become her husband, pianist Keith Tippett. Their first album together, *1969* (1969), was released under her name. Featuring original songs with inventive arrangements for horns, *1969* was a jazz-rock album with touches of the British folk-rock revival sung by Driscoll with quiet power.

Afterward, she took on a variant of her husband's name and became known as Julie Tippetts. She worked prolifically in jazz and experimental venues, often in large bands led by her husband or in collaboration with Carla Bley and other jazz musicians. She remains active in the 21st century.

Suggested Album: 1969 (1969)

DYLAN, BOB (1941–)

Rooted in the immigrants' quest to escape the past and of pioneers building their future on the frontier, reinvention is at the heart of the American experience. With the closing of the frontier at the end of the 19th century and the passage of restrictive immigration quotas in the 1920s, reinvention became a matter of social and

DYLAN, BOB

Rising from his origins in the folk-blues revival of the early 1960s, Bob Dylan became the single most influential individual in rock music by the middle of the decade. By infusing modernist poetry into his lyrics, he raised the expectation that rock could aspire to become art. (Photofest)

cultural role-playing. One of America's signature novels, F. Scott Fitzgerald's *The Great Gatsby*, concerns a Midwesterner of obscure origin who changed his name and transformed himself into the toast of East Coast society.

Born Robert Zimmerman, Bob Dylan was doubtless aware of Gatsby when he followed that character's path from Minnesota to New York. Reinvention and its corollary, concealment, are integral to Dylan's nature. Perhaps the origins can be sought in his upbringing. As a Jew in Hibbing, a small town in Lutheran Minnesota, he may have felt a need to blend in. Like many teenagers in the 1950s, Dylan embraced the new sound of rock and roll, and like other musicians of his generation drawn to the nonconforming outskirts of American culture, he put his early rock and roll band behind him, took up acoustic guitar, and made for the cultural frontier, the mecca of the folk-blues revival, Greenwich Village, in 1961.

By that time, he had already adopted his new surname, honoring Welsh poet Dylan Thomas while phonetically invoking the dusty American past beloved by folklorists. Matt Dillon was one of America's best-known fictional heroes of the Old West as the protagonist of the popular television series *Gunsmoke*. Many performers have opted for new names in tune with the public image they hope to establish, but few have been as imaginative as Dylan, who invented a shifting set of pasts to buttress his standing as a voice from the heartland, a young protégé of

Woody Guthrie who left home, worked in a circus, and rambled town to town in search of the real America. Dylan would remain a fabulist and purveyor of red herrings. Even with the publication of his memoirs, *Chronicles, Volume 1* (2004), he remained the unreliable narrator of a remarkable life, comfortable behind masks and contemptuous of the press whose reporting he deliberately confounded.

Dylan came to Greenwich Village with more chutzpah than talent. His sandpaper voice rubbed raw even in the ears of folk purists, but he was an eager student of the music and literature of his milieu. With the pluck and good fortune of a Horatio Alger protagonist, he earned favorable notice from the *New York Times* within months of arriving and an audition with John Hammond, the Columbia Records producer who had signed Billie Holiday. Before long he had a recording contract. Joan Baez, the Village's leading light, championed and shared stages with him. His self-titled debut album (1962) was a thin collection of folk-blues revival material. The tune for his original, "Song to Woody," was borrowed from Guthrie's "1913 Massacre."

Talent came later, but came quickly. If Dylan's development had stopped with his first recording, he would scarcely merit a footnote in any account of music or popular culture in the 1960s. To switch literary comparisons from Fitzgerald and Alger to Walt Whitman, the Dylan who emerged over the next three years contained multitudes. He spurred the shift from folk music as historic preservation and reenactment into the self-expression of the singer-songwriters who followed in his wake; along with John Lennon and Paul McCartney, he set the imperative for rock musicians to perform their own material rather than rely on the product of professional songsmiths. By raising expectations, he set conditions for the emergence of art rock as the conscious effort to lift rock and roll from its vernacular origins and endow it with greater scope and the power to illuminate reality more profoundly than even the greatest narrator of everyday life in early rock and roll, Chuck Berry.

Dylan's second album, *The Freewheelin' Bob Dylan* (1963), documented his increasing poetic sophistication. It opened with his first significant song, "Blowin' in the Wind," with rhymes reminiscent of one of his favorite poets, Robert Burns, and melody adapted from an old spiritual, "No More Auction Block." Dylan had a folklorist's appreciation for music as common property. Three weeks after its release, "Blowin' in the Wind" was covered by pop folk act Peter, Paul and Mary, who turned it into a hit. *Freewheelin'* also included "A Hard Rain's A-Gonna Fall," whose surreal sequence of post–atomic war images was set to the Child ballad "Lord Randall," and the jeremiad "Masters of War," with music borrowed from another medieval British ballad, "Nottamun Town." The music for the album's love song, "Girl from the North Country," was drawn from the same source as Simon & Garfunkel's "Scarborough Fair."

With *The Times They Are a-Changin'* (1964), Dylan stepped back from poetry in favor of the hoary folk tradition of broadsides, rhyming the news of the day and setting the dispatches to familiar tunes. With its rousing call to arms for the civil rights movement, the title number elevated Dylan into America's leading protest singer, the new voice of a generation. He chafed at the role. *Another Side of Bob Dylan* (1964) abruptly shifted the terms with "My Back Pages," which consigned his protest singing to history's ashcan and broke with politically motivated folk music. Some folk purists condemned Dylan for becoming "inner directed" rather than the bugler for the cause.

Dylan outgrew the confines of the folk-blues revival without losing touch with its aesthetics. He was ready to reembrace his first love, rock and roll, but in a new form. Inspired by the Beatles' music and popularity, he was eager to climb onto a higher stage than the folk scene offered.

Dylan was uninterested in the potential of the recording studio to create unique sonic artifacts. Like a folk singer, he preferred to be documented in the moment. He drew at all times from existing idioms in rock, folk, blues, and country. Dylan's breakthrough, and his larger importance in the development of rock music, was to endow popular songs with the possibility of art by investing them with poetry. Some of the great songwriters of the 1930s, such as Harold Arlen and George Gershwin, also thought they were creating art, not merely entertainment, but this self-consciousness felt new to the youth culture that came of age under Dylan's spell. Dylan had long been aware of the archaic poetry of Anglo-Celtic balladry, but he had a revelation upon hearing *King of the Delta Blues Singers* (1961), an LP collection of 1930s recordings by Robert Johnson. Unlike British rock contemporaries Keith Richards and Eric Clapton, who were inspired by Johnson's uncanny guitar playing, Dylan focused on the poetry Johnson forged from vernacular material. He also found inspiration farther afield in modernist verses of T.S. Eliot and the Symbolism of Arthur Rimbaud and Charles Baudelaire. At the same time, Dylan understood that his lyrics lived beyond the printed page. Like playwrights or ancient bards, his words were meant to be performed.

With *Bringing It All Back Home* (1965), Dylan brought all of his influences together from rock and roll through the folk-blues revival and combined poetry with the power of post–British Invasion rock. Half of the album remained in the solo folk format, with Dylan's voice accompanied by acoustic guitar and harmonica. He was backed on the other half by rock musicians. Even the album cover represented a step into greater complexity. Like the gatefold that would surround the Beatles' *Sgt. Pepper's Lonely Hearts Club Band* (1967), it was an object worth studying not only for the information it conveyed but also for the series of suggestions it inferred. The density of images surrounding Dylan on the cover evoked the objects a painter might array around himself in a self-portrait, and mirrored the density of the lyrical images within.

The times were changing and changing fast. In January 1965 the Byrds, a band of Los Angeles folk singers who defected to rock after hearing the Beatles, were given an advance copy of a new Dylan song, "Mr. Tambourine Man," and began recording a rock rendition. Their abbreviated take, issued in April, a month after the release of Dylan's version on *Bringing It All Back Home*, became a hit. By then, Dylan had already moved on musically. In July, he released "Like a Rolling Stone," which reached number two on the singles chart, an astonishing breakthrough for a six-minute sequence of bitter metaphors. It was a full-tilt rock song, with guitarist Michael Bloomfield serving as bandleader and Al Kooper improvising the memorable part for carnival organ.

On July 25, 1965, five days after the release of "Like a Rolling Stone," Dylan reached a watershed with his performance at the Newport Folk Festival. Instead of performing as usual in work shirt and jeans, he came attired in the Carnaby Street togs favored by British rock bands. Rather than accompany himself on acoustic guitar and harmonica, Dylan brought along the Paul Butterfield Blues Band. Although blues appreciation was integral to the folk-blues revival, the purists preferred their music unplugged, as Muddy Waters had already discovered when touring the United Kingdom with his electric band. Greeted with boos and shouts of "traitor," Dylan stalked offstage. Peter Yarrow of Peter, Paul and Mary coaxed him back to perform a few crowd-warming numbers on acoustic guitar. Although revisionists assert that the crowd reacted poorly because they could not hear the words through the amplified guitars, the event became legendary as Dylan's breaking point with the folk scene; indeed, as that scene's eventual accommodation with changing times. Two nights after Newport, Dylan gave a concert with Kooper on organ, Bloomfield on guitar, and two members of the Band, drummer Levon Helm and guitarist Robbie Robertson. In what became his concert format for years to come, Dylan performed an acoustic and an electric set. Before long, the Band became Dylan's regular backing band.

In August 1965, Dylan released *Highway 61 Revisited*, its name a tribute to the road connecting the blues country of Mississippi with his home state of Minnesota. Along with "Like a Rolling Stone," the album contained such masterpieces as "Desolation Row," a bleak 10-minute tour of a society that had lost its connection with the life force, and "Ballad of a Thin Man," interpreted as a sardonic depiction of an older generation incapable of comprehending the changes around them.

The final album in this groundbreaking phase of Dylan's career, *Blonde on Blonde* (1966), was rock's first two-LP set, a format formerly reserved for classical music, and the inclusion of a 20-minute song, "Sad-Eyed Lady of the Lowlands." The album encouraged rock musicians to paint on larger canvases, albeit most of them lacked Dylan's breadth. Two months after its release, Dylan suffered a serious motorcycle accident near his home in Woodstock, New York. Rumors flew that he met a James Dean end, an artist dead before his time or at least paralyzed or incapacitated.

Dylan disappeared from view for 18 months, retreating from the tumultuous cultural milieu he had helped inspire. He could have traveled to San Francisco for the Summer of Love and been lauded as an oracle. Instead, he withdrew into seclusion with the Band and recorded many hours of original songs and traditional numbers reimagined for the rock era. Recordings soon circulated among the rock elite, inspiring a tilt toward Band-like Americana among some British musicians. The music fell into the hands of illicit entrepreneurs and helped launch an underground industry of "bootleg albums," often of dodgy sonic quality. Demand for an official release led to *The Basement Tapes* (1975), an incomplete record of the sessions. The whole of Dylan's work from those years with the Band finally saw light as *The Basement Tapes Complete: The Bootleg Series Vol. 11* (2014).

Although shying away from public performance, Dylan reemerged as a recording artist with *John Wesley Harding* (1968), a bare-boned acoustic album that ran counter to such highly produced LPs as the Beatles' *Sgt. Pepper's Lonely Hearts Club Band* as well as the trend toward louder, heavier rock. The stark imagery of "All Along the Watchtower" could have been at home on *Blonde on Blonde*, but "I'll Be Your Baby Tonight," which sounded like a popular tune from the era of parlor pianos, was a deliberate affront to the counterculture that honored Dylan as its poet laureate. He moved even further from expectations with *Nashville Skyline* (1969). Recording with guest star Johnny Cash in Nashville, Dylan enveloped his raspy voice with reverb and emulated the polished "countrypolitan" style of Eddy Arnold and other country music professionals. The album's "Lay Lady Lay" became a pop hit and has often been covered by other artists.

Dylan remained determined to break the constraints to which his audience would bind him. He delivered his most perplexing album, the double LP *Self Portrait* (1970), followed by one of his most nondescript, *New Morning* (1970). *Self Portrait* was disorderly in its eclecticism. Live performances with the Band from one of his rare concerts from the era, Britain's Isle of Wight Festival, were mixed with new originals and a grab bag of folk, country, and pop covers. His rendition of "The Boxer," harmonizing badly with himself on a Simon and Garfunkel song reputedly written about him, supports the idea that *Self Portrait* was a self-parody. However, on many songs, Dylan sounds entirely sincere. *Self Portrait* might also have been the first album by a rock artist conceived as a tribute to the performer's influences. The songs gathered for *New Morning* are unconvincing in their depiction of Dylan as a serenely married country gentleman. Olivia Newton-John covered the album's love song, "If Not for You," turning it into a pop hit. Dylan's music from that era is best served by *Another Self Portrait (1969–1971): The Bootleg Series Vol. 10* (2013), a listenable collection of demos and alternate takes.

Dylan was selling briskly to a pop audience. His dirge-like "Knockin' on Heaven's Door" from the Sam Peckinpah film *Pat Garrett and Billy the Kid* (1973) was a Top 20 hit. However, longtime fans continued to be dismayed by the path of his career and greeted the following two albums as something of a return to expectations. The studio album *Planet Waves* (1974) and the live *Before the Flood* (1974) reunited him with the Band. Only now, with his songs subsumed into their sound, Dylan seemed more a member of the Band than its leader. Documenting his first concert tour since his motorcycle accident, *Before the Flood* was Dylan's hardest rock effort to date, an exuberant reinvention of familiar songs and one of rock's greatest live albums.

The previous two albums gave no sign of what was coming. If his 1960s albums helped to shape their time, *Blood on the Tracks* (1975) remains timeless. Inspiration for its deceptively simple profundity came from his marital turmoil, yet Dylan transcended finger pointing, including himself in the album's epic track, "Idiot Wind." The upbeat "Lily, Rosemary, and the Jack of Hearts," an outlaw ballad whose trickster hero is the human heart, tells its story cinematically with tarot symbolism in every scene. *Blood on the Tracks* was folkish but not folk, drawing from rock and blues but transmuting those elements into something new.

For *Desire* (1976), Dylan took inspiration from his encounter with a Gypsy encampment in the south of France and built the sound around the swirling violin of

Scarlet Rivera. The album was unusual for Dylan's collaboration with a lyricist, Jacques Levy, an off-Broadway theater director who had previously written "Chestnut Mare" with Roger McGuinn. "Isis," a hero's quest for the feminine archetype, is *Desire*'s peak. The album contains a pair of broadsides: "Joey," a curiously sympathetic account of murdered Mafioso Joey Gallo, and "Hurricane," which helped propel the cause célèbre surrounding the conviction of boxer Rubin "Hurricane" Carter for murder.

Desire led into the Rolling Thunder Revue, a freewheeling concert tour whose shifting lineup included associates from the 1960s such as Joan Baez, Allen Ginsberg, and Roger McGuinn along with new colleagues Joni Mitchell and Mick Ronson. The tour was documented by *Hard Rain* (1976) and was the basis for a money-losing cinematic folly, Dylan's audacious four-hour film *Renaldo and Clara*. As Dylan's marriage finally came apart, he embraced Protestant fundamentalist Christianity and was baptized in Pat Boone's swimming pool.

Dylan's next albums were unlike anything he had done. For *Street Legal* (1978), he went for an almost Bruce Springsteen saxophone-driven sound. On the live *Bob Dylan at Budokan* (1979), he emulated Neil Diamond. He shifted again with a trilogy of overtly Christian albums, *Slow Train Coming* (1979), *Saved* (1980), and *Shot of Love* (1981). Dylan professed his new belief in no uncertain terms. Some fans responded with the outrage of folk purists when Dylan embraced rock in 1965.

Dylan's interest in Christianity was a logical outcome of his fascination with Americana. His debut album included a traditional spiritual, "Gospel Plow," and his lyrics had drawn from the religious imagery of the folk-blues tradition. Intimations of a spiritual quest could be heard in many of his earlier songs. Dylan's conversion experience can be read as another chapter in a life built around breaking preconceptions.

Stepping back from fundamentalism and proselytizing, Dylan seemed to find equanimity between Judaism and Christianity. After *Shot of Love*, he withdrew into the commercial backwaters with a series of misguided or indifferent albums, most containing at least one or two gems. Forever restless, he recorded a pair of albums (1988, 1990) with the Traveling Wilburys, a supergroup featuring Tom Petty, George Harrison, Jeff Lynne, and before his death, Roy Orbison. Dylan ended the decade with *Oh Mercy* (1989), embracing a contemporary sound with the help of U2 producer Daniel Lanois.

Acknowledging that he suffered from writer's block, he reconnected with his folk-blues roots on a pair of solo acoustic albums recorded in his garage. *Good as I Been to You* (1992) and *World Gone Wrong* (1993) drew material from the traditional songs he heard and performed in Greenwich Village. Dylan's muse returned for *Time Out of Mind* (1997), the album that inaugurated yet another renaissance for the songwriter that continued through *Love and Theft* (2001), *Modern Times* (2006), *Together through Life* (2009), and *Tempest* (2012). Dylan returned to the methodology of his youth by making something new out of old songs and connecting lines of lyrics from the public domain to tell new tales. Discernible are traces of the blues of Charlie Patton and Robert Johnson, the country of the Carter Family, the balladry of Robert Burns and Walter Scott, and even the 19th-century verse of Henry

Timrod, "the poet laureate of the Confederacy." For *Together through Life*, Dylan collaborated with Grateful Dead lyricist Robert Hunter.

In 1988 Dylan commenced a series of ongoing concert tours rock critics dubbed the "Never-Ending Tour." His backing band evolved over those years and included many musicians heard on his latter-day albums. The concerts have been eclectic, drawing from Dylan's deep grab bag of songs. Determined to connect with new audiences, Dylan appeared in television ads for Victoria's Secret (2004), Cadillac (2008), and Pepsi alongside rapper will.i.am (2009); and he has been inducted into the Rock and Roll Hall of Fame. Dylan was awarded the Nobel Prize for Literature in 2016.

Suggested Albums: The Freewheelin' Bob Dylan (1963); *The Times They Are a-Changin'* (1964); *Another Side of Bob Dylan* (1964); *Bringing It All Back Home* (1965); *Highway 61 Revisited* (1965); *Blonde on Blonde* (1966); *John Wesley Harding* (1968); *Nashville Skyline* (1969); *Planet Waves* (1974); *Before the Flood* (1974); *Blood on the Tracks* (1975); *Desire* (1976); *Street Legal* (1978); *Slow Train Coming* (1979); *Shot of Love* (1981); *Infidels* (1983); *Good as I Been to You* (1992); *World Gone Wrong* (1993); *Time Out of Mind* (1997); *Love and Theft* (2001); *Modern Times* (2006); *Together through Life* (2009); *Tempest* (2012); *Tell Tale Signs: The Bootleg Series Vol. 8* (2008); *Another Self Portrait (1969–1971): The Bootleg Series Vol. 10* (2013); *The Basement Tapes Complete: The Bootleg Series Vol. 11* (2014)

EAGLES

Southern California has long maintained a mythic status in American culture, representing golden promises of beauty, wealth, and fame but with a dark undercurrent lurking beneath the shimmering surface. The entertainment industry headquartered in Los Angeles promulgated both the dream and reality of the region since the inception of Hollywood in the 1910s. By the early 1960s rock music had become an integral part of creating and chronicling the area's culture, beginning with Dick Dale and other surf instrumental bands, building with the Beach Boys' odes to the sun and surf culture of suburban Los Angeles, through Guns N' Roses' journey into the seething decadence of Sunset Strip in the late 1980s. The region's rock bands represented both the ideal and at times stark reality of Southern California, but perhaps no other band captured its essence as did the Eagles in the 1970s.

The Eagles were founded in 1971 by guitarist Glenn Frey and drummer Don Henley, who had been playing in Linda Ronstadt's backing band. Henley and Frey recruited former Flying Burrito Brothers guitarist Bernie Leadon to join them and plucked bassist Randy Meisner from Rick Nelson's Stone Canyon Band. Like so many Southern Californians, none of them hailed from the Golden State. Frey was from Detroit, where he cut his teeth playing in local rock bands and was mentored by Bob Seger (Frey's background vocals can clearly be heard in Seger's original recording of "Ramblin' Gamblin' Man"). Henley was a Texas native, and Leadon was a Floridian. The members adapted quickly to the region's lifestyle and soon fell into the burgeoning local country rock scene. Driven by the hugely ambitious Frey, the group secured a recording contract with Asylum Records, attracted by owner David Geffen's promise of a nurturing atmosphere of creative freedom.

British producer Glyn Johns (who had worked with the Who and the Faces) was recruited to produce the Eagles' eponymous debut album, which was recorded in London and released in 1972. The band's sound did not come together immediately, as there was conflict between Frey's vision of the Eagles as a rock band and Leadon's strong country leanings. Leadon's approach won, with the help of Johns, who chose to emphasize the band's remarkable vocal harmony blend. Along with the vocals, Leadon's country-flavored guitar and banjo playing dominate the sound. The first single, "Take It Easy," became an anthem of the country rock movement and the post-1960s mindset. Co-written by Frey and Jackson Browne (with Frey adding the upbeat second verse), the song seemingly provided a

The Eagles were already well established hitmakers before the addition of guitarist Joe Walsh (second from left). With a gift for endearing melodies, vocal harmonies, and insightful lyrics, the Eagles reflected and critiqued the hedonism of southern California in the 1970s. (Pictorial Press Ltd/Alamy Stock Photo)

soothing alternative to a nation roiled by the Vietnam War and the Watergate scandal. The album sold well, and the Eagles were recognized as a band on the rise.

Henley and Frey felt considerable pressure to produce an epic second record, and they decided they needed to become the principal songwriters. The duo's efforts paid off handsomely, as the first two songs they wrote, "Tequila Sunrise" and "Desperado," become the centerpieces of *Desperado* (1973). Frey sang the lead on "Tequila Sunrise," a lovely Latin-flavored country number. However, it was the title track that became the album's standout, a piano-based ballad that caught the emotional weariness of a generation that had survived the 1960s and now was seeking a way home. The album itself was a loosely based concept album centered around the dubious, although often echoed theme of the rock star as a modern-day Wild West outlaw. The effort was critically well received, but did not sell as well as the band's debut album. The follow-up, *On the Border* (1974), showed Frey asserting his leadership of the band. Johns was sacked as producer, and lead guitarist Don Felder was brought in to provide a harder rocking edge. However, the country-influenced ballad "Best of My Love" proved to be the album's biggest hit.

As the Eagles' success grew, they began to be recognized as *the* Southern California band. Part of it was their look. Their long hair, bellbottom jeans, prominent facial hair—all seemed emblematic of the public perception of a California rock star. Beyond that, the group simply sounded like Southern California, with a polished (some would say sterile) sound, never a note missed or out of place. Then there were the vocal harmonies, with the trademark high vocal part that had become identified with Southern California beginning with Brian Wilson's falsetto and Chris Hillman's high harmony with the Byrds and that would continue through Michael Anthony's background vocals with Van Halen in the 1980s. The Eagles also heavily indulged in the Southern California lifestyle of free sex, profligate drug use, and nonstop partying, and they seemed to enjoy their image as the epitome of that lifestyle. However, by the time of the group's fourth album, *One of These Nights* (1975), it became apparent that they were beginning to take a more critical look at Southern California. The album had a darker feel and tone, with a more contemporary reverberated production that further distanced the band from its country rock origins; the lyrics began to cast a critical eye on the seamier aspects of the Los Angeles scene. The album was a smash hit, and the band was reaching the heights of the rock stratosphere.

Once again, the Eagles felt the need for a powerful follow-up album, and signaled a changed of direction by replacing the country-influenced Leadon with guitarist Joe Walsh, who had been leader of the hard rock James Gang. The fruits of their labors was a truly standout album, *Hotel California* (1976), a full-scale examination and critique of the Southern California lifestyle and culture. The album's title track became an instant classic, a reggae-influenced journey that highlighted the tantalizing allure and dangerous pitfalls of succumbing to the lifestyle. The track was lifted to new heights by the closing guitar solo, a tour de force between Felder and Walsh that provided a dramatic climax to an already memorable song. Other songs such as "Life in the Fast Lane," "New Kid in Town," and "Wasted Time" showed the band moving from skepticism to cynicism as they asked fundamental questions about the Los Angeles scene and showed growing maturity as songwriters. The album achieved huge commercial success, pushing the Eagles to true superstardom.

With one of the biggest albums of the decade in tow, the band yet again faced the challenge of surpassing previous expectations with their next album. This time they buckled under the pressure. Songs began to come more slowly, as the group began to deal with burnout from years of relentless touring and partying. Meisner left the band in favor of Poco bassist Timothy B. Schmidt, and personal tensions within the band began to escalate as the creative output slowed to a snail's pace. Compounding the difficulty was the fact that the Eagles had begun to fall out of favor with critics who thought that their heavily produced sound lacked passion, and they faced attacks from the emerging punk and new wave scene that saw the band's music and lifestyle as the epitome of the corporate rock dinosaurs they sought to replace. *The Long Run* (1979) took more than three years to deliver and landed with a thud. The album was an uninspired collection of disparate tunes, far removed from the searing insight and intensity that typified *Hotel California*. Despite strong sales, the band broke up following an acrimonious tour in 1980, with Henley vowing they would reunite "when hell freezes over."

The 1980s saw the individual members achieve varying degrees of commercial and artistic success. Frey and Henley became significant solo artists, mastering the video format and becoming staples on the new MTV network (Frey also established a side career as a television and film actor). Walsh battled substance abuse issues while continuing to release solo albums; Schmidt took part in a vast array of musical projects. Seemingly against all odds, the band reunited for a series of concerts in 1994 and released a live album (with four new studio originals) appropriately titled *Hell Freezes Over* (1994). The band then took to the road once more, touring for several years before taking another hiatus. Creatively, the band took to the studio (minus Felder, who had been fired by the band) and emerged with *The Long Road Out of Eden* (2007), an effort that redeemed the band's creative reputation tarnished by the debacle that was *The Long Run*.

A series of tours followed, ending with a farewell tour in 2015, made final by Frey's death due to complications from arthritis in early 2016. His passing, only weeks after David Bowie's, resulted in an outpouring of grief that indicated that the Eagles' music had touched fans far more than critics had realized. While it is true that the Eagles seldom took chances with their music, they also took the time and trouble to make sure their music was consistently strong. The Eagles were not originators or innovators, but they were professionals in the best sense of the word, and they produced a body of work that deserves to be considered apart from the sometimes bland Southern California sound that they helped to develop.

Suggested Albums: Eagles (1972); *Desperado* (1973); *On the Border* (1974); *One of These Nights* (1975); *Hotel California* (1976); *The Long Road Out of Eden* (2007)

EASTERN BLOC ROCK

Control of cultural life was a priority for Eastern Europe's Communist regimes focused on marshaling public enthusiasm and troubled by the power of unfettered expression to question the status quo. The general line among Western commentators is that rock music was repressed throughout the Soviet bloc. While this is not incorrect, repression fails to explain the surprisingly large number of albums released behind the Iron Curtain by local rock bands in many genres.

Even the Soviet Union, which may have been more eager to keep out rock than some of its satellites, countenanced the inclusion of a few rock and roll songs in officially sanctioned ensembles, sponsored by trade unions and other institutions, as early as 1960. Given the paucity of electric guitars, accordion often became the lead instrument. As the 1960s continued, the state-owned record label, Melodiya, issued pirated Rolling Stones and Beatles recordings without attribution, calling it "English people's music." By the 1970s the cultural Cold War had thawed, evidenced by the inclusion on Radio Moscow of shows devoted to Anglo-American rock and the official release of Beatles albums. Most Western LPs were still scarce and remained desirable on the black market.

Unabashed rock bands surfaced in the USSR during the 1970s, sponsored by factories and other state enterprises. A few groups drew from local influences, including Arnika, which transposed Ukrainian folk music into a rock idiom, and Arsenal, which performed similar transformations with Russian folk. Underground rock bands also existed. Notable among them, Machina Vremeni (Time Machine) began by furtively circulating tapes and performing at private gatherings. Their experience illustrated the vagaries of rock in the face of Soviet policy. In 1980 Machina

Vremeni were awarded official status, a recording contract, and permission to stage concerts. Three years later, they were forced to disband when the Communist Party's Central Committee launched a campaign against Western influences.

In the Soviet bloc, as in the West, outbreaks of moral panic occurred periodically over lyrics, the message conveyed by the music itself, and the existence of autonomous youth culture. However, in the USSR, the clampdowns could result in penalties more severe than any meted out in the United States.

Although the satellite states of Eastern Europe were not unconcerned with the subversive potential of rock music, they often pursued a more tolerant policy punctuated by periodic efforts to repress or restrain. Poland, Czechoslovakia, Hungary, and Romania nurtured rosters of recording acts, their album covers showing a progression from beat groups resembling the Beatles in their scuffling Hamburg days through elaborate psychedelic spreads with flowing Art Nouveau fonts and bands clad in Carnaby Street togs. By the early 1970s, album covers by Eastern European progressive rock bands mirrored the sleeve designs of Yes and similar acts.

Some Soviet bloc bands managed to find a following beyond the Iron Curtain. After attracting attention in Japan and Western Europe, Hungary's progressive rock band Locomotiv GT was allowed to record in London on their first release outside their homeland. Jack Bruce played harmonica on the session. Although guitarist Tamas Barta defected while touring the United States in 1974, the Hungarian authorities continued to tolerate their country's most popular rock band. Locomotiv GT continued to record and perform after the fall of communism. However, Barta never achieved success as a solo artist and was murdered in Los Angeles in 1982, allegedly over a drug deal.

The Plastic People of the Universe became rock's famous dissidents from the Eastern bloc. The Czech band formed in 1968 after Soviet troops crushed their country's liberal Communist administration and imposed a hardline regime. Taking their name from a Frank Zappa song, the Plastic People were heavily influenced by the Velvet Underground after playwright Vaclav Havel returned from New York with a copy of that band's album, *White Light/White Heat*. The Plastic People's key album, *Egon Bondy's Happy Hearts Club Banned*, was recorded in 1974 but released in France in 1978. Egon Bondy, a dissident Czech poet, became their principal lyricist.

Police broke up the Plastic People's concerts. In 1976 band members and fans were convicted for "organized disturbance of the peace" and sentenced to prison. As a result of the trial, playwright Havel and other intellectuals and artists organized the Charter 77 human rights movement, which gained media attention in the West and helped delegitimize the Eastern bloc in the eyes of many Western leftists. Havel became the first post-Communist president of Czechoslovakia. The Plastic People reunited in 1997 at Havel's suggestion to commemorate the anniversary of Charter 77.

EIRE APPARENT

Jimi Hendrix's sole production job, *Sunrise* (1969), was the lone album by this Northern Irish band that opened his 1968 U.S. tour. Occasionally Eire Apparent sounded a little like Van Morrison when they dipped into similar American soul influences. For the most part they performed tuneful psychedelic rock. Contrary to expectations, *Sunrise* sounded nothing like the funky heavy rock of its producer, even though Hendrix played guitar on several tracks. By the time of *Sunrise's* release, the direction of music had begun to move away from psychedelia. Eire Apparent disbanded, although its members continued their careers in other bands. The album's most memorable track, "Mr. Guy Fawkes," deserves another hearing in light of the appropriation of Guy Fawkes imagery by 21st-century protest movements.

Suggested Album: Sunrise (1969)

ELECTRIC FLAG

The Electric Flag were at the forefront of the horn-driven jazz-rock that emerged toward the end of the 1960s. Unlike Chicago or Blood, Sweat & Tears, they were firmly grounded in the era's soul music. The original lineup could have competed with confidence in a battle of the bands against most 1960s rhythm and blues revues.

Founded by guitarist Mike Bloomfield, formerly of the Paul Butterfield Blues Band, the Electric Flag was a multiracial group of top-flight young musicians. Bassist Harvey Brooks had played in Bob Dylan's band, drummer Buddy Miles with soul legend Wilson Pickett, and keyboardist Barry Goldberg already had extensive experience in the recording studio. The Electric Flag debuted on the soundtrack for Roger Corman's film *The Trip* (1967). Written by Jack Nicholson and starring Peter Fonda and Dennis Hopper, *The Trip* was superior to contemporaneous counterculture movies for affording a glimpse of psychedelia flourishing amidst the ruins of old Hollywood. The soundtrack included Paul Beaver on Moog synthesizer, one of the instrument's earliest appearances on record.

Beaver lent a hand on the Electric Flag's first proper album, *A Long Time Comin'* (1968). An extraordinary collection of mostly original songs by Bloomfield, the album is built on the supple yet powerful playing of its rhythm section and is held together by Nick Gravenites's expressively soulful voice. The horn section provides memorable riffs as well as concisely inventive solos. Arrangements and textures drew from many sources, including psychedelia, musique concrète, and classical music as well as jazz and soul, yet the diverse influences never sounded eclectic for their own sake but came together in a seamlessly contemporary sound.

Several songs had Top 40 potential and the album sold well. However, drug and other personal problems hampered the band's progress. After the departure of Bloomfield and other original members in 1968, Miles helmed the Electric Flag through a self-titled album (1969). Bloomfield reunited with Gravenites and Miles for *The Band Kept Playing* (1974), but the Electric Flag's moment had passed.

In the aftermath, Miles formed the short-lived Buddy Miles Express and played on Jimi Hendrix's *Band of Gypsys* (1970). He went on to work with Carlos Santana and maintain an active career before his death in 2008.

Suggested Album: A Long Time Comin' (1968)

See also: Bloomfield, Mike

ELECTRIC LIGHT ORCHESTRA

The Electric Light Orchestra sprang from the fertile creative mind of Roy Wood. The eccentric leader of the Move had become interested in forming a new band centered around classical string and horn instruments. Wood plucked guitarist Jeff Lynne and drummer Bev Bevan from the Move and set about developing the new group, dubbed Electric Light Orchestra, although contractual obligations required the trio to remain with the Move for an additional year, delaying ELO's debut until 1971.

Electric Light Orchestra's eponymous first album (1971) showed Wood's vision to full effect. Cellos, violins, oboes, and clarinets abound, with dramatic overtures and orchestral swells, often with a baroque flavor and at times recalling British composer Edward Elgar. There were also more than a couple of Wood's offbeat touches, making one wonder if at times there weren't a tongue-in-cheek element to a project that otherwise verged on the pretentious. The album sold decently in the United Kingdom but nowhere else. Wood departed after apparent business conflicts with the rest of the band, leaving Lynne at the helm.

The next several albums saw the band continue to explore Wood's vision of playing rock with classical instruments, although over time the classical influence

The Electric Light Orchestra was one of many bands that sought to incorporate classical music influences into rock. By the time of this 1977 concert, they had arrived at a formula that brought them onto the pop music charts. (Pictorial Press Ltd/Alamy Stock Photo)

114 ELECTRIC LIGHT ORCHESTRA

was increasingly deemphasized. *ELO2* (1973) had a classical progressive rock feel, although it did yield one Top 40 hit, a cleverly chosen cover of Chuck Berry's "Roll Over Beethoven," which interwove Beethoven's Fifth Symphony with Berry's rock and roll masterpiece. The single was far more successful than the entire album, but the band soldiered on and sales improved with their third album, *On the Third Day* (1973), which featured contributions from T-Rex leader Marc Bolan. The U.S. edition of the album contained another successful single, "Showdown," a rhythm and blues–styled rock song with a melody line that bore a more than passing resemblance to Marvin Gaye's "I Heard It Through the Grapevine."

The next two albums, *Eldorado* (1974) and *Face the Music* (1975), yielded more hit singles, although pop elements began to prevail over classical. Lynne's songwriting owed heavily to the Beatles (John Lennon counted himself an ELO fan), and his prowess in the recording studio led the strings to become more of an accompaniment than a featured component of the band's sound.

If ELO was moving away from Wood's original vision, the public wasn't complaining, and the band's direction was commercially validated with the hit album *A New World Record* (1976). Lynne began to feel his oats as a producer, and the effects-laden album yielded three hit singles: "Livin' Thing," a new version of the Move's "Do Yam," and the Bee Gees–influenced ballad "Telephone Line." Keyboards now dominated the group's sound, and Lynne's increasingly high-pitched singing was either perfect pop fare or gratingly cloying, depending on one's taste.

The album went multi-platinum and paved the way for the even more commercially successful *Out of the Blue* (1977). That album, with its distinctive spaceship cover, moved the band into superstar status, as hit singles such as "Turn to Stone," "Sweet Talkin' Woman," and "Mr. Blue Sky" became staples of AM radio. *Out of the Blue* was even more heavily produced than its predecessor, and Lynne's voice was so effect heavy as to sound almost robotic at times. Along with the album's popularity came a perhaps predictable backlash, as the group's slick production techniques drew the ire of punk and new wave devotees who longed for a back-to-basics approach (although some in the power pop camp admired Lynne's Beatles-influenced songwriting). The album's pulsing rhythms and chirping synthesizers resembled disco, considered by many to be the archenemy of everything rock.

ELO's next album, *Discovery* (1979), was a bit less successful, and by the early 1980s the band's commercial fortunes began to wane as the strings were completely replaced by synthesizers. One would have thought that the synth-dominated 1980s would have been tailor-made for this approach, but ELO never really made the transition to the video era, albeit their soundtrack to the film *Xanadu* (1981) sold well. The band was forced to fend off bizarre charges of subliminal satanic messages hidden in backing tracks. Album sales slipped. ELO broke up in 1986, despite a Top 20 U.S. hit, "Calling America."

As ELO ended, Lynne began to enjoy a fruitful second act as both an artist and producer. Lynne became a member of the part-time supergroup the Traveling Wilburys and became a prominent producer, working on albums with the likes of Brian Wilson, Paul McCartney, Ringo Starr, Joe Walsh, Dave Edmunds, and fellow Wilburys George Harrison, Roy Orbison, and Tom Petty.

ELO reformed in 2001 and released two solid albums, *Zoom* (2001) and *Alone in the Universe* (2015). Electric Light Orchestra seems to be a band that fans either love or loathe, but there is no denying the group's initial ambition, Lynne's knack for a catchy pop hook, or the fact that ELO always did things to the verge of, and perhaps at times past the point of excess.

Suggested Albums: Electric Light Orchestra (1971); *On the Third Day* (1973); *Face the Music* (1975); *A New World Record* (1976); *Out of the Blue* (1977); *Zoom* (2001); *Alone in the Universe* (2015)

EMBRYO

Formed in 1969, Germany's Embryo was a rock band whose vision encompassed the world. Their recordings were far superior to most of the "world music" marketed under that handle in the 1990s. Rock-based but expansive, the various fusions they achieved sounded organic rather than preconceived. Along with the usual lineup of guitars, bass, drums, and keyboards, Embryo's members played woodwinds, vibraphone, marimba, violin, and such Near Eastern string instruments as the oud and the Persian hammered dulcimer called the *santur*. The band recorded some of their music on off-road tours through India and Afghanistan.

Embryo was also in tune with the introduction of electric instruments into jazz that began with Miles Davis's *In a Silent Way* (1969), performing jazz-rock fusion at a higher energy level than most practitioners of that genre. They recorded with pianist Mal Waldron, an African American expatriate who had played with John Coltrane and Eric Dolphy, and with saxophonist Charlie Mariano, a sideman for Stan Kenton and Charles Mingus. Although several core members left in 1981 to form Dissidenten, Embryo remains active in the 21st century.

Suggested Albums: Opal (1970); *Embryo's Rache* (1971); *Father Son and Holy Ghosts* (1972); *Steig aus* (aka *This Is Embryo*) (1972); *Rocksession* (1973); *We Keep On* (1973); *Surfin'* (1975); *Bad Heads and Bad Cats* (1976); *Live* (1977); *Apo Calypso* (1977); *Embryo's Reise* (1979)

EMERSON, LAKE & PALMER

"Welcome back, my friends, to the show that never ends," began the lyrics to one of Emerson, Lake & Palmer's best known songs. Those words aptly describe the mindset that made ELP one of the best known and commercially successful groups in the annals of progressive rock. Unlike many of their more earnest progressive rock contemporaries, ELP approached their music with a sense of flair, showmanship, and even a pop sensibility of sorts that proved accessible to a public that often found progressive rock boring and difficult to relate to. That accessibility led the band to become a mainstay on FM rock radio, granting them a level of stardom matched in 1970s progressive rock circles only by Yes, and exceeded only by Pink Floyd.

Keith Emerson, Lake & Palmer were a progressive rock supergroup. Emerson was a former piano prodigy who had made a name for himself as a flamboyant

EMERSON, LAKE & PALMER

keyboardist with the jazz and classical–influenced British group, the Nice. It was during a Fillmore West performance with the Nice that he met King Crimson bassist Greg Lake. They decided to form a new band, enlisting Atomic Rooster drummer Carl Palmer (formerly of the Crazy World of Arthur Brown) to join them. The new group's notable appearance at the 1970 Isle of Wight festival apparently caught the eye of the ever-canny Atlantic Records president Ahmet Ertegun, who signed the band to a record contract.

The band's eponymous debut album arrived in 1970, and from the first track to last it was apparent that this was a band of high purpose. Grandiose classically based arrangements, dramatic passages and swells, and elaborate instrumentation marked the effort. Most of the tracks lacked guitar. Emerson's keyboard was the lead instrument on most tracks, although Lake's bass and Palmer's drumming were not buried in the mix. "Classical rock" fit ELP like a glove. An exception to the rule was the album's single, the more commercially friendly "Lucky Man," an English folk-style ballad. "Lucky Man" broke the *Billboard* Top 50 and showed the band's commercial as well as artistic ambition.

Tarkus (1971), the live *Pictures at an Exhibition* (1971), and *Trilogy* (1972) followed a similar path, with Emerson's accomplished but often overly busy keyboard work driving the sound. Emerson made frequent use of synthesizers, which were becoming increasingly popular in the early 1970s and would prove to be a progressive rock mainstay. Classical music was the chief influence, especially Bach, Wagner, Ravel, and Mussorgsky (whose music was featured in *Pictures at an Exhibition*). Jazz influences also became more prominent, and the Little Richard–styled piano raver "Ready Eddie" that closed *Tarkus* was an astonishing departure from the band's formula. The public responded approvingly, propelling the group's albums to the Top 10 on the charts and making them one of progressive rock's most commercially successful acts.

Emerson's wild onstage antics were true showmanship, far beyond the stolidly earnest stage presence of most of his progressive rock contemporaries. Melodies began to become more accessible and at times were truly catchy. Songs became more up-tempo and Emerson's keyboard arrangements became less complex and more pleasing to the ear. Some songs even displayed a playful sense of humor, a trait not often associated with progressive rock. Bassist Lake provided their most accessible music, demonstrating a knack for writing haunting acoustic guitar ballads such as "From the Beginning" and "Still . . . You Turn Me On" that received consistent airplay on FM radio.

Still, the band never abandoned its classical roots and tried to bring it all together with *Brain Salad Surgery* (1973), an album clearly intended to be their magnum opus. Opening with the magisterial "Jerusalem," which references British hymnody as well as William Blake, the album closes with "Karn Evil," a four-part piece with lengthy instrumental passages fusing jazz and classical music.

They returned in 1977 with the ambitious *Works Volume 1*, a double album with each member's work receiving one side and the entire band coming together for the final. Predictably, Emerson's was a lengthy piano-based instrumental, Lake's a more accessible and melodic collection of mostly acoustic-based songs, and Palmer's a surprising set of harder rocking tunes that displayed a more contemporary than expected taste in music. The final side was vintage ELP, comprised mostly of a lengthy rendition of Aaron Copland's "Fanfare for the Common Man."

The album had less impact than their previous work, and the coming of disco and punk did not auger well for ELP's commercial prospects. Their next album, *Love Beach*, would prove to be their Waterloo, showing the band losing direction and caught between musical eras as they sought to maintain relevance. The album sold poorly and the group broke up in 1979.

Lake made a disastrous attempt to re-form the band with Rainbow drummer Carl Powell providing the "P" in the name. They released an eponymous album in 1986. The original trio re-formed in the early 1990s, touring steadily and releasing a couple little-noticed studio albums and a host of live albums. Sadly, the curtain fell on the show that never ends with Emerson's suicide in March of 2016 and Lake's death from cancer nine months later.

Without question, Emerson, Lake & Palmer were polarizing. Mention their name, and one will likely receive a strong reaction, whether positive or negative. Critics called the band's music "grandiose" and "pretentious," often with considerable justification. There is no doubt that the band was never far from over the top, and at times the epic seriousness with which the group approached their more classically influenced pieces bordered on being laughable. However, their pop tendencies are often overlooked, and their music at times was quite listenable and occasionally enjoyable, even to those not inclined to like progressive rock.

Suggested Albums: Trilogy (1972); *Brain Salad Surgery* (1973)

ENO, BRIAN (1948–)

Brian Eno is one of rock's most fascinating figures, albeit rock even broadly defined is a category scarcely wide enough to contain him. While a member of one of the 1970s' most venturesome British bands, Roxy Music, Eno was spotted eagerly working with pencil and notebook while his bandmates remixed a track in the studio. "I woke up this morning with a theory about prime numbers," Eno explained, covering his sheets with columns of figures.

And yet he was never a geek, but rather one of glam rock's most outrageous showboats before withdrawing into an image of mysterious black or bohemian beret chic. For Eno, the glamour of Roxy Music was never a way of life but a game ultimately less interesting to play than spinning tape loops or working out the theory of ambient music, which set the template for the chill rooms of 1990s rave culture. A professed "nonmusician," Eno's chief instruments were tape recorders and his compositional method often involved assembling organic-sounding performances from splices and edits. He was more concerned with the process of creativity, systems in which ideas could be generated, than in playing music. Through his prolific if oblique solo career and his producer's role with U2, Talking Heads, and David Bowie, Eno influenced the shape of music as much as anyone of his generation.

Eno's full name arrested attention when he surfaced in the public spotlight. Brian Peter George St. Jean le Baptiste de la Salle Eno suggested some hopelessly cosmopolitan scion of aristocracy from a Nabokov novel, its polysyllables enhancing an elusive sense of identity. Actually, Eno was a Catholic boy from provincial England who slipped the confines of his parochial education while retaining a Roman Catholic scholastic's love of systems and order.

As an art student in London during the heady 1960s, Eno absorbed ideas from all over while maintaining an aloof lack of commitment. Unlike some graduates of that open-ended epoch, he applied himself with rigorous discipline to whatever interested him. He'd rather have pored over a philosophical tome than a book of guitar chords, argue aesthetics than share a joint. In younger years his sexual proclivities were voracious, which was perhaps the one thing he shared with most 1970s rock stars. He became more comfortable in the company of the smarter musicians who emerged from punk such as Bono and David Byrne.

Before clashing with Roxy Music's frontman Bryan Ferry and departing as the band's synthesizer player after their second album (1973), Eno straddled pop and progressive rock. Once out of Roxy Music, Eno began to collaborate with King Crimson's Robert Fripp, who had grown bored with the conventions of rock, and to work on his first solo album. The sessions resulted in Fripp and Eno's *No Pussyfooting* (1973) and Eno's *Here Come the Warm Jets* (1973). With Fripp, Eno helped develop the tape-delay echo system dubbed Frippertronics. For both projects, Eno derived inspiration from German electronic bands such as Can, Cluster, Faust, Kraftwerk, and Tangerine Dream. He was fascinated by their use of repetition as a form of change and their penchant for sustaining a mood that required an "immersive" state of listening. *Here Come the Warm Jets* was recorded with members of Roxy Music (minus Ferry) along with Fripp and Hawkwind's hypnotic drummer Simon King. The rhythmically jerking, abstractedly funk garage rock anticipated the early Talking Heads.

Warm Jets was still easily definable as rock, but after a record label–organized live album with Kevin Ayers, Nico, and John Cale, *June 1st, 1974* (1974), Eno delved more deeply into ostensibly random strategies for composing and recording rooted in the I Ching and John Cage. Inspired by postcards of a Maoist opera (but not the opera itself), *Taking Tiger Mountain (By Strategy)* (1975) was a transitional album between rock and the terra incognita to come.

By *Another Green World* (1975) and *Discrete Music* (1975), Eno had crystalized the concept of ambient music meant to be listened to (or not) as a stimulating yet unobtrusive backdrop for creative activities. On the albums that followed, Eno remained alert to the potential of unintended consequences and happy accidents; he spotted opportunities in raw material or mistakes other artists had been trained to overlook or discard. His chief influence came less through his own recordings than his production and collaboration with other artists, starting with the albums he made with David Bowie that dramatically expanded the sonic range of rock music.

After Bowie's "Berlin Trilogy" of *Low* (1977), *Heroes* (1977), and *Lodger* (1979), Eno became much sought-after as a producer. He guided in-the-moment albums such as the noisy punk-jazz compilation *No New York* (1978) and helped plot the rising stardom of Devo on their debut album (1978). Eno produced Talking Heads' *More Songs about Buildings and Food* (1978), *Fear of Music* (1979), and *Remain in*

Light (1980) and became David Byrne's congenial partner, first on *My Life in the Bush of Ghosts* (1981) and later on *Everything That Happens Will Happen Today* (2008). Eno reached the pinnacle of his role as sonic consultant in working with U2. Usually in tandem with Daniel Lanois, Eno co-produced *The Unforgettable Fire* (1984), *The Joshua Tree* (1987), *Achtung Baby* (1991), *Zooropa* (1993), and *All That You Can't Leave Behind* (2000).

Eno acted as the coolly detached uncle of punk and the mysterious grey eminence of postpunk. He anticipated new age music, and he could have been its most interesting practitioner had he wanted. He was at the vanguard of remixing, electronica, and world music but lingered long in none of those fields, preferring to discuss psychology and art history than music. Unlike some rock artists who dabbled in visual arts, Eno achieved respect in the hermetic world of museum curators and art critics. His audiovisual works were displayed in the British Pavilion of the Venice Biennale, Paris's Pompidou Centre, Amsterdam's Stedelijk Museum, and St. Petersburg's Pavlovsk Palace. He could be called a Renaissance man but Eno dislikes the Renaissance for, as he explains, "ignoring part of our psyche—the part that's a bit messy and barbarian."

Suggested Albums: Here Come the Warm Jets (1973); *Another Green World* (1975); *Discrete Music* (1975); *Before and After Science* (1977); *Ambient 1: Music for Airports* (1978); *Music for Films* (1978); *My Life in the Bush of Ghosts* (1981); *Ambient 4: On Land* (1982)

ENTWISTLE, JOHN (1944–2002)

Bassist John Entwistle's solo career was the most distinctive among his mates in the Who. Always under the shadow of Pete Townshend's songwriting, Entwistle had contributed occasional numbers to Who albums and amassed a small stockpile of good material by the time he began recording under his own name. His best solo albums came first, *Smash Your Head Against the Wall* (1971) and *Whistle Rymes* (1972). Both featured the sardonic, offbeat humor that first became apparent on his tune "Boris the Spider" from *A Quick One* (1966); both were bottom-ended, produced and mixed to draw attention to his aggressive yet melodic bass playing. *Smash Your Head* was heavier sounding than the Who and nudged against heavy metal on some tracks; *Whistle Rymes* was hard rock but with a lighter, even cheerful tone as it offered a sometimes heartfelt, sometimes sardonic take on domestic life.

With covers of "Hound Dog" and "Lucille," and pastiches of the 1950s, *Rigor Mortis Sets In* (1973) and *Mad Dog* (1975) were part of the era's rock and roll revival, a nostalgia-driven trend that manifested the periodic tendency of rock music to get back to basics. He gave up solo recording for many years and produced only two albums before his 2002 death, *Too Late the Hero* (1981) and *The Rock* (1996). While much of his energy was spent with the Who since the 1970s, he toured in Ringo Starr's All-Star Band and engaged in other nostalgic projects.

Suggested Albums: Smash Your Head Against the Wall (1971); *Whistle Rymes* (1972)

See also: Who

FACES

The Faces were the quintessential 1970s British band. Elegantly louche, often heavy but never metal, they were rooted in the blues without being blues-rock. The band evolved out of a 1960s group more popular in the United Kingdom than the United States, the Small Faces. They outgrew their original name when they lost singer Steve Marriott to Humble Pie in 1969 and stole a pair of rising stars from the Jeff Beck Group, guitarist Ron Wood and singer Rod Stewart. On their debut album, *First Step* (1970), the Faces' tough mid-tempo rock flowed into finger-picked acoustic songs, which sounded as if preserved in Appalachian aspic, and numbers whose controlled fervor was derived from gospel music. They transformed Bob Dylan's "Wicked Messenger" into a doomy rock song driven by Ian McLagan's organ. Drummer Kenny Jones and bassist Ronnie Lane propelled the music with muscular rhythms.

The Faces successfully mixed different influences with original songs and powerful cover versions. Wood was an adept slide guitar player, conjuring the spirit of the Mississippi Delta in an amped-up context. As lead vocalist, Stewart invested ballads with ragged vulnerability and whooped-and-hollered through the hard rockers.

Long Player (1971) continued in the direction of *First Step*. Half the album was recorded live at the Fillmore East, capturing their loose coherence, a combustion of talent without polish. Among the highlights was a fervent rendition of Paul McCartney's "Maybe I'm Amazed." By the time of *A Nod Is as Good as a Wink . . . To a Blind Horse* (1971), the favorite album for many of the band's fans, the Faces sounded increasingly like the Rolling Stones without ceasing to sound like themselves. The album includes their signature song, "Stay With Me," a brilliantly nasty put-down of a one-night sexual partner written by Wood and Stewart. There would be no morning after, the singer insisted as the guitarist laid down a blistering lead.

The final album by the Faces, *Ooh La La* (1973), included one of their biggest hits, Wood-Stewart-McLagan's "Cindy Incidentally." However, by then, Lane had quit the band and Stewart's successful solo career began to eclipse them, even as they performed his hits on tour. In 1976 Wood left to join the Rolling Stones and McLagan became the Stones' regular keyboardist. After a brief Small Faces reunion, Jones joined the Who, filling Keith Moon's seat.

Suggested Albums: First Step (1970); *Long Player* (1971); *A Nod Is as Good as a Wink . . . To a Blind Horse* (1971); *Ooh La La* (1973)

See also: Small Faces; Stewart, Rod

FERRY, BRYAN
See Roxy Music

FAIRPORT CONVENTION

Fairport Convention was the springboard for the careers of guitarist Richard Thompson, singer Sandy Denny, and a cadre of musicians devoted to coupling Britain's folk traditions with rock music. The band was founded in 1967 by guitarist Simon Nicol and bassist Ashley Hutchings, who quickly added Thompson to the lineup. Although they primarily covered contemporary American songs by Bob Dylan and the Jefferson Airplane, they were quickly signed to a record deal. Their eponymous first album (1968) contained suggestions of the future in their dynamic rock revamp of Joni Mitchell's "Chelsea Morning," infused with Englishness through the crystalline voice of Judy Dyble.

The singing style was continued by her replacement, Sandy Denny, on *What We Did on Our Holidays* (1969). Denny guided the band into the Middle Ages through the doorway of the psychedelic 1960s with her song "Fotheringay," which rued the imprisonment of Mary Queen of Scots. Hutchings also wrote, though his blues-rock "Mr. Lacey" was uncharacteristic of Fairport's direction. The band's third songwriter, Thompson, began to find his unique voice with the defiantly despondent "Meet on the Ledge."

By *Unhalfbricking* (1969), Fairport had arrived at its distinctive sound, a grave and unmistakably British folk-rock propelled by Thompson's elegantly fluid electric guitar playing, often psychedelic in tone but eschewing the usual blues influences for something more ancient. The 18th-century broadside "A Sailor's Life" became a platform for Thompson's endlessly inventive soloing. Denny contributed a song that has become the enduring standard of the British folk revival, "Who Knows Where the Time Goes." The gently reflective ballad had already been recorded by Judy Collins and has more recently been covered by Cat Power and Sinead O'Connor.

Liege & Lief (1969) is regarded as Fairport's greatest work and as a classic among British folk-rock albums. It was instrumentally enriched by the addition of violinist and violist Dave Swarbrick, who began co-writing with Thompson. The album's characteristic song, the Denny-Hutchings collaboration "Come All Ye," evoked the age of traveling minstrels in an electric rock context. Denny and Hutchings left after *Liege & Lief* to form their own folk-rock bands, Fotheringay and Steeleye Span, respectively. Fairport carried on with *Full House* (1970), a strong body of songs by Thompson and Swarbrick including one of the band's best excursions into medieval rock, the sinister "Doctor of Physick."

American-born producer Joe Boyd lent a guiding hand as the band found its path over the rapid evolution of those first five albums. After *Full House*, Boyd and Thompson departed, leaving behind an accomplished ensemble that continued with virtuosity if little brilliance. Denny rejoined to record *Rising for the Moon* (1975) but left the following year. Fairport Convention remains a fixture on the British folk scene in the 21st century and continues to tour and record. Nicol is the only original member.

Suggested Albums: Fairport Convention (1968); *What We Did on Our Holidays* (aka *Fairport Convention*) (1969); *Unhalfbricking* (1969); *Liege & Lief* (1969); *Full House* (1970); *Angel Delight* (1971); *Rising for the Moon* (1975)

See also: Denny, Sandy; Steeleye Span; Thompson, Richard

FAMILY

Popular in their British homeland but never finding a significant audience in the United States, Family was one of the most interesting progressive rock bands. Although usually relegated to a footnote in rock history for the 1969 defection of their bassist, Rick Grech, to the short-lived supergroup Blind Faith, Family left behind a handful of fascinating albums. Largely avoiding the lure of classical music and the emotional tone of blues-rock, Family employed jazz rhythms seldom heard in hard rock and occasionally echoed British folk music in compositionally unpredictable songs. They were capable of being heavy and metallic but were not classed with the early generation of heavy metal acts.

Family began in 1966 as a rhythm and blues band but soon embraced the possibilities suggested by the fluorescence of psychedelic rock. Violin, flute, and vibraphone were featured on many of their recordings, but the most distinctive instrument was Roger Chapman's vibrato voice, capable of projecting emotions from vulnerable to outraged but often suggesting a man at the end of his rope. The whisper to scream dynamics of many Family songs was unusual at the time; their unconventional chording put them at the cusp where familiar rock tropes met unknown sonic landscapes.

By the time of *Bandstand* (1972), Family had become less aggressively unconventional, albeit the snaky guitar lines heard on some tracks suggested some of the more ambitious guitar bands to emerge from punk rock. Their final album, *It's Only a Movie* (1973), traded progressive rock for quirky pop and was roundly ignored.

Calling Family quits in 1973, Chapman and guitarist Charlie Whitney formed a band of less distinction, Streetwalker. John Palmer became a session musician and appeared on Pete Townshend's solo albums. In the 2010s Family regrouped for occasional concerts, drawing large audiences in Great Britain.

Suggested Albums: Music in a Doll's House (1968); *Family Entertainment* (1969); *A Song for Me* (1970); *Anyway* (1970); *Fearless* (1971); *Bandstand* (1972)

FAUST

Germany's Faust began in 1971 with an uncompromising attitude toward the aesthetics of rock. Installed in a private studio with producer Uwe Nettlebeck, they recorded prolifically, splicing and editing the results into tracks for albums (with much material remaining unreleased for decades).

Their music was often a sonic stream of consciousness flirting with elements of many genres including the experimental reggae called dub music, the musings of postpsychedelic rock, and the minimalism of Philip Glass. Faust recorded an album of droning minimalism, *Outside the Dream Syndicate* (1972), with Tony Conrad, the American avant-garde composer with whom John Cale served his apprenticeship before the Velvet Underground. Their most accessible album, *Faust IV* (1973), was recorded in London and included a knockout song, a caustic indictment of a violent youth subculture set to an ironically twisted reggae beat, "The Sad Skinhead."

Faust's noisier music set an example for industrial bands such as Throbbing Gristle that emerged in the postpunk 1980s. Faust disappeared without explanation from 1975 through 1990, when they resurfaced in light of a changed musical culture that allowed more space for musicians with their proclivities. After 1990 members of the band performed and recorded together in various configurations, sometimes under the Faust banner.

Suggested Albums: Faust (1971); *Faust So Far* (1972); *Outside the Dream Syndicate* (1972); *The Faust Tapes* (1973); *Faust IV* (1973)

FISCHER, WILD MAN (1944–2011)

Rock music has always had its share of eccentric characters, but perhaps none more so than Larry Wayne Fischer, better known as Wild Man Fischer. Fischer grew up in Los Angeles, where his lifelong struggles with mental illness began at an early age and led to him being institutionalized as a teenager. By the late 1960s Fischer had become a Los Angeles street performer. He was noticed by fellow eccentric Frank Zappa, who recorded *An Evening with Wild Man Fischer* (1968), a truly unique piece of work that captured the essence of Fischer's street performances.

The songs are mostly a cappella, often rambling with barely any recognizable structure, but at times recall the form of early rock and roll. Fischer shrieks, howls, and laughs indiscriminately, while almost rapping usually nonsensical and at times childlike free-form poetry. The result is fascinating and disturbing, an uninhibited look at a greatly troubled yet apparently creative mind. The album was released on Zappa's Bizarre Records label, but eventually Zappa grew weary of dealing with Fischer's odd and at times frightening behavior, and a dispute over royalties led to their eventual split.

Fischer resurfaced in 1975 and recorded the first release by fledgling Rhino Records, the *Go to Rhino Records* anthology, which established the label as a haven for the offbeat and interesting. He later released two little noticed but equally strange albums, *Pronounced Normal* (1981) and *Nothing Scary* (1983). Fischer continued to be plagued by psychological disorders and was eventually placed in a psychiatric facility where he died from heart failure in 2011.

Suggested Album: An Evening with Wild Man Fischer (1968)

FLAMIN' GROOVIES

Amidst the thunder of heavy metal, the flash of glam rock, and the bombast of progressive rock, the Flamin' Groovies navigated a different course in the 1970s, flying under the radar and showing a new path to invigorate rock music by drawing inspiration from its past. The Groovies' most immediate influence came from the British Invasion and garage band sound of the mid-1960s, but their sound also looked all the way back to the 1950s roots of rock and roll. By the time punk and new wave hit in the late 1970s, the Groovies were recognized as trailblazers who helped lead the way to a musical revolution based on a more immediate, energetic, and relevant form of rock music.

The Flamin' Groovies hailed from San Francisco, but it was clear from the start that the musical and cultural trends sweeping through their hometown in the 1960s were entirely irrelevant to their music. Albums such as *Supernazz* (1969) and *Flamingo* (1970) rocked with a primitive fury and raw energy that was as far removed from the Summer of Love and psychedelia as east was from west. Loud, overdriven guitars and a relentless 4/4 drumbeat provided the backbone of the group's powerful sound. The band performed garage band–styled covers of Little Richard, Fats Domino, and Chuck Berry, while songwriters Cyril Jordan and Roy Loney proved adept at penning numbers that recalled the Beatles and Rolling Stones.

It was the Groovies' fondness for the British Invasion (along with a much more raw approach and sound) that separated the band from more Americana-influenced back to basics contemporaries such as Creedence Clearwater Revival and the Band. The band's Dave Edmunds–produced album *Shake Some Action* (1976) is often hailed as a pioneering power pop effort. The 12-string electric guitars recalled the Byrds, and the often Beatlesque sound represented a departure from their garage band beginnings. It seemed as though the times had finally caught up to the Groovies, who were being recognized as a seminal influence on punk and new wave. The group broke up in 1992 and has never fully reunited.

Suggested Albums: Supernazz (1969); *Flamingo* (1970); *Teenage Head* (1971); *Shake Some Action* (1976); *Jumpin' in the Night* (1979)

FLEETWOOD MAC

Aside from lending his name to the band, Mick Fleetwood is the only original member remaining through Fleetwood Mac's many changes. Although often overlooked, Fleetwood is a musical drummer whose lively rhythmic sense has been the one constant as the band made its way from blues-rock to pop rock and obscurity to platinum stardom.

Fleetwood Mac's prime period of creativity divides neatly into three phases. In the early years (1967–1970), the crucial figure was blues-rock guitarist Peter Green. The middle period (1971–1974) saw many lineup changes and a move away from blues. The band reached its pinnacle of popularity (1975–1977) with the addition of Lindsey Buckingham and Stevie Nicks.

Green had been Eric Clapton's replacement in John Mayall's Bluesbreakers. Upon forming his own group in 1967, Green took along the Bluesbreakers' drummer, Fleetwood, and several months later recruited Mayall's bassist, John McVie.

Supported by an agile rhythm section that sidestepped the plodding thud of many blues-rock bands, Green shone for the sharp stinging tone and good vibrato of his guitar playing. He executed eccentric licks with an edgy intensity that may have echoed the psychological unease of a musician wrestling with mental illness.

Fleetwood Mac's self-titled debut album (1968) was a blues-rock effort. The follow-up, *Mr. Wonderful* (1968), featured a session pianist who later became prominent in the band, Christine Perfect. Known as Christine McVie after marrying Fleetwood Mac's bassist, she joined the band in 1970.

The band's early discography is confusing. A U.S. release, *English Rose* (1969), was compiled from half of *Mr. Wonderful* plus miscellaneous tracks including Green's spooky "Black Magic Woman," transformed into a Latin rock hit a year later by Santana. Many of those same songs also appeared on a British compilation of singles and B-sides, *The Pious Bird of Good Omen* (1969). Although little known in the United States, Fleetwood Mac sold well in the United Kingdom, where Green's dreamy instrumental "Albatross" (1969) became a number one hit. Still invested in the blues, the band traveled to the famed Chess Records Studio to record *Fleetwood Mac in Chicago* (1969), a jam session featuring Willie Dixon, Buddy Guy, and Otis Spann.

Then Play On (1969) marked a leap in sophistication as the band opened itself to new influences and showcased the stunning interchange between Green and the band's other two guitarists, Danny Kirwan and Jeremy Spencer. However, Green's mental health declined with some witnesses blaming a bad dose of LSD. Diagnosed with schizophrenia, he was admitted to psychiatric hospitals after leaving Fleetwood Mac in 1970 and endured electroshock treatment. He reemerged by decade's end, released several recordings, and made guest appearances on latter-day Fleetwood Mac albums. Some of his extraordinary guitar playing during his last months with the band was later released on a CD set, *Live in Boston* (1985).

The first post-Green album, *Kiln House* (1970), was also the first to include Christine McVie as a band member and the last to feature Spencer, who dominated the album with paeans to 1950s rock and roll. On the tour that followed, Spencer disappeared one night and turned up days later at a sectarian commune called the Children of God. American guitarist Bob Welch replaced him in time for *Future Games* (1971), an album that marked the band's move toward a more pop sound. *Bare Trees* (1972) was the final album for Kirwan, fired on tour for his alcoholic rages. It featured Welch's "Sentimental Lady," which he later remade during his late 1970s solo career. Other personnel came and went through *Penguin* (1973). *Mystery to Me* (1973), the band's final British album, included the track that finally gained them a consistent presence on American FM. Featuring one of rock's most familiar drumbeats, Welch's "Hypnotized" was a jazz-tinged tour of the paranormal set to a mesmeric rhythm.

Opting to be closer to the center of the music industry, Fleetwood Mac moved to Los Angeles in 1974. Welch departed after *Heroes Are Hard to Find* (1974) and was replaced by American guitarist Lindsey Buckingham and his girlfriend, singer Stevie Nicks. They came to Mick Fleetwood's attention through their album *Buckingham Nicks* (1973), a tuneful exercise in Southern California pop rock. The arrival of Buckingham and Nicks transformed a band with a checkered past and an uncertain identity into a hit machine.

Although they had released an eponymous album seven years earlier, the band apparently thought no one remembered it and reused the title for their breakout LP. *Fleetwood Mac* (1975) amounted to a restart for the group and raced to number one on the American album chart on the strength of McVie's jubilant love songs "Over My Head" and "Say You Love Me" and Nicks's autumnal "Rhiannon." The phenomenal success of *Fleetwood Mac* is attributable to a pop sensibility in tune with the era, articulated by a trio of individually distinctive songwriters and the blend of three voices represented by Christine McVie's unthreatening sultriness, Buckingham's melodic and unaffected singing, and Nicks's ethereal witchy tone.

The aural buffet continued on *Rumours* (1977), whose name was derived from the imploding personal lives of band members, including the divorce of the McVies and the split-up between Buckingham and Nicks. *Rumours* became one of the best selling LPs ever with no less than seven Top 10 hits including "Go Your Own Way," "The Chain," "Dreams," "Don't Stop," "You Make Loving Fun," "Second Hand News," and "Gold Dust Woman."

Flush with the success of *Rumours*, Fleetwood Mac took a path less obvious on their follow-up, *Tusk* (1979). A double LP with 20 songs, *Tusk* opened with the mellow pop rock that had become their brand but lurched into mutant rockabilly and a title track that incorporated all 112 members of the University of Southern California marching band. With Buckingham egging them on, Fleetwood Mac

Fleetwood Mac underwent dizzying changes in membership and musical direction after debuting in 1967 as a blues-rock band. They are seen here during their late 1970s peak as a platinum-selling pop-rock act with (left to right) John McVie, Lindsey Buckingham, Christine McVie, and Stevie Nicks. (Peter Still/Getty Images)

decided to be quirky while hedging their bets. The formula worked, sort of. *Tusk* sold in the millions, but the critics were mostly baffled, the record label was nonplussed, Fleetwood Mac fans didn't really dig it, and the brave new world of punk and postpunk—to which *Tusk* was a response—didn't buy it.

While Fleetwood Mac remained popular in the 1980s, they never entirely regained the zenith they had enjoyed in the late 1970s. Nicks, Buckingham, and Christine McVie pursued solo careers while regrouping periodically for Fleetwood Mac albums such as *Mirage* (1981) and *Tango in the Night* (1987). Their *Rumours* hit "Don't Stop" became the theme song for Bill Clinton's 1992 presidential campaign. With shifting lineups, the band continued touring and performing in the 1990s, 2000s, and 2010s. Fleetwood Mac has been inducted into the Rock and Roll Hall of Fame.

Suggested Albums: Fleetwood Mac (1968); *Mr. Wonderful* (1968); *English Rose* (1969); *The Pious Bird of Good Omen* (1969); *Fleetwood Mac in Chicago* (1969); *Then Play On* (1969); *The Original Fleetwood Mac* (1971); *Mystery to Me* (1973); *Heroes Are Hard to Find* (1974); *Fleetwood Mac* (1975); *Rumours* (1977); *Tusk* (1979); *Live in Boston* (1985)

FLO & EDDIE
See Turtles

FLOCK
The Dionysian potential of the violin reached a febrile height in rock music when violinist Jerry Goodman placed the instrument at the forefront of the Flock. The Chicago jazz-rock band featured intricate arrangements for a small brass and woodwind section reminiscent of the band Chicago, but infused their sound with a bluesy soulfulness that approached that of the Electric Flag. Goodman's electric violin, along with the group's vocal harmonies, lent the Flock a note of distinction.

The Flock's self-titled debut album (1969) includes a handful of original songs that showcased the band's ability to jam along with a mammoth version of the Kinks' "Tired of Waiting," a whirling dervish psychedelic rendition propelled by funky brass and heavy rhythms but with baroque moments. The follow-up, *Dinosaur Swamps* (1971), was, if anything, even more eclectic. After Goodman left to join Mahavishnu Orchestra, the Flock underwent other personnel changes before issuing a final album, *Inside Out* (1975), featuring Mountain's Felix Pappalardi on vocals.

Suggested Albums: The Flock (1969); *Dinosaur Swamps* (1971)

FLYING BURRITO BROTHERS
The Flying Burrito Brothers are regarded as pioneers of country rock for combining country instrumentation and songwriting with a slightly more intense rock sensibility. Country enthusiast Gram Parsons formed the California-based group in 1968

after leaving the Byrds, following their seminal country rock album *Sweethearts of the Rodeo*. Fellow Byrd and country fan Chris Hillman joined Parsons in forming the new band, which was dedicated to marrying country with rock, rhythm and blues, psychedelia, folk, and gospel in a new and eclectic mix Parsons called "Cosmic American Music." And to be sure, while Hillman's contributions were critical to the Burrito Brothers' music, the group was primarily a reflection of Parsons's mission to fuse all things American into one new musical form that would defy categorization and bring down labels that he saw as forcing pointless and needless divisions.

The band's debut, *The Gilded Palace of Sin* (1969), is perhaps the best expression of Parsons's musical vision, a classic collection of well-crafted, country-influenced songs, rhythm and blues covers, and expressive ballads. The instrumentation was pure country, featuring pedal steel guitar, banjo, and mandolin, but the electric guitar and assertive drumming provided more rock punch than anything that was coming out of Nashville. Parsons's emotional singing worked well in a country setting, even if his vocals barely had a twang and demonstrated only a slight command of traditional country phrasing. His sincerity was sufficient to provide country credibility, but his vocal limitations actually served his purpose of breaking down walls and creating a fresh and original blend of musical styles.

The album's original material, mostly penned by Parsons and Hillman, toe the country line more, but are more complex than typical country songs of the era and expand upon the verse-chorus structure favored by the Nashville songwriting establishment. The album sold only modestly, but it struck a chord with countless rock musicians who suddenly saw the virtues in the once disparaged country music.

Perhaps due to Parsons's growing friendship with the Rolling Stones' Keith Richards, the band's second album, *Burrito Deluxe* (1970), focused more on the rock side of the band's sound. Future Eagle Bernie Leadon was brought in to play lead guitar, although given his country leanings he was unlikely to push the band too far astray from that form of music. Nevertheless, the album rocked more than its predecessor, and songs like "High Fashion Queen" and "Cody, Cody" could aptly and accurately be called country rock. The song quality was not quite as strong as on *Gilded Palace of Sin*, but the album was a strong follow-up, notable for including the first recorded version of "Wild Horses," which became a centerpiece on the Stones' classic 1971 album *Sticky Fingers*.

The Burrito Brothers' influence was spreading rapidly, especially in Southern California where scores of young musicians began following their path into country rock. However, things were not going as well within the band itself. Frustrated by the group's lack of commercial success and beset by drug and alcohol problems, Parsons departed in hopes of finding better fortunes in a solo career. The rest of the band continued on, releasing the truly country rock album *The Flying Burrito Bros* (1971). A pleasant collection of tunes, it sorely missed the distinctive elements and visionary credibility provided by Parsons. Leadon left to join the more commercially rewarding Eagles, and Hillman kept the Burrito Brothers alive, releasing two more albums of original music, with increasingly diminishing artistic returns.

Hillman was next to leave the band, although original bassist Chris Etheridge kept the group going as the Burrito Brothers, and eventually scored some country crossover success in the 1980s. However, the Flying Burrito Brothers will best be remembered as a seminal band in the development of country rock, and no matter how distasteful Parsons found the term, most people today consider the Burrito Brothers to be synonymous with the genre.

Suggested Albums: The Gilded Palace of Sin (1969); *Burrito Deluxe* (1970)

See also: Parsons, Gram

FM RADIO

FM radio not only promoted classic rock but helped define it during the late 1960s and early 1970s. After the mid-1970s, however, FM radio helped end the era of classic rock by diminishing it as a viable art form.

FM stations always had the advantage of higher fidelity than stations on the AM band, but the popularity of frequency modulation grew only slowly after its introduction in the late 1930s. By the early 1960s FM stations were able to broadcast in stereo, making them attractive venues for classical music. However, AM radio remained predominant and unchallenged. Many radios received only AM signals. FM was the preserve of colleges that used the facilities for educational purposes and commercial stations that carried nothing but simulcasts of their AM sister stations. But in 1967, the Federal Communications Commission took steps to reduce such simulcasting in a ruling that coincided with the rise of the counterculture and the tendency of college students to bring their own albums to the studio and play music unheard on the AM dial.

Before long free-form FM rock stations proliferated across the United States. Often taking their cue from low-key, late-night jazz programs, FM rock DJs were often mellow as opposed to their hyperactive AM counterparts; they played music they believed in and often engaged in exegesis of the songs they played. Entire sides of albums by Bob Dylan or the Beatles might be featured, obscure foreign bands could be heard, and even Arlo Guthrie's interminable "Alice's Restaurant" was played unedited. Commercial FM stations mostly ran advertisements for concert promoters and other countercultural enterprises. FM rock radio provided listeners with a sense of adventure impossible on Top 40–driven AM. FM opened new worlds as DJs played sequences of music that conveyed particular moods or connected ideas.

The golden years of free-form FM were short lived. By the early 1970s, a creep toward tighter formats was already evident on many stations as program directors sought larger audiences and greater advertising revenue. By the middle of the decade more and more FM stations adopted playlists based on the pseudo-science of market research. The shrinking creativity of FM rock programming arrived alongside the beginning of consolidation in the broadcast industry as media chains purchased privately held local stations.

The restrictive new format was called Album Oriented Rock (AOR), which countenanced airplay only for a slender number of album tracks rotated with boring inevitability. AOR programming directors often hesitated to try new bands and were openly hostile to such newer forms of music as punk rock and new wave. The stultifying boredom of AOR drove many otherwise contented middle-class American youth toward punk and other radical alternatives.

During the 1980s, noncommercial rock programming came full circle as college stations once again took the lead in exposing music that could not be played elsewhere. Many of those stations were, like their forebears in the 1960s, free-form or quasi-free-form and gave DJs great liberty to explore music from beyond the mainstream.

FOCUS

The Dutch rock band Focus gained worldwide success in 1973 with their hit single "Hocus Pocus," becoming yet another in rock's long list of one-hit wonders, but with the added distinction of being one of the few progressive rock acts to earn that status. The band had its genesis as the backing group for the Dutch production of the musical *Hair*. Their first album, *In and Out of Focus* (1970), was a mostly gentle collection of dreamy ballads that wouldn't have sounded out of place on Pink Floyd records. The flute-based single, "House of the King," recalled fellow progressive rock band Jethro Tull.

Focus's follow-up, *Moving Waves* (1971), opened with "Hocus Pocus." Although released as a single, the song had little chart success until an edited version caught on in 1973. "Hocus Pocus" was an inventive track, featuring a monster rock riff and a virtuoso guitar solo that was a precursor to what became recognized as neoclassical playing. Interspersed is a playfully yodeling vocal and flute solo, all backed by powerfully busy drumming. The song was one of the most original singles of the early 1970s and stood out amidst much of the inane pop all too common to the era. The rest of the album was largely contemplative instrumentals, often centered around wistful flute and keyboard melodies.

The band would never again achieve the commercial success of "Hocus Pocus," although the next album, *Focus 3* (1972), sold decently. Subsequent work offered thoughtful, melodic, and at times baroque-sounding instrumentals with occasional rockers leavened with a sense of humor. Focus began to add harder rock elements and vocals to their songs, with not always interesting results. Eventually jazz fusion entered the band's sound, leading to their eventual split.

Focus re-formed in 2002 and continue to record and tour. They will be remembered for "Hocus Pocus," but what set them apart from other progressive rock groups was their willingness to forego the bombast typical of the genre and take a more delicate and quiet approach, giving their music a less dated feel that has aged surprisingly well.

Suggested Albums: In and Out of Focus (1970); *Moving Waves* (1971); *Focus 3* (1972); *Hamburger Concerto* (1974)

FOGERTY, JOHN (1945–)

In many people's minds, John Fogerty is synonymous with Creedence Clearwater Revival. His status as primary songwriter, singer, and lead guitarist left the impression that the other band members were simply backup players supporting Fogerty's genius. His autocratic control of the band was a contributing factor in the group's breakup in 1972. Given Fogerty's dominance of all things CCR, it's not surprising that his subsequent solo career often reminded listeners of his legendary band. Fogerty has rarely ventured far afield from the memorable sound he helped create during his sporadic and sometimes solo career.

Fogerty's first solo offering, a well-made collection of country and bluegrass covers titled *The Blue Ridge Rangers* (1973), may have been an attempt to distance himself from his former band. He played all the instruments, yet there was no mention of him on the album cover, and the title and cover art created the impression that the album was the work of a band. And while the music seemed to be a departure from CCR, that appearance was deceiving, as Creedence songs such as "Lookin' Out My Back Door" and "Lodi" displayed a clear country bent. Any attempt by Fogerty to maintain anonymity went out the window the minute listeners heard his trademark voice on the album's minor hit, a cover of Hank Williams's "Jambalaya." The album was a solid start to Fogerty's solo career, but CCR fans did not take to the record, which barely cracked the Top 50 in the charts. A strong but little noticed Fogerty original, "You Don't Owe Me," followed under the Rangers' name.

Perhaps in reaction to the tepid sales, Fogerty's name was front and center on his eponymous second album (1975). There was no attempt to distance himself from the CCR sound on songs that could have been culled from virtually any CCR album. The joyous "Almost Saturday Night" echoed the freewheeling roadhouse abandon of CCR classics like "Around the Bend," while the bluesy stomper "The Wall" had the feel of many of Fogerty's earlier songs. The album represented a strong return to expected form, but sold even less well than *The Blue Ridge Rangers*. However, Slade scored an international hit in 1976 with a cover of the album's first single, the rousing anthem "Rockin' All Over the World."

Fogerty stumbled badly on his next album, *Hoodoo*. The listless collection of tunes, some of which seemed an attempt to create a more contemporary version of the CCR sound, was of such low quality that his record label refused to release it. *Hoodoo* has yet to officially see the light of day. Fogerty retreated from the public eye, with commercial failure, an acrimonious dispute with his label, Fantasy Records, and the ugly aftermath of the CCR breakup sapping his creative energy and will to record. As CCR became an institution on oldies radio and 1960s-based film soundtracks, Fogerty seemed content to live quietly in what seemed to be permanent retirement.

However, 1985 saw Fogerty's unexpected return to recording with the release of his first single in 10 years, "The Old Man Down the Road." The song, a swamp-drenched rocker reminiscent of CCR classics like "Green River" and "Run Through the Jungle," was a triumphant return to creative and commercial relevance for Fogerty. The subsequent album, *Centerfield*, solidified his first popular success as a solo artist. Once again, Fogerty played all the instruments, and if the music clearly harkened back to CCR, the public was finally receptive to Fogerty as the vehicle for delivering that sound. There were some sour notes associated with Fogerty's comeback, as he once again found himself embroiled in legal wrangling with Fantasy over the label's claim that similarities between "The Old Man Down the Road" and "Green River" (to which Fantasy owned the rights) amounted to copyright violation. Additionally, former Fantasy president Saul Zaentz sued Fogerty for defamation, alleging that Fogerty's song "Zanz Kant Danz" was slanderous. Fogerty won the intellectual property battle but was forced to change the title of "Zanz Kant Danz" to "Vanz Kant Danz."

Following the artistic and commercial success of *Centerfield*, Fogerty once again took a stab at updating the Creedence sound, this time working with other musicians on *Eye of the Zombie* (1986). Fogerty's efforts proved unsuccessful, as the album's polished production and overdriven guitars smothered all that was unique about his sound and produced a bland and generic result. Fogerty toured behind the album and seemed intent on remaining in the public eye.

This was not to be, as it took 11 years for Fogerty to release another album. On *Blue Moon Swamp* (1997), an updated version of CCR proved to be creative lightning with its unbridled energy, crack songwriting, and musicianship. The polished production added sonic depth and integrity that enriched Fogerty's material, as if he had taken the Creedence vehicle into the shop for a tuneup and emerged with a completely refurbished, road-ready model. *Blue Moon Swamp* was a commercial success, earning Fogerty a Grammy Award for Best Rock Album of 1997. A confident and energized Fogerty hit the road to promote the album, permanently ending a self-imposed ban on playing CCR songs, and releasing a strong live album, *Premonition* (1998).

Fogerty then took yet another break from recording, returning in 2004 with the release of *Deja Vu All Over Again,* and again in 2007 with *Revival. Deja Vu* saw Fogerty emerge as a full-fledged critic of the Iraq War, taking a harder rocking and at times heavier approach than usual with decidedly mixed results, while *Revival* was a more traditional-sounding Fogerty album in a decidedly CCR vein. The album's title was a clear nod to his famous band; the collection even included a track called "Creedence Song." Fogerty continued to look to his past with a 2009 reboot of his first solo project, the highly listenable *The Blue Ridge Rangers Rides Again.* Fogerty continues to tour, and in 2013 he released *Wrote a Song for Everyone*, a well-received collection of duets of prominent songs from all points of Fogerty's career.

It seems that despite a solo career filled with twists, turns, and long periods of isolation, Fogerty has finally found the creative and commercial equilibrium he has been searching for since the breakup of CCR.

Suggested Albums: The Blue Ridge Rangers (1973); *John Fogerty* (1975); *Centerfield* (1985); *Blue Moon Swamp* (1997); *Revival* (2007); *The Blue Ridge Rangers Rides Again* (2009); *Wrote a Song for Everyone* (2013)

See also: Creedence Clearwater Revival

FOLK-BLUES REVIVAL

The folk-blues revival, a movement led by white college-educated youth in the late 1950s and early 1960s, sought to recover endangered musical traditions,

134 FOLK-BLUES REVIVAL

especially rural music by white and black performers. American folk music was a category identified at least as far back as the "song collectors" of the early 20th century, including ethnographer John Lomax and poet Carl Sandburg. Following the example of American folklorist Francis James Child's seminal collection, *English and Scottish Ballads* (1857–1858), they began by setting down the words from balladry withering in the glare of urbanization and the industrialization of entertainment. Lomax and his son, Alan, journeyed together through the South beginning in 1933, commissioned by the Library of Congress to document vernacular performers on cumbersome yet mobile recording machines for the Archive of American Folk Song. By this time, the everyday music of white Southerners, which overlapped to an extent with their black neighbors, began to separate from its folk origins into a commercial industry, country and western, based in Nashville.

The idea of folk music as a living tradition of working-class lives and aspirations was embodied by Woody Guthrie in the late 1930s and embraced by the political left. He addressed social and political topics in ballads drawn from campfire melodies and the broadsides of the anarcho-syndicalist Industrial Workers of the World, whose organizers led strikers in song during the labor struggles of the early 1900s. Guthrie rose to attention as a "singing cowboy" on Los Angeles radio and was drawn into the orbit of Communist organizations.

By 1940 Guthrie had moved to New York City and became prominent in the culture of the Popular Front, which sought to bring Communists, Socialists, and New Deal liberals together in the name of social reform. More than anyone, Guthrie set the template for American folksingers, dressed in work clothes and singing in a Dust Bowl voice accompanied by acoustic guitar and harmonica. His image as a wandering minstrel of dissent inspired young Bob Dylan's trek into folk music. Guthrie's son Arlo carried on his legacy.

During the 1940s Guthrie kept company with actor-singers Paul Robeson and Burl Ives and, more importantly, the African American performer Lead Belly. According to legend, Lead Belly was pardoned from Louisiana's Angola prison farm on the strength of his singing. White liberals embraced him after John and Alan Lomax brought him to New York, but the urban black audience wanted nothing to do with an old Southern man who reminded them of everything they wanted to escape. Labeled "King of the Blues" and a "Negro minstrel," Lead Belly was a hard to categorize repository of African American song from an earlier era. He knew spirituals and work songs, children's numbers, and the juke joint tunes that set the stage for the blues. His performances were rugged yet dignified. Influenced by the café society milieu of his final years, he wrote protest songs such as "The Bourgeois Blues," but more enduring were his Southern-rooted songs that later entered the rock music canon, including "The Midnight Special" and "House of the Rising Sun."

Pete Seeger, son of Communist ethnomusicologist Charles Seeger, was another crucial inseminator of folk music. His party comrades, however, did not initially embrace Pete's concept of proletarian music transplanted from Appalachia to urban America. One Communist Party official scolded him, "If you are going to work with the workers of New York City, you should be in the jazz field." Seeger persisted, toting his banjo and kitbag of hillbilly tunes to nightclubs and concert halls. He even marched into the hit parade with his group the Weavers, topping the charts with a rendition of Lead Belly's "Goodnight, Irene" (1950).

Blacklisted during the McCarthy era, Seeger toured a circuit of fundraisers and rented halls. He considered himself the Johnny Appleseed of folk music during those years. One of those scattered seeds fell at the feet of 13-year-old Joan Baez when her aunt brought her to a Seeger performance. "Sing with me," he told audiences. "Sing by yourself. Make your own music. We don't need stars. You can sing."

Others responded to the call. By the last years of the 1950s most big cities and college towns harbored European-style coffeehouses serving espresso, poetry readings, and folk music by young amateurs like Baez, who knew the Blue Ridge Mountains and the Mississippi Delta only from picture books and sound recordings. The appeal of folk, transcending strictly political associations, signaled a rejection of the commodification and suburbanization of America, and a search for values that felt more "authentic" or grounded. Folk shared affinities with the Beat literary movement of Jack Kerouac and Allen Ginsberg, and introduced the partial rejection of modernism that characterized the counterculture in the 1960s.

Many devotees turned to a set of albums called *The Anthology of American Folk Music* (1952) for material and inspiration. Harry Smith, an artist and follower of occultist Aleister Crowley, produced the *Anthology* as a cross-section of country, blues, and gospel music released by commercial record labels from 1927 through 1932. Although most were scarcely more than 20 years old at the time, he approached those songs like an archeologist rooting through the ruins of buried civilizations. The music he unearthed had been released to niche markets and was already forgotten, if it had ever been known at all. The independent Folkways label released the *Anthology* with covers designed by Smith to correspond with the hermetic elements of earth, air, fire, and water, and an etching of the "Celestial Monochord," a musical instrument ascribed to Pythagoras, being tuned by the hand of God. Smith also wrote and gathered illustrations for an accompanying booklet that contextualized the album's 84 sections within a mysterious, arcane system. Aspiring folksingers regarded the *Anthology* as the Rosetta Stone to a lost world.

Smith also inspired a generation of blues researchers who fanned out across African American districts in search of fragile 78-rpm blues recordings as well as those who performed on them. They recorded memories of black Southern life in the 1920s and 1930s and tracked down surviving musicians such as Son House, Skip James, and Fury Lewis, who found new opportunities to perform for largely white audiences on the growing folk-revival circuit. Many of the songs they recovered were reissued on LP and entered the repertoire of rock bands in the 1960s.

The folk-blues revival gathered momentum beyond the radar of popular culture, but surfaced soon enough in mainstream society. In 1958 the Kingston Trio, also Seeger acolytes, reached number one on the charts with a 19th-century ballad, "Tom Dooley." In 1959, the inaugural run of the Newport Folk Festival, which set a precedent for the rock festivals of the 1960s, presented an impressive array of hoary veterans and fresh faces including bluegrass banjoist Earl Scruggs, bluesmen

136 FOLK-ROCK

Sonny Terry and Brownie McGhee, along with the Kingston Trio, Seeger, and Baez. The New York press flocked to the event and elevated the folk movement to greater prominence.

Many participants in the folk scene, intolerant of change, were dismayed to learn that contemporary African American blues performers preferred electric over acoustic guitars, and were angered when Dylan amped up his songs to reach a wider audience. And yet, the folk-blues revival also provided a nurturing environment for nonconformists, including musicians such as Dylan, Roger McGuinn, and Jerry Garcia who jumped from folk to rock in the mid-1960s. By insisting that vernacular music could be artful as well as entertaining, the folk-blues revival set the stage for the aspirations of the classic rock era. They provided the DNA for attitudes that have persisted in progressive rock, punk rock, and other musical subcultures, including distrust of commercialism, the notion of popularity as the mark of selling out, a quest for obscurity, a concern with maintaining "authenticity," and the stubborn but demonstrably false idea that rock musicians and fans are inevitably left of center.

FOLK-ROCK

Prior to early 1965, the union of rock and roll and folk music seemed nearly unthinkable. Devotees considered folk music as intelligent, lyrically deep, and socially conscious, while rock was more often perceived as raw, crude, and generally lacking in substance. The early 1960s saw the rise of the folk-blues revival, in which traditional folk music's simple acoustic sound and songs passed down generationally by oral tradition were fused with a more polished commercial approach and liberal social and political perspective. Folk revival artists such as Peter, Paul and Mary and the Kingston Trio competed for chart position with the more sanitized, industry-driven music that passed for rock and roll at the time, while "protest singers" such as Pete Seeger and (especially) Bob Dylan were at the forefront of a more politicized version of folk. The arrival of the Beatles in 1964 and the subsequent British Invasion reestablished rock's chart primacy and led some folk musicians to reassess their commercial and artistic fortunes.

Two such young folkies, Jim McGuinn (later known as Roger McGuinn) and Gene Clark, formed the Byrds. Their cover of Dylan's "Mr. Tambourine Man" (1965) was a hit that defined one particular stream of folk-rock through McGuinn's distinctive, jangling 12-string electric guitar (an instrument already heard on recordings by the Beatles and the Searchers), coupled with harmonies inspired by folkloric American recordings. Later that year, Dylan plugged in his guitar and went electric at the Newport Folk Festival to a decidedly cool reception from the folk purists but to commercial acclaim. His music was also called folk-rock but was considerably closer to the roots of blues and rock and roll than the Appalachian folk sources of the Byrds. Folk-rock had entered the popular lexicon but its definition was vague.

The Byrds' style of folk-rock influenced contemporary bands such as the Beau Brummels and was a factor along with Dylan in inspiring a distinctly British folk-rock led by Fairport Convention. The Byrds' early sound endured as a source for a younger generation of bands, starting with Tom Petty and the Heartbreakers in the 1970s but reaching prevalence in the alternative rock scene of the 1980s through bands such as R.E.M. and the Bangles. The label of folk-rock was also attached to many acoustic performers with ostensibly folk roots who added a drum kit and electric instruments to their repertoire.

See also: Byrds; Dylan, Bob; Folk-Blues Revival

FOOL

In Tarot, the Fool card represents the fringe. He is a figure dressed in many colors to denote his multiplicity and carries a bag at the end of a stick symbolizing the mind and its burden. The Dutch art-music commune called the Fool sprang out of Amsterdam's anarchist avant-garde and embodied the elements represented on the Tarot card. They were best known for designing densely visual psychedelic album covers for the Move and the Hollies, stage costumes for Cream and Procol Harum, and for painting John Lennon's Rolls Royce as well as the mural outside the Beatles' Apple Boutique in London.

The Fool also released a self-titled album (1968) that mixed futuristic electronic bleeps with the strings and pipes of medieval minstrels, Sunday hymns to an unknown God, field recordings of nature, and psychedelic folk songs. Producer Graham Nash stirred the elements together in a cauldron of whimsy. Before breaking up, the Fool moved to Los Angeles and painted theaters for performances of the musical *Hair*.

Suggested Album: The Fool (1968)

FOTHERINGAY

See Denny, Sandy

FRAMPTON, PETER (1950–)

Peter Frampton's career trajectory was unusual, to say the least. After spending the first half of the 1970s chasing stardom, he suddenly found himself catapulted to superstardom on the basis of one of the bestselling live albums of all time, only to plummet from the pinnacle of career success to near has-been status by the end of the decade. And while Frampton never again achieved significant chart success, the ensuing decades saw him forge a solid, workmanlike career, mostly playing as a sideman for other artists.

Frampton first tasted success as a member of a barely successful British Invasion band, the Fray. The band didn't attract much attention, but Frampton's teen idol looks did, earning him a measure of fame beyond his group's modest level of success. The 18-year-old Frampton then teamed up with Small Faces' Steve Marriott to form a prominent hard rock group, Humble Pie. By 1971 Frampton left after

138   FREE

growing tired of Humble Pie's power rock approach. His first solo album, *Winds of Change* (1972), relied more on mid-tempo melodic rock songs. The album sold poorly. His next two albums, *Frampton's Camel* (1973) and *Somethin's Happening* (1974), featured harder rocking songs, often with a noticeable rhythm and blues feel. He returned to a more melodic approach with *Frampton* (1975) and hit the road to promote the album.

Frampton Comes Alive (1976) was recorded during that tour. Within two months the album topped the charts, and soon it produced three hit singles, "Show Me the Way," "Baby, I Love Your Way," and "Do You Feel Like We Do." The material was drawn from his solo albums, but the mid-tempo numbers rocked a bit harder and featured Frampton's guitar skills, particularly his distinctive use of voice box during his solos. *Frampton Comes Alive* was set apart from previous live albums for featuring the audience almost as much as the artist. The crowd's raucous response to Frampton's playing was prominently displayed in the mix, even during some of the songs, creating the feel of an actual live show.

On the charts for nearly two years, *Frampton Comes Alive* gained the guitarist his long-sought superstardom. Frampton's angelic looks proved to be a hit with young women, but had the unintended consequence of alienating many male fans first drawn by his prowess on guitar. This double-edged sword doomed his much anticipated follow-up studio album, *I'm in You* (1977), which emphasized his soft rock tendencies at the expense of guitar playing skills and saddled him with a pretty boy image that put him in the crosshairs of the emerging punk rock revolution. The album sold well initially, but lacked sustained appeal. Frampton's role in the wretched film adaptation of *Sgt. Pepper's Lonely Hearts Club Band* (1978) subjected him to ridicule. His star fell quickly.

Frampton would never have much chart success after the 1970s, although he continued to record and tour in support of artists like David Bowie, Ringo Starr, and Bill Wyman. The years have seen Frampton earn respect as a skilled guitarist, but he will best be remembered for *Frampton Comes Alive*, which remains one of the bestselling live albums of all time.

Suggested Albums: Winds of Change (1972); *Frampton's Camel* (1973); *Frampton* (1975); *Frampton Comes Alive* (1976)

See also: Humble Pie

FREE

British rock band Free was a steady presence on radio airwaves in the first half of the 1970s thanks to their signature hit "All Right Now," a single that proved to be their only significant chart success. However, the fame of lead singer Paul Rodgers and the legacy of guitarist Paul Kossoff has ensured that the band is perhaps better appreciated by serious music fans nowadays than they were by the public at large during their existence.

The members of Free were still in their teens when they released their first album, *Tons of Sobs* (1968), but the work was stronger and more sophisticated than recordings by groups several years their senior. The music was strongly, but not slavishly blues influenced, with Rodgers's muscular and assertive vocals commanding immediate attention. The songwriting was fresh and melodic, but also brooding and intense, and the music was performed with power and youthful confidence. Kossoff's lead guitar work was outstanding, featuring a rich, over-driven tone and highlighted by a unique, brilliantly controlled vibrato. Despite this auspicious debut, the album sold poorly, as did the more blues-based follow-up, *Free* (1969).

Free's fortunes changed with the release of *Fire and Water* (1970). The band transcended its influences and created a new and original hard rock sound based on chunky power chords, passionate vocals, and songwriting that retained the passion of the blues but broke clear of the 12-bar structure that handcuffed many lesser similarly influenced artists. The album contained "All Right Now," a memorable and energetic rocker that put the band's strengths firmly on display. While the song was a worldwide hit, radio-friendly editing deprived many listeners of the full brilliance of Kossoff's vibrato-laden guitar solo. The album also sold well, and it seemed that Free was about to achieve stardom.

However, it was not to be, as conflicts between Rodgers and Kossoff began to escalate, probably stoked by Kossoff's increasingly out of control drug problems. The band's next album, *Highway* (1970), lacked the vitality of their first few efforts, although the group did recover and release two quality and commercially successful albums, *Free at Last* (1972) and *Heartbreaker* (1973). Unfortunately, Kossoff's downward spiral continued, and Free broke up in 1973 with Kossoff forming a new band, Back Street Crawler. He died in 1976 due to complications from his longstanding battle with drugs. After Free, Rodgers went on as a member of the supergroup Bad Company.

The new millennium saw a renewed recognition for Kossoff's guitar genius, as rising blues-rock guitarist Joe Bonamassa proclaimed him a seminal influence, and even took to playing Kossoff's legendary Les Paul onstage as a tribute to his hero. A new generation of guitarists was inspired by Kossoff's spectacular playing and the recordings he made with the underappreciated Free.

Suggested Albums: Tons of Sobs (1968); *Free* (1969); *Fire and Water* (1970); *Free at Last* (1972); *Heartbreaker* (1973)

FRIPP, ROBERT

See King Crimson

FUNK

The etymology of *funk* includes the African American vernacular for "bad smell," which came to connote earthy authenticity. By the 1950s jazz with a gospel backbeat, as opposed to the era's more cerebral cool jazz genre, was sometimes described as funky.

Funk as a specific genre was born with James Brown's "Papa's Got a Brand New Bag" (1965), which marked the emergence of music where groove was everything and each instrument was percussive and rhythmic. Bass tends to be the prominent instrument. Although funk's primary purpose was to get people moving, the irrepressible grooves were immediately associated with the Black Pride movement for their association with African polyrhythms.

In the 1960s and 1970s, funk was more assertively black than even soul music, a fact that did not prevent white performers from trying to be funky. Their efforts often fell short. The beats are easy enough to play, but the spirit behind them is harder to emulate without deep emersion in the culture that gave rise to the rhythms. African American bandleader George Clinton and his group Funkadelic found it easy to embrace rock elements, while for most rock groups funk was beyond their grasp. Despite bringing funky rhythms together with metallic guitar rock, Funkadelic was ignored by FM rock radio in the classic rock era and waited to find a significant multiracial audience until the 1980s, a time when rock and rap came together in Run-DMC's cover of Aerosmith's "Walk This Way."

FUSION
See Jazz-Rock

GABRIEL, PETER
See Genesis

GALLAGHER, RORY (1948–1995)

Rory Gallagher made a name for himself in the 1970s as a powerful blues-rock guitar player with a particularly strong reputation as a live performer. Armed with his trusty Fender Stratocaster, Gallagher was a constant presence on the road, touring steadily and always ready to showcase his fine playing and dynamic stage presence. While he had a solid career as a recording artist, the three live albums released during his 19-year career demonstrate that his skills were best showcased before a live audience.

Born and raised in Ireland, Gallagher followed a familiar path to music stardom, beginning in skiffle bands and eventually graduating to the sort of blues-based bands that had become standard fare in mid-1960s Britain. His first group, Taste, attracted attention in the late 1960s as an opening act for Cream and Blind Faith. The band didn't last, and Gallagher set off for a solo career, landing a record company and releasing a series of well-received albums throughout the 1970s and 1980s.

Gallagher is often pigeonholed as a "blues boogie" artist, but in truth his work was more eclectic than that label would suggest. To be sure, blues was a primary influence and never far from the surface, but he assimilated that influence and formed a more individual hard rock style that at times trod a path similar to that of Blind Faith–era Eric Clapton, while also delving into such diverse realms as Irish folk and country music. His albums were uniformly solid, but none established a level of true excellence. Gallagher's guitar playing was what attracted the most attention for his sturdy and passionate style, with a full tone and solid command of both traditional and country blues.

While an accomplished player, Gallagher was too similar to the scores of blues-based players filling the airwaves in 1970s to truly stand out, and it was his energetic stage presence that attracted the most attention. Gallagher's music popped in front of a crowd, a fact best seen on the standout live sets *Live in Europe* (1972) and *Irish Tour* (1974).

Gallagher's albums never topped the charts, but still had respectable sales, and he remained a concert attraction deep into the 1980s, but problems with alcohol

142 GENESIS

began to affect his health and eventually led to his death following an unsuccessful liver transplant in 1995. While he was never a superstar, or perhaps even especially well known during his prime, Gallagher's guitar playing proved more influential than one would expect, and it has been noted as inspirational by players such as U2's The Edge, Slash, Joe Bonamassa, and Brian May.

Suggested Albums: Rory Gallagher (1971); *Deuce* (1971); *Live in Europe* (1972); *Tattoo* (1973); *Calling Card* (1976); *Jinx* (1982)

See also: Taste

GENESIS

Genesis began in 1967 at Charterhouse, a British public school (equivalent to an American college preparatory academy), at a time when popular music seemed to advance with every week and every new album. Charterhouse was a good school for aspiring musicians with a legacy that already included at least one prominent graduate, composer Ralph Vaughan Williams.

Co-founder Peter Gabriel spoke of the early inspiration of Otis Redding rather than classical music, and their earliest demos reveal an echo of rhythm and blues. But their debut album *From Genesis to Revelation* (1969), which satisfied none of the band members and sold few copies, pointed the way toward the grand, elaborate, sprawling ethos of progressive rock. If Charterhouse imposed lines and limits, its rebellious students were determined to break out and embrace wider possibilities.

Personnel changes helped define the band as they entered the British album charts and found a small but avid American following. When Phil Collins joined in 1970, the drummer brought professionalism and proficiency, anchoring a band still in search of their sound. Also joining that same year was Steve Hackett, who took Genesis forward with accomplished but never flashy lead guitar lines. Along with the surviving original members Gabriel, keyboardist Tony Banks, and bassist Mike Rutherford, this became the classic lineup on such signature progressive rock albums as *Nursery Cryme* (1971), *Fox Trot* (1972), and *Selling England by the Pound* (1973). Their distinct, often lengthy and involved compositions were presented with characteristic English reserve.

During those years, Gabriel began slipping onstage in his wife's frocks or wearing a fox's head and other costumes. He explained the introduction of theatricality as simply something to do during the band's long instrumental passages and tuneups. Others have proposed that Gabriel was reticent and masked himself through stage personae. Whatever the inspiration, the effect was entirely different from the transgressive androgyny of David Bowie or Marc Bolan.

The Lamb Lies Down on Broadway (1974), conceived by Gabriel as a Pilgrim's Progress set on the streets of New York, marked the summit and the end of the classic lineup as Banks came to blows with Gabriel over the band's direction. Unaccountably, Genesis launched an American tour with the album barely released. Audiences were puzzled by the unfamiliar music along with the frequent failure of

Genesis made its most innovative music before the departure of their original vocalist, Peter Gabriel, but achieved mainstream popularity under his replacement, Phil Collins. Collins is seen here fronting the band during a British concert in the 1980s. (Simon Dack Archive/Alamy Stock Photo)

the rear-screen slide show and the difficulty of miking Gabriel's cumbersome, grotesque masks. At the end of the tour, Gabriel left the band and embarked on a commercially successful, aesthetically challenging solo career.

Genesis auditioned singers but chose Collins as their new vocalist. On *A Trick of the Tail* (1976) the band compressed progressive rock into tighter songs. Their popularity increased after Hackett's departure in 1977. With their 1978 hit "Follow You, Follow Me," Genesis became the once-progressive band that supplied the slow dance number on prom night.

Genesis carried on with two drummers. Weather Report's Chester Thompson played opposite Collins, and American fusion guitarist Daryl Stuermer filled Hackett's spot. The melodically inoffensive Collins devoted increasing time to his solo career, even as Genesis filled stadiums and reached the pinnacle of the charts. During the 1980s Collins alone or with his band seemed ubiquitous. And then, as the 1990s began, the hits stopped coming. Collins left Genesis in 1996 and regrouped with the 1980s lineup for a 2006 final tour.

Meanwhile, Gabriel cultivated a solo career, beginning with the first of many eponymous albums (1977) that crossed boundaries rather than colored within them. Insisting the masks he wore were tools of revelation rather than objects of concealment, he brought the staging of rock concerts to new heights during the 1980s and was a determined promoter of non-Western music through his Real World record label, the WOMAD music festival, and the influences he

144   GENTLE GIANT

incorporated into his own albums. He was proficient at the nascent art of MTV videos and enjoyed several hits in the 1980s, starting with "Shock the Monkey" (1982). "Sledgehammer" (1986) knocked Genesis's "Invisible Touch" from the top of the U.S. charts.

While the band led by Collins provided a soundtrack to the late 1970s and 1980s for mainstream audiences, the band's work during the Gabriel era left a deeper impression as evidenced by the re-creations of popular tribute bands such as Britain's ReGenesis and Canada's the Musical Box, the latter touring with a production of *The Lamb Lies Down on Broadway*. Genesis has been inducted into the Rock and Roll Hall of Fame.

Suggested Albums: From Genesis to Revelation (1969); *Trespass* (1970); *Nursery Cryme* (1971); *Foxtrot* (1972); *Selling England by the Pound* (1973); *The Lamb Lies Down on Broadway* (1974)

GENTLE GIANT

Three Scottish-born brothers formed the British progressive rock band Gentle Giant after they failed to make it big in the 1960s as a rhythm and blues act. Phil, Derek, and Ray Shulman were multi-instrumentalists with high musical aspirations who had become frustrated with various attempts at fashioning a commercially successful sound (one such effort sounded sufficiently Beatlesque to spark rumors that it was a surreptitious Fab Four recording). Fed up with trying to find a lucrative formula, the brothers formed Gentle Giant in 1970 and set about recording ever more complex progressive rock that pleased them and a devoted fan base, but never achieved the mass success they initially longed for.

From their first album, *Gentle Giant* (1970), it was clear that this band was cut from no common cloth, even by the high-minded standards of progressive rock. Eschewing the grandiosity of many such bands, Gentle Giant composed songs of intricate complexity while never truly abandoning a blues-influenced heavy rock approach. It was common to call progressive rock bands "classical rock," but the label appropriately fit Gentle Giant more so than most. Their music at times sounded classical, but the term was apt more for the approach the group took. Gentle Giant made copious use of polyphonic melodies, frequently shifting odd time signatures, diverse chord voicing, and highly complex and well-defined structured themes, all techniques heavily utilized by classical composers. The music was often dissonant, but rarely unpleasantly so, and that dissonance was often used to fascinating effect.

The band's multi-instrumental approach ensured that they would never form a truly definable sound, which led to the music staying fresh but often lacking coherence. Like most progressive rock, there was an undeniable sense of self-indulgence, and the music was far removed from the urgency and passion associated with the roots of rock and roll. They lyrics were often abstract and complex. The band's approach probably reached full fruition with *Free Hand* (1975), which puts the band's considerable strengths and noticeable weaknesses on full display.

Gentle Giant's creative heyday had passed by the time punk hit in the late 1970s, and the group broke up in 1980. However, they are fondly recalled by many lovers of progressive rock and should be noted for a genuine creative spirit and an original and fresh approach. While none of their albums rank as a true masterpiece, virtually every Gentle Giant record has more than a few moments of inspiration and interest.

Suggested Albums: Gentle Giant (1970); *Acquiring the Taste* (1971); *Three Friends* (1972); *Octopus* (1972); *In a Glass House* (1973); *Free Hand* (1975)

GLITTER ROCK

It has been said that glitter or glam rock began in March 1971 when T. Rex's Marc Bolan appeared on British television's *Top of the Pops* in glitter and flowing satin, yet the impulse began in the 1960s with the foppish fashions of the Who and the Rolling Stones and the countercultural bend toward sartorial transgressions such as long hair for men. Evidence of androgyny can be found in the togs worn by early Alice Cooper and even by Gram Parsons, a leading figure in the more traditionalist genre of country rock.

Bolan's appearance on TV galvanized the trend, but David Bowie became its most visible proponent. Soon enough, rising star Elton John was rigged up in high heels, outrageous glasses, and Liberace costumes. Art rock bands such as Roxy Music flirted with the look. Glitter rock was never a musical genre but described an image and an attitude with its teasing suggestion of all things gay and forbidden. Once the movement was underway, the United States responded with the New York Dolls, and Lou Reed applied mascara and nail polish, yet in America glitter remained marginal. However, it was the rage in England where cross-dressing was already associated with entertainment and drew on the decadent tradition of Oscar Wilde and Aubrey Beardsley with its intimations of forbidden love and fawn-like young men.

As with any movement, glitter's bandwagon was soon crowded with the likes of Alvin Stardust, Gary Glitter, and other late adopters. After Bowie abandoned glitter following *Diamond Dogs* (1974), the trend lost its creative edge. Although disdained by punk rock, the impulses reemerged in such new wave acts as Adam Ant and Culture Club. In the 1980s, glam rock was resuscitated by a host of heavy metal bands better remembered for their hairdos than their music.

GOLDEN EARRING

Dutch bands counted for nothing beyond the borders of the Netherlands until the late 1960s. The visual art-music collective the Fool were known to psychedelic cognoscenti in the United Kingdom and the United States, but the first international hit by a Dutch group was the Shocking Blue's Brazilian-infused "Venus" (1970). The progressive–hard rock band Focus climbed charts around the world with the novelty instrumental "Hocus Pocus" (1971). The mini Dutch wave continued and concluded with Golden Earring's "Radar Love" (1973).

Golden Earring was obscure in most countries before then but had been stars in their homeland for nearly a decade. As the Golden Earrings, they first tasted local acclaim with "Please Go" (1965), the first in a string of pop hits. By the end of the 1960s Golden Earring shifted toward hard rock and were called heavy metal by critics as late as 1980. The Who employed Golden Earring as opening act for a European tour and they crisscrossed the United States, opening for any headlining band that would have them. But "Radar Love" from *Moontan* (1973) was what broke them in America.

A standout whether heard in edited form on AM or complete with long instrumental bridge on FM, "Radar Love" was a road song whose protagonist was linked psychically to his girlfriend. The music and lyrics vividly conjured up scenes from a long nocturnal drive with the car radio keeping the exhausted driver awake. The bass line sounded like wheels hitting pavement while the vocal was oddly passionless, probably because the singer delivered the narrative in a language learned from school textbooks. Like many Golden Earring recordings, "Radar Love" borders on cool and clichéd, a modestly intriguing idea delivered by a band with limited range.

Although their follow-up, *Switch* (1975), received FM airplay, it failed to sell in the United States. Golden Earring briefly returned to widespread attention with one of MTV's early video hits, "Twilight Zone" (1982), a new wave song inspired more by Robert Ludlum than Rod Serling. Since then, Golden Earring has maintained their European fan base through a succession of LPs.

Suggested Album: Moontan (1973)

GONG

Gong began in 1967 as a freewheeling psychedelic experiment in music and imagination. The band's visionary, Daevid Allen, was an Australian Beat who wandered to Great Britain in the early 1960s, played free jazz in London, and was an early member of Soft Machine. Allen fell under the spell, romantically and intellectually, of Welsh poet-vocalist Gilly Smyth. The couple founded Gong in France with local musicians after Allen was denied reentry to the United Kingdom because of visa problems. While Allen was tripping on LSD, a whimsical mythology unfolded in his consciousness that became the basis for many lyrics and storylines on Gong albums. Illustrative of Allen's ethos was the nonviolent protest he staged in Paris during the 1968 riots, which involved handing out teddy bears to strangers. A stay in an ashram in the south of France buttressed the mystical leanings evident in Gong.

Gong's debut, *Magick Brother* (1970), alternates between manic and reflective, with lovely acoustic melodies, raving rock, collages of voices and sounds, experiments in tape manipulation and electronics. Allen's LSD-inspired mythos, hinted at on early albums such as *Camembert Electrique* (1971) and his solo LP *Bananamoon* (1971), came to full fruition on the "Radio Gnome Trilogy." *Flying Teapot* (1973), *Angel's Egg* (1973) and *You* (1974) featured guitarist Steve Hillage and a story involving the Good Witch Yoni, Zero the Hero, and the Pot Head Pixies from

Planet Gong. Allen and Smyth, citing psychic concerns, left Gong in 1975. The band continued in ever morphing forms and lineups, veering into jazz-rock fusion under the leadership of French drummer Pierre Moerlen.

For Allen, the exploration of his personal mythos had only begun. Recording under his own name and as Planet Gong and other band monikers, he continued to record prolifically, often with Smyth and their son, drummer Orlando Allen. Exemplifying Allen's endeavors was the Gong Family Unconvention, a series of multiday, semiannual events held in Glastonbury or Amsterdam and involving musicians from dozens of Gong-related bands that had spun off from his original vision. Afflicted with cancer, Allen sat out Gong's 2014 European tour. He died in 2015, expressing the hope that Gong could continue without him.

Suggested Albums: Magick Brother (1970); *Camembert Electrique* (1971); *Bananamoon* (1971) (by Daevid Allen); *Continental Circus* (1971); *Flying Teapot* (1973); *Angel's Egg* (1973); *You* (1974)

GRATEFUL DEAD

During the 1970s, the Grateful Dead, a pure product of the 1960s counterculture, became a subculture unto themselves. If the phenomenon of the Dead threatened to eclipse the music, the music was always integral to the phenomenon.

With the exception of classically trained bassist Phil Lesh, the original band members were part of the dialectic that produced many memorable American rock bands in the mid-1960s. They played rock and roll in high school, and as young adults were drawn to the folk-blues revival before embracing the new rock that emerged in the wake of Bob Dylan and the Beatles. Jerry Garcia played banjo and guitar with bassist Robert Hunter, who later became the Dead's lyricist, in bluegrass and jug bands. By 1962 they performed regularly at West Coast coffeehouses and folk festivals. In 1965 Garcia, Lesh, guitarist Bob Weir, keyboardist Ron "Pigpen" McKernan, and drummer Bill Kreutzmann formed a rock band, the Warlocks, which became the Grateful Dead. They took their name from a figure in the folklore of many cultures, a ghost that appreciated the generosity of a stranger who paid for the burial of his corpse.

By the close of 1965, the Grateful Dead were the house band at the Acid Tests, the psychedelic dance parties hosted by Ken Kesey, author of *One Flew Over the Cuckoo's Nest*. The novelist had recently returned to the West Coast after leading a group of adventurers, the Merry Pranksters, on a legendary road trip across the United States in a bus whose destination plate read FURTHER. In their early months, the Dead mixed folk-blues repertoire, including Slim Harpo's "I'm a King Bee" and the 1920s jug band tune "Viola Lee Blues," with contemporary hits such as Them's "Gloria" and a few original songs. The time-disorienting effects of the Acid Tests, with their flashing strobe lights and liberal use of LSD, encouraged endless versions of songs made elastic through improvisation. Tom Wolfe referred to them in his memorable account of Kesey and the Pranksters, *The Electric Kool-Aid Acid Test* (1968).

Unlike any other band to emerge from the 1960s West Coast counterculture, the Grateful Dead maintained their allegiance to the era's values in the face of changing times. Their devotion won them an audience that endured even after the death of their leader, Jerry Garcia, shown here (background) with Bob Weir (front), also a founding member of the band. (Eautographhunter/Dreamstime.com)

The Grateful Dead's self-titled debut album (1967) only hints at how they sounded at the Acid Tests. With the exception of a 10-minute take of "Viola Lee Blues," the songs clocked in at five minutes or less. Most of the original songs were Americana transformed in the DayGlo of psychedelia. *The Grateful Dead* was the band's hardest rocking album while still suggesting the shambolic looseness that would characterize future recordings as well as live shows.

Garcia's emblematic guitar playing was compounded from folk, bluegrass, country, and Chuck Berry. He played with the looseness of jazz and an exploratory spirit inspired by the psychedelic experience. As a soloist, he was less prominent on record than in concert, where his famed lengthy excursions were brilliant or not depending on his lucidity. His playing and the Dead's music were notable for their lack of aggression. They represented the antithesis of punk and heavy metal, yet had too much electric sizzle to be classed with the "soft rock" of the 1970s. On record the drumming was low in the mix on earlier albums, keeping time but never pushing the music hard.

Mickey Hart joined on drums for *Anthem of the Sun* (1968), and Robert Hunter commenced his songwriting collaboration with Garcia on *Aoxomoxoa* (1969). Both albums were psychedelic collage experiments in tape editing with multitracked layers of sounds and songs spliced together from live performances and studio recordings. The expense of recording *Aoxomoxoa* left the Dead in debt to their record label, Warner Brothers. They were determined from then on to keep it simple in the studio.

In 1970 they released their finest albums, *Workingman's Dead* and *American Beauty*. Both LPs sat comfortably alongside the Band and Creedence Clearwater Revival in their search for authentic American roots with vocal harmonies and pedal steel that linked their sound to country rock. The sunny lyric and lovely Latin melody of "Uncle John's Band," which opened *Workingman's Dead*, was heard as a call to relax after the upheavals of the decade just ended. The low-key blues-rock of "New Speedway Boogie" was interpreted as an abstract comment on the fiasco of Altamont, the 1969 rock festival that saw the killing of a concertgoer by Hells Angels. The country shuffle of "Casey Jones" recalled the long tradition of balladry concerning a railroad engineer involved in a storied turn-of-the-century train wreck.

American Beauty was stronger still, matching poetry with country rock on "Box of Rain" and the outlaw spirit with Appalachian string band music on "Friend of the Devil." The jubilant paean to high times and love, "Sugar Magnolia," and the paranoid boogie of "Truckin'" were standards on FM radio. "What a long strange trip it's been," a line from "Truckin'," became the band's motto.

The Grateful Dead never released an album as strong as *American Beauty*. Future recordings had moments of interest but seemed conceived to provide grist for live jams. From 1970 on, the Dead existed primarily to perform live, especially at mammoth outdoor concerts. As their generational peers fell by the wayside or accommodated themselves to changing times and shifting fashions, the Dead held on to a communal vision of camaraderie framed by music and often sustained through the shared experience of marijuana.

Long before anyone else, the Dead recognized the community-career building value of allowing fans (called Deadheads) to record their concerts and share the tapes. They even smiled benignly on the cottage industry of bootleg Grateful Dead concert LPs, tolerating the modest earnings of their underground producers for the interest those recordings generated among fans. Following the Dead on tour became a subcultural pastime or even obsession. Like the seminomadic court of Central Asian chieftains, the Dead seemed continually on the move along with a tribe of camp followers. The band encouraged Deadheads to be entrepreneurial by becoming vendors at concerts of food, tie-dyed T-shirts, and other paraphernalia.

While the Dead maintained its fan base through the 1970s, by the 1980s they attracted a younger audience in large numbers. Many were weekenders seeking escape from the monotony of everyday life, drawn to the Dead as the survivors of a past more colorful than the present. The growth of Dead fandom and the band's rising profile probably accounted for the greatest surprise from their later years, a Top 10 single, "A Touch of Gray" from *In the Dark* (1987), an album whose production was more pop-oriented than was usual for them.

The 1995 death of Garcia from a heart attack while staying at a drug rehabilitation center devastated his fans. Surviving band members engaged in solo projects or collaborations with one another, including Weir, Lesh, and Hart's band the Other Ones, known as the Dead after 2002. During the 1990s a new generation of jam bands such as Phish, String Cheese Incident, and Widespread Panic tried to reinvent the Dead's music and spirit for a new era.

To mark the anniversary of the band's founding, Hart, Kreutzmann, Lesh, and Weir toured in 2015 under the banner "Fare Thee Well: Celebrating 50 Years of the Grateful Dead." Some fans grumbled at a Dead without Garcia, but most accepted Phish guitarist Trey Anastasio as a respectable substitute and turned out in tie-dyes to witness what was promised as the last hurrah for a communal hippie experience that survived into the culturally fragmented 21st century.

Suggested Albums: The Grateful Dead (1967); *Anthem of the Son* (1968); *Aoxomoxoa* (1969); *Workingman's Dead* (1970); *American Beauty* (1970); *In the Dark* (1987)

GROUNDHOGS

The Groundhogs took their name from John Lee Hooker's "Groundhog's Blues," so it's little surprise that their music was firmly grounded in and paid homage to the sort of gritty blues Hooker helped make famous. However, the Groundhogs accomplished the difficult task of taking the blues as inspiration and putting their own stamp on the form while never fully erasing its imprint on their sound.

Formed in the early 1960s and led by guitarist Tony McPhee, the Groundhogs hit the music scene in 1968 with the release of their debut album, *Scratching the Surface*. The follow-up *Blues Obituary* (1969) established the band's aggressive blues-based approach with loud heavy bass and drums providing a pulverizing rhythmic base while a Chicago blues–influenced harp dominates throughout. The debt owed to the likes of Hooker and Willie Dixon is obvious, and the vocals are sung rough-hewn blues style in a similar but more accessible vein than that being adopted across the Atlantic by Captain Beefheart. The Groundhogs played with a volume and power beyond that of more reverent blues enthusiasts, establishing a more distinct and fresh sound, much in the manner of fellow British blues rockers the Pretty Things.

The group began to experiment with more complex arrangements with the release of *Thank Christ for the Bomb* (1970), especially with the title track, a tempo-shifting paean to the Pax Atomica. Their fourth album, *Split* (1971), saw the group develop a far less blues-based songwriting style as they further stretched their musical boundaries. *Split* displayed a more progressive, psychedelic take on blues-rock that was creative, but must have sounded a bit quaint by the early 1970s. However, the band's albums sold well in the United Kingdom, despite having little chart success elsewhere.

The Groundhogs broke up in 1974, although McPhee eventually reformed the band. They toured and recorded off and on for the better part of three decades with a revolving door of lineup changes while moving in a harder-edged direction that bordered at times on metal and punk. McPhee's health issues eventually forced him to retire. The Groundhogs broke up again in 2014.

Suggested Albums: Scratching the Surface (1968); *Blues Obituary* (1969); *Thank Christ for the Bomb* (1970); *Split* (1971); *Who Will Save the World* (1972); *Hogwash* (1972); *Razor's Edge* (1985)

GUESS WHO

The Guess Who placed a string of singles on AM radio as the 1960s turned into the 1970s while maintaining a presence on FM. They grew out of early 1960s rock and roll bands playing in Winnipeg, Manitoba, and fronted by singer Chad Allan. Early rock and roll roots were audible on their first hit, an uncharacteristically bone-rattling cover of Terry and the Pirates' "Shakin' All Over" (1965). Their record company slapped "The Guess Who?" on the single's label, hoping to arouse suspicion that it was the work of moonlighting British Invasion stars. After Burton Cummings replaced Allan, the renamed Guess Who released garage psychedelic singles written primarily by guitarist Randy Bachman and became familiar throughout Canada through prominent attention on CBC radio and television.

By the late 1960s the Guess Who had grown into a band of considerable musical scope. Their U.S. profile rose with the jazz-accented pop-soul number "These Eyes," a Cummings-Bachman collaboration from *Wheatfield Soul* (1969) in an idiom Tom Jones or even Vic Damone could understand. Cummings had already honed a vocal style capable of anguish and calm within the same number. *Canned Wheat* (1969) brought Cummings-Bachman's sophisticated songcraft to the fore with "Laughing," a dramatic pop production with dynamic harmonies, and the Wes Montgomery–influenced "Undun," which became a minor standard among jazz musicians.

With *American Woman* (1970), the Guess Who reached their pinnacle of popularity in a more hard rock format that often featured guitar played through the howling distortion of a Leslie amplifier. The title cut was a scathing rebuke to U.S. politics unmatched in Canadian music until Rufus Wainwright ruefully declared, "I'm so tired of you, America," in "Going to a Town" (2007). The enigmatic "No Time" could have been sung from the perspective of a draft dodger seeking refuge in Canada or could have concerned a love affair brought to a painful end. "No Sugar Tonight" contained several distinct movements, including baroque acoustic guitar and a surging rock chorus, within the framework of a pop song.

Bachman, whose musicianship and songwriting was crucial, left in 1970 to form the band that eventually became Bachman-Turner Overdrive. A pair of guitarist-songwriters, Kurt Winter and Greg Leskiw, replaced him. Cummings's distinctive voice helped the Guess Who stay the course for *Share the Land* (1970) with its pair of hits, Winter's annoyed "Hand Me Down World" and the utopian dream of Cummings's title number.

Although holding on to popularity in Canada, the Guess Who's visibility diminished south of the border and their musical direction suffered as members came and left. Their final American hit, "Clap for the Wolfman" (1974), was a novelty tribute to gravel-voiced DJ Wolfman Jack. The Guess Who broke up in 1975 with Cummings opting for a career as a mainstream pop singer. Because their name had never been legally registered, bands calling themselves the Guess Who surfaced regularly, occasionally with Cummings and Bachman participating.

Suggested Albums: Wheatfield Soul (1969); *Canned Wheat* (1969); *American Woman* (1970); *Share the Land* (1970)

GURU GURU

Although he played drums, Guru Guru's leader Mani Neumeier never let his kit get in the way of showmanship and became an antic performer after forming Guru Guru in 1968. Part of the tempestuous German scene soon dubbed "Krautrock" by players and fans, Guru Guru were intimately involved with the political upheavals and alternative lifestyles of Germany in that era.

Guru Guru's early albums attracted comparisons with Jimi Hendrix through guitarist Ax Genrich's heavy playing as well as Newmeier's jazz-influenced drumming. Sometimes employing odd devices such as the Mani-Tom, an inflatable drum, Neumeier brought Frank Zappa levels of zaniness to his shows. By the mid-1970s Guru Guru drifted toward jazz-rock fusion. Popular in their homeland, Guru Guru attracted a small following of Krautrock fans elsewhere. Through many lineup changes, Guru Guru remains active and prolific in the 21st century.

Suggested Albums: UFO (1970); *Hinten* (1971); *Kangaru* (1972); *Guru Guru* (1973); *Don't Call Us, We Call You* (1973)

GUTHRIE, ARLO (1947–)

Woody Guthrie was temperamentally as well as politically adverse to establishing a dynasty, yet he sired one that began with his son, Arlo. Arlo eventually emerged from the shadow of his father, America's greatest folksinger from the mid-20th century, to become his own artist.

The younger Guthrie gained prominence with "Alice's Restaurant," which occupied an entire side of the album of the same name (1967). The song was not unlike something his father might have sung, if Woody had a mind to perform an 18-minute epic. A humorously rambling story of the Vietnam War draft and the inanity of rules and regulations, "Alice's Restaurant" boasted an irresistible chorus that could have been sung around a hobo's campfire and was heard often on FM radio. The song inspired the Arthur Penn–directed film *Alice's Restaurant* (1969). Guthrie starred in this counterculture comedy-drama, which mocked the squares without flinching from the drug addiction, complications of free love, and low status of women that flourished amidst the counterculture's fine talk of freedom.

By the time of the film's release, Guthrie had developed his own voice as a performer. He embraced a taut contemporary folk-rock sound for *Running Down the Road* (1969), which included a minor hit, "Coming into Los Angeles." With *Alice's Restaurant* elevating him into a countercultural celebrity, Guthrie performed at Woodstock (1969). Three years later, he saw his greatest hit with a version of Steve Goodman's "City of New Orleans," a country-folk number in the long tradition of American railroad songs. Guthrie transformed Goodman's wistfully nostalgic ballad into a standard that has since been covered by Willie Nelson, Lynn Anderson, and dozens of other performers.

However, Guthrie was so associated with the late 1960s that the 1970s left him in the pop culture backwater. The success of "City of New Orleans" was an anomaly rather than the harbinger of his future. A competent songwriter and a likable performer, Guthrie led a band called Shenandoah in the 1970s. He performed with Ry Cooder, Emmylou Harris, John Prine, and Cyril Neville, appeared occasionally in movies and television shows, and continued working but never regained the attention he enjoyed at Woodstock.

In recent years Guthrie purchased the desacralized church featured in *Alice's Restaurant* and turned it into an interfaith center serving families with HIV and other illnesses. Guthrie's family has followed him into music. He tours with his son, Abe. Daughter Cathy plays in Folk Uke with Amy Nelson, daughter of Willie Nelson. Daughter Annie is a songwriter and Sarah Lee records with her husband Johnny Irion. Arlo's grandson, Krishna, plays drums in Modest Me.

Suggested Albums: Alice's Restaurant (1967); *Running Down the Road* (1969); *Hobo's Lullaby* (1972)

HAMMILL, PETER
See Van der Graaf Generator

HARPER, ROY (1941–)
It is tempting to say that the British folk guitarist Roy Harper has marched to the beat of a different drummer, but if Harper's 50-year recording career has proved anything, it is that he is far too much of an individualist to follow anyone's lead. Harper has always kept time to his own beat, and in the process has earned the admiration of countless artists, some of whom likely wish they could forge a path as distinct as his.

Harper was writing poetry by the time he was 12. He took up guitar and joined the skiffle craze of 1950s Britain before taking to the road as a street musician through Europe and North Africa. He landed a recording contract and released his first album, *Sophisticated Beggar* (1966). The album featured largely acoustic music, but it was immediately apparent that Harper was cut from a different cloth than other folk artists populating the scene. The acoustic guitar was strummed with a force and power unlike the standard folk fare, creating a more folk-rock feel, but usually without an accompanying amplified band. His melodies were often ornate, but never delicate, with hints of Eastern music droning through. His second album, *Come Out Fighting Ghengis Smith* (1968), showed him experimenting with other instruments while retaining a predominately acoustic sound. Harper's lyrics were also original, with inventive and offbeat musings and observations that could be described as eccentrically Dylanesque, although any similarity was likely due to a shared interest in poetry and Beat culture (Harper listed Keats and Kerouac among his influences). *Folkjokeopus* (1969) saw Harper's music become less overtly folk and at times vaguely psychedelic as he began to try different instruments and arrangements, at times at the expense of coherence as his music and lyrics began to become a bit disjointed.

In the 1970s Harper was squarely back in the acoustic camp, recording a series of folk albums that highlighted his maturing songwriting and mesmerizing finger-picked guitar playing. Other artists began to take notice of Harper and began to express admiration for his unique and uncompromising style. Led Zeppelin paid homage to him with "Hats Off to Harper," a track from their 1975 album *Physical Graffiti*. That same year Pink Floyd took the unusual step of enlisting him as guest lead vocalist on one of their best known songs, "Have a Cigar," from *Wish You Were Here*.

Public attention lagged behind, although Harper did score the occasional minor hit single in the United Kingdom. For the most part though, Harper's records were never big sellers, and he never showed the slightest inclination to accommodate the public's taste. Harper's planned lyrical collaboration with Led Zeppelin fell through when the album was scratched due to the death of singer Robert Plant's son. Harper's recording career carried on throughout the 1980s and 1990s, sometimes with a band and sometimes not, always with a broad lyrical range that touched on issues of aging, psychological struggles, and social criticism.

Harper continues to record and perform live, releasing most of his recent work on his own record label, Science Fiction. His 22nd studio album, *Man and Myth* (2013), showed Harper in good form, with his lyrical edge undiminished in a pleasing mix of acoustic and electric tracks. Harper averted disaster when he was acquitted of child sex abuse charges in 2015, charges the artist angrily denied. Harper's long and influential career received its greatest public recognition in 2013 when BBC Radio awarded him a Lifetime Achievement Award at its Radio 2 Folk Awards.

Suggested Albums: Sophisticated Beggar (1966); *Come Out Fighting Ghengis Smith* (1968); *Lifemask* (1973); *Valentine* (1974); *HQ* (1975); *Bullinamingvase* (1977); *Whatever Happened to Jugula?* (1985); *Once* (1990); *Death or Glory* (1992); *The Dream Society* (1998); *The Green Man* (2000); *Man and Myth* (2013)

HARRIS, EMMYLOU (1947–)

It is often difficult to think of Emmylou Harris apart from the legendary Gram Parsons, the country rock pioneer who brought the dulcet-toned singer to prominence when he signed her on as a duet partner at the beginning of his solo career. Harris herself is partly responsible for this perception, as she continued to thoroughly identify with Parsons following his death in 1973, recording many of his songs and repeatedly acknowledging her debt to him in interviews. And while she has never stopped paying tribute to her mentor, she has managed to build a separate artistic identity and has forged a highly successful and influential career in the field of country music that in some ways fulfilled the vision Parsons never lived to fulfill.

Harris was raised in the American south and developed a strong interest in music while attending college in North Carolina. She took up guitar and began playing folk music, eventually releasing a surprisingly diverse debut album, *Gilded Bird* (1969), which highlighted her lovely voice and mixed country and pop songs with Judy Collins–sounding folk. Flying Burrito Brother Chris Hillman saw her perform live and was sufficiently impressed to recommend her to his band co-founder Parsons, who brought her on board to sing with him on his debut solo album *GP* (1973). The pair established immediate vocal (and some have suggested romantic) chemistry, with Parsons's vulnerable tenor perfectly complemented by Harris's reassuring soprano. Their duets on songs such as "We'll Sweep Out the Ashes in the Morning" and "That's All It Took" are pure magic, as the two establish a vocal rapport that sounds as if they had been singing together for years. Parsons and Harris's chemistry translated well to the stage (aided by Harris's stunning beauty), but their collaboration came to a halt when Parsons died of a drug overdose in 1973.

Harris appeared with Parsons on his posthumous release *Grievous Angel* (1973), but the singer's death left Harris an emotional wreck. Her *Pieces of the Sky* (1975) seemed in part an effort by Harris to come to terms with the loss. The eclectic album shifts effortlessly between bouncing country rock, deeply emotional country balladry, and songs that recall her folk roots, all carried by Harris's beautifully aching vocals. The ballad "Boulder to Birmingham" is her tribute to Parsons and became one of her best-known songs.

The album received critical raves, but didn't sell well. The follow-up, *Elite Hotel* (1975), yielded several country hits. Harris soon began finding consistent success on the country charts, where she established a long and highly respected career that landed her in the Country Music Hall of Fame. Harris's often outstanding country output consistently merged a traditional approach with a willingness to cross boundaries that paid homage to Parsons's dream of creating a new musical melting pot from the myriad forms of American music. And in fitting tribute, a popular Internet music site uses Parsons's original term "American Cosmic Music" to classify Harris's work, a fact that doubtless would put a smile on the face of the man whose legacy Harris has always sought to carry on.

Suggested Albums: Gilded Bird (1969); *Pieces of the Sky* (1975); *Elite Hotel* (1975); *Quarter Moon in a Ten Cent Town* (1978); *Roses in the Snow* (1980); *Cowgirl's Prayer* (1993); *Wrecking Ball* (1995)

HARRISON, GEORGE (1943–2001)

Known as "the quiet Beatle," George Harrison's contributions to the band were often underheralded. As a songwriter he was always in the shadow of John Lennon and Paul McCartney and was allowed to contribute only a small number of songs to the Beatles' catalogue. However, he was always influential. Harrison was initially the biggest proponent within the Beatles of Bob Dylan, whose example made the band aware of rock and roll's potential for creative expression. He influenced the sound of folk-rock, especially that of the Byrds, by favoring a 12-string electric guitar. Harrison was also crucial for the introduction of Eastern modes into rock, beginning with his sitar playing on "Norwegian Wood."

As a guitarist, Harrison played sparsely with an audible twang indebted to Chet Atkins. With Chuck Berry as another early inspiration, Harrison never chose a wrong note and played impeccably. Harrison's scope as a guitarist grew through his friendship with Eric Clapton; in turn, Harrison may have endowed Clapton with a pop sensibility.

Harrison's first ventures outside the Beatles were *Wonderwall Music* (1968), the raga-flavored soundtrack to the eccentric period film *Wonderwall*, followed by

Electronic Sound (1969), which consisted of two compositions for Moog synthesizer. His first significant solo album was the first three-LP set in rock history. *All Things Must Pass* (1971) contained a wealth of material, much of it amassed during the Beatles years. Produced by Phil Spector, *All Things Must Pass* featured musical support from Clapton, Ringo Starr, and Badfinger mixed into Spector's characteristic "Wall of Sound," a mammoth rock orchestral effect, but without eclipsing Harrison's unique sweet-sounding, slide-guitar sound. The album included a number one hit, "My Sweet Lord." While expressing Harrison's Hindu faith, the syncretic lyric positioned the Judeo-Christian "hallelujah" alongside "Hare Krishna" to achieve a more universal significance. The song became an early battleground over music as intellectual property when he was sued for the melody's similarity to the Chiffons' 1963 hit "He's So Fine." In 1976 a U.S. federal judge concluded that Harrison had "subconsciously" plagiarized "He's So Fine," a ruling that left Harrison frightened about writing new songs and opened a floodgate of suits over allegedly similar melodies and chord progressions.

A man of conscience, Harrison decided to put his stardom to good purpose with concerts, a documentary film, and a live album to raise money for victims of a cyclone that ravaged East Pakistan as well as a savage campaign by Pakistan's military to put down a rebellion in the territory. The resulting *The Concert for Bangladesh* (1971), also a three-LP set, brought together a cast of stars including Clapton, Starr, Billy Preston, Badfinger, Leon Russell, and Dylan's first public appearance in several years. Although an IRS audit of the Beatles' Apple Records label froze most of the proceeds until long after East Pakistan gained independence as Bangladesh, Harrison's concert set a precedent for Live Aid, Farm Aid, and a wave of rock benefit concerts beginning in the mid-1980s.

Living in the Material World (1973) found Harrison comfortably settled in his musical style and produced another number one hit, the earnest plea "Give Me Love (Give Me Peace on Earth)." The following year Harrison established Dark Horse Records, which released albums by his mentor, sitar maestro Ravi Shankar, as well as several rock and soul acts that never rose beyond obscurity. Dark Horse eventually became the vehicle for his own solo work. The catchy title number from the album *Dark Horse* (1974) made the Top 15 but Harrison's new music seemed increasingly inconsequential, especially in light of his legal troubles over "My Sweet Lord" and the debacle of the 1974 Dark Horse tour of North America. Expectations were high for the first tour by an ex-Beatle, but Harrison resolutely refused to perform any Beatles song except for one of his own, "Something." Opening act Shankar was booed by impatient audiences, Harrison's voice was described as rough, and media coverage was often negative. Afterward, Harrison retreated from live performances for many years.

Although he often appeared as the most serious Beatle, Harrison took an active interest in the Monty Python comedy troupe, acting as executive producer of their films *Life of Brian* (1979) and *Time Bandits* (1981). He even appeared in Monty Python's parody of the Beatles, *All You Need Is Cash* (1978). He continued to release albums but sales were disappointing and airplay diminished. His greatest chart success in later years was a single featuring McCartney and Starr, "All Those Years

Ago" (1981), which rose to the top of the charts in honor of the recently slain Lennon.

Harrison later found renewed inspiration in the company of the Traveling Wilburys, the supergroup featuring him, Dylan, Roy Orbison, Tom Petty, and Jeff Lynne. The Wilburys recorded two albums (1988, 1990) and managed a pair of hit singles with "Handle with Care" and "She's My Baby." The final studio album released during his lifetime, *Cloud Nine* (1987), also included a hit, "Got My Mind Set on You." Harrison enjoyed a quiet, largely secluded life in his last years before dying of cancer in 2001. His posthumous studio album, *Brainwashed* (2007), was a spry-sounding, good-humored album. Recorded from 1988 through 2000, it was not unlike *All Things Must Pass* in drawing from a gradually building stockpile of strong material.

Suggested Albums: Wonderwall Music (1968); *All Things Must Pass* (1971); *The Concert for Bangladesh* (1971); *Living in the Material World* (1973); *Cloud Nine* (1987); *Brainwashed* (2007)

See also: Beatles

HAWKWIND

Co-founded by London busker Dave Brock in 1969, Hawkwind quickly became a leading exponent of space rock. In future years the primal beat of their music and against-the-grain attitude formed a bridge between psychedelia and punk. Through their collaborations with prominent British science fiction and fantasy author Michael Moorcock, Hawkwind achieved notice in literary circles.

Hawkwind attracted attention early on for provocative gestures such as setting up a free concert outside the gates of the Isle of Wight Festival (1970). Their eponymous debut album (1971), produced by the Pretty Things' Dick Taylor, contained remnants of Brock's street musician days, especially on the folk-trance opening number, "Hurry on Sundown." The influence of other members was felt on space rock jams such as "Be Yourself" and "Seeing It as You Really Are" with pulsating mesmeric rhythms, the spacy yet hard-edged solos of guitarist Huw Lloyd, the chilly synthesizers of Dik Mik, and Nik Turner's freewheeling saxophone.

Brock would survive as the sole continuing member through almost innumerable personnel changes. One of the most significant on and off members was Robert Calvert, who first turned up on *In Search of Space* (1971) as a contributor to the science fiction *Hawkwind Log* booklet packaged with the original release. Calvert was a poet in Moorcock's circle and became Hawkwind's principal lyricist through the end of the 1970s. He co-wrote with Brock their biggest British hit, the single "Silver Machine" (1972), inspired by an essay by Symbolist playwright Alfred Jarry. Calvert also enjoyed a solo career, including a Brian Eno–produced concept album on Viking voyages to the New World, *Lucky Leif and the Longships* (1975). The participatory nature of Hawkwind rotated members into lead vocals and other key roles. The band's recently added bassist, Ian "Lemmy" Kilmister, sang "Silver Machine."

The 1972 Space Ritual Tour, documented on the double album *The Space Ritual Alive in Liverpool and London* (1973), gave full rein to the band's theatrical tendencies. The audiovisual experience included a dance troupe, costumes, and a science fiction story concerning Starfarers traveling in suspended animation through time and space. With the exception of "Master of the Universe" from *In Search of Space* (1971), most of the material came from *Doremi Fasol Latido* (1972). The songs were linked in concert by electronic and spoken word segues, including Calvert's recitation of Moorcock's poem "Sonic Attack."

Popular in Great Britain, the band attracted some notice on tour in the United States and received FM airplay for *Warrior on the Edge of Time* (1975). The album's concept was based on Moorcock's ideas about the "multiverse," a reality of many dimensions and parallel worlds. Several songs were credited to Moorcock. Underscoring the piping woodwinds and eerie electronics was an aggressive garage rock beat. While touring in support of the album, the band fired Kilmister, who went on to form one of the leading influences on post-1970s heavy metal, Motorhead. His new band was named for a Hawkwind song.

With the rise of punk rock, Hawkwind stood as one of the few long-haired bands accepted by Johnny Rotten and other British punks, yet ongoing personnel changes and management problems sidetracked them. The album *25 Years On* (1978) was recorded under a transparent pseudonym, Hawklords. By the following year Brock regrouped as Hawkwind, recording *Levitation* (1980) with drummer Ginger Baker. A flurry of albums and tours followed with Brock maintaining course through shifting lineups. Moorcock wrote lyrics, occasionally performed with the band, and continued as an influence. *The Chronicle of the Black Sword* (1985) was based on Moorcock's Elric of Melnibone, the protagonist in a series of sword and sorcery novels. Hawkwind recruited a woman, Bridget Wishart, as vocalist for *Space Bandits* (1990) and *Palace Springs* (1991). Turner, an on again, off again member, toured the United States under the Hawkwind name even as Brock's Hawkwind attempted to mount an American comeback.

Brock remained prolific through the first decades of the new millennium, occasionally reuniting past members into an aggregation called the Hawkestra. He won a lawsuit against Turner for using Hawkwind or similar monikers; Turner now performs under the name Space Ritual. Latter-day incarnations of Hawkwind have included eclectic guest stars such as Arthur Brown and Lene Lovich.

Suggested Albums: Hawkwind (1971); *In Search of Space* (1971); *Doremi Fasol Latido* (1972); *The Space Ritual Alive in Liverpool and London* (1973); *Hall of the Mountain Grill* (1974); *Warrior on the Edge of Time* (1975); *Astounding Sounds, Amazing Music* (1976); *Quark, Strangeness and Charm* (1977); *Levitation* (1980); *The Chronicle of the Black Sword* (1985)

See also: Space Rock

HEAVY METAL

The Kinks' "You Really Got Me" (1964) has been called the starting point of heavy metal, but like most phenomena, the history of metal has a prehistory. Kinks guitarist Dave Davies's heavy riffing was anticipated by Link Wray's instrumental hit

"Rumble" (1958), and Wray's eerily ominous guitar sound was probably inspired by some of the blues recordings coming out of the Chess Records studio in the early 1950s. For the aesthetics of heavy metal, one might even cite Richard Wagner's groundbreaking operas for their orchestrated percussion and leitmotifs that pulled at the low end of tonality.

As the world grew louder in the 20th century, music followed suit with the advent of the electric guitar by the 1930s. Amplification became more essential for musicians to be heard above the din of modernity. Rock bands played through suitcase-size Fender amplifiers and were inaudible above cheering stadium-size crowds until the late 1960s when larger, more powerful Marshall amps enabled performers to obliterate audience noise; music could strike concertgoers with the blunt force of a freight train. Technology made heavy metal possible, but the music's creation and reception involved other factors, including the embrace of machine-tooled sounds as predicted by the Italian Futurists (hence, metal) and a growing tendency toward "heaviness" in music, which may have been spurred in part by the mood-altering effect of barbiturates, whether used medically or recreationally.

Heavy metal's most obvious roots were in the electric blues of the 1950s. The joyful sadness of traditional blues was being supplanted by the gravity of such Muddy Waters discs as "I'm Ready" and "I Just Want to Make Love to You." Heavy metal can be separated from such predecessors by greater aggression, amplification, and guitar and bass chords struck more powerfully on the lower strings. Electric guitar became the prominent instrument, and the introduction of the electric bass made a heavier bottom easier to achieve. Although the term *heavy metal* may have found its way into cultural discourse through William S. Burroughs's novel *Soft Machine* (1961), the likely source for the musical genre's name was the "heavy metal thunder" lyric in Steppenwolf's hit "Born to be Wild" (1968), a reference to the roar of Harley-Davidson motorcycles, sometimes referred to as "American iron" by riders. The sound of unmuffled motors was not unrelated to the high decibel roar characteristic of the music.

If rock music became harder during the 1960s, hard rock was not always the same thing as the nascent genre of heavy metal. The Rolling Stones were often hard but never heavy. British bands took the lead toward heaviness. The Troggs' "Wild Thing" (1966) was a steppingstone in the genre's evolution. Cream solidified the heavy sound with their second album, *Disraeli Gears* (1967). Even as guitarist Eric Clapton objected in the name of blues purism, vocalist-bassist Jack Bruce and drummer Ginger Baker infused Cream's songs with a heavy, brooding downbeat. Cream's colleague Jimi Hendrix was often heavy and influenced the development of metal through masterful command of distortion, but his music was too funky and rhythmic to be contained within the genre. In the United States, a pair of bands contributed to the cacophony. Performing at eardrum bursting volume, Blue Cheer managed to crack the hit parade with an aggressively heavy cover of Eddie Cochran's "Summertime Blues," while the MC5's *Kick Out the Jams* (1969) pushed rock into the red zone of noisy confrontation.

Donovan became an unlikely link in the evolution of heavy metal when guitarist Jimmy Page and bassist John Paul Jones, the session musicians who conceived Led

Zeppelin, commandeered his raga-inspired "Hurdy Gurdy Man" (1968). One year later, the Jeff Beck Group, which had shifted into heavy blues-influenced rock, backed Donovan on "Barabajagal."

The genre's pivotal years were 1968 and 1969 as two defining lines of heavy metal began rolling down divergent tracks. Led Zeppelin and Black Sabbath formed at that time under dissimilar circumstances, a hundred miles apart but worlds away. Zeppelin emerged from Swinging London, crewed by some of Britain's top session players and a tangent of the counterculture, while Sabbath were unknowns from the grungy factory town of Birmingham and might be understood as a contra-counterculture. Both bands shared roots in the blues and an interest in the occult, though, characteristically, Jimmy Page collected leather-bound first editions of Aleister Crowley while Ozzy Osbourne was happy to catch horror movies in second-run cinemas. In the deep background lurked a story unknown to most teen-age fans of those seminal metal bands, the legend that bluesman Robert Johnson sold his soul in exchange for the power to play guitar as it had never been heard before.

Led Zeppelin maintained the questing spirit of the 1960s amidst Page's serrated guitar solos and the pile-driving drumming of John Bonham. In a nod to the distant sources of heavy music, vocalist Robert Plant emulated the Valkyrie chorus in "The Immigrant Song." It was music that could carry the imagination to far places.

Black Sabbath, on the other hand, hewed to basics with an often dirgey sound and cast-iron riffing. Guitarist Tommy Iommi lost the tips of two fingers in an industrial accident; the prosthetics he wore surely affected his sense of tone. Much of Sabbath's music was built from drawn-out notes and conveyed the menacing sense of a behemoth slowly moving. There was no Wagner, but perhaps a touch of Gilbert and Sullivan in the eccentric melody of "Iron Man" and a sense that Osbourne was having a good laugh.

Heavy metal proved to be one of the most virulent and adaptive strains of music after the classic rock era ended. By the close of the 1970s new bands such as Iron Maiden and Def Leppard had absorbed the up-tempo fury of punk rock; Twisted Sister and other 1980s "hair metal" bands took a page from the 1970s glam rock. Many metal bands have followed Black Sabbath's path of diabolic simplicity, while "progressive metal" is indebted to Led Zeppelin by emphasizing virtuosity, eclecticism, and profundity. When it emerged as a distinct entity by 1970, heavy metal was defiantly anti–pop music regardless of how popular many of its bands became. Ironically, later decades would see the emergence of "pop metal."

HENDRIX, JIMI (1942–1970)

Widely regarded as one of rock music's outstanding guitarists and visionaries, Jimi Hendrix grew up in Seattle and learned guitar by copying early rock and roll songs. He was drawn, however, to the blues, which he learned by listening intently to recordings by B.B. King, Howlin' Wolf, and especially Muddy Waters, whose voodoo-sounding records such as "Louisiana Blues" and "Got My Mojo Working" must have made a profound impression. He enlisted in the army and served in the 101st

Airborne Division. Some have speculated that the sonics of high-altitude parachute jumping might have influenced his sensibility. "'Scuse me while I kiss the sky," as he sang in one of his most familiar songs, "Purple Haze."

Discharged from the service in 1962, Hendrix began his musical career in earnest, forming a band based in Nashville that toured the "Chitlin' Circuit" of Southern venues set aside for black audiences. He also picked up gigs backing soul singers such as Jackie Wilson, Sam Cooke, and Wilson Pickett. In 1964 he moved to Harlem where he joined the Isley Brothers' band and, later, Little Richard's band, the Upsetters. He cut a few records along the way, playing on the Isleys' "Testify" (1964), Don Covay's "Mercy Mercy" (1964), and Little Richard's "I Don't Know What You Got (But It's Got Me)." Most of his recordings from this period were later gathered on *West Coast Seattle Boy: The Jimi Hendrix Anthology* (2010). He then joined the New York rhythm and blues band Curtis Knight and the Squires, whose 1965–1966 sessions were finally released in good order as *You Can't Use My Name* (2015). Hendrix's guitar playing behind Knight is superb and gives evidence that he was on his way to the distortion-shaping sounds for which he is remembered.

By 1965 Hendrix moved from Harlem to Greenwich Village where his deep blues roots were appreciated by a mostly white audience weaned on the folk-blues revival. By this time young African Americans had largely traded blues as a vestige of an oppressive past for the redemptive promise of soul music. Hendrix was an outlier among young blacks for his fascination with the blues and apparent disconnection from the gospel music tradition. He was discovered in Greenwich Village by Chas Chandler, formerly the Animals' bassist and now a manager-producer. Chandler brought him to London in 1966 and teamed him with a pair of British musicians, bassist Noel Redding and drummer Mitch Mitchell. Together, they formed rock's most dynamic power trio, the Jimi Hendrix Experience.

Hendrix arrived in Britain with the force of a cyclone and fulfilled a half-perceived need among rock musicians and fans for the coming of a black bluesman of their own generation who could update the music while respecting its integrity. He played traditional blues licks but performed them with newfound volume and intensity. Brightly dressed like Sgt. Pepper before the Beatles recorded *Sgt. Pepper*, Hendrix exuded confident sexuality and played with enough furious finesse to put even Eric Clapton in the shade. The presence of Mitchell and Redding was as much a token that white musicians could keep pace with Hendrix as a gesture of integration.

Chandler produced their debut album, the provocatively titled *Are You Experienced* (1967). Rock was shaken on both sides of the Atlantic by Hendrix's mammoth riffs and mind-bending distortion. Mitchell's nimble drumming helped shape the music while Redding's bass kept it anchored to earth. "Purple Haze" and "Foxy Lady" were heavy blues-rock but were too funky for heavy metal. The musical aggression of "Manic Depression" almost overpowered the despondency of the lyrics. Hendrix showed he was capable of playing softly with "The Wind Cries Mary," whose poetic metaphors reveal a debt to Bob Dylan. The past was the palette from which Hendrix painted the future of music and the primary color was blue. On many tracks the band operated essentially like a jazz trio in a highly electrified setting. Miles Davis was listening.

Jimi Hendrix brought the electric guitar to unprecedented heights of expression during the late 1960s and added unforgettable showmanship to his performances. Hendrix would die of a drug overdose shortly after this 1970 concert in Germany. (Stormarn/Dreamstime.com)

Hendrix's showmanship was almost as outstanding as his music. He had been playing guitar behind his back and with his teeth since the early 1960s for hard-to-please audiences on the Chitlin' Circuit and employed everything he learned from his erstwhile employer, Little Richard. Even before the spectacular conclusion of his show at the Monterey Pop Festival (1967), Hendrix was setting his instrument on fire, making tangible the element he conjured through his playing.

On *Axis: Bold as Love* (1968) and *Electric Ladyland* (1968), Hendrix continued to explore the untapped potential of electric guitar through feedback, sustain, and volume with the backing of the Experience. Psychedelic visions abounded and science fiction themes were prevalent; he understood fantasy as a way of shedding light on reality. *Electric Ladyland* was Hendrix's strongest collection of new songs. "Crosstown Traffic" amplified his tendency toward making blues-rock funky. With "Voodoo Chile" he recreated the uncanny side of Muddy Waters complete with a murmuring gypsy and a blood-red moon hovering over the lyric. The album included Hendrix's sole Top-20 hit in America (he had enjoyed greater success with singles in the United Kingdom), his apocalyptic rendering of Dylan's "All Along the Watchtower."

Hendrix tried to stay arm's length from the racial and political turmoil of the late 1960s, but in the United States black power advocates called him out for playing with white musicians for white audiences. By the end of 1968 Hendrix disbanded the Experience. At Woodstock (1969), backed by a large ensemble dubbed the Electric Sky Church, Hendrix was responsible for one of the festival's indelible scenes when he played "The Star Spangled Banner" as a wrenching electric guitar solo. Afterward, he led the short-lived all-black Band of Gypsys featuring army buddy Billy Cox on bass and the Electric Flag's Buddy Miles on drums. Some critics have interpreted the band's sole album, the concert recording *Band of Gypsys* (1970), as a musically abstract gesture toward contemporary rhythm and blues.

Within months Hendrix returned to a primarily trio format, retaining Cox and rehiring Mitchell on drums. The ensemble toured the burgeoning rock festival circuit with stops at the Atlanta International Pop Festival, the New York Pop Festival, and the Isle of Wight. With Cox, Mitchell, and various guests, he began recording a double-LP in his own New York studio, Electric Ladyland. He was unable to complete the project. Having abused alcohol and other drugs for several years, Hendrix succumbed to an accidental overdose of sleeping pills in 1970.

Hendrix's catalog of albums expanded voluminously after his death. Along with numerous bootleg concert recordings came the live album *Hendrix in the West* (1972) and the BBC broadcast album *Radio One* (1988). Producers Alan Douglas and Eddie Kramer were responsible for assembling a welter of posthumous releases from hundreds of hours of demos and songs in progress. Sometimes they appeared to work at cross-purposes. Douglas's decision to overdub new parts onto incomplete tracks was denounced by some Hendrix fans who viewed this as akin to completing unfinished canvases found in Picasso's studio after the artist's death. Years later producer Eddie Kramer expunged Douglas's overdubs and, working with the master tapes, compiled a plausible version of the album Hendrix was working on at the time of his death, *First Rays of the New Rising Sun* (1997).

Battles over Hendrix's intellectual property began as early as 1967 when low-budget labels began issuing shoddily packaged, often dubious recordings made prior to the Jimi Hendrix Experience. During the early 1990s the Hendrix estate, led by the guitarist's father, battled for control over the guitarist's recordings and song publishing. By 1995 Al Hendrix won and a series of authorized albums followed.

Among the prominent rock star deaths at the turn of the 1970s, Hendrix's was the most tragic from an artistic perspective. The Doors' Jim Morrison sounded spent and Janis Joplin seemed at the top of her game while by all indications Hendrix had gone only a short way down the path he could have followed. One can easily imagine him dueling with great jazz musicians, pulling the fusion jazz of the 1970s away from pop and back to the blues; he might have embraced hip-hop and infused it with musicality; he probably would have served as a living inspiration to rock guitarists by continuing to defy the limits of his instrument.

Suggested Albums: Are You Experienced (1967); *Axis: Bold as Love* (1968); *Electric Ladyland* (1968); *Band of Gypsys* (1970); *The Cry of Love* (1971); *Rainbow Bridge* (1971); *Hendrix in the West* (1972); *War Heroes* (1972); *Loose Ends* (1974); *Crash Landing* (1975); *Midnight Lightning* (1975); *Nine to the Universe* (1980); *Radio One* (1988); *First Rays of the New Rising Sun* (1997); *West Coast Seattle Boy: The Jimi Hendrix Anthology* (2010); *Valleys of Neptune* (2010); *People, Hell and Angels* (2013); *You Can't Use My Name: The RSVP/PPX Sessions* (by Curtis Knight and the Squires) (2015)

HOLLIES

The British Invasion band the Hollies took their name during the Christmas season of 1962. Filled with the Yuletide spirit as well as admiration for the late Buddy

166   HOLLIES

Holly, they dubbed themselves the Hollies and soon obtained bookings at Liverpool's legendary Cavern Club. Not surprisingly, record companies had set their sights on the Beatles' home club as a breeding ground for talent. The Hollies obtained a record deal and began releasing a series of singles.

The group's initial focus was on cover versions of early rock and roll songs. Their first two albums, *Stay with the Hollies* (1964) and *In the Hollies Style* (1964), bore a distinct vocal and instrumental resemblance to the Beatles. However, bandleaders Graham Nash, Allen Clarke, and Tony Hicks began to write original material under the pseudonym "L. Hansford." In 1964 they scored their first original hit single, "We're Through."

While the band started out aping the Beatles, by 1965 they had begun to develop a more distinct musical identity. The Hollies' sound featured three-part vocal harmonies as well as bright, chiming arpeggiated guitar riffs that caught the ear, provided a repeated musical reference point, and are best heard on their first U.S. hit single, "Look Through Any Window" (1965). While the band's songwriting progressed, they continued to rely on covers for singles (1966's "Stop, Stop, Stop" was an exception), even as their albums were heavy on original songs. An outside songwriter, future 10cc member Graham Gouldman (writer of "Look Through Any Window" as well as the Yardbirds' "Heart Full of Soul"), provided the group with perhaps its finest song, the 1966 hit single "Bus Stop," a tale of summer romance leading to marriage centered around a memorable minor chorded melody. The albums *Evolution* (1967) and *Butterfly* (1967) showed the band's maturing songwriting, including several songs with touches of psychedelia and Eastern music. Their 1967 single "Carrie Anne" would prove to be their final American hit with Nash, as he left shortly thereafter to form the supergroup Crosby, Stills and Nash.

The Hollies initially stumbled a bit without Nash, but returned to the charts in 1969 with the sappy hit ballad "He Ain't Heavy, He's My Brother," a song that set the band on its future soft rock course. They fared much better with the John Fogerty–inspired rocker "Long Cool Woman in a Black Dress," which soared up the singles charts in 1972.

The grittier style of "Long Cool Woman" was not a harbinger of things to come, as the Hollies returned to their soft rock ways for the 1974 worldwide hit "The Air That I Breathe," a syrupy ballad centered around an evocative guitar riff and overly soothing melody. The song would prove to be the band's last significant chart success in the United States or Great Britain, although they did find a more receptive audience in Europe.

The Hollies toured with an ever-changing lineup and continued on after Clarke's retirement in 2001. The band also proved to be an inspiration for numerous power pop bands of the 1970s and 1980s, with groups such as the Romantics and the XTC side project Dukes of the Stratosphere recording Hollies-influenced material. The Hollies were inducted into the Rock and Roll Hall of Fame.

Suggested Albums: Hollies (1965); *For Certain Because* (1966); *Evolution* (1967)

HOT TUNA

One of several side projects by members of the Jefferson Airplane, Hot Tuna was formed in 1969 by bassist Jack Casady and guitarist Jorma Kaukonen. Esteemed for his fingerstyle guitar playing, Kaukonen was a blues purist before joining the Jefferson Airplane and remained grounded in the blues through his tenure with the band. "Embryonic Journey," his fingerstyle instrumental from the Airplane's *Surrealistic Pillow* (1967), received much airplay on FM and introduced a new audience to a style rooted in early 20th-century blues guitarists emulating the piano-based approach of ragtime.

Hot Tuna showcased Kaukonen's writing and playing, usually in acoustic settings during the early years. After 1974 Hot Tuna became a hard rock power trio, which allowed Kaukonen to play with distortion and effects in an overdriven blues style not unlike that of Eric Clapton or Jeff Beck. In concert, the band's mid-1970s performances featured lengthy jams built around Kaukonen's improvisations.

Hot Tuna disbanded in 1977 but briefly reunited for a 1983 tour and came back together in 1986 as the principal creative outlet for Kaukonen and Casady. They continue to perform and record in both electric and acoustic modes.

Suggested Albums: Burgers (1972); *The Phosphorescent Rat* (1974); *America's Choice* (1975); *Yellow Fever* (1975); *Hoppkorv* (1976)

See also: Jefferson Airplane/Jefferson Starship

H.P. LOVECRAFT

During his lifetime, Howard Phillips Lovecraft was little known beyond a small coterie of readers who discovered him in the pages of pulp fiction magazines. After his death in 1937, his writings were kept in circulation by a slowly growing network of fans. In the 1960s he finally found a wide audience for his stories of cosmic horror, redolent of dimensions beyond the capacity of human understanding. Lovecraft might have been horrified had he lived to see the psychedelic era, convinced as he appeared to be in his fiction that there are doors that must remain locked, books that should never be read, and even music that human ears should never hear.

The Chicago band that adopted Lovecraft's name in 1967 was a manifestation of the author's unexpected embrace by the 1960s counterculture. With classically trained keyboardist Dave Michaels setting an eerie mood for guitarist George Edwards's songs, H.P. Lovecraft's high harmonies and borrowings from American folk songs reveal their roots in the folk-blues revival as well as Lovecraft's unsettling fiction. The band often suggested the Jefferson Airplane in a macabre frame of mind. Edwards's earlier stints in a jazz trio can be heard in the rhythmic flexibility of their performances.

H.P. Lovecraft moved to the San Francisco Bay Area in 1968 and shared bills with the era's top psychedelic groups, but neither of their albums sold well. The original band separated by the end of 1969, albeit various iterations regrouped through the mid-1970s.

Suggested Albums: H.P. Lovecraft (1967); *H.P. Lovecraft II* (1968)

HUMBLE PIE

Humble Pie was a British hard rock band whose popularity was elevated by the growth of rock concerts as we know them today, a generally large venue musical event featuring a full set by a headlining act with supporting artists opening the show. Rock concerts differed from the largely ensemble revues of earlier times where numerous bands played short sets. Rock concerts grew in popularity due to the growing market for the music and the rise of venues such as Bill Graham's Fillmore East in New York and its sister venue, San Francisco's Fillmore West, along with a growing public appreciation for hearing the entire work of serious artists. The larger venue called for bands that projected larger images, thought bigger, and often played louder. Humble Pie fit the bill, crisscrossing the world for years as a popular concert attraction.

The band was formed by Small Faces singer Steve Marriott, who had tired of his band's pop-oriented approach and longed to perform harder rock. He connected with a young guitarist named Peter Frampton, who left his band the Fray to join the new group. They christened the band Humble Pie and released their debut album, *As Safe as Yesterday Is* (1969). The album was dominated by power guitar–driven rock with a loud, heavy drumbeat that easily sat alongside albums by contemporaries such as Free and Led Zeppelin. The album sold well in the United Kingdom, and Humble Pie's hard rock sound began to attract attention.

The surprisingly pastoral acoustic sound of the band's follow-up, *Town and Country* (1969), proved to be an anomaly. *As Safe as Yesterday Is* set the template for the rest of the band's career. Loudly amplified guitars, heavy riffing, and thunderous roof-raising drums became the group's musical trademarks. The group's arrangements were well structured with rhythms perfect for fist pumping, and often featured anthemic sing-along choruses designed to promote the communal spirit of early rock concerts. But it was Marriott's voice that carried the day, a remarkable instrument capable of ragged screaming and soulful exhortation, helping set the tone for future artists fronting rock bands. Humble Pie's approach is best heard on albums such as *Smokin'* (1972), which, despite the departure of Frampton for a successful solo career, was their bestselling effort and contained their best known song, "30 Days in the Hole."

The band toured relentlessly in the early 1970s, playing raucous shows and establishing a strong live reputation, although their hard rock riffing sound could border on the sort of bombastic excess that would later be parodied in the film *This Is Spinal Tap* (1984). The group broke up in 1975 following the release of two lackluster albums, although Marriott would re-form the band and release a largely forgotten album, *On to Victory* (1980). Original drummer Jerry Shirley obtained the rights to the band's name and has toured and recorded as Humble Pie. Marriott had a longstanding solo career prior to his death in 1990. Frampton continues to tour and record to this day.

Suggested Albums: As Safe as Yesterday Is (1969); *Town and Country* (1969); *Rock On* (1971); *Smokin'* (1972)

HUNTER, IAN (1939–)

Ian Hunter's work as leader of Mott the Hoople was sufficiently influential to establish a lasting legacy as a pioneering artist who influenced the development of punk and new wave. Hunter left Mott in 1974, burned out from the music industry and suffering from a nervous breakdown, so it would have been no surprise had he simply turned his back on a recording career and never been heard from again. However, Hunter joined forces with his friend, guitarist Mick Ronson, and entered the studio to begin a lengthy solo career that never quite captured his previous band's artistic and commercial success, but had its share of memorable moments.

On his eponymous debut solo album (1975), Hunter established an edgy hard rock sound louder and heavier than that of Mott the Hoople, but with his biting wit and jaded sensibility firmly intact. Ronson's overdriven guitar work dominates the album and contains some of his finest post-Bowie moments, while Hunter's songwriting is uniformly strong. "Once Bitten, Twice Shy" kicks off the album with a punk swagger that is only slightly dimmed by the song's unfortunately misogynist bent (a cover of the song would become a hit single for the 1980s hair band Great White). Hunter waxes Dylanesque at times in songs like "Boy" and "The Truth, the Whole Truth, Nuthin' But the Truth," and in retrospect the exuberant rocker "I Get So Excited" sounds like a lost hit single. The album was well received and enjoyed steady FM rock airplay.

Hunter's solo career looked to be off to a promising start, but the enigmatic artist tossed a curveball with his next album, *All American Alien Boy* (1976), a departure from hard rock to a more soulful horn-dominated sound. Many of the songs were softer, although Hunter's jagged lyrical perspective remained unchanged. *Overnight Angels* (1977) saw Hunter return to hard rock, but his work was beginning to lack inspiration even as he was being hailed as a pivotal influence on the burgeoning punk rock movement. The sound became more generic and the lyrics began to lose their characteristic bite. Hunter enjoyed a brief resurgence with *You're Never Alone with a Schizophrenic* (1979, helped in part by the inclusion of half of Bruce Springsteen's E Street Band, who gave the album a vitality lacking in Hunter's previous couple of efforts. The album sold well, but Hunter adapted awkwardly to the 1980s with a bland contemporary sound that only vaguely echoed the intensity of his finest work and at times threatened to devolve into self-parody.

Hunter teamed up yet again with Ronson for *YUI Orta* (1990), a solid updating of Hunter's sound and lyrical perspective, but their longstanding artistic collaboration ended with Ronson's death from cancer in 1993. Hunter has continued to record and tour into the new millennium, releasing a strong album, *Shrunken Heads* (2007), and performing with a reformed Mott the Hoople in 2009. Hunter achieved a permanent place in popular culture when a cover of his song "Cleveland Rocks" became the theme song for the popular 1990s American sitcom *The Drew Carey Show*.

Suggested Albums: Ian Hunter (1975); *You're Never Alone with a Schizophrenic* (1979); *Short Back 'n' Sides* (1981); *YUI Orta* (1990); *Dirty Laundry* (1995); *Shrunken Heads* (2007)

IDES OF MARCH

The Ides of March are remembered for their Top 10 hit "Vehicle" (1970), a relentlessly funky yet darkly enigmatic number about a roving child molester. The Chicago band began in 1965, inspired by the British Invasion. The album that included "Vehicle" was surprisingly eclectic. "Symphony for Eleanor (Eleanor Rigby)" reinvented the Beatles' classic as a suite of contrasting musical colors that pushed through psychedelia to progressive rock. The Ides also turned a medley of Stephen Stills's "Wooden Ships" and Jethro Tull's instrumental "Dharma for One" into a masterpiece of orchestral rock. Their funky, poppy, jazz-rock album fell between the cracks of AM and FM. After disbanding, guitarist Jim Peterik formed 1980s arena rock act Survivor. The Ides of March have regrouped in recent years.

Suggested Album: Vehicle (1970)

INCREDIBLE STRING BAND

Edinburgh musicians Robin Williamson, Clive Palmer, and Mike Heron formed Incredible String Band in 1966. Of a piece with the rural, archaic side of the 1960s counterculture, their original material was a surreal field trip through Anglo-American folk traditions while touching on the outskirts of India. Palmer left after their self-titled debut album (1966), but Williamson and Heron continued under the benign guidance of producer Joe Boyd.

Their most admired albums, *The Hangman's Beautiful Daughter* (1968) and *Wee Tam and the Big Huge* (1968), drew from a wider palette of themes and instrumentation, including organ, piano, and Jew's harp along with pipes and acoustic stringed instruments. Illustrative of their songwriting was an outstanding song from *The Hangman's Beautiful Daughter*, "The Minotaur's Song," in which the mythic monster boasted of its misdeeds in the form of a British music hall number. With their 1968 albums, Incredible String Band achieved an avid following in Great Britain (Paul McCartney called himself a fan). They performed in the United States at the Newport Folk Festival and at San Francisco's psychedelic hub, the Fillmore Ballroom. Incredible String Band appeared at Woodstock, but the audience was puzzled and their performance was omitted from the documentary film that defined memory of the event.

Incredible String Band developed ambitious concepts for theatrical and multimedia performances, but their efforts were greeted with critical disdain and public

172   IT'S A BEAUTIFUL DAY

disinterest. Even before Boyd severed ties with them in 1970, they began writing under the influence of Scientology while drifting toward a more folk-rock format with drum kits and electric bass and guitar. After Incredible String Band disbanded in 1974, Williamson and Heron recorded prolifically as solo artists, often combining Anglo-Celtic folk with avant-garde tendencies. Several reunions occurred in the late 1990s and early 2000s.

Suggested Albums: The Incredible String Band (1966); The 5000 Spirits or the Layers of the Onion (1967); The Hangman's Beautiful Daughter (1968); Wee Tam and the Big Huge (1968); Changing Horses (1969); I Looked Up (1970); Liquid Acrobat as Regards the Air (1971)

IT'S A BEAUTIFUL DAY

The violin turned up as a lead instrument in several rock bands during the late 1960s, but it was seldom played with such classical finesse as in It's a Beautiful Day. David LaFlamme, a former soloist with the Utah Symphony Orchestra, founded the San Francisco band in 1967. On their most widely heard release, their eponymous debut (1969), LaFlamme's training was audible. The album's best-known song, "White Bird," had all the attributes of classical program music as his violin emulated avian flight. LaFlamme's wife Linda played a supporting role on backup vocals and keyboards. Several other tracks achieved airplay, especially "Hot Summer Day," another ambitious composition whose music reflected the lyrical theme.

The carefully cultivated chamber rock of It's a Beautiful Day was unlike anything proffered by their peers in the San Francisco scene. The best tracks are timeless. It's a Beautiful Day also embraced exotic influences on the instrumental "Bombay Calling" and the dreamily lyrical "Bulgaria." By 1970 the LaFlammes had separated; she left the group in the hands of her ex-husband. Personnel changes continued and several albums were released before the band broke up in 1974. David LaFlamme launched a solo career and enjoyed modest chart success with a new version of "White Bird" (1976). In recent years LaFlamme has performed under the It's a Beautiful Day banner.

Suggested Album: It's a Beautiful Day (1969)

IVEYS

See Badfinger

JADE WARRIOR

The members of Jade Warrior, veterans of the British rock scene since the mid-1960s, had played in various mod and psychedelic bands. Founded in 1970, the original Jade Warrior was a progressive rock trio consisting of guitarist Tony Duhig; Jon Field on flute, percussion, and keyboards; and Glyn Havard on bass and vocals. The music on the three albums released by the band's original incarnation, *Jade Warrior* (1971), *Released* (1971), and *Last Autumn's Dream* (1972), was compared to Jethro Tull recordings from the period. Although they toured the United States with Dave Mason and sold modestly in their homeland, the original Jade Warrior dissolved by the end of 1973 due in part to disinterest from their record label.

The following year, at the urging of Stevie Winwood, Island Records signed Duhig and Field under the Jade Warrior name. The quartet of albums they recorded for Island, *Floating World* (1974), *Waves* (1975), *Kites* (1976), and *Way of the Sun* (1978), were multilayered studio creations, ambient in texture, softly punctuated by rock guitars, and woven from strands of Japanese, Chinese, Latin American, Indonesian, and African music. Winwood guest-starred on their albums along with Fred Frith, guitarist from the mercurial avant-garde rock band Henry Cow.

Although esteemed by Brian Eno and admired by some music critics, the Zen-like music of Jade Warrior's second period won few listeners. At the time of their release they seemed to fit nowhere in the taxonomy of the music industry. Jade Warrior was years ahead of trends such as new age and world music and produced music that was superior to most of what would be hawked under those monikers.

Jade Warrior fell silent until the release of *Horizen* (1984), largely a Duhig effort with minimal contributions from Field. Duhig died in 1990 but Field continued the band with various musicians including Havard and members of Gong and King Crimson.

Suggested Albums: Jade Warrior (1971); *Released* (1971); *Last Autumn's Dream* (1972); *Floating World* (1974); *Waves* (1975); *Kites* (1976); *Way of the Sun* (1978)

JAMES GANG

The James Gang emerged from Cleveland, Ohio, in the late 1960s and immediately began to attract attention as an up-and-coming band with an original take on blues and country–influenced hard rock. The band today is best remembered for introducing the world to the powerful playing and offbeat antics of guitarist Joe Walsh, as well as for providing a couple of album tracks that became staples on FM rock radio in the 1970s.

Drummer Jim Fox formed the band after leaving Cleveland garage rock band the Outsiders, who had scored a hit single in 1966 with the bouncy "Time Won't Let Me." Walsh asked for an audition with Fox's new group, and the drummer was sufficiently impressed to hire Walsh as lead guitarist, vocalist, and principal songwriter. Initially a five-piece, the group was forced to play a gig opening for Cream with only three available members, and henceforth decided to go forward as a power trio in the manner of the show's headlining act. A recording contract soon followed, the band joined forces with a young Los Angeles producer named Bill Szymczyk (who later went on to fame producing the Eagles), and a productive professional partnership was formed.

From their first release, *Yer Album* (1969), the James Gang stood out among their hard rock cohorts for the verve and vitality of their recordings and live shows. Songs like "Funk 49" from *James Gang Rides Again* (1970) and "Walk Away" from *Thirds* (1971) are emblematic of the band's hard rock style. Both tracks adopt a familiar blues-boogie shuffle, but Walsh's percussive rhythm guitar and Fox's spirited drumming infuse the songs with a swing and snap more commonly associated with country music. Walsh's vocals, while a bit thin and reedy, had a comfortable drawl and stood out from the sometimes forced soulful bluesy bellowing of far too many boogie bands. His quirky sense of humor provided a pleasant, if at times distracting touch. Walsh's lead playing was more melodic and drew from a wider range of influences than the average blues-based guitarist, while his smoothly power-chorded rhythm playing provided a muscular but not overbearing edge to the band's sound.

Walsh left the band to pursue a successful solo career before joining the Eagles. The remaining members continued on, but Walsh's absence was keenly felt, as they released four fairly insubstantial albums, although *Bang* (1973) introduced the world to future Deep Purple guitarist Tommy Bolin. The James Gang's music lacked sufficient depth to be significant, but the band will be remembered as a launching pad for several successful musical careers.

Suggested Albums: Yer Album (1969); *James Gang Rides Again* (1970); *Thirds* (1971)

JAZZ-ROCK

The roots of rock and roll and jazz overlap in the blues, and many musicians from the early days of rhythm and blues, one of the streams that fed the birth of rock and roll, came from jazz. Before rock and roll was proclaimed as the music of the rising generation, jazz was associated with juvenile delinquency as well as the Beat subculture. Marlon Brando's motorcycle gang in *The Wild One* (1953) smashed up the town as bebop blared from the jukebox. Bop was an alternate name for rock and roll in the early days. Jazz musicians sometimes found themselves playing on rock and roll sessions, and swing riffs turned up in rockabilly. And yet, a line was drawn early on between rock and roll and jazz; post–World War II jazz had grown too complex, "like a symphony" as Chuck Berry claimed in his genre-defining hit "Rock and Roll Music" (1957). The kids sought something simpler.

By the 1960s some of the kids of the 1950s were ready for complexity. Rock music of the classic era was open to influences from anywhere, including jazz. A milestone was set by the Byrds' hit "Eight Miles High" (1966) when Roger McGuinn emulated the sound of John Coltrane's soprano saxophone on his 12-string electric guitar and quoted a short passage from Coltrane's "India." The influence of avant-garde jazz contributed to the cacophony of the Velvet Underground and was always a component in Frank Zappa's musical synthesis. The looseness of jazz rhythms was audible in many psychedelic recordings because many of the players had been exposed to jazz.

At the same time, three movements were explicitly bringing jazz together with rock, two of them inside rock and the other within jazz. The Electric Flag opened the way for the music popularly termed "jazz-rock" in the late 1960s and early 1970s with their horn-driven album *A Long Time Comin'* (1968). Blood, Sweat & Tears, Chicago, the Flock, and Chase were among the bands that followed in their wake.

Meanwhile, the great jazz trumpeter Miles Davis considered his next move. Like Pablo Picasso and other visual artists who set the pace for aesthetic movement in the 20th century, Davis, unsatisfied with resting on his already considerable laurels, opted to push his music into another phase. He was also acutely aware that jazz had lost touch with popular audiences in the 1960s.

With the release of his groundbreaking albums *In a Silent Way* (1969) and *Bitches Brew* (1970), Davis "crossed over" from jazz to rock, straddling both worlds in precarious, fascinating unbalance. As much as anything, the music he made during that period was an abstraction of funk and soul, amplified and played in part with electric instruments. The sidemen on those albums took a prominent role in the development of "jazz-rock fusion" or "fusion" as it was later called. Guitarist John McLaughlin maintained a level of energy and improvisation in his post-Davis band, the Mahavishnu Orchestra. Most of those players, including Chick Corea, Lenny White, and Joe Zawinul, inched away from the hard edges of Davis's fusion, leading the genre away from its always tenuous roots in rock.

The third movement occurred in Great Britain where rock musicians connected directly to avant-garde jazz with or without Davis's mediation. Prominent among them were Soft Machine and East of Eden along with King Crimson, whose "21st Century Schizoid Man" shredded harmonic structures in ways Ornette Coleman might have appreciated.

JEFFERSON AIRPLANE/JEFFERSON STARSHIP

The Jefferson Airplane epitomized San Francisco psychedelia in the late 1960s more than any other band, even the Grateful Dead. Unlike most of their peers, the Airplane was successful on AM as well as FM radio. Briefly, they became their city's chief musical ambassador to the outside world.

Named for blues guitarist Blind Lemon Jefferson, the Jefferson Airplane was formed by a pair of San Francisco folk-blues revivalists, guitarists Marty Balin and Paul Kantner. They recruited friends from the coffeehouse scene for their project, including guitarist Jorma Kaukonen, drummer Skip Spence, bassist Jack Casady, and singer Signe Anderson. The band debuted with *The Jefferson Airplane Takes Off* (1966), a trebly, tentative folk-rock album featuring Balin's already accomplished vocals and incongruous knack for pop melodies (especially their Byrdsy single "It's No Secret") amidst the dolefully strummed minor chords. Spence left after the album's release and formed Moby Grape. Jazz drummer Spencer Dryden filled his seat. Anderson was replaced by a more distinctive female vocalist, Grace Slick.

Slick had sung with a similarly inclined folk-rock band, the Great Society, and brought two Great Society songs with her to the Jefferson Airplane, "Somebody to Love" and "White Rabbit." They proved to be the hits from her first album with her new band, *Surrealistic Pillow* (1967). An epochal album, *Surrealistic Pillow* defined San Francisco psychedelia in sharp tones. "Somebody to Love" was unsettling in its urgency. In gentler hands, it might have been a warm paean to free love; here, Slick's almost scornful yet sexual vocals took the song somewhere else. "White Rabbit" drew on imagery from Lewis Carroll for its description of the psychedelic

Unlike most psychedelic bands from the San Francisco scene, the Jefferson Airplane enjoyed occasional success on AM radio despite concerns over drug references in their lyrics. Fronted by singer Grace Slick, their performances included a psychedelic light show. (Interfoto/Alamy Stock Photo)

experience. However, a certain menace in Slick's delivery prevented the record from sounding like a whole-hearted endorsement of the lyric's call to try LSD.

Surrealistic Pillow benefited from the contributions of several distinctive song-writers. Balin and Kantner's "Today" was almost medieval in cadence and presaged the British folk-rock of the Airplane's London admirers, Fairport Convention. Kaukonen and Balin collaborated on the enigmatic, acid-edged rocker "She Has Funny Cars." Spencer provided a lighter touch with the sunny "My Best Friend" while Kaukonen explored the intricacies of fingerstyle guitar on his instrumental "Embryonic Journey."

Although much of *Surrealistic Pillow* had a wintry sound, it became the sound-track for San Francisco's fabled Summer of Love before the utopian dream descended into a nightmare of addiction, exploitation, and disease. Although the Airplane dove headfirst into the Bay Area's counterculture, the music on *Surrealistic Pillow* cast an ominous if unintended shadow over the future.

Mirroring the dissolution of San Francisco's hippie milieu, the Jefferson Airplane began their slow crack-up after *Surrealistic Pillow*. *After Bathing at Baxter's* (1967) included no hits, sold poorly, and echoed the sound of egos butting against each other. Although uneven, *Crown of Creation* (1968) was something of an improvement musically and in sales. It featured "Triad," a David Crosby ballad about a ménage à trois that had been rejected by Crosby's band, the Byrds.

The Jefferson Airplane embraced full-tilt political radicalism on the title track from *Volunteers* (1969), probably the most primal rock and roll song in their catalogue thanks to the piano of British session musician Nicky Hopkins. *Volunteers* also included Kaukonen's lovely arrangement of the traditional spiritual "Good Shepherd" and Kantner's collaboration with Crosby and Stephen Stills, the postapocalyptic "Wooden Ships." The Airplane performed at Woodstock and at the festival's antithesis in the mythology of the 1960s, Altamont. Band members began to leave, starting with Dryden, who joined New Riders of the Purple Sage. Kaukonen and Casady focused on their new band, Hot Tuna. Balin felt increasingly pushed aside from the band he cofounded. The Airplane's copilots became Kantner and Slick, lovers and now parents of a baby girl.

The science-fiction concept album *Blows Against the Empire* (1970) was released under the name Paul Kantner and the Jefferson Starship. Kantner and Slick regrouped with Kaukonen and Casady as the Jefferson Airplane for *Bark* (1971), an album whose most remarkable song, "Pretty as You Feel," was a more-or-less band collaboration with contributions from Carlos Santana. *Bark* marked the debut of violinist Papa John Creach, a respected jazz musician who had appeared with Nat King Cole in Fritz Lang's film noir *The Blue Gardenia* (1953).

A plethora of unsuccessful solo albums and forgotten collaborations escorted the transformation of the Jefferson Airplane into the Jefferson Starship. Led by Kantner and Slick, the Starship was an effort to reinvent their previous band, retaining enough of the old name while developing a more polished, radio-friendly sound for their debut, *Dragonfly* (1974). Creach's violin added a distinctive tone to "Ride the Tiger," which became the album's FM hit. Balin was coaxed back, contributing lyrics and vocals to Kantner's "Caroline." Balin returned as a full member for their top-selling LP, *Red Octopus* (1975), featuring his schmaltzy hit "Miracles."

Despite platinum sales for *Spitfire* (1976) and *Earth* (1978), and pop hits "With Your Love" and "Count on Me," the band's chemistry remained unstable. Slick's alcoholic outbursts on stage prompted Kantner to obtain her resignation from the band. Balin also departed. What followed through the 1980s and into the 2010s was a shifting mélange of replacement vocalists and reunions with old members, punctuated by fluctuating sales and occasional hits and sustained by the lure of concert receipts. One of Balin's replacements, Mickey Thomas, led a rival version of the band called Starship. Even after Kantner's death in 2016, a version of the Jefferson Starship continued to tour.

Although they were the most popular San Francisco psychedelic band in the late 1960s, the Jefferson Airplane squandered its legacy by recording music that was either ill-conceived or conceived altogether too well for mainstream success. As touchstones of their era, they were supplanted by 1980 by the Grateful Dead, who remained true to the spirit of their times.

Suggested Albums: The Jefferson Airplane Takes Off (1966); *Surrealistic Pillow* (1967); *Crown of Creation* (1968); *Volunteers* (1969)

See also: Hot Tuna

JETHRO TULL

Among the score or more of wildly creative rock bands to emerge from Great Britain in the late 1960s, Jethro Tull was one of the most diverse in musical direction. Early albums included blues and proto-heavy metal alongside jazz, British folk, and the brain-searing distortions of psychedelia. Their leader, Ian Anderson, wielded an unusual lead instrument in rock, the flute. Dressed for the part in long overcoats and a wild mane of beard and hair, Anderson gladly played the role of pied piper.

The core of the original group, with Anderson on vocals, Jeffrey Hammond on bass, and John Evan on drums and keyboards, had played together under various names in Blackpool since the early 1960s. By 1967 they had moved to London where they recruited Mick Abrams on guitar and Clive Bunker on drums. In the counterculture fashion for antique-sounding rock band monikers, they adopted the name of an influential eighteenth-century British agronomist and became Jethro Tull.

Their first album, *This Was* (1968), was heavily indebted to the London blues-rock scene they were drawn into as well as the influence of Abrams, who vied with Anderson for leadership. The guitar workout of "Cat's Squirrel," a traditional blues number popularized by Cream, was a concession to Abrams. The LP's other cover, Roland Kirk's "Serenade for a Cuckoo," showcased Anderson's flute and love of jazz.

Abrams soon left to form the blues-rock band Blodwyn Pig, leaving Anderson's direction unchallenged. Jethro Tull's follow-up, *Stand Up* (1969), was among the most impressive albums from the period. More successfully than most groups with similar inclinations, they were, in essence, a jazz combo playing rock and playing it well. Even the skull-crushing heavy metal of "A New Day Yesterday" had jazz in its genome. The instrumental "Bouree" was a flute arrangement for a J. S. Bach melody but carried on a jazz rhythm. Anderson's affinity with British folk-rock was also heard on "Jeffrey Goes to Leicester Square." On "Fat Man," Jethro Tull ventured farther afield into raga. While Anderson was the sole songwriter, *Stand Up* was clearly a group effort based on the organic tempi of Bunker and bassist Glenn Cornick. Lead guitarist Martin Barre made emotionally expressive use of distortion. Anderson's flute kept pace and led the band into the psychedelic rave-up that concluded "Back to the Family."

By *Benefit* (1970), Jethro Tull had settled into a more straightforward rock sound, though not without fascinating tempo changes and a heavy admixture of British folk-rock. *Aqualung* (1971) broke the band in America as their sound hardened into the two directions that would be predominant on several later albums, hard rock and acoustic ballads. The title track's ominous lead guitar intro, a riff almost as primal as Deep Purple's "Smoke on the Water," brought the band FM airplay. The album also included "Mother Goose," an enchanting acoustic ramble spiked with Anderson's pungent wit, and "Wond'ring Aloud," a sensitive, not saccharine ballad redolent of mystic-ancient influences shared with Led Zeppelin. Perhaps not coincidentally, Zeppelin was in the studio down the hall during the recording of *Aqualung*, building "Stairway to Heaven." Lyrically, *Aqualung* explored Anderson's struggle to locate spirituality within religion and to find God within each person, even those as bedraggled and socially despised as the old man of the title track.

Gathering stray singles and unreleased tracks, the double-LP *Living in the Past* (1972) was one of rock's greatest collections of odds and ends. The title number was a surprise American hit, a call to ignore the era's revolutionary upheavals set to a Dave Brubeck 5/4 beat and laced with subtle Latin percussion. "Sweet Dream" brilliantly wrapped its narrative of an illicit love affair in spy movie guitars and a James Bond orchestration.

Jethro Tull digressed with a pair of concept albums that took progressive rock grandiosity to a dead end, *Thick as a Brick* (1972) and *A Passion Play* (1973). *Brick* had the advantage of an album cover that parodied the contents of a newspaper with mordant Monty Pythonesque humor. *Passion Play* had a few good moments but sagged in many sections. Even Anderson later conceded that his opuses fell short.

Most fans were relieved when Jethro Tull returned to succinct songs instead of lengthy compositions on *War Child* (1974). With a bright pop polish, the loose concept album included the band's second AM hit, "Bungle in the Jungle." The most enduring track was engagingly upbeat British folk-rock with a touch of raga, "Skating Away on the Thin Ice of the New Day." *Minstrel in the Gallery* (1975) followed *Aqualung*'s formula of mixing hard rock with balladry. In light of punk rock's challenge to the previous generation of stars, *Too Old to Rock'n'Roll* (1976) sounded like an honest confession to many listeners.

Afterward, Jethro Tull albums focused on Anderson's penchant for folk-rock with *Songs from the Wood* (1977), *Heavy Horses* (1978), and *Stormwatch* (1979). Lineup changes left Anderson as Tull's sole original member and with no certain direction in the changing musical climate of the 1980s. His attempts at electronica,

Jethro Tull was not the only rock band to introduce flute to their music, but the instrument became the trademark of Tull's frontman, Ian Anderson (left). Anderson was happy to play up a pied piper image as he led his band from blues to progressive rock and British folk music. (Philip Buonpastore/Alamy Stock Photo)

whether on albums credited to the band or to him as a solo artist, received little attention. In one of the decade's greatest music industry kerfuffles, Jethro Tull's return to hard rock, *Crest of a Knave* (1987), defeated Metallica's . . . *And Justice for All* for Best Heavy Metal Performance at the Grammy Awards to the dismay of many in the audience. Anderson responded to his unwanted trophy with good humor.

Whether as Jethro Tull or under his own name, Anderson continues to tour and record into the 21st century. He remains an engaging performer with a raconteur's sensibility and a keen sense of humor.

Suggested Albums: This Was (1968); *Stand Up* (1969); *Benefit* (1970); *Aqualung* (1971); *Living in the Past* (1972); *War Child* (1974)

JOEL, BILLY (1949–)

Billy Joel was forever self-identified by his first hit single, "Piano Man." Much like his contemporary Elton John, the piano-playing singer-songwriter's sound and persona have been shaped and defined by his instrument of choice. Pianists have long been crucial to the sound of rock music, beginning with the frenetic playing of pianists like Little Richard and Jerry Lee Lewis and continuing with highly stylized sidemen such as the E Street Band's Roy Bittan and Tom Petty and the Heartbreakers' Belmont Tench. However, the guitar quickly gained predominance with the piano often ending up playing a secondary role in rock music, resulting in piano-based artists being pigeonholed as pop. Such tensions were on display throughout Joel's long and highly successful career.

Joel was born in New York during the height of the Baby Boom and grew up in the Long Island suburb of Levittown. A "bridge and tunnel" New Yorker to the core, Joel's upbringing left a lasting imprint on his music. Like millions of others, Joel took to music after seeing the Beatles on the *Ed Sullivan Show*. Joel played in a series of bands, but later admitted that his piano playing proved an awkward fit in rock's increasingly guitar-dominated culture. However, his chops were too good to be ignored.

Billy Joel's first hit, "Piano Man," established his initial reputation as a thoughtful singer-songwriter in the Bob Dylan mode. He achieved greater popular success by the end of the 1970s singing cleverly written, melodically mellow love ballads. (Photofest)

On his first solo album, *Cold Spring Harbor* (1971), the serious approach and probing lyrics led some critics to saddle Joel with the "new Dylan" label. However, the album's opening McCartneyesque track, "She's Got a Way," demonstrates that Joel was more influenced by the Fab Four (he would have a hit with a remake of the song in 1981). A mastering error resulted in Joel's vocals sounding unnaturally high and the album flopped, but it did result in his being signed to the powerhouse Columbia Records.

Backed by a major label, Joel's career took off with the release of his second album, *Piano Man* (1973). Sales were solid, and the album's title track garnered considerable attention. The song's harmonica intro revived the "new Dylan" talk as Joel spun a tale of an aspiring musician reduced to playing bars and scratching out a living on tip money from lounge lizards. The album saw Joel expand his musical horizons to include bluegrass, honky-tonk blues, and funky soul, although it was burdened at times by an overly earnest lyrical approach. The focal point was clearly Joel's prodigious piano work, drawing inevitable comparisons to the fabulously popular Elton John. Joel's next two albums, *Streetlife Serenade* (1974) and *Turnstiles* (1976), failed to replicate the sales of *Piano Man*, albeit *Turnstiles* contained

182 JOEL, BILLY

two of his best songs, the Phil Spector–inspired "Say Goodbye to Hollywood" and the Sinatra-worthy tribute to the Big Apple, "New York State of Mind."

It appeared that poor album sales would doom Joel's once promising career, but things turned around when he successfully transitioned to a more pop-oriented approach with *The Stranger* (1977) and *52nd Street* (1978). Joel began a string of hit singles with "Just the Way You Are," a schmaltzy ballad culled from *The Stranger*. The song sold millions, but despite a clever lyric, the mellow electric piano gave it a hotel lounge quality that robbed Joel of any semblance of street credibility.

This duality proved to be emblematic as Joel's late 1970s success became a double-edged sword. While his soaring vocals and strong melodies proved popular, he was too often dragged down by lyrics that revealed an artist who took himself far too seriously. Even worse, the lyrical perspective seemed to be that of an angry young suburbanite who had the world handed to him. Worse still, Joel reacted defensively to critical brickbats labeling his pop tendencies as hopelessly unhip compared to edgier punk and new wave sounds. Joel's battle with critics reached its nadir on *Glass Houses* (1980). The album's sound cynically aped new wave, even as one of its biggest hits, "It's Still Rock and Roll to Me," petulantly sneered at the musical usurpers trying to unseat rock stars like Joel.

Joel's critical reputation came closer to matching his commercial success as the 1980s rolled on. Even his worst critics had to take a second look at the artist with the release of the musically and lyrically sophisticated *The Nylon Curtain* (1982), in which Joel finally found his creative voice. The failing state of his marriage led to introspection. Joel pointed a finger at himself and his fellow Baby Boomers instead of the world at large as he began to come to terms with the effects of marital discord, stress and anxiety, Rust Belt disintegration, and the Vietnam War. An even bigger hit album followed, *An Innocent Man* (1983). Joel's second marriage to the stunning supermodel Christie Brinkley clearly elevated his spirits, and he responded with a joyous album celebrating the early rock and roll, doo-wop, and Motown records that he loved growing up. Surprisingly, the unprepossessing Joel became a star on the new MTV video format, with multiple hit singles from *An Innocent Man* earning regular rotations on the upstart network.

Seemingly at ease with his new role as the bard of Baby Boomers on the cusp of middle age, Joel went on a run of tuneful and at times insightful looks at adulthood, resulting in strong singles such as "A Matter of Trust," "I Go to Extremes," "River of Dreams," and a stellar duet with rhythm and blues legend Ray Price on "Baby Grand." In 1986 Joel also played his part in cracking the Iron Curtain, becoming one of the first American rock musicians to tour the Soviet Union.

The 1990s saw Joel achieve respected elder status, retaining a legion of loyal fans and earning grudging respect as a stellar pop songwriter from critics who had historically disdained him. His marriage to Brinkley ended in amicable divorce in 1994, but that same year saw him embark on the successful "Piano Men" tour with his former 1970s rival Elton John. Country crossover superstar Garth Brooks listed Joel as a major influence and appeared onstage with him. Joel's 1999 induction into the Rock and Roll Hall of Fame was controversial, more for the nature than the quality of his music, as some believed he was more pop than rock, sparking a useful debate as to where those lines should be drawn. While he stopped releasing pop records in the 1990s, Joel continues to play his greatest hits live, and he remains a popular concert attraction.

Joel achieved one of the greatest honors of his career in 2016 when his first hit, "Piano Man," was selected for preservation by the Library of Congress in the National Recording Registry.

Selected Albums: Piano Man (1973); *Turnstiles* (1976); *The Stranger* (1977); *The Nylon Curtain* (1982); *An Innocent Man* (1983); *Storm Front* (1989)

JOHN, ELTON (1947-)

Born Reginald Dwight, Elton John is one of the world's top-selling recording artists with no less than 58 Top 40 singles in the United States. Writing music with lyricist Bernie Taupin, John was half of a two-man hit factory dominant in the 1970s and successful through the end of the century. Like Jerry Lee Lewis and Little Richard, he was a flamboyant stage performer who refused to be imprisoned behind his piano. Unlike them, he was a classically trained pianist possessing the ability to execute virtually any style of music.

An adolescent prodigy, John won a scholarship to London's Royal Academy of Music. The city's burgeoning blues scene gave him access to audiences outside the world of classical recitals. By the mid-1960s his band Bluesology served as backing band for visiting African American singers as well as early British blues singer Long John Baldry. In 1967 he responded to a newspaper advertisement for songwriters and was paired with Taupin. Working for Dick James Music as staff writers, they became legendary for their ability to knock out tunes to order. Although Taupin was sometimes a clumsy lyricist, John already had a remarkable facility with melody. In his recording career, John would prove to be the Irving Berlin of his generation, producing melodic miracles even from base material.

His debut album, *Empty Sky* (1969), was the blueprint that promised the breadth of his future. On the title track, John delivered solid piano-powered rock with progressive flourishes sung in a high nasal tenor that gave no clue of his Englishness. Avoiding the tendency of 1960s British singers to emulate the blues, he sang in a straightforward, unaffected American voice. John transformed Taupin's Nordic fantasy "Valhalla" into an exercise in baroque chamber rock. However, Taupin's imagination traveled more often to the American South and West. On "Western Ford Gateway," John obliged him by turning in an impressive pastiche of the Band. *Empty Sky* also contained the wistfully hopeful hymn-like "Skyline Pigeon," a song that long remained in his repertoire.

John was a musical omnivore famous for descending on record stores and carting away crates full of albums and for amassing an enormous collection of singles. His music always echoed the diversity of his tastes, yet was held together by the recognizable consistency of his voice and piano playing. John was never an innovator. Unlike David Bowie, he was never ahead of the curve but always on the curve in the 1970s as the right performer at the right time. He straddled many borders, appealing to fans of hard rock, pop, rhythm and blues, and introspective singer-songwriters.

His career ascended with his eponymous follow-up album (1970), which included his first Top 10 hit, the poignant "Your Song," along with the secular gospel of "Border Song," which also received American airplay. John was a model of success in the 1970s recording industry, gaining fans with every single, building his career album by album and year by year. Each effort showcased different aspects of his protean songcraft. John fully embraced Taupin's passion for Americana with *Tumbleweed Connection* (1971), an album of country rock and Band-derived songs. Taupin's proclivities were occasionally farcical, notably on *Tumbleweed's* most familiar track, "Country Comfort," with its references to patching barns and rocking chairs creaking on the porch. On the bare-boned live album *11-17-70* (1971), John was backed only by bassist Dee Murray and drummer Nigel Olson, musicians who served him well through the peak years of his career.

The heavily orchestrated *Madman Across the Water* (1971) was constructed around outstanding arrangements by another of John's frequent collaborators, Paul Buckmaster. Buckmaster used pedal steel guitar as a solo orchestral instrument for "Tiny Dancer" and was able to infuse even Taupin's most banal or puzzling lyrics with unwarranted drama and expectation. *Honky Chateau* (1972) featured John's touring band of Murray, Olson, and guitarist Davey Johnstone, and opened with the New Orleans–flavored "Honky Cat." *Honky Chateau's* other hit, the dreamy "Rocket Man (I Think It's Going to Be a Long, Long Time)," was based on a Ray Bradbury story and employed synthesizer for futuristic sound. John's capacity for contrast was also heard on *Don't Shoot Me I'm Only the Piano Player* (1973) whose hits included the nostalgic rock and roll revival of "Crocodile Rock" along with the restrained melancholy of "Daniel," set to one of Taupin's most touching lyrics.

By the end of 1973 John had shed blue jeans and T-shirts for frocks, platform boots, feather boas, and spangled spectacles. He could have been the clown prince of glitter rock, but his songs carried too much weight for any glib dismissals. John's new image was on full display across the gatefold of *Goodbye Yellow Brick Road* (1973), a double-LP packed with hits in every flavor. The title cut was orchestral rock reminiscent of Phil Spector's emendations for the Beatles; "Funeral for a Friend/Love Likes Bleeding" digressed through progressive rock; "Saturday Night's Alright for Fighting" proved John could rock as hard as anyone; "Candle in the Wind," Taupin's tribute to Marilyn Monroe, was part of the era's nostalgic mood yet has survived as a standard. Incongruously, "Bennie and the Jets" became a hit on American rhythm and blues radio, prompting John's appearance on television's *Soul Train*, a rare feat for a white performer at the time.

The following year saw John organizing a boutique label, Rocket Records, with releases by British soul singer Kiki Dee ("I've Got the Music in Me") and one-time American teen idol Neil Sedaka ("Bad Blood"). John recorded a twee version of the Beatles' "Lucy in the Sky with Diamonds" with John Lennon and sang on Lennon's "Whatever Gets You Thru the Night." He also found time to record *Caribou* (1974),

Elton John became one of the world's top-selling recording artists by amassing a formidable array of hit singles from the 1970s through the end of the 20th century. During the peak of his influence in the mid-1970s, John was known for flamboyant stage attire. (Photofest)

another musical broad tent encompassing the Spector-influenced pop grandeur of "Don't Let the Sun Go Down on Me" as well as "The Bitch Is Back," a hard rock tune that slyly played with his sexual identity.

Captain Fantastic and the Brown Dirt Cowboy (1975) was an autobiographical album recounting experiences from the John-Taupin career. The high point was "Someone Saved My Life Tonight," whose lyric reflected gratefully on a romance that failed. After firing Olson and Murray, he made *Rock of the Westies* (1975). Although the album entered the charts at number one, its most familiar songs, the Caribbean tourist tale "Island Girl" and the offensive Mexican narrative of "Grow Some Funk of Your Own," were indicators of creative decline.

Afterward, John's juggernaut slowed. Some attribute the career reversal to his candid admission of bisexuality in a *Rolling Stone* interview (1976), which lifted few eyebrows among the rock elite but shocked some mainstream pop fans. He may also have been tired, creatively spent, after several hard-charging years of recording and touring. The maudlin "Sorry Seems to Be the Hardest Word" from the otherwise forgettable *Blue Moves* (1976) summed up his situation. John toyed with retirement, broke with Taupin, and worked with a new lyricist on the undistinguished *A Single Man* (1978). With the emergence of disco and punk rock, John seemed passé.

And yet, the 400,000 fans who turned out for his free concert in New York's Central Park (1980), an event broadcast on the Home Box Office channel, proved his enduring appeal. Although he would no longer influence the direction of rock music and was increasingly regarded as pop rather than rock, John continued to sell out arenas. Reuniting with Taupin, he posted new hits to the singles chart with "Empty Garden (Hey Hey Johnny)" (1982), "I Guess That's Why They Call It the Blues" (1983), "Sad Songs (Say So Much)" (1984), "Nikita" (1986), "I Don't Want to Go On with You Like That" (1988), and "The One" (1990).

John established a second career in soundtracks for animated movies with Disney's *The Lion King* (1994) and won an Oscar and a Golden Globe for one of the film's hit songs, "Can You Feel the Love Tonight." In 1997 he performed "Candle in the Wind" with revised lyrics at the much-publicized funeral of Princess Diana. The single "Candle in the Wind 1997" set sales records. By then, John had become a favorite of Britain's royal family, appearing at weddings, performing at the Queen's Jubilee Concert in Buckingham Palace, and accepting a knighthood. He has also become a prominent gay rights activist and remains a celebrity as likely to be featured in *Architectural Digest* as in *People* magazine. John has been inducted into the Rock and Roll Hall of Fame.

Suggested Albums: Empty Sky (1969); *Elton John* (1970); *Tumbleweed Connection* (1971); *11-17-70 (aka 17-11-70)* (1971); *Madman Across the Water* (1971); *Honky Chateau* (1972); *Don't Shoot Me I'm Only the Piano Player* (1973); *Goodbye Yellow Brick Road* (1973); *Caribou* (1974); *Captain Fantastic and the Brown Dirt Cowboy* (1975); *Too Low for Zero* (1983); *Reg Strikes Back* (1988); *Sleeping with the Past* (1989); *The One* (1992); *Made in England* (1995); *Peachtree Road* (2004); *The Union* (with Leon Russell) (2010); *The Diving Board* (2013); *Wonderful Crazy Night* (2016)

JOPLIN, JANIS (1943–1970)

Born in Port Arthur, Texas, Janis Joplin was drawn to Beat poetry and the folk-blues revival and was always a misfit until she settled in the counterculture mecca of San Francisco in 1966. She became an avatar of nonconformity for a generation that professed the desire to find its own way beyond the paths laid out by their parents. Singing provided her creative outlet. An early live recording of Lead Belly's "Careless Love" shows Joplin firmly grounded in the blues, not just the mannerisms but the emotional heart. In a blindfold test, many listeners might have mistaken her for a pre–World War II blueswoman with guitar along the lines of Memphis Minnie.

However, her prewar blues emersion was no cul-de-sac but the highway leading to new horizons. She was drawn to the ear-splitting deep end of rock as singer for Big Brother and the Holding Company, where she was seen as a woman playing a man's game in the largely white, male-dominated hard rock of the 1960s. The band sometimes came across as garage rock built on the blues, but even on the relatively simple "Down on Me," Joplin carried the performance over the top with a fiercely expressive voice. Big Brother was underrated, as shown on the spacious yet adamant groove of

"Ball and Chain" or the Bach-like electric guitar line for "Summertime." During her tenure with Big Brother, Joplin cemented her reputation as a blues-rock powerhouse, rising from low-key to a shriek in a heartbeat. She achieved stardom fronting the band at the Monterey Pop Festival (1967).

Unsatisfied by blues-rock, Joplin left Big Brother in 1968 for what proved to be a short solo career emulating the Southern soulfulness issuing from Memphis's Stax-Volt label. Her reputation was indelibly stamped by her performance at Woodstock (1969). Joplin would record only two solo albums, backed by the Kozmic Blues Band for *I Got Dem Ol' Kozmic Blues Again Mama!* (1969) and the Full Tilt Boogie Band for *Pearl* (1971). Never a prolific songwriter, Joplin relied on contemporary material in her solo years, often by African Americans such as Clarence Carter, Bobby Womack, and Eddie Floyd.

Janis Joplin brought the pain and exuberance of the blues to life in her dynamic performances. While earning a worldwide reputation as a live performer among the era's counterculture, her sole hit single, "Me and Bobby McGee," charted after her 1970 death from a heroin overdose. (Photofest)

Waging a war against conventional notions of female beauty, Joplin became the ugly duckling who reinvented herself as a swan on her own terms, her frizzy hair and peacock frocks helping broaden female fashion. At the same time her persona was often interpreted in tomboy terms as the hard-playing woman who was "one of the guys" in a succession of all-male bands.

Joplin was one in a trio of rock stars (along with Jimi Hendrix and Jim Morrison) who fell to heroin as the 1970s began. She died of an overdose in 1970. Her only number one hit, which climbed the charts after her death, was a country-soul rendition of Kris Kristofferson's "Me and Bobby McGee" whose regretful tone stands at odds with many of her earlier songs and raises intriguing questions about the artist she might have become.

After her death, Joplin's image and recordings helped inspire new possibilities for women in rock music. The Oscar-winning film *The Rose* (1979) retold her life story with Bette Midler as the unlikely star in the lead role; the schmaltzy theme song, bearing no resemblance to Joplin's music, became a hit. She has been the subject of several biographies, documentary films, and a successful musical that began Off-Broadway in the 1990s, *Love, Janis*. Joplin was inducted into the Rock and Roll Hall of Fame.

Suggested Albums: I Got Dem Ol' Kozmic Blues Again Mama! (1969); *Pearl* (1971); *Early Performances* (1975); *This Is Janis Joplin 1965* (1995)

See also: Big Brother and the Holding Company

KALEIDOSCOPE

The diversity of Kaleidoscope's influences was exceeded only by the band's ability to harmonize the array into a coherent sound. Kaleidoscope emerged in 1966 out of the Los Angeles folk-blues revival. They were led by a pair of multi-instrumentalists with multiple interests, David Lindley and Solomon Feldthouse.

Kaleidoscope's debut album, *Side Trips* (1967), included vocal harmonies and jangling guitars reminiscent of Beau Brummels' folk-rock ("If the Night"), Beatlesque folk-rock ("Pulsating Dream") and moody Middle Eastern psychedelia ("Keep Your Mind Open"). They ventured through time and space for old-time blues ("Hesitation Blues"), a creative interpretation of Cab Calloway ("Minnie the Moocher"), doleful Appalachian folk ("Oh Death"), and a spin on Mediterranean tradition that would have sounded at home at a Greek Orthodox church festival ("Egyptian Gardens").

The title number from *A Beacon from Mars* (1968) evoked the ominous organ-driven blues-rock of the Doors but otherwise traveled Kaleidoscope's usual paths through the Middle East ("Rampe Rampe"), easy-going psychedelic rock à la Buffalo Springfield ("Love Games"), and unique fusions of raga, blues, and American folk ("Nobody"). Their cover of Buck Owens's "Hello Trouble" was an indicator of the band's increasing interest in country music and Americana on their final albums, *Incredible! Kaleidoscope* (1969) and *Bernice* (1970).

Kaleidoscope disbanded by the start of 1970. While never winning many fans, they earned admirers among fellow musicians. Lindley had no trouble securing session work during the 1970s, recording with Jackson Browne, Linda Ronstadt, and others. In the 1980s he began a solo career that continues today. Other members of Kaleidoscope went on to interesting projects. Chris Darrow also became a sought-after session musician. Chester Crill wrote for the underground comic series *Mickey Rat*. Stuart Brotman became a leading figure in the klezmer revival. Kaleidoscope briefly reunited in 1976 and again in 1990.

As the first to play electric guitar with a bow, Lindley inspired Jimmy Page, whose bluesy–Middle Eastern solo albums were presaged by Kaleidoscope. Kaleidoscope's globe-spanning sound set a precedent for the late 1980s direction of Camper van Beethoven, who also included "Oh Death" in their repertoire, and 21st-century bands such as TriBeCaStan.

Suggested Albums: Side Trips (1967); *A Beacon from Mars* (1968); *Incredible! Kaleidoscope* (1969); *Bernice* (1970)

KANSAS

Progressive rock band Kansas can be described as a serious group, particularly during the zenith of their career in the early to late 1970s. In an era when bands tended toward the earnest, there seemed to be something especially weighty about Kansas in both their philosophical approach and musical direction. While critics often expressed disdain for the band, the group's music found a widespread audience, leading to strong album sales and even a series of unlikely hit singles.

As one might surmise, the group hailed from the state from which they took their name. Landing a recording contract with music impresario Don Kirshner's label in 1974, they released their eponymous debut album that same year. The album was firmly in the progressive rock camp, as dramatic organ swirls and arpeggios cascade throughout lengthy and often complex musical passages. At times the sound seemed closely related to the busy keyboards of British progressive rockers Emerson, Lake & Palmer, but Kansas added its own unique touches to the genre. A persistent blues-boogie beat energized and drove the music, making songs like their cover of J. J. Cale's "Bringing It Back" and the original "Can I Tell You" solid radio fare. Robby Steinhart's violin gave their music a touch of Americana, hinting at country and Appalachian music.

The band's blending of boogie and progressive rock kept Kansas on the airwaves for the next several years, as songs such as the title track to *Song for America* (1975) and "It Takes a Woman's Love to Make a Man" from *Masque* (1975) received FM airplay. Eventually, boogie took a back seat to progressive rock, robbing the band's music of anything resembling a lighter touch. Kansas seemed to have found its niche in progressive rock, but it seemed that lack of accessibility would prevent the group from achieving widespread success. However, the band's biggest days were yet to come.

The band's big break came thanks to the surprising success of "Carry On, Wayward Son," the first single from *Leftoverture* (1976). With disco gaining steam, punk just around the bend, and soft rock dominating the Top 40, the song's ponderous lyrics and changing time signatures made it an odd fit for AM radio, but the chorus had a hook and the heavy blues-based guitar riff caught on with a public in the mood for a taste of middlebrow intellectualism. Bigger things were in store for Kansas with the release of *Point of Know Return* (1977), which produced two more hit singles in the form of the organ-based title track and the haunting acoustic ballad "Dust in the Wind." Kansas was now a headlining act, successfully touring and scoring another hit single, "People of the South Wind," from the live set *Monolith* (1979).

However, Kansas had hit its peak, and creative and personal tensions created rifts in the band's chemistry. By the 1980s, the public had begun to lose its taste for progressive rock, and the band's sales began to plummet. Leading member Kerry Livgren's conversion to Christianity caused further dissension within the group, as some members expressed displeasure with his increased proselytizing. Christian themes began to dominate Kansas's lyrics, and this change in direction led to newfound fans in the rising contemporary Christian music scene. The addition of ace

Despite their name, Kansas soon outgrew any associations with music from the American heartland and became a progressive rock band in the British mode. They had achieved steady sales on the album and singles charts by the time of this 1980 concert. (Philip Buonpastore/Alamy Stock Photo)

guitarist Steve Morse added instrumental heft to the group's sound, but did little to improve their commercial fortunes.

Kansas continued touring and releasing albums throughout the 1990s and into the new millennium, but its greatest days were in the past. Replacement member John Elefante became a successful producer and a force in contemporary Christian music thanks to his production of popular act Petra. The last decade saw the band release a series of compilation and live albums. They continue to tour and record original material.

Suggested Albums: Kansas (1974); *Masque* (1975); *Point of Know Return* (1977)

KING, CAROLE (1942–)

Born Carol Klein in Brooklyn, she anglicized her name as was not uncommon for American entertainers before the mid-1960s. She was a teenager when she married her first important collaborator, Gerry Goffin. It was a fruitful marriage of sensibilities. Raised on a diet of Rodgers and Hammerstein musicals, King wrote unself-conscious yet sophisticated little masterpieces, often imbuing her husband's melancholic lyrics with a brighter tone. Goffin and King worked in the Brill Building, headquarters for many New York music publishers, from a cramped office furnished with a piano, two chairs, and an ashtray. They wrote to order at a time when few singers penned their own material. Goffin's genius was to write believably from a woman's perspective; together they composed songs that were often deeply personal yet somehow universal.

The catalogue of their accomplishments through the mid-1960s is extensive. Goffin and King came to attention with the Shirelles' "Will You Still Love Me Tomorrow" (1961), whose understated melody conveyed a girl's emotional anxiety following her initial sexual encounter. Their succeeding hits included the Cookies' "Chains" (1962), the Drifters' "Up on the Roof" (1962), Herman's Hermits' "I'm into Something Good" (1964), the Animals' "Don't Bring Me Down" (1966), Aretha Franklin's "(You Make Me Feel Like) a Natural Woman" (1967) and the Monkees' "Pleasant Valley Sunday" (1967). Discovering talent in their 17-year-old babysitter, Little Eva, they wrote and produced her hit, "The Loco-Motion" (1962).

Although John Lennon and Paul McCartney admired Goffin and King (the Beatles covered "Chains" on an early album), their success changed the music industry through the example of rock bands recording their own songs rather than relying on professional writers. In 1968 with the Brill Building's influence fading, Goffin and King moved to the burgeoning music scene in Los Angeles as their marriage was dissolving. King formed a combo, the City, with her new collaborator-husband, Charles Larkey. The band's lone album, *Now That Everything's Been Said* (1969), sold few copies but yielded two songs that became hits in other hands, "Hi-De-Ho" as covered by Blood, Sweat & Tears and "You've Got a Friend" by James Taylor, who became a frequent collaborator.

The City's producer, Lou Adler, saw greater potential for King as a soloist. The first album released under her name, *Writer* (1970), sold modestly. However, her second release, *Tapestry* (1971), set new sales records for an LP. Adler set an intimate mood by turning the lights low in the studio during the recording sessions. The resulting sound was warm and comfortable, and together with King's songs, *Tapestry* became a relaxed coda to the chaos of the 1960s. The album had special appeal to women finding their way out of the sexism of the era's culture and counterculture. *Tapestry*'s number one hit, "It's Too Late," addressed the impermanence of marriage in post-1960s society through the lyrics of Toni Stern. Also included were new versions of "You've Got a Friend" and "A Natural Woman."

Finally overcoming stage fright, King began touring in support of a string of successful albums, albeit none sold as well or had the impact of *Tapestry*. She continued to enjoy hit singles through the mid-1970s, including "Sweet Seasons" from *Carole King: Music* (1971), "Been to Canaan" from *Rhymes and Reasons* (1972), and "Jazzman" from *Wrap Around Joy* (1974). She has recorded and performed prolifically through the present day, authored an autobiography, and received many prizes and awards including the Gershwin Prize (2013) and Kennedy Center Honors (2015).

Suggested Albums: Writer (1970); *Tapestry* (1971)

KING CRIMSON

The Who's Pete Townshend famously called King Crimson's debut album "an uncanny masterpiece." *In the Court of the Crimson King* set a high bar for progressive rock, one that most pretenders to the throne could never approach. There were other bands in their time with equivalent ambition and talent, but none ever reached as wide a public as King Crimson.

Although it was not clear at the onset that guitarist Robert Fripp would be the dominant force in King Crimson, he soon enough became its visionary-in-chief and the sole connecting cord between the band's several incarnations. A theorist as well as a disciplined virtuoso, Fripp was an eager adopter of new ideas in technology. Determined to avoid the trap of endless repetition that afflicted artists in the popular arena, Fripp pushed himself and King Crimson through distinct artistic phases that promised continued evolution.

As a teenager, Fripp was an avid listener to Charlie Parker and Charlie Mingus. By 1964 he played in a jazz trio as well as his own rock band, the League of Gentlemen, a name he would dust off for a project in the early 1980s. Fripp attended Bournemouth College, where he studied economic and political history. He would bring a scholarly perspective and tone to his musical undertakings. In 1967 he became part of his first recording group, the eccentric pop trio of Giles, Giles and Fripp. A year later drummer Michael Giles accompanied Fripp into King Crimson. Other original members included Fripp's friend from Bournemouth, vocalist-bassist Greg Lake; multi-instrumentalist Ian McDonald; and lyricist Pete Sinfield, who coined the King Crimson name and played an important early role in the band's aesthetics.

In the Court of the Crimson King (1969) was startling upon release, challenging the status quo that had already overtaken the ostensibly daring, rebellious subculture of 1960s rock. Sinfield drew from a palette of fantasy and science fiction to paint a panorama of disillusionment in a world governed by fools. The opening track, "21st Century Schizoid Man," delivered anxiety in the starkest terms. As Lake's astringent, electronically processed vocals taunted hearers, the music charged through jazz cadences fused with metallic timbres; the song's structure had more to do with Bela Bartok than the Beatles while Fripp's incendiary solos blazed with the fire of John Coltrane and Ornette Coleman.

The music quickly turned pastoral on succeeding tracks, but even the lovely "I Talk to the Wind" conveyed unease, as if the autumn breeze whispered a downbeat riddle to all who cared to listen. The eerie dream world of "Moonchild" probably alluded to Aleister Crowley's novel of the same name. Throughout, Giles's drumming was important not just as a timekeeper but as a lead instrument, integral to the ensemble without digressing into the interminable soloing beloved by many rock drummers of the era. *In the Court of the Crimson King* concluded on a darkly majestic note with its title track, a sterling example of rock's symphonic potential. Inspired by the Moody Blues, McDonald's mellotron carried the weight of an orchestral string section while every note on guitar and flute and each drumbeat was itself carefully orchestrated to contribute to a mood of despondent grandeur.

The original lineup did not survive the band's 1969 U.S. tour. McDonald and Giles left and released an album, *McDonald and Giles* (1970), emulating King Crimson's sound. McDonald went on to co-found Foreigner in 1976. Fripp carried on, reprising King Crimson's debut with *In the Wake of Poseidon* (1970). Personnel continued to change, including the departure of Lake for a new supergroup,

194 KING CRIMSON

Emerson, Lake & Palmer. The next incarnation under Fripp's leadership barely survived the recording of *Lizard* (1970), and yet another imploded after a U.S. tour in support of *Islands* (1971).

Afterward, Fripp recruited a dynamic lineup ready to reinvent progressive rock once again. Bill Bruford left Yes to join Crimson on drums. Also on board were bassist John Wetton from Family, violinist David Cross, drummer Jamie Muir (who employed found objects for percussion), and a new lyricist, Supertramp founding member Robert Palmer-Jones. Bruford recalled that instead of a list of songs to learn, Fripp handed him a reading list that included the Armenian mystic and mythmaker G. I. Gurdjieff, who preached that humans must awaken from their slumber and pursue their full potential; Gurdjieff's Russian disciple P. D. Ouspensky; his British disciple, psychologist J. G. Bennett; and Carlos Castaneda, the American anthropologist who popularized shamanism with his bestseller, *The Teachings of Don Juan* (1968).

For the new lineup's first album, *Larks' Tongues in Aspic* (1973), Fripp delved deeper into musical esoteria, crafting metallic rock music from free improvisation as well as modernist classical music. Muir resigned and became a Buddhist monk before the recording of *Starless and Bible Black* (1974). Ambitiously knit together from live and studio tracks, *Starless* glowed with the fierce dueling of Cross's violin and Fripp's guitar and continued the thorny trajectory *of Larks' Tongues*. The title of one of the album's instrumentals, "Fracture," described much of the music.

Despite breaking with all expectations for rock music, even at its most progressive, Fripp fretted over artistic dead ends and broke up the band following *Red* (1974), an album with a mixed roster of personnel (including the brief return of McDonald) and a mix of studio and concert tracks.

Fripp had long chafed under the demands of the record industry, the logistical burdens of massive rock tours (which by then had come to resemble military incursions), his disdain for the hedonism and drugs of the mainstream rock lifestyle, and what he saw as the musical straightjacket he had helped tailor in the form of progressive rock. He proposed something radical, replacing rock bands with "small, independent, mobile and intelligent units," essentially one-man shows armed with sophisticated technology. He had already recorded outside King Crimson by collaborating with Brian Eno on *No Pussyfooting* (1973), which in hindsight has been seen as the birth of ambient music but at the time was greeted with incomprehension by most rock fans. Along with Eno, he developed "Frippertronics," a looping multitrack taped performance process anticipated a decade earlier by avant-garde composer Terry Riley. He recorded again with Eno on *Evening Star* (1975).

For several years Fripp reduced his visibility. He played guitar on Peter Gabriel's first solo album (1977) and toured with the former Genesis frontman, but played from the wings or behind a curtain. Fripp played on David Bowie's groundbreaking album *Heroes* (1977) and produced an eclectic handful of albums including efforts by Daryl Hall and the Roches. His first solo album, *Exposure* (1979), began with a wry preface expressing his attitude toward the music industry in which he asks, "Could I play you some of the new things I'm doing, which I think could be commercial?" Next comes a buzz saw punk take on Chuck Berry, "You Burn Me Up I'm a Cigarette," but what follows are further excursions into the angular metallic blocks of sound first explored on *Larks' Tongues* and *Starless*. With *Exposure*, Fripp found himself in communion with the more daring wing of punk rock.

While executing session work for Talking Heads and Blondie, Fripp released *God Save the Queen/Heavy Manners* (1980), followed by an album with his short-lived group, the League of Gentlemen, a self-described "new wave instrumental dance band."

Although he had once declared that King Crimson was over forever, Fripp decided to perform under that name for a trio of albums, *Discipline* (1981), *Beat* (1982), and *Three of a Perfect Pair* (1984). For those projects, Fripp recruited Bruford; guitarist Adrian Belew, whose resume included Bowie, Talking Heads, and Frank Zappa; and a sideman from *Exposure*, guitarist–Chapman Stick player Tony Levin. The sound was contemporary postpunk with synthesizers and minimalist influences.

Disbanding King Crimson, Fripp kept busy developing a music course called Guitar Craft and recording several Frippertronic albums using updated digital technology. He collaborated with David Sylvian from the late-1970s art rock group Japan and recorded with a variety of younger artists. In 1994 he re-formed King Crimson with an augmented version of the band's 1980s lineup. The ever-shifting Crimson roster along with satellite projects continued into the 21st century with albums such as *The Power to Believe* (2003) and *A Scarcity of Miracles: A King Crimson ProjeKct* (2011). Fripp's long and varied discography with King Crimson plus session work, side projects, and collaborations testifies to his ongoing artistic restlessness.

Suggested Albums: In the Court of the Crimson King (1969); *In the Wake of Poseidon* (1970); *Lizard* (1970); *Islands* (1971); *Larks' Tongues in Aspic* (1973); *Starless and Bible Black* (1974); *Red* (1974); *Discipline* (1981); *Beat* (1982); *Three of a Perfect Pair* (1984)

KINKS

It is impossible to ignore the Kinks. From their arrival at the zenith of the British Invasion and throughout their long and frequently memorable career, the Kinks set standards, confounded expectations, and created some of the most significant music in an era of giants. Guided by the songwriting genius of the band's creative leader, Ray Davies, they put an indelible stamp on rock music, inspiring their contemporaries and influencing artists decades younger. And while their greatest and most influential work is compressed within a relatively short period, the quality of their creative output more than justifies the consistent high praise lavished on the band.

The Kinks are the product of brothers Ray and Dave Davies, who grew up in the Muswell Hill suburb of London. Their upbringing was musically richer than most, as their parents hosted Saturday night parties that exposed the brothers to many musical styles. Older brother Ray's horizons were further expanded by a stint in the creative incubator of British art school, where he studied film, theater, and various forms of music. He returned home to form the Ravens with brother Dave, and the group began playing locally. The band signed a record deal in 1964 and set about searching for a more distinctive name. They settled on the Kinks, a moniker that set them apart from the multitude of groups taking their name from the animal kingdom or blues records. A couple of undistinguished singles threatened to scuttle their career, but things changed with their third single for both the band and all of rock music.

Looking back through the prism of history, it's difficult to imagine just how revolutionary that single, "You Really Got Me," must have sounded in 1964. Ray Davies had begun writing songs, mostly innocuous numbers that reflected the early rock and roll and rhythm and blues that was pervasive in early 1960s England. "You Really Got Me" was nothing like anything he, or anybody else had written before. Built around a savage two-chord riff, the song rocks with a primal force descended from the Kingsmen's "Louie, Louie" but taken to a far more explosive conclusion. The record's fuzz guitar sound was the product of Dave Davies taking a razor blade to the speaker of his amplifier, creating a distorted sound that set rock on a course that eventually led to heavy metal and punk. Dave Davies's solo, a wildly improvised exercise in chaos, often misattributed to then sessions man Jimmy Page, would set the stage for more frenetic players such as Jimi Hendrix.

The manic energy and feral quality of the single was both exhilarating and perhaps a bit frightening to audiences just getting used to the sound of the Beatles and the rest of the British Invasion. Still, the song became a worldwide hit, and the similarly pulverizing follow-up "All Day and All of the Night" established the Kinks as a force to be reckoned with as the band began touring, attracting almost as much attention for internal tumult that often spread to the stage as for their music.

Like so many of their mid-1960s contemporaries, the Kinks' early career focused on singles, with albums filled out by covers or throwaway originals. Those singles chronicled Ray Davies's rapid growth as a songwriter. He quickly moved from the ferocious rock of the band's first two hits and began developing a catalogue of songs demonstrating astonishing breadth and depth. His first foray into deeper creative waters was the biting "A Well Respected Man." Set to rolling acoustic guitars, Davies's picture of a smug British upper-class snob teetered on the edge of caricature. The song was saved by a strong melody and acerbic wit, and captured the socially conscious temper of the times. Davies did better with the band's follow-up, the humorous "Dedicated Follower of Fashion," a music hall–inspired acoustic send-up of swinging London's burgeoning mod scene. The next single, "Sunny Afternoon," showed Davies's further maturation as he took the measure of another denizen of Britain's upper class, but the intended scathing portrayal was leavened by Davies's perhaps unintended empathy for the subject's plight at the hands of Britain's confiscatory tax policies. Satire, searing wit, and increasing social and personal insight became trademarks of Davies's writing. He stood alongside the likes of Bob Dylan, John Lennon and Paul McCartney, Brian Wilson, and Pete Townshend as a songwriting titan.

After a series of extraordinary singles, the Kinks set about recording their first truly classic album, *Something Else by the Kinks* (1967), which saw Ray fully realizing his promise as a songwriter and moving the band into a new and even more ambitious phase of their career. With a novelist's eye for detail, Davies delved deeper into the human condition, populating his songs with characters that sprang fully to life within the confines of three- to four-minute songs. Whether it was the hero-worshipping schoolboy teen of "David Watts," the jealous sister of "Two Sisters," or the unambitious middle-class bloke of "Autumn Almanac," the characters were treated with insight, empathy, and wit. The album reaches a crescendo with the brilliant "Waterloo Sunset," a poignant tale of an aging man who lives vicariously through a young couple's romance. The ballad is not only Davies's finest song, it ranks as one of the greatest songs in rock history.

Outstanding as *Something Else* was, the band topped themselves with *The Kinks Are the Village Green Preservation Society* (1968), a concept album dealing with time, change, and loss of stability and tradition. A nostalgic hue pervades the album and can be seen as a metaphor for a society coming to terms with a much too rapidly changing world.

Despite poor sales, *Village Green Preservation Society* was a watershed in the development of concept albums, and Davies would repeatedly return to its themes. The gender-confused narrator of their 1970 hit "Lola" and the escapist figure in "Apeman," both from *Lola versus Powerman and the Moneygoround, Part One* (1970), show characters trying to cope with bewilderingly confusing times. The nostalgia of *Village Green* was revisited in the oddly touching tribute to Hollywood's Golden Era, "Celluloid Heroes," from *Everybody's in Showbiz* (1972). By the late 1960s no other British Invasion act was as distinctly British as the Kinks. Concept albums became their norm, ranging from the strong *Arthur (or the Decline and Fall of the British Empire)* (1969) to the vapid *Preservation Act 1* (1973). Perhaps a bit of a Fabian Socialist at heart, Ray Davies began to rail at the corrupting influence of money and seemed to yearn for an imagined more egalitarian world. The band hit a low spot with the dreary *Soap Opera* (1975) and *Schooboys in Disgrace* (1975), and it seemed that Davies's fascination with concept albums was beginning to verge on self-parody. A rare mid-1970s highlight was the holiday single "Father Christmas," a rocker deriding class inequities with equal parts "bah humbug" and "season's greetings."

Had their trajectory continued, the Kinks would have been relegated to oblivion by the late 1970s, but instead their fortunes revived. *Sleepwalker* (1977) saw Davies abandon concept albums and return to writing self-contained rock songs. Respectable sales and radio play brought the band back into the public eye. They followed up with the even stronger *Misfits* (1978), which reestablished Davies as a creative force. Punk rock and new wave had made the band relevant again, as many artists cited the Kinks as a major influence, and it was apparent that they were revitalized by the musical revolution that they had foreshadowed more than a decade before. New wave artists began paying open homage to the Kinks. The Jam's searing cover of "David Watts" (1978) and Nick Lowe's sparkling Phil Spector–styled production of the Pretenders' cover of "Stop Your Sobbing" (1980) paid tribute to and actually surpassed the quality of the originals. Meanwhile, in America's hard rock milieu, Van Halen's plodding version of "You Really Got Me" (1978) kickstarted their superstar career. The Kinks responded to all this by releasing a hard rock album, *Low Budget* (1979), that contained several hit singles and saw the band return to the top of the charts and airwaves.

As the 1970s gave way to the 1980s, the Kinks rode a commercial and artistic high. They had developed a tightly constructed and performed stage act and were a headlining arena attraction. The live *One for the Road* (1980) was a radio staple that brought songs like "Lola" and "Sunny Afternoon" to a new audience. The band remained a popular concert act throughout the decade, but unfortunately, Davies was unable to match commercial success with further artistic triumphs. His songwriting edge, while never dull, began to lose its sharpness as the years wore on. The work was never bad but seldom outstanding, and the overall impression was that of a band treading water. An exception was the hit "Come Dancing" (1983), which saw Davies yet again waxing nostalgic in wistful recollection of growing up at the end of the big band dance hall days.

Tensions began to rise within the band, as Dave Davies chafed in his brother's shadow and eventually recorded his long promised solo album (1980). The brothers began bickering in the press, and Ray became absorbed in writing and directing the film *Return to Waterloo* (1985). A consistent slide in popularity led to the band's dissolution in the mid-1990s even as their music was being rediscovered yet again, this time by the Britpop generation led by bands such as Blur and Oasis.

Both Davies brothers released a series of solo albums of varying quality, and the band talked about re-forming in the early 2000s. Sadly, Dave's health problems put an end to such speculation, although the brothers did play together onstage in 2015. The Kinks were inducted into the Rock and Roll Hall of Fame, a fitting tribute for one of the most important rock acts of all time. Scores of artists list Ray Davies and the Kinks as seminal influences, including the Clash, the Jam, Elvis Costello, XTC, Madness, Oasis, and Blur as a few of the most prominent. Whenever one hears intelligently written and incisive British rock music, one hears a bit of the Kinks' legacy.

Suggested Albums: The Kinks (1964); *Kinda Kinks* (1965); *Kinkdom* (1965); *The Kink Kontroversy* (1965); *Face to Face* (1966); *Something Else by the Kinks* (1967); *The Kinks Are the Village Green Preservation Society* (1968); *Arthur (or the Decline and Fall of the British Empire* (1969); *Lola versus Powerman and the Moneygoround, Part One* (1970); *Muswell Hillbillies* (1971); *Sleepwalker* (1977); *Misfits* (1978); *Low Budget* (1979); *Give the People What They Want* (1981); *State of Confusion* (1983)

KOOPER, AL (1944–)

Al Kooper spent virtually his entire life in the music industry. At age 15 he joined the Royal Teens, the group with the 1958 hit "Short Shorts." He then found session work as a guitarist and pianist and wrote "This Diamond Ring," a number one pop hit for Gary Lewis and the Playboys (1965). A friend of Bob Dylan's producer Tom Wilson, he was admitted to the recording studio as a "standby" guitarist during the session for "Like a Rolling Stone" (1965), only to be thrust behind the organ, an instrument he did not play. Intuitively, he put together the organ part that helped define one of the signal songs of the 1960s.

He stayed in touch with Dylan, backing him at the Newport Folk Festival (1965) performance where he was legendarily booed by folk purists for embracing rock, and recorded with him on *Blonde on Blonde* (1966) and *New Morning* (1970). In 1965 Kooper co-founded his own band, the innovative Blues Project, and went on in 1967 to form the original incarnation of Blood, Sweat & Tears. He organized *Super Session* (1968), an all-star blues and rock album featuring dueling guitarists Mike Bloomfield and Stephen Stills, supported by his keyboard playing.

Kooper recorded prolifically as a solo artist in the 1970s and early 1980s. As a producer he worked with Lynyrd Skynyrd, Nils Lofgren, and the Turtles but is most remembered for his memoir of rock in the 1960s, *Backstage Passes* (1977). He later toured with fellow writers Stephen King, Dave Barry, Amy Tan, and Matt Groening as the Rock Bottom Remainders. Kooper continues to perform.

Suggested Album: Super Session (1968)

See also: Blood, Sweat & Tears; Blues Project

KORNER, ALEXIS (1928–1984)

Alexis Korner is a pivotal figure in the development of the 1960s British blues scene despite never producing any recordings of great popularity. While widespread recognition eluded Korner, his legacy lies in the startling number of prominent artists whom he mentored and whose careers were shaped in the London blues scene he helped create in the early 1960s.

The French-born Korner grew up in London in the 1940s, where he developed a love for American jazz and blues. He picked up the guitar and began playing in blues and jazz groups, and it was in one of these bands that he developed a friendship with blues harmonica player Cyril Davies. The duo began playing in local jazz clubs and soon opened their own, the London Blues and Barrelhouse Club. Korner and Davies headlined and developed a devoted clientele by booking American blues acts. Most significantly, they formed Alexis Korner's Blues Incorporated and released a series of competent, faithfully executed blues albums. The records are not well remembered, but the list of the band's membership reads like a Who's Who of 1960s British rock. Charlie Watts, Jack Bruce, Ginger Baker, Graham Bond were regular members, and Steve Marriott, Manfred Mann, Paul Jones, and Ian Stewart sat in with the band. Korner became a mentor for Rolling Stones Mick Jagger and Keith Richards, both of whom list their time spent with Korner at his club and the London Marquee Club (where Korner's group often headlined) as formative experiences.

Korner continued to perform and record to little notice, even as many of the acts he helped nurture went on to shape the direction of rock music in the 1960s and 1970s. By the 1980s Korner had been relegated to the status of respected elder, recognized by the historically aware for the artists he helped develop, but rarely for his own interpretations of the blues for which he so zealously proselytized. A longtime smoker, Korner died of lung cancer in 1984.

Suggested Album: Alexis Korner's Blues Incorporated (1965)

KRAFTWERK

The duo at the heart of Kraftwerk, Florian Schneider and Ralf Hutter, came from the culturally and musically turbulent German scene that nurtured Amon Duul II, Can, and Cluster. Unlike their peers from that early 1970s milieu, Kraftwerk enjoyed Top 40 singles, Top 10 albums, and wide-reaching influence beyond the borders of their homeland. Kraftwerk inspired most of the synthesizer-powered rock bands that came forth from Great Britain in the late 1970s and early 1980s, and their influence extended into America's nascent hip-hop culture. Even in the 21st century, many groups with electronic inclinations remain indebted to Kraftwerk.

Steeped in avant-garde music and visual art, and fascinated by the potential of new technology, Germany's Kraftwerk set the stage for several musical revolutions. Kraftwerk influenced everyone from David Bowie and his followers to the nascent hip-hop genre in the 1980s. (Photofest)

As with many of their comrades in the "Krautrock" scene, Kraftwerk cited thorny avant-garde German composer Karlheinz Stockhausen as a source, yet once they got past the improvisational space rock of *Kraftwerk* (1970) and *Kraftwerk 2* (1972), Schneider and Hutter arrived at a largely electronic sound as futuristic yet polite and unthreatening as R2-D2 and C-3PO from *Star Wars*. *Ralf und Florian* (1973) was mostly instrumental, generating melody with analog synthesizers and rhythm with drum machines while processing the minimal vocals through a vocoder, a sound wave synthesizing device whose musical application was pioneered by German researchers. Conny Plank, Germany's best known recording engineer, co-produced the earliest Kraftwerk albums as well as their breakout, *Autobahn* (1974), and is credited with guiding them into the new technology of music-making.

Autobahn's title track, stretching for 22 minutes across one side of the LP, was an aural representation of a ride along Germany's freeway system famed for its lack of speed limits. The sunny motor tour with its simple German-language refrain (translating as "Driving, driving, driving on the autobahn") was abbreviated into a three-and-a-half–minute single, which became an unlikely hit in the United States, Great Britain, continental Europe, and Australia. It was the first exposure many listeners had to original music composed and performed electronically without recourse to conventional instruments and was a signal of things to come in popular music.

In the wake of their success, Schneider and Hutter toured Kraftwerk as a four-piece unit deploying Mini Moog and ARP Odyssey synthesizers alongside homemade electronic percussion devices. *Autobahn*'s sales also enabled them to construct the Kling Klang recording studio in their hometown, Dusseldorf, where they recorded a follow-up, the bilingual *Radio-Activity* (1975). The lyrics were punning deadpans on commerce and science. The title track could be interpreted as reflecting either on nuclear decay or radio airplay. Afterward, Kraftwerk issued most of their albums in two forms, one sung in rock's lingua franca of English and the other, released in Central Europe, in the group's native German.

Trans-Europe Express (1977) appeared as David Bowie began work on his "Berlin Trilogy"; Bowie tipped his hat to Kraftwerk's influence with "V-2 Schneider" from *Heroes* (1977). *Trans-Europe Express*'s title track used repetitive electronic drum patterns to suggest the steady rumble of a train on the railbed while synthesizers simulated acceleration and the countryside passing by in the windows of the train carriage. Electronically processed vocals repeated the song's title hypnotically. For the cover, Kraftwerk was photographed in suits and ties, their sartorial rejection of the 1960s counterculture in keeping with fashions emerging from the new wave about to issue forth from the United Kingdom.

With its striking Russian Supremacist cover design, including group members posed in red shirts and black neckties, *The Man-Machine* (1978) sent ripples through the musically adventurous edge of Britain's punk scene and provided a well of ideas for the likes of Gary Numan, Soft Cell, Orchestral Manoeuvres in the Dark, Human League, Ultravox, New Order, and Depeche Mode. In America, Kraftwerk similarly inspired Blondie's turn toward the pulsating electro-pop of "Heart of Glass" (1979). "Trans-Europe Express" was sampled on "Planet Rock" (1982), the influential hip-hop single by Afrika Bambaataa & the Soul Sonic Force. The electronic dance genre known as techno coalesced in Detroit during those years from a mixture of Kraftwerk, disco, and funk influences.

As the rest of the world absorbed their lessons, Kraftwerk quietly worked in the seclusion of Kling Klang studio on an album whose theme as well as its music proved remarkably prescient, *Computer World* (1981). As robotic rhythms kept time and synthesizers maintained a cool reserve, the group sang of a global society whose border-spanning institutions, from the FBI to Deutsche Bank, were linked by chains of numerical data. The emotionally blank vocals offered no clue to

Kraftwerk's feelings on globalization and digitalization, albeit the upbeat single "Pocket Calculator" seemed to celebrate the dawn of handheld electronic devices. In concert, Kraftwerk made full use of available technology with visuals synchronized to the music and mannequins of the group's members performing on stage.

Committed to transportation as a theme, Kraftwerk released a single about cycling, "Tour de France" (1983), that was featured in the hip-hop movie *Breakin'* (1984). Kraftwerk continued to tour and released an album in what by then had become their trademark style, *Electric Café* (1986). *The Mix* (1991) was a collection of remixed tracks. They released no new music afterward until *Tour de France Soundtracks* (2003), which included a fresh recording of the 20-year-old title track. Kraftwerk toured in support of *Tour de France* using four custom laptop computers to generate much of the music. Despite the long gap between new recordings, Kraftwerk endured no loss of career momentum and appeared as part of the warp and weave of the new millennium. Although Schneider left Kraftwerk in 2008, Hutter continues to tour under that name. Kraftwerk's 3D concert visuals have been exhibited in museums, and the unit has enjoyed the distinction of performing at New York's Museum of Modern Art and London's Tate Modern.

Suggested Albums: Kraftwerk (1970); *Kraftwerk 2* (1972); *Ralf und Florian* (1973); *Autobahn* (1974); *Radio-Activity* (aka *Radio-Aktivitat*) (1975); *Trans-Europe Express* (aka *Trans-Europa Express*) (1977); *The Man-Machine* (aka *Die Mensch-Maschine*) (1978); *Computer World* (aka *Computerwelt*) (1981); *Electric Café* (aka *Techno Pop*) (1986); *The Mix* (1991); *Tour de France Soundtracks* (2003)

LE ORME

Briefly, in the early 1970s, British and American record labels took an interest in progressive rock bands from Italy. Several groups were signed to short-lived recording contracts, including PFM (Premiata Forneria Marconi), Banco (Banco del Mutuo Soccorso), and the Italian band most esteemed by progressive rock fans, Le Orme.

Beginning in Venice in 1966, Le Orme evolved apace with the British bands that inspired them from "beat music" into psychedelia. Their first album, *Ad gloriam* (1969), was a magical mystery tour whose 13 short numbers flowed together in an appealing sequence. *Ad gloriam* featured dreamy, churchy organ and Carnaby Street harmonies sung in Italian. Years later a sample from the title track, embedded in David Holmes's "69 Police," was heard in the soundtrack of *Ocean's Eleven* (2001).

Like many European psychedelic bands that endured into the 1970s, Le Orme shifted into progressive rock under the spell of Emerson, Lake & Palmer and Gentle Giant. Their albums *Collage* (1971) and *Uomo di pezza* (1972) were Top 10 in Italy. A tour with Peter Hammill led to an unusual collaboration. *Felona e Sorona* (1973) was issued in Italian for the band's homeland while an English-language version, *Felona and Sorona*, with lyrics by Hammill derived from the original Italian texts, was released elsewhere. Largely keyboard-powered with a muscular yet melodic sound, *Felona and Sorona* is ranked by aficionados as a great if overlooked progressive rock album.

Afterward, Le Orme fumbled in trying to find new directions. Their live album *In concerto* (1974) was derided by progressive rock pundits; *Smogmagica* (1975) was recorded in Los Angeles with prominent guitar parts in a bid for mainstream rock. *Verita nascoste* (1976) was heard as a return to form, yet the sort of classical music–based rock that had been their trademark was receding against the rise of punk and newer genres. Le Orme set aside electric instruments altogether for *Florian* (1979), a set of folk chamber music performed on violin, cello, clavichord, and vibraphone.

In the early 1980s Le Orme stumbled backward into unsuccessful pop music before disbanding in 1982. They returned after 1986, touring and recording with a mix of older and newer band members. Le Orme continue to work the worldwide circuit of progressive rock festivals in the 21st century.

Suggested Albums: Ad gloriam (1969); *Collage* (1971); *Uomo di pezza* (1972); *Felona e Sorona / Felona and Sorona* (1973); *Florian* (1979)

LED ZEPPELIN

As the 1970s biggest selling and most pervasively influential rock band, Led Zeppelin became an easy target for punk rock upstarts as the decade came to a close. Zeppelin's guitarist Jimmy Page was especially annoyed by accusations that his music strayed too far from the roots of rock. After all, Page was integral to the roots of British rock. As his country's top session guitarist during the 1960s, he played on seminal recordings by the Rolling Stones, the Who, the Kinks, Them, and Donovan, as well as the theme from the James Bond movie *Goldfinger* (1964). During those years he often worked in tandem with the man who became Led Zeppelin's bassist, John Paul Jones. In those years Jones was a studio keyboard player, arranger, and producer who worked with the Rolling Stones, Jeff Beck, Donovan, Cat Stevens, Tom Jones, and many other acts. Led Zeppelin's other half were relative novices. Singer Robert Plant and drummer John Bonham came from Band of Joy, which mixed rhythm and blues covers with songs by popular American psychedelic bands.

Led Zeppelin's roots grew out of the Yardbirds, the innovative band that introduced guitarists Eric Clapton, Beck, and Page to the general public. In 1966 Page joined the band and briefly shared the stage with Beck, their violent dynamism captured in the concert scene from Michelangelo Antonioni's film *Blow-Up* (1966). After Beck's departure in late 1966, the Yardbirds began to falter. Although they played their final show in the summer of 1968, the Yardbirds were contractually committed to a Scandinavian tour. Page was authorized by the other Yardbirds to use the band's name to fulfill those obligations. Page recruited Plant, Jones, and Bonham and they toured as the New Yardbirds.

Within months they adopted the Led Zeppelin moniker, recording and mixing their first album in a nine-day session. Atlantic Records soon signed them. A respected rhythm and blues and jazz label, Atlantic, eager to capitalize on the explosion of new rock bands, granted them a large advance and virtually complete artistic control.

Their eponymous debut (1969) proved that the label's confidence was well advised. Rising into the Top 10 album chart without the aid of a single (a medium the band disdained), *Led Zeppelin* was a towering milestone on the road of heavy metal. Hard rock bands then and since have envied the rhythmic power of such tracks as "Communication Breakdown" and "Good Times Bad Times."

Page always went for the most exciting performance even if it included flubbed notes. He was not a technical perfectionist, despite his obvious proficiency, but aimed for emotional impact. Page cultivated a particular sound in the studio, creating depth through astute arrangement of amplifiers and microphones. He was not alone among his bandmates for bringing unique talents into play. In Bonham's hands heavy metal was no metaphor. His thundering drumming resulted from muscular physicality, yet he was also an intelligent player, carefully listening to Page's playing and echoing his riffs percussively. Jones, always the most overlooked band member, played bass with uniquely rounded tones that never overpowered the songs. His background as an arranger helped to shape Led Zeppelin's mountainous sound. Plant's high-pitched wail was the most easily caricatured aspect of the band, yet he was able to transmute the personal pain and perseverance of the blues into a universal cry of anguish and defiance. Already they displayed the capacity to produce a ballad that ascended from the mystic into loud catharsis on their version of Anne Bredon's "Babe I'm Gonna Leave You," a song that originated in the folk-blues revival of the early 1960s.

Led Zeppelin II (1970) was recorded while on tour in the United States with the band dropping into various studios in between concerts. However, the results were fully coherent as they continued to solidify their sound. "Whole Lotta Love" was blues-rock at a mind-blowing, chord-crunching supersonic level never heard before.

One of the biggest selling and most pervasively influential rock bands of the 1970s, Led Zeppelin transmuted blues and British folk influences into a sound of Wagnerian dimensions. They were fronted by guitarist Jimmy Page and singer Robert Plant. (Photofest)

In preparation for *Led Zeppelin III* (1970), Page and Plant, the band's primary songwriters, secluded themselves in a remote cottage tucked into the Welsh mountains, a place of foreboding in the stories of Arthur Machen, a writer whose circle overlapped with Aleister Crowley, the occultist whose writings became such a prevalent influence on Page that the guitarist purchased Crowley's house overlooking Loch Ness. Nordic mythology resounded on the album's most played track, "Immigrant Song," propelled by Plant's one-man Wagnerian Valkyrie chorus. Also explored were the commonalities between Indian and Arabic music and the bent notes of the blues along with killer rock riffs and Anglo-Celtic balladry.

Led Zeppelin exerted the artistic control granted by their label to the fullest with the release of their fourth album (1971). The LP had no title, though it is usually referred to as *Led Zeppelin IV*. Even the band's name was omitted from the enigmatic cover, replaced by a set of four symbols representing each band member in a foretaste of Prince's notorious glyph. The inside sleeve bore the image of the Hermit, derived from the early 20th-century tarot deck designed by Crowley's rival, British occultist A. E. Waite. The album included a track that became the most played song on FM radio, "Stairway to Heaven."

Unlike such future bands as Nirvana, who prided themselves on going from a whisper to a scream, "Stairway to Heaven" mounted with gradual logic from acoustic to electric, from ballad to hard rock, with each verse a step on the ascending ladder before reaching an exhilarating climax unmatched in rock. Page nailed the electric guitar solo in one take, improvising it by feel. "Stairway to Heaven" was British folk-rock, psychedelically tinged hard rock, and heavy metal within an eight-minute composition.

Had "Stairway to Heaven" never been recorded, *Led Zeppelin IV* would still be a great album whose bounty of memorable tracks included the ominous hard rock of "Black Dog," the J.R.R. Tolkien–derived ballad "The Battle of Evermore" (featuring bewitching vocals by British folk singer Sandy Denny), the nuclear-powered cover of Memphis Minnie's despairing blues song "When the Levee Breaks," and the ebullient rock and roll of "Rock and Roll."

By contrast, *Houses of the Holy* (1973) seemed almost low key as it picked up the trajectory of *Led Zeppelin III* rather than continue in the direction of *IV*. *Houses* included the uncharacteristic "D'yer Mak'er," which introduced American rock fans to reggae rhythms a year before Clapton's "I Shot the Sheriff" but without identifying the music's Jamaican origins. Most stateside listeners were pleasantly baffled.

Few albums were as hugely anticipated as *Physical Graffiti* (1975), a two-LP set played in its entirety upon release on some FM stations. A rich, varied, and tuneful work, it included psychedelia ("The Inner Light"), a cinematic tour of India's far frontier ("Kashmir"), a blues-rock take on spooky pre–World War II Mississippi Delta blues ("In My Time of Dying"), hard metallic rock ("Houses of the Holy"), rock and roll ("Boogie with Stu"), and even metallic funk echoing the sound of Stevie Wonder's "Superstition" ("Trampled Under Foot").

Even under the best of circumstances, the high standards set by *Physical Graffiti* would have been hard to follow, and the circumstances following its release were anything but favorable. Plant was injured in a car crash and was forced to record *Presence* (1976) while seated, which affected his singing. Page began using heroin. *Presence* was easily their most dispirited album, as if recorded under the influence of the bad drugs alluded to on the best track, the "monkey on my back" in the bluesy "Nobody's Fault But Mine."

Hobbled by Plant's injury, Led Zeppelin did not tour to support *Presence* but instead completed postproduction on a concert documentary shot at the close of their 1973 tour. The resulting film, *The Song Remains the Same* (1976), reveals a band understandably fatigued after an extensive American road trip. Supplementing the concert footage were silly "fantasy sequences." The movie provided a strong argument for those who thought Led Zeppelin and the superstar rock bands of the 1970s were artistically spent.

Stung by criticism of their musical grandiosity and high-flying rock star lifestyle, Led Zeppelin shifted course dramatically for *In Through the Out Door* (1979), rolling out synthesizers, snappier beats, and more sharply written tunes in response to the new wave that threatened to dim the luster of many 1970s rock stars. It proved to be their final album of new material. In 1980 Bonham died at Page's home after a heavy bout of drinking. Unlike many of their generational peers, Led Zeppelin saw the death of a key member as a sign to retire. Their posthumous *Coda* (1982) collected strong unreleased tracks recorded during the 1970s.

Led Zeppelin regrouped for the Live Aid benefit concert (1985). In 1988 they reassembled for Atlantic Records' 40th Anniversary Concert with Bonham's son Jason on drums. That lineup came together again in 2007 for a concert honoring Atlantic Records' founder Ahmet Ertegun. Plant and Page recorded a largely acoustic album together, *No Quarter: Jimmy Page and Robert Plant Unledded* (1994). Both have enjoyed highly regarded solo careers. Page pursued the aesthetic of his former band on a series of albums that brought blues together with Middle Eastern influences. Plant was more eclectic, scoring a hit with a cover of the rhythm and blues standard "Sea of Love" (1985) with an act called the Honeydrippers, and recording an album with bluegrass singer Alison Krauss, *Raising Sand* (2007).

After they disbanded, Led Zeppelin attracted charges of plagiarism, many of them from rock critics with no sense of how music is created or disseminated. Page and Plant were sometimes careless about attribution, but, like Bob Dylan, operated as if they were folk musicians drawing from a common body of melodic and lyrical motifs. Just as Delta bluesman Robert Johnson borrowed from Son House and Chicago bluesman Willie Dixon borrowed from Johnson, Page and Plant borrowed from Dixon, albeit the Chicago artist had the savvy to copyright his songs, fencing off material that had been evolving in public domain and triggering a lawsuit. In most cases Led Zeppelin substantially reworked material they derived from older sources. Perhaps the most egregious example of actual plagiarism was "Boogie with Stu," which replicated Ritchie Valens's "Ooh My Head." A recent accusation concerns alleged links between Spirit's "Taurus" and "Stairway to Heaven." While the guitar lines are not unrelated, they are substantially different songs.

Led Zeppelin's legacy is incalculable. In their own time and in their aftermath, there has hardly been a hard rock or heavy metal band that did not derive something from them even if indirectly. If one wanted to draw an analogy between rock in the 1960s and the 1970s, it could be said that Led Zeppelin were the Rolling Stones of the latter decade in their pursuit of a hard-edged vision of rock while David Bowie was the Beatles in the breadth of his ambition and cultural influence. Led Zeppelin's aura of decadent mystery, including much exaggerated salacious accounts of their behavior on tour, helped establish the image of 1970s rock stars as demigods beyond the law and above the fray of everyday life. Led Zeppelin has been inducted into the Rock and Roll Hall of Fame.

Suggested Albums: Led Zeppelin (1969); *Led Zeppelin II* (1970); *Led Zeppelin III* (1970); *Led Zeppelin IV* (1971); *Houses of the Holy* (1973); *Physical Graffiti* (1975); *In Through the Out Door* (1979); *Coda* (1982)

LEFT BANKE

Rock and roll and classical music were antithetical, or so Chuck Berry asserted in "Roll Over Beethoven" (1956). But after the Beatles crossed the barrier with the sonorous string quartet of "Yesterday" (1965), a new generation of musicians saw no reason not to combine the contemporary verve of rock with the sophisticated musicality of the concert hall. Classical rock bands were more prevalent in the

United Kingdom than the United States, but the movement received a push from an American group, the Left Banke.

Despite classical leanings, recordings by the New York group were firmly rooted in the verities of the era's Top 40 pop. Their songs were short and told a story in less than four minutes. From their inception, bickering and lawsuits plagued the Left Banke. While many of their songs lacked distinction, the band's musical mastermind, pianist Michael Brown, was responsible for a pair of superb "baroque pop" hits. "Walk Away Renee" (1966) was sung in a voice of emotional exhaustion whose roiling was tempered by the steady beat; a string quartet deepened the sorrow and the tinkling harpsichord set the sad story of resignation in environs more elegant than was usual in Top 40 love songs. More remarkable was "Pretty Ballerina" (1966), a dreamy piano etude accompanied by strings. Here, the contented narrator delivers a surprise ending indicating that the ideal woman described in the song was a pleasant figment of his imagination.

The Left Banke's album *Walk Away Renee/Pretty Ballerina* (1967) contained both hits along with a mixed bag of material whose strongest songs also folded classical influences into compact pop-rock formats. The band broke up in 1969 after releasing a second album. Brown was later involved in several recording acts, including the Stories, and several short-term reunions have occurred in recent years. The Scottish alternative rock band Belle & Sebastian are indebted to the Left Banke.

Suggested Album: Walk Away Renee/Pretty Ballerina (1967)

LENNON, JOHN (1940–1980)

John Lennon, the most ambitious and artistically multifaceted Beatle, was also the band's most controversial member. Bored with being one of the world's biggest pop stars, he became determined to turn his stardom into a platform for promoting ideas about world peace and vague utopian visions. Lennon took greater chances than his fellow Beatles and sometimes fell far from the mark of his ability. However, he left behind a stronger body of work than any of his erstwhile bandmates.

Even before meeting Yoko Ono in 1966, Lennon was restless with the role he played in the Beatles and found other outlets including authoring books of comical stories and drawings. His relationship with Ono, who eventually became his second wife, helped trigger the growing separation between him and co-songwriter Paul McCartney. Ono brought entirely new ideas to Lennon. She was part of New York's Fluxus art scene, which followed the example of composer John Cage, honored the art of randomness, and valorized anything avant-garde.

Ono began to supplant McCartney as Lennon's creative partner. Lennon's first non-Beatles albums were a pair of electronic tape-loop experiments recorded with Ono in the Fluxus manner. *Unfinished Music No. 1: Two Virgins* (1968) and *Unfinished Music No. 2: Life with the Lions* (1969) attracted little notice save for the full frontal nudity of *Two Virgins'* front cover. Lennon and Ono then organized the Plastic Ono Band with guitarist Eric Clapton; drummer Alan White, later of Yes; and bassist Klaus Voorman, a friend of the Beatles from their Hamburg club days.

They famously performed with Ono singing inside a plastic bag at the Toronto Rock and Roll Revival, a one-day festival that brought together 1950s rock and roll acts with contemporary bands and proponents of the "rock and roll revival" that sought to return the music to an earlier era. The Plastic Ono performance, Lennon's first concert since the Beatles stopped touring in 1966, was released as *Live Peace in Toronto, 1969*. The Plastic Ono Band also recorded "Cold Turkey" (1969), an agonizing hard rock depiction of the effects of heroin addiction. A minor hit single, "Cold Turkey" did not appear on an LP until its inclusion on Lennon's greatest hits compilation, *Shaved Fish* (1975).

While conducting a clever media campaign against the Vietnam War around the slogan "War Is Over! If You Want It," Lennon and the Plastic Ono Band released a single with a shimmering reverberant production by Phil Spector. Like "Cold Turkey," "Instant Karma" (1970) was a hit that later appeared on *Shaved Fish*. Shortly after its release, the Beatles' break-up was announced amidst much rancor, especially between Lennon and McCartney. In the aftermath it became clear that the two songwriters had less in common than their fans supposed. Where McCartney was comfortable as an entertainer, Lennon saw himself as an adventurer. Lennon was a genius and McCartney a great talent. As their business empire unraveled into a morass of recriminations, the arguments became personal with McCartney hurling javelins at Ono. In the public mind, Ono was routinely blamed for the demise of the Beatles. The truth was more complicated and also involved the death of their manager Brian Epstein and conflicts over the direction of their Apple Records label as well as boredom and envy.

Lennon's next album, *John Lennon/Plastic Ono Band* (1970), was profoundly influenced by his sessions with American psychologist Arthur Janov, author of *The Primal Scream* (1970). In Janov's theory, neurosis could be cured by peeling away layers of defenses to reveal the true self. According to Lennon, Janov's primal therapy helped him confront childhood trauma, especially the loss of his parents. Primal therapy enabled him to feel his own fear and pain. He channeled those emotions into the album on soul-baring songs such as "Mother," "God," and "Working Class Hero." With "Love," a song that would be covered by Barbra Streisand and other artists, he proved himself equal to McCartney as a romantic balladeer. A stark recording despite Spector's involvement, the album was focused on Lennon's vocals and piano with accompaniment by Ono, Voorman, and fellow ex-Beatle Ringo Starr.

Janov's influence continued on *Imagine* (1971), whose dreamy, utopian title track remains the song most associated with Lennon. Co-produced by Spector, the album's instrumentation was more characteristically lush, buffering the themes of pain and suffering on "Jealous Guy" and "Crippled Inside" as well as the scathing anger of "Give Me Some Truth." Lennon vented his bitterness against McCartney in "How Do You Sleep?" George Harrison played guitar on some songs. Heard on *Imagine* was George Harrison on guitar along with legendary rhythm and blues saxophonist King Curtis and members of Badfinger.

With the release of *Imagine*, Lennon and Ono moved to New York's Greenwich Village, which still seethed with revolutionary sentiments. They were greeted as cultural heroes by New Left activists such as Jerry Rubin and Abbie Hoffman from Students for a Democratic Society (SDS). Comfortable in these environs, Lennon produced an album for leftist street band David Peel and the Lower East Side, best remembered for "Have a Marijuana." Lennon also released his worst album under the spell of neighborhood politics, recording the heavy-handed, slogan-ridden *Some Time in New York City* (1971) with a local hard rock band, the Elephant's Memory. During this time Lennon began to fight a court battle to obtain permanent residence in the United States, problematic because of his conviction in Britain for possession of marijuana and the Nixon administration's campaign to deport him as a political troublemaker. Lennon was finally granted a green card in 1975.

With *Mind Games* (1973), Lennon returned to the melodicism of *Imagine*. He produced the album's strongest number, the title track, in the Spector style. However, much of *Mind Games* suffered from spotty inspiration. His next effort was up to his highest standards. *Walls and Bridges* (1974) included the hit "#9 Dream," which continued along the melodically and lyrically dreamy path of "Imagine" and "Mind Games." Shifting the mood was the spirited hit "Whatever Gets You Through the Night," sung with Elton John. It proved to be the anthem for Lennon's alcohol-sodden 18-month separation from Ono. During this lengthy "lost weekend," he worked with Spector on *Rock'n'Roll* (1975), an album of old rock and roll songs. Recorded with Spector's trademark "wall of sound," the album included Lennon's renditions of Gene Vincent's "Be-Bop-a-Lula" and Chuck Berry's "Brown-Eyed Handsome Man" and "You Can't Catch Me." His version of Ben E. King's "Stand By Me" almost eclipses the original in its passionate plea. Faithful to the originals while putting his own stamp on them, Lennon's *Rock'n'Roll* helped renew interest in the best music of the 1950s, which had suffered from a wave of insipid nostalgia in the early 1970s.

Reunited with Ono, Lennon lived quietly for the next years in New York's famed Dakota, the Gothic apartment tower that served as the setting for Roman Polanski's film *Rosemary's Baby*. He popularized the term "house husband" as he cared for their child, the future recording artist Sean Lennon, while Ono attended to business. His absence from music was a source of unending fascination among writers and fans who wondered if he would ever record or tour again.

Double Fantasy (1980) was the welcome break from the silence. Among the most striking comeback albums ever recorded, *Double Fantasy* was the work of a sometimes irresponsible man who had matured. Unlike McCartney's musical musings on domesticity, Lennon's happiness had a hard-won edge on songs such as "(Just Like) Starting Over," "Watching the Wheels," and "Beautiful Boy (Darling Boy)." Tragedy cut short Lennon's return when, on December 8, 1980, he was killed outside the Dakota by a demented ex-fan.

On *Double Fantasy*, Ono displayed her growing command over the idioms of songwriting with "Kiss Kiss Kiss." She reflected on Lennon's death with *Season of Glass* (1981), her first album to receive attention outside avant-garde circles. Since then her quirky, chirping vocals have been acknowledged as an influence on new wave acts such as the B-52s and Lene Lovich, and the strength of her songwriting was credited by a tribute album, *Every Man Has a Woman* (1984), with contributions by artists as varied as Elvis Costello and Roberta Flack. She continued to record with growing success, scoring a number one dance club hit with "Everyman . . . Everywoman" (2004) and collaborating with contemporary alternative rock bands such as the Flaming Lips, Cat Power, and Porcupine Tree. Ono continued as the primary steward of Lennon's legacy, arranging the release of an album of unreleased tracks recorded in the months before his death, *Milk and Honey* (1984), and organizing exhibits of his visual artwork.

Suggested Albums: Live Peace in Toronto, 1969 (1969); *John Lennon/Plastic Ono Band* (1970); *Imagine* (1971); *Mind Games* (1973); *Walls and Bridges* (1974); *Rock'n'Roll* (1975); *Shaved Fish* (1975); *Double Fantasy* (1980); *Milk and Honey* (1984)

See also: Beatles

LES VARIATIONS

Formed by a trio of Moroccan-born French Sephardic Jews, Les Variations began in 1966 as a rock and roll cover band touring Europe. Singing primarily in English during their recording career and playing in an otherwise undistinguished hard rock format, their best tracks represented a unique convergence of rock with Moroccan-Arab-Berber influences.

Popular in France, Les Variations were signed by an American label in 1974 and appeared on their way to breaking into the U.S. market. They headlined television's *The Midnight Special* concert show and the syndicated FM rock program *King Biscuit Flower Hour* while touring the states. Although Les Variations broke up by the end of 1975 before capitalizing on their inroads, they set a sonic precedent for 21st-century "Oriental metal" bands such as Myrath, a Franco-Tunisian group balancing progressive power-metal with traditional orchestral music of North Africa.

Suggested Albums: Take It or Leave It (1971); *Moroccan Roll* (1974); *Café de Paris* (1975)

LITTLE FEAT

Like Captain Beefheart and Wild Man Fischer, the California-based Little Feat owe some of their career development to the eccentric vision of Frank Zappa. Guitarist Lowell George was finishing a brief stint with Zappa's Mother's of Invention (accounts differ whether George was fired from the band or urged by Zappa to pursue a solo career), while keyboardist Bill Payne had failed an audition with the band. After meeting, George and Payne decided to form Little Feat and Zappa helped the group secure a recording contract, leading to the release of their eponymous debut album (1971).

In some ways it's hard to reconcile that album's roots Americana sound with George's previous band, but George and Payne's songwriting and arrangements showed a quirky sensibility that likely would have appealed to Zappa. Strong musicianship pervades the album, and a muscular attack featuring George's raspy aggressive vocals add power to what could have been yet another down home–sounding rootsy record that became common in the wake of the Band, Creedence Clearwater Revival, and country rock. The album's best known song, "Willin,'" was a loose-feeling ballad featuring Ry Cooder's slide guitar and drug culture lyrics that would make it a favorite of 1970s stoners.

A shift in direction was in store for the band's follow-up album, *Sailin' Shoes* (1972). The bucolic feel of the debut was replaced by a tougher, funkier approach featuring louder guitars and drums, and a harder, slightly heavier feel. Boogie, New Orleans funk, and rhythm and blues influences moved to the front, making it a not inappropriate companion to the album the Rolling Stones released the same year, *Exile on Main St.* The more aggressive guitars pointed the way to the pub rock being born in England, and the driving "Teenage Nervous Breakdown" foreshadowed the rise of punk. *Sailin' Shoes* set the table for the band's next album, *Dixie Chicken* (1973), which saw the band fully realize their New Orleans influences. The pounding jazzy piano, infectious bass lines, and strutting rhythms created the feel of a rowdy night in the Big Easy, and the melodic swagger of the title track helped make it the band's signature song.

A certain predictability crept into the band's music following *Dixie Chicken* as they settled into a comfortable groove of rhythm and blues, funk, and early rock and roll, with bits of country tossed into the mix. The results were solid if unspectacular, providing reassuring listening for longtime fans but not the dynamic energy needed to attract a larger audience. The band ratcheted up the funk for several tracks from *Time Loves a Hero* (1977), but the move seemed forced and robbed the music of some of its more distinctive elements. The advent of punk and its back to basics approach might have invigorated the band, but Little Feat continued with the uninspired *Down on the Farm* (1979). The album would be their last with George, who died of a heart attack a few months prior to the album's release.

Little Feat broke up and would not re-form until the end of the next decade when Payne debuted a reconstituted band. *Let It Roll* (1988) was pleasant retelling of the classic Little Feat sound minus the trademark edge provided by George. The new lineup began touring and developed a good-time rock and boogie sound that resulted in a resurgence in popularity and was on display in a series of competent but not overly compelling albums. Health problems for various members have sidelined the band in recent years, although they did manage to release an album of new material, *Rooster Rag* (2012).

Suggested Albums: Little Feat (1971) ; *Sailin' Shoes* (1972); *Dixie Chicken* (1973); *Feats Don't Fail Me Now* (1974); *Let It Roll* (1988)

LOVE

It is said that Burt Bacharach was outraged when he heard what Love did with his "My Little Red Book." The sophisticated jazz-accented New York songwriter had yet to reconcile himself to the rock revolution that had broken out all over the world. Love's rendition of "My Little Red Book" preserved the melody while reinventing the song in a rock idiom with slashing guitars, a determined drum and tambourine beat, and a thumping bass line that qualifies as lead instrument.

Love was among the few racially integrated rock bands of the mid-1960s, splitting ethnicity down the middle with a black as well as a white frontman-songwriter, Arthur Lee and Bryan Maclean, respectively, plus a black lead guitarist, Johnny Echols, and a white rhythm section. Although the original lineup crackled with collaborative energy, Lee was always the predominant figure.

Lee grew up in the Los Angeles neighborhood of West Adams, a middle-class district where many of the businesses were black-owned. From his musician father he inherited an interest in jazz that was sometimes audible in Love; his mother, a schoolteacher, provided him with the stability and comfort of a room of his own. Lee attended Dorsey High School, one of Los Angeles's few integrated schools in those years. The Beach Boys' Mike Love was another alumnus. While admiring black music, Lee not only was entirely at home in predominantly white genres but mastered them.

As early as 1963 Lee released his first single with the LAGs, a surf instrumental group with a touch of Booker T. and the MGs. A year later he recorded with his own garage rock band, Lee's American Four, and became known around LA for penning songs for other groups. Later in 1964 the original lineup of Love came together as the Grass Roots, the name chosen by Lee from Malcolm X's reference to "grass roots people" bettering themselves. They were forced to become Love when prominent songwriter P.J. Sloan released a single under the Grass Roots name.

Living together in the Laurel Canyon house once owned by Bela Lugosi, Love worked out a fusion of folk-rock and the British Invasion, rehearsing songs by the Byrds and the Kinks and developing their own repertoire. Theirs was a distinctly Anglophile folk-rock from the tougher than usual rhythmic push of their music to their appearance. Maclean looked the part of the Rolling Stones' Brian Jones from his haircut to his choice of sport coats.

"My Little Red Book" was included on Love's eponymous debut (1966) but did not overshadow the original songs. "Can't Explain" was folk-rock in all its jangling glory, topped by Lee's pleading vocal. "My Flash on You" was folk-rock with punk rock swagger. Their version of the 1960s rock standard "Hey Joe" captured the emotional frenzy of homicide in ways competing versions never did. Love was also capable of unschmaltzy sensitivity on the jazz-inflected "Softly to Me" and dreamy psychedelic harmonies on "You'll be Following." The dire ballad "Signed DC" was a warning against the slavery of heroin addiction whose narrator was resigned to die alone and uncared for.

Da Capo (1967) was a superb follow-up. The album's Top 40 single, "Seven and Seven Is," was a furious hard rock psychedelic rave-up that would translate well as a punk rock staple a decade later. "Stephanie Knows Who," baroque rock with punk intensity rather than fey reserve, broke into a wild jazz instrumental midway through. "She Comes in Colors" was moody psychedelia with a tough rock edge.

Love shifted direction with *Forever Changes* (1967), an orchestral song cycle with acoustic guitar at its core. Maclean's "Alone Again Or," a pledge of monogamy

214   LOVE SCULPTURE

amidst an acknowledgment of free love, is the standout. As a devotee of Miles Davis's *Sketches of Spain*, Lee must have inspired the Latin arrangement complete with horns and a string section.

Afterward, a bevy of personal problems fractured Love's original lineup. In 1968 Lee fired everyone and continued Love with a new lineup responsible for two albums, *Four Sail* (1969) and *Out Here* (1969). The lack of collaborative energy dampened the recordings, which disappointed most fans and sold few copies. A final album with the second version of Love, *False Start* (1970), included one track recorded with Jimi Hendrix. Lee called Love quits. What followed was a broken string of solo albums and abortive attempts to use the Love name.

Lee spent 1995 through 2001 in prison for weapons offenses. Then, billed as Love with Arthur Lee, he toured with Echols playing their old songs, including *Forever Changes* in its entirety. After Lee's death in 2006 from leukemia, Echols continued to work the nostalgia circuit as Love Revisited.

Love's first three albums were discovered by a new generation of fans after 1980 and became touchstones of musical integrity and innovation. Those recordings were especially beloved by punk and neo-psychedelic bands such as the Damned and the Jesus and Mary Chain. The Love tribute album *We're Not Normal and We Want Our Freedom* (1994) included contributions by Teenage Fan Club, the Television Personalities, and other alternative bands.

Suggested Albums: Love (1966); *Da Capo* (1967); *Forever Changes* (1967)

LOVE SCULPTURE

The Welsh trio Love Sculpture began as a beat group called the Image featuring guitarist Dave Edmunds. Renamed the Human Beans in 1967, they released a psychedelic single that received airplay on the North Sea pirate station Radio London but sold few copies. Rechristened as Love Sculpture in 1968, they were encouraged by their record label to become a blues-rock power trio. Edmunds later claimed he knew little about the blues but was enthusiastic about the chance to make an album. *Blues Helping* (1968) was largely composed of blues covers but featured fine guitar work by Edmunds, who scrambled to copy Eric Clapton's licks from Bluesbreakers and Cream albums.

Incongruously, Love Sculpture achieved notice on the concert circuit and BBC radio for a version of Aram Khatchaturian's "Sabre Dance," which was released as a single. The supercharged interpretation of the Armenian composer's already frenetic piece appeared on Love Sculpture's follow-up, *Forms and Feelings* (1970). Their bluesy and psychedelic second album featured more original songs and was a showcase for Edmunds's pyrotechnic metallic yet sometimes classically steeped guitar playing, which anticipated Yngwie Malmsteen by more than a decade.

Although they toured the United States, played San Francisco's famed Fillmore West ballroom, and scored a Top 5 British hit with "Sabre Dance," Edmunds tired of Love Sculpture and was eager to move on. Steeping himself in the reverberant production values of rockabilly recordings from the 1950s, Edmunds had a hit with his cover of New Orleans rhythm and blues singer Smiley Lewis's "I Hear You Knocking" (1970). He became a mentor to the pub rock movement, producing albums by Ducks Deluxe and Brinsley Schwarz, and a role model for the roots-oriented wing of punk rock with his band Rockpile. During the 1980s he produced recordings for the Stray Cats and the Fabulous Thunderbirds. Edmunds toured with Ringo Starr and His All Star Band in 1992 and 2000. He has been semiretired in recent years but performs occasionally.

Suggested Album: Forms and Feelings (1970)

LOVIN' SPOONFUL

The folk-rock revolution of the mid-1960s is most often associated in California with the Byrds, the Mamas & the Papas, and the Beau Brummels emerging from the Golden State to bring the genre's joyful jangle and socially conscious lyrics to the top of the charts. However, New York's Lovin' Spoonful showed that folk-rock was not the sole domain of the West Coast. They brought a unique take on the form and enjoyed a brief but successful career before going their separate ways by the decade's end.

The Lovin' Spoonful was founded by John Sebastian, a Greenwich Village native and son of a professional musician. Sebastian grew up surrounded by folk music and joined with local folk guitarist Zal Yanovsky to form the Spoonful (Yanovsky's previous band included future Mamas & Papas members Cass Elliott and Denny Doherty). The band initially lacked skill, but became sufficiently proficient to land a recording contract in 1965. Success was quick in coming. The Lovin' Spoonful hit the Top 10 with their first single, the vibrant "Do You Believe in Magic" (also the title of their 1965 debut album). The song's carefree celebration of the liberating power of music caught the spirit of an era when it seemed that rock could change the world.

The Spoonful's next single, the catchy "Did You Ever Have to Make Up Your Mind," also distinguished them as a unique entry in folk-rock circles. The songs established their cheerful, upbeat outlook, setting them apart from their more introspective and serious contemporaries. Their New York upbringing led them to lean on the blues and rock a bit harder at times than their West Coast rivals, and Sebastian's frequent use of the autoharp gave them an individual sound and stage presence. A carefree, wistful quality pervaded their music, exemplified on singles such as 1966's "Daydream" and "You Didn't Have to Be So Nice."

The 1966 smash "Summer in the City" provided an edgier, more rocking contrast, as the song's minor chording and searing rhythm brought both the romance and danger of a long, hot, and potentially riotous summer to life. The band's three albums were strong, but the Lovin' Spoonful are best remembered for their singles, most of which were Sebastian originals.

The Spoonful spent the latter part of the 1960s trying their hands at soundtracks for Woody Allen's debut, *What's Up, Tiger Lily?* (1966) and Francis Ford Coppola's *You're a Big Boy Now* (1967), and dealing with multiple lineup changes.

Sebastian left the band in 1968 to begin a moderately successful solo career, while the remaining members released their final album, the undistinguished *Revelation: Revolution '69* (1969). The Lovin' Spoonful was inducted into the Rock and Roll Hall of Fame.

Suggested Albums: Do You Believe in Magic (1965); *Daydream* (1966); *Hums of the Lovin' Spoonful* (1966); *You're a Big Boy Now* (1967); *Everything Playing* (1967)

LYNYRD SKYNYRD

Lynyrd Skynyrd was not the first prominent Southern rock band, but they are likely the most important. While the Allman Brothers predated their arrival and were on the vanguard of the Southern rock movement of the early 1970s, Lynyrd Skynyrd best embodied the genre, defining its sound, look, and attitude. Bound inextricably with the rise of the New South in the 1970s, the "Skynyrd boys" defined the early stages of the postsegregationist American South and furthered the region's cultural reunification with the rest of the nation. The tragic plane crash that claimed the life of several key members moved the group to legendary status to such an extent that if you asked the average rock listener to name a Southern rock band, "Lynyrd Skynyrd" would be the most likely response.

The original members formed the group while attending Robert E. Lee High School in Jacksonville, Florida, and took their name from Leonard Skinner, a physical education teacher who kicked back in resistance against the trend of boys growing long hair (in keeping with the changes in the region, Skinner himself would later become a fan of the band). In a clever move, the band changed the spelling of the name, leading to many comical mispronunciations throughout the course of their career. The strong voice of lead singer Ronnie Van Zant and the guitar playing of Gary Rossington helped them establish a local following, and their discovery by veteran musician Al Kooper (then with Blood, Sweat & Tears) led to a recording contract with MCA Records.

Kooper produced their debut album *(Pronounced Leh-nerd Skin-nerd)* (1973), which displayed a young band that both typified and deviated from the expanding corps of Southern rockers landing recording contracts. Their mix of blues and country was by no means unusual, but they were capable of a heavier sound thanks to a dual guitar attack that was more aligned with British hard rock. Songs such as the humorous "Gimme Three Steps" and "I Ain't the One" evoke Saturday night in a roadhouse saloon, the more gentle "Tuesday's Gone" and the defiantly proud "Simple Man" hinted at greater depth. The album's centerpiece was "Freebird," a wistful ballad that concluded with a lengthy dual guitar solo that had more in common with Led Zeppelin than Muscle Shoals and would become an FM radio mainstay. The overall impression was of a band that could provide good-time rock and roll, while also offering intelligent lyrics and a perspective that belied Southern redneck stereotypes.

The band's follow-up album, *Second Helping* (1974), was one of the pivotal works of Southern rock and one of the most important albums of the early 1970s.

Improved songwriting certainly played a part in its success, as Van Zant developed a lyrical outlook not unlike that of country singers such as Merle Haggard and Johnny Cash who championed the often forgotten (and sometimes scorned) common man. Van Zant became a working-class hero through songs like "Don't Ask Me No Questions" that celebrated the ornery defiance of the Southern male, but he also sang a tender tale of a poor elderly black man in "The Ballad of Curtis Lowe." A cover of J. J. Cale's "They Call Me the Breeze" and the record industry dig "Workin' for MCA" were also radio hits, but it was the album's first single, "Sweet Home Alabama," that forever etched Lynyrd Skynyrd in the American consciousness.

"Sweet Home Alabama" was nothing less than a cultural milestone. Driven by an irresistible three-chord melody and a chugging beat evocative of Hank Williams or Sun Sessions Elvis Presley, "Sweet Home Alabama" proudly raised the Confederate banner, thumbing its nose at Yankee sensibilities by singing unabashed praises to Dixie culture, giving a seeming thumbs-up to Alabama's notorious segregationist governor George Wallace, and putting that same thumb in Neil Young's eye for "Southern Man" (Young later agreed that his song was an unfair portrayal of the region). "Sweet Home Alabama" became a huge hit, but not without controversy, as its evocation of a then dishonored culture was seen as a call to a second Southern uprising in counterrevolution to the hard-earned gains of the civil rights movement. The band was having none of it, pointing out that a chorus of boos follows the mention of Wallace, and that the song was intended to be ambiguous.

Steeped in their Southern heritage but appealing to hard rock audiences across the U.S., Lynyrd Skynyrd contributed the oft-played "Freebird" to the repertoire of FM classic rock radio. Vocalist Ronnie Van Zant and three other members died in a 1977 plane crash. (Pictorial Press Ltd/Alamy Stock Photo)

218   LYNYRD SKYNYRD

Some critics defended the band, pointing to songs such as "The Ballad of Curtis Lowe" and antiracist statements by Van Zant as exonerating evidence. However, the band itself complicated matters by displaying a Confederate flag on the single's sleeve, and fans regularly waved the flag and donned Confederate regalia at their concerts. The success of the song and Skynyrd's image led to the eventual national furor over the role of the Confederate flag in American culture, which critics saw as a legacy of slavery, racism, and secession. Supporters claimed it represented nothing more than regional pride divorced from a reprehensible past and was now the banner of a more enlightened generation.

Regardless of controversy, Lynyrd Skynyrd marched on to greater success, adopting an even more British hard rock sound along the lines of the Rolling Stones and Humble Pie. Subsequent albums *Nuthin' Fancy* (1975) and *Gimme Back My Bullets* (1976) rocked with more overdriven guitar riffs and heavier rhythms, while the lyrics became less nuanced and evocative. What had been a pleasing combination of sounds now gave way to simple good old rock and roll, although often with equally pleasing results.

The group's image of the long-haired, bearded, denim-wearing rockers established the Southern rock look, while songs like the anti-handgun anthem "Saturday Night Special' played against that stereotype. Each album brought in more fans, and it seemed that Lynyrd Skynyrd had the potential to become an American version of the Rolling Stones. The band released its most polished album yet, *Street Survivors* (1977), but days later tragedy struck when an airplane carrying the band ran out of fuel and crashed in a Mississippi forest. Van Zant and three other band members were killed (along with both pilots and one of the group's managers), while the rest of the band miraculously survived. The accident was eerily reminiscent of the 1959 crash that killed Buddy Holly, Ritchie Valens, and the Big Bopper, and sent shock waves throughout the music world.

The surviving members would not perform as a band for 10 years, although they eventually re-formed, first with a female vocalist and eventually with Van Zant's younger brother Johnny as lead singer. The regrouped band has toured and recorded ever since and has released several albums that continue the group's sound, but lack the unique perspective of Ronnie Van Zant's songwriting.

Lynyrd Skynyrd's influence remains strong to this day, as virtually every Southern rock act pays some homage to their legacy. In one of the most notable examples, Southern rockers Drive By Truckers used the Skynyrd story to weave a tapestry of regional culture in their album *Southern Rock Opera* (2002). *Sweet Home Alabama* was the title of a hit movie starring Reese Witherspoon (2002), and the song has provided bumper music to scores of stock car auto races. The band's greatest influence is probably on modern country music, which often sounds more like a slightly twangier version of the Southern rock defined by the band. Lynyrd Skynyrd was inducted into the Rock and Roll Hall of Fame.

Suggested Albums: (Pronounced Leh-nerd Skin-nerd) (1973); *Second Helping* (1974); *Nuthin' Fancy* (1975); *Gimme Back My Bullets* (1976); *Street Survivors* (1977); *God & Guns* (2009)

MAGMA

Progressive rock was meant to give wide scope for ambition, but it's safe to say that no progressive rock artist was as ambitious as Christian Vander, guiding light of the French band Magma. Vander sings in a language he devised, Kobaian, drawn from Slavic and Germanic sources. In the future sagas that unfold across Magma's albums, Kobaian is the tongue of refugees from Earth who colonized a planet called Kobaia.

The epics of J. R. R. Tolkien may have inspired Vander's linguistic interests. Embraced across Europe and North America by the 1960s counterculture, *The Hobbit* and *Lord of the Rings* were populated by speakers of invented languages. Vander, a classically trained drummer, founded Magma in 1969. Their music covered considerable range. Near folk-rock balladry could explode into dynamics reminiscent of King Crimson. An echo of Debussy's impressionism was heard, along with the mechanical Weimar rhythms of Kurt Weill, the savage chorales of Carl Orff, and the high-wire anxiety of post–World War II modernism. On other occasions Magma became an excellent jazz-rock fusion band with an accent on a rock beat and an emphasis on improvisatory solos inspired by John Coltrane from the period of *A Love Supreme*.

After their initial period of innovation in the 1970s, Magma fell relatively quiet for several years. In the 1990s neo-progressive rock bands such as Porcupine Tree and Spock's Beard sparked interest in their venturesome forebears, and the development of a circuit of progressive rock festivals and the effect of the World Wide Web gained them new ears. Magma is credited with becoming a genre unto itself under the name "Zeuhl," a word from the Kobaian language. Zeuhl has been used to describe solo albums by Christian Vander, his wife Stella Vander, the Japanese duo Ruins, the Belgian chamber rock band Univers Zero, and others.

Suggested Albums: Magma (aka *Kobaia*) (1970); *1001 Degrees Centigrades* (1971); *Mekanik Destruktiw Kommandoh* (1973); *Wurdah Itah* (1974); *Kohntarkosz* (1974); *Udu Wudu* (1976); *Attahk* (1978)

MAHAVISHNU ORCHESTRA

Jazz-fusion was on the rise in the early 1970s, drawing sufficient notice to prompt some critics to label it the "next big thing" that would alter the course of rock music in the coming decade. Of all the artists fusing jazz and rock, few gained as much

220   MAHAVISHNU ORCHESTRA

fame and respect as the Mahavishnu Orchestra, the progeny of guitar virtuoso John McLaughlin. And while jazz-fusion never reached the heights hoped for by its enthusiasts, Mahavishnu Orchestra established a legacy—particularly through McLaughlin's guitar work—that inspired jazz-influenced rock for decades to come.

McLaughlin had already compiled an impressive resume by the time he formed the band in 1971. An early devotee of jazz, McLaughlin played multiple instruments as a child before focusing on guitar. His skill landed him gigs with rhythm and blues and jazz–influenced acts such as Graham Bond, Georgie Fame, and Brian Auger, and he jammed with the likes of Jimi Hendrix. He also developed a career as a sideman, and he received his biggest break in 1970 when the legendary jazzman Miles Davis tapped him to play on his groundbreaking fusion album, *Bitches Brew*. Davis suggested that McLaughlin form a band, and McLaughlin turned to another Davis sideman, drummer Billy Cobham, to help him form Mahavishnu Orchestra. Their debut album, *The Inner Mounting Flame* (1971), shows Davis's jazz-fusion influence, but also draws on funk and Hendrix-style hard rock to create a much harder blend of musical styles.

McLaughlin's inspired guitar work drives the band much the same way that wind instrumentalists such as Davis, Charlie Parker, and John Coltrane did in jazz orchestras. His playing had the free-form experimentalism of jazz, but included fuzz-distorted rave-ups and incorporated a rich variety of tones that pushed the boundaries of the instrument. Violinist Jerry Goodman and keyboardist Jan Hammer were also integral to the album's eclectic experimentalism.

The Orchestra scaled even greater heights with its next album, *Birds of Fire* (1973), an advance in sonic and musical possibilities that ranks as perhaps the finest jazz-fusion album of the era. McLaughlin's mind-bending guitar work on the title cut takes the listener to places only a Coltrane could go, and "Celestial Terrestrial Commuters" hints at the direction Hendrix could have easily taken had he lived. Cobham's musical drumming sets the pace, providing a thrilling backdrop for McLaughlin's guitar genius and Hammer's textured playing. The follow-up live album *Between Nothingness & Eternity* (1973) is entirely composed of original lengthy conceptual pieces. Violinist Jean-Luc Ponty came on board a revamped Orchestra for *Apocalypse* (1974), and McLaughlin has expressed great fondness for the new incarnation. The material now seemed less groundbreaking and at times was a tad overly dramatic, but the album was still strong musically and helped refine the jazz-fusion landscape.

The unfocused *Visions of the Emerald Beyond* (1975) was a step backward, but the band rebounded with the more soulful *Inner Worlds* (1976). Tensions between McLaughlin and Ponty pushed the band toward dissolution. *Inner Worlds* would be the Orchestra's last album until a re-formed version of the band released the solid if uninspired *Mahavishnu* (1984). They would tour off and on for years, although McLaughlin's main focus seems to be on his solo career.

Mahavishnu Orchestra, and McLaughlin in particular, never sold vast quantities of records, but they achieved a lasting legacy thanks to the scores of artists inspired by their creative mix of jazz, rock, funk, rhythm and blues, and soul. Eric Johnson, Al Di Meola, Shawn Lane, and Steve Morse either credit McLaughlin as an influence or have expressed admiration for his work. Hammer and Cobham have also had long and successful careers working with a plethora of artists. Hammer is perhaps best known in the United States for having composed the fusion-based theme for the 1980s hit television drama *Miami Vice*, finally bringing a touch of his band's jazz-fusion influences to the masses.

Suggested Albums: The Inner Mounting Flame (1971); *Birds of Fire* (1973); *Between Nothingness & Eternity* (1973); *Apocalypse* (1974); *Inner Worlds* (1976)

MAHOGANY RUSH

The Canadian hard rock band Mahogany Rush is probably best known for the Jimi Hendrix–influenced guitar style of its eccentric leader, Frank Marino. Marino got his start in the late 1960s when in keeping with the times he tuned in by getting into rock guitar (after starting out on drums), was turned on to LSD, and dropped out of school in the seventh grade. Fully immersed in hippie culture, Marino formed Mahogany Rush, and within a few years acquired a record deal and released the band's debut album, *Maxoom* (1972).

As *Maxoom* aptly demonstrates, Mahogany Rush was built almost exclusively on Marino's vision dominated by the spirit of Hendrix, the guitar genius who had died only a couple years before. Marino's acid-drenched blues guitar licks were straight from the Hendrix songbook, and he took emulation one step further by skillfully adopting Hendrix's unique vocal style. Marino and the band played well, but were scorned by some as mere imitators. Those who felt Mahogany Rush lacked originality could double down on the criticism with the band's next album, *Child of the Novelty* (1974), an even more Hendrix-inspired collection that sounded as if it could have included outtakes from *Are You Experienced*. Those longing for Hendrix would find a suitable substitute in Marino, and Mahogany Rush developed a relatively small but devoted following.

The band's best album was their third, *Strange Universe* (1975), in which Marino incorporated his Hendrix influences into a more original form and included some longer progressive rock passages that gave the record a more distinct identity. The popularity of guitar heroes helped Marino and the band gain some attention, and they often appeared at large rock festivals. The band had passed its peak by the early 1980s, although they continue to tour with Marino as the sole original member.

Suggested Album: Strange Universe (1975)

MAMAS AND THE PAPAS

John Phillips, the mastermind and songwriter behind the Mamas and the Papas, honed his skills in high school singing doo-wop. By the early 1960s he was active in the music industry, cutting a lush ballad that landed him on *American Bandstand* (1960). A year later he joined the Journeymen, playing Greenwich Village dates on the same bill as Bob Dylan. Phillips married a much younger model,

Michelle Gilliam, who became one of the voices of the Mamas and the Papas. Phillips completed the group by recruiting Cass Elliot and Dennis Doherty from the Mugwumps, a folk-barely-rock group with pronounced pop proclivities. By 1965 the foursome was in Los Angeles as the Mamas and the Papas.

They had no difficulty crossing over from the folk-rock scene to mainstream popularity. The Mamas and the Papas were a visually appealing set of opposites: the daunting beauty of Gilliam Phillips paired with the friendly and obese Elliot; the bohemian Phillips with the rock star–looking Doherty. They were contemporary yet many of their songs evoked the era of parlor pianos and Tin Pan Alley. Each voice was distinct and arranged by Phillips with the cut-crystal precision of a mini Mormon Tabernacle Choir. Their first hit, "California Dreaming," was folk-rock perfectly realized as a pop single, its melancholy harmonies coupled with an ultimately hopeful lyric expressing the 1960s fantasy of the Golden State as a land of endless summer and opportunities.

The Mamas and the Papas followed with a string of Top 10 hits, including the happy-sad "Monday, Monday," the old-time pop of "Words of Love," the earnest purity of "Dedicated to the One I Love," the exuberant "I Saw Her Again," and the self-referential "Creeque Alley." Their albums *If You Can Believe Your Eyes and Ears* (1966), *The Mamas and the Papas* (1967) and *The Mamas & the Papas Deliver* (1967) were bestsellers. Comfortable performing at the countercultural Monterey Pop Festival (1967), the foursome were welcome guests on network television. They were Hollywood celebrities, running with the Jack Nicholson, Dennis Hopper crowd. All doors were open.

It ended quickly. By 1968 the Phillipses' marriage had fractured, the foursome's latest singles weren't rising in the charts, and solo opportunities beckoned. Elliot had a hit with the 1930s pop tune "Dream a Little Dream of Me" (albeit the single was billed as by Mama Cass with the Mamas and the Papas, to Phillips's dismay). Early efforts at reunions fumbled badly. Doherty released a few records before returning to Canada, where he became a successful thespian and television host. Gilliam Phillips enjoyed a successful movie career, co-starring with Rudolf Nureyev in director Ken Russell's biographical picture *Valentino* (1976). Elliot continued to perform until her death in 1974.

Afflicted with drug and alcohol problems, Phillips had difficulty finding his creative footing. By the early 1980s he launched the New Mamas and the Papas with his ex-wife and Doherty plus Elaine McFarlane of the 1960s pop act Spanky and Our Gang standing in for Elliot. They were not well received and membership fluctuated. Phillips died in 2001 and Doherty followed in 2007.

Suggested Albums: If You Can Believe Your Eyes and Ears (1966); *The Mamas and the Papas* (1967); *The Mamas & the Papas Deliver* (1967)

MAN

In 1968 the Welsh cover band the Bystanders transformed themselves into an original music group called Man. *Revelation* (1969) and *2 Ozs. of Plastic with a Hole in the Middle* (1969) were pretentious pop psychedelia whose best tracks were reminiscent of the Jefferson Airplane. By the time of *Do You Like It Here, Are You Settling In* (1971), they became known as a jam band and were compared with the Grateful Dead for playing for hours on end. Fans consider *Be Good to Yourself at Least Once a Day* (1972) and *Christmas at the Patti: Live at the Padget Rooms, Penarth* (1973) as documents of Man at its peak. Their affinities with West Coast psychedelic jamming brought them to the attention of Quicksilver Messenger Service's guitarist John Cippolina, who produced *Maximum Darkness* (1975).

Man broke up after the disappointing *Welsh Connection* (1976) and *All's Well That Ends Well* (1977), albeit various members began playing under the Man name beginning in 1983. Drummer Terry Williams joined Dave Edmunds's band Rockpile and later became a member of Dire Straits.

Suggested Albums: Be Good to Yourself at Least Once a Day (1972); *Christmas at the Patti: Live at the Padget Rooms, Penarth* (1973)

MANN, MANFRED (1940–)

Manfred Mann emerged during the British Invasion, scoring hit singles with an upbeat organ-based sound and romantic spirit. The South African–born keyboard player had already made a name for himself in London blues clubs, playing in a band that for a time included scene fixture Graham Bond. Bond moved on, but Mann picked up a soulful singer named Paul Jones and named his new band after himself.

The band Manfred Mann caught a quick break in 1964, as they were commissioned to compose the theme song "5-4-3-2-1" for the British pop music show *Ready Steady Go*. The band was now being heard by British teens on a weekly basis, and the song hit the Top 10. The momentum continued with a run of exuberant hit singles, "Do Wah Diddy Diddy," "Sha La La," and "Come Tomorrow." Mann's organ rippled with high-end optimism and Jones sang with joyous abandon on songs that celebrated the joys of being young, in love, and surrounded by fantastic music. The band's best single was the ebullient "Pretty Flamingo" (1966), a sunny hit that exuded the joy of simply being in the presence of an unattainable woman. The band had a notable fan in a New Jersey teen named Bruce Springsteen, who would cover "Pretty Flamingo" and modeled his early vocal style partly on Jones. Albums such as *The Five Faces of Manfred Mann* (1964) and *Mann Made* (1965) were more varied than indicated by the singles and included uncompromising blues, rowdy rhythm and blues, and jazz.

Jones left the group in 1966, and his successor, Mike d'Abo, ushered in a new era for the band, as their focus began to switch from singles to albums. The arrangements became more elaborate, and the subject matter on *As Is* (1966) dealt with weightier, more socially conscious topics. *Soul of Mann* (1967) was an instrumental album comprised of current hits like the Rolling Stones' "(I Can't Get No) Satisfaction" and the Who's "My Generation" as well as traditional songs like "God Rest Ye Merry Gentlemen." *Mighty Garvey* (1968) was an exercise in psychedelic pop that yielded a hit with a charmingly goofy hit single, a cover of Bob Dylan's "Mighty Quinn."

The band rebranded as Manfred Mann Chapter Three following d'Abo's departure in 1969, exploring intriguingly written jazz-rock with free jazz soloing on *Manfred Mann Chapter Three* (1970) and *Manfred Mann Chapter Three Volume Two* (1970). The band adopted yet another name in 1972, calling themselves Manfred Mann's Earth Band and releasing an eponymous album that same year. This incarnation leaned toward progressive rock mixed with boogie and funky rhythm and blues. Mann profitably turned to Bruce Springsteen for some of his biggest later career hits, gaining airplay and sometimes chart success in the 1970s with covers of Springsteen's "Spirit in the Night," "Blinded by the Light," and "For You." The band broke up in 1987, but resumed recording, releasing their most recent album, *Manfred Mann 06,* in 2006.

Suggested Albums: Mann Made (1965); *Pretty Flamingo* (1966); *As Is* (1966); *Soul of Mann* (1967); *Mighty Garvey* (1968); *Manfred Mann Chapter Three* (1970); *Manfred Mann Chapter Three Volume Two* (1970)

MANZAREK, RAY (1939–2013)

Despite his gifts as a keyboardist and his role in shaping the sound of the Doors, Ray Manzarek never achieved great success in his post-Doors career. He issued a pair of albums, an aural essay in Egyptology called *The Golden Scarab* (1974) followed by the back to basics *The Whole Thing Started with Rock & Roll Now It's Out of Control* (1974), before launching a band, Nite City (the name alludes to a line from the Doors' "L.A. Woman"), which released a pair of albums (1977, 1978) to little attention. Manzarek continued to promote the idea that Morrison's death might have been staged. He spent much of the last years of his life before cancer in nostalgic tours focused on the Doors' music.

Manzarek's best post-Doors album involved music he did not write. In an unusual collaboration with minimalist composer Philip Glass, Manzarek recorded *Carmina Burana* (1983), a rock rendition of Carl Orff's cantata. For all his shortcomings as a songwriter, Manzarek can be credited with possessing an open mind toward music. He chose the then-unknown Patti Smith to recite a fragment of Morrison's poetry on "I Wake Up Screaming" from *The Whole Thing Started with Rock & Roll.* He also produced the first albums by punk rockabilly pioneers X, *Los Angeles* (1980) and *Wild Gift* (1981). X covered a Doors song, "Soul Kitchen," on their debut.

Suggested Album: Carmina Burana (1983)

MARK-ALMOND

Formed in 1970, Mark-Almond's titular members were a pair of veteran British session musicians, guitarist Jon Mark and saxophonist-flautist Johnny Almond. Notably, Mark had accompanied Marianne Faithfull on her early recordings and Almond played with the Alan Price Set. As Mark-Almond, they released a pair of albums in the jazz-rock field (1971, 1972) that had little recognition in the United States. After receiving steady American FM airplay for the melancholic "What Am

I Living For" from *Mark-Almond '73* (1973), they broke up. Mark moved to New Zealand and eventually became successful in ambient music. Almond played saxophone in San Francisco before his death from cancer in 2009.

Suggested Albums: Mark-Almond (1971); *Mark-Almond II* (1972); *Mark-Almond '73* (1973)

MARSHALL TUCKER BAND

The Marshall Tucker Band would likely be one of the first acts named when compiling a list of early 1970s Southern rock bands, despite the fact that they were scarcely the first to release an album and their success never placed them among the most popular artists of the day. Their prominence is due more to the fact that there were qualities about the band that seemed so distinctly Southern that they epitomized the movement more than many of their contemporaries did. They garnered a fairly consistent level of FM airplay and solid album sales.

The Marshall Tucker Band did not have a member named Marshall Tucker, but rather took their name from a local Spartanburg, South Carolina piano tuner. The original members had previously formed a band and reconnected after four of them served during the Vietnam War. They earned a reputation as a strong live act and released their eponymous debut album (1973) to generally good reviews and respectable sales. What immediately set the band apart was their willingness to sound identifiably "Southern." While Gregg Allman's bluesy vocals owed as much to Chicago as the Mississippi Delta, and Lynyrd Skynyrd interpreted blues and roots rock through the eyes of the Rolling Stones as much as Muddy Waters or Chuck Berry, the Marshall Tucker Band always played and sang with a cheerful twang and drawl that sounded comfortably and authentically down-home. Frequent use of the flute gave their music a distinctive flair and made their songs easily identifiable. Their best-known songs, "Can't You See," "This Old Cowboy," and "Fire on the Mountain," bore the imprint of country, but also added elements of blues and even jazz.

Lacking a charismatic frontman or superstar guitar hero, the band had a bit of a faceless quality that limited their commercial appeal. However, they did manage to score a hit single in 1977 with the pleasantly country-styled "Heard It in a Love Song," but that would prove to be their last significant commercial success. Later years saw the band follow the familiar pattern of constant recording and touring through numerous lineup changes. The Marshall Tucker Band continues to record and tour as of this writing.

Suggested Albums: The Marshall Tucker Band (1973); *Where We All Belong* (1974); *Searchin' for a Rainbow* (1975); *Carolina Dreams* (1977)

MARTYN, JOHN (1948–2009)

Singer and guitarist John Martyn achieved a degree of prominence in the 1970s as he developed an eclectic take on traditional British folk music that earned him the respect of a number of musicians and critics. His beginnings were not quite so auspicious, as his early albums contained the sort of acoustic British music that comedian Eric Idle might have parodied on *Monty Python's Flying Circus*. The fleet guitar playing was strong, but the songs created the impression that Martyn yearned for some long-lost country garden scene where fair-haired maidens roamed and a visit from an elf or fairy was not out of the question. The occasional foray into the blues provided some respite and hinted at greater potential.

That potential began to be realized on his third album, *Stormbringer!* (1970), in which Martyn enlisted the help of the Band's Levon Helm and began to add a heavier dose of blues and rock into the acoustic mix. Martyn was the rare folk artist who experimented with guitar tone, adding fuzz and echoplex effects to create texture and add power to his sound. *Bless the Weather* (1971) saw Martyn begin to add jazz elements to his music, using more complex chords to create a dreamy and reflective mood for one of the most expressive and inventive albums of the British folk revival. Probably his best album was the follow-up, *Solid Air* (1973), which continued the jazz influences, but in a more emotional context and energized with some harder rocking blues and effects-laden songs. Gone were the stereotypical English folk touches that hampered his earlier work. Martyn had emerged as an artist with a distinct musical vision.

The success of *Solid Air* gave Martyn a following. He achieved another artistic triumph with the heavily reverberated jazz and reggae–influenced album *One World* (1977).

By the 1980s marital problems and alcohol abuse began to affect Martyn's music, although it did provide inspiration for the starkly emotional album *Grace and Danger* (1980). An unsuccessful stab at rock with *Sapphire* (1984) showed an artist increasingly beginning to lose focus. Martyn eventually came out of his funk, and despite health problems continued to record and perform live until his death in 2009, at times dabbling in the hip electronic genre known as trip-hop. While never a commercial force, Martyn was a respected artist who collaborated with Helm, David Gilmour, Eric Clapton, Paul Weller, and most notably his good friend Phil Collins.

Suggested Albums: Stormbringer! (1970); *The Road to Ruin* (1970); *Bless the Weather* (1971); *Solid Air* (1973); *One World* (1977); *Grace and Danger* (1980); *Glorious Fool* (1981); *On the Cobbles* (2004)

MASON, DAVE (1946–)

British guitarist Dave Mason should be best known as a co-founder of Traffic, but left the band prior to the release of their debut album. As a result, Mason is better remembered for a long and sporadically successful solo career.

Mason was born in Worcester, England, and met future Traffic bandmate Jim Capaldi while playing in local bands as a teenager. Mason's skill on guitar landed him some prime sessions on the Rolling Stones' *Beggars Banquet* (1968), and he also added 12-string acoustic guitar to Jimi Hendrix's cover of "All Along the Watchtower." After leaving Traffic for good in 1969, he played with Delaney &

Bonnie and Friends and launched a solo career. Mason's debut album, *Alone Together*, established him as a solid songwriter grounded in rhythm and blues and adept with upbeat melodies and mid-tempo rock that featured his steady rhythm guitar and tasteful lead playing. The album featured a minor hit with "Only You Know and I Know" (also covered by Delaney & Bonnie). It would remain one of his best-known songs, although tracks such as "Show Me Some Affection" from *Dave Mason* (1974) also got some FM airplay. Later albums saw Mason branch out into country, funk, and Caribbean influences. He had his greatest success with the 1977 soft rock hit single "We Just Disagree."

Mason's career continued with diminishing commercial success into the 2000s. In 2016 he released *Traffic Jams*, an album mixing new material with remakes of songs from Traffic and his solo career.

Suggested Albums: Alone Together (1970); *Dave Mason* (1974); *Let It Flow* (1977)

MASTERS APPRENTICES

The Masters Apprentices began as the Mustangs in Adelaide, South Australia, in the early 1960s. By 1966, their heads turned by the British Invasion, they became the Masters Apprentices, their name a gesture of humility toward their influences. They were especially enamored of harder blues-based bands such as the Rolling Stones, the Pretty Things, and the Yardbirds. The Masters Apprentices were at the center of a thriving local scene that drew slight recognition elsewhere until their demos caught ears at a Melbourne record label. Their first single, "Undecided," went Top 10 across Australia in 1966, driven by a savage rhythm, a lead guitar line in the manner of the Kinks' Dave Davies, and the punk snarl of lead vocalist Jim Keays.

The self-titled album that followed (1967) included minor-key melodies in Eastern modes à la the Yardbirds and short outbursts of psychedelic garage rock. They benefited from the songwriting of guitarist Mick Bower, who was capable of compelling chord progressions and adroit time shifts. American rock critic Greg Shaw proclaimed the Masters Apprentices' "Wars or Hands of Time" as one of the "Top 10 Power Pop Songs of All Time," which belatedly brought the band worldwide attention among aficionados of 1960s rock.

The notice came too late for the Masters Apprentices. After Bower suffered a breakdown while on tour in 1968, they enjoyed airplay for a new single, the psychedelic "Elevator Driver." Keays kept the band going for a few months, but they were unable to sustain their enthusiasm past the end of the year.

Suggested Album: The Master's Apprentices (1967)

MAYALL, JOHN (1933–)

John Mayall's impact on the development of British blues-rock has been profound, both as an originator of the form and for bringing to prominence some of the greatest and most important musicians of the classic rock era. An early exposure to the music of Lead Belly, Lonnie Johnson, Sonny Boy Williamson, and Little Walter instilled in Mayall a lifelong love of the blues, and he took up piano, guitar, and most significantly harmonica by the time he was a teenager. The first incarnation of his band the Bluesbreakers (featuring future Fleetwood Mac bassist John McVie) began playing London nightspots by the early 1960s. With help from blues mentor Alexis Korner, the band began its pursuit of a recording contract.

Although the Bluesbreakers' first single fizzled, the band continued to develop a following in the ever-growing London blues scene. A huge break came when guitarist Eric Clapton quit the Yardbirds and joined the Bluesbreakers. A blues purist, Clapton left the Yardbirds because he thought the band had become too pop, and the Bluesbreakers' commitment to the blues helped them land the biggest name among British blues guitarists. Their revelatory debut album *Blues Breakers with Eric Clapton* (1966) set the course for blues-based rock. Mayall's passionate singing and steam-powered harp playing alone would have made the album a powerhouse, but without question, Clapton's sizzling guitar work put the album over the top. From the tension-packed distorted arpeggio of "All Your Love" to the rollicking romper "Hideaway" and the searing "Steppin' Out," Clapton raised the bar for what was expected of rock lead guitar. Mayall gave Clapton room to explore, and he took full advantage to stretch out on extended solos. Clapton's playing was louder and more stinging than anything that had been heard before. Although the album consisted mostly of blues standards (with only a few Mayall originals), the Bluesbreakers had created something new and original.

Just as Mayall and the Bluesbreakers were coming to prominence, Clapton bolted the band to join the supergroup Cream. Undeterred, Mayall found another guitar genius, this time in the form of 20-year-old Peter Green. Now billed as John Mayall and the Bluesbreakers, the band released *A Hard Road* (1967). Green's confident, soulful guitar work proved a worthy replacement for Clapton, and the album was another strong interpretation of modern blues. However, Green was also not long for the band, as he left to help form Fleetwood Mac. Replacing him was another dazzling young guitar player, Mick Taylor. Taylor stayed for three strong albums, but when the Rolling Stones hired him away, it was obvious that Mayall's Bluesbreakers had become a farm system providing talent for other bands. Perhaps tired of having band members stolen from him, Mayall switched to a more acoustic blues direction featuring guitarist Jon Mark and sax player John Almond. The one constant throughout the lineup changes was Mayall himself, with his strong vocal and harp work providing a steadying force for the band's sound.

Mayall relocated to Los Angeles as the 1970s dawned. Recording without the Bluesbreakers, he embarked on a more laid-back jazz-blues sound, releasing his first American record, *USA Union* (1970). Solid playing and singing was not sufficient to lift Mayall's new sound past the mundane, and his work lacked the dynamic energy of the Bluesbreakers. Perhaps realizing this, Mayall brought Clapton and Taylor back for the harder rocking *Back to the Roots* (1971). After this, as Mayall drifted from the blues and worked in a more jazz-fusion context, it was apparent that his most significant days were behind him. Mayall re-formed the Bluesbreakers with varying lineups in the 1980s, albeit the band's most famous guitarists, Clapton, Green, and Taylor, were never part of the lineup. Mayall will be forever linked with the development of three great guitar players who shaped the sound of rock music in the 1960s and beyond, and for that alone Mayall's legacy is secure.

Suggested Albums: Blues Breakers with Eric Clapton (1966); *A Hard Road* (1967); *Crusade* (1967); *Bare Wires* (1968); *Blues from Laurel Canyon* (1968); *Empty Rooms* (1969); *Back to the Roots* (1971)

See also: Clapton, Eric; Fleetwood Mac

MCCARTNEY, PAUL (1942–)

For several years Paul McCartney was in danger of being defined by one of his characteristic hits of the 1970s, "Silly Love Songs." He did himself no favors by distancing himself from the breadth of his accomplishments with the Beatles. As researchers sorted through the John Lennon–Paul McCartney catalogue of songs to decide who really wrote what, it became clear that McCartney was primarily responsible for the proto–heavy metal of "Helter Skelter" as well as the hymnody of "Let it Be," the majestic "Hey Jude," the juvenile "Maxwell's Silver Hammer," the groundbreaking "Eleanor Rigby," and the British music hall of "When I'm 64." Throughout the Beatles' decade of recording he was an innovator as well as a traditionalist. Some of that breadth was still audible as his solo career began, but after a few years McCartney seemed almost to conspire against the memory of his great accomplishments from the 1960s by producing a plethora of trivial material.

McCartney's self-titled debut album, released in 1970 but recorded while the Beatles were still intact, was an engagingly homespun affair featuring him on all instruments. It included his greatest non-Beatles song, "Maybe I'm Amazed," which became a hit as news of the band's breakup was fresh. His wife, Linda McCartney, received co-credit on his next album, *Ram* (1971). Some have suggested that his collaboration with Linda, a modestly talented singer and keyboardist, was in response to Lennon's work with Yoko Ono. One can also imagine instead that Linda's musical contributions were born of genuine affection and were an outgrowth of their domesticity. *Ram* included a pair of hits, "Another Day," an empathetic glimpse into the life of an everyday office girl, and "Uncle Albert/Admiral Halsey," a whimsical descendant of "Maxwell's Silver Hammer" whose nonsense lyrics were carried by a fetching tune and just-right arrangement.

Afterward, as if to distance himself from his former group by submerging into a new band, McCartney formed Wings with Linda and Denny Laine, guitarist for the original Moody Blues. Their first album, *Wild Life* (1972), was recorded in a week's time, sold modestly, and included no songs that lived on in memory. Wings scored a British hit with "Give Ireland Back to the Irish" (1972), released in reaction to the "Bloody Sunday" incident in which British troops killed 12 Roman Catholics during the Northern Ireland troubles. It has the distinction of being the only McCartney record banned by the BBC. Perhaps intended as a sly comment on airplay for controversial lyrics, he followed with "Mary Had a Little Lamb," setting the nursery rhyme to a twee melody. His third single from 1972, the hard rocking "Hi Hi Hi," was the only one to stir much interest in the United States.

His next effort with Wings, *Red Rose Speedway* (1973), yielded the lackluster "My Love," which reached number one in America. Later that year he enjoyed a second hit with the clever title song from the James Bond movie *Live and Let Die*. McCartney and Wings finally reached their pinnacle with *Band on the Run* (1974), a platinum-selling album that displayed most of his strengths and few of his weaknesses. He alluded to serious subjects in "1985," which set dystopia against the joy of sex and somehow made the tandem work. Included were several endearing rock tunes boasting lyrics of no substance, including "Helen Wheels" and more so "Jet," which made no sense even if the subject was McCartney's pet dog. As if to beat Lennon at his own game, "Let Me Roll It" replicated his erstwhile partner in writing and vocal style.

Venus and Mars (1975) contained some good numbers, including the hard rock warning against drug abuse, "Medicine Jar," the sexually urgent "Letting Go," and an exuberant celebration of McCartney's regained joy in touring, "Rock Show." The album was also home to the silly "Magneto and Titanium Man" and the lyrical nonstarter, "Listen to What the Man Said." The descent continued with *Wings at the Speed of Sound* (1976), a true band effort with lead vocals and songwriting from Laine and other members but with some of McCartney's worst efforts, including the inane "Let 'Em In" and the defensive self-explanatory "Silly Love Songs."

Through this time McCartney added gold records to his wall, selling in quantity to the pop mainstream but alienating the hardcore rock audience. Hits such as the Scottish-flavored "Mull of Kintyre" led rock critics to compare McCartney to McDonald's, selling the sonic equivalent of fast food by the millions. McCartney's biggest hits in the early 1980s were duets with African American artists, "Ebony and Ivory" with Stevie Wonder (1982) and "The Girl Is Mine" with Michael Jackson (1983). His film *Give My Regards to Broad Street* (1984) was dismissed as insipid. He continued to score occasional hit records while setting records for highest grosses on his concert tours, which pulled material from the Beatles as well as his solo and Wings years.

His venture into classical music, *Liverpool Oratorio,* recorded by the Royal Liverpool Philharmonic Orchestra (1991), was routinely dismissed, but he won praise for his unplugged concert on MTV (1991). After spending many months working with George Harrison, Ringo Starr, and George Martin on *The Beatles Anthology*, a series of albums documenting their career (1995–1996), McCartney seemed creatively rejuvenated. *Flaming Pie* (1997) featured his best songwriting in years, and *Run Devil Run* (1999), his tribute to 1950s rock and roll, was well received. Tragedy struck his personal life, first with the death of Linda from cancer (1998) and later with the acrimonious divorce from his new wife, Heather Mills (2008). Marking McCartney's status in British culture were a pair of high-profile performances in 2012 at Queen Elizabeth's Diamond Jubilee concert at Buckingham Palace and the opening ceremony of the London Summer Olympic Games. McCartney is probably the most beloved surviving figure from the classic rock era. His concert tours sell out with no difficulty.

Suggested Albums: McCartney (1970); *Ram* (1971); *Band on the Run* (1974); *Venus and Mars* (1975); *Unplugged: The Official Bootleg* (1991); *Flaming Pie* (1997); *Run Devil Run* (1999); *Chaos and Creation in the Backyard* (2005)

See also: Beatles

MC5

If revolutionary times demand revolutionary music, no band was more suited for the incendiary times of the late 1960s than Detroit's MC5. Steeped in radical left-wing politics and armed with a combustible garage rock sound, the band initially known as the Motor City Five led a short-lived attack on the political and musical establishment, and planted the seeds of future musical revolutions that would give rise to punk and heavy metal. While never hugely popular, the MC5 accomplished far more in a few years than many bands did over the course of decades.

The band had its genesis in the early 1960s, when Detroit high schoolers Wayne Kramer and Fred "Sonic" Smith became friends over a shared love of early rock and roll. Kramer taught Smith guitar and the pair began playing in local bands, eventually forming the Motor City Five in 1964. They quickly added an unconventional frontman in the pudgy Rob Tyner, who brought a left-wing political bent to the group. At Tyner's suggestion, the band shortened its name to MC5, and they began making a name for themselves in the gritty Motor City music scene with their frenetically energetic live performance, often supporting big name national acts and proceeding to blow them off the stage. Their music had garage band rawness, but more sophistication than most thanks to Smith and Kramer's interest in free jazz, which led them to try to emulate the saxophone tones of artists like John Coltrane.

The band took the unusual step of recording its debut album, *Kick Out the Jams* (1969), before a live crowd at Detroit's Grande Ballroom. With Tyner leading the way, the band became advocates for the radical Black Panther Party and adopted the group's Marxist philosophy. That radicalism permeates *Kick Out the Jams*, although it comes through most explicitly in banter between songs. More implicitly, the band's revolutionary spirit is fully expressed through the music, a high-energy, distortion-filled version of garage rock, slamming through a set of unrelenting hard rock tunes. The powerful riffing of the title track sets the tone for the album, and the energy never lets up, fueled by Smith's piercing lead guitar work. A fierce version of John Lee Hooker's "Motor City Is Burning" feels like a call to urban violence, and the pseudo-psychedelia of "Starship" quotes a Sun Ra poem, earning the radical jazzman a co-writing credit.

The devastating heaviness of "I Want You Right Now" is every bit a piece of proto-metal as anything Black Sabbath was doing at the time, and the band's rebellious attitude would be labeled "punk" when practiced by a younger generation in the late 1970s. Decades later, the album still feels like the musical equivalent of a street riot, and given the group's mindset at the time, it's likely what was intended.

Armed with radical politics and a high-decibel approach to performing, the MC5 were at home at protest rallies as well as concert halls. They eventually softened their rough edges and toned down the politics before disbanding in 1973. (Leni Sinclair/Michael Ochs Archives/Getty Images)

Prominent rock critic and future Bruce Springsteen mentor and producer Jon Landau was brought in to produce the band's next album. *Back in the USA* (1970) took its title from the Chuck Berry song (covered on the album) and was less overtly political than their debut. Landau smoothed out a few of the band's rough edges and created a more controlled if no less energetic sound that served as a full antecedent to punk rock. Chunky power chords dominate the spirited "High School," which seems like a celebration of adolescent culture but hints of a breeding ground for future radicals. "Shakin' Street" and "Call Me Animal" are more overt conventional rockers, but the band returns to political radicalism in "The American Ruse" and "The Human Being Lawnmower." Smith's pentatonic-based lead guitar work lights up the record with stellar playing worthy of better-known guitar heroes. The more focused sound was a clear attempt to improve the band's commercial fortunes, but sales proved disappointing. Their next album was the musically more sophisticated *High Time* (1971), in which the band developed a heavier sound that was often more overtly heavy metal, and included some free jazz and psychedelic experimentation.

Drug problems and frustration with the band's lack of commercial success led to their breakup in 1973. But it didn't take long for their rediscovery, as the emergence of punk rock made it clear that MC5 had established a legacy that exceeded its popularity. Punk's raw energy and revolutionary spirit was a clear descendant of *Kick Out the Jams*, and power chorded, roots-oriented music owed a debt to *Back in the USA*. Left-wing punk bands like the Clash acknowledged MC5's influence, and Smith's Sonic Rendezvous Band was widely accepted in underground clubs across the United States. Smith's marriage to proto-punk queen Patti Smith furthered the band's connection with punk, and Kramer made inroads into the scene between stints in jail on drug charges.

Tyler and Smith both died of heart-related problems in the 1990s, but the band has re-formed around Kramer, with a rotating lineup that has featured Dictators lead singer "Handsome" Dick Manitoba on vocals. A truly fitting tribute came in 2000, when Rage Against the Machine, possibly the most overtly radical band since the MC5, recorded a popular cover of "Kick Out the Jams" on their album *Renegades*. Given the band's influence and legacy, MC5 are a glaring omission from the Rock and Roll Hall of Fame.

Suggested Albums: Kick Out the Jams (1969); *Back in the USA* (1970); *High Time* (1971)

MCLAUGHLIN, JOHN
See Mahavishnu Orchestra

MCLEAN, DON (1945–)
Don McLean is best known as the composer and performer of "American Pie," one of rock's biggest hit singles and one of the best-known American songs of the 20th century. Without a doubt, being associated with such a generational milestone has proved to be a blessing and a curse for McLean, as it has earned him a lasting place in modern cultural history while overshadowing the rest of his decades-long career.

McLean was born in a suburb of New York City in 1945 on the verge of the post–World War II baby boom. Hence, McLean was witness to almost all of the stunning changes that would alter the cultural landscape over the next several decades. Like many well-educated young Americans, he became fascinated with the folk-blues revival that swept the nation in the late 1950s and early 1960s. He took to playing folk festivals across the country before releasing his debut album, *Tapestry* (1970). Bright, spirited songs and energetic fingerpicked guitar set *Tapestry* apart from the more earnest music being produced by many of McLean's singer-songwriter contemporaries. In fact, the songs making use of a backing band bore more than a passing resemblance to some of the Byrds' early folk-rock albums.

If the general public ignored McLean's debut album, almost no one overlooked his phenomenally successful follow-up, *American Pie* (1971). Of course, that was due almost entirely to the title cut, which dominated the charts upon its release in early 1972 and has never left the public consciousness since. A rollicking rhythm backed an intricate symbolic history of rock music, beginning with the death of Buddy Holly and culminating with the horrors of Altamont and the subsequent burnout of the ideals of the 1960s generation. Every line includes a reference to a key player in rock history and their meaning has been the subject of endless speculation. The song's repeated refrain, "the day the music died," became a catch phrase describing rock's lost innocence. "American Pie" was such a musical powerhouse that it obscured the album's second-best song, "Vincent," a beautifully crafted tribute to the art and personal struggles of the painter Vincent Van Gogh.

The aftermath of "American Pie" shows McLean struggling to live up to that song's promise and live down its expectations. It is often forgotten that he didn't simply go away, and in fact had a Top 40 single with the assertive horn-backed folk-rock of "Dreidel" from the album *Don McLean* (1972). In 1973, easy listening crooner Perry Como lined McLean's pockets with a hit cover of McLean's "And I Love You So," taken from McLean's debut album. McLean also had occasional chart success in later years, including a hit single with a cover of Roy Orbison's "Crying" (1978).

However, he never came remotely close to achieving the impossible task of replicating the success of "American Pie," despite never losing his perspective and fine songwriting skills. McLean's pure tenor remained strong and he sang with an honesty that never slipped into the self-absorption that bedeviled too many singer-songwriters. But he remains best known for his biggest hit, performing to this day to audiences that repeatedly shout requests for "American Pie," to his consternation. McLean was inducted into the Songwriters Hall of Fame in 2004.

Suggested Albums: Tapestry (1970); *American Pie* (1971); *Don McLean* (1972); *Homeless Brother* (1974); *Addicted to Black* (2009)

MILES, BUDDY (1946–2008)

Buddy Miles became a professional drummer in his adolescence when he went on tour with his father's jazz band. Session work followed. He came to the attention of the rock audience as a member of the Electric Flag (1967–1968). Following their breakup, he formed his own jazz-rock band, the Buddy Miles Express. Miles had known Jimi Hendrix before the guitarist left for England and became a star. Hendrix contributed a poem to the back cover of the Express's debut, *Expressway to Your Skull* (1969), and produced a few tracks on their second album, *Electric Church* (1969). Miles drummed on guitarist John McLaughlin's seminal fusion album, *Devotion* (1969).

Miles joined with drummer Billy Cox in Hendrix's short-lived Band of Gypsys and continued with the Express on *Them Changes* (1970), whose title track received much airplay. Although he was never without work or collaborators, even during a stint in prison and a halfway house, Miles was unable to capitalize on his early success or associations. Performing and working through the end of his life, his most widely circulated accomplishment in later years was as vocalist for the California Raisins Claymation television campaign, where he sang "I Heard It Through the Grapevine" (1986). He died of congestive heart failure in 2008.

Suggested Albums: Expressway to Your Skull (1969); *Electric Church* (1969); *Them Changes* (1970)

MILLER, STEVE (1943–)

Given Steve Miller's upbringing, it seems almost a given that he would have found a career in music. He was born in Milwaukee, Wisconsin, to jazz enthusiast parents who were good friends with guitar pioneer and inventor Les Paul, who reportedly encouraged young Steve's interest in guitar. Miller began playing in bands as a teenager and found another young musician named Boz Scaggs, whom Miller recruited for his band. A family relocation to Texas enriched his musical points of reference, and time spent in Chicago gave him an in-depth exposure to the blues. Further encouraged by the likes of Muddy Waters and Buddy Guy, Miller headed west in the mid-1960s where he fell in with the burgeoning San Francisco music scene.

Once in San Francisco, Miller set about forming the Steve Miller Band. Their debut, *Children of the Future* (1968), featured Miller as lead guitarist with Miller and Scaggs sharing lead vocals. Miller had begun to make his mark playing the blues, but *Children of the Future* was an organ-drenched exercise in psychedelia with blues informing and ornamenting the music. The band's next album, *Sailor* (1968), followed an even more psychedelic path, and it would be the band's last album with Scaggs, as he left to pursue a solo career and future stardom. The album is best known for the songs "Gangster of Love" (a Johnny Watson cover that would feature a recurring character in Miller's songwriting) and his first hit, "Living in the USA," a protest song that demonstrated Miller's growing knack for writing a hook. Miller struck up a friendship with Beatle Paul McCartney while recording the band's next album, *Brave New World* (1969) in London. McCartney played and sang on the album under the pseudonym "Paul Ramon" (he also seemingly lent the riff to "Lady Madonna" to the album's best known song, "Space Cowboy"). Miller remained mired in psychedelia as the 1960s drifted to a close, although the band's next album, *Your Saving Grace* (1969), began a transition to rhythm and blues–flavored hard rock. *Number 5* (1970) added touches of pop, country, and Latin music to the mix.

By 1973 Miller was ready to make a full go at pop rock. His efforts met with stunning success, as the title track from the album *The Joker* (1973) became a worldwide hit. Co-written with music impresario Ahmet Ertegun, the song referenced previous Miller characters "Maurice," "Gangster of Love," and "the Space Cowboy" in a strange set of lyrics with nonsensical lines such as "I speak of the pompatus of love." What the song had above all else was an irresistibly catchy chorus that was impossible to shake from the mind. The album was slickly produced, with little of the bluesy guitar playing that had brought him to fame.

Miller seemed content to rest on his laurels, waiting until 1976 to release *Fly Like an Eagle*. For Miller, it was certainly worth the wait, as the album was a smash hit, producing such hit singles as the pleasantly rolling "Rock'n Me," the country rock–influenced "Take the Money and Run," and the title track that reprised the dreamy psychedelic touches of his first few albums. *Book of Dreams* (1977) furthered the band's run of success with "Jet Airliner" and "Jungle Love" becoming chart hits.

The Steve Miller Band was a Top 40 mainstay throughout the second half of the 1970s, but like so many popular acts, Miller was forced to endure his share of critical barbs. Some noted that he had a tendency to "borrow" riffs from other artists, pointing out that the riff for "Rock'n Me" bore a distinct similarity to Free's "All Right Now," and the lead line to "Jet Airliner" seemed lifted from Cream's cover of Robert Johnson's "Crossroads." In truth, Miller seemed to be doing nothing more than making sly nods to past hits, a time-honored tradition in rock music, and the rest of the songs were different enough for him to dodge charges of plagiarism. Miller's polished pop rock didn't sit well with devotees of punk and new wave, who gleefully pointed out his abandonment of his blues roots.

Miller's output dwindled in the 1980s, although he did score hits with the Buddy Holly–influenced "Heart Like a Wheel" from *Circle of Love* (1981). An even bigger hit was the title track from *Abracadabra* (1982), a hook-laden cross between disco and new wave that was an international number one hit. The song would prove to be Miller's last hit, although he occasionally recorded and continued to tour. Steve Miller has been inducted into the Rock and Roll Hall of Fame.

Suggested Albums: Children of the Future (1968); *Sailor* (1968); *Brave New World* (1969); *The Joker* (1973); *Fly Like an Eagle* (1976)

MITCHELL, JONI (1943–)

Joni Mitchell emerged from the folk-blues revival and plotted a course into jazz. Cajoled into the contemporary pop arena, she regained her artistic equilibrium but eventually decided that the music business was hopeless. However, no shorthand description does full justice to her unique gifts. Mitchell was one of a kind, starting with her unusual guitar tunings, which allowed her to write songs that seldom fit conventional molds in any genre.

Born Roberta Joan Anderson in Alberta, Canada, she studied art and would later paint several of her own album covers. She found her footing playing in Toronto's folk scene, where she married folksinger Chuck Mitchell. They moved across the border to Detroit, where she gained notice and ended her marriage. In her first years, Mitchell was best known through other artists' renditions of her songs, especially Judy Collins's hit with "Both Sides Now" (1967). Successful engagements in New York led to a contract and her debut album, *Song to a Seagull* (1968), produced by David Crosby.

Mitchell finally recorded "Both Sides Now" on her second album, *Clouds* (1969). Although she was a fresh face for record buyers, her perspective was already that of an older narrator reflecting on a long life. Little wonder Frank Sinatra added "Both Sides Now" to his repertoire, tailoring it to his autumnal melancholy. *Clouds* and her other early acoustic guitar–based albums such as *Ladies of the Canyon* (1970), *Blue* (1971), and *For the Roses* (1972) showed her ability to make oddly metered lines work in song. The lyrics for "Carry," "My Old Man," "A Case of You," "The Last Time I Saw Richard," and "You Turn Me On (I'm a Radio)" were sophisticated reflections on relationships.

Settling in Los Angeles, Mitchell was at the center of the city's music scene and was viewed with reverence by her colleagues. She was seen as a force in the "soft rock" that emerged in Southern California during the early 1970s. However, her songs were on a higher level than those of her confessional singer-songwriter companions, written with intelligence as well as an open heart and with melodies as personal as her lyrics. Mitchell's soprano voice hit the high notes from unusual angles. She sang like a jazz horn player rather than a vocalist.

The jazz influence became more pronounced on her bestselling album, *Court and Spark* (1974), recorded with a gamut of musicians ranging from the Jazz Crusaders to Jose Feliciano and the Band's guitarist Robbie Robertson. The album netted a pair of hit singles sung in a voice that glided across scales, "Help Me" and "Free Man in Paris." *Court and Spark* also contained a cover of "Twisted," a sophisticatedly humorous 1952 song by jazz singer Annie Ross.

Jazz was on full display with *Miles of Aisles* (1974), recorded live with the L.A. Express fusion band. Mitchell quickly transcended fusion conventions for an idiosyncratic, esoteric path into jazz. Albums such as *The Hissing of Summer Lawns* (1975), *Hejira* (1976), and *Don Juan's Reckless Daughter* (1977) were generally lambasted by rock critics and met with incomprehension by folk, pop, and rock fans lacking the context to understand her new music. With *Mingus* (1979), she wrote lyrics to some of the final melodies written by jazz bassist-composer Charles Mingus, dying of Lou Gehrig's disease. The last album in her jazz sequence, *Shadows and Light* (1980), was recorded live with guitarist Pat Metheny and bassist Jaco Pastorius. She was rewarded for her musical innovation with declining sales, albeit in recent times her jazz albums have been discovered by new audiences and reevaluated by critics and fans who found them baffling upon release.

Doubtlessly under pressure to sell albums again, Mitchell spent the 1980s trying to adjust to the changing face of music. *Wild Things Run Fast* (1982) yielded an unlikely minor hit with a synth-pop rendering of Elvis Presley's "(You're So Square) Baby I Don't Care." Mitchell at least sounded as if she was having fun with the old Presley tune. The rest of the album forced her into awkward juxtapositions with hard rock and commercial pop. Synth pop hit maker Thomas Dolby helped produce *Dog Eat Dog* (1985), less sonically excruciating than its predecessor but filled with topical songs that have not aged well. In what looked suspiciously like another record label ploy, Mitchell made an album of duets, *Chalk Mark in a Rain Storm* (1988). Willie Nelson was among the singing partners who made sense for Mitchell. On the other hand, Billy Idol was a jarring choice. The album's single, "My Secret Place," was sung with Peter Gabriel.

With *Night Ride Home* (1991), Mitchell inched back toward her acoustic roots. *Turbulent Indigo* (1994) signaled her comeback by winning a pair of Grammys and the respect of a younger generation of female performers and fans in light of Lilith Fair. Mitchell continued to tour and record, and she experimented with playing guitar synthesizer. *Both Sides, Now* (2000) was a Grammy-winning album of jazz

238   **MOBY GRAPE**

standards. After *Travelogue* (2002), which reinterpreted her older songs with orchestral arrangements, Mitchell announced her retirement from the music industry. She returned nevertheless with *Shine* (2007). Released on the label associated with the Starbucks coffee shop chain, *Shine* was her highest charting album in the United States since *Hejira*. A tribute album, *River: The Joni Letters* (2007), featured contributions by Norah Jones, Tina Turner, and Leonard Cohen.

Health problems have put the future of her musical career in doubt, including a reported brain aneurysm in 2015.

Suggested Albums: Song to a Seagull (aka *Joni Mitchell*) (1968); *Clouds* (1969); *Ladies of the Canyon* (1970); *Blue* (1971); *For the Roses* (1972); *Court and Spark* (1974); *The Hissing of Summer Lawns* (1975); *Hejira* (1976); *Don Juan's Reckless Daughter* (1977); *Mingus* (1979); *Turbulent Indigo* (1994); *Both Sides, Now* (2000)

MOBY GRAPE

The jokey literary allusion of their name aside, Moby Grape's story could be the basis for a great novel on the dashed hopes of the 1960s. The talented San Francisco band became a magnet for record labels and were thoroughly mishandled by the company they signed with. Struggling to overcome the sour aftertaste of failed hype and an uncertain well of inspiration, they were at work on their follow-up album when a band member went violently berserk. By the time of their fourth album, one member was in the service. It was 1970 and time had run out for Moby Grape.

Their self-titled debut album (1967) was dynamic and bursting with ideas from the band's four songwriters. Moby Grape's best-known songs, "Hey Grandma" and "Omaha," were rollicking rock and roll shading into psychedelic discord. ("Hey Grandma" has been covered by several bands, including the Black Crowes [2009].) They were also capable of folk-rock with a hard edge thanks to the confluence of two antipodal members. Guitarist Peter Lewis, privileged son of actress Loretta Young, emerged from folk-rock, while bassist Bob Mosley came up playing garage rock in San Diego's tough bars. Moby Grape had diverse lead vocalists and harmonies to rival Crosby, Stills & Nash. Unfortunately, Columbia Records took the unprecedented step of simultaneously releasing five singles from *Moby Grape*. None of them sold well, and the flamboyant marketing failure diminished the band's countercultural credibility.

Moby Grape persisted. While recording *Wow/Grape Jam* (1968) in New York, guitarist Skip Spence (formerly the Jefferson Airplane's drummer) attacked the hotel room of a fellow band member with a fire ax while deranged from the effects of drugs and was sentenced to six months at Bellevue. *Wow* was eclectic if less exuberant than its predecessor and suffered from a phenomenon that would become common among rock bands in the 1970s, the "sophomore jinx." Many bands found that they had a lifetime to write their first album but only a few hectic months to develop their second.

Following the country rock–tinged *Moby Grape '69* (1969), Mosley left to join the Marines, leaving the remnants to record the mediocre *Truly Fine Citizen* (1970) and the lovely but overlooked *20 Granite Creek* (1971). Band members re-formed several times over the decades and engaged in a lengthy legal battle with their former manager over rights to their name. At some points they performed as Maby Grope.

Suggested Albums: Moby Grape (1967); *Moby Grape '69* (1969); *20 Granite Creek* (1971)

MODS

After World War II, Great Britain nurtured a succession of male-oriented youth subcultures. Their numbers were drawn from the lower or lower-middle classes, enabled by the relative prosperity that trickled down the social ladder under Britain's postwar quasi-socialism of strong trade unions, state-owned enterprises, and a flourishing network of art schools, and driven by the desire to escape the bleakness of a nation that felt defeated in victory. Like their predecessors from the 1950s, the Teddy Boys, the Mods, prevalent in the mid-1960s, established a group identity through a shared sartorial sensibility. While the Teds favored retrospective, almost Edwardian fashions, the Mods embraced the most current looks, including sharp-lapelled Italian suits. They wanted to dress as well as if not finer than their social betters. The Mods' favorite mode of transportation was the sleek Italian Vespa motor scooter, inexpensive to fuel and easy to park on narrow British streets.

While the Mods began with a love for American rhythm and blues, they soon became important as an audience for a particular emerging style of rock bands including the Who, the Creation, and the Move. Favoring songs as short and sharp as the Mods' lapels, those bands were known for songs with a defiant and sardonic take on society. The Mods were the subject of the Who's rock opera *Quadrophenia* (1973). With the Police's Sting in the main role, the film based upon it (1979) depicted the Mods' struggle against a rival subculture, the Rockers, who rode motorcycles and dressed like 1950s cinematic depictions of American juvenile delinquents.

By 1966 the Mods had begun to run their course as many of its dedicated followers of fashion dripped into hippie psychedelia. The Mods enjoyed a short-lived revival for a new generation in the late 1970s, spurred by the Jam, a punk rock band steeped in the dress and ethos of the early Who.

MONKEES

German sociologist Theodor Adorno, a famous foe of the "culture industry," understood all popular music, even jazz, as the product of a capitalist system. For him, recording artists were not artists at all but factory workers on an assembly line of banality. Although he lived until 1969, Adorno left no comment on the Monkees, who indeed began as a product of the music industry designed to capitalize on the popularity of the Beatles. Adorno might have been surprised to learn that the factory workers in question, Peter Tork, Mickey Dolenz, Davy Jones, and

240 MONKEES

Michael Nesmith, revolted against their overseers. If the Monkees did not exactly seize the means of production, they were able to wrest a degree of artistic control over their phenomenally successful if short career. From 1966 through 1968 they amassed a dozen Top 40 hits and collectively occupied the number one spot on the charts for 12 weeks with "Last Train to Clarksville," "I'm a Believer," and "Daydream Believer." Contrary to popular memory, the Monkees were not merely a singles band. Their albums sold 16 million copies within a two and a half year period.

Bob Rafelson, an aspiring filmmaker who went on to direct *Five Easy Pieces*, was inspired by Richard Lester's film *A Hard Day's Night* (1964). He imagined a weekly television series about a fictitious band that would capture the madcap energy of Lester's depiction of Beatlemania. Early on the Lovin' Spoonful were considered for the show's band. According to legend, Stephen Stills was among the applicants who failed the audition. After a casting call, Rafelson and producer Bert Schneider chose Jones, the Tony-nominated Englishman who played the Artful Dodger in the Broadway musical *Oliver!*, along with a trio of Americans. Dolenz was a former child actor while Nesmith and Tork were musicians from the folk-blues revival.

While the Monkees played on television when their show debuted in 1966, studio musicians handled most of the instruments heard on their early recordings. Although Nesmith was permitted to contribute a few songs, their hits were the work of professional songwriters such as Neil Diamond ("I'm a Believer"), Carole King and Jerry Goffin ("Pleasant Valley Sunday"), Tommy Boyce and Bobby Hart ("Last Train to Clarksville"), and John Stewart ("Daydream Believer"). They were not initially expected to play live shows, but the success of the TV show prompted a U.S. tour with an unlikely opening act, Jimi Hendrix. Disputes over artistic direction eventually led to the firing of producer Don Kirshner in 1967 and the release of the first Monkees album over which the band had control, *Headquarters* (1967). For his next project, Kirshner dispensed with human musicians and created an animated television series with a cartoon band, the Archies.

During its two-season run, the Monkees television show included segments in which particular songs were enacted, setting a precedent for music videos. Although the program was the reason for the Monkees' existence, its ratings, while good, were overshadowed by the band's record sales. At their peak, the Monkees outsold the band that inspired them, the Beatles. After gaining independence from their overseers, the Monkees headed in a country rock direction under Nesmith's leadership. After the cancellation of their TV show in 1968, Rafelson directed the band in *Head*, a stream of psychedelic consciousness film co-written by Jack Nicholson. It sold few tickets. The Monkees' television audience was shocked by its departure from the band's carefully manicured image, while the hippie counterculture addressed in the film rejected the band on Adorno's terms, regarding the Monkees as industry product rather than a true rock group.

Tork left the band in 1969, followed by Nesmith in 1970. The remaining original members struggled on for another year before disbanding. Jones pursued a career in acting through his death in 2012 while the other members followed music with varying degrees of success. The pop and retrospective wing of the late

1970s new wave fostered renewed interest in the Monkees, leading to occasional reunions into the 21st century and a television show, *The New Monkees* (1987), with a young cast and updated settings.

The appetite for nostalgia continues to serve the Monkees well. The three surviving members released a 50th anniversary album, *Good Times!* (2016), which reached the Top 10. Working as they did in the 1960s, the Monkees mixed their own originals with bespoke songs from top contemporary songwriters, including Weezer's Rivers Cuomo, XTC's Andy Partridge, and Death Cab for Cutie's Ben Gibbard.

Suggested Albums: The Monkees (1966); *More of the Monkees* (1967); *Headquarters* (1967); *Pisces, Aquarius, Capricorn & Jones Ltd.* (1967); *The Birds, the Bees and the Monkees* (1968); *Head* (1968)

MOODY BLUES

In 1964, when the Moody Blues began in Birmingham, England, they were one of countless local bands influenced by American music and inspired by the phenomenal success of the Beatles. They had a number one hit in their homeland with "Go Now" (1965), a well-done cover of a recent U.S. rhythm and blues song. Following the 1967 departure of guitarist Denny Laine (who eventually joined Paul McCartney and Wings), the group's classic lineup gathered around the heady promise of progressive rock. *Days of Future Passed* (1967) was an early effort at melding rock with classical music. Featuring recited poetry and recorded with the so-called London Festival Orchestra, actually an aggregation of studio players, the album belatedly yielded a U.S. hit with the autumnal-sounding "Nights in White Satin," which reached number two on the charts in 1972.

By the time "Nights in White Satin" reached the ears of AM listeners, the Moody Blues had already established themselves as a prominent progressive rock band on FM with much-played tracks such as "Question," "The Story in Your Eyes," "Isn't Life Strange," "Melancholy Man," and "I'm Just a Singer (In a Rock and Roll Band)." They were not the first band to employ a mellotron, a keyboard capable of simulating an orchestra of strings and woodwinds, but made the chilly-sounding instrument into their trademark. Melodic and musically uncomplicated despite their penchant for suites and lengthy numbers, their songs expressed despair over the human condition and maintained a cosmic mood. Their most popular albums were *Every Good Boy Deserves Favor* (1971) and *Seventh Sojourn* (1972).

The Moody Blues went dormant for several years as drummer Graeme Edge and guitarists Justin Hayward and John Lodge pursued solo careers. They regrouped for *Octave* (1978), the last album featuring mellotron player Mike Pinder. Replacing him was former Yes keyboardist Patrick Moraz. The vaguely new wave–influenced *Long Distance Voyager* (1981) included the hits "The Voice" and "Gemini Dream." The Moody Blues continued recording in a contemporary, more commercially driven vein through the 1990s and into the new millennium. The retirement in 2002 of flautist Ray Thomas, who had been with the Moody Blues from the late 1960s, left the group in the hands of Hayward, Lodge, and Edge.

Suggested Albums: The Magnificent Moodies (aka *Go Now: The Moody Blues #1*) (1965); *Days of Future Passed* (1967)

MORRISON, VAN (1945–)

Van Morrison began his recording career as a teenager with the Northern Irish group Them. If he had done no more than write and sing their ecstatic narrative of sexual experience, "Gloria," his place in rock history would be assured. But as many of his contemporaries faded into repetition, Morrison moved on and established a remarkable solo career, beginning in 1967 with "Brown Eyed Girl." A perfect rock single, "Brown Eyed Girl" sketches a coming of age story in three minutes, driven by a striking guitar line improvised in the recording studio by a session musician and lifted on a joyous Latin-Calypso melody. "Brown Eyed Girl" went Top 10 in the United States (albeit in a bowdlerized edit) and was included on an album of demos released without Morrison's consent, *Blowin' Your Mind* (1967).

He considered *Astral Weeks* (1968) as the start of his solo vocation. By then he was well under way to inventing his own kind of soul music, and his lyrics were blossoming into poetry. Morrison recorded *Astral Weeks* in New York in a few quick takes with several of the city's finest jazz sidemen. The resumes of his

Van Morrison was among the most singular creative forces to emerge from the classic rock era. Beginning his career with the garage rock of his 1960s band Them, Van Morrison expanded his scope to include jazz, rhythm and blues, Celtic folk, and intimations of new age music. (Pictorial Press Ltd/Alamy Stock Photo)

accompanists include gigs with Eric Dolphy, Charles Mingus, Kenny Burrell, and the Modern Jazz Quartet. They received no instruction from their impromptu bandleader but like good jazzmen improvised and created enduring performances in the moment. *Astral Weeks* was an acoustic session, its themes of romantic, erotic, and spiritual love flowing easily from song through song.

During the first half of the 1970s, Morrison released a sequence of classic albums more focused than *Astral Weeks* on the verities of conventional writing filled with songs distinct in tone and texture. The characteristic Morrison sound coalesced during those years as a reinvention of 1950s rhythm and blues with jazz inclinations and passages of charismatic gospel. The piano-based title song from *Moondance* (1970) has become a jazz standard. However, the alto, soprano, and tenor saxophones of Jack Schroer and Collin Tilton defined much of the album. Morrison played his tenor voice like an instrument, fitting it to the needs of each song. He was not a jazz singer but an echo of jazz was often heard. "Into the Mystic" may have referred to the river flowing through Boston, where he sojourned at the time, but a double meaning was evident. Morrison's lyrics often gave the sense that the physical world was a symbol of something greater. "Come Running" was the hit single from *Moondance*, while "Crazy Love," "Caravan," and "Moondance" were heard often on FM. Through the mid-1970s Morrison was a regular presence on both radio bands.

The next several albums built on the Hibernian-Harlem path set by *Moondance* as Morrison became the first genuine Irish soul man. He had absorbed the spirit of rhythm and blues without trying to sound like an African American singer. He was natural, comfortable in the organic fusion he achieved. *His Band and the Street Choir* (1970) included a pair of hits, the fervent "Domino" and the jazzy "Blue Money."

Tupelo Honey (1971) opened with "Wild Night," which transmuted his influences into an ideal rock song about being young and alive, delivered with the perfect snap of rhythm and blues drumming and the twang of pedal steel guitar moving at a rock tempo. The title song was a poetic evocation of romantic devotion that freed the language of love from cliché. Morrison's voice verged on scatting in "Tupelo Honey" as the music suggested an ancient Celtic air infused with loose yet solid soul by Modern Jazz Quartet drummer Connie Kay. The fetching "I Wanna Roo You" was Morrison's take on old-time country music, an interest that would surface again.

Saint Dominic's Preview (1972) was another Irish soul masterpiece starting with his tribute to a powerful rhythm and blues singer, "Jackie Wilson Said (I'm in Heaven When You Smile)." With "Redwood Tree," Morrison found a mystic oneness with nature expressed with gospel undertones. The album included two songs that clocked in at over 10 minutes each, "Almost Independence Day" and "Listen to the Lion," whose stream of impressions were reminiscent of *Astral Weeks*.

For *Hard Nose to the Highway* (1973) and the live *It's Too Late to Stop Now* (1974), Morrison worked with the dozen members of the Caledonia Soul Orchestra, whose name spoke to his musical-cultural ambitions. Influenced by a short stay in the Irish Republic, written in the shadow of his divorce from singer Jane Planet and recorded quickly, *Veedon Fleece* (1974) was comparable to *Astral Weeks* in its

244 MOTT THE HOOPLE

acoustic texture and visionary poetry. The title was a term of Morrison's invention and refers to the spiritual object of his pursuit, a Holy Grail of wisdom and enlightenment.

Afterward, Morrison fell silent for several years. He surfaced for *The Last Waltz* (1976), the film and album documenting the Band's farewell concert, where he encountered New Orleans pianist Dr. John. They collaborated on *A Period of Transition* (1977), one of Morrison's lesser works. In a transparent bid for airplay, he called his next album *Wavelength* (1978). A livelier effort, closer in sound to albums from the early 1970s, it included a rousing reflection of his Jehovah's Witness upbringing, "Kingdom Hall." *Into the Music* (1979) closed the decade in a fusion of Celtic folk and Philadelphia soul.

Since then, Morrison has carved a singular path, exploring in poetic metaphor the inner life and the silence at the heart of existence on albums such as *Common One* (1980), *Beautiful Vision* (1982), *Inarticulate Speech of the Heart* (1983), and *A Sense of Wonder* (1985). *Avalon Sunset* (1989) included a duet with early 1960s British pop singer Cliff Richard, "Whenever God Shines His Light." There were tangents, including an album of largely Irish folk songs recorded with the Chieftains, *Irish Heartbeat* (1988), and albums of country music, *You Win Again* (2000) and *Pay the Devil* (2006). Morrison has not toured as extensively as his reputation would warrant, but continues to record prolifically. His thirty-fifth studio album, *Duets: Re-working the Catalogue*, was released in 2015.

An esteemed figure in Great Britain and Ireland, Morrison sang at the signing of the Good Friday Agreement (1998) that brought peace to Northern Ireland. Few Irish performers, from Thin Lizzy and U2 through the Boomtown Rats and Dexy's Midnight Runners, have escaped his inspiration. Morrison's influence as a writer and vocalist spans both sides of the Atlantic and can be heard in Bruce Springsteen, Graham Parker, Tom Petty, John Mellencamp, and even Rickie Lee Jones. Morrison was inducted into the Rock and Roll Hall of Fame.

Suggested Albums: Blowin' Your Mind (1967); *Astral Weeks* (1968); *Moondance* (1970); *His Band and the Street Choir* (1970); *Tupelo Honey* (1971); *Saint Dominic's Preview* (1972); *Hard Nose the Highway* (1973); *It's Too Late to Stop Now* (1974); *Veedon Fleece* (1974); *Wavelength* (1978); *Into the Music* (1979); *Common One* (1980); *Beautiful Vision* (1982); *Inarticulate Speech of the Heart* (1983); *A Sense of Wonder* (1985); *Irish Heartbeat* (1988); *Avalon Sunset* (1989); *Hymns to the Silence* (1991); *The Healing Game* (1997); *Back on Top* (1999); *You Win Again* (2000); *Pay the Devil* (2006)

See also: Them

MOTT THE HOOPLE

Producer Guy Stevens discovered the British band and came up with their quizzical name from a character in a Willard Manus novel. He convinced guitarist Mick Ralphs and the rest of the group that a stronger frontman was needed if they were going to get anywhere in the music business, hence a talent hunt that found vocalist Ian Hunter. It was the band's good fortune to land Hunter, who proved to be an imaginative songwriter and charismatic frontman. His arrival launched a career that touched on glam and influenced scores of young British musicians who would later form the core of punk rock in the late 1970s.

Hunter's talents were not much on display on the band's self-titled debut (1969), which opened with a heavy instrumental version of the Kinks' "You Really Got Me." Hunter took a backseat as a writer to cover versions of songs written by the likes of Sonny Bono and Doug Sahm, employing Dylanesque vocals over backing that often sounded borrowed from *Highway 61 Revisited*. An exception was the rowdy rocker "Rock and Roll Queen," which although penned by Ralphs would prove to be a better predictor of the band's future direction. Hunter was clearly in charge by the second album, *Mad Shadows* (1970), writing all but two of the songs and pushing the group in a more distinctive hard rock direction. No longer aping Dylan, Hunter sang in an increasingly British accent as the band turned up the volume with noisier guitars and more aggressive drumming. The songs were largely reflective as Hunter seemingly struggled to find his voice as a songwriter.

He began to find his voice in the band's next two albums, *Wildlife* (1971) and *Brain Capers* (1971). Hunter wrote only three songs on *Wildlife*, but they were evocative tales of the rock lifestyle and telling portrayals of hardened street survivors. *Brain Capers* was where Hunter emerged as an artistic presence, writing several rough and ready songs as the band rocked with a newfound swagger that would provide increasing credibility with young listeners quickly becoming bored with the high-mindedness of progressive rock.

The band had developed a following in the United Kingdom, but had little presence in the United States and elsewhere. Their profile was elevated with the release of *All the Young Dudes* (1972), the album and song most associated with Hunter and the band. The title track, written by David Bowie and replete with sexually ambiguous allusions, provided Mott the Hoople with its first hit single and gave them an entry point into the world of glam rock, as did a cover of the Velvet Underground's "Sweet Jane." Hunter was now singing in a full British accent, and the songs developed a harder edged punk perspective filled with street smarts and cynical observations on the riff-raff surrounding a rock band. The music hit harder than ever, making Mott the Hoople a critical favorite and increasing their following.

Onstage the band moved further toward glam, and they dandied up a bit, but never adopted the androgynous look favored by Bowie and others. The band shifted to a more polished approach for their next two albums, *Mott* (1973) and *The Hoople* (1974). "All the Way from Memphis," the leadoff track to "Mott," was a spirited radio-friendly rocker about life on the road, with a soaring sax and hook-laden chorus (and some sadly racially insensitive lyrics). Songs like "Whizz Kid" and "Drivin' Sister" also had considerable commercial appeal, but the brutal "Violence" showed that Hunter had not gone soft in the pursuit of fame. *The Hoople* was more overtly commercial, but its merits included the ebulliently melodic "Roll Away the Stone," the nostalgic "The Golden Age of Rock and Roll," and the tortured rebelliousness of "Marionette." While sales were strong, some critics groused over the band's new, slicker direction. Guitarist Ariel Bender (nee Luther Grosvener) had replaced Ralphs, and internal dissension as well as Hunter's desire to start a solo career led to the band's dissolution in 1974, just as they approached the height of their popularity.

Hunter quickly put the band behind him with a solo record, and Ralphs did the same by forming the supergroup Bad Company. The remaining band members put out two desultory albums under the name Mott before breaking up to form British Lions. Mott the Hoople would quickly return to prominence with the advent of punk, as the rowdy aggressiveness of songs like "Violence" and "Death May Be Your Santa Claus" provided inspiration for the new generation of rock rebels. Bands like the Clash clearly owed a debt to Hunter and the band in both sound and lyrical approach, and Hunter was hailed as a pre-punk pioneer. However, the band is probably best known for "All the Young Dudes," the song that has probably become the leading anthem of glam rock and has remained a staple of FM radio since its release. The band re-formed in 2009 and has played a limited number of dates since then.

Suggested Albums: Mott the Hoople (1969); *Mad Shadows* (1970); *Wildlife* (1971); *Brain Capers* (1971); *All the Young Dudes* (1972); *Mott* (1973); *The Hoople* (1974)

See also: Hunter, Ian

MOUNTAIN

When Long Island guitarist Leslie West stepped outside his garage rock band, the Vagrants, to record a solo album called *Mountain* (1969), he called on Felix Pappalardi to play bass. Pappalardi was a classically trained musician who emerged from the Greenwich Village folk-blues revival to become an inventive producer, notably for Cream and the Youngbloods. Pleased with their collaboration, West and Pappalardi formed the band Mountain with keyboardist Steve Knight to explore heavy, post-Cream rock. One of their first appearances was at the Woodstock Festival (1969), where they were well received.

Their debut album, *Climbing!* (1970), included a staple of early 1970s hard rock, "Mississippi Queen," with a heavy guitar riff and clanging cowbells. By contrast, the title number from *Nantucket Sleighride* (1971) demonstrated the potential of a rock band, without pretentious compositional tricks or the aid of an orchestra, to achieve a symphonic sound through the unique timbres and power of electric guitar and organ. Mountain was capable of grit and grandeur and West was able to pronounce emotionally powerful solos but often chose to stick to the basics.

Mountain released a half-live, half-studio LP, *Flowers of Evil* (1971), before briefly disbanding. West joined the power trio West, Bruce and Laing (with ex-Cream bassist Jack Bruce), but regrouped with Pappalardi as Mountain for a pair of live and studio albums (1974). They played their final show together at the end of 1974.

West continued with little notice as a solo artist and worked the nostalgia circuit under the Mountain name. The respect he achieved as a guitarist is evidenced by

MOVE 247

his invitation to play with the Who on sessions for their album *Who's Next* (1971). However, those tracks were omitted from the LP and only surfaced years later as bonus tracks. Hearing problems aggravated by Mountain's high-decibel concerts forced Pappalardi to withdraw from music. In 1983 his wife shot him to death.

Suggested Albums: Climbing! (1970); *Nantucket Sleighride* (1971)

MOVE

The Move's name suggested the dynamism of the Mod subculture as well as unwillingness to stand still musically. They formed in 1966 in Birmingham, England, an unfashionable industrial city that nourished a flourishing music scene with the Moody Blues, the Spencer Davis Group, and dozens of bands that never found an audience beyond the English Midlands. Already veterans of several of those local bands, the Move's members had honed their harmonies singing Motown covers, always a popular draw among Mods. The falsetto vocals of the Move's guitarist and songwriter, Roy Wood, added distinction to their recordings.

Wood was already a formidable writer on the band's first singles from 1967, "Night of Fear," "Disturbance," and "I Can Hear the Grass Grow." At this stage he was to psychedelia what Brian Wilson was to surf. Both were able to vividly articulate an experience they had never had. Stylistically, Wood and the Move were often comparable to Pete Townshend and the early Who in their ability to set short and often amusing vignettes to sharply chiseled three-minute songs propelled by busy bass lines and a heavy beat.

None of their early singles appeared on their eponymous debut album (1968), and there was no sign that Wood's inspiration was flagging. The irresistible "Fire Brigade," a humorous aside on smoldering sexuality, rode on an Eddie Cochran riff. The melodically memorable "Useless Information" was a prescient complaint against media overload. Had Gilbert and Sullivan lived long enough to pen an operetta about England in the 1960s, it might have included the cheeky "Flowers in the Rain." "Walk Upon the Water" was emblematic of English psychedelic pop with its inventive whimsy and harmless eccentricity. *The Move* already included hints of the string quartets and baroque influences that came to fluorescence in Wood's next band, Electric Light Orchestra.

Their only number one British single was drenched in the influence of *Rubber Soul* Beatles. "Blackberry Way" (1968) was released in between albums, part of the Move's disorganized discography, which left many of their finest moments waiting to be collected years later on anthology albums.

The Move's next album, *Shazam* (1970), was an about-face from the snappy Mod psychedelic pop of its predecessor. Most tracks were longer in length and were hard rock verging on heavy metal, largely bereft of blues but infused with idiosyncratic pop aspirations. Jeff Lynne joined the Move for *Looking On* (1970) and *Message from the Country* (1971), albums that developed the band's sound along *Shazam's* lines. During this time, Wood and Lynne began planning their next move, the Electric Light Orchestra, and experimented with cello as a substitute for electric bass and oboe as a lead instrument in hard rock. They continued to produce quality work under the Move's name until their contractual obligations were fulfilled. Their final release was a three-song recording featuring Lynne's "Do Ya," later a hit for Electric Light Orchestra (1977), and Wood's "California Man," familiar to American rock fans from Cheap Trick's version (1978), which quoted the riff from an earlier Move song, "Brontosaurus."

Suggested Albums: The Move (1968); *Shazam* (1970); *Looking On* (1970); *Message from the Country* (1971); *The Best of the Move* (1974)

See also: Electric Light Orchestra; Wood, Roy

MURPHY, ELLIOTT (1949–)

In the early 1970s, New York's Elliott Murphy was one of several recording artists dubbed "a new Bob Dylan" by rock critics eager to replace the great songwriter of the 1960s, who seemed to have let them down. The release of one of Dylan's greatest albums, *Blood on the Tracks* (1975), began to make their point seem moot, as did the changing cultural landscape, which assured that any new Dylan would never gain influence comparable to the old one.

Murphy was an intelligent, literate singer-songwriter whose early albums echoed a sense of lost opportunities, of having missed the golden age, on songs such as "Last of the Rock Stars" from his debut, *Aquashow* (1973), or the title of its follow-up, *Lost Generation* (1975). His greatest rock song, the anthemic "Drive All Night" from *Just a Story from America* (1977), received some airplay.

Overshadowed by Bruce Springsteen and the rise of punk rock, Murphy never connected with a wide American audience but found more success in Europe. He has been living in Paris for many years, where he became noted for his fiction and essays. Murphy was admitted to the Legion of Honor as a Chevalier des arts et des Lettres (2015), a distinction he shares with artists such as Philip Glass and Uma Thurman. Murphy continues to record prolifically and has released more than 25 albums.

Suggested Albums: Aquashow (1973); *Lost Generation* (1975); *Night Lights* (1976); *Just a Story from America* (1977)

NAZZ

Todd Rundgren's long, productive, and often individualistic career began in the late 1960s with Nazz, a band that oddly enough tended to sound like other artists. Formed in 1967, Nazz took their name from a Yardbirds song, and the cover of their eponymous debut album (1968) bore a more than passing resemblance to *Meet the Beatles*. The music was melodic garage rock, more hook-laden than most, but often lacking in originality. The power chord opening to the riff-dominated "Open My Eyes" bore great similarity to the Who's "I Can't Explain," while other songs brought to mind Hendrix, Cream, and of course the Beatles. The piano-driven ballad "Hello, It's Me" showed Rundgren in more original form, and it was clear that he had a way with melodic pop that would come to greater fruition later in his career. Rundgren would have a hit single with a re-recorded version in 1972. Rundgren split vocal duties with keyboardist Robert "Stewkey" Antoni.

While some of the songs on the follow-up, *Nazz Nazz* (1969), continued to echo Cream and the Beatles, a number of more original-sounding, piano-based Rundgren numbers found their way to the record. Rundgren's pop instincts were evolving and the album showed greater sophistication in songwriting, pointing to a way beyond the garage band psychedelia of their debut.

Rundgren eventually felt confined by the band and departed in 1969 to pursue an at times quirky but often artistically and commercially successful career as a recording artist and producer. A third album, *Nazz III*, was released in 1971 without the band's knowledge and boasted a postproduction swap of Rundgren's vocals in favor of Antoni's. The band broke up for good in 1971. One song, "Open My Eyes," was included on Lenny Kaye's well-regarded compilation of garage band classics, *Nuggets* (1972). Drummer Thom Mooney following his stint with Rundgren had another brush with the soon to be famous in his next band, Fuse (whose original name, oddly, was also Nazz). Fuse included two young Illinois rockers, Rick Nielsen and Tom Petersson, who would later enjoy superstardom with Cheap Trick.

Suggested Albums: Nazz (1968); *Nazz Nazz* (1969)

NEKTAR

British expatriate musicians formed Nektar in Hamburg in 1969. Their American fans could be forgiven for assuming they were German, given the spelling of their name and their debut as a recording act on German labels. A postpsychedelic guitar-keyboard band, Nektar edged into the concept album compositional complexity of Gentle Giant–style progressive rock. Buoyed by a brief surge of American interest in German bands beyond the hardcore "Krautrock" fans, Nektar's *Remember the Future* (1973) gained a wide audience and *Down to Earth* (1974) reached the Top 40 album chart in the United States.

Although left behind by fashion, Nektar continued to record before breaking up in 1980. Banking on the renewed interest in progressive rock, Nektar regrouped in 2002 and resumed recording and performing.

Suggested Albums: Journey to the Centre of the Eye (1971); *A Tab in the Ocean* (1972)

NEU!

Formed in Dusseldorf in 1971, Neu! consisted of former Kraftwerk drummer Klaus Dinger and guitarist Michael Rother with Kraftwerk's engineer-producer Conny Plank providing technical support. Their name ("Neu!" is German for "New!") commented on the advertising industry's manipulation of the public's appetite for novelty. Neu!'s eponymous debut (1972) was among the influences on Brian Eno and David Bowie that culminated in Bowie's "Berlin Trilogy" of albums (1977–1979). Running out of money during the recording of *Neu! 2* (1973), they resorted to producing tape-manipulated variations of previously recorded music, resulting in an early example of a "remix" recording. Some of that music found its way into the soundtrack of Taiwanese director Jimmy Wang Yu's martial arts flick *Master of the Flying Guillotine* (1976) and from there to Quentin Tarantino's tribute to the earlier movie, *Kill Bill Volume 1* (2003).

Essentially two solo albums packed together, *Neu! 75* (1975) exemplified the growing split between Rother and Dinger. Rother's side was ambient; Dinger's was aggressive and an influence on the more adventurous wing of punk rock. Neu! broke up after the album's release. Rother had already begun collaborating with other musicians, including a project with fellow German electronic artists Cluster under the name Harmonia. After the breakup, he recorded a trio of albums produced by Plank (1977–1979). Dinger formed a superb rock band with punk proclivities, La Dusseldorf, which issued three albums (1976–1981).

In 1985 and 1986, Rother and Dinger recorded together with the results released years later as *Neu! 4* (1995). They continued to bicker, even as odds and ends from their time together were released alongside tribute albums with contributions from Oasis, Primal Scream, and other contemporary bands.

Suggested Albums: Neu! (1972); *Neu! 2* (1973); *Neu! 75* (1975)

See also: Cluster; Kraftwerk

NEW RIDERS OF THE PURPLE SAGE

The early days of the New Riders of the Purple Sage were intertwined with the Grateful Dead. Both had roots in the northern California folk-blues revival of the early 1960s, and the Dead's mastermind Jerry Garcia frequently gigged with members of the New Riders. Future New Riders guitarists John Dawson and David Nelson remained friends with the Dead after the band broke big, and eventually a mutual love of country music (and the Bakersfield scene in particular) led Garcia to sit in and play steel guitar with the duo after they formed the New Riders of the Purple Sage.

The new band's country and bluegrass proclivities coincided with the rise of country rock. The Byrds' *Sweethearts of the Rodeo* was a fresh memory and Gram Parsons's Flying Burrito Brothers were making waves. The New Riders began by touring in conjunction with the Dead and landed a recording contract on the strength of that tour.

The Dead's fingerprints were all over the New Riders' eponymous debut (1971). Garcia played on the album and was credited as a band member, although he would leave before the release of the next album. The Dead's drummer Mickey Hart also played on some tracks, and bassist Phil Lesh was given a credit as executive producer. The music itself was pleasing country rock, more comfortably, authentically country than *Sweethearts of the Rodeo* but lacking the genre-bending originality of Parsons's Burrito Brothers. *Workingman's Dead* was a solid reference point, but the New Riders stuck much more closely to a country path than the Dead did on their masterpiece.

That country direction determined the direction of the band's career, as they seldom changed over the course of the next several decades. *The Adventures of Panama Red* (1973) featured a snappy cover of Peter Rowan's "Panama Red" that became the band's most popular song. The New Riders opened a number of shows for the Dead in the late 1970s, but were overshadowed by the Eagles, Poco, and other more commercially successful country rock acts. Had the New Riders played their cards differently they might have attached themselves to the burgeoning "outlaw country" movement, but the band continued to move in rock circles to increased public indifference. The New Riders continue to tour and occasionally record in the new millennium, despite the 2009 death of founding member John Dawson.

Suggested Albums: New Riders of the Purple Sage (1971); *Powerglide* (1972); *The Adventures of Panama Red* (1973)

NEW YORK DOLLS

During their short run together, the New York Dolls sold few records and were mocked when not ignored by mainstream media. They were classified as thrift store glitter rock because of their androgynous togs and as a caricature of the Rolling Stones for their hard rock sound as well as the resemblance both between the Dolls' lead singer David Johansen and the Stones' Mick Jagger and between the

Dolls' guitarist Johnny Thunders and the Stones' Keith Richards. But they were embraced by a segment of the rock press for bringing fun and irony to rock at a time when the music had grown deadly serious. The New York Dolls helped set the stage for the punk rock scene that emerged at the CBGB's club in the Bowery, and their tour of the United Kingdom planted seeds that would sprout in the form of the Sex Pistols.

The classic lineup of the New York Dolls was in place by 1972 with Johansen and Thunders joined by drummer Jerry Nolan, guitarist Sylvain Sylvain, and bassist Arthur "Killer" Kane. Chaotic, out of tune, and unpredictable, the Dolls were brought into the studio to record their self-titled debut (1973) under producer Todd Rundgren. Rundgren was unable to do much but document a glorious mess that could not eclipse (and perhaps enhanced) a wonderful batch of witty, hard rocking originals. Most were written by Johansen and Thunders, though usually separately and not in collaboration as with Jagger and Richards. For their follow-up, *Too Much Too Soon* (1974), their label brought in George "Shadow" Morton, a producer best known for early 1960s hits with the girl group the Shangri-Las. By this time the well of original songs was nearly tapped out. Along with three of the Dolls' finest songs, "Babylon," "Who Are the Mystery Girls," and "Chatterbox" (the latter with lead vocals by Thunders), the album was filled out with doo-wop and blues covers.

Beginning the final leg of their career, the New York Dolls hooked up with British Svengali Malcolm McLaren, soon to be notorious as the Sex Pistols' manager. Pronouncing glitter rock passé, McLaren dressed the Dolls in red costumes, hung a Communist banner above their stage, and sent them on the road, apparently assuming that revolution would spread in their wake. Drug abuse and bickering caused a gradual implosion with Thunders and Nolan leaving the band. The remnants struggled on through 1977, long enough to greet the arrival of punk rock, whose adherents regarded the Dolls as heroic forerunners.

Thunders and Johansen went on to noteworthy careers, with the latter enjoying his greatest acclaim under the guise of swing-era nightclub singer Buster Poindexter. Thunders eventually joined with Nolan and punk rock recording artist Richard Hell as the Heartbreakers, a hard rock band drenched in passion and heroin. Thunders died in 1991 and Nolan followed a year later.

In 2004 Smiths vocalist Morrissey, who as a teenager had headed the New York Dolls' British fan club, coaxed Johansen, Sylvain, and Kane to reunite for a London festival documented on CD and film. Although Kane died later that year, Johansen and Sylvain decided to continue to tour and record as the New York Dolls. Rundgren produced a reunion album, *Cause I Sez So* (2009).

Suggested Albums: The New York Dolls (1973); *Too Much Too Soon* (1974)

NEWMAN, RANDY (1943–)

Randy Newman grew up at the interstices where Hollywood in the sunset of its golden era met the nascent music industry rising in Los Angeles. With 10 Academy

Awards and many more Oscar nominations between them, his uncles Alfred, Lionel, and Emil Newman were prolific composers of film scores, writing orchestral music for *All About Eve, The Grapes of Wrath, Wuthering Heights,* and *The Hunchback of Notre Dame,* among others. The father of his childhood friend, Lenny Waronker, headed Liberty Records. Waronker grew up to produce Newman and become president of Warner Brothers Records.

Newman took up the family trade in the early 1960s and by the end of the decade had penned songs for recording artists as diverse as Peggy Lee, Gene Pitney, Petula Clark, Three Dog Night, Dusty Springfield, the O'Jays, the Alan Price Set, Peggy Lee, and Harpers Bizarre. His mordant humor was apparent on his self-titled debut (1968), which opened with "Love Story (You and Me)," which predicted that love and marriage would end in death at a Florida nursing home. The album sounded like the work of a man from another time with Newman playing the part of Oscar Levant or Hoagy Carmichael on piano as he arranged and conducted the accompanying orchestra. For his follow-up, Newman showed that he could move between his uncles' era and his own. *12 Songs* (1970) was an eccentric album of Americana with Ry Cooder adding inventive bottleneck guitar on the spooky "Let's Burn Down the Cornfield" and Newman rewriting a Stephen Foster antislavery song, "Old Kentucky Home."

With great powers of observation and the ability to express himself economically, Newman invented narrators for his songs with disturbing perspectives but endowed them with understanding if not sympathy. Some of his songs reflected on the irony of America, a nation hard pressed to fulfill the promise of its lofty ideals. The greatest example, the title number from *Sail Away* (1972), was a sales pitch from a slave trader to his unwitting West African victims. The pitchman promised freedom and adventure in the New World as the orchestra painted an Aaron Copland sonic panorama. *Sail Away* also included a nod to Kurt Weill in the sardonic "Lonely at the Top." In "Political Science," an exasperated and ugly American spoke of blowing up the rest of the word in a tune Phil Silvers could have sung in a 1940s Hollywood musical.

Good Old Boys (1974) was another pointed critique of America. A loose song cycle about the South, it opened with the rollicking ragtime of "Rednecks," a naked assertion of Dixie racism that also called out Northern hypocrisy. "Birmingham" was amusing local boosterism set to parlor piano blues. "Louisiana 1927," a cinematic retelling of the flood that inundated the South during the Coolidge administration, mingled sympathy with fatalism as the waters rose. "Kingfish" was a straight-faced celebration of the accomplishments of Louisiana's demagogue Governor Huey Long.

Newman's sharp irony limited his audience until his fluke hit, "Short People" from *Little Criminals* (1977). Intended as a parody of mindless bigotry but widely embraced for its catchy nastiness, "Short People" was the silliest song on an otherwise serious album. With its rueful depiction of urban decay, "Baltimore" attracted jazz singer Nina Simone, who added it to her repertoire. Newman employed a synthesizer instead of an orchestra and was backed by the Eagles' Glenn Frey, Don Henley, and Bernie Leadon.

His song-oriented albums were a mixed bag afterward as Newman fell into the banality of 1980s studio production. There was a sense that he had reached the final pages of his joke book. Although he had already dabbled in writing for movies and television, Newman began to receive the most attention for his work in cinema, following the path of his uncles by winning Oscars for the Pixar Studio animated features *Monsters Inc.* (2001) and *Toy Story 3* (2010) as well as nominations for *Toy Story, A Bug's Life, Toy Story 2, Cars,* and *Monsters University*. He also won an Emmy for the theme song from television's *Monk*.

Suggested Albums: Randy Newman (1968); *12 Songs* (1970); *Randy Newman Live* (1971); *Sail Away* (1972); *Good Old Boys* (1974); *Little Criminals* (1977)

NICE

The members of the Nice were veterans of Britain's rhythm and blues–aspiring rock bands of the mid-1960s, but there was little evidence of that in their music. Their debut album, *The Thoughts of Emerlist Davjack* (1967), was a mixed bag. "Rondo," a heavy-handed, rhythmically simplistic variation on Dave Brubeck's "Blue Rondo a la Turk" and Mozart's "Rondo Alla Turca," served keyboardist Keith Emerson's irrepressible desire to show off his speed. However, on that first album, he shared writing credits with guitarist Davy O'List and bassist-vocalist Lee Jackson, who ameliorated his worst tendencies. The title track (co-written by List and Emerson) and "Flower King of Flies" (Emerson and Jackson) were magnificent examples of psychedelic pop rock.

List abandoned the Nice midway through recording their second album, *Ars Longa Vita Brevis* (1968). He was briefly a member of Roxy Music and played on Bryan Ferry's album *Another Time, Another Place* (1974) before joining the proto–power pop band Jet. With List gone, the Nice became Emerson's show, whose overheated classical rock became a model for his contributions to the supergroup Emerson, Lake & Palmer. The Nice ended in 1970.

Suggested Album: The Thoughts of Emerlist Davjack (1967)

NICO (1938–1988)

Nico was a singular presence in music. Born Christa Paffgen, she grew up in Berlin as the Third Reich crumbled under Allied bombings and the Soviet army closed in. She became a veritable Cassandra of ill omen on record and stage. Nico was part of the European jet set in the early 1960s with a small role in Federico Fellini's epochal *La Dolce Vita* (1961) and a modeling job in Paris. Befriending Rolling Stones guitarist Brian Jones, she entered the music scene with a single produced by Jimmy Page before leaving for the postwar world cultural capital, New York. There she met Andy Warhol, spent her nights at the endless parties in his Factory studio, and appeared in his film, *Chelsea Girls* (1966). Warhol connected her with the rock band he managed and was given equal time on their debut album, *The Velvet Underground and Nico* (1967).

She soon went solo. *Chelsea Girl* (1967) was a lovely album of chamber pop. Nico was the expressionless mannequin voice of elegant emotional isolation, accompanied by a string quartet on a handful of songs by her erstwhile Velvet Underground colleagues and three by her youthful guitar accompanist, the then-unknown Jackson Browne.

Beginning with *The Marble Index* (1969) and continuing through *Desertshore* (1970) and *The End* (1974), Nico found her unique style. Sometimes she sang alone with her harmonium, conjuring images of an abandoned church on the heaths of Northern Germany whose gaps in the roof revealed a cold starry sky. Her voice had become more anxious, edged in the trepidation of doomed emotional isolation. Some of her cadences suggested the late medieval hymnody of Martin Luther, but bereft of any hope of salvation. Her enduring friend from the Velvet Underground, John Cale, produced those albums, adding eerie touches of guitar and percussion but often leaving her alone. She is notable for investing the Doors' pretentious epic "The End" with Gothic sincerity.

Nico devoted most of the 1970s to acting in the films of French director Philippe Garrel and contributing to their soundtracks. She performed occasionally with guitarist Lutz Ulbrich from the German band Ash Ra Tempel and was much admired by the progenitors of punk rock. The punk scene provided her with a new audience after 1977. Her first album in nearly a decade, *Drama of Exile* (1981), mixed rock with Middle Eastern influences and included covers of the Velvet Underground and David Bowie as well as originals. Nico's final album, *Camera Obscura* (1985), included a beautifully doomed rendition of Richard Rodgers and Lorenz Hart's standard "My Funny Valentine." She died of a brain hemorrhage after a bicycling accident in 1988.

Nico's demeanor and music provided inspiration for the "Goth" subculture that emerged from punk rock with British bands such as Bauhaus and Siouxsie and the Banshees leading the way. Bjork and the Cult have covered her songs. Nico has been portrayed in several films and plays, starting with director Oliver Stone's *The Doors* (1991).

Suggested Albums: Chelsea Girl (1967); *The Marble Index* (1969); *Desertshore* (1970); *The End* (1974); *Drama of Exile* (1981); *Camera Obscura* (1985)

NILSSON, HARRY (1941–1994)

Singer-songwriter Harry Nilsson topped the charts in 1972 with his cover of Badfinger's "Without You," but that success was the fruit of an already extensive career that had begun in the mid-1960s. The Brooklyn-born Nilsson had performing in his blood as the son of circus entertainers. When his father walked out on the family, it fell to an uncle to nurture Nilsson's already obvious musical skills. Inspired by a love for rhythm and blues, Nilsson took up songwriting at a relatively early age, honing his craft with help from musical acts he met while working as an assistant manager at the Paramount Theater in Los Angeles, where he had finally settled after a transient childhood.

Nilsson's debut album, *Pandemonium Shadow Show* (1967), featured his powerful intense voice and finely tuned songwriting. The material was largely pop oriented, but the subject matter was darker than the average Top 40 tune, and the sound at times resembled Broadway and cabaret more than rock music. The album didn't chart well, but Nilsson picked up some important fans in the form of the Beatles, who reportedly were quite taken with his work. His next album, *Ariel Ballet* (1968), mixed folk-styled songs with pop and took on even darker subject matter such as parental abandonment and suicide. Most songs were written by Nilsson, but not his first hit single, the folky soon-to-be-a-standard "Everybody's Talkin'," featured in the soundtrack of director John Schlesinger's *Midnight Cowboy* (1969).

Critics sang praises for *Nilsson Sings Newman* (1970), an album of strong interpretations of Randy Newman songs, accompanied by the composer himself on piano. Nilsson scored another critical hit with his concept album *The Point!* (1971), which included narrative interludes and whose sophisticated pop songwriting and arrangements evoked the vocal harmonies of the Beatles and the Hollies.

The general public discovered Nilsson with *Nilsson Schmilsson* (1971) and its smash single "Without You." The deeply emotional piano ballad bordered on melodrama as Nilsson crooned a trembling tenor vocal, singing of the devastating effects of lost love in lyrics that seemed to contemplate suicide. The calypso-based "Coconuts" and guitar rocker "Jump Into the Fire" also received airplay. Suddenly Nilsson was a star. He formed a fast friendship with recent Los Angeles arrival John Lennon and the two proceeded to paint the town in an orgy of excessive drinking and generally boorish behavior.

Nilsson seemed to turn his back on commercial success, recording an album of standards from the Great American Songbook, *A Little Touch of Schmilsson in the Night* (1973), which nevertheless yielded a popular cover of "As Time Goes By." A co-starring role with Ringo Starr in the film *Son of Dracula* (1974) allowed Nilsson to try his hand at acting, although the movie was not well received. Things took a turn for the worse when Nilsson badly damaged his vocal cords recording his next album, *Pussy Cats* (1974), shielding the information from producer Lennon. The injuries would plague Nilsson for the rest of his life, and his voice would never truly be the same. The subsequent album sounded more like a Lennon record and was Nilsson's hardest rocking effort.

From that point Nilsson's career went on a downward trajectory. His last album was the soundtrack to the film *Popeye* (1980). Nilsson's later life was often troubled, forced to deal with the murder of close friend Lennon and beset by financial difficulties. He rallied to begin work on a new album, but in 1994 he died of complications from a heart attack before it could be completed.

Nilsson will be forever remembered for "Without You," a pop classic that has been frequently covered, most notably by Mariah Carey who had a hit with her even more melodramatic version (1994). "Everybody's Talkin'" remains a touchstone of the late 1960s counterculture, and while both songs were covers, Nilsson was a sufficiently respected songwriter to be ranked No. 62 on *Rolling Stone* magazine's list of "The 100 Greatest Songwriters of All Time."

Suggested Albums: Pandemonium Shadow Show (1967); *Ariel Ballet* (1968); *Harry* (1969); *Nilsson Sings Newman* (1970); *The Point!* (1971); *Nilsson Schmilsson* (1971); *Son of Schmilsson* (1972); *Pussy Cats* (1974)

NRBQ

Begun in 1966 as the New Rhythm and Blues Quintet, the enigmatic acronym they soon adopted was better suited for a band that considers the breadth of American music as fair game. Pianist Terry Adams is the only original member, but the shifting lineup has not disrupted their musical evolution. Roots rock and roll is the grounding for NRBQ's explorations of mid-20th-century jazz, Tin Pan Alley pop, and Beatlesque rock. Their breadth was already apparent on their self-titled debut album (1969), which included covers of Eddie Cochran and Sun Ra. Their second album, *Boppin' the Blues* (1970), was in collaboration with rockabilly pioneer Carl Perkins.

NRBQ never amassed a large audience but developed a devoted following for their eclectic recordings, unpredictable live repertoire, and sense of humor. Their original songs have attracted attention from other artists. "Me and the Boys," a classic rock and roll tune from *Tiddlywinks* (1980), has been covered by Bonnie Raitt and Dave Edmunds. NRBQ's brush with stardom occurred when they appeared live and as animated figures in seasons 10 through 12 (1998–2001) of the popular Fox network show *The Simpsons*.

Suggested Albums: NRBQ (1969); *Boppin' the Blues* (with Carl Perkins) (1970); *Scraps* (1972); *Workshop* (1973); *All Hopped Up* (1977); *At Yankee Stadium* (1978); *Kick Me Hard* (1979); *Tiddlywinks* (1980); *Grooves in Orbit* (1983)

NUGGETS

When it was first released in 1972, nobody really knew what to call the music collected on *Nuggets: Original Artyfacts from the First Psychedelic Era 1965–1968*. The album's compiler, rock critic Lenny Kaye (who soon became Patti Smith's guitarist), approached the task like an archaeologist. Instead of excavating in the sands of the Near East, he dug through bins of "cut out" albums deleted from record label catalogues, through stacks of singles and boxes of discs at rummage sales and resale stores. Kaye was trying to reconstruct an overlooked facet of recent history, the fluorescence of American rock bands responding to the British Invasion. Calling it the "First Psychedelic Era" implied anticipation for a second coming. But "Psychedelic Era" proved a misleading title, as the consciousness-altering properties of LSD may have inspired some but not all of the music Kaye collected. The bracketed dates defined a time when teenage Americans digested the startling arrival of the Beatles and their compatriots and embraced the heady possibilities of new rock. Unlike the Jefferson Airplane or the Grateful Dead, none of the *Nuggets* bands enjoyed success past 1968.

The impact of *Nuggets* on 1970s rock fans was comparable to Harry Smith's *Anthology of American Folk Music* on folk-blues revivalists of the previous generation.

It was a window on a recent but already forgotten past, a period distant enough from the present to assume romantic hues. Like Smith's *Anthology*, *Nuggets* was not a collection of field recordings but was gleaned from the debris of the record industry, the music discarded by the corporations as worthless.

Nuggets stimulated interest in a parallel line of development in rock music that largely fell outside the FM radio canon of the Beatles, the Doors, the Jefferson Airplane, and the Rolling Stones. Many of the singles anthologized on *Nuggets* were the work of bands that never displayed more than three minutes of inspiration. Most did not produce a body of work comparable to the great bands of the classic rock era but testified to the possibility that the creative spark existed everywhere.

Aside from being young, American, and often forgotten outside their localities, the bands Kaye selected shared more differences than commonalities. Some were truly psychedelic, like the dynamic yet ethereal Electric Prunes. Mouse were mediocre Bob Dylan impersonators while the Knickerbockers were just as good at being the early Beatles as the early Beatles themselves. A few bands were models for punk rock, an idea just taking root in the pages of cutting-edge rock magazines. In that camp lived the snarling blues-based rave-ups of the Shadows of Knight. And then came psychedelic punks such as the Seeds and the 13th Floor Elevators.

When punk rock finally happened in the late 1970s, many bands turned to *Nuggets* for repertoire and songwriting ideas. *Nuggets* inspired *Pebbles* and other compilations of obscure and forgotten rock bands. Rhino Records, a reissue label whose existence owes some debt to Kaye's vision, released an expanded four-CD *Nuggets* box set (2012).

NYRO, LAURA (1947–1997)

Laura Nyro (born Laura Nigro) grew up amidst a variety of music. Her mother was an opera and classical music buff; her father was a jazz trumpeter. She attended Manhattan's High School of Music and Art, drank up Motown hits from the radio, and, as a teenager, found her way into the Greenwich Village's folk-blues revival.

She was only 19 when she recorded *More Than a New Discovery* (1966), which sold poorly but was a trove of hits for other artists. The 5th Dimension recorded "Wedding Bell Blues" and "Blowin' Away," Barbra Streisand had a hit with "Stoney End," and Blood, Sweat & Tears with "And When I Die." Nyro found an audience in her own right with *Eli and the Thirteenth Confession* (1968). Chock-full of sophisticated melodies with jazz inflections, Broadway-worthy tunes delivered with pop gospel fervor, and echoes of early Carole King sung in a powerful voice with penetrating range and a warm tone, the album included more songs that became hits in other hands. The 5th Dimension returned for "Stoned Soul Picnic" and "Sweet Blindness," and Three Dog Night reached the Top 10 with "Eli's Comin'."

Nyro seldom toured but concentrated on writing and recording. *New York Tendaberry* (1969) featured poetic lyrics, intense phrasing, and one of her most familiar songs, "Save the Country." *Christmas and the Beads of Sweat* (1970) was an eclectic outing backed on some numbers by Duane Allman and the Muscle Shoals studio band and by free jazz musician Alice Coltrane on others. She changed direction again with *Gonna Take a Miracle* (1971), an album of rhythm and blues covers accompanied by the soul group Labelle.

Uncomfortable with the public spotlight, she retired from music in 1973 but restarted her recording career three years later and began to perform more often. Nyro died in 1997 of ovarian cancer. She influenced the songwriting of several notable artists, including Todd Rundgren, Elvis Costello, and Rickie Lee Jones.

Suggested Albums: More Than a New Discovery (aka *The First Songs*) (1966); *Eli and the Thirteenth Confession* (1968); *New York Tendaberry* (1969); *Christmas and the Beads of Sweat* (1970); *Gonna Take a Miracle* (1971)

OLDFIELD, MIKE (1953–)

Mike Oldfield seized the attention of pop as well as progressive rock fans when an excerpt from his 49-minute album-length composition, *Tubular Bells* (1973), became a hit single after its inclusion in the soundtrack of William Friedkin's *The Exorcist*. The album and the single sold so well that Oldfield is credited for launching the career of Virgin Records' Richard Branson, who emerged from the music industry to found Virgin Airways and a host of other enterprises.

The parallel paths of Oldfield's early musical life converged on latter-day albums that combined electronic and acoustic moods. In the 1960s Oldfield played guitar in a band influenced by British instrumental rock group the Shadows as well as a folk duo with his sister, Sally. Drawn to the quirky edges of Britain's progressive rock scene, Oldfield joined Kevin Ayers's band in 1970 and began work on his magnum opus, *Tubular Bells*.

Oldfield played guitar, bass, keyboards, and other instruments, recording *Tubular Bells* in multiple layers. Indebted to minimalists such as Philip Glass, the music is composed of repetition inching forward toward resolution. As a single, it caught attention, as utterly unfamiliar sonically yet strangely melodic; vaguely eerie, it established an unsettling mood for *The Exorcist* and spoke to the Top 40 audience of the time.

Hergest Ridge (1974) and *Ommadawn* (1975) continued Oldfield's exploration of texture and minimalism in a long-form rock context. Although he never regained the level of worldwide attention that greeted *Tubular Bells*, Oldfield remained popular in Great Britain, especially after moving in the direction of pop music and disco. Tipping the hat to his influences, *Platinum* (1979) included a disco version of Philip Glass's "North Star." Oldfield enjoyed Top 10 singles in his homeland during the 1970s, scored music for British television, and composed the anthem for the royal wedding of Prince Charles and Princess Diana (1981). He wrote music for Roland Joffe's *The Killing Fields* (1984) and other films and recorded albums that found favor in the new age market. He continues to work prolifically.

Suggested Albums: Tubular Bells (1973); Hergest Ridge (1974); Ommadawn (1975)

OS MUTANTES

In 1964 Brazil's military overthrew their country's government and the Beatles' music reached Latin America. The coincidence became the context for Tropicalia

("Tropicalism"), a Brazilian countercultural aesthetic that produced some astonishingly good music and became the alternative for a rebellious generation trapped in a cycle of political thuggery.

A movement whose members distrusted movements, Tropicalia brought Brazil's longstanding heritage of blending Africa with Europe, the street with the salon, into the decade of flower power and electric guitars. Tropicalia involved avant-garde visual art and theater, but music became its prominent facet. Many musicians associated with Tropicalia, including Gilberto Gil and Caetano Veloso, may have been inspired by the Beatles but had little audible connection with rock. On the other end of Tropicalia, Os Mutantes were a rock band that drew the indigenous sounds of their country into the swirling psychedelic currents of contemporary rock.

Os Mutantes began as a trio consisting of bassist Arnaldo Baptista and his younger brother, guitarist Sergio, along with singer Rita Lee, the latter a descendant of Confederates who fled the South after the Civil War. The older Baptista had played in surf instrumental bands and Lee had sung popular American hits, but their heads were turned by the arrival of the Beatles. Os Mutantes debuted in 1966 and became associated with Gil and Veloso. They drew a wary eye from the military regime and condemnation from leftists who considered rock bands the shock troops of Anglo-American imperialism.

Gil and Veloso were imprisoned and exiled by the regime. Less overtly political, Os Mutantes carried on and released no less than seven albums in their homeland under the military dictatorship. The first five were the work of the original trio. Singing largely in Portuguese, Os Mutantes incorporated Brazilian rhythms into an easy-going aural kaleidoscope, a sonic funhouse enlivened by self-invented guitar pedals and the deployment of bug spray cans as percussion.

After *Mutantes e Seus Cometas no Pais do Baurets* (1972), Lee left to pursue a solo career. The band devolved into a more conventional progressive rock sound, releasing several albums before dissolving in 1978.

A U.S. compilation CD derived from their first five LPs, *Everything Is Possible: The Best of Os Mutantes* (1999), was released on David Byrne's Luaka Bop label and exposed them to the wider world. In 2006 the Baptista brothers (without Lee) reunited Os Mutantes and found a new audience among alternative rock and trip-hop fans.

Suggested Albums: Os Mutantes (1968); *Mutantes* (1969); *A Divina Comedia out Ando Meio Desligado* (1970); *Jardim Electrico* (1971); *Mutantes e Seus Cometas no Pais do Baurets* (1972)

OTIS, SHUGGIE (1953–)

Shuggie Otis is the son of a remarkable figure in rhythm and blues, Johnny Otis. Johnny was a dark-complexioned Greek American who, in a reversal of the era's racial hierarchy, passed for black. The elder Otis led a big band in the mid-1940s and easily transitioned by decade's end to the rhythm and blues that helped herald the birth of rock and roll. Johnny Otis produced Big Mama Thornton's "Hound Dog" (1953) and scored a hit with his "Willie and the Hand Jive" (1958), which became an FM staple in the early 1970s through Eric Clapton's cover version.

Shuggie took up guitar in childhood, playing in his father's bands and recording with him through the early 1970s. He also recorded with Al Kooper before launching his solo career with *Here Comes Shuggie Otis* (1970). Produced by his father, the album combined baroque psychedelia with country blues guitar. Inspired by Jimi Hendrix and Sly Stone as well as the Beatles and the Brothers Grimm, Otis's second album, *Freedom Flight* (1971), included "Strawberry Letter 23," a hit when covered by the funk act Brothers Johnson (1977).

With *Inspiration Information* (1974), Otis became an early adopter of the drum machine, which allowed him to work more independently. He produced the album, playing guitar, bass, keyboards, and vibraphones while supervising imaginative orchestrations that drew on 20th-century classical music, cool jazz, funk, and rock in a manner that predicted Prince's most ambitious recordings of the 1980s. But in the 1970s, Otis's vision was unsupported by the preconceptions of the record industry, radio programmers, and music fans. Aside from appearing with his father before the latter's death in 2012, Otis largely disappeared from view. In 2013 an album composed of recordings Otis made from 1975 through 2000, *Wings of Love*, was packaged with the CD release of *Inspiration Information*.

Suggested Albums: Here Comes Shuggie Otis (1970); *Freedom Flight* (1971); *Inspiration Information* (1974)

PARKS, VAN DYKE (1943–)

Brian Wilson's song for the Beach Boys, "I Just Wasn't Made for These Times," could have been written about his occasional collaborator, Van Dyke Parks. Although part of the generation that grew up with rock and roll, Parks seemed largely oblivious and sometimes hostile to the music even after he was drawn into its circles. He associated with the stars of the 1960s without appearing star-struck. A teenage actor, he played in the film *The Swan* (1956) with Grace Kelly. After her, the new stars must have seemed a little dim.

Parks sang soprano with the Metropolitan Opera at age 10 and worked regularly as a TV actor in his teens. George Gershwin and Arnold Schoenberg, Les Paul and Spike Jones defined his musical world. He moved to Los Angeles in 1963 and became a probably reluctant part of the folk music revival along with his older brother, Carson Parks. Curmudgeonly in his disregard for the Beatles, Bob Dylan, the hippie movement, and almost every development of his era, Parks was truly idiosyncratic, yet somehow maintained a recording career against the tide of all trends.

Although he disliked the Beach Boys, he was impressed by their album *Pet Sounds* (1966) and fell in with Brian Wilson. He is probably most remembered for working with Wilson on an ambitious Beach Boys album that was never completed, *Smile*. He also played organ for the Byrds on *Fifth Dimension* (1966) and was briefly a member of the Mothers of Invention, leaving because "I didn't want to be screamed at."

Although his debut album, *Song Cycle* (1968), had psychedelic overtones, his songwriting owed more to Tin Pan Alley than Haight-Ashbury. And yet, despite his retrospective inclinations, he owned one of the first Moog synthesizers. Recent decades found him exploring calypso music, accepting occasional acting jobs, writing scores for film and television, composing arrangements for the Australian alternative rock band Silverchair, and working on and off with Wilson. Parks was successful in many formats and has accumulated enough good stories to fill a fascinating memoir.

Suggested Albums: Song Cycle (1968); *Discover America* (1972); *Clang of the Yankee Reaper* (1975); *Jump!* (1984); *Tokyo Rose* (1989); *The Fisherman & His Wife* (1991); *Orange Crate Art* (1995) (with Brian Wilson); *Moonlighting: Live at the Ash Grove* (1998)

See also: Beach Boys

PARSONS, GRAM (1946–1973)

Gram Parsons, one of the most influential artists of the late 1960s, was a visionary who reunited country music with rock and roll and helped ignite the country rock genre in the 1970s. However, Parsons's influence, whether as a member of the Byrds or the Flying Burrito Brothers, has extended beyond that musical movement and era, touching a variety of artists, some only tangentially attached to country music. While he was little known at the time of his death in 1973, Parsons's influence has grown and continues to impact both rock and country music to this day.

Despite being born and raised in the American South, Parsons was a relatively late convert to country music. He became captivated by rock and roll after seeing Elvis Presley play live in 1956 and began to perform in rock bands as a teenager. Later, the folk revival of the early 1960s caught his attention, and he was playing in folk groups when he became hooked on country music after hearing Merle Haggard for the first time while a student at Harvard University. He transformed his group, the International Submarine Band, into a country-influenced outfit. The band relocated to Los Angeles, where they cut *Safe at Home* (recorded in 1967 and released in 1968), an album of barely rock-tinged country that consisted of covers highlighted by a few Parsons originals.

During this time Byrds' bassist Chris Hillman recruited Parsons to join the band to replace David Crosby. The band had planned an ambitious double-album history of American popular music, but Parsons quickly began steering the project in a more country direction. The resulting album, *Sweethearts of the Rodeo* (1968), is widely hailed as a groundbreaking marriage of country and rock. The Byrds briefly toured in support of the record, but Parsons left the band later in 1968, reportedly over his refusal to join their planned tour of South Africa. Hillman left along with Parsons and they set about forming the Flying Burrito Brothers.

The Flying Burrito Brothers are regarded as pioneers of country rock for combining country instrumentation and songwriting with a slightly more intense rock and roll sensibility. However, Parsons disliked the term country rock, preferring to call the band's sound "cosmic American music," which in his mind was an eclectic blend of rock, country, R&B, psychedelia, folk, and gospel. The band's 1969 debut, *The Gilded Palace of Sin,* is perhaps the best expression of Parsons's musical vision, a classic collection of well-crafted country-influenced songs, R&B covers, and expressive ballads. While there is little in the way of true rock and roll on the record, several songs have more drive than the average country tune, and innovations such as fuzz box–distorted steel guitar furthered the connection between rock and country.

The band's follow-up, *Burrito Deluxe* (1970), brought more rock into the mix, leading to the creation of a truer country rock sound. The Burrito Brothers didn't fare well commercially, but the band developed a cult following and began inspiring other musicians to take up the country rock banner. During this time Parsons developed a friendship with Keith Richards of the Rolling Stones, leading to a musical collaboration that briefly pulled the Stones toward country music. Time spent with the Stones, as well as Parsons's increasingly erratic behavior due to drug and alcohol use, took a toll on his relationship with the Burrito Brothers. Parsons left the band in 1970 to pursue a solo career.

As a solo artist, Parsons continued to develop his cosmic American music, although with a decidedly more country emphasis. He recorded two well-regarded albums, *GP* (1973) and the posthumously released *Return of the Grievous Angel* (1974), a strong collection of tunes featuring vocal collaborations with Emmylou Harris, a young discovery who would later become a country music star in her own right. The albums featured few new Parsons originals (possibly a reflection of his drug use), but demonstrated strong vocals, an increasingly introspective maturity, and hints of a move toward a purely country sound. Sadly, Parsons died of a drug overdose in 1973 before he could fully develop his musical vision.

Parsons's death was little noted at the time, but in subsequent years his reputation and influence began to grow to almost mythical proportions. Countless country and alternative country rock acts have cited Parsons as a seminal influence, and noncountry artists such as Elvis Costello, Tom Petty, Beck, and Sheryl Crow have acknowledged their musical debt. The outlaw country movement of the mid-1970s furthered the connection between country and rock, and it's not impossible to imagine Parsons playing with Waylon Jennings and Willie Nelson had he lived. And while Nashville may have turned a cold shoulder to Parsons during his lifetime, thanks in part to Harris's constant proselytizing, the country establishment has at least grudgingly admitted his influence in promoting country music. Parsons was a strong songwriter and vocalist, but his true legacy is as a visionary and facilitator, an artist who saw connections between musical genres others missed and broke down barriers, influencing diverse artists to discover common ground they might have otherwise overlooked.

Suggested Albums: GP (1973); *Return of the Grievous Angel* (1974)

See also: Byrds; Flying Burrito Brothers; Harris, Emmylou

PENTANGLE

Often classed with the Anglo-Celtic folk revival, Pentangle occupied a unique position for their baroque, jazz, and blues influences. Much of their music appealed to fans of Led Zeppelin's acoustic songs and drew from the same zeitgeist. Pentangle was formed in 1967 by virtuoso guitarists Bert Jansch and John Renbourn, drummer Terry Cox, and bassist Danny Thompson. They were impressive for being able to recast blues influences into an emotional key that sounded entirely English, with nary a hint of straining to reach the Mississippi Delta or Chicago's South Side. Jansch and Renbourn enjoyed prolific solo recording careers before, during, and after Pentangle.

Suggested Albums: The Pentangle (1968); *Sweet Child* (1968); *Basket of Light* (1969); *Cruel Sister* (1970); *Reflection* (1971); *Solomon's Seal* (1972); *History Book* (1972)

PINK FAIRIES

The Pink Fairies emerged from the anarchic edge of Britain's 1960s counterculture. An outgrowth of a previous band, the Deviants, the Pink Fairies had an unstable lineup but a consistent approach to prankish provocation and stripped-down, energetic rock and roll. Members and guest musicians included Twink, formerly the drummer for the Pretty Things; Mick Farren, who gained recognition as a rock critic; Trever Burton, formerly of the Move; and Paul Rudolph, who replaced Lemmy in Hawkwind. The Pink Fairies were recognized as a precursor by the punk rock movement that emerged in late 1970s Britain, and they have occasionally regrouped in various configurations to tour and record.

Suggested Albums: Never Never Land (1971); *What a Bunch of Sweeties* (1972); *Kings of Oblivion* (1973)

PINK FLOYD

In the aesthetics of Friedrich Nietzsche, Pink Floyd's history could be divided into the short-lived Dionysian phase with Syd Barrett followed by the long Apollonian aftermath under Roger Waters. In other words, Barrett fits the romantic conception of the artist as a mad visionary whose work was more appreciated in death than in life, albeit Barrett's "death" was psychological; he lived on in seclusion for 35 years after recording his final song. If Barrett was rock's Vincent Van Gogh, Waters was closer to Claude Monet, who earned a comfortable living and a place in the pantheon, but lived long enough to become old-fashioned in the eyes of younger artists.

Barrett, an art student, formed Pink Floyd in 1965 with a trio of architecture students, Waters, Nick Mason, and Richard Wright. Emerging from London's mid-1960s blues scene, Pink Floyd was named by Barrett for two folkloric African American musicians, Pink Anderson and Floyd Council. But Pink Floyd's blues roots were barely audible on their first album, *The Piper at the Gates of Dawn* (1967). Named for a chapter from Kenneth Grahame's Edwardian children's novel, *Wind in the Willows*, the LP featured Barrett's exquisite pop psychedelic masterpieces "Arnold Layne" and "See Emily Play" along with such improvisation-fueled space rock jams as "Interstellar Overdrive" and "Astronomy Domine."

Barrett approached songwriting with a child's sense of wonder, filling his lyrics with magical cats, pet mice, and eccentric cross-dressers, yet the "You could lose your mind at play" refrain from "See Emily Play" sounds ominous in hindsight. In an earlier epoch Barrett might have been another Lewis Carroll or J. M. Barrie, content to evoke wonders through smoking opium in an ornate meerschaum pipe from the comfort of his study. In his own time, the hurly-burly of rock music, the peculiar demands of stardom, and the dangerous seduction of repeated trips on LSD proved his undoing. Barrett's behavior became increasingly erratic. He sometimes stood and stared onstage, his guitar hanging limply from its strap. When Pink Floyd appeared on the Pat Boone show during their first U.S. tour, Barrett refused to lip sync "See Emily Play" in a symptom of madness or an unwelcome gesture of subversion. At the end of 1967, the other band members added a second guitarist, David Gilmour. Pink Floyd began to play gigs without bothering to invite Barrett.

Pink Floyd completed its second album, *A Saucerful of Secrets*, by the end of April 1968, just as Barrett's departure from the band was announced. Recollections of Barrett's role on *Saucerful* are contradictory; he is credited with only one song, and Waters began his ascent as Pink Floyd's primary songwriter. The album continued the band's psychedelic trajectory, but psychedelia, fading by the end of the 1960s, was already morphing into progressive rock.

Pink Floyd would take a role in defining progressive rock but seemed uncertain of its direction after Barrett. The movie soundtrack *More* (1969) included stately acoustic ballads and blistering hard rock. *Ummagumma* (1969) was a double-LP, half recorded live and half consisting of one contribution from each band member. The extended compositions on *Atom Heart Mother* (1970) solidified Pink Floyd's popularity in the United Kingdom but were dismissed by band members as "rubbish." *Meddle* (1971) and the soundtrack LP *Obscured by Clouds* (1972) found the band moving toward the sonic landscape of their signature album, *The Dark Side of the Moon* (1973).

Spacious and contemplative, *Dark Side of the Moon* was the apotheosis of music meant to be heard on headphones with the listener enraptured in a personal experience. For many, the LP served as a dreamy companion to quiet time spent with a bowl of marijuana or brownies laced with hashish. The production at London's Abbey Road Studio, with future recording artist Alan Parsons as engineer, was an audiophile's delight, the zenith of high fidelity and the multitracked recording studio as an orchestra of timbres and instruments in the hands of a producer-conductor with a control board as his baton. Not unlike a movie director composing a coherent narrative from many reels of raw film, the end product was constructed from splicing and editing tapes.

Word of mouth was crucial to the album's unanticipated popularity. *Dark Side of the Moon* broke sales records and remained on the *Billboard* charts for 14 years. One track after another entered the playlists of U.S. FM rock stations, including the single, "Money," with its rare echo of the band's R&B roots. Posters of the album's enigmatic front cover, featuring a pyramid refracting light, became a fixture in bedrooms and dorm rooms around the world.

The album's mood of quiet desperation found a vast youthful audience beyond the progressive rock circles that had sustained Pink Floyd. With its title evoking space rock, *Dark Side of the Moon* was a journey through inner space where treacherous passages could lead to madness. Erudite listeners noted that in Jungian psychology, the moon represents the unconscious where archetypes dwell, adding a double meaning to the more obvious references to Barrett's psychological state. Few of Pink Floyd's millions of new fans were aware of Barrett, but the band's absent founder was clearly on Waters's mind. "And when the band you're in starts playing different tunes . . ." ran the lyric from "Brain Damage."

Regret over Barrett's collapse and the band's response had been an undertow in Pink Floyd's career. The theme was made explicit on the band's much-anticipated follow-up to *Dark Side of the Moon*. *Wish You Were Here* (1975) was a sympathy card to their founder and a rebuke to the music industry that contributed to his breakdown. Less dependent on studio atmospherics than its predecessor, *Wish You Were Here* contains some of Waters's best songwriting, especially the moving tribute to Barrett, "Shine on You Crazy Diamond."

Animals (1977) marked Waters's shift to sociopolitical analogies. Drawn from George Orwell's classic satire of Soviet communism, *Animal Farm*, *Animals* sounded tired and despondent compared to previous albums. Its release coincided with the explosion of punk rock, whose leading figures derided Pink Floyd as an example of everything they despised in rock stars gone creatively inert and comfortably numb. Many punks, however, expressed admiration for Barrett even as they derided what his band had become. *The Wall* (1979) cannot be called a punk album, but its anger and alienation against the seemingly unmovable systems governing the world seemed a rejoinder to punk rock. The single, "Another Brick in the Wall (Part II)," topped the charts in the United States and United Kingdom.

In their early days as a London club band, Pink Floyd featured prominent visuals in the form of psychedelic lightshows. As their popularity grew, so did the size of their venues and the scale of their presentation. Pink Floyd concerts became logistically complicated with giant inflatable effigies of characters from *Animals* and *The Wall* hovering over stadiums. Tensions roiled within the band, much of it

Pink Floyd survived the departure of founder Syd Barrett in the 1960s and became one of the leading lights of European progressive rock in the 1970s. They became known for elaborate stage presentations, as at this 1975 concert in the Netherlands. (Pictorial Press Ltd/Alamy Stock Photo)

spurred by resentment over Waters's dominance. Wright was expelled from Pink Floyd in 1979 but hired as a sideman on *The Wall* tour. He played keyboards and collected his fee, watching as his erstwhile bandmates lost more than $500,000 on the expensive tour.

Problems worsened during the recording of *The Final Cut* (1983), Waters's critique of Margaret Thatcher and the Falklands War. Waters went solo with the bestselling album *The Pros and Cons of Hitch Hiking* (1984) while Wright and Mason engaged in unsuccessful projects. Afterward, much of the creativity associated with Pink Floyd was diverted from the recording studio to the courtroom over contested royalties, breaches of contract, and legal rights to the band's name. Gilmour, Mason, and Wright recorded and toured as Pink Floyd, dogged by Waters's sharply worded jabs in the media and his legal challenges.

In 2005, Bob Geldorf, who years earlier had reluctantly agreed to play Waters's stand-in character in the movie version of *The Wall* (1982), coaxed Waters, Gilmour, Wright, and Mason to reunite for a benefit concert in London's Hyde Park. After Barrett's death in 2006, the quartet performed a tribute concert for their founder. Wright died in 2008, leaving the remaining members to regroup occasionally for charity events.

Pink Floyd sold more albums than any band of the classic rock era, yet their most popular LPs influenced relatively few musicians aside from U2's guitarist The Edge. Although he completed only one album with the band, Barrett's inspiration proved greater and more enduring. His creativity was admired by David Bowie and the first generation of punk rock bands, and emulated by a host of postpunk and neo-psychedelic artists from Robyn Hitchcock through XTC and Echo and the Bunnymen.

Suggested Albums: The Piper at the Gates of Dawn (1967); *A Saucerful of Secrets* (1968); *More* (1969); *Meddle* (1971); *The Dark Side of the Moon* (1973); *Wish You Were Here* (1975); *The Wall* (1979)

See also: Barrett, Syd

POCO

Poco was one of the seemingly innumerable bands riding the wave of the country rock movement after the 1960s. Formed by Buffalo Springfield members Richie Furay and Jim Messina following that group's disintegration in 1968, Poco began a long, steady, if largely unremarkable career that has spanned more than four decades. The band debuted in 1969 with *Pickin' Up the Pieces*, and rarely strayed from that album's core sound of pleasant, usually relaxed country-influenced rock with a strong emphasis on vocal harmonies. Despite only occasional commercial success, Poco has survived almost constant lineup changes and continues to tour and release albums into the new millennium. Several members found fame after leaving Poco; Furay with the Souther-Hillman-Furay Band, Messina with early 1970s soft rock duo Loggins and Messina, and Randy Meisner and Timothy B. Schmidt with the Eagles.

POP, IGGY (1947–)

James Osterberg was nicknamed Iggy while drumming in an Ann Arbor, Michigan band, the Iguanas. After a short stint on the Chicago blues scene, he became Iggy Stooge for the band he formed in 1967 after returning to Detroit, the Stooges. Soon enough, he settled on an even more sardonic surname and became known as Iggy Pop. As the antithesis of pop music, he represented rock pushed to the far end of the red zone and became the embodiment of every threat implicit in rock and roll since Elvis Presley left the world all shook up. And yet, he played golf with his parents and, after attaining wealth, happily moved into a Beverly Hills mansion. Perhaps Jimmy Osterberg lived on behind the persona of Iggy Pop even during the early 1970s, when heroin addiction threatened to engulf the man and his image.

Pop formed the Stooges after seeing a Doors concert, motivated by the example of Jim Morrison, whose performances promised to bring down the structure of order and authority. Pop went further in breaking the wall between performer and audience by aggressively diving into the crowd; he demanded a visceral response as he cut himself onstage with broken glass. In those dangerous years, Pop's performances turned rock into a theater of cruelty. He went beyond Antonin Artaud's call to awaken audiences from their complacent consumption of culture.

If Morrison was Pop's launch point, the Doors inhabited a world of musical endowment the Stooges could never reach. Pop turned his band's limitations into a virtue by honing in on the primitive power and urgency inherent in garage rock. Signposts on the road to the Stooges include the Sonics' "Psycho" and the Troggs' "Wild Thing," yet the Stooges' self-titled debut album (1969) was cut from strikingly new fabric. Although one of its memorable songs is called "1969," the fuzz-tone setting on some of Ron Asheton's short guitar solos harkens to acid rock, and the longest track, "We Will Fall," is built on a raga-like drone, the LP sounds strangely timeless. Janus-like in its arrival on the cusp of decades, it looked to the future as well as the past.

At the time of its release, most rock critics, FM DJs, and audiences outside the Stooges' hometown had no idea what to make of them. Recently departed from the Velvet Underground, John Cale produced their debut, yet the link with the Velvet Underground's dark and obscure second album, *White Light/White Heart* (1968), endeared few commenters at a time when the Velvets were considered outré by the counterculture. The Stooges' primal fury of menacing riffs and archetypal drumbeats contradicted progressive rock. The band's urban identity pointed away from country rock. The Stooges' alienation set them apart from the politics of the time. While fellow Detroit rock band MC5 raged against "the System," the Stooges remained aloof. As for free love, Pop responded with the abasement of "I Wanna Be Your Dog." The peace proffered by the Woodstock generation was a matter of indifference to the Stooges, who resembled neither hippies nor squares, but the scary people at the back of the bus no one would sit near.

The Stooges followed with *Fun House* (1970). Harder and faster than their debut, *Fun House* brought their music deeper into aggressively organized metallic chaos, courtesy of the free jazz of guest saxophonist Steven Mackay. Dropped by their record label, Elektra, the Stooges broke up and might have remained a footnote with few fans but for the enthusiasm of one highly placed fan, David Bowie. Now billed as Iggy & the Stooges, the band that recorded *Raw Power* (1973) featured the proficient James Williamson on guitar; Ron Asheton was demoted to bass, playing alongside his brother, drummer Scott Asheton. Greater sophistication in songwriting, especially the lyrical images, was evident. "Gimme Danger" recalled the mood of Pop's inspiration, the Doors, while much of the music was rock and roll sharpened to a hard point. Bowie mixed the album with an ear for making it as radio friendly as his other recent protégés, Lou Reed and Mott the Hoople. The association with Bowie allowed the music industry to misfile Pop with glam rock.

Although the bid for commercial success failed, Pop's London concert drew an audience whose members, including the Sex Pistols' John Lydon and the Clash's Mick Jones, shaped the direction of punk rock a few years later. Selling few records, the second incarnation of the Stooges broke up after a 1974 Detroit concert documented on *Metallic K.O.* (1976). Pop's antagonistic furor triggered a storm of bottles from the audience. While checked into a neuropsychiatric clinic, Pop recorded a superb album with Williamson, later released as *Kill City* (1978), which coincided with the proliferation of a movement that embraced him as its godfather, punk rock. Pop's apparent opposition to everything seemed a bracing alternative to the increasingly formatted, by-rote rock culture of FM playlists and concerts that resembled military operations more than spontaneous events. Alienation was cool and Pop was alienation's most articulate spokesman.

While Detroit's influential *Creem* magazine kept his name before the public and punk gave him a dependable audience, Pop retreated to West Berlin with Bowie, who produced a pair of masterpieces drenched in German electronic progressive rock, *The Idiot* (1977) and *Lust for Life* (1977), companions to Bowie's groundbreaking albums *Low* (1977) and *Heroes* (1977). Pop offered a detached commentary on decadence with "Nightclubbing," a warning about heroin on "Street of Chance," and a deeply felt love song that became a hit for its co-author, Bowie, "China Girl."

Revitalized, Pop returned to more conventional guitar-based rock settings with *New Values* (1979), *Soldier* (1980), and *Party* (1981). During the 1980s, Pop's music was characterized by a pleasant deep-voiced croon but inconsistent songwriting, and was plagued by the bland, compressed production sound of eighties mainstream rock. He enjoyed a U.K. and Australian hit covering an obscure 1950s rock and roll song, "Real Wild Child" (1986).

The 1990s and 2000s found Pop with as much work as he could handle, opening concerts for Madonna, contributing songs to movie soundtracks, and collaborating with a host of other artists, including B-52s singer Kate Pierson on the hit single "Candy" (1990). Pop also turned to acting, notably a guest appearance on *Star Trek: Deep Space Nine*. He toured and recorded with the surviving original members of the Stooges until Ron Asheton's death in 2009. Since then, Williamson has resumed his role as the Stooges' guitarist. Inspired by the writings of controversial French novelist Michel Houellebecq, and professing fatigue with guitar rock, Pop released an interesting jazz-inflected solo album, *Preliminaires* (2009), and worked with a singer he inspired, Josh Homme of Queens of the Stone Age, on *Post Pop Depression* (2016).

Suggested Albums: The Stooges (1969); *Fun House* (1970); *Raw Power* (1973); *The Idiot* (1977); *Lust for Life* (1977); *Kill City* (1978); *New Values* (1979); *Soldier* (1980); *Party* (1981); *American Caesar* (1993); *Preliminaires* (2009); *Post Pop Depression* (2016)

POPOL VUH

Named after a Mayan sacred text, Popol Vuh's music belonged to no specific time or place. The German group formed in 1969 in the midst of their nation's musically creative countercultural fluorescence, but followed its own trajectory. The first album, *Affenstunde* (1970), could be called space rock except for the lack of discernible rock influences. The pulsating hum of Florian Fricke's synthesizers was coupled with echoes of tribal percussion from Holger Trulzch. A dedication to emerging technology was underscored by their third member, Frank Fielder, whose role was as recording engineer, not instrumentalist.

Unmoored from traditional melody, rock rhythms, and pop structure, Popol Vuh often suggested the minimalism of Steve Reich or Terry Riley, as well as traditional music from around the world. Popol Vuh found a measure of international attention from their scores for a series of films by German director Werner Herzog, including *Aguirre: The Wrath of God* (1975) and *Nosferatu* (1978).

Suggested Albums: Affenstunde (1970); *In den Garten Pharaos* (1971); *Hosianna Mantra* (1972)

POWER POP

The Who's Pete Townshend coined "power pop" in a 1967 interview as a description of his band's music. Drawing from his art school education, Townshend may have intended to categorize the Who as pop art infused with the power of rock music. Power pop was a dormant concept until revived in the late 1970s by critic Greg Shaw as a platonic ideal for rock music. By his definition, everyone from Abba to Slade and the Ramones produced power pop recordings at one time or another. However, power pop soon narrowed in popular understanding to a genre of bands committed to the succinct energy of Beatles-influenced mid-1960s Top 40. Power pop was applied retroactively to the Raspberries, Badfinger, Big Star, and other early 1970s bands influenced by mid-period Beatles.

PRETTY THINGS

The Pretty Things emerged out of Little Boy Blue and the Blue Boys, a London band with vocalist Mick Jagger and guitarists Keith Richards and Dick Taylor. Taylor played bass in an early lineup of the Rolling Stones but left and formed the Pretty Things in 1963 with vocalist Phil May. His new band never attained the stardom or U.S. sales of the Stones or other leading British Invasion acts, but the high level of their music coupled with their obscurity ensured them an avid American cult following.

Their first two albums, *The Pretty Things* (1965) and *Get the Picture?* (1965), traveled the same American musical byways as the early Stones, but with greater assurance. Taking their name from a Bo Diddley recording, "Pretty Thing," they conjured a bluesy sound more primal and feral than that of the Stones. Even on their debut album, the Pretty Things were not content to emulate their African American heroes, although they did that well, but pushed their influences into rock and roll. And yet, as the Stones gained momentum, pushed by a well-cultivated image as the "bad boys" of the British Invasion, the Pretty Things were unable to make an impression on the huge American record-buying audience. They had hit singles in the United Kingdom, Australia, New Zealand, and in Europe, but never in the United States.

Emotions (1967) was a largely failed compromise between the pop market and the movement in British rock toward complexity. As psychedelia took hold, however, the Pretty Things reached their second artistic peak. Some of their best recordings from the period, including the magnificent "Walking Through My Dreams" (1967), were originally released only as singles and were later collected on various album anthologies.

If the Beatles might never have achieved their extraordinary innovations without producer George Martin, the Pretty Things likewise grew to maturity at Abbey Road Studio during their psychedelic period under the tutelage of their new producer, Norman Smith. Like Martin, Smith was older and had a wide grasp of music. He had been a jazz musician and conducted orchestral scores, and he was willing to experiment with the percussive qualities of ashtrays and chairs in search of sonic wonders. With Smith's encouragement, and a sitar borrowed from George Harrison, the Pretty Things recorded the first rock opera, *S.F. Sorrow* (1968), painting a gorgeous aural canvas through full use of Abbey Road's four-track studio and a new musical instrument, the mellotron, a keyboard polyphonic tape replay mechanism. Despite Pete Townshend's denials, most authorities believe the war-themed *S.F. Sorrow* led the way to *Tommy* (1969), the first rock opera to reach a wide audience.

Commercial success continued to elude the Pretty Things. *S.F. Sorrow* was belatedly released in the United States by a Motown subsidiary with no idea how to market British rock. The Pretty Things remained prolific, recording soundtracks for low-budget movies under the name Electric Banana and juggling a shifting roster of personnel.

With Smith directing the sessions, the Pretty Things began the new decade with their third summit of artistic success, *Parachute* (1970). If *S.F. Sorrow* reached the climax of the sixties' psychedelic sensibility, *Parachute* was the epilogue that questioned what had gone before. Although it was not a story album, a concept could be discerned amidst the refined hard rock and Beatlesque melodies. Not unlike the postpsychedelic LPs by the Stones and the Beatles, *Parachute* was a partial return to basics, a synthesis of primitive rock and roll with the developments of the past half-decade. The titular "parachute" referred to the escape by many of the era's British rock stars to country estates and to the countercultural "back to the land" movement. The implication was that parachutes sometimes fail and escape can be a blind alley. *Rolling Stone* magazine named *Parachute* the album of the year, choosing it over contenders by the Beatles, the Stones, Led Zeppelin, the Who, and the Kinks. Like *S.F. Sorrow*, it failed to find a wide public.

Afterward, Taylor left the band and Smith embarked on a solo career as Hurricane Smith. With Taylor on guitar, he enjoyed a number one U.S. hit with a song evoking 1930s dance bands and catching a trend of prerock nostalgia, "Oh, Babe, What Would You Say?" (1972). May led the Pretty Things on *Freeway Madness* (1972), a hard rock album whose title alluded to their unsuccessful pursuit of fame on the American touring circuit. Signed by Led Zeppelin's Swan Song label, the Pretty Things released a capable effort, *Silk Torpedo* (1974), which garnered a measure of FM airplay in the United States but only modest sales. The band broke up in 1976.

As with many rock groups, the end was not the end, but rather the beginning of a long half-life. Since 1980, various versions of the Pretty Things have appeared, most led by Taylor and May; tours, new albums, reissues, and lawsuits over unpaid royalties ensued. Taylor and May's greatest late career accomplishment was the release of canonical CD versions of their essential albums, complete with non-LP tracks.

Suggested Albums: The Pretty Things (1965); *Get the Picture?* (1965); *S.F. Sorrow* (1968); *Parachute* (1970); *Freeway Madness* (1972); *Silk Torpedo* (1974)

PRICE, ALAN (1942–)

Alan Price cemented a niche in classic rock history by providing the powerful, churning organ that, along with Eric Burdon's relentless vocal snarl, defined the Animals' fierce sound of the mid-1960s. However, in 1965 Price left the band at the height of its popularity to pursue a lengthy, quirky solo career.

His first post-Animals band, the Alan Price Set, had a U.K. hit with a cover of Screamin' Jay Hawkins's "I Put a Spell On You" that echoed the Animals' rendition of "House of the Rising Sun." It was their last nod to the Animals, as the Alan Price Set featured a brassier, more diverse sound touching on R&B, soul, calypso, and British music hall, with hints of vaudeville and show tunes. The group is perhaps best remembered for introducing the public to the music of Randy Newman, recording seven of his songs on their second album. Later in his career, Price recorded with U.K. pop star Georgie Fame, participated in a few Animals reunions, and embarked on a career composing film and television scores.

Suggested Albums: The Price to Play (1966); *A Price on His Head* (1967)

See also: Animals

PRINE, JOHN (1946–)

John Prine was a success among the many singer-songwriters dubbed "New Dylans" by critics in the 1970s. A down-to-earth Chicago letter carrier who "made up songs" and performed in local folk clubs, Prine came to the attention of Atlantic Records through Kris Kristoffersen, who recognized a kindred spirit. Prine leaned toward country music but with a worldview grounded in the sixties generation. Unlike many "folkies" who emerged as the seventies began, Prine received a great deal of FM rock airplay. His eponymous debut album (1971) was recorded at Memphis's American Recording Studio with musicians who had backed Elvis Presley.

Prine brought a unique perspective to his lyrics, which he delivered in a neighborly voice. He was irreverent toward institutions but seldom toward people. His sympathy for the human condition encompassed lonely hearts whose paths might never cross in "Donald and Lydia," but also situations seldom addressed in song, including the plight of the elderly in "Hello in There" and the struggle with heroin addiction among Vietnam veterans in "Sam Stone" at a time when veterans of that war were ignored or depicted as psychopaths in popular culture. In "Illegal Smile," life's drudgery is brightened by marijuana; "Spanish Pipedream" is a lighthearted counterculture idyll narrated by a draft dodger ("a soldier on the way to Montreal"). Prine's debut also included a song that became a standard, the wistful "Angel from Montgomery."

Although many of his most recognized numbers were packed onto his first album, Prine continued along the same arc, writing with humorous tolerance and understanding and setting words to homespun Americana melodies. *Common Sense* (1975), produced by rhythm and blues guitarist Steve Cropper with deliberately radio-friendly intentions, cracked the *Billboard* Top 100. *Bruised Orange* (1978), produced by old friend and fellow folkie Steve Goodman, returned to rustic form. Prine co-wrote the country hit "You Never Even Call Me By My Name" with Goodman, but refused to take credit. He also wrote a hit for country singer Don Williams, "Love Is on a Roll." *Pink Cadillac* (1979) had rockabilly echoes with some tracks produced by Sam Phillips at Memphis's Sun Studios.

In 1984, Prine took charge of his career, releasing albums through his own Oh Boy imprint and sallying forth on periodic solo tours. *The Missing Years* (1991), produced by Tom Petty's bassist Howie Epstein, earned a Grammy. Cancer slowed but never halted Prine, who survived into the 21st century as an inspiration to a new generation of Americana and acoustic artists.

Suggested Albums: John Prine (1971); *Diamonds in the Rough* (1972); *Sweet Revenge* (1973); *Common Sense* (1975); *Bruised Orange* (1978); *Pink Cadillac* (1979); *German Afternoons* (1986); *The Missing Years* (1991)

PROCOL HARUM

As the musical signifier for 1967, the Beatles' *Sgt. Pepper* had at least one rival, Procol Harum's "A Whiter Shade of Pale." Solemn, not celebratory, the song cast a long shadow over the Summer of Love. The lyrics were embraced for their "acid trip" associations, yet a close listen suggests that "A Whiter Shade of Pale," as with many of the group's early songs, struck a cautionary note against the rampant enthusiasm for LSD. Procol Harum listed lyricist Keith Reid as a band member, an indicator of the importance of words in late 1960s rock as lyrics strived for poetry. The melody was based on J. S. Bach, which spoke to rock's aspiration of becoming art. All around the world, rebellious music students forced their teachers, hostile to rock, to listen to "A Whiter Shade of Pale." The older generation was often forced to concede.

Procol Harum was the archetypical British classical rock band for its debt to Bach and its often majestic playing of organist Matthew Fisher, yet most of the genre's exponents, songwriter-pianist-vocalist Gary Brooker's roots in rhythm and blues, were often evident. The band's range was remarkable, with credible approximations of John Lee Hooker, rueful ballads suggestive of Nick Drake, and scorching echoes of Jimi Hendrix. Guitarist Robin Trower left the band in 1971 to pursue a solo career in the Hendrix manner. Procol Harum recorded one of the most successful collaborations between a rock band and a symphony orchestra, *Live in Concert with the Edmonton Symphony Orchestra* (1971), which yielded a hit single, the Latin-tinged "Conquistador."

After a prolific recording career, Procol Harum's stock of ideas was nearly empty by the time of *Procol's Ninth* (1975), whose only memorable track was a cover of Mike Leiber and Jerry Stoller's rhythm and blues song "I Keep Forgetting." Leiber and Stoller were tapped to produce the album, in a nod to their influence on the band, but they were unable to work much magic from the uninspired material.

After a decade's hiatus, Procol Harum regrouped in the 1990s and has toured and recorded with various groupings of musicians in the years since. Brooker has been the only consistent member remaining from the classic lineup.

Suggested Albums: Procol Harum (1967); *Shine on Brightly* (1968); *A Salty Dog* (1969); *Home* (1970); *Broken Barricades* (1971); *Live in Concert with the Edmonton Symphony Orchestra* (1971); *Grand Hotel* (1973); *Exotic Birds and Fruit* (1974)

PRODUCERS

In the music industry, producers are generally in charge of recording sessions. Some producers consider themselves documentarians making a record of musical performances; some are collaborators with the musicians; and others impose a particular vision much as a conductor dictates to a symphony orchestra. The term *producer* was unknown during the first 70 years of recorded music, when the artist and repertoire (A&R) man usually supervised recordings.

Steve Sholes, head of RCA's country and western division, began crediting himself as producer shortly after signing Elvis Presley. Popular music historian Michael

Jarrett speculated that Sholes's inspiration came from the original soundtrack album for Presley's movie *Love Me Tender* (1956), which listed Lionel Newman as producer, even though the film's credits read "Music by Lionel Newman." In the movie industry, producer referred to the person in charge of the financial and business arrangements for a film, while the director supervised the making of the film. Sholes and some future music producers were likewise responsible for keeping projects within budget and representing the record label to the artists. In the music industry after the late 1950s, the business role of producer and artistic role of director has often been combined under the heading of producer.

The early A&R men in charge of recording sessions had relatively little to do aside from scheduling time in the studio, hiring musicians if necessary, and in some cases selecting songs to be recorded. A recording engineer hung a single microphone overhead, whether for a solo pianist or a big band, and adjusted the volume meter. As technology increased the complexity and potential of recorded sound, production and A&R became separate fields, with the latter acting as talent scouts and the former assuming the role of aural artist.

Les Paul played a crucial role in the development of sound recording, leaving an incalculable influence on the production and consumption of music and on the way music is performed, recorded, and appreciated. His achievements were extraordinary. As inventor of the solid-body electric guitar, he made the sound of rock music possible. Paul was among the first musicians to recognize the potential of magnetic recording tape and broke ground with overdubbing, tape delay, and multitrack recording.

Paul was a regular on Bing Crosby's radio show, and the singer encouraged Paul to set up a recording studio in his garage and experiment with the newly developed reel-to-reel tape recorder based on technology developed in Nazi Germany and introduced in the United States after World War II. Paul recognized the new technology's potential to transform recording from the act of documenting actual performances into the creation of music that could never exist in real time through multitracking.

Paul's recording with singer Mary Ford of the jazz standard "How High the Moon," which reached number one on the charts in 1951, was a breakthrough for its dazzling use of the multitrack potential of recording tape. The novelty of hearing a singer harmonize with herself and one guitarist playing what sounded like a dozen guitars struck a receptive chord with an audience with a vision of a bright future through technology.

During the 1950s Paul continued to develop multitracking and was commissioned by Ampex to build the first eight-track recording studio. The effect of "How High the Moon" and Paul's other technically innovative recordings on the ways music would be produced, consumed, and understood was both immediate and gradual. Paul's influence reached new peaks years later with such carefully crafted sonic artifacts as the Beatles' *Sgt. Pepper's Lonely Hearts Club Band* (1967) and Pink Floyd's *Dark Side of the Moon* (1973).

Paul was not the lone pioneer in the shift from the dry documentary studio sound of early recordings to a richer aural palette facilitated by recording tape,

280   PRODUCERS

encouraged by the emergence of "high fidelity" phonographs and long-playing albums, and pushed by the decline of big brass and woodwind–powered orchestras in favor of smaller guitar-driven combos. Reverb was prominent in the drive toward a "wetter" sound that filled the tonal space and endowed recordings with an aura difficult to recreate on stage. The Harmonicats' "Peg O' My Heart" (1947) and Vaughn Williams's "Ghost Riders in the Sky" (1949) were among the early pop hits made possible by the new technology.

In the early 1950s, two exemplary producers (even if they only called themselves producers in hindsight) enveloped many of their recordings in a scrim of reverb, Leonard Chess and Sam Phillips. Both headed independent record labels, Chicago's Chess and Memphis's Sun, and ran inventive studios within tight budgets. Chess was at the forefront of electric blues with Muddy Waters and Howlin' Wolf, and Sun was already developing the genre that would be called rockabilly by the time Phillips recorded Elvis Presley in 1954.

The drive toward bigger, wider sound was led in the early 1960s by Phil Spector, whose dream of composing "little symphonies for the kids" spurred his development of the "Wall of Sound" on recordings such as the Ronettes' "Be My Baby" (1963), the Righteous Brothers' "You've Lost That Lovin' Feeling" (1964), and Ike and Tina Turner's "River Deep, Mountain High" (1966). The Wall of Sound was built from massed guitars and other string instruments, horns, and a profusion of percussion, cemented by reverb and endowed with additional force through Spector's appreciation for the unique power of monophonic recording. Not unlike Charlie Chaplin's rear-guard action on behalf of silent cinema in the 1930s, Spector continued to champion mono as the public raced to embrace stereo. He became an anachronism, but caught a second wind as the 1970s began, producing the Beatles' *Let It Be* (1970), George Harrison's *All Things Must Pass* (1970), and John Lennon's *Imagine* (1971).

Spector was an authoritarian producer, molding his recording acts from the early 1960s in his image and imposing his Wall of Sound on prominent artists later in his career. By contrast, George Martin was the producer as open-minded collaborator and mentor. He deserved his accolade as "the fifth Beatle." Martin's ambition was to become a classical composer, but he helped reinvent popular music instead. He studied at Guildhall School of Music and took a job in 1950 at London's Abbey Road Studio supervising baroque, Latin, children's, orchestral pop, and jazz recordings. After becoming head of EMI subsidiary Parlophone Records in 1955, Martin was known for recording the Goons, the inventive comedy group starring Peter Sellers.

Abbey Road, Britain's state of the art studio, became Martin's sonic laboratory. Inspired by Degas and the great impressionist painters whose canvases conveyed sensations beyond photography's reach, Martin compared old-style documentary recording to photography and the new studio technology to a painter's palette.

In 1962 Martin began the most important phase of his career when he signed the Beatles to Parlophone and began working with them at Abbey Road. The band members were fans of the Goons and Martin heard something in the young group. Any generation gap was instantly bridged. "It was their genius that made the songs work," Martin said of the Beatles, and his humility is borne out by comparison with his other recording projects. Martin produced a slew of other British Invasion acts, including Gerry and the Pacemakers, Billy J. Kramer, and Cilla Black, and dominated the U.S. and U.K. charts through the mid-1960s, but few of those recordings measure up to his work with the Beatles.

However, the Beatles might never have flourished musically without a producer of Martin's scope and empathy. Martin imagined things just beyond the Beatles' horizon, summoning Bernard Hermann as inspiration for "Eleanor Rigby's" spiky string arrangement that struck like hard piano keys to emphasize the syncopation; his grasp of avant-garde techniques for prepared piano and tape manipulation enabled the construction of tracks such as "Rain" and "Tomorrow Never Knows."

Unlike many producers that followed in the 1970s, Martin was never indulgent or pretentious. Like a crack newspaper columnist, he was brilliant on deadline when handed great material. Most of the Beatles' early recordings were knocked out in an hour or two. *Sgt. Pepper's Lonely Hearts Club Band* was recorded in sessions lasting only 34 hours.

During the 1960s African American producers such as Motown Records' Berry Gordy supervised recording sessions for other African Americans; more often, whites produced African American recording artists. Tom Wilson was exceptional as a black producer working primarily with white rock acts. He exemplified the school of producers whose mission was to encourage the potential of the artists they served. For Simon & Garfunkel, Wilson surrounded "The Sound of Silence" (1964) with a reverential sonic chapel; his recording of Bob Dylan's "Like a Rolling Stone" (1965) emphasized the rough edges; during the Velvet Underground's two-day session for *White Light/White Heat* (1968), he gave the band free rein for noisy improvisation.

The trend toward self-production by rock artists was well underway before the end of the 1960s with the Beach Boys' Brian Wilson in the lead. Many musicians realized that they could do the job themselves and, as was the case with the Rolling Stones, had been doing it despite the pretense of their manager, Andrew Loog Oldham, in claiming production credit. By assuming the producer's role, rock bands received money that otherwise would have gone to outside hands.

And yet, many artists have benefited from the presence of another set of ears, a disinterested mentor in the control booth who might hear things the musicians missed or imagine the songs in new settings. Examples of the positive results of good production continued to be found after the end of the classic rock era, especially Butch Vig's transformation of Nirvana on *Nevermind* (1991) into a fuller sounding, radio-ready band. Elvis Costello's recordings never sounded as good as when Nick Lowe was at the controls.

PROGRESSIVE ROCK

Art rock and *progressive rock* are terms that have often been used interchangeably. Art rock properly describes any conscious effort to elevate rock and roll from its vernacular origins and endow it with wider musical range and the power to illuminate reality more profoundly than even the greatest narrator of everyday life in 1950s rock and roll, Chuck Berry. Progressive rock is a genre that coalesced within the boundaries of art rock.

Bob Dylan played a crucial role in the development of art rock. By bringing the allusive imagery of 20th-century poetry into his lyrics, he encouraged rock song-writers to think beyond the well-tried themes of romantic and erotic love. Even the album cover for Dylan's *Bringing It All Back Home* (1965) represented a step into greater complexity. Like the gatefold that enclosed the Beatles' *Sgt. Pepper's Lonely Hearts Club Band* (1967), it was an object worthy of study not only for the information it contained but also for the suggestions it implied. Dylan's *Blonde on Blonde* (1968) was rock's first double-LP (a format that had been largely reserved for classical music) and included the first composition in a rock context to occupy an entire side of an album, "Sad-Eyed Lady of the Lowlands." Even musicians with no obvious debt to Dylan were inspired by the possibilities he suggested.

Progressive rock developed from the convergence of two overlapping trends, classical rock and psychedelia. Few noticed the birth of classical rock when Roger McGuinn drew from Bach for the guitar passage opening the Byrds' version of Dylan's "Mr. Tambourine Man" (1965). The more obvious turning point was the Beatles' "Yesterday" (1965), whose dolorous George Martin arrangement for string quartet signaled a rapprochement between rock and the European classical music tradition. The Beatles' rival, the Rolling Stones, answered with a string arrangement on their ballad "As Tears Go By" (1965). Baroque influences surfaced often in mid-sixties pop. The speeded-up piano of the Beatles' "In My Life" (1965) sounded like a harpsichord, and the Rolling Stones evoked the Elizabethan age with Brian Jones's dulcimer on "Lady Jane" (1966).

Aside from such American outliers as the Left Banke, classical rock was less associated with the United States than the United Kingdom. America's vigorous vernacular musical tradition pointed young middle-class musicians to the folk-blues revival rather than the concert hall, while their British counterparts seemed unaware, until the Anglo-Celtic folk revival of the late sixties, of distinctly local influences other than the music hall. Most British progenitors of classical rock grew up in a culture of piano lessons and periodic visits to the philharmonic. Genesis was formed at Charterhouse, the exclusive school whose music department had once nurtured Ralph Vaughan Williams.

Classical rock came into its own with the worldwide success of Procol Harum's Bach-based "A Whiter Shade of Pale" (1967). The trippy surrealism of the lyrics suggested psychedelia, the other strain in progressive rock's DNA. By evoking alternate states of consciousness through the use of emerging electronic technology or non-Western modes, psychedelic rock's openness to all sorts of influences provided an expansive template for the ambitions of progressive rock. Pink Floyd emerged from psychedelia through the space rock subgenre to become the world's most popular progressive rock band.

By 1970 a quartet of bands had emerged to define the various directions taken by progressive rock. Emerson, Lake & Palmer borrowed liberally from 19th-century classical music. Yes drew less obviously from concert-hall melodies but delved into classical-like suites and ambitious concept albums. King Crimson was unique in balancing the fury of avant-garde jazz with the symphonic majesty of the mellotron, an electro-mechanical keyboard capable of suggesting an orchestra. Mellotron was also the key to the Moody Blues, framing their cosmic utterances with quasi-orchestral sweep.

With few exceptions, progressive rock's trajectory moved as far as possible from rock's roots in country, blues, and rhythm and blues. By the 1970s its encouragement of ambitious self-expression often resulted in pretentiously bombastic music and lyrics with no emotional pulse. By the end of that decade progressive rock became a lumbering target for the punk rock rebellion.

Although the original wave of progressive rock receded, it retained fans and provided inspiration for ambitious musicians. Alternate tunings, ambitious harmonies, and conservatory-level playing of metal bands such as Kings X betray progressive influences. A new wave of progressive rock took shape. "Prog," as fans affectionately call the movement, rebounded by the end of the 1990s with a plethora of festivals and specialty record labels along with new bands such as Spock's Beard, Porcupine Tree, and Dream Theater. Tributes to the original progressive rock era have surfaced, notably the Quebec band the Music Box, specializing in replicating concerts by Peter Gabriel–era Genesis.

PSYCHEDELIA

The lotus-eaters of Homer's *Odyssey* were not the only ancient culture engaged in altering consciousness with organic chemicals. Throughout the world, psilocybin mushrooms and psychoactive plants were part of shamanistic rites and mystery religions and often were accompanied by chant or other music. The visionary power of opium was well known in the romantic period, with Hector Berlioz's *Symphonie fantastique* (1830) as the most familiar nineteenth-century musical work inspired by the narcotic. In the early 20th century, occultist Aleister Crowley and philosopher Walter Benjamin sought visionary intoxication in consciousness-altering drugs.

After World War II, the intersection of age-old practices, modern science, and popular culture led to what essayist Daniel Pinchbeck called the "failed mass-cultural voyage of shamanic initiation" of the 1960s counterculture. It began in the late 1940s when a minority of scientists and poets went in search of a new kind of high. The literary Beat movement was fueled by drugs of all sorts, sometimes for kicks, sometimes for the satori of momentary enlightenment. Anthropology's popularization by Margaret Mead and other writers led down one avenue. Poet Allen Ginsberg and novelist William Burroughs went to South America looking for yage, an indigenous hallucinogen brewed from local plants. The greatest development, however, occurred in a petri dish when Switzerland's Sandoz laboratory synthesized a new substance from fungus called LSD-25 (1943). LSD interested psychiatrists as a tool for understanding the chemistry of consciousness and the CIA as an instrument of mind control. Government agencies and universities supported LSD research. Timothy Leary, a Harvard psychologist, conducted LSD trials, preached

284 PUB ROCK

the drug as a shortcut to enlightenment, anointed himself as the prophet of a psychedelic revolution, and tried to bring down the establishment. Author Ken Kesey, exposed to LSD during an experimental program, bought an old school bus, filled it with friends calling themselves the Merry Pranksters, and set out on the road. Leary thought he had a message and Kesey wanted to have fun. Their attitudes formed the opposing poles of the psychedelic movement.

In rock music, psychedelia was the sonic response to the popularity of LSD, dubbed "acid" for its ability to strip away the layers of conformity. Psychedelic rock was already evident in 1966, the year LSD became illegal in the United States, and echoed many tendencies from the childlike awareness of Pink Floyd's "See Emily Play" (1967) to the towering sense of oneness with the universe in Jimi Hendrix's "Purple Haze" (1967). Given the association of the psychedelic experience with Eastern religions and non-Western culture, modes and instruments from India and the Middle East were embraced. The aural distortions of an acid trip were replicated by fuzz-tone guitars, wah-wah pedals, and effects achieved through tape manipulation in the recording studio. Because of LSD's tendency to suspend the normal sense of time and distance, psychedelic bands such as the Grateful Dead tended toward long jams and improvisations on stage; the vivid visual sensations of an acid trip were simulated through the morphing lights and multimedia shows accompanying concerts.

Lyrically, psychedelic-tinged rock had no necessary association with drug use. The Electric Prunes' "I Had Too Much to Dream Last Night" (1966) was a song of love lost in a psychedelic setting; the Beatles' "Strawberry Fields Forever" (1967) may have been inspired by drugs, meditation, childhood memories, or adult ennui. A remarkable recording that later surfaced on several anthologies of 1960s garage rock, the Shag's "Stop and Listen" (1967), set an anti-LSD lyric to powerful acid rock.

As a mass movement, psychedelia burned itself out as the 1960s transitioned into the 1970s, yet psychedelic music left a mark on the development of progressive rock. Psychedelia has undergone periodical revivals, notably in the 1980s with artists such as Robyn Hitchcock, the Rain Parade, and Plasticland. Even Prince dipped into neo-psychedelia with his album *Around the World in a Day* (1985). The impulse toward sounds that suggest transcendence of everyday reality could be discerned in music associated with the rave culture, dance club music, and electronica in the late 20th and early 21st centuries.

PUB ROCK

A British phenomenon of the early to mid-1970s, pub rock reflected a backlash against the hedonistic excesses of glam rock, the pretentiousness of progressive rock, and the star-driven music industry. Most pub rock bands failed to make a dent commercially, yet their reach extended beyond their initial impact and their influence on popular music would be felt long after it ceased to exist as a musical movement.

The catalyst for pub rock's development was an early 1970s visit to Great Britain by American country rock band Eggs Over Easy. The tour's success led to revived interest in local live rock music, as roots-oriented bands began popping up with increasing frequency in the London area. These bands lacked sufficient audiences to play larger venues and wound up playing in pubs. Their sound echoed the simplicity of early rock and roll, with influences from Chuck Berry, R&B, country music, and even hints of the Band and the Grateful Dead. Dr. Feelgood, Brinsley Schwarz, Ducks Deluxe, and Ace were among pub rock bands signed to major labels, but Ace's soulful 1974 hit single "How Long" proved to be the movement's only significant chart success.

By 1975, pub rock had largely waned as a movement, but its influence was only beginning to be felt. Its "back to basics" ethos and unpretentious style paved the way for the more revolutionary punk rock of the late 1970s. Moreover, pub rock proved to be a valuable farm system, as artists with pub rock ties such as Nick Lowe, Dave Edmunds, Elvis Costello, Graham Parker, Paul Carrack, Ian Dury, and Joe Strummer achieved varying degrees of commercial success and artistic influence, establishing pub rock's legacy far beyond its modest commercial impact.

PULSAR

Members of Pulsar had been playing together under various names since the mid-1960s, and their evolution from rhythm and blues cover band through psychedelia and into progressive rock paralleled that of many British acts. The band's direction changed after witnessing Pink Floyd in concert. Their first album, *Pollen* (1975), featured long synthesizer-driven instrumental space rock and lyrics sung in French. Perhaps in a bid for international attention, *The Strands of the Future* (1976) drew more noticeably from Pink Floyd influences and was sung in rock's lingua franca, English. On later albums, Pulsar attempted to evoke the doomed romanticism of Gustav Mahler.

Key original members, including keyboardist Jacques Roman, drummer Victor Bosch, flutist Roland Richard, and guitarist Gilbert Gandil, have been with the band through most of its phases. Like many progressive rock acts, Pulsar moved toward musical theater. They adapted a story by the controversial Austrian novelist Peter Handke into an album staged under the direction of Bruno Carlucci, *Bienvenue au Conseil d'Administration* (1981).

Suggested Albums: Pollen (1975); *The Strands of the Future* (1976)

PUNK ROCK

Critic Dave Marsh coined the term *punk rock* in a 1971 article for *Creem* magazine on Question Mark and the Mysterians, an otherwise obscure Latino band from Michigan who scored a gold record with "96 Tears" (1966). The neologism was a case of inverting the negative meaning of a word, punk, turning a mark of shame into a badge of distinction. Marsh celebrated Question Mark as refreshingly obnoxious, untutored and unpretentious, a treasure unearthed from the trash heap of recent pop culture.

Soon enough, rock critics such as Lester Bangs, Richard Meltzer, and Greg Shaw advocated punk rock as they railed against the tendency of early 1970s rock bands toward self-important artiness, sterility, and loss of connection with the music's vital roots. Those critics sought an alternative to the canon of classic rock as defined by FM radio and *Rolling Stone* magazine, and were handed one in 1972 when critic (and future Patti Smith guitarist) Lenny Kaye compiled *Nuggets*, an album of mostly regional hits by American garage bands of the 1960s such as the Blues Magoos and the Standells. Question Mark and the Mysterians was not included, but could have been. The bands collected on *Nuggets* emulated the British Invasion, sometimes within a limited musical range. The compilation inspired a punk rock aesthetic stressing expression over skill, emotional punch over grand ambition. The theoreticians of punk embraced several current bands, especially the Stooges and New York Dolls, as exemplary of no-frills, no-holds-barred rock. Somehow, the avant-garde and poetic ambitions of the Velvet Underground were trimmed to fit the theory of punk rock.

Ironies abounded. Question Mark and most of the acts labeled "proto-punk" were trying to make hit records and break into the music industry. If they were considered outsiders by mainstream society, so were more successful generational peers not deemed punk by the critics, such as the Doors and Jefferson Airplane. Ironically, Dave Marsh was generally nonplussed by punk rock when the genre actually emerged, circa 1975, around New York's CBGB club and spread to the United Kingdom one year later in the wake of the Ramones' first overseas tour.

Although commercially marginal in the 1970s and 1980s, punk rock proved the maxim that history is often made by minorities. Its influence is incalculable. The punk aesthetic made a virtue of limitations and found power in simplicity, promoted a do-it-yourself spirit; and created new spaces for creativity. With its appeal to rock and roll's primitive roots, punk represented a rejection of much of what classic rock had stood for; its rise coincided with (but did not cause) the closing of the classic rock era. And yet, punk rock often justified itself in aesthetic terms, recruited adherents from art schools, was led by critical discourse, and nurtured bands such as Television and Talking Heads whose ambitions were as great as those of any classic rock act. The ambition of classic rock to be taken seriously as an art form created the conditions for punk rock, whose advocates often shared Marcel Duchamp's denunciations of art while reveling in the distinction of being artists.

PURE PRAIRIE LEAGUE

Among the many country rock bands signed in the wake of the Byrds' seminal *Sweethearts of the Rodeo*, few emphasized the country side of the genre more than Pure Prairie League. Although the band's original members hailed from Ohio, the feel of the Grand Ole Opry was present in their eponymous 1972 debut release and continued throughout their next several albums. The use of steel guitar was a prominent feature in the band's sound, along with sweet country-influenced

PURE PRAIRIE LEAGUE 287

melodies and pleasant vocals with a rural feel that sounded far less forced than those of many of their contemporaries.

Pure Prairie League scored a hit single in 1974 with the buoyant "Aime," culled from their second album, *Bustin' Out*. The song's catchy melody and likable vocals made "Aime" one of the highlights of country rock and remains the band's most enduring achievement.

By the late 1970s, the band began to alter its strict reliance on country. They earned a footnote in music history when future country superstar Vince Gill joined for the 1979 album *Can't Hold Back*. Gill's contributions drove the band in a slightly more rock-influenced direction, but did not result in greater album sales. Nevertheless, Pure Prairie League carried on and continues to tour. While their music is lacking in originality, the band's strong songwriting and pleasing vocals make Pure Prairie League one of the most listenable groups to come out of the country rock movement.

Suggested Albums: Pure Prairie League (1972); *Bustin' Out* (1972); *Can't Hold Back* (1979)

QUATERMASS

Two guitars, bass, and drums were solidified as the classic rock band lineup with the Beatles and the British Invasion. By the end of the 1960s a countertrend became audible in rock groups led by keyboardists instead of guitarists or that dispensed with guitars altogether. One of the best guitarless bands, the keyboard, bass, and drums trio Quatermass, took its name from the professorial protagonist of several British science-fiction films. On their sole album, recorded at London's Abbey Road Studio, the British group achieved cathedral-like grandeur on Hammond organ, traveled the jazz-rock road of Soft Machine, deployed the futuristic Moog synthesizer, and balanced long instrumental passages with fist-pounding rock. Ritchie Blackmore later covered "Black Sheep of the Family." Quatermass's self-titled album was an excellent representation of progressive rock at the start of the 1970s.

Suggested Album: Quatermass (1970)

QUATRO, SUZI (1950–)

Throughout its first 20 years, rock and roll was largely male dominated. While there were any number of prominent women performers during that time, most were confined to the role of lead singer in bands or producer-driven vocal groups. In the early 1970s, Suzi Quatro was one of the few artists to challenge the notion that women were unable to rock as hard as men, both as musicians and vocalists.

A native of Detroit, Quatro moved to England in 1971 after failing to achieve success with her first two bands, the Pleasure Seekers and Cradle. She was quickly discovered by British producer Mickie Most, who hooked her up with the glam rock songwriting team of Nicky Chinn and Mike Chapman. A string of U.K. hits soon followed. While her music was unexceptional guitar-driven rock similar to other early 1970s bands such as Slade and the Sweet, Quatro was unusual for fronting her band and serving as bass player. Her leather-clad image, while clearly sexual, was tougher and more assertive than most previous women in rock, and she projected the image of bandleader, a true rarity for that time.

Quatro's glam rock music never caught on in the United States. She eventually traded in the tough rocker image for a more laid-back approach. "Stumblin' In," her 1978 soft rock duet with Smokie's Chris Norman, became a Top 10 U.S. hit. She also had a successful acting career, and she is best remembered for her recurring role as Leather Tuscadero on the television series *Happy Days*. While her music was hardly influential, she served as a role model for a generation of aspiring female rockers such as Chrissie Hynde and Joan Jett, who were inspired by Quatro's belief that women "could play as well if not better than the boys."

QUEEN

Few bands of the classic rock era are as difficult to label as Queen. The British four-piece group swung between thunderous arena rock, tender ballads, metal-based riffing, and music hall camp, all seemingly without contradiction. The band was capable of shocking brilliance and maddening excess. They were quintessentially British yet highly accessible to international audiences. There were distinctive elements to Queen's music, yet there was no truly identifiable "Queen sound." Queen began its career as barely indistinguishable from a host of other hard rock bands, yet eventually broke from the pack to emerge as one of the most diverse acts of the classic rock era. While the band's music eventually came to be derided as "pomp rock," that term only reflects a portion of Queen's creative output.

Part of the band's diversity resulted from the fact that each of the four members was a contributing songwriter, almost always without collaboration. This led to many Queen songs having a stand-alone quality, self-contained pieces reflecting the work of a band with common goals but no common musical vision. Queen's musical trademarks were based on lead singer Freddie Mercury's astonishing vocal range and dynamics, and Brian May's distinctive, elegantly powerful guitar tone produced by his homemade "Red Special" guitar, created by a teenaged May and his father from household odds and ends.

The band formed in 1970 following the breakup of May and drummer Roger Taylor's previous band, Smile. They quickly started a new group, adding vocalist Mercury (who suggested calling the group Queen), as well as bassist John Deacon. The band recorded a demo in 1972 and signed a record deal in 1973, releasing the driving rocker "Keep Yourself Alive" as a debut single. Queen's first two albums were passable but, beyond the distinctive elements provided by Mercury and May, were standard riff-based hard rock records typical of the era. The songs were mostly derivative of metal and progressive rock, often featuring fantasy-based lyrics and choruses that hinted at bombastic tendencies to come. Change arrived in 1974 with the release of the Mercury-penned single "Killer Queen," a campy, piano-based hit that owed more to the British music hall and Noel Coward than to rock arenas and Led Zeppelin. The subsequent album, *Sheer Heart Attack*, saw the band exploring diverse musical horizons while not fully abandoning its hard rock origins.

That musical exploration was a harbinger of the group's follow-up album, *A Night at the Opera* (1975), a potpourri of hard rock, country, vaudeville, ragtime, emotive ballads, and progressive rock. The album's centerpiece was the nearly six-minute-long "Bohemian Rhapsody," surely one of the most unusual hit singles in the annals of popular music. After beginning as a Dostoevskyesque ballad of crime and punishment leading to a regal May guitar solo, the song unexpectedly breaks into a minute of multitracked comic opera (sung by Mercury, May, and Taylor),

Quintessentially British yet gaining a worldwide audience, Queen proved equally adept at thunderous arena rock, opera parody, and music hall camp. Shown here are bassist John Deacon, vocalist Freddie Mercury, and guitarist Brian May from a 1980 concert. (Photofest)

before transitioning to thunderous riff-driven rocker and concluding with Mercury's quiet piano and vocal. The song was unlike anything heard on the radio before or since. "Bohemian Rhapsody" was the international hit that propelled the band to megastardom and remains a staple of rock radio to this day. While a classic single, it also fully introduced the elements of over-the-top musical excess that would eventually lead to Queen's sound being labeled "pomp rock."

The classic rock era concluded just as Queen was achieving widespread success, and they would become one of the most popular bands in the world by the end of the 1970s. As the decade wore on, the band became increasingly reliant on operatic pomp and bombast. However, the bombast was often leavened with tongue-in-cheek humor and a refusal to take themselves entirely seriously. By the 1980s, Queen began to remove the more excessive elements from their music and achieved new highlights with an engaging rockabilly tune, "Crazy Little Thing Called Love" (1980), and an inspired collaboration with David Bowie, "Under Pressure" (1981). The band remained popular through the 1980s but broke up following Mercury's death from complications due to AIDS in 1991. May and Taylor have since reformed the group with various lead singers taking Mercury's place, and they continue to tour as of this writing.

Suggested Albums: Queen (1973); Queen II (1974); Sheer Heart Attack (1974); A Night at the Opera (1975); News of the World (1977); The Game (1980)

QUICKSILVER MESSENGER SERVICE

One of the most distinctive bands to emerge from San Francisco psychedelia, Quicksilver Messenger Service was among the precursors of more recent generations of jam bands for their loose concert improvisations around intricate guitar solos. Devoid of the era's dominant clichés, Quicksilver's self-title debut album (1968) tapped into a darker sonic vein than the Grateful Dead or the Jefferson Airplane. "Pride of Man" opened the album on a prophetic tone with a jeremiad against human vanity.

Initially built around the trebly guitars of John Cipollina and Gary Duncan, Quicksilver's sound was sharp and glassy, precise as a scalpel in a surgeon's hands. While a jazz rhythmic sensibility was audible, their musical inspiration was also derived from the folk revival of the early 1960s. However, they were so unlike Bob Dylan or the Byrds that the folk-rock label cannot apply. With their high-lonesome sound, Quicksilver suggested an Appalachian string band transmuted into a rock group.

The band's playful intelligence was indicated by the hermetic significance of their name, and they proved as mercurial as their namesake. Quicksilver underwent continual shifts in personnel. Acclaimed British keyboardist Nicky Hopkins joined the band for *Happy Trails* (1969) and *Shady Grove* (1970), putting piano at the center of many songs and bringing the sound closer to British rock of the period. Cipollina departed and returned. Quicksilver managed a Top 40 hit with "Fresh Air" (1970) and received sporadic FM airplay into the mid-1970s. Band members occasionally regrouped or went on to other bands. Cipollina played with the Welsh psychedelic jam band Man while bassist David Freiberg joined the Jefferson Starship.

Suggested Albums: Quicksilver Messenger Service (1968); *Happy Trails* (1969); *Shady Grove* (1970); *Just for Love* (1970); *What About Me* (1971)

RASCALS

The overused term "blue-eyed soul" was never more appropriate than when describing the Rascals, the band that that graced the airwaves in the late 1960s with songs drenched in rhythm and blues style, emotion, and most certainly soul. Few all-white bands conveyed the essence of contemporary black American music as genuinely as the Rascals while at the same time transcending their roots and making that music their own. Much of this was owed to the voice and organ of Felix Cavaliere, who sang and played with a passion and conviction that eluded many similar frontmen. And while the band didn't last into the 1970s, they left a strong body of work, much of which has never failed to feel fresh and relevant.

Initially dubbed the Young Rascals, the band was the creation of a group of New Jersey school friends, notably Cavaliere and fellow vocalist and eventual songwriting partner Eddie Brigati. Their debut album, *The Young Rascals* (1966), consisted mostly of rhythm and blues covers, including "Good Lovin,'" their first hit. Cavaliere's churning organ drove the song as he sang of sexual desire with fervor of a street corner preacher. The verse built to the climactic release of the chorus, and the sheer energy and exuberance made the single an instant classic.

Cavaliere and Brigati stepped up as songwriters on the band's next album, *Collections* (1967), and the duo came into their own with the third album, *Groovin'* (1967). *Collections* solidified the band's authentic but original rhythm and blues–based sound, while *Groovin'* saw them swerve toward an East Coast version of psychedelia, sunny and optimistic but with a streetwise feel often absent from San Francisco bands. The sound was best captured on the blissfully copacetic title track and the cabaret groove of "How Can I Be Sure." The Rascals went more fully psychedelic with mixed results with *Once Upon a Dream* (1968), but hit the mark with the soulful stand-alone single "A Beautiful Morning" (1968) and the joyously utopian soul shouter "People Got to Be Free" from *Freedom Suite* (1969). Both singles stood as symbols of hope amidst that era's roiling societal waters.

The Rascals managed a few minor hits to close out the 1960s, but Brigati left the band in 1971 before the group's last album, *The Island of Real* (1972). With Cavaliere in full control, the band experimented with a jazzier sound to little positive effect. Cavaliere pursued a lengthy solo career. The Rascals reunited in 2014 for a multimedia show co-directed by E Street Band member Steven Van Zandt, who had inducted the band into the Rock and Roll Hall of Fame. The show had a limited Broadway run and a brief East Coast tour followed.

Suggested Albums: The Young Rascals (1966); *Collections* (1967); *Groovin'* (1967); *Freedom Suite* (1969)

REED, LOU (1942–2013)

After leaving the Velvet Underground in 1970, Lou Reed went on to work at his father's office. While he had no immediate prospects for employment as a musician, life as a white-collar worker held no promise, and despite the commercial failure of his previous band, the record industry was willing to give him another chance. Reed's self-titled solo album (1972) was a strong collection of songs that attracted little notice. Reed was on his way to becoming a footnote in rock history if not for the timely intervention of a rising star, David Bowie. A Velvet Underground fan, Bowie and his guitarist, Mick Ronson, co-produced *Transformer* (1972), which earned critical respect and netted an unlikely Top 10 single, "Walk on the Wild Side."

Although released at a time when boundaries were being pushed in all areas of popular culture, "Walk on the Wild Side" left many listeners wondering if they misheard the lyrics. After all, a song that not only explicitly referenced sex but also transsexuality and amphetamine use was not the usual fodder for AM radio. Perhaps the song sneaked onto playlists through its lulling, disarming melody, riding on what became rock's most memorable bass line, actually a spacious jazz line by bassist Herbie Flowers. "Walk on the Wild Side" was not the end of the riches on *Transformer*. "Satellite of Love" and "Perfect Day" were ballads in various shades of bittersweet that no one could mistake for soft rock. Reed's sensitivity was too hard won, his vocals were often detached bordering on deadpan, and his lyrical tone achieved resignation without bitterness. *Transformer* also included "Vicious," classic hard rock lashed forward by Ronson's guitar. "Walk on the Wild Side" and many other songs included allusions to Andy Warhol's circle, references that would continue long into Reed's career.

Reed flew against commercial considerations for the thematically downbeat *Berlin* (1973). A harrowing concept album about a doomed couple sinking into violence, drug abuse, prostitution, and suicide, *Berlin* was written with unusual emotional intelligence. The song cycle was not set in Berlin. Reed chose the title for its image of foreboding dating from the Third Reich and the Cold War.

For much of his solo career, Reed was a man of two minds, intrigued and repelled by rock stardom, drawn to pop culture as well as the bohemian demimonde, to gay life and straight marriage. The touch of eyeliner he wore on the photograph filling the front cover of *Transformer* hinted of his leanings toward the Bowiesque world of glitter rock. However, the cover of his concert album *Rock'n'Roll Animal* (1974), with Reed's hair bleached and nails blackened, suggested Frankenstein's monster more than Ziggy Stardust. The live album sold well and received much FM airplay, especially for hard rock renditions of "Vicious" and the Velvet Underground's "Sweet Jane," exposing the latter to many new listeners. The bestselling *Sally Can't Dance* (1974) was one of the most slickly produced albums of his career, and although he is credited as co-producer, he soon repudiated it.

As if sickened by commercialism, Reed released a two-LP set of feedback and electric noise, *Metal Machine Music* (1975). Some saw it as a sardonic joke or a jibe against his record label; the concept may have been rooted in the experimentalism of avant-garde composer LaMonte Young, an influence on the Velvet Underground's most abrasive recordings. In hindsight, *Metal Machine Music* is seen as pointing the way toward post-1980 industrial music.

Coney Island Baby (1976) was an about-face, finding Reed in a nostalgic mood, reflecting on high school football as well as cheerful recollections of drug busts and the sex trade. The album's title referred to a local New York doo-wop hit from Reed's adolescence, the Excellents' "Coney Island Baby." The largely acoustic texture of the recording gave no indication that Reed was aware of the punk rock scene taking hold in Lower Manhattan around the CBGB's nightclub. On *Rock and Roll Heart* (1976) *and Street Hassle* (1978) he greeted the movement that found inspiration in his work with the Velvet Underground, relishing his role as godfather of punk while putting the movement down for its simple-minded inability to create the sort of fully alive characters that populated his songs. As if answering Bowie's "Berlin Trilogy," Reed ended the decade with *The Bells* (1979), incorporating disco rhythms, synthesizers, and a wide palette of instrumentation.

After the openly gay performer surprised fans by marrying British designer Sylvia Morales, Reed released a reflection on love and domesticity, *Growing Up in Public* (1980). He shifted gears again for the starkly powerful *The Blue Mask* (1982), an album whose paranoia was fueled by the playing of guitarist Robert Quine, formerly of the art punk band Richard Hell and the Voidoids. Afterward he released a series of unremarkable albums whose often-cheerful tone and inane lyrics gained him a modest following among mainstream rock fans. He threw himself into benefit concerts and ended the decade with the somber concept album *New York* (1989), which reflected on the toll of the AIDS epidemic.

The new decade began in a reunion with his long-estranged Velvet Underground partner, John Cale. They collaborated on *Songs for Drella* (1990), a warmly felt tribute to Warhol, their mentor. *Drella's* success led to a short-lived Velvet Underground reunion. *Magic and Loss* (1992) was a moving contemplation on mortality featuring jazz singer Little Jimmy Scott. After divorcing Morales, Reed married performance-recording artist Laurie Anderson, with whom he collaborated, and engaged in projects such as director Robert Wilson's *Time Rocker*, a rock musical based on H. G. Wells's *The Time Machine*.

The Raven (2003), a double CD inspired by Edgar Allan Poe, included contributions from David Bowie and avant-garde saxophonist Ornette Coleman as well as actors Willem Dafoe and Steve Buscemi. During his final years Reed published several books of photography, guest-starred on alternative rock albums, made cameo appearances in films, released an album of ambient music, and witnessed Groovefinder's remix, "Satellite of Love '04," reach the Top 10 in Britain. Reed continued to confound fans through the end of his life. His last album, *Lulu* (2011), was recorded with Metallica and was based on the work of proto–German Expressionist playwright Frank Wedekind. Reed died of liver disease in 2013. As a result of his songwriting, rock music became as suitable as literature for investigating the difficult undercurrents of contemporary life.

Suggested Albums: Lou Reed (1972); *Transformer* (1972); *Berlin* (1973); *Coney Island Baby* (1976); *Rock and Roll Heart* (1976); *Street Hassle* (1978); *The Bells* (1979); *Growing Up in Public* (1980); *The Blue Mask* (1982); *New York* (1989); *Songs for Drella* (with John Cale) (1990); *Magic and Loss* (1992); *The Raven* (2003)

See also: Cale, John; Velvet Underground

REGGAE

In the 1950s, on the eve of Jamaican independence from Great Britain, American rhythm and blues heard on powerful Miami and New Orleans radio stations began to influence mento, the island's indigenous folk music. Rhythm and blues, mento, and the calypso and merengue rhythms from neighboring islands coalesced at Kingston's Studio One, where producer Clement Dodd is said to have instructed his musicians to make a specifically Jamaican sound.

The result, the fast-paced genre called ska, was propelled by the drummer coming in on the second and fourth beats, not unlike many swing blues recordings, and the guitarist retaining the cadences of mento. The first ska records appeared circa 1960. Emerging from the early 1960s ska scene, Bob Marley and the Wailers were crucial to the evolution of Jamaican music. Marley became his nation's musical superstar well before his death in 1981.

Ska was immediately exported to Great Britain's growing Jamaican diaspora. Ironically, as Jamaican expatriates accepted newer sounds coming from their homeland as the 1960s progressed, ska was embraced by Britain's racist skinhead youth subculture. Shorn of right-wing associations, ska would be revived, often by biracial bands, as an outgrowth of Britain's punk rock scene in the late 1970s.

Meanwhile in Jamaica, the tempo of ska slowed into the short-lived rocksteady genre, a shift either blamed on a heat wave that struck the island in 1966 or credited to the spread of the Rastafarian sacrament of smoking marijuana. Rocksteady was the bridge between ska and the even slower tempo of reggae, which became Jamaica's distinct contribution to world music.

Awareness of reggae spread slowly in the United States. Often mistaken for Jamaican, the African American singer Johnny Nash enjoyed a pair of reggae hits with "I Can See Clearly Now" (1972) and a cover of Marley's "Stir It Up" (1973), but few Americans understood the music as reggae or recognized Marley's name. Led Zeppelin's "D'yer Mak'er" (1973) boasted a reggae rhythm, but the Jamaican connection did not register with American hard rock fans. The turning point came with Eric Clapton's hit version of Marley's "I Shot the Sheriff" (1974), which finally awakened interest in the genre among rock fans and musicians. Reggae influences were soon heard in artists such as 10cc, Elvis Costello, and the Police. During the 1980s reggae became universal in popularity while being identified around the globe as the music of Third World struggle.

RENAISSANCE

The Yardbirds split in 1969 with guitarist Jimmy Page forming the proto-metal blues-rock band Led Zeppelin and guitarist-vocalist Keith Relf and drummer Jim McCarty founding the classical rock group Renaissance. Under their leadership, Renaissance released two albums (1969, 1971) that attracted little notice. A drastic shift in membership resulted in the Renaissance that became familiar to progressive rock fans in the 1970s. Only the name remained from the original incarnation.

The classic lineup brought an unusual feminine dimension into the male-dominated culture of progressive rock. The band was fronted by the octave-leaping, opera-trained vocalist Annie Haslam singing lyrics by poet Betty Thatcher. Guitarist Michael Dunford was the primary composer, sending sheet music by post to the reclusive Thatcher. Pianist John Tout was integral to the sound. The classic lineup debuted with *Prologue* (1972) and continued through the studio albums *Ashes Are Burning* (1973), *Turn of the Cards* (1974), and *Scheherazade and Other Stories* (1975). Their music echoed sources as diverse as Chopin, Gershwin, Bach, and Khachaturian, albeit some songs veered close to soft rock. Haslam released a solo album, *Annie in Wonderland* (1977), produced by Electric Light Orchestra's co-founder Roy Wood.

Renaissance found a more receptive audience among American progressive rock fans than in their homeland. But after *Novella* (1977) and *Song for All Seasons* (1978), changing personnel and misguided efforts to keep abreast of changing fashions doomed the band. Old fans did not accept their early 1980s synth-pop incarnation and contemporary music fans regarded their move as farcical. Various lineups led by Haslam and Dunford carried on through the end of the millennium. Tout rejoined for *Tuscany* (2001). After several years of silence, Haslam and Dunford toured as Renaissance in 2009. By 2015 Thatcher, Dunford, and Tout had died, but Haslam continued to perform under the Renaissance name.

Suggested Albums: Prologue (1972); *Ashes Are Burning* (1973); *Turn of the Cards* (1974)

REO SPEEDWAGON

REO Speedwagon became superstars of soft rock in the early 1980s, riding a string of high-charting singles and one big hit album. However, they started off quite differently before arriving at the formula that made them one of the world's biggest-selling acts. Formed by Illinois college students Alan Gratzer and Neal Doghty in the late 1960s, the band took its unique name from a 1930s-era flatbed truck. A talented young guitarist named Gary Richrath later joined and after paying their dues playing the Midwest club circuit, they were signed to a record deal. Their eponymous debut (1971) was heavy and hard rocking, serious in purpose with politically and socially charged lyrics mixed with romantic themes. The album made little impact and the band struggled through three different lead vocalists over the course of their first five albums.

A permanent solution to the lead singer problem was found in high-voiced Kevin Cronin. Cronin had sung on the band's second album, *REO/T.W.O.* (1972), which included one of their best-known early songs, the heavy-handed protest song "Golden Country." Cronin departed before the next album, *Ridin' the Storm Out* (1973), whose apocalyptic title cut would later become one of the band's best-known songs. Singer Michael Murphy's strong hard rock voice failed to elevate the band's profile. Cronin returned for their sixth effort, *R.E.O* (1976).

With the lineup finally stabilized, the band proceeded to tour tirelessly while adopting a more melodic hard rock sound that emphasized tightly structured songs with better-defined choruses. That approach was refined with the band's next two studio albums, *You Can Tune a Piano, but You Can't Tuna Fish* (1978) and *Nine Lives* (1979), and came to fruition with the enormously successful *High Infidelity* (1980). With that album, REO hit upon the perfect soft rock mix of sensitive high-pitched vocals and hook-filled pop melodies, with an electrifying Richrath guitar solo thrown in to keep the band's rock credentials barely intact.

REO filled the early to mid-1980s with such hit singles as "Keep on Loving You," "Take It on the Run," and "Can't Fight This Feeling." Strong sales were countered with widespread critical disdain, as the band had to fight off charges that their music had slipped into a soft rock bordering tepid pop act. Cronin's vocals could be cringe worthy, although Richrath was an energetic and at times inspired guitarist. The band's best music could be described as power pop. REO's commercial fortunes dropped as the 1980s went on and one member after another left the group. They continued, touring with a variety of lineups throughout the 1990s and into the new millennium. Richrath, the band's anchor musician, died in 2015.

Suggested Albums: Ridin' the Storm Out (1973); *High Infidelity* (1980)

ROCK AND ROLL

No one was surprised when in 1934 the Boswell Sisters recorded a swinging vocal number called "Rock and Roll." The phrase "rock and roll" was heard on recordings during the swing era and earlier, explicitly referring to dancing but implicitly to sexual intercourse. By the mid-1940s rhythm and blues began to spin out of swing orchestras as small combos began to shift their rhythm toward the heavier beats that would be associated with rock and roll. Rhythm and blues was African American music, but a parallel phenomenon occurred in country music with genres such as hillbilly boogie and rural rhythms that presaged rockabilly. Audiences for those emerging forms of music were usually found outside the mainstream, facilitated by independent record labels rather than the major corporations that dominated the recording industry.

The search for the first rock and roll record has stirred much debate and produced many candidates. The roster is long and includes Roy Brown's "Good Rockin' Tonight" (1947), the Dominoes' "Sixty Minute Man" (1951), Jackie Brenston's "Rocket 88" (1951), and Bill Haley and the Comets' "Crazy Man, Crazy" (1953). The aforementioned all appeared before the release of Elvis Presley's first single on Sun Records, "That's All Right" backed with "Blue Moon of Kentucky" (1954).

Thanks to the promotion of Elvis Presley through the nascent medium of television, he was usually the first exposure white Northern teenagers had to rock and roll. However, Southerners of all races along with Northern blacks and white hipsters had a notion of what was happening. The new genre had already been named "rock and roll" by DJ Allan Freed in 1951. An influential broadcaster and impresario first in Cleveland and then New York, Freed promoted the emerging youthful variant of rhythm and blues as rock and roll in an effort to find a broader multiracial audience. When the news media crowned Presley the King of Rock and Roll, black artists such as Little Richard and Chuck Berry felt cheated.

Rock and roll drew from vital, long-running currents in American music and society but was intended as entertainment. Early performers were not self-conscious as artists. With the greater ambitions of the 1960s borne out of Bob Dylan and the Beatles came the abbreviated term *rock*, which stood for the idea that rock and roll had developed into an art form capable of greater musical range and lyrical commentary. Rock and roll continued to be used as a description of rock music that hewed closer to pre-1960s roots.

ROCK CRITICISM

Although early rock and roll attracted the alarmed concerns of sociologists and psychologists, it received little serious attention from musical or cultural perspectives until the 1960s when rock established its claim as an art form. By the 1970s rock critics were often more than mere observers and helped set trends and determine the direction for many bands. This was especially true in Great Britain, where publications such as *Melody Maker* and *New Music Express* exerted a powerful influence; in the United States *Creem* and *Rolling Stone* also helped define how the music was understood.

By the late 1960s the musical ambitions of the Beatles and the poetic depth of Bob Dylan triggered the rise of professional rock critics at mainstream newspapers, the "underground press," and specialized rock magazines. Record labels considered critics vital to promoting the careers of their recording artists. The first serious rock magazine, *Crawdaddy*, was established by Paul Williams in 1966 and was inspired by science-fiction fanzines that plugged a gap in critical appreciation for an undervalued literary genre. Williams saw a parallel between the academy's disdain for science fiction and its dismissal of rock. *Crawdaddy* was followed in 1967 by *Rolling Stone*, established by Jann Wenner with the aid of respected jazz critic Ralph J. Gleason, and *Creem*, founded in 1968 by Barry Kramer. By 1968 the *New York Times* began reviewing the Beatles as cultural criticism rather than news reporting, and in that same year the *Village Voice* added rock to its roster of film and theater criticism, employing Ellen Willis for her perceptive analysis of the rapidly developing music scene. Books followed, starting with Lillian Roxon's *Rock Encyclopedia* (1969), Richard Meltzer's *The Aesthetics of Rock* (1970), and a classic exegesis of vernacular music as cultural criticism, Greil Marcus's *Mystery Train* (1975).

In an era before MTV and the Internet, rock critics encouraged interest in music that would not be broadcast on the increasingly restricted playlists of FM stations as they devolved from free-form programming into the "album-oriented rock" format. Rock critics, especially Lester Bangs (*Creem*) and Robert Christgau (*Village Voice*), can claim a measure of credit for the rise of punk rock in the late 1970s. At least two critics successfully transformed words into action. Lenny Kaye produced the influential anthology of 1960s garage punk, *Nuggets* (1972), and Jon Landau produced Bruce Springsteen's hallmark album, *Born to Run* (1975).

ROCK FESTIVALS

The late 1960s saw the rise of large-scale live concert events that came to be known as rock festivals. While live music had always been experienced communally, rock concerts were larger, longer, more ambitious, and at times more self-important than previous concert experiences. Rock festivals were always outsized in scale, featuring huge mass gatherings of fans in open-air venues watching a large lineup of musical acts performing over the course of several days. Woodstock was the most important of such festivals, and it set the course for live event settings that remain popular to this day.

Jazz provided the earliest form of the modern music festival with the Newport Jazz Festival, billed as the "First Annual American Jazz Festival," commencing in 1954. Lasting two days, the festival attracted a star-studded lineup of jazz greats, and it provided a bonding experience for young jazz aficionados from various scenes across the country. More festivals followed in the United States, Great Britain, and Europe, and grew to include blues and folk music as well on the model of the Newport Folk Festival, which began in 1959. The runaway popularity of rock music in conjunction with the large generational cohort of baby boomers made providing outlets for large gathering of rock fans almost a necessity. One of the first and most famous rock festivals was the Monterey International Pop Festival (1967), pushed to legendary status by the breakout performance of Jimi Hendrix, who made headlines with his dynamic act and by famously lighting his guitar on fire. Canny promoters saw dollar signs in the new way to present live music, and music festivals began to pop up throughout the late 1960s (although some boasted free admission).

Without a doubt, rock festivals would not be what they are today without Woodstock (1969), the gathering of flower children in upstate New York. For three days festivalgoers endured torrential downpours, muddy terrain, inadequate rest rooms and food to witness a series of landmark musical performances by many of the era's top artists. To the surprise of many, the gathering was largely peaceful, leading some to speak of the birth of a new utopian "Woodstock Generation." Such dreams were dashed later that year when the Rolling Stones headlined the disastrous Altamont Free Concert, where the promoter's disastrous decision to hire the Hells Angels motorcycle gang as security resulted in the stabbing death of an audience member. The debacle, while sobering, did nothing to deter rock festivals' popularity, and they proliferated in the United States and throughout the world during the 1970s and 1980s. While most were intended simply as entertainment, festivals developed a conscience in the mid-1980s with the massive Live Aid, staged simultaneously in the United States and Great Britain and designed to raise money to ease the plight of drought- and war-ridden Ethiopia.

By the 1990s rock festivals were part of the cultural landscape. The annual touring caravan that was the Grateful Dead took on the air of a moveable festival, with "Deadhead" fans and their retinue of vendors, artists, and sideshow acts becoming almost as much a part of the festival as the Dead's music. As rock festivals grew in size and scope, many began to feature multiple stages, permitting fans to see a more diverse set of artists. Festivals became more specialized, with heavy metal getting into the act in venues such as Germany's gigantic Wacken Open Air Festival. A planned farewell tour for alternative rock band Jane's Addiction took on more acts and grew into the annual Lollapalooza music festival, a traveling festival that features alternative rock acts and includes performance booths for other art forms such as dance and comedy, as well as political and social activists.

In much the same manner, Lilith Fair was a festival that crisscrossed the United States in the 1990s featuring only female artists. Both festivals provided career boosts to countless otherwise neglected musical acts. And while a 30th anniversary Woodstock festival proved to be far less successful than the original event, rock festivals remain a mainstay of today's entertainment industry, with events taking place almost every year to showcase virtually every form of rock music.

ROCK OPERA

The ambition of 1960s bands to be taken seriously as artists led to the conception of rock opera. However, according to the Who's biographer Mike Segretto, producer Kit Lambert coined the term *rock opera* as a half-joking description of Pete Townshend's long-form aspirations. Although many albums have been carelessly called rock operas, most do not have the recurring characters or definable plot that are essential in defining a work of music as opera. Curiously, *Hair* (1967) was called a "rock musical," not a rock opera. Composer Galt MacDermot was content to break into Broadway, not the Metropolitan, and in any event, his songwriting could best be described as pop, not rock.

The first rock opera was Townshend's 10-minute "A Quick One While He's Away" (1966), whose plot of comic misadventure could have been penned by one of Mozart's librettists. "A Quick One" filled out the Who's second album. Townshend continued to talk about rock operas; in a 1967 interview he spoke of writing *Rael*, about Communist China's takeover of the world in futuristic 1999. Snatches of *Rael* have surfaced over the years. Fortunately, Townshend went on to pursue better ideas, starting with *Tommy* (1969), inspired by the Pretty Things' concept album *S.F. Sorrow* (1968). A song cycle of an everyone's odyssey through the early 20th century, *S.F. Sorrow* has been claimed as the first full-length rock opera, but hardly anyone heard it upon release. With its story of a deaf, dumb, and blind boy who becomes a rock star–like messianic figure, *Tommy* introduced rock opera to a wide audience. Briefly rivaling the popularity of the original album was an LP of

Tommy (1972) as performed by the Who and the London Symphony Orchestra with Rod Stewart, Richie Havens, and other singers playing roles.

In 1970 Townshend floated the idea of *Lifehouse*, a rock opera about a future society where rock music was banned. The project never came to fruition but some of the songs found their way onto the album *Who's Next* (1971). The Who returned to rock opera with a story set in the British mod scene of the mid-1960s, *Quadrophenia* (1973). Townshend tired of writing rock opera, but not of performing them. The Who performed *Tommy* and *Quadrophenia* in their entirety and both were turned into movies, the latter more successfully than the former.

On the heels of *Tommy* came Andrew Lloyd Webber and Tim Rice's *Jesus Christ Superstar* (1970), which was turned into a forgettable movie but has endured in the musical theater repertoire. Their follow-up, *Evita* (1976), was conceived as a rock opera but was reinvented as a Tony-winning West End musical, revived on Broadway, and turned into a motion picture starring Madonna as Evita Peron. Webber enjoyed great success as he moved away from rock toward contemporary musicals such as *Phantom of the Opera* and *Les Misérables*.

The Kinks released a series of song cycles and thematic albums, some of them with theatrical tendencies. *Preservation Act 1* (1973) and *Preservation Act 2* (1974), with its story of England devoured by corporate greed, heedless competition, and other malign forces, are generally regarded as rock operas. Other groups released concept albums that lent themselves to multimedia theatrical performances. Genesis's *The Lamb Lies Down on Broadway* (1974) is a character-based narrative described as a Pilgrim's Progress on the streets of New York, but has eluded classification as an opera. Story albums continue to be released in the 21st century. Inspired by *Tommy* and *Jesus Christ Superstar*, Green Day called its album *American Idiot* (2004) a rock opera, but Neil Young never applied the term to his equally elaborate narrative, *Greendale* (2003).

In the post–classic rock era, rock opera rings pretentious and bombastic in many ears. Opera composers who emerged after the 1960s, such as Philip Glass (*Einstein on the Beach*) and John Adams (*Nixon in China*), have eschewed rock influences in favor of the gradual movement and steady pulse of minimalism. However, Townshend continues to champion the sketchy idiom he helped create. Under the name *The Who's Tommy*, a theatrical production of his first full-length rock opera won several Tony Awards after its debut in 1993. The Who did not participate in the performances.

ROCKABILLY

New York DJ and impresario Alan Freed coined the word *rockabilly* in 1956 to describe what for him seemed the dubious phenomenon of hillbillies playing rock and roll. Rockabilly's roots grew from the long history of white Southern musicians combining their folk and country music with black innovations such as swing, blues, and rhythm and blues. The 1930s western swing of Bob Wills and other orchestras, which fired up traditional string-band lineups with jazz rhythms and a drum kit, laid the groundwork. In the 1940s and early 1950s such historically forgotten genres as hillbilly boogie and rural rhythm were apparent in country music and shaped the direction of Elvis Presley's early recordings for Sun Records, under the tutelage of producer Sam Phillips. In the wake of Presley's success with "That's All Right" (1954), copycats and innovators proliferated throughout the South.

Rockabilly was relatively short-lived and regional in its original incarnation, and it had largely faded from popular memory by the early 1960s. Echoes of rockabilly can be discerned in Creedence Clearwater Revival. One rockabilly song, "The Train Kept a-Rollin'," made its way into the repertoire of several classic rock bands. First recorded by R&B singer Tiny Bradshaw, the 1956 rendition by the Johnny Burnette Trio transformed the number into one of rockabilly's greatest moments and featured an early example of fuzz-tone guitar. The Yardbirds and Aerosmith covered the song, which became heavier with each rendition. Spurred by punk rock's interest in the music's primitive roots, a rockabilly revival began in the United States and Great Britain in the late 1970s.

ROLLING STONES

The Rolling Stones were the most enduringly influential band to emerge from London's burgeoning blues scene of the early 1960s. Mick Jagger, Keith Richards, Charlie Watts, and Brian Jones had all previously played in Alexis Korner's seminal band, Blues, Inc. The Rolling Stones debuted in 1962 with Jagger on vocals, Richards and Jones on guitars, Dick Taylor on bass, and Mick Avory on drums. Taylor left to found the Pretty Things and Avory joined the Kinks. They were replaced by year's end by Bill Wyman and Watts, respectively. In 1963 the Stones were booked for a long residency at London's Crawdaddy Club, where they attracted attention at a time when British lads playing blues covers with rock energy were still considered boundary crossing. The Stones were not necessarily the best of the London blues-rock bands, but their unpremeditated, vaguely threatening aura attracted the managerial skills of Andrew Loog Oldham. Oldham produced their early recordings and is credited with marketing the Stones as the anti-Beatles, the antiheroes of rock.

In 1964 the Stones stood out sullenly from their eager-to-please compatriots in the British Invasion. However, an observer detached in space and time, a rock fan from Mars or the 21st century, might find little to differentiate the Beatles of *A Hard Day's Night* from the Super 8 footage of the Stones traveling by train to a gig, cutting up in their compartment, and outracing shrieking fans on their way to the concert hall. Their haircuts were almost Beatlesque, and sometimes the Stones even wore neckties.

Except when acting dumb for the press, whose minions were often none too bright, the Stones were sophisticated actors, capable of being polite and polished. Jagger studied at the prestigious London School of Economics and, along with David Bowie, had one of the shrewdest minds in rock. Although he loved to play the role of untutored savage, Richards was a bibliophile who later studied library science to better catalogue his book collection. Watts, who worked in advertising

With good reason, the Rolling Stones dubbed themselves "the world's greatest rock and roll band." Working from blues roots, they had by 1970 achieved a hard rock sound uniquely their own, grounded in large part on the drumming of Charlie Watts, the guitar playing of Keith Richards, and the vocals and showmanship of Mick Jagger. (AP Photo)

before committing himself to a full-time career in music, was a jazz fan with a keen sense for cutting a groove. Wyman was the least colorful member, but played his part well as the stone-faced anchor for the music and the wild abandon of the band's frontman. Jagger and Richards later conceded that Jones was the musical genius early on. A quick study on virtually any instrument, Jones taught Richards his distinctive style of playing and in some accounts showed Jagger how to be a dangerous-looking performer by emulating African American showmen.

Their earliest recordings were mostly covers of American blues, rhythm and blues, and rock and roll that inevitably fell short of the originals. They had a U.K. hit with a Beatles tune, "I Wanna Be Your Man" (1963). When Jagger and Richards began writing and recording original songs, the Stones came into their own with a hard rock sound distilled from blues influences. The fruits of the band's rapid development were initially appreciated as a series of remarkable singles. The albums issued from 1964 through 1966 were a hotchpotch of conflicting and overlapping U.S. and U.K. releases, and some singles went uncollected on LP for several years.

The Stones began their claim to distinction with "The Last Time" (1965), which featured chiming guitars, loud blues echoes, and vocals that reached for ecstasy as the band held the performance to earth in a tight grip. "(I Can't Get No) Satisfaction" (1965) became the Stones' signature, a bemused protest against the artificially induced, insatiable desires of consumer society set to wiry fuzz-toned lead guitars and a relentless drumbeat. Swinging on a Latin rhythm, "Get Off of My Cloud" (1965) was another expression of irritation at contemporary life. In all cases, the lyrics made no claim to poetry but worked in rhythmic lockstep with the guitars.

Poetry came into play on "Play with Fire" (1965), credited to Nanker Phelge (a pseudonym for group compositions). A sinister baroque masterpiece with Jones on tinkling harpsichord, it was unlike anything previously heard in popular music. With restrained menace, Jagger threatened a wealthy young London socialite in lyrics specific in reference yet enigmatic in what was left unsaid. With Jones playing sitar against Richards's guitar, the anguished "Paint It, Black" (1966) fused rock and raga as Jagger's vocal shifted effortlessly between vaguely Asian modes and a hard rock rasp. On "Lady Jane" (1966), the Renaissance modal melody on Richards's acoustic guitar offset Jones as he plucked a dulcimer with a quill. Jagger played straight-faced like a character in an Elizabethan drama, pronouncing regret while alluding to the economic and social underpinnings of marriage. Marimba took the lead on the hard-driving, man's-world misogyny of "Under My Thumb" (1966).

With its surreal stream of images, "19th Nervous Breakdown" (1966) was the Stones' response to "Like a Rolling Stone"–era Bob Dylan. The folk-rock "Mother's Little Helper" (1966) addressed a topic previously unknown in pop music, prescription drug abuse, while "Have You Seen Your Mother, Baby, Standing in the Shadow?" (1966) was a dynamic production number. Exuberant yet oddly innocent, "Let's Spend the Night Together" (1967) was a delightful song of sexual encounter, while in "Ruby Tuesday" (1967), performed with Jones piping on a recorder and Richards bowing a double bass, Jagger achieves resignation in the face of loss. During this time, the Stones toured internationally, even crossing the Iron Curtain into Poland, and were at the center of young London's social life. They also drew controversy and tabloid headlines following arrests for marijuana possession. Harder drugs would dog Richards for many years.

At the close of 1967 the Stones released their response to the Beatles' *Sgt. Pepper's Lonely Hearts Club Band. Their Satanic Majesties Request* tipped the hat to *Sgt. Pepper* through colorful cover design and elaborate production on songs that alluded to one another without quite telling a story. It was maligned as a Beatles rip-off or an unworthy digression. However, *Satanic Majesties* can also be seen as a mild spoof of the Beatles, with whom they coexisted in friendly rivalry, and as an intriguing period piece credited for the inception of space rock with "2000 Light Years from Home." *Satanic Majesties* was also the first Stones album released in identical form in the United States and United Kingdom.

Beggars Banquet (1968) was an abrupt shift from psychedelia to hard rock with country and blues roots. Unlike its fey predecessor, *Beggars Banquet* included much aggression along with softer moments. "Street Fighting Man" was an ambivalent shrug at the era's political turmoil, while "Sympathy for the Devil" was a percussive recounting of the history of violence. Lightening the mood was "Jumpin' Jack Flash's" hard-driving anthem of perseverance. *Beggars Banquet* was the last album Jones completed. Sapped by drugs and unable to tour, he was quietly edged out of

306 ROLLING STONES

the band he had cofounded. Less than a month later, in July 1969, he was found dead in his swimming pool under cloudy circumstances.

Mick Taylor replaced Jones in time to record some tracks for *Let It Bleed* (1969), its title a sardonic rejoinder to the Beatles' recently released *Let It Be*. It included "Gimme Shelter," which reinvented the blues in a new rock idiom, as well as an authoritative if uncredited rendition of Robert Johnson's "Love in Vain." The album contained material shocking to popular audiences, especially "Midnight Rambler," sung from a serial killer's perspective. "You Can't Always Get What You Want," a signature song welcoming the end of the 1960s and the beginning of an era of lowered ambitions, featured a sardonically voiced Jagger and a guest appearance by the London Bach Choir. The Stones ended the 1960s, literally in the minds of many Utopians, by presiding over the disastrous Altamont rock festival at which Hells Angels, employed as security on the Grateful Dead's recommendation, killed a black concertgoer. The debacle was documented in Albert and David Maysles's film *Gimme Shelter* (1970).

The Stones marked time at the start of the new decade with a live album, *Get Yer Ya-Ya's Out!* (1970). Andy Warhol's cover for *Sticky Fingers* (1971) was emblematic of their status on the international jet set. The album opened with the thundering hard rock classic "Brown Sugar," which seemed to celebrate sex between plantation owner and slave in the old South. *Sticky Fingers* found the Stones at the height of their powers as a blues-derived rock band that had long since slipped the boundary of any genre but their own. The album also featured the exquisite country-rock of "Wild Horses" and a soul jazz coda to "Can't You Hear Me Knocking."

Britain's punitive tax rates for high earners sent the Stones to the French Riviera, where they recorded *Exile on Main Street* (1972) in a rented villa and a druggy haze. Loose and louche, the double-LP yielded "Happy" (sung by Richards) and "Tumbling Dice." By now the Stones were billed as "the World's Greatest Rock & Roll Band," selling out stadiums and flying through world tours on their own jet. But their next album, *Goat's Head Soup* (1973), was a muddled letdown to fans while containing a number one pop hit, the incongruously sensitive love ballad "Angie." *It's Only Rock 'n' Roll* (1974) was a return to form with a memorable title track and a commanding interpretation of the Temptations' "Ain't Too Proud to Beg." Taylor left, replaced by Faces guitarist Ron Wood as the band fumbled for new directions on *Black and Blue* (1976). The album included comical attempts at reggae ("Cherry Oh Baby") along with a sensitive soul ballad ("Fool to Cry") and, bowing to trends, disco ("Hot Stuff").

After a decade of mixed accomplishments, the Stones ended the 1970s on a high with *Some Girls* (1978). Regenerated by the challenge of punk rock, some of whose adherents branded Jagger and company as out-of-touch socialites, they responded with the blistering hard rock of "Shattered" and a successful disco-blues fusion, "Miss You," featuring bluesman Sugar Blue on wailing harmonica.

They started the new decade with a bestselling batch of new songs along the lines of *Some Girls, Emotional Rescue* (1980). *Tattoo You* (1981) included one great single, "Start Me Up," but was comprised largely of outtakes. It proved to the their final number one album in the United States. A deepening rift between Jagger and

Richards left the band adrift during much of the decade with the former focusing on a solo career and the latter left to run recording sessions. *Steel Wheels* (1989) was embraced as a comeback with the upbeat "Mixed Emotions" as the hit single and one track recorded in Morocco with the Master Musicians of Jajouka, a traditional ensemble for which Jones had produced an album shortly before his death.

Steel Wheels led to a renewed round of tours with comfortable breaks in between that continued into the 21st century. Wyman retired from the band in 1993 and was replaced by Miles Davis sideman Darryl Jones starting with *Voodoo Lounge* (1994), an admirable effort under the watchful gaze of producer Don Was. Although they continue to release albums of new material, the concert stage has become their primary platform, a showcase for Jagger's unflagging athleticism and a long repertoire of hits as polished and sharp as gems. Each Stone has engaged in solo projects that suited his tastes, with Richards receiving the greatest acclaim for his memoir, *Life* (2010). The Rolling Stones have been inducted into the Rock and Roll Hall of Fame.

Suggested Albums: The Rolling Stones (aka *England's Newest Hit Makers*) (1964); *12 × 5* (1964); *The Rolling Stones No. 2* (1965); *The Rolling Stones, Now!* (1965); *Out of Our Heads* (1965); *December's Children (And Everybody's)* (1965); *Aftermath* (1966); *Got Live If You Want It!* (aka *Have You Seen Your Mother Live!*) (1966); *Between the Buttons* (1967); *Flowers* (1967); *Their Satanic Majesties Request* (1967); *Beggars Banquet* (1968); *Let It Bleed* (1969); *Get Yer Ya-Ya's Out!* (1970); *Sticky Fingers* (1971); *Exile on Main Street* (1972); *It's Only Rock 'n' Roll* (1974); *Some Girls* (1978); *Emotional Rescue* (1980); *Steel Wheels* (1989); *Voodoo Lounge* (1994)

RONSON, MICK (1946–1993)

As a child Mick Ronson wanted more than anything to play cello, but he was too small. In adulthood he often played guitar with long legato notes as if it were a cello. After playing in bands around his hometown, Hull, England, he came to London in 1970 and quickly fell in with David Bowie. His lead guitar added a hard metallic edge to Bowie's *The Man Who Sold the World* (1970). Ronson continued to work with Bowie, writing string arrangements for *Hunky Dory* (1971) and becoming integral to his glitter rock band, the Spiders from Mars. He was involved in Bowie's production projects, providing guitar on Lou Reed's *Transformer* (1972) and arrangements for Mott the Hoople's *All the Young Dudes* (1972). After leaving Bowie's entourage, he continued as a session guitarist and producer-arranger for acts as various as David Cassidy, Pure Prairie League, Roger Daltrey, John Mellencamp, and Bob Dylan. He played an important role in Ian Hunter's career on record and on tour.

Like many electric guitarists of his era, Ronson was fascinated by the orchestral power of his instrument to summon and convey a variety of emotions. He put his talent to use on a pair of solo albums. The first received the most attention in the United States. *Slaughter on Tenth Avenue* (1974) included *Ziggy Stardust*–like songs given him by Bowie and a gorgeous instrumental version of Richard Rodgers's

"Slaughter on Tenth Avenue," originally written for a 1936 George Balanchine ballet. *Play Don't Worry* (1975) was an eclectic collection of originals and covers.

Ronson played on Bowie's album *Black Tie White Noise* (1993). He died that year of cancer.

Suggested Albums: Slaughter on Tenth Avenue (1974); *Play Don't Worry* (1975)

RONSTADT, LINDA (1946–)

Perhaps it's inevitable that an artist whose career spans the course of six decades will undergo more than a few transformations along the way. Such is the case with Linda Ronstadt, whose long, often celebrated (and sometimes criticized) career has had more than its share of changes. Those changes reflect both the shifting nature of public taste as well as the maturation of an artist who began as a young woman and continued performing into her sixties. Ronstadt experienced the highs of superstardom, the double-edged sword of celebrity, and finally settled into a comfortable role that allowed her to age rather gracefully.

Ronstadt was born in 1946, the daughter of an affluent Arizona couple from locally prominent families. She began singing publicly with her brother and sister, landing gigs while only in her mid-teens. Blessed with a voice both lovely and powerful, the young Ronstadt joined the ranks of ambitious musicians who flocked to the musical Promised Land that was Los Angeles in the middle 1960s. Her first foray into pop music was with the folk-rock group the Stone Poneys, who owed at least a part of their local notoriety to Ronstadt's habit of performing barefoot clad in a miniskirt. Their eponymous 1967 debut album was eclectic, with dashes of bluegrass and country alongside some rather somber folk-oriented songs. The album was lost amidst a sea of folk-rock releases, but the follow-up, *Evergreen, Volume 2* (1967), featured a hit single, the sparkling "Different Drum," written by the Monkees' Michael Nesmith. Set amidst a pristine pop production, Ronstadt's voice soars over lyrics that described troubled romance, but also served as a metaphor for a young generation eager to break from the shackles of societal conformity. Unsurprisingly, Ronstadt quickly eclipsed the other members of the band and embarked on a solo career by 1968.

Ronstadt's first solo album, *Hand Sown . . . Home Grown* (1969), shows a young artist growing in confidence while exploring new terrain. Despite a residue of Stone Poneys folk influences, the music rocked harder and Ronstadt's voice had become a true powerhouse. The album's country rock leanings were demonstrated in the standout "Silver Threads and Golden Needles." Ronstadt's vocals transitioned easily to more country-flavored material, and she proved adept at both rockers and aching ballads, such as her first prominent single, "Long, Long Time" from *Silk Purse* (1970).

She moved quickly up the ranks of Southern California's country rock scene of the early 1970s, becoming one of the faces of the movement. Ronstadt projected the image of the cowgirl next door, singing with grace and force, all the while exuding a healthy, vibrant sexuality that was alluring but nonthreatening. She befriended rising young talent. By hiring young musicians Glenn Frey and Don Henley for her touring band, she became instrumental in forming future superstar band the Eagles. Two more albums, *Linda Ronstadt* (1971) and *Don't Cry Now* (1973), served to further her status as a country rocker on the rise, and a re-recorded rocked-up version of "Silver Threads and Golden Needles" gained solid FM airplay.

By 1974, Ronstadt was ready to expand her horizons, hiring producer Peter Asher to record more rock and pop–oriented material. The resulting album, *Heart Like a Wheel* (1974), proved to be her finest work. Ronstadt took command of the diverse material, singing with a relaxed and confident maturity that gained her notice in the male-dominated world of FM rock radio. Ronstadt put her own stamp on Betty Everett's "You're No Good," which became a hit single. The album's other standout track was the title cut, a ballad that showed how far she had progressed from the innocent-sounding girl of the Stone Poneys. *Heart Like a Wheel* was a breakout hit. Ronstadt had become a star.

Stardom turned into superstardom as the 1970s moved on. Backed by an ace crew of LA session musicians, Ronstadt racked up one chart success after another, becoming a veritable one-woman hit machine. Always an interpreter rather than a writer of songs, Ronstadt scored hits with covers of Buddy Holly and the Crickets' "That'll Be the Day," Roy Orbison's "Blue Bayou," Warren Zevon's "Poor, Poor, Pitiful Me," and Martha and the Vandellas' "Heat Wave." However, unlike Ronstadt's work on *Heart Like a Wheel*, these covers had a more generic vocal treatment, as Ronstadt took to bellowing the hits with the gusto of a college cheerleader working the crowd at a big game. To her credit, Ronstadt did expose a new generation of listeners to rock's formative artists. She also promoted fresh talent by covering Elvis Costello's "Alison" on *Living in the USA* (1978), although Costello initially scorned her version (he later characterized his ungracious reaction as "punky and horrible").

Ronstadt became an international celebrity, dating a presidential candidate in California, Governor Jerry Brown, gracing the covers of all the major magazines of the time, and becoming an acknowledged sex symbol (despite insecurity regarding her appearance). Along with success came often withering attacks from critics who charged that her work was overly slick and superficial, and that she had become a marketed commodity like Coca-Cola and McDonald's hamburgers. Ronstadt attempted to silence the critics with the new wave–styled *Mad Love* (1980), but despite strong sales the album was dismissed as cynical opportunism.

Perhaps burned out by the stress of celebrity, Ronstadt moved away from pop stardom in the 1980s. A lead role in a Broadway production of Gilbert and Sullivan's operetta *The Pirates of Penzance* (1980) opened the door to theater and eventually a short but unsuccessful detour into opera. *Trio* (1987), a collaboration with country legends Emmylou Harris and Dolly Parton, bought Ronstadt fully into country music and earned the three singers a Grammy award. Now choosing material that interested her rather than for its commercial appeal, Ronstadt dabbled in jazz, recorded an album of pop standards, and released an album of Mexican mariachi music.

Cry Like a Rainstorm, Howl Like the Wind (1989) included her first hit single in almost a decade, a duet with Aaron Neville on the tender ballad "Don't Know Much." After that, Ronstadt returned to releasing albums that pleased her without regard for public acclaim. She began to record more roots-oriented material and increased her range to include an album of Cajun music, the well-regarded *Adieu False Heart* (2006). Ronstadt's remarkable voice was silenced in 2015, when the effects of Parkinson's disease made it impossible for her to sing.

While many critics have derided Ronstadt as a sellout who squandered her considerable talent, she deserves recognition as a pioneer who paved the way for women to achieve a more prominent place in the rock hierarchy. While most of her most popular music was her least interesting, she nevertheless brought attention to country rock, as well as to new artists and underappreciated legends.

Suggested Albums: Evergreen, Volume 2 (with the Stone Poneys) (1967); *Hand Sown . . . Home Grown* (1969); *Silk Purse* (1970); *Linda Ronstadt* (1971); *Don't Cry Now* (1973); *Heart Like a Wheel* (1974); *Prisoner in Disguise* (1975); *Hasten Down the Wind* (1976); *Adieu False Heart* (2006)

ROTARY CONNECTION

Rotary Connection was an experiment in psychedelic soul rock conceived by Marshall Chess of Chicago's famed blues label, Chess Records. Born as a studio project under producer-arranger Charles Stepney, Rotary Connection drew from an eclectic multiracial cast of players including local rock band the Proper Strangers, esteemed Chess session musicians Phil Upchurch and Morris Jennings, and the Chess label's receptionist Minnie Riperton, an octave-spanning soprano vocalist. The self-titled debut album (1967) featured sitar and Stepney's dreamy string arrangements executed by members of the Chicago Symphony Orchestra. It included Stepney originals along with soulfully baroque covers of songs by the Rolling Stones and Bob Dylan.

Rotary Connection attracted a measure of attention, released several follow-up albums, and played at rock festivals. Indicative of their eclecticism was their performance of a Roman Catholic "rock mass" at a 1969 liturgical convention. Although Rotary Connection lasted into 1971, Riperton's solo career began in 1970 with the Stepney-produced *Come to My Garden* album. She enjoyed a successful career before her death from cancer in 1979.

Suggested Album: Rotary Connection (1967)

ROXY MUSIC

Breaking with the direction set for rock by the 1960s counterculture, Roxy Music's eponymous debut album (1972) and their Top-10 British single, "Virginia Plain," were startling for freshness of vision in image as well as music. Model Kari-Ann Moller posed provocatively on the album's cover, an incongruous gesture for an early 1970s rock release that harkened to the cheesecake that often adorned pop jazz LPs from an earlier generation. Sonically discordant yet entirely coherent, *Roxy Music* galloped into the future of rock. The rich surfaces of their songs enveloped minimal frameworks with many pastiches. "Re-make/Re-model" quoted the Beatles, Henry Mancini, and Richard Wagner.

Bryan Ferry's trebly, almost irrepressibly ironic vocals were rimmed with an aura of quizzical experimentation courtesy of Brian Eno, credited with synthesizer and tape effects. During his tenure with the band, the androgynous Eno added a touch of glitter rock to Roxy Music's image. The creative push and pull between Ferry and Eno generated dynamic tension on *Roxy Music* and its follow-up, *For Your Pleasure* (1973), which featured "Do the Strand," whose inside-out boogie-woogie was edged with squawking jazz. Eno exited afterward for an influential career as a solo recording artist and producer, leaving the band fully in Ferry's hands.

But despite Eno's challenge to his authority and occasional songwriting contributions from other members, Roxy Music was largely Ferry's creation all along. The child of frugal circumstances in Britain's coal-mining country, Ferry was drawn to the imagery of affluence. At art school he learned to use the world around him as his palette and absorbed pop art's premise of appropriating commercial culture. While not averse to rock, Ferry was more a fan of soul music, which he admired as much for the sharp-suited look of the early soul revues as for the power of their music. He knew he could never reach the latter but was happy to draw from the former. Ferry was an artist of artifice.

Although Eno made a virtue of amateurism as a strategy for undercutting clichés, Ferry was otherwise keen to choose professionals to provide a sturdy foundation for his ideas. Saxophonist Andy Mackay, a graduate of the National Youth Jazz Orchestra, brought the possibility of avant-garde improvisation into play, as did guitarist Phil Manzanera, formerly of the rhythmically complicated jazz-rock band Quiet Sun. Drummer Paul Thompson's no-frills urgency propelled the songs.

Such was his suave demeanor that early on some fans took Ferry for a continental European. As the only member of Roxy Music who looked at home in suit and tie, his manner suggested a regular at Monte Carlo who traveled between dates first class on the Orient Express. Ferry's image was as crucial to Roxy as their harmonically diffuse music. Roxy Music was entertaining and important, and in the United Kingdom they easily jumped across the high wall separating art rock from pop in the early 1970s. Unlike many progressive rock bands, they had style as well as substance and were ahead of almost everyone except David Bowie for their postmodern willingness to recontextualize historical styles with ironic flair.

Ferry's parallel career as a soloist, which continued throughout the Roxy Music years and often involved members of Roxy, began with *These Foolish Things* (1973). Like Bowie's *Pin-ups* from that same year, *These Foolish Things* was an album of covers at a time when rock artists enthralled by the cult of originality rarely did such things. Some fans were shocked by Ferry's juxtaposition of ephemeral pop and poetic folk by putting Leslie Gore's "It's My Party" alongside Bob Dylan's "Hard Rain's a-Gonna Fall."

RUNDGREN, TODD

With *Country Life* (1974), Roxy Music finally broke through on American FM with the sardonic decadence of "The Thrill of It All" and "Out of the Blue," soaring on violin solos by Eno's replacement, Eddie Jobson. American AM discovered them a year later with "Love Is the Drug" from *Siren* (1975). The disco rhythm set the pace for Ferry's frank exploration of singles-bar sex as a chemical addiction. "Love Is the Drug" brilliantly reduced disco to its grim essentials and became something almost unthinkable, a deliberately joyless dance record. Addiction is no fun.

Roxy Music split after *Siren*, releasing a live album with the hopeful title *Viva! Roxy Music* (1976). During their time off, Mackay, Manzanera, and Ferry released several solo albums each, and Ferry tasted international celebrity during his affair with model Jerry Hall before she left him for Mick Jagger. By the time Roxy reunited for *Manifesto* (1979), their music had become lush sophisticated pop with Ferry's irony shading into doomed romanticism on hit singles such as "Angel Eyes" and "Dance Away." With *Flesh + Blood* (1980), Ferry, Mackay, and Manzanera were the only remaining members from Roxy Music's classic period. By this time Roxy Music had become living inspiration to a new wave of style-conscious, carefully coiffed, ready for MTV acts led by Duran Duran.

The lovely *Avalon* (1984) with the hit "More Than This" was relaxed in pace and texture, a shock of tranquility when compared with Roxy Music's early albums. Ferry continued to release exquisitely tailored solo albums. *Boys and Girls* (1985) included "Slave to Love," a quiet emotional sequel to "Love Is the Drug." On the darker *Bête Noire* (1987), Ferry played the role of the doomed romantic trapped in the flashbulb world of celebrity culture. *Taxi* (1993) featured cover songs delivered with haunting understatement and mature weariness.

In 2001 Ferry re-formed Roxy Music with Manzanera, Mackay, and Thompson as an occasional touring band. His solo career continued in collaboration with musicians as diverse as Robin Trower, the Eurythmics' David Stewart, and his old rival, Eno. Ferry was one of the outstanding figures to emerge from rock music in the 1970s and like old scotch whiskey, he has aged well. With Roxy Music and in his long solo career, Ferry created pop art statements more emotionally engaging than any picture hanging on a wall: his music enveloped listeners in a world of style, illusion, the longing of romance, and the dangers of sex, power, and compulsion.

Suggested Albums: (Roxy Music): *Roxy Music* (1972); *For Your Pleasure* (1973); *Country Life* (1974); *Siren* (1975); *Manifesto* (1979); *Flesh + Blood* (1980); *Avalon* (1984); (Bryan Ferry): *These Foolish Things* (1973); *Another Time, Another Place* (1974); *Let's Stick Together* (1975); *In Your Mind* (1977); *The Bride Stripped Bare* (1978); *Boys and Girls* (1985); *Bête Noire* (1987); *Taxi* (1993); *The Jazz Age* (2012)

See also: Eno, Brian

RUNDGREN, TODD (1948–)

When Todd Rundgren said goodbye to his early garage rock band Nazz and began his solo career, even his fertile imagination could not have predicted the many paths he would take. Rundgren has pursued a diversity of directions that made him difficult to label, categorize, pigeonhole, and most certainly to anticipate. There have been three tracks to Rundgren post-Nazz: Rundgren the solo artist; Rundgren the band member in his brainchild Utopia; and Rundgren the producer. Had he simply pursued one of those paths he would have had a full career, but his insatiable curiosity and eccentric personality could not be fenced in. Rundgren would likely disagree with F. Scott Fitzgerald's contention that life is best looked at through a single window.

His solo career began conventionally enough as a pop singer-songwriter. He had begun experimenting with keyboard-based songs while still in Nazz, so it wasn't a huge stretch to find his piano dominating his first two solo albums, *Runt* (1970) and *Runt: The Ballad of Todd Rundgren* (1971). Quiet piano numbers were interspersed with harder rock, experimental chants, a tribute to singer-songwriter Laura Nyro, and one quirky pop hit, "We Gotta Get You a Woman."

The albums were well received, but Rundgren had bigger things in mind for his next release, the double-LP pop masterpiece *Something/Anything* (1972), on which Rundgren played the majority of instruments. All of Rundgren's many influences are there for the listening, from the Beatles and the British Invasion through Brian Wilson, Jimi Hendrix, Cream, and *Tapestry*-era Carole King. The album's first hit, "I Saw the Light," recalled King with a healthy dose of the Fab Four tossed in for good measure. Another single, "Hello, It's Me," was first recorded with Nazz; his less psychedelic solo version yielded another hit. The pop experimentation of *Something/Anything* was just the start, as the concept album *A Wizard, A True Star* (1973) would demonstrate. The dreamlike and varied music of *A Wizard* could be described as progressive pop, as Rundgren played with studio effects and an eclectic set of melodies, some of which had the feel of Broadway show tunes.

Todd (1974) saw Rundgren experiment with synthesizers and comedic material along the lines of Gilbert and Sullivan, but also included the pop single "A Dream Goes On Forever." From then on, Rundgren veered between pop conventions and experimentation. While comfortable with such commercial singles as the poignant "Can We Still Be Friends" (1978) and the rousing "Bang the Drum All Day" (1983), he would lurch into an album such as *A Cappella* (1985), consisting entirely of his voice, or the electronic rap of *No World Order* (1993). Few artists traveled as many creative roads.

Not content with pursuing a solo career, Rundgren also formed the band Utopia, which debuted with *Todd Rundgren's Utopia* (1974). Unlike his solo efforts, Utopia started out as pure progressive rock with lengthy and complex instrumental passages, often centered around an organ that gave the band a sound not unlike early Kansas. Jazz and classical elements added further complexity, and there was barely a hint of the pop genius animating his concurrent solo work.

Ra (1977) was an even more ambitious trip to the world of classical and progressive rock, with Rundgren slipping into the truly pretentious and inaccessible with some lovely soft piano passages keeping the album from going completely over the edge. Always one to confound and perplex, Rundgren's Utopia shifted gears to more accessible pop with *Oops! Wrong Planet* (1977), rock and easy listening pop for *Adventures in Utopia* (1979), and British Invasion on the delightful

314   RUSH

Deface the Music (1980) with its Beatlesque single "I Just Want to Touch You." Then it was back to more progressive hard rock for the politically charged *Swing to the Right* (1982).

Utopia (1984) sounded at home in the slickly produced synthesized world of the 1980s while still maintaining a pop eclecticism. *Oblivion* (1984) fell into the same mainstream as Genesis and Robert Palmer. It seemed Rundgren was eager to try virtually all that the musical world had to offer, with every expectation that his fans would follow along the way. Utopia's journey ended with *P.O.V.* (1985), the band's final studio album.

Rundgren also carved out a significant niche as a producer for other artists, as well as himself. He helped set the table for punk rock with the New York Dolls' eponymous debut album (1972), capturing their decadent swagger with an energetic live-sounding record. Rundgren had a Midas touch as a producer, working on hit records for groups as diverse as Grand Funk Railroad, Meat Loaf, Patti Smith, XTC, Tom Robinson Band, Bad Religion, and Cheap Trick. Rundgren also dabbled in music videos and television and film scores, adding further to an already exhaustive musical resume.

The new millennium saw Rundgren remain active, releasing new solo material, producing a New York Dolls reunion album, and playing in a re-formed version of new wave superstars the Cars. Rundgren continues to tour, conducts university lectures on music, and performs with symphony orchestras. Amazingly, Rundgren has not been inducted into the Rock and Roll Hall of Fame as of this writing.

Suggested Albums: Runt (1970); *Runt: The Ballad of Todd Rundgren* (1971); *Something/Anything* (1972); *A Wizard, A True Star* (1973); *Todd* (1974); *Hermit of Mink Hollow* (1978); *The Ever Popular Tortured Artist Effect* (1982); *Nearly Human* (1989); *Liars* (2004); *Arena* (2008); *Global* (2015); *(With Utopia): Oops! Wrong Planet* (1977); *Adventures in Utopia* (1979); *Deface the Music* (1980); *Swing to the Right* (1982)

See also: Nazz

RUSH

To some Rush fans they are a thinking person's rock band, writing and performing intelligent progressive music with virtuoso skill and precision while making complex lyrical subject material accessible to millions. To others, their music is sterile and pretentious, the epitome of uncool, appealing to a fan base consisting of nerdy technophiles. It seems odd that Canada's popular rock export would prove to be so polarizing, as the band has never courted controversy and their music lacks the threatening aspects of heavy metal, punk, or rap. But nevertheless, rock fans seem prepared to draw the line at Rush. What almost all can agree on is that since their arrival, Rush has carved out a long and highly successful career with a cohesive and stable lineup despite wildly changing music trends, strong critical aversion, and immense personal tragedy.

Rush was formed in the early 1970s by guitarist Alex Lifeson and bassist Geddy Lee, school classmates in a suburb of Toronto, Ontario. Original drummer John Rutsey filled out the lineup, and the group quickly picked up a local following. Their self-released debut album *Rush* (1974) was eventually distributed by Mercury Records and the group immediately drew comparisons to Led Zeppelin. Without doubt, there were similarities between the two bands. Lifeson's heavy guitar riffing brought Jimmy Page to mind, and Lee's high-pitched vocals were highly reminiscent of Robert Plant. Rush was a second-generation rock group, influenced by Led Zeppelin, but lacking the organic blues and roots influences that animated Zeppelin's music. However, the riff dominated "What You're Doing" and "Take a Friend" could pass for outtakes from *Led Zeppelin II*. And, as if to underscore the point, Rush's big break came when they were added to a prominent Cleveland radio station's playlist after listeners flooded the lines with requests for Rush's thundering "Working Man," mistakenly thinking it was a new Zeppelin song.

Comparisons with Zeppelin would continue to haunt the band in its early days, but they already were moving in a more progressive direction for their second album, *Fly By Night* (1975). The opening track, "Anthem," set the pace, starting with a Page-styled riff before unexpectedly breaking into power chords and a more complex arpeggio-oriented verse. Other tracks featured similarly complex song structure, often with dynamic arrangements and tempo changes. One of the main reasons for the band's musical growth was the arrival of new drummer Neil Peart, who had signed on after health issues forced Rutsey to leave. Peart's active and inventive drumming challenged Lifeson and Lee and gave the band room to stretch musically.

Peart also took over lyric writing, and his unconventional literary themes included fantasy, science fiction, and the objectivist philosophy of Ayn Rand. Rush's permanent lineup was set, and the Pete Townshend–styled title track gained the band attention with considerable FM rock airplay. Their next album, *Caress of Steel* (1975), was a full-fledged progressive rock exploration with lengthy highly involved songs, extensive soloing, and highly original and at times fanciful lyrics. Although poor sales checked their career momentum, the band rejected record label pressure to produce a more commercial follow-up, opting instead for the progressive double album *2112* (1976), an over-the-top masterpiece of excess based on Peart's continued fascination with Rand's philosophy.

What could have been a career killer turned into Rush's big break, as the band gained new fans with *2112* and the live album *All the World's a Stage* (1976). Still heavily grounded in progressive rock, *A Farewell to Kings* (1977) gave Rush its first hit single, the chiming "Closer to the Heart." Rhythmically and lyrically complex, *Hemispheres* (1978) was ambitious, but seemed out of touch with the emergence of punk and new wave. Critics lambasted the band as pretentious and out of touch with the concerns of everyday fans.

Rush responded with *Permanent Waves* (1980), whose shimmering production set the stage for tracks colored by touches of new wave, metal, and reggae. Melodic songs such as "The Spirit of Radio" and "Freewill" displayed Peart's ability to make

Canada's Rush have often been considered a "thinking person's hard rock band" for writing and performing with intelligence and virtuoso skill. By the time of this 1976 performance, the band's classic lineup had jelled around guitarist Alex Lifeson, bassist Geddy Lee, and drummer Neil Peart. (Fin Costello/Redferns/Getty Images)

cerebral lyrics accessible. The album was a tremendous commercial success. Rush became an arena-filling act building on the strength of hit albums *Moving Pictures* (1981) and *Signals* (1982). Radio-friendly songs such as "Tom Sawyer," "Limelight," and "Red Barchetta" showed the band had become adept at pairing complex, progressive-oriented music with highly listenable melodies. Rush's musical virtuosity was always up front. Peart and Lee were ranked among the most highly ranked players of their respective instruments.

Rush's sound continued to evolve throughout the 1980s as Lee made increasing use of keyboards to the delight and consternation of fans. Their fan base had become increasingly devoted, with stories of some logging thousands of miles to see show after show. The band remained a popular live act into the 1990s even as album sales slowed. Tragedy almost ended their long run in the late 1990s when Peart's wife and teenaged daughter died within a year of each other. Peart announced his retirement and dealt with his grief by embarking on a prolonged motorcycle trek across North America, returning to the band almost two years later and writing a well-regarded memoir of his journey. After his return, the band recorded *Vapor Trails* (2002) followed by a triumphant comeback tour. Rush continued to record and tour, playing to pack houses until 2015, when the band embarked on what they hinted would be their final full-scale tour. They have been inducted into the Rock and Roll Hall of Fame.

Suggested Albums: Fly By Night (1974); *2112* (1976); *Permanent Waves* (1980); *Moving Pictures* (1981); *Signals* (1982); *Grace under Pressure* (1984); *Power Windows* (1985); *Vapor Trails* (2002); *Clockwork Angels* (2012)

RUSSELL, LEON (1942–2016)

Leon Russell achieved notice with his Top 20 U.S. single "Tightrope" (1972), but his keyboard playing had been heard on a host of prominent songs. Beginning with his work in the legendary Los Angeles sessions ensemble the Wrecking Crew in the early 1960s, Russell enjoyed a long and varied career in the music business.

The Oklahoma-born Russell learned piano as a child and headed to Los Angeles as a young adult, where he quickly caught on as a sessions musician, first with the Wrecking Crew, and then playing on records by Gary Lewis and the Playboys, Glen Campbell, Delaney & Bonnie, Bob Dylan, and Badfinger, and helping organize Joe Cocker's *Mad Dogs and Englishmen* tour (1970), of which he was a featured musician. Russell began a solo career later in 1970 with a self-titled solo album, a heavily rhythm and blues–flavored effort that featured his blues and gospel–influenced keyboard playing and hinted at what would become known as Southern rock.

George Harrison invited him to play at *The Concert for Bangladesh* (1971). Russell also enjoyed success as a songwriter, most notably as co-writer of the Carpenters' hit "Superstar" (1972) and "The Masquerade," which became a standard in jazz and pop after George Benson's hit version (1976). He also helped launch Shelter Records, whose roster included such acts as Tom Petty and the Heartbreakers and J. J. Cale. Russell's music career eventually gravitated more toward country music, where he enjoyed some success, but he returned to rock with *The Union* (2010) a collaborative album with Elton John. Despite battling health issues, he continued to tour before his death. Russell has been inducted into the Rock and Roll Hall of Fame.

Suggested Albums: Leon Russell (1970); *Carney* (1972); Elton John and Leon Russell: *The Union* (2010)

RYDER, MITCH (1945–)

Few musical environments can boast the breadth and depth of talent as Detroit in the 1960s. From the pop soul of Motown, the guitar pyrotechnics of Ted Nugent's Amboy Dukes, and the turbulent prepunk of the Stooges and MC5, Detroit seemed to provide one great act after another. Even admitting that staggering array of talent, Mitch Ryder and the band he fronted, the Detroit Wheels, stood out for their sheer energy, passion, and intensity. Ryder and the Wheels' run at the top was relatively short-lived, but the records they made were dynamic and remain fresh and vital sounding.

Born William Levise Jr., Ryder displayed early talent and was fronting bands in his teens. At 17 he recorded his first single and became a local sensation singing for

Billy Lee & the Rivieras. Ryder and the band's high-energy shows became the stuff of legend, leading to a recording contract. A conflict with the surf band of the same name resulted in the Rivieras being rechristened Mitch Ryder and the Detroit Wheels, a name apropos of their Motor City roots and high-powered live performances. What followed were some of the most electrifying singles in rock history. The furious organ-driven rock ravers "Jenny Take a Ride," "Devil with a Blue Dress On/Good Golly Miss Molly," "Sock It to Me Baby," and "Little Latin Lupe Lu" exploded out radio speakers with a kinetic energy that was almost unparalleled.

It mattered little that the songs were covers. Ryder's impassioned raw power made them his own as he screamed with a rugged snarl and emotional force that rivaled James Brown and Little Richard. Lead guitarist Jim McCarty matched Ryder for intensity, playing stinging, distorted solos that pushed the band to a fever pitch. Ryder's unrelenting blue-eyed soul singing and rugged appearance brought to mind the Animals' Eric Burdon, and the Wheels' urban feel made them almost an American version of Burdon's band. The Wheels' white-hot intensity brought them consistent chart success, but that success was short-lived. Ryder left the band in 1968.

Ryder then turned to Memphis to record *The Detroit/Memphis Experiment* with rhythm and blues legends Booker T & the MG's. Ryder seemed inspired to be singing with a genuine rhythm and blues group, and the MG's reciprocated his hard rock electricity. The album didn't sell well, and Ryder formed the heavier band Detroit, releasing a strong eponymous album in 1971 that was most known for its power chord–driven cover of the Velvet Underground's "Rock & Roll." After that album failed to chart, Ryder left the music industry for most of the remainder of the decade, returning to release the starkly confessional *How I Spent My Vacation* (1979). He attracted some commercial attention with the John Mellencamp–produced *Never Kick a Sleeping Dog* (1983), which included his last charting single, a cover of Prince's "When You Were Mine." Ryder still records and tours, but he is best remembered for his classic singles with the Detroit Wheels. Bruce Springsteen has done much to keep Ryder's music in the public eye, covering Ryder's best-known material in his "Detroit Medley," one of the Boss's concert staples. Ryder's most recent album is the rhythm and blues–infused *The Promise* (2012).

Suggested Albums: Take a Ride (with Detroit Wheels) (1966); *Breakout* (with Detroit Wheels) (1966); *Sock It to Me* (with Detroit Wheels) (1967); *The Detroit/Memphis Experiment* (1969); *Detroit* (1971); *How I Spent My Vacation* (1979); *Never Kick a Sleeping Dog* (1983); *The Promise* (2012)

SADISTIC MIKA BAND

Formed by songwriter-producer Kazuhiko Kato and his wife, singer Mika Fukui, Sadistic Mika Band was one of the most popular rock acts in Japan during the early 1970s. They enjoyed flash-in-the-pan notoriety in Great Britain where the idea of a Japanese glitter rock band appealed to British tastemakers at a moment when Japan was in vogue in popular culture for its prominence in the electronics industry and as a venue for touring Anglo-American rock bands. The wonders of Tokyo were mentioned in band interviews. Deep Purple even recorded a tribute, "Woman from Tokyo." Sadistic Mika Band recorded in England, opened for Roxy Music, and appeared on British radio and television before breaking up in 1975. Since then, various lineups have performed under the Sadistic Mika name.

Suggested Albums: Kurofune (The Black Ship) (1974); *Hot! Menu* (1975)

SAINTE-MARIE, BUFFY (1941–)

A Cree Indian born in Canada but raised by foster parents in the United States, Buffy Sainte-Marie gravitated to the folk-blues revival as a college student and attracted attention playing coffeehouses in Boston, Greenwich Village, and Toronto. Her debut album, *It's My Way* (1964), included an antiwar song, "The Universal Soldier," popularized by Donovan and recorded by artists from many countries. The album also contained "Cod'ine," a stark anti–hard drug song performed by a host of psychedelic and garage bands such as the Charlatans, Quicksilver Messenger Service, and Man and later by Courtney Love. Her second album, *Many a Mile* (1965), included the lovelorn ballad "Until It's Time for You to Go," a hit when covered by Elvis Presley in 1972.

Sainte-Marie's *Illuminations* (1969) was a fascinating experiment in electronic music with producer Maynard Solomon using early synthesizers to conjure eerie soundscapes from Sainte-Marie's vocals and acoustic guitar. *Illuminations*' best known song, "God Is Alive, Magic Is Afoot," was co-written by Leonard Cohen and received FM airplay. On *She Used to Wanna Be a Ballerina* (1971), Sainte-Marie performed a mix of originals and covers backed by Ry Cooder along with Neil Young and Crazy Horse. She later married the album's producer, Jack Nitzsche, a one-time protégé of Phil Spector. Sainte-Marie and Nitzsche shared an Oscar for writing the pop tune "Up Where We Belong" from *An Officer and a Gentleman* (1982).

320   SANTANA

Sainte-Marie continues to record and perform and is active in Native American causes.

Suggested Albums: It's My Way (1964); *Many a Mile* (1965); *Illuminations* (1969); *She Used to Wanna Be a Ballerina* (1971)

SANTANA

Possibly no one sitting on the muddy fields of the Woodstock festival (1969) had heard of Santana, but the band made its career that day with a memorable performance that peaked during Michael Shrieve's climactic drum solo on "Soul Sacrifice." Word fanned out from Woodstock that Santana was a band to watch.

Their last-minute addition to the festival's lineup was the work of their manager, San Francisco impresario Bill Graham, who had been booking the band at his Fillmore West ballroom. Like much of the music on Santana's eponymous debut album (1969), "Soul Sacrifice" was an instrumental riding on Gregg Rolie's soul jazz organ with Shrieve's drumming coupled with congas and other percussion, and adorned with the melodic cry of the band's namesake guitarist, Carlos Santana. Although he was Mexican American, the bandleader drew his primary influences from Puerto Rico and the blues. Vocals were sparse on the album. On "Jingo," the only words are a chorus shouted in an unfamiliar language.

"Jingo's" inclusion spoke to the breadth of Santana's influences. They derived the song from Nigerian drummer Babatunde Olatunji's *Dreams of Passion* (1959), a seminal album that introduced America to African music and influenced the direction of jazz. *Santana's* hit single, the lyrically laconic "Evil Ways," came from an album by jazz percussionist Willie Bobo and concluded in a furious Afro-Caribbean percussive jam.

Growing out of jam sessions, not poetry readings or pop songwriting workshops, Santana's music was loose yet kept in a tight groove. Their second album, *Abraxas* (1970), a more fully realized production, explored the map laid out on its predecessor. Echoes of Miles Davis's fusion could be heard on "Singing Winds, Crying Beasts." On Santana's reinvention of Fleetwood Mac's "Black Magic Woman," Rolie's organ added a gothic suggestion and the rolling thunder of the tribal tom-tomming maintained anxiety as Carlos Santana soared on electric guitar, achieving symphonic majesty with his instrument. Their faithful yet rock-accented rendition of "Oye Como Va" by mambo percussion master Tito Puente received much FM airplay. *Abraxas* could wax with the driving Latino rock of "Se a Cabo" and wane with the mellow Latin fusion of "Incident at Neshabur." Carl Jung defined *abraxas*, a word found in ancient Gnostic and magical texts, as the supreme union of all opposites, God and Satan, good and evil. Its choice as an album title signaled the spiritual quest of the band's namesake leader that would soon become the driving force behind his music.

Santana III (1972) continued in a similar vein with the Latin rock hit "No One to Depend On." Appearing soon afterward, *Caravanserai* (1972) set the pattern for many future Santana releases. Much of the music was Latin fusion jazz with a few tracks definable as funky Latin rock. By this time the band Santana consisted of whomever the guitarist by that name chose. Carlos Santana began releasing albums under his own as well as the band's name and became a disciple of Hindu guru Sri Chinmoy alongside his future collaborator, Mahavishnu Orchestra guitarist John McLaughlin. Now known as Devadip ("the light, the eye of God") Carlos Santana, he recorded an album with McLaughlin called *Love, Devotion, Surrender* (1973). More esoteric still was an album of Indian-influenced jazz with keyboardist Alice Coltrane, *Illuminations* (1974). With an omnivore's interest in world music, he recorded *Borboletta* (1974) under the band name Santana with Brazilian percussionist Airto Moreira and vocalist Flora Purim.

By this time Role and second guitarist Neal Schon left to form

Guitarist Carlos Santana has recorded as a soloist while also lending his name to the band Santana. He reached widespread attention through an electrifying performance at Woodstock and continues to refine his Afro-Caribbean influences, often in a jazz or pop vein. (Paul Warner/AP Photo)

Journey, a progressive rock band bereft of progress. Shrieve became a session drummer and eventually joined Stomu Yamashta's Go. Santana continually shifted between esoteric fusion projects and more commercially oriented funky Latin jazz-rock albums, the latter netting a hit cover of the Zombies' "She's Not There" from *Moonflower* (1977) and "Winning" and "Hold On" from *Zebop!* (1981). Breaking with Chinmoy over his guru's strict prescriptions for living in 1982, Santana found his way into interesting projects in the following years. Country singer Willie Nelson and blues-rock band the Fabulous Thunderbirds were guest stars on *Havana Moon* (1983). Santana produced the score for *La Bamba* (1987), the biographical film on 1950s Latino rock and roll star Ritchie Valens, and continued to record prolifically with jazz artists.

Encouraged by his record label to make a commercial comeback, Santana recorded *Supernatural* (1999) with a cast of younger musicians including Dave Matthews, Matchbox Twenty's Rob Thomas, and Lauryn Hill, along with contributions from his generational peer Eric Clapton. Crossing many genre boundaries, *Supernatural* included the number one hit "Smooth," became one of rock's best-selling albums, and won nine Grammy awards. In the aftermath, Santana played guitar on Michael Jackson's album *Invincible* (2002) and collaborated with musicians as

SAVOY BROWN

diverse as rhythm and blues singer Seal, Latin pop star Shakira, and Chad Kroeger from Canadian alternative rock act Nickelback. PRS Guitars has produced a line of Santana Signature Guitars. Carlos Santana is a character in the Guitar Hero 5 game and has been inducted into the Rock and Roll Hall of Fame.

Suggested Albums: Santana (1969); *Abraxas* (1970); *Santana III* (1972); *Caravanserai* (1972); *Love, Devotion, Surrender* (1973) (Carlos Santana and John McLaughlin); *Illuminations* (1974) (Carlos Santana and Alice Coltrane); *Supernatural* (1999)

SAVOY BROWN

Kim Simmonds had the misfortune of founding Savoy Brown too late. By the time the London guitarist formed the band and released the first album under that name, *Shake Down* (1967), the blues scene that gave rise to the Rolling Stones and Cream was already dissipating. As a result, Savoy Brown never achieved stardom in their homeland, but by dint of hard touring and prolific recording found mid-level success in the United States, where by 1970 every city was home to white blues bands playing predominantly white blues bars for predominantly white audiences.

A hard taskmaster, Simmonds hired and fired musicians continually. By Savoy Brown's second album, *Getting to the Point* (1968), few members remained from the original incarnation. Simmonds was a talented guitarist, an able soloist with wide musical scope. *Raw Sienna* (1970) opened with the FM hit "A Hard Way to Go," a Latin-tinged rock song that could be mistaken for Santana. Simmonds emulated the funky side of Jimi Hendrix with "That Same Feelin'," ventured into piano-driven soul jazz with "Master Hare," the droll Mose Allison–style shuffle of "Needle and Spoon," and tuneful basic blues-rock with "A Little More Wine."

In 1971 three of Savoy Brown's members, guitarist Dave Peverett, drummer Roger Earl, and bassist Tone Stevens, broke away to form the popular blues-boogie band Foghat. Other members of Savoy Brown have gone on to join Fleetwood Mac, Blodwyn Pig, and UFO. Simmonds continues to lead a band called Savoy Brown in the 21st century.

Suggested Albums: Shake Down (1967); *Getting to the Point* (1968); *Blue Matter* (1969); *A Step Further* (1969); *Raw Sienna* (1970); *Looking In* (1970); *Street Corner Talking* (1971); *Hellbound Train* (1972)

SCAGGS, BOZ (1944–)

Born William Royce Scaggs, Boz Scaggs grew up in Texas where he was exposed to blues guitarist T-Bone Walker and inspired by the big rhythm and blues bands of Ray Charles and Jimmy Reed. By 1960 he was drawn into the blues end of the folk-blues revival, playing coffeehouses around Dallas while leading a double musical life as a member of the Marksmen, a band led by Steve Miller, who became Scaggs's pole star. He followed Miller to the University of Wisconsin at Madison, where they played rhythm and blues–based music in bars and at fraternity parties. Scaggs led a peripatetic life for several years as a busker in Western Europe and released a folk-blues album in Sweden (1965). In 1967 he received a postcard from Miller, who was forming a band in San Francisco. Scaggs accepted his invitation to join the Steve Miller Blues Band.

By the time he arrived in San Francisco's Summer of Love, Scaggs had already explored and rejected drugs and derided the hippie subculture as dangerously silly. Although often mistaken for a police detective for his short hair and suits, Scaggs became integral to Miller's psychedelically tinted blues project, sharing songwriting, lead vocals, and guitar playing with his mentor. He left after Miller's second album to pursue his own direction.

Boz Scaggs (1969) was co-produced by *Rolling Stone* editor Jann Wenner at Alabama's famed Muscle Shoals Studio and pitted Scaggs against the studio's ace guitarist, Duane Allman. The album's magnum opus was a slowly unwinding 13-minute-plus organ-guitar blues workout, "Loan Me a Dime." Afterward, Scaggs recorded several albums indebted to the big rhythm and blues he loved while growing up.

Scaggs did not achieve commercial success until *Silk Degrees* (1976), which caught the peppy string-sweetened taste of Philadelphia soul and launched several hit singles, including the disco-friendly "Lowdown," the florid pop of "We're All Alone," and the brightly polished rhythm and blues of "Lido Shuffle." Unlike many veteran singers who turned up around this time with a disco LP, Scaggs arrived through natural evolution, sounded entirely at home in the dressed-up world of glittering disco balls, and brought a wealth of musical knowledge and emotional experience to the best of his material.

Scaggs reached platinum sales again with *Down Two Then Left* (1977) and *Middle Man* (1980), racking up hit singles such as "Hard Times," "Jojo," and "Look What You've Done to Me" from the movie *Urban Cowboy* (1980). A divorce and custody battle led him to withdraw from the music business for several years before returning with *Other Roads* (1986) with its Top 40 hit, "Heart of Mine," and several songs co-written with an unlikely collaborator, punk rock poet Jim Carroll. In the early 1990s he performed with a project organized by Steely Dan's Donald Fagen, the all-star New York Rock and Soul Revue. Scaggs continues to tour and record in the 21st century. His collection of jazz standards, *But Beautiful* (2003), rose to number one on the jazz album charts.

Suggested Albums: Boz Scaggs (1969); *Silk Degrees* (1976); *Other Roads* (1986); *But Beautiful* (2003)

SCHULZE, KLAUS (1947–)

Although Klaus Schulze was briefly a member of the estimable German groups Ash Ra Tempel and Tangerine Dream, as well as Japanese composer Stomu Yamashta's supergroup Go, his greatest significance has been as a solo artist. He has released some 40 albums under his own name plus numerous collaborations as well as LPs of techno and dance music under the pseudonym Richard Wahnfried, a reference to the burial place of Richard Wagner. An early adopter of synthesizers, Schulze's dreamy soundscapes from the 1970s forecast the direction of Brian Eno's ambient music along with the new age instrumental genre that emerged in the 1980s. Keeping abreast of changing technology, Schulze adapted to digital synthesizers in the 1980s and experimented with sampling in the 1990s. He recorded a trio of albums in the 21st century with Lisa Gerrard, vocalist from the Australian medieval-Middle Eastern-Celtic–inspired group Dead Can Dance.

Suggested Albums: Irrlicht (1972); *Cyborg* (1973); *Blackdance* (1974); *Picture Music* (1975); *Timewind* (1975); *Moondawn* (1976); *Mirage* (1977); *X* (1978); *Dune* (1979); *Trancefer* (1981); Klaus Schulze and Lisa Gerrard: *Farscape* (2008); *Rheingold* (2008); *Dziekuje Bardzo* (2009)

SEARCHERS

The birth of folk-rock is most often credited to the Byrds' cover of Bob Dylan's "Mr. Tambourine Man" (1965), but a case can be made that Britain's the Searchers beat them with their hit single, "Needles and Pins" (1964). The song contained all the elements of folk-rock: jangling 12-string guitar, beautifully intricate harmonies, and a wistful melody over a steady 4/4 beat. It was a new sound that emerged from Merseybeat and would be widely copied, giving the Searchers a limited but notable legacy.

As with so many British Invasion bands, the Searchers had their earliest roots in skiffle, eventually morphing into a more conventional rock band and taking their name from a classic John Wayne western film. Starting in their hometown of Liverpool, they followed the path trod by fellow Liverpudlians the Beatles with a stint in Hamburg, Germany. Returning home, they made their first recordings, releasing innocuous Merseybeat singles in the wake of the Beatles' success. The Searchers' "Sweets for My Sweet" temporarily dislodged the Beatles from the top of the U.K. charts.

Next they chose "Needles and Pins," a song that had been recorded by American folk singer Jackie DeShannon and was written by legendary engineer Jack Nitzsche and future star Sonny Bono. The song's sparkling sound with its chiming 12-string guitar was pivotal in the formation of folk-rock. "Needles and Pins" went to number one in Great Britain and just missed the Top 20 in the United States, establishing the Searchers as significant players in the British Invasion with a unique and captivating sound at once bright, melodic, and uplifting. They followed with "Don't Throw Your Love Away," "Some Day We're Gonna Love Again," and a cover of the Rolling Stones' "Take It or Leave It," which stood alongside the top American folk-rock records. Possibly the band's finest moment was their cover of Jackie De-Shannon's "When You Walk in the Room," an ode to unrequited love centered around a memorable guitar riff and set to the Searchers' characteristic "big jangle." While covered by many artists, the Searchers put their stamp on a song that would later become a huge 1980s hit for Phil Collins.

Strong as their output was, the Searchers were always a singles band and never made a significant album. They were almost solely a covers group, never writing any of their hits, putting them at the mercy of finding quality material by other artists. Lacking the songwriting genius and musical vision of the Beatles, the raw charisma of the Stones, and the epic power of the Who, the Searchers could go so far and no farther. As the British Invasion gave way to psychedelia, the Searchers' fortunes waned and the band released nothing of note until a comeback in 1979. The British Invasion sound was back in vogue, thanks to the rise of new wave and power pop, and the Searchers decided to show the new generation how it was done with a less than stellar eponymous 1979 album and the much stronger pop album *Love's Melodies* (1981). Despite its high quality, the album didn't sell well, and the Searchers were largely viewed as a nostalgia act. The band continued to tour on the oldies circuit with a revolving lineup. Their legacy is their sound through their influence on Tom Petty, Bruce Springsteen, the Flamin' Groovies, and countless power pop bands.

Suggested Albums: Meet the Searchers (1963); *Searchers Smash Hits* (1967); *Love's Melodies* (1981)

SEEDS

The Seeds were most often characterized as a garage rock band; the primitive, raw intensity of their music was typical of many similar bands from the mid to late 1960s. But the Seeds, led by their dynamic and eccentric leader Sky Saxon, were set apart from the garage rock pack by a greater degree of intensity in Saxon's voice and in the band's playing. The Seeds projected an attitude that would be much appreciated a decade later by the nascent punk rock band scene. However, like many other garage rock bands, the Seeds were short-lived and experimented with psychedelia before breaking up.

Saxon was born in Salt Lake City, Utah, and started as a doo-wop singer before moving to Los Angeles and forming the Seeds, playing bass, singing, and becoming the band's main songwriter. The band's first single, "I Can't Seem to Make You Mine" (1965), was not atypical of garage rock with aggressive guitars and assertive vocals singing of the frustrations of young love. Their next single, "Pushin' Too Hard" (1966), went further. The beat was hard and insistent, the guitars tougher, and Saxon sang with a sneeringly defiant tone that matched the lyrics. This was true protopunk, and "Pushin' Too Hard" became a popular cover song for punk rock bands of the 1970s and thereafter.

Their self-titled debut album (1966) continued the rebellious onslaught. Song titles like "You Can't Be Trusted," "Nobody Spoil My Fun," and "It's a Hard Life" could have fit just as easily on any late 1970s punk release. Touches of psychedelia can be detected in the band's next album, *Web of Sound* (1967), with its whirling and trippy organ sound and songs that carried a glimpse of what would become acid rock. On the intriguing "Up in Her Room," Saxon sang highly suggestive lyrics over 14 minutes of a groove derived from Them's "Gloria."

Saxon took the Seeds fully psychedelic for their next album, *Future* (1967), which brought other instruments such as piano and trumpet into a more experimental sound. The flower-showered album artwork and songs like "Travel with Your Mind" and "A Thousand Shadows" show a band ready and willing to blow minds. More significantly, "March of the Flower Children" created an identifying label for the new generation seeking peace, love, sex, drugs, and rock.

Saxon took a detour from the Seeds to record *A Full Spoon of Seedy Blues* (1967), a fine album of raunchy blues driven by his gritty vocals and given credibility by the presence of members of Muddy Waters's band. The Seeds' live album *Raw & Alive: The Seeds in Concert at Merlin's Music Box* (1968) would be their swan song as the album tanked commercially. Saxon went his own eccentric way, joining the Yahowa religious sect and largely disappearing from the public eye. Punk rock revived interest in the Seeds and Saxon was recognized as a prepunk hero. Several versions of the band re-formed sans Saxon, and any hopes of a reunion were dashed when Saxon died of an infection in 2009.

Suggested Albums: The Seeds (1966); *Web of Sound* (1967); *Future* (1967); *A Full Spoon of Seedy Blues* (1967) (by Sky Saxon)

SEGER, BOB (1945–)

By the time Bob Seger finally reached a national audience with a pair of bestselling albums in 1976, he had already passed the age of 30 and was writing songs reflecting on youthful memories and the passage of time. Seger had been playing around his hometown, Detroit, since 1961, initially inspired by early rock and roll and rhythm and blues but absorbing the influence of Bob Dylan and the British Invasion after 1964. His regionally released singles earned him local hero status, but he played in the shadow of Motown as well as MC5, the Stooges, Mitch Ryder, and other rock bands with major label contracts.

Seger began attracting a small audience outside his hometown with a trio of superb albums recorded as the Bob Seger System, *Ramblin' Gamblin' Man* (1969), *Noah* (1969), and *Mongrel* (1970). With future Eagle Glenn Frey on backup vocals, "Ramblin' Gamblin' Man" was classic Detroit rock with a pile-driver rhythm, soulful organ, and Seger's already distinctively expressive raspy voice, which moved easily between gravelly hard rock and profound emotional sympathy. The albums he recorded with the System included great variety without succumbing to mere eclecticism. Wiry psychedelic rock songs such as "Tales of Lucy Blue" and "Evil Edna" flowed easily into dreamy ballads such as "Gone" and "Big River" and on to the growling blues-rock of "Down Home." *Ramblin' Gamblin' Man* included what was perhaps the best anti–Vietnam War song, "2 + 2 = ?," a powerfully delivered burst of anger and anxiety by a blue-collar candidate for the draft.

Disbanding the System, Seger recorded a solo acoustic album, *Brand New Morning* (1971), which failed to find an audience. He returned to a full-band format with *Smokin' OP's* (1972), which yielded a minor hit in Seger's cover of "If I Were a Carpenter," a song that had recently seen greater success in the hands of Johnny Cash and June Carter. Several tracks on *Back in '72* (1973) were recorded at Alabama's Muscle Shoals studio, but Seger backed out after discovering the high cost of working at the famed facility. *Back in '72* included "Rosalie," which became a hit in the United Kingdom several years later for Irish band Thin Lizzy. On *Seven* (1974), Seger introduced his new backing band, the Silver Bullet Band, recruited from top Detroit musicians. The album included "Get Out of Denver," later popularized by Dave Edmunds.

With *Beautiful Loser* (1975), Seger began to gain nationwide attention on FM radio. Named for the Leonard Cohen novel, the album boasted the ready for the road yet radio-friendly sound that would soon carry him to fame. *Beautiful Loser* showcased Seger's tendency toward balancing reflective mid-tempo musings ("Beautiful Loser") with rollicking rock and roll ("Katmandu"), depression ("Black Night"), and paeans to the rambling life ("Travelin' Man").

Bob Seger was a local hero in Detroit for a decade before finally achieving national success as a recording artist with his 1976 album *Night Moves*. Seger brought a mixture of gritty authenticity and empathy for the human condition to his best songs. (Photofest)

Seger and the Silver Bullet Band finally achieved widespread fame with a pair of LPs released during America's bicentennial year. *Live Bullet* (1976), a lively concert recorded before an enthusiastic Detroit audience, gained airplay. Successful on AM as well as FM, the studio album *Night Moves* (1976) finally established him as a star. It included three hits, two of them melancholy reflections on the past, "Night Moves" and "Mainstreet," and the other the infectiously upbeat and nostalgic "Rock and Roll Never Forgets."

Seger stayed in form with *Stranger in Town* (1978), buoyed by the popularity of the melancholy "Still the Same," the ebullient "Hollywood Nights," and the anti-disco anthem "Old Time Rock and Roll." The ballad "We've Got Tonight" later became a huge hit in a duet by Kenny Rogers and Sheena Easton. Seger added a bullet point to his songwriting resume by co-authoring "Heartache Tonight," a popular number from the Eagles' *The Long Run* (1979).

Seger continued to mount the charts with *Against the Wind* (1980) and its singles, "Fire Lake" (featuring the Eagles on backup vocals), "You'll Accomp'ny Me," and "Against the Wind," which forecast his career direction by crossing over onto Billboard's adult contemporary chart. As the membership of the Silver Bullet Band began to dissipate in favor of studio musicians, Seger found success in marketplaces beyond rock. His cover of country singer Rodney Crowell's

"Shame on the Moon" from *The Distance* (1982) sold well in country as well as adult contemporary venues. He did not forget his rock and roll or Detroit roots on "Making Thunderbirds," his jeremiad on the decline of America's auto industry.

As the 1980s wound down, Seger remained in the spotlight through popular music videos and contributions to movie soundtracks, including the Oscar-nominated "Shakedown" from *Beverly Hills Cop* (1987). Although in recent years he received relatively little airplay for new material or attention from the mainstream media and the music press, his new recordings continue to sell and he remains a popular live attraction.

Suggested Albums: Ramblin' Gamblin' Man (1969); *Noah* (1969); *Mongrel* (1970); *Brand New Morning* (1971); *Smokin' OP's* (1972); *Back in '72* (1973); *Seven* (1974); *Beautiful Loser* (1975); *Live Bullet* (1976); *Night Moves* (1976); *Stranger in Town* (1978); *Against the Wind* (1980); *The Distance* (1982)

SIMON, CARLY (1945–)

Born into the sort of affluent New York family featured in many Woody Allen films, Carly Simon and her sister Lucy waded into the Greenwich Village folk scene as the Simon Sisters. They released albums during the 1960s and enjoyed a minor hit before ending their act when Lucy married. Although she was a frequent visitor on the adult contemporary and pop charts through the 1980s, Simon made her most significant music on her first three albums, *Carly Simon* (1971), *Anticipation* (1971), and *No Secrets* (1972). Her greatest songs can be described as upper middle-class young adult pop. Like Edith Wharton's stories from the turn of the century, her lyrics took the pulse of the privileged caste.

Her first hit, "That's the Way I've Always Heard It Should Be" (1971), expressed ambivalence over the prospect of marriage. Simon had become such a topic among columnists that speculation swirled over the identity of the swain in "Anticipation" (1971), the lonesome pop star of "Legend in Your Own Time" (1971), and the high-flying cad of "You're So Vain" (1972). Although Mick Jagger sang backing vocals on the latter, some whispered that he was the song's subject.

Simon's marriage to James Taylor produced a hit duet, their cover of the early 1960s rhythm and blues hit "Mockingbird" (1974), and ended in divorce (1981). Simon seldom toured but maintained a prolific recording career. She continued to place singles on the charts in the 21st century.

Suggested Albums: Carly Simon (1971); *Anticipation* (1971); *No Secrets* (1972)

See also: Taylor, James

SIMON, PAUL (1941–)

When folk-rock superstars Simon & Garfunkel went their separate ways in 1970, neither member of the duo planned on a permanent split. Both Paul Simon and Art

Garfunkel foresaw only a brief hiatus from performing together while pursuing solo projects. It didn't work out that way, as Simon found solo work instantly successful and rewarding, while Garfunkel began to eye a film career.

Simon's early success was not heavily anticipated, as many thought Garfunkel held more promise as a solo act. Certainly Garfunkel's ringing tenor was a superior instrument to Simon's thinner and softer voice, but Simon had been the songwriting genius responsible for some of the 1960s' greatest songs. His creative muse was a renewable resource providing a constant supply of stellar material, while Garfunkel was forced to rely on the talents of other songwriters. That prowess, coupled with an ever-expanding musical curiosity, would serve Simon well as he set himself to the task of building a catalogue worthy of his status as a classic American songwriter.

Simon succeeded with his first solo single, "Mother and Child Reunion," from his excellent album, *Paul Simon* (1972). Simon recorded the song in Jamaica; its fresh beat and appealing melody became a hit (despite somewhat downbeat lyrics), as Simon introduced America to the island's rhythms three years before Eric Clapton hit the charts with "I Shot the Sheriff." The captivating calypso of "Me and Julio Down by the Schoolyard" with its mysterious lyrics and pop culture references was also a hit. The two songs pointed to Simon's eventual preoccupation with what would soon be marketed as "world music."

Any concerns with a sophomore slump were put to rest with *There Goes Rhymin' Simon* (1973), an album of stunning variety and quality. From the bouncy jaunt of "Kodachrome" and a melody borrowed from Bach for the elegiac "American Tune" through the upbeat gospel of "Loves Me Like a Rock," Simon took his writing to a new level of imagination and inventiveness. The lyrics were becoming deeper but without losing the universal appeal of his best work with Simon & Garfunkel. The album was met with widespread critical acclaim that was matched with equally strong sales.

Fully established as a solo star, Simon reunited with Garfunkel on the single "My Little Town" from his next album, *Still Crazy After All These Years* (1975). Many fans were disappointed that the duo's reunion wasn't permanent, but they were not disappointed in the record. Among the highlights were the effervescent gospel of "Gone at Last," the jazzy poetry of "50 Ways to Leave Your Lover," and the wistful title track. Simon took a major step forward as a lyricist, wedding genuine poetry with highly tuneful and accessible melodies. Simon also entered the popular culture as a television performer, beginning a frequently recurring role as guest host of NBC's groundbreaking new comedy show *Saturday Night Live*, beginning with a legendary duet with musical guest George Harrison.

Seemingly at the top of his game, Simon inexplicably took the rest of the decade off, releasing the lilting hit "Slip Slidin' Away" as a single from a 1977 greatest hits album, but not issuing another album until *One Trick Pony* (1980). That album contained the bouncy hit "Late in the Evening" but overall was not up to the standards of his earlier solo recordings. The confessional *Heart and Bones* (1983) was more of a return to form and recalled some of his work with Simon & Garfunkel.

330 SIMON & GARFUNKEL

Simon reached new levels with his next album, *Graceland* (1986), partially recorded in South Africa with local musicians. Having put his toes in the water of world music with his first two solo singles, Simon now dove right in on a magnificent album heavily steeped in South African "township music" as well as Cajun, rock, Caribbean, and American folk. The music is filled with joy and wonder, and Simon made a successful return to the charts with a critically acclaimed work. Some critics ripped Simon for violating the UN-sanctioned boycott of South Africa's apartheid regime as well as exploiting African culture, but *Graceland* has stood up as a work of art and can be seen as a turning point in putting an end to South Africa's oppressive white majority rule.

World music remained Simon's stock in trade for *The Rhythm of the Saints* (1990), which explored Latin America with a focus on Brazil. Simon's output slowed in the 1990s and into the new millennium as he focused on touring and took part in a concert reunion with Garfunkel. A foray into theater failed. His Broadway musical *The Capeman* (1998) was a critical flop and closed after only 68 performances. He returned to recording and released the pleasantly relaxed *You're the One* (2000) and a sonically intriguing collaboration with Brian Eno, *Surprise* (2006). Still traversing new creative terrain, Simon's most recent album, *Stranger to Stranger* (2016), finds the singer merging electronica with a potpourri of African and Latin beats. With more than 50 years as a recording artist behind him, Simon's work remains rich and rewarding. Simon has been inducted into the Rock and Roll Hall of Fame.

Suggested Albums: Paul Simon (1972); *There Goes Rhymin' Simon* (1973); *Still Crazy After All These Years* (1975); *Heart and Bones* (1983); *Graceland* (1986); *The Rhythm of the Saints* (1990); *You're the One* (2000); *Surprise* (2006); *So Beautiful or So What* (2011); *Stranger to Stranger* (2016)

SIMON & GARFUNKEL

In early 1964, Paul Simon and Art Garfunkel were two young folksingers working the clubs of New York's Greenwich Village. By the end of the decade, they were a superstar duo with a string of hits that deeply touched millions and carried a cultural impact that helped define a generation. Profoundly intelligent, emotionally vulnerable, and sung with passion, conviction, and even an air of mystery, Simon & Garfunkel's music had a mythic quality that distinguished it from the era's ocean of brilliant songs. Their music was often timeless, yet was a product of and relevant to their time. Both Simon and Garfunkel retained strong individual identities yet performed as a cohesive unit to the point that it was difficult to think of one without the other. Their music was rooted in folk, rock, doo-wop, and later incorporated rhythms from other cultures to create a recognizable but unique folk-rock sound. Simon's exceptional songwriting was the cornerstone, decorated by the duo's sweet two-part harmonies.

Legends most often spring from humble beginnings, and such was the case with Simon & Garfunkel. The two met in the 1950s while grammar school students in the New York suburb of Forest Hills. A shared love of early rock and roll and doo-wop formed the basis of a friendship, and they discovered their voices harmonized well when singing together. Simon got the songwriting bug and was composing by the time they were in high school. At the age of 15 they released a Simon-penned single, "Hey Schoolgirl," under the name Tom & Jerry. Record company payola bought some radio airplay, and the song made a small dent in the charts.

However, dreams of stardom clashed with practical concerns, and their music career was put on hold as they pursued college. Neither stopped performing. By the early 1960s, they were playing Greenwich Village, where Bob Dylan's producer Tom Wilson discovered them.

Wilson produced their first album, *Wednesday Morning, 3 A.M* (1964), a standard-sounding folk affair, but notable for four eye-opening Simon originals. "Bleecker Street," "Sparrow," and the title track were literate and sophisticated, a cut above ordinary folk songs. Even more so was "The Sounds of Silence," a song of such dramatic impact that a folk-rock version was recorded for their second album, *Sounds of Silence* (1966), and became a chart-topping hit single. Inspired by the Byrds' "Turn, Turn, Turn," Wilson employed brittle, chiming guitar and a persistent drumbeat with inspired fills. The duo added evocative harmonies to Simon's despairingly cynical lyrics to create a close to perfect folk-rock anthem. Almost as great was another Simon original, "I Am a Rock," a deceptively cheery sounding folk-rock gem whose shimmering guitars sweetened the bitter alienation of Simon's romantically disillusioned narrator.

Simon was emerging as a rock poet like Dylan, and Simon & Garfunkel played folk-rock equal to that of the Byrds. *Parsley, Sage, Rosemary, and Thyme* (1966) turned more toward the folk side of the ledger. Simon's lyrics became more intricate and insightful, with a biting edge in the more rocking "Big, Bright, Green Pleasure Machine." At times the songs veered toward pretentious, but Simon hit the mark with the road-weary folk-rock single "Homeward Bound" and the pleasantly idyllic "The 59th Street Bridge Song (Cancion Del Puente De La Calle)."

As their popularity grew, a distinctive Simon & Garfunkel sound became apparent, always with one foot firmly in folk but with varying degrees of rock keeping the music from crossing the line from poetic to precious. A familiar division of vocal responsibilities emerged, with Simon usually singing lead and Garfunkel accompanying on harmonies. Not always appreciated was the role of Simon's acoustic guitar playing in their sound. Often fingerpicked, but always precise and involved, Simon's guitar was never powerful but bristled with a subliminal tension that added another layer of complexity.

The next phase of Simon & Garfunkel's career saw them move from mere stardom to cultural significance, thanks to director Mike Nichols overcoming Simon's initial objections to include the duo's music in the soundtrack to the groundbreaking film *The Graduate* (1967). The soundtrack featured a reprise of "Sounds of Silence" as well as a stunning new song, "Mrs. Robinson." Also included on the duo's next album, *Bookends* (1968), "Mrs. Robinson's" memorable chorus and lyrics of lost innocence and lack of meaning in everyday life captured the frustration of a generation that came of age with the hope of the New Frontier and felt the betrayal of failed promises. The album contained other standout tracks. The searing rocker "Hazy Shade of Winter" casts a bleak and ominous shadow over the changing seasons, while "America" is a road story worthy of Beat novelist Jack Kerouac. The album also shows how far Simon and Garfunkel had come as singers. Their vocal chemistry had developed to the point that their voices seemed interchangeable, making it at times difficult to tell who was singing which part.

All seemed well for Simon & Garfunkel, but trouble was on the horizon. Their relationship began to fray as they clashed over musical direction. Recording sessions for their next album, *Bridge over Troubled Water* (1970), were difficult. The end product was worth the effort, as the hymn-like title track became one of their biggest and best-known hits. The song had a touch of melodrama, but its soothing message resembled that of the Beatles' "Let It Be." Garfunkel's soothingly emotional vocal brought hope and comfort to a society torn apart by war and social discord. Simon's seemingly autobiographical "The Boxer" portrayed the struggles for artistic integrity as comparable to that of a beaten-down prizefighter. Their expanding musical palette was represented with the Latin sounds of "Celia" and the Peruvian folk tradition of "El Condor Pasa (If I Could)."

Despite the album's success, Simon and Garfunkel were drawing apart. Garfunkel began flirting with movie acting and Simon was itching to leave the duo for a solo career. In 1971 Simon announced the duo's breakup, and although the split

Simon & Garfunkel exemplified the positive aspirations of the 1960s generation through a series of singles and albums that articulated the mood of their times. They reunited after an 11-year separation for this 1981 concert in New York's Central Park. (Nancy Kaye/AP Photo)

was not intended to be permanent, *Bridge Over Troubled Water* was to be their last studio album. They briefly reunited in 1975, releasing the elegant single "My Little Town," a critique of the frustrations of small town life that began quietly and built to a powerful horn and string–dominated fade out. The duo would do sporadic live appearances over the years, notably a 1981 free concert in New York's Central Park and a limited concert tour in 2003.

Personal tension between them seems to make any full-scale reunion extremely unlikely. Simon became a successful and influential solo artist, selling millions of records and earning critical acclaim. Garfunkel has acted, notably in *Catch-22* (1970) and *Carnal Knowledge* (1971). He resumed his recording career with *Angel Clare* (1973), containing "All I Know," whose dramatic vocal earned him play on FM and AM. In recent decades Garfunkel has maintained success on the adult contemporary charts. Simon & Garfunkel were inducted into the Rock and Roll Hall of Fame.

Suggested Albums: Wednesday Morning, 3 A.M. (1964); *Sounds of Silence* (1966); *Parsley, Sage, Rosemary and Thyme* (1966); *Bookends* (1968); *Bridge over Troubled Water* (1970)

See also: Simon, Paul

SIR DOUGLAS QUINTET

The Sir Douglas Quintet introduced the world to Doug Sahm, the American guitarist whose mix of rock, blues, and Tex-Mex would shape the popular music of his native Texas and exert an influence beyond the Lone Star State. Sahm was already a music veteran by the time he formed the Quintet in 1964, starting as a country guitar child prodigy and gaining experience playing blues and country as a teen, forming a lifelong friendship with future Tex-Mex country star Freddie Fender. Many career paths were open but Sahm saw opportunity in the British Invasion sounds popularized by the Beatles and the Rolling Stones. They initially adopted a similar style and a British-sounding moniker. However, the band's roots and influences were too varied to be trapped by following trends, and while their music's raw energy and spirit is often labeled garage rock, they transcended such categorization.

The Quintet's first album was given the misleading title *The Best of the Sir Douglas Quintet* (1966) and is highlighted by their first single and best known song, "She's About a Mover." A pumping 12-bar blues rocker featuring an organ riff bearing a resemblance to the blues standard "See See Rider," "She's About a Mover" was equal parts Ray Charles and Rolling Stones. Rooted in early rock but with a timeless quality, it is one of the most enduring garage rock singles of the mid-1960s. The rest of the album is eclectic and accomplished as Sahm takes the Quintet on a tour of modern American music, touching on blues, Tex-Mex, bluesy country, and Cajun music, all wrapped up in the Quintet's distinctive keyboard and sax sound. Bob Dylan was said to have counted the Quintet as one of his favorite bands of the period, and Sahm was on his way to becoming a legend in his home state. Moving

334   SKIFFLE

to San Francisco, the band inevitably drifted toward psychedelia and recorded interesting but somewhat disjointed jazzy material. Sahm and company inevitably fared better with songs that evoked their native state, like the infectious Tex-Mex singles "Mendocino" and "Dynamite Woman."

The group broke up in 1972, with Sahm going solo and becoming an influence on ZZ Top, Steve Earle, Jimmie Vaughan, and Delbert McClinton. He hit the country charts in the 1990s as a member of the Tex-Mex supergroup Texas Tornados. The Quintet carried on without Sahm to little notice or acclaim, working together in various forms throughout the 1980s and 1990s. Sahm died of a heart attack in 1999.

Suggested Albums: The Best of the Sir Douglas Quintet (1966); Mendocino (1969)

SKIFFLE

During the 1950s skiffle music influenced a generation of young British musicians who would have a profound impact on the development of rock a decade later. Skiffle's roots lay in American music, drawing from rural blues, jug bands, traditional jazz, ragtime, Dixieland, and boogie-woogie. Music called "skiffle" first appeared in America in the 1920s, but became a fad in Great Britain in the 1950s as young musicians were drawn to its energetic up-tempo shuffle beat and acoustic guitar–driven sound. Skiffle's use of homemade instruments such as cigar box guitars, washboards, and jugs made it affordable in a country struggling to recover from the ravages of World War II.

Lonnie Donegan became skiffle's biggest star with his 1955 U.K. hit cover of Lead Belly's "Rock Island Line," which showcases the spoken word intro and rapidly increasing tempo often employed in skiffle records. Skiffle's popularity faded in the United Kingdom by end of the 1950s, but John Lennon and Paul McCartney, Jimmy Page, Mick Jagger, Ron Wood, Ritchie Blackmore, and David Gilmour all cut their teeth in skiffle bands, giving skiffle a legacy that helped shape the course of the classic rock era and has lasted beyond skiffle's brief and regionally confined run of popularity.

SLADE

During their peak years, Slade was a British band that attracted a fiercely loyal following in their homeland but attained little attention in the United States. They grew out of the N'Betweens, a quartet from the industrial city of Wolverhampton in the West Midlands, and became known as Ambrose Slade by the time of their first album, *Beginnings* (1969). The tuneful, complicated chording of their psychedelic pop rock gave little indication of their future direction. In 1970 they reemerged as Slade, their name suddenly clipped as short as their hair. Shorn of flowing locks and paisley, Slade adopted the boots and braces look of Britain's skinhead youth subculture.

Their new music was as hard-nailed as their appearance. Led by the shrill howl of singer Noddy Holder, Slade charged along on roaring guitar chords and a boot-stomping beat. They were metallic rock stripped to its studs but without sacrificing melody. From 1971 through 1973 Slade enjoyed a remarkable string of hits in their homeland, many written in working-class British patois, including "Coz I Luv You" (1971), "Look Wot You Dun" (1972), "Take Me Bak 'Ome" (1972), "Mama Weer All Crazee Now" (1972), "Gudbuy T' Jane" (1972), "Cum on Feel the Noize" (1973), and "Skeeze Me, Pleeze Me" (1973). Along the way the members grew their hair back and adopted a sci-fi glitter rock look.

Hungering for success in the all-important American market, Slade began tempering their distinctive sound with piano and ballads and moved to the United States, where they recorded and opened for popular touring acts. The venture gained them nothing except hostility from British fans who accused them of selling out.

Slade enjoyed a second run as part of the new wave of heavy metal that swept out of Britain in the early 1980s, and they scored a hit single with "We'll Bring the House Down" (1981). Interest in the United States was piqued after the American neo-glam band Quiet Riot had a hit with a cover of "Cum on Feel the Noize" (1983). Slade's album *Keep Your Hands Off My Power Supply* (1984) sold well in North America but afterward, they once again lost their direction and their audiences in the United States and United Kingdom. Various versions of Slade continued to perform in recent years.

Suggested Albums: Beginnings (aka *Ballzy*) (1969); *Play It Loud* (1970); *Slade Alive* (1972); *Slayed?* (1972); *Old New Borrowed and Blue* (1974)

SLY AND THE FAMILY STONE

As a DJ on San Francisco's KSOL, Sylvester Stewart displayed broad tastes and stepped over boundaries by playing Bob Dylan and the Beatles on his soul music show. He sang and recorded with a family gospel quartet as a teenager before moving on to doo-wop. While working as a producer for San Francisco's Autumn Records, he supervised albums by the folk-rock bands the Beau Brummels and the Great Society while working local clubs at the head of a rhythm and blues band, Sly and the Stoners. The band provided him with his enduring stage name and the nucleus of the group that brought him fame and influence, Sly and the Family Stone.

His previous experiences suggested the parameters for his new biracial, bigender, genre-crossing group, which included trumpeter Cynthia Robinson, brother Fred Stewart on guitar, bassist Larry Graham, drummer Greg Errico, and saxophonist Jerry Martini. Like Stone, his band members all had formal musical training. "Underdog," which opened their debut, *A Whole New Thing* (1967), was a denunciation of racial injustice driven by a furious rock drumbeat and funky bass line delivered with a ravaging soul vocal. The album leaned more heavily toward rhythm and blues than rock, but the organic blend of influences challenged assumptions in both camps and inspired ambitious albums in the coming years by Marvin Gaye and Stevie Wonder as well as the genre-defying funk-rock of Funkadelic.

Sly and the Family Stone's follow-up, *Dance to the Music* (1968), elevated them to stardom with the chart-climbing title track and established their sound. As well drilled as a soul revue, the Family Stone were at the leading edge of rhythm and blues. They borrowed from the creative examples of psychedelia and progressive rock without succumbing to either. Graham's bass lines became both heavier and funkier. The carefully channeled exuberance and camaraderie extended to the shared responsibility for the vocals.

Life (1968) continued the band's direction but was roundly ignored. They roared back into the charts with their crowning achievement, *Stand!* (1969). The title cut was an anthemic call to the younger generation in the form of a new model for black pop built from sophisticated chord progressions and suffused with funkiness. The relentless "I Want to Take You Higher" reinvented funk, suggesting the Pentecostal testifying of Stone's childhood churchgoing, and pulled forward on a monstrous, almost tribal rhythm. Proselytizing for tolerance, the ebullient "Everyday People" was a plea for mutual respect and unfurled a big tent that encompassed all races and cultures. Sly and the Family Stone were a hit at Woodstock (1969).

Afterward, Stone sank into a toxic milieu of paranoia-inducing drugs and the disillusionment that settled in as Woodstock shifted to Altamont and the 1960s stumbled into a new decade with many dreams unfulfilled. While locked in recording studios laboring over the album he hoped would be his masterpiece, he kept in the public eye by releasing singles, the sunny "Hot Fun in the Summertime," the enigmatically funky "Thank You Falettinme Be Mice Elf Agin," and the sophisticated black pop of "Star." The new songs were collected with previously released tracks as *Greatest Hits* (1970), one of the best albums of its kind ever released.

Sly and the Family Stone's much-belabored masterpiece, *There's a Riot Goin' On* (1971), was downbeat funk, the trademark sound in place but largely drained of joy and spiked with edgy dissonance. The lone hit single was the sonically murky "Family Affair." Graham left to form the successful funk act Graham Central Station. Stone continued recording under the Family Stone name. "If You Want Me to Stay" from *Fresh* (1973) was a hit, but his recordings diminished in sales and innovation and he became unreliable on tour, passing out or not appearing as scheduled. He finally went into drug rehabilitation in 1984 but was convicted of cocaine possession in 1987. His most recent album, *I'm Back! Family & Friends* (2011) featured an all-star cast of rock and rhythm and blues musicians performing new versions of old Family Stone hits. Sly and the Family Stone have been inducted into the Rock and Roll Hall of Fame.

Suggested Albums: A Whole New Thing (1967); *Dance to the Music* (1968); *Life* (1968); *Stand!* (1969); *Greatest Hits* (1970); *There's a Riot Goin' On* (1971); *Fresh* (1973)

SMALL FACES

Along with the Who, the Small Faces were a quintessential mod band. Sharp in dress and appearance, the Small Faces represented the mod fashion ethic and their rhythm and blues–influenced sound was perfectly aligned with mod musical taste.

But while the Who was able to transcend their mod roots and achieve international impact, the Small Faces' influence was largely limited to the British Isles. Certainly there was musical growth, but without a colossally ambitious creative leader like Pete Townshend, the Small Faces were destined to remain in the Who's shadow.

A product of London's tough East End, the Small Faces was formed in 1965 by vocalist Steve Marriott and bassist Ronnie Lane. United by a love of rhythm and blues, the two young musicians enlisted drummer Kenney Jones and keyboardist Jimmy Winston. Marriott's amazingly powerful gritty voice and the band's abundant energy attracted attention in London's vibrant blues club scene. Their smart suits and trendy hairstyles made them a favorite around swinging London and put them in competition with fellow mods the Who. The Who had a distinct advantage in Townshend, a gifted writer who penned songs that gave voice to the feelings and frustrations of young mods, while the Small Faces were initially forced to look outside the band for material.

However, the Small Faces were able to make that material their own on the exuberantly soulful "Sha-La-La-La-Lee," the song that became their first hit single (1966). The band quickly developed as songwriters, writing half the songs on their eponymous debut album (1966). Winston was replaced by Ian McLagan, whose distinctive rhythm and blues–flavored organ stands out as a sturdy counterpoint to Marriott's passionate singing.

The Small Faces' next two albums were released within a short time of each other. *From the Beginning* (1967) included the memorable pop ballad "All or Nothing." A second eponymous album was released a few weeks later and displayed the growing prowess of the songwriting team of Marriott and Lane. The duo began to push the band in a more pop direction.

With 1967 came the Beatles' *Sgt. Pepper's Lonely Heart's Club Band*, and the Small Faces were caught up in the spirit of the times, releasing the cheerful psychedelic single "Itchycoo Park." With its idyllic bounce and distinctively British vocals, "Itchycoo Park" moved away from the band's mod roots and into a psychedelic period. "Here Comes the Nice" and "Tin Soldier" showed the band expanding its range with more involved subject matter and complex arrangements. *Ogden's Nut Gone Flake* (1968) was truly experimental, with Cockney music hall numbers standing alongside heavier hard rock and tuneful pop. The second side was a concept piece based around a modern fairy tale regarding a boy's search for the meaning of life. The album was well received, but Marriott's dissatisfaction with the group's pop approach led him to quit abruptly at the end of 1968, effectively breaking up the band.

Marriott quickly found success with the hard rocking Humble Pie, while Jones and McLagan plucked singer Rod Stewart and guitarist Ron Wood from the Jeff Beck Group to form the even more successful Faces. The Small Faces reunited in 1975, releasing two listenable but relatively insubstantial albums, *Playmates* (1977) and *78 in the Shade* (1978). In an interesting twist, drummer Jones joined forces with erstwhile mod rivals the Who, replacing Keith Moon after the legendary drummer's death in 1978. Lane died of complications from multiple sclerosis in 1997, six years after the tragic death of vocalist Marriott. McLagan died in 2014.

Suggested Albums: Small Faces (1966); *From the Beginning* (1967); *Small Faces* (1967); *Ogden's Nut Gone Flake* (1968)

SMITH, PATTI (1946–)

Patti Smith is crucial to what happened after the classic rock era ended, but unlike most figures who emerged at the inception of punk, Smith was an unabashed acolyte of classic rock, waxing enthusiastically over the Rolling Stones and Bob Dylan. She was Janus-like, facing past and future with equanimity. Her debut album, *Horses* (1975), was remarkable for its barebones breakthrough sound, including a startling reinvention of Them's 1964 hit "Gloria." *Horses* was the nexus for several worlds. Hard rock guitarist Allen Lanier from Blue Oyster Cult was a guest star; and the androgynous cover photo by Robert Mapplethorpe spoke to the New York punk scene's ties with Manhattan's edgy visual art underground. The Patti Smith Group guitarist, Lenny Kaye, was already significant for assembling *Nuggets*, a collection from the forgotten underside of 1960s American rock that inspired a revival of interest in garage bands.

Like the 1960s artists she admired, Smith changed and grew with succeeding albums and even entered the Top 40 with a song she co-wrote with Bruce Springsteen, "Because the Night" (1978). After her 1980 marriage with one of her heroes from the previous epoch, MC5 guitarist Fred "Sonic" Smith, she went into semiretirement to raise a family. With her husband's death in 1994, she resumed recording and performing, touring with Dylan (1995), exhibiting her photographs, and writing well-regarded memoirs, *Just Kids* (2010) and *M Train* (2015). She was inducted into the Rock and Roll Hall of Fame in 2007.

Suggested Albums: Horses (1975); *Radio Ethiopia* (1976); *Easter* (1978); *Wave* (1979); *Twelve* (2007)

SOFT MACHINE

Soft Machine began as a manifestation of the vibrant bohemian scene in Canterbury, England, during the 1960s. Vocalist Kevin Ayers, drummer Robert Wyatt, and bassist Hugh Hopper played together from 1964 through 1966 as the protopsychedelic Wilde Flowers. Wyatt, Ayers, keyboardist Mike Ratledge, and Australian guitarist Daevid Allen grouped together in 1966 as Soft Machine after the title of a William Burroughs novel. In 1967 they released an exuberant Dadaist psychedelic rock single and became as integral to London's psychedelic scene as Pink Floyd. Connections with the wider world of culture were reinforced when they provided music for a performance in St. Tropez of Pablo Picasso's play *Le Desir attrape par le queue* (1967). When visa problems prevented Allen from reentering the United Kingdom, he stayed in France and formed Gong. Soft Machine carried on.

Recorded in New York under Velvet Underground producer Tom Wilson, Soft Machine's eponymous debut album (1968) was keyboard-driven psychedelia whose jazz-accented rhythm section was amplified into a sonic boom. Although straining at the seams, *The Soft Machine* retained the outlines of pop song structure. When Ayers departed to pursue a solo career, Soft Machine pursued its jazz inclinations more intensely on *Volume Two* (1969) while remaining fully cognizant of the liberating potential of electric instruments and tape editing. By *Third* (1970), Soft Machine had recruited saxophonist Elton Dean, trumpeter Marc Charig, trombonist Nick Evans, and saxophonist-flautist Lyn Dobson in a full embrace of avant-garde fusion jazz.

Many personnel changes ensued over the course of *Fourth* (1972) and *Fifth* (1973), including Wyatt's departure for a solo career. After *Bundles* (1975), Ratledge, the last original member, left to pursue film soundtracks. In the 21st century various musicians associated with the band continued playing fusion-oriented music as Soft Ware, Soft Works, Soft Machine Legacy, and even as Soft Machine.

Suggested Albums: The Soft Machine (1968); *Volume Two* (1969); *Third* (1970); *Fourth* (1972); *Fifth* (1973)

See also: Ayers, Kevin; Gong

SOUL MUSIC

In the American music industry, marketing and distribution had been segregated since the 1920s, with recordings for African American audiences tracked on separate sales charts by the trade magazine *Billboard* as "race music." By 1950 rhythm and blues became the accepted term, and it began to refer generically to small combo bands emerging from the swing era. Rhythm and blues was embraced by adventurous white listeners bored with the blandness of much of early 1950s pop music, and it was often indistinguishable from early rock and roll being produced in the northern cities of the United States. In the 1950s the audience for rock was more racially mixed than is often assumed.

Rhythm and blues continued to evolve and by the early 1960s was identified as soul music. The term derived from the dominant influence of black gospel music on singers such as Sam Cooke and Aretha Franklin, and on the ensemble playing of musicians whose earliest performances were on the chancels of African American churches. The Isley Brothers' "Shout" (1959), much covered by rock bands in the 1960s because of its relentless energy, was an edited version of the musical "testifying" that occurred in many black churches. Soul songs often had gospel roots; a few changes in lyrics shifted the ecstasy of the Holy Spirit to the ecstasy of sexuality or love.

Soul music became associated with the rise of the Black Pride and Black Power movements, and was a conscious attempt to define African American music as not easily coopted by a white-controlled industry or white performers. This did not prevent the phenomenon of "blue-eyed soul," a term applied to the all-white Righteous Brothers and their hit, "You've Lost That Loving Feeling" (1965), or the idea that a white singer could sound "soulful" if she tried. However, the best soul music captured a cultural experience particular to African Americans. Performers from other backgrounds were usually imitative, not innovative. The young African American audience of the 1960s embraced soul in preference to the blues, which they rejected as the music of an oppressive time, while the audience for classic rock adopted blues as a touchstone of authenticity.

By the 1970s the cultural impetus behind soul music, not unlike the forces behind the largely white counterculture, began to fade. *Billboard* belatedly changed the name of its R&B chart to Hot Soul Singles in 1973, but the term would soon become anachronistic. By the time *Billboard* dropped soul and returned to R&B in 1982, disco had already come and gone and soul music endured as a memory and an influence.

SOUTHER-HILLMAN-FURAY BAND

Supergroups were all the rage in the early 1970s, but the Souther-Hillman-Furay Band was one of the few to work in the milieu of country rock. J. D. Souther was an established songwriter who had already written for the Eagles and would go on to write for Linda Ronstadt, Dan Fogelberg, and Christopher Cross. Chris Hillman and Richie Furay had even more impressive resumes. Hillman had time with folk-rock pioneers the Byrds and Flying Burrito Brothers to his credit, while Furay came to fame with Buffalo Springfield. While the three artists were between projects, Asylum Records impresario David Geffen recruited them to record an album of country rock titled *The Souther-Hillman-Furay Band* (1974).

Not surprisingly, the album featured the strong songwriting and excellent musicianship one might expect from a group of accomplished veterans. What was more surprising was the group's cohesive teamwork in singing and playing, a quality not always found in the somewhat ad hoc nature of supergroup albums. They sounded as if they were an actual band with years of touring behind them. The trio turned up the volume on the amps and rocked a little harder than was becoming the norm in the increasingly mellow realm of country rock, infusing the music with a refreshing level of energy. What was missing was passion and inspiration; the overall impression created was of friends hanging out and enjoying playing music.

The Souther-Hillman-Furay Band stuck together for one more album, the less country and more run-of-the-mill rock–sounding *Trouble in Paradise* (1975). It was apparent that the three were ready to move on, and they did just that, disbanding their partnership and moving on to solo careers.

Suggested Album: The Souther Hillman-Furay Band (1974)

SOUTHERN ROCK

The southern United States has always been a cradle for American popular music. Blues, jazz, country, and many types of folk music had their genesis in that rich racial and cultural milieu of the Deep South, and those forms of music combined to give birth to rock and roll. However, despite rock's clear Southern heritage, a host of historical, cultural, political, and commercial factors caused rock music to distance itself from its Dixie roots to such an extent that by the late 1960s, the South seemed disconnected from the music it helped to create. But in the early 1970s a wave of young Southern musicians sought to reclaim rock music and bring it back home to the South, creating a new genre under the mantle of "Southern rock."

Beginning with Elvis Presley, Sam Phillips's Memphis-based Sun Studio presented a roster of Southern-born rock and rollers that helped create the rockabilly sound and proved to be a catalyst in the burgeoning world of rock music. However, rockabilly's rowdy rebel yell proved to be too provincial and at times threatening to enjoy a sustained national audience, and rockabilly stayed a largely regional genre confined to the South. In the 1960s the British Invasion and the rise of psychedelia further distanced rock music from its Southern origins to such an extent that by decade's end most people viewed the South as country music's domain, with little connection to what was happening in the world of rock. The painful legacy of the American Civil War, Reconstruction, and Jim Crow were at odds with the more inclusive spirit adopted by rock artists influenced by the civil rights movement. Southern rockers such as Gram Parsons left for Los Angeles to establish their careers.

While the South seemed divorced from rock music in the 1960s, under the surface things began to change. Muscle Shoals Studio featured an all-white rhythm section that helped produce scores of soul hits by black artists. Muscle Shoals guitarist Duane Allman formed an integrated blues-based rock band, the Allman Brothers Band, and the band's success inspired other younger, often more inclusive Southern rock musicians to follow their lead. By the early 1970s, the term *Southern rock* began to describe this wave of musicians reasserting their region's place in rock. Macon, Georgia–based Capricorn Records signed the Allmans and became the epicenter for Southern rock.

In truth, there was no truly Southern rock sound. Blues and rhythm and blues inspired the Allman Brothers and Wet Willie, while the Marshall Tucker Band and Charlie Daniels drew inspiration from country music. The most popular Southern rock band, Lynryrd Skynyrd, played a hard, boogie-based brand of rock that owed as much to the Rolling Stones as either blues or country. What Southern rock artists had in common was a shared sense of identity, their heritage proudly proclaimed in their music and image. The Charlie Daniels Band declared that "The South's Gonna Do It Again" in a hit single (1974), but while the song called for Southern rockers to stand up and be counted, its spirit was not of secession, but rather inclusion with the rest of the world of rock music. Ironies abounded in Southern rock, as many acts adopted regalia such as the Confederate flag that reminded many of the region's troubled history and caused some to look on such acts with at least a modicum of suspicion. However, most Southern rockers espoused more racially tolerant attitudes than their ancestors; their stance probably helped advance the cause of Southern integration.

Southern rock dovetailed with the rise of the "New South" as the former Confederacy began to shed the legacy of segregation. This movement culminated in 1976, as former Georgia governor Jimmy Carter was elected president with the

342 SPACE ROCK

financial backing of Capricorn's president Phil Walden and the support of many Southern rock bands. As artists like Skynyrd, Elvin Bishop, and the Marshall Tucker Band began to rack up hits, Southern rock climbed to a commercial success. However, that momentum halted with the 1997 plane crash that claimed the lives of key members of Lynyrd Skynyrd. While newer Southern artists such as 38 Special and Molly Hatchet gained prominence in the 1980s, they displayed a more homogenized, album-oriented radio sound that was less reflective of their Southern heritage. Southern rock became more of a catch-all term for bands that hailed from the South and sang with a bit of a twang, rather than describing a distinct musical or cultural phenomenon.

SPACE ROCK

During the early 1960s, surf instrumental bands occasionally released singles evoking the space race in title and sound. However, space rock as a defined concept emerged out of psychedelia and became a subset of progressive rock in the late 1960s, with the Rolling Stones' "2000 Light Years from Home" and Pink Floyd's "Interstellar Overdrive" leading the way. The fascination with the Apollo program, the success of Stanley Kubrick's film *2001: A Space Odyssey,* and the heady promises of Timothy Leary converged, as it was never entirely clear whether space rock celebrated the exploration of outer or inner space. With boundaries too imprecise for it to be labeled a genre, space rock sometimes described music built around synthesizers (still considered futuristic in the early 1970s) or songs with science-fiction references such as David Bowie's "Space Odyssey." Space rock's defining band became Hawkwind, whose hypnotic, droning music sometimes accompanied lyrics by science-fiction author Michael Moorcock. A space rock revival became audible after the 1980s, complete with outdoor festivals and independent record labels.

SPARKS

Like many of the most creative groups to emerge in the classic rock era, Sparks refused to stand in place and repeat themselves for the entertainment of unimaginative fans. Led by brothers Ron and Russell Mael, Sparks began in 1968 as the Los Angeles band Halfnelson. In revolt against the nascent Southern California soft rock, country rock culture, they preferred to emulate British bands such as the Who and the Move and often pretended to be English. Halfnelson released an eponymous album produced by Todd Rundgren (1971), later reissued as *Sparks* after the band changed its name in 1972. Their love of humor and wordplay was manifested in the title of their second album, *A Woofer in Tweeter's Clothing* (1972).

Anglophiles to the core, Sparks moved to Great Britain in 1973 and became eccentric fellow travelers in the glitter rock scene. Singing in a plummy aristocratic voice, Russell Mael looked like a rock star. Nattily attired like a 1940s golf pro, Ron was probably the only public figure since World War II to sport a close-cropped Hitler mustache. Their classic album from the period, *Kimono My House* (1974), was a tuneful outing in falsetto operatic cabaret rock and surely an influence on Queen's Freddie Mercury.

"This Town Ain't Big Enough for Both of Us" from *Kimono* became a number two hit in the United Kingdom. *Kimono My House*, *Propaganda* (1974), and *Indiscreet* (1975) received FM airplay in some U.S. cities. Sparks toured the United States and appeared on *American Bandstand* but would always be more popular in Britain.

In 1976 the brothers returned home to Los Angeles and recorded a pair of Sparks albums with session musicians. They were disappointed with the results. Changing direction again, Sparks recorded an early predecessor of synth-pop, *In Heaven* (1979), with Giorgio Moroder, the producer behind Donna Summer's disco hit "Love to Love You Baby." As usual, they found their greatest acceptance abroad. "When I'm with You" from *Terminal Jive* (1980) was a massive hit in France, where the brothers sojourned for a year.

By the early 1980s, Sparks were accepted as quirky progenitors of new wave and had their first U.S. hit with "Cool Places," a collaboration with the Go-Gos' Jane Wiedlin from *Sparks in Outer Space* (1983). Later albums such as *Gratuitous Sax and Senseless Violins* (1994) provided oddly tuneful European hits such as "When I Kiss You (I Hear Charlie Parker Playing)." *Lil Beethoven* (2002) was an experiment in classically derived orchestral and choral arrangements. Their musical *The Seduction of Ingmar Bergman* (2009) was based on the Swedish director's uncomfortable experience in Hollywood. Sparks continue to make imaginative music and have toured as a duo in the 21st century.

Suggested Albums: Sparks (aka *Halfnelson*) (1971); *A Woofer in Tweeter's Clothing* (1972); *Kimono My House* (1974); *Propaganda* (1974); *Indiscreet* (1975); *In Heaven* (1979); *Terminal Jive* (1980); *Sparks in Outer Space* (1983); *Gratuitous Sax and Senseless Violins* (1994); *Lil Beethoven* (2002); *The Seduction of Ingmar Bergman* (2009)

SPIRIT

Spirit emerged from the psychedelic landscape of late 1960s California to enjoy a brief run of success that included a hit single and record several well-regarded albums. The band became better known recently for a well-publicized legal battle with legendary rock band Led Zeppelin, but Spirit left a strong enough body of work to justify recognition in their own right.

Spirit was formed in Los Angeles by guitarist Randy California, bassist Mark Andes, and vocalist Jay Ferguson. With their hometown becoming the center of the mid-1960s music world, it didn't take long to attract attention. Legendary music producer Lou Adler signed them to a record deal. Some songs on their eponymous debut album (1968) follow the acid-laced psychedelia of the time, but strategic use of tempo changes, improvised jazz passages, and lengthy instrumental breakouts pushed the music closer to progressive rock. A haunting ethereal quality pervades many tracks, largely thanks to a plethora of minor chord melodies and Ferguson's vaguely mystical singing. Sales were solid.

344 SPOOKY TOOTH

The band's next album, *The Family That Plays Together* (1968), sold more copies thanks to the catchy single "I Got a Line on You." The song's funky groove was eminently danceable, and Spirit found itself with a Top 40 hit. The rest of the LP was decidedly less commercial, as the psychedelia of their debut gave way to a more experimentally jazzy sound with longer instrumental jams. More confident instrumentally, California began double-tracking guitar parts in much the same way as Zeppelin's Jimmy Page would come to do. The aesthetic was highlighted on Spirit's next album, *Clear* (1969). California's intense blues-based jams highlight perhaps the band's best album.

Spirit followed with *Twelve Dreams of Dr. Sardonicus* (1970), a complex exploration of jazz and progressive rock filled with imaginative arrangements and melodic songwriting. The moody acoustic ballad "Nature's Way" failed as a hit single, but earned a solid level of FM airplay. With sales slipping, members began drifting away, with Andes leaving to form Jo Jo Gunne and California dropping out to begin a solo career. The remaining members released and toured behind the surprisingly listenable album *Feedback* (1972), but the public ignored it and Spirit broke up in 1973. California joined a reunion of the band in 1974, and they released the pleasantly laid-back double album *Spirit of '76* (1975). The band continued to release a series of little-noticed albums into the 1990s, ending with California's death in 1997.

After decades of obscurity, Spirit recently gained attention after Randy California's estate filed an intellectual property lawsuit against Led Zeppelin's Page and Robert Plant, claiming the superstars plagiarized their classic "Stairway to Heaven" from "Taurus," an instrumental on Spirit's debut album. While "Taurus's" main riff is similar to "Stairway," the songs differ greatly when taken in their entirety. After a 2016 trial in federal court, a jury cleared Page and Plant of copyright infringement.

Suggested Albums: Spirit (1968); *The Family That Plays Together* (1968); *Clear* (1969); *Twelve Dreams of Dr. Sardonicus* (1970); *Feedback* (1972); *Spirit of '76* (1975)

SPOOKY TOOTH

Britain's Spooky Tooth centered their music around dual keyboards rather than the dominant guitar sound of their time. The band was initially and rather presumptuously called Art, and became Spooky Tooth after organist Gary Wright joined in 1967. As Art, they released a heavy album of psychedelic blues, *Supernatural Fairy Tales* (1967), but the first Spooky Tooth album, *It's All About* (1968), leaned more on the keyboards of Wright and Mike Harrison.

Wright's organ created a bit of a classical feel, but the music itself was traditional hard rock thanks to guitarist Luther Grosvenor's blues-based riffing. Oddly, songs such as "Bubbles" and "Weird" displayed a bit of a silly side not commonly heard in the music of the rather serious late 1960s. The band struck an incongruous note with a close to carbon copy cover of the Band's "The Weight," investing their debut with perplexing variety. Such unpredictable diversions from the expected heavy rock became a Spooky Tooth trademark. They dabbled in soul and pop balladry on a couple of songs from *Spooky Two* (1969), which stands as the group's best.

A collaboration with French electronic composer Pierre Henry saw the band move in a more progressive direction. Their work with Henry resulted in a Roman Catholic mass as concept album, *Ceremony* (1969). Electronic effects produce haunting chimes, chirps, and bleats that at best create an eerie tension. Strangely beautiful at times, and just plain strange at others, *Ceremony* sounded nothing like Spooky Tooth's earlier work and alienated Wright, who bristled over Henry's influence over the album. Wright and Harrison left the band after *Ceremony*, leaving Grosvenor to release the listless *The Last Puff* (1970). Wright and Harrison returned in 1972 to record the humorously titled but inconsequential *You Broke My Heart So . . . I Busted Your Jaw* (1973). After two more albums, Spooky Truth finally broke up in 1974.

Grosvenor would go on to play with Stealers Wheel, best known for their humorously Dylanesque hit "Stuck in the Middle" (1973). He also did a short stint with Mott the Hoople under the stage name Ariel Bender before forming his own band. Wright had an international hit in 1976 with the spacy ballad "Dream Weaver." Spooky Tooth re-formed for the hard rock album *Cross Purpose* (1999), and versions of the band continue to perform on occasion.

Suggested Albums: It's All About (aka *Tobacco Road*) (1968); *Spooky Two* (1969); Pierre Henry and Spooky Tooth: *Ceremony* (1969)

SPRINGSTEEN, BRUCE (1949–)

Few artists have had as much expected of them as Bruce Springsteen. As a young man carrying phenomenal promise, Springsteen was hailed as nothing less than the savior of rock and roll, and over the course of his long and substantial career he has been compared to Bob Dylan, Elvis Presley, and Woody Guthrie, all the while analyzed in light of the hopes and wishes of his many devoted fans. While at times recoiling from the role of cultural standard-bearer, Springsteen also shared and sought to live up to such expectations. As he has noted, he at times sought greatness above fame, fortune, and even personal happiness. Such are the makings of a complex and sometimes controversial artist, and while many will debate his ranking among rock's all-time greats, few can question his importance.

Springsteen was the son of working-class parents in Long Branch, New Jersey. The family struggled financially, and the bleak blue-collar environment of his upbringing would profoundly shape his artistic perspective. Rebellious by nature, Springsteen fell in love with rock and roll and frequently clashed with his restrictive father. A Roman Catholic education gave him a spiritual nature and a literary bent, although he chafed under some of the church's restrictions. A loner by nature, Springsteen only truly felt comfortable playing music, and from the mid-1960s on, his prowess on guitar made him a local legend along the Jersey shore. Springsteen made a name for himself playing in a series of local bands, notably the hard rock outfit Steel Mill. With a gift for storytelling inherited from Italian American ancestors, Springsteen developed as a songwriter capable of vivid imagery and striking detail.

While still in high school, he had met fellow guitarist Steve Van Zandt, finding a lifelong friend and musical collaborator. Another important piece in Springsteen's musical puzzle came in the form of former football star turned sax player Clarence Clemons, who teamed up with Springsteen in the early 1970s and whose playing became integral to Springsteen's sound.

Springsteen's big break came in 1972, when manager Mike Appel arranged an audition with legendary Columbia Records talent scout John Hammond, the man who had discovered Robert Johnson and Bob Dylan, and would later spot blues guitar genius Stevie Ray Vaughan. The prolific Springsteen readily reeled off a string of original music that stunned Hammond, who signed him to a record deal. Hammond envisioned Springsteen as a solo acoustic act, but the artist had other things in mind, and Springsteen brought in a group of musical compatriots (soon dubbed the E Street Band) from New Jersey to play on his debut album, *Greetings from Asbury Park, New Jersey* (1973). The album's wildly imagistic lyrics prompted critics to label Springsteen as yet another "New Dylan," and certainly Dylan factored into Springsteen's writing. However, a plethora of influences were on display, as Springsteen roamed through a musical landscape that included Van Morrison, Sam Cooke, Fats Domino, and the Band. "Blinded by the Light," "Growing Up," and "For You" were clearly the work of a great talent, but many of the lyrics were overly verbose and the album's production failed to capture the energy of Springsteen's live shows. Critics loved the album and hyped Springsteen as possibly rock's next great artist, but despite heavy promotion it sold poorly.

The Wild, the Innocent & the E Street Shuffle (1973) was a step forward creatively. Springsteen wrote with greater depth and insight, capturing the world of the Jersey shore populated with colorful and recognizable characters. The music was at times derivative of Van Morrison, but "4th of July, Asbury Park (Sandy)," "Incident on 57th Street," and the crowd-pleasing set closer "Rosalita (Come Out Tonight)" told wistfully captivating stories filled with romantic promise and puckish wit. While critics raved again, another poor production job caused the album to tank commercially, and whispers began circulating that if sales didn't improve, Springsteen's next album could be his last.

With his career on the line, Springsteen faced enormous pressure as he reentered the studio. He enlisted Jon Landau as producer. A prominent critic who had called Springsteen "the future of rock and roll," Landau had previously produced MC5's *Back in the U.S.A* and sold himself as the person who could finally unleash Springsteen's spirit fully and clearly on record. The album took a wearying 14 months to record, as Springsteen became a studio perfectionist, searching for the ideal performance, production, and mix. The final product, *Born to Run* (1975), was an epochal masterpiece heard as the culmination of the first 20 years of rock music. Springsteen's goal was to combine Phil Spector's "Wall of Sound," Dylan's lyrical intelligence, and Roy Orbison's vocals, and while he succeeded in achieving the first two goals he didn't quite have the pipes to fully pull off the third.

Still, brilliant songwriting and crackling rock energy abounded as the album's title cut rumbled across the Top 40 airwaves, and tracks such as "Thunder Road," "Tenth Avenue Freeze Out," "Backstreets," and the 10-minute "Jungleland" became instant FM radio classics. Clemons's sax provided a soulful accompaniment to Springsteen's ambitious lyrics, and the "Big Man" became Springsteen's onstage foil as "The Boss" toured in support of the album. Springsteen was now the talk not only of the music world but the mainstream media. He appeared on the covers of *Time* and *Newsweek* magazines in the same week, resulting in charges of out of control hype. A deeply conflicted Springsteen struck back against the critics, iconoclastically torpedoing record company promotions to the point of tearing down concert posters while touring London.

It seemed that Springsteen had finally lived up to his early promise, but he disappeared from the public eye and would not release another album for three years. While some began to label him a has-been and one-hit wonder, it was not common knowledge that Springsteen was engaged in a bitter legal battle over control of his songs with manager Appel. After successfully settling a lawsuit many consider a landmark victory for artistic integrity, Springsteen got to work recording dozens of songs for the next album, *Darkness on the Edge of Town* (1978). The album is a highly complex, thematically intertwined work, as Springsteen grappled with themes of class conflict, betrayal, failed dreams, and paternal conflict, with characters based on people he knew well from his native New Jersey. Stripped-down arrangements and a harder rocking, guitar-driven sound propelled songs like "Badlands," "The Promised Land," and "Prove It All Night." Springsteen's marathon concerts rocked with a reckless abandon that placed him at the pinnacle of live performers. Songs rejected for the album became hits for Patti Smith, the Pointer Sisters, and Southside Johnny and the Asbury Jukes, further enhancing Springsteen's reputation as a songwriter. An enormous batch of outtakes from the session was eventually released on a multi-CD set, *The Promise: The Darkness on the Edge of Town Story* (2010).

After *Darkness,* Springsteen adopted a unique artistic perspective. Inspired by the novels of Flannery O'Connor and John Steinbeck, and the western films of director John Ford, Springsteen saw his albums as part of a continuing saga with loosely recurring characters. *The River* (1980) was a sprawling double album that took its characters into adulthood and examined the struggles of working-class America. The album had many stellar moments, but lacked the electric tension of *Darkness* and at times suffered from a generic roots-based sound that enhanced Springsteen's everyman image but failed to rise above the ordinary. After another successful tour, a depressed and alienated Springsteen released the all-acoustic *Nebraska* (1982), a stark and at times frightening installment in Springsteen's story. Characters first introduced in *Darkness* were now exiled on the margins of society and eventually crossed the line into violence and criminality. The album was seen as a metaphor for recession-ravaged America in the early 1980s and stands as one of Springsteen's crowning achievements.

America was booming in time for *Born in the U.S.A.* (1984), and Springsteen's career followed suit with his first true hit single, the synth-laden "Dancing in the

Known to his fans as "the Boss," Bruce Springsteen built a reputation in the 1970s on marathon energetic concerts as well as songs that recapitulated the spirit of 1950s and 1960s rock. In the 21st century his music became more political as he assumed the role once played by activist singers such as Woody Guthrie. (Scott Anderson/Dreamstime.com)

Dark." The music was as close to pop as Springsteen ever got with slick production and bright melodies masking the sometimes dark lyrics. The album spawned hit single after hit single, including the title track, which outlined the travails of a Vietnam vet but was mistaken by many for a jingoistic anthem. Despite some excellent songs, Springsteen's thematic approach was threatening to become redundant, and he teetered on the edge of self-caricature.

Springsteen had finally reached the long-predicted superstardom, selling out stadiums and becoming a video star on MTV. His 1985 wedding to actress Julianne Phillips surprised and perplexed fans who feared the Boss was going Hollywood. But Springsteen's fundamental restlessness led him down a different artistic road, as he broke up the E Street Band to record a largely self-performed album, *Tunnel of Love* (1987). The thematic approach was dropped in favor of a collection of highly personal looks at the ups and downs of love, marriage, and adulthood. Many were not surprised when Springsteen divorced Phillips in 1988 and entered a successful marriage to New Jersey singer and E Street band member Patti Scialfa.

Ensconced in domestic tranquility, Springsteen moved to Los Angeles and simultaneously released two lackluster albums, *Human Touch* (1992) and *Lucky Town* (1992). The 1990s was a lost decade artistically as Springsteen spent much of his time with his wife and children, recording only sporadically and becoming more active in his left-wing political interests. Springsteen reunited with the E Street Band in the 2000s, taking them on the road in an ongoing series of highly successful tours. He brought his family back to New Jersey and released the excellent album *The Rising* (2002), a wrenching look at the effects of the September 11, 2001, terrorist attack that affected his neighbors in New York City and the surrounding New Jersey area.

Increasingly politically active, Springsteen took part in the historic 2008 presidential campaign of Senator Barack Obama. *Working on a Dream* (2009) is filled with the sense of optimism gained during Obama's rise to the presidency. He took a break from the E Street Band to record the fine folk album *We Shall Overcome: The Seeger Sessions* (2006). The E Street Band endured two tragic losses with the deaths of organist Danny Federici (2008) and Clemons (2011). Undeterred, Springsteen carried on, with Clemons's nephew Doug replacing him on sax, and adding another key figure to the band, former Rage Against the Machine guitarist Tom Morello.

More musically eclectic than in the past, Springsteen continues to tour and record as he approaches his late 60s, working with an energy many younger performers would do well to emulate, and he continues to record. Springsteen has been inducted into the Rock and Roll Hall of Fame.

Suggested Albums: Greetings from Asbury Park, New Jersey (1973); *The Wild, the Innocent & the E Street Shuffle* (1973); *Born to Run* (1975); *Darkness on the Edge of Town* (1978); *The River* (1980); *Nebraska* (1982); *Born in the U.S.A.* (1984); *Tunnel of Love* (1987); *The Ghost of Tom Joad* (1995); *The Rising* (2002); *We Shall Overcome: The Seeger Sessions* (2006); *Working on a Dream* (2009); *The Promise: The Darkness on the Edge of Town Story* (2010); *Wrecking Ball* (2012); *High Hopes* (2014)

STARR, RINGO (1940–)

Ringo Starr was the Beatle of whom the least was expected when the Fab Four went their separate ways in 1970. A number of factors played into the low expectations for the former Richard Starkey, beginning with the fact that he only joined the group shortly before they hit it big and in some people's minds had only a tenuous claim on the band's considerable legacy (a 1990s film went so far as to suggest that there were "Three Beatles, plus Ringo"). Beyond that, Starr possessed only a pedestrian voice, hadn't shown much in the way of being a songwriter, and while considered a capable drummer was nobody's idea of a virtuoso. It would have surprised few had Starr simply disappeared from public prominence while his more creative bandmates went on to success apart from the Beatles. What was overlooked was the fact that Starr had charisma, charm, and some highly talented friends who proved eager and able to help him carve out a post-Beatles niche that maximized his abilities and provided some highly listenable and likable moments.

Starr's solo career got off to a less than propitious start with an album of standards from the Great American Songbook, *Sentimental Journey* (1970), followed in short order by a collection of country songs, *Beaucoups of Blues* (1970). *Beaucoups* was the better of the two albums, but both suffered from the unfortunate decision to choose material that highlighted Starr's less than compelling vocal skills. Just when it seemed as if he was headed straight toward self-parody, he rebounded with a strong hit single co-written with George Harrison, "It Don't Come Easy" (1971). The driving rocker featured a classic Harrison descending guitar riff and a memorable hook-laden melody. The song became a hit single, as was the 1972 rocker "Back Off Boogalo," which some took as a dig at Paul McCartney ("Boogalo" allegedly being one of his nicknames). Suddenly, Starr's solo career didn't seem to be so much of a joke and offered possibilities beyond original expectations.

Those expectations were raised considerably when Lennon and Harrison's participation at recording sessions for Starr's next album sparked rumors of a possible Beatles reunion. Speculation ran rampant when McCartney sent a song (he wasn't able to make the session). The much-anticipated album *Ringo* (1973) featured crack pop production by Carly Simon producer Richard Perry and appearances by all four Beatles plus an all-star cast including Billy Preston, Harry Nilsson, Steve Cropper, and several members of the Band. Not surprisingly, it was Starr's former bandmates that provided the album's highlights, especially the Phil Spector–influenced hit single "Photograph," co-written by Starr and Harrison. The album soared to the top of the charts, although the hoped-for Beatles reunion never materialized. Starr followed this success with *Goodnight Vienna* (1974), a solid but less star-studded album, although Lennon and Elton John contributed songs to the effort. Starr followed Lennon's suggestion and scored a hit with an endearing cover of the Platters' "Only You."

After *Goodnight Vienna*, it appeared that Starr had found a comfort zone, and he rarely diverted from the formula of recording other people's songs and adopting an inoffensive mid-tempo pop rock sound (an exception was 1977's dreadful *Ringo the 4th*, which saw him dabbling in disco). Starr vacillated between using studio musicians as well as more famous friends, but the albums generally lacked artistic inspiration and were coolly received by public and critics alike.

However, Starr did manage to successfully update his sound to greater effect with *Time Takes Time* (1992) and *Choose Love* (2005), two of his better latter career releases. He scored some success with the formation of Ringo Starr and His All Starr Band, a traveling revue featuring an ever-changing cast of some of his well-known musical friends. The group has toured steadily and generally successfully, and has included such luminaries as Joe Walsh, Nils Lofgren, Dr. John, Levon Helm, Clarence Clemons, Dave Edmunds, John Entwistle, and Peter Frampton. The All Starrs backed Starr in performing his hits, as well as chipping in with versions of their own songs.

More than anything, Starr is quite comfortable in his own skin, content with his legacy and basking in the warmth and support of friends and fans. Perhaps the most notable thing about his post-Beatles career is that regardless of their feelings toward each other, all three former Beatles seemed eager to contribute to Starr's solo career.

Suggested Albums: Ringo (1973); *Goodnight Vienna* (1974); *Time Takes Time* (1992); *Choose Love* (2005)

STATUS QUO

Great Britain's Status Quo began as a psychedelic band that scored a Top 40 hit single. They successfully transitioned from psychedelia to hard rock boogie, paving the way for a long and successful career in their homeland, although they never matched that success elsewhere.

Originally called Traffic, legal complications with the better known band headed by Steve Winwood forced them to take a different name. In 1968 the group now known as Status Quo released their debut album under the ornate title *Picturesque Matchstickable Messages from the Status Quo*. The first single, "Pictures of Matchstick Men," began with a droning guitar riff and chord progression reminiscent of Jeff Beck–era Yardbirds, and the hypnotically melodic hook propelled the song into the Top 20 of the American charts. The rest of the album showed a strong pop sensibility and can be considered a forgotten classic of psychedelia. The follow-up, *Spare Parts* (1969), failed to connect with the public.

Abruptly changing gears to a blues boogie style, the band released the single "Down the Dustpipe" (1970), providing them with a return to the U.K. charts. Following that success, Status Quo found their footing and stuck to the blues boogie course that would provide them a steady stream of successful British albums. *Dog of Two Head* (1971), *Piledriver* (1972), and *Hello!* (1973) are all brimming with cheerful energy and enthusiastically rollicking blues-based rockers. Status Quo differed from some earnestly bluesy contemporaries by paying a bit more attention to the lyrics, often employing an entertaining wit. The band retained a pop sensibility, adding playful melodies that made for radio-friendly hard rock. The British public responded, making Status Quo one of Great Britain's bestselling bands. Sales were also strong in the rest of Europe, yet Status Quo's American success was limited to "Pictures of Matchstick Men."

The band's albums were consistently solid, but one tended to blend into another, and there was precious little musical growth. *Rockin' All Over the World* (1977) is distinguished by its hit cover of the John Fogerty–penned title track, and the album heralded a slicker hard rock direction, as the band began to veer from its formula of blues boogie. Status Quo transitioned to an energetic hard rock band and continued to sell well in the United Kingdom, just as they failed to sell in the United States. Status Quo continues to record and tour, and retains a surprising number of original members.

Suggested Albums: Picturesque Matchstickable Messages from the Status Quo (1968); *Spare Parts* (1969); *Dog of Two Head* (1971); *Piledriver* (1972); *Hello!* (1973); *Quo* (1974); *On the Level* (1975)

STEELEYE SPAN

Founded in 1969 by Ashley Hutchings, the bassist from Fairport Convention, Steeleye Span began as a British folk-rock band determined to hew closely to traditional material played with electric instruments. Irritated by the gravitational pull of the 20th century over fellow band members, Hutchings left in 1971 to form

352 STEELY DAN

the more resolutely traditional Albion Country Band. This left Steeleye Span in the hands of vocalist Maddy Prior, who steered the band to a measure of success in their homeland. Steeleye Span added a drummer to *Parcel of Rogues* (1973). *Now We Are Six* (1974), produced by Jethro Tull's Ian Anderson with guest star David Bowie on saxophone, yielded a British hit in "Thomas the Rhymer." Steeleye Span reached a commercial plateau with *Commoner's Crown* (1975), featuring guest star Peter Sellers on ukulele, and *All Around My Hat* (1976), which gained some American FM airplay. The band never attracted as much attention again, but has maintained a loyal following in their homeland through shifting lineups and sporadic recordings.

Suggested Albums: Hark! The Village Wait (1970); *Please to See the King* (1971); *Ten Man Mop, or Mr. Reservoir Butler Rides Again* (1971); *Below the Salt* (1972); *Parcel of Rogues* (1973); *Now We Are Six* (1974); *Commoner's Crown* (1975); *All Around My Hat* (1976)

STEELY DAN

Although Steely Dan began as a band, even in the earliest days all decisions came down to the duo of Walter Becker and Donald Fagen. Graduates of exclusive Bard College, Becker and Fagen were determined to find a career in music. Obsessed with jazz and the technology of recording, they were perfectionists who labored long over every recording.

Becker and Fagen served an apprenticeship in the touring band of singing group Jay and the Americans. They tried to become professional songwriters and provided music for the soundtrack of a movie seen by few filmgoers, *You've Got to Walk It Like You Talk It or You'll Lose That Beat* (1971). Calling themselves Steely Dan after the name of a sex toy from William Burroughs's novel *Naked Lunch*, their debut album *Can't Buy a Thrill* (1972) contained a pair of remarkable hit singles, "Do It Again" and "Reelin' in the Years," along with other songs that achieved FM airplay.

"Do It Again" opened the album on a mysterious note. With unconventional jazz-derived harmonies slipped inside the pliable shell of a pop song, "Do It Again" revealed no perspective on its enigmatic story, which possibly concerned a compulsive petty criminal. Briskly paced and hurried along by studio guitarist Elliott Randall's memorable solo that introduced and concluded the song, "Reelin' in the Years" handled one of the oldest topics in song lyrics, love gone wrong. However, the perspective of the jilted lover was unlike anything previously heard in popular music. The bitter narrator hurls recriminations at an ex-girlfriend who could have emerged from a J. D. Salinger story, a self-described genius without common sense. An aura of upper-class privilege clung to many of their songs, whether the aging gentlemen friends seeking kicks in "Midnight Cruiser" or the portrait of infidelity sketched out in "Dirty Work," where the impulse of desire trumps all other considerations.

The jaunty but joyless samba of "Only a Fool Would Say That" mocks the utopian aspirations of the 1960s while sympathizing with ordinary people, trudging home from work, too tired for revolution. Like David Bowie's *The Man Who Sold the*

During most of their peak years, Steely Dan was a recording studio project led by Walter Becker (left) and Donald Fagen. Obsessed with jazz and the technology of recording, the duo's perfectionism led to a series of exquisitely crafted top-selling LPs. (Chris Walter/WireImage/Getty Images)

World (1970) or Roxy Music's *For Your Pleasure* (1973), *Can't Buy a Thrill* marked a pop culture turning point away from the heady futurism of the 1960s toward accommodation with the reality of the 1970s.

David Palmer sang on *Can't Buy a Thrill*. The follow-up, *Countdown to Ecstasy* (1973), was the first Steely Dan album featuring Fagen's lead vocals on all songs. Although containing no hit singles, many songs were aired often on FM with lyrics that established Fagen and Becker as the Nathaniel West of rock, writing about the failures and illusions in the shadow of the American Dream.

The mysterious lyric of "Rikki Don't Lose That Number" from *Pretzel Logic* (1974) didn't prevent the song from rising into the American Top 10 singles chart. Musically, "Rikki" defined Steely Dan with its polished union of pop, rock, and jazz, wrapping a dark story in a bright and inoffensive package. "Rikki's" bass line was borrowed from jazz pianist Horace Silver's "Song for My Father." While some of *Pretzel Logic*'s tracks leaned toward a power guitar–powered funk sound, the inspiration of jazz from earlier eras was never far away. "Parker's Band" works from Charlie Parker riffs. Steely Dan even covered Duke Ellington's "East St. Louis Toodle-oo."

The departure of guitarist Jeffrey "Skunk" Baxter and keyboardist Michael McDonald for the Doobie Brothers made little audible difference on future Steely Dan

354 STEPPENWOLF

albums, so firmly were Fagen and Becker in control of every aspect. After 1974, the duo withdrew from concert halls to the studio where they applied tracks to their sonic canvases with the care of a painter in no hurry to complete his masterpieces.

Katy Lied (1975) produced another Top 40 hit that resolutely refused to explain itself, "Black Friday." "Don't Take Me Alive," an oft-played track on FM from *The Royal Scam* (1976), was clear enough in its story of a mad sniper lashing out at the world. *Aja* (1977) became Steely Dan's first platinum album, its sales buoyed by the hits "Peg" and "Deacon Blues." An audiophile's delight, *Aja* won a Grammy for Best Engineered Album. *Gaucho* (1980) ended their trek through the 1970s with "Hey Nineteen," a complaint about the musical ignorance of the younger generation. Their love of jazz finally became problematic when pianist Keith Jarrett sued Becker and Fagen for plagiarizing *Gaucho*'s title track.

The duo dissolved in 1981. Becker became a gentleman farmer in Hawaii while Fagen released occasional bestselling solo albums in the mode of Steely Dan and organized an all-star touring band, the New York Rock and Soul Revue. Becker and Fagen began working together sporadically from the late 1980s and reunited Steely Dan for the platinum-selling, Grammy-winning *Two Against Nature* (2000) and the less commercially successful *Everything Must Go* (2003). Unlike in their heyday, the reunited Becker and Fagen enjoyed touring. Steely Dan has been inducted into the Rock and Roll Hall of Fame.

Suggested Albums: Can't Buy a Thrill (1972); *Countdown to Ecstasy* (1973); *Pretzel Logic* (1974); *Katy Lied* (1975); *The Royal Scam* (1976); *Aja* (1977); *Gaucho* (1980)

STEPPENWOLF

The "heavy metal thunder" reference in Steppenwolf's "Born to Be Wild" gave an emerging genre its name. In the decades since that 1968 hit, heavy metal's definition has morphed several times, but Steppenwolf's uncompromising hard rock remains one of the roots. They were the band bikers partied to in the 1960s, and "Born to Be Wild" remains a biker culture anthem for its placement in the 1969 road movie *Easy Rider*.

Steppenwolf was more than a one-song band and represented an unusual convergence of influences and places. Singer John Kay was an East German refugee who moved his blues-rock group the Sparrows from Toronto to Los Angeles. Renamed for the Hermann Hesse novel popular with the counterculture, Steppenwolf went playfully psychedelic on their second hit from 1968, "Magic Carpet Ride." Mostly, however, Steppenwolf stayed hard, forging a sound called heavy metal in their day and maintaining an image tough enough to give the Hells Angels pause.

Like many 1960s bands, Steppenwolf broke up and re-formed several times. Kay may be the only original member from the time when Steppenwolf achieved both AM hits and underground FM airplay, but as the band's voice, frontman, and leader, it was always his show.

Suggested Albums: Steppenwolf (1968); *The Second* (1968)

STEVENS, CAT (1947–)

London-born Cat Stevens has lived a three-act musical life. In act one, he was a heavily produced pop singer, something of a teen idol, whose "Matthew and Son" became a number two hit in Great Britain (1967). In act three, he converted to Islam (1977), took the name Yusuf Islam, and renounced fame and all its trappings, only to return cautiously to music in the 2000s.

Act two contains the songs for which he is remembered. From 1970 through 1974, Stevens was one of the world's most successful singer-songwriters in the soft rock field. Beginning modestly with the muted folk-rock of *Mona Bone Jakon* (1970), with Peter Gabriel accompanying on flute, Stevens amassed a series of pretty but earnest albums whose covers were often adorned with his own paintings. *Tea for the Tillerman* (1971) yielded the hit "Wild World" and *Teaser and the Fire Cat* (1971) contained "Morning Has Broken," derived from an Anglican hymn; the anguished yet hopeful protest song "Peace Train"; and the zesty "Moonshadow." *Catch Bull at Four* (1972) included the dark "Sitting," *Foreigner* (1973) boasted "The Hurt," and *Buddha and the Chocolate Box* (1974) had "Oh Very Young." Afterward, Stevens's sales fell.

Stevens's lyrics were always indicative of a seeker, and a religious conversion experience should have been no surprise to attentive fans. Worried about prohibitions of secular music in Islamic law, he stuck with Muslim-themed music into the new millennium. After singing "Peace Train" on a post-9/11 benefit concert on VH 1 (2001), he returned to recording and performing on a more regular basis, careful to exclude anything from his old repertoire that was forbidden under Islam. Cat Stevens has been inducted into the Rock and Roll Hall of Fame.

Suggested Albums: Mona Bone Jakon (1970); *Tea for the Tillerman* (1971); *Teaser and the Fire Cat* (1971); *Catch Bull at Four* (1972)

STEWART, AL (1945–)

Al Stewart rose out of London's folk music scene in the mid-1960s, where he knew Paul Simon during the New Yorker's brief British sojourn and associated with Roy Harper, Bert Jansch, and other luminaries of British folk. His first album, *Bedsitter Images* (1967), was issued only in the United Kingdom. His second album, *Love Chronicles* (1969), received a wider release, featured Jimmy Page and Richard Thompson on guitar, and was voted folk album of the year by Britain's influential *Melody Maker* magazine. He recorded with little commercial success until *Past, Present and Future* (1974) and *Modern Times* (1975), where he found his voice as a narrator of historical subjects as well as the usual topics favored by songwriters. His breakthrough album, *Year of the Cat* (1976), was a moody and highly polished production whose enigmatic title cut became a Top 10 hit. He sustained his popularity with *Time Passages* (1978) but began to slip from the pop music spotlight during the 1980s. He continues to record and perform.

Suggested Albums: Love Chronicles (1969); *Year of the Cat* (1976)

STEWART, ROD (1945–)

Few singers possess a voice as ideal for rock as Rod Stewart. Raspy and ragged, powerful and expressive, Stewart is capable of conveying the suffering of the blues, the raging energy of rock and roll, and the gentle sympathy of folk, allowing him to shift styles with credibility and seemingly little effort. Stewart was adept at any kind of rock, and although he never truly sang heavy metal, one imagines he could have done so. After leaving the Jeff Beck Group, Stewart began a solo career filled with great possibilities, some of which he realized. However, in many ways Stewart squandered his immense talent, choosing the lure of stardom over artistic integrity, making money rather than the brilliant rock music of which he was eminently capable.

The British singer began as a teenager, although his initial ambition was to become a professional footballer. After starting in the folk-blues revival, Stewart became a mod and sang blues with Long John Baldry as well as for keyboard ace Brian Auger. His big break came when Jeff Beck hired him for the Jeff Beck Group, where his frayed singing was a perfect complement to Beck's heavy blues guitar. Although Stewart departed from Beck after two albums (1968, 1969) to start a solo career, he simultaneously squeezed in time as lead singer for Ron Wood's new band, the Faces.

Stewart surpassed previous work on his debut solo album, *An Old Raincoat Won't Ever Let You Down* (1969). Acoustic guitars dominated the sound, but they rocked hard and steady, providing an interesting contrast to Stewart's expressive vocals. A daring cover of the Rolling Stones' "Street Fighting Man" got things off to a rousing start, and the tender ballad "Handbags and Gladrags" showed Stewart could turn down the volume as well. Heavy blues and bucolic folk existed side by side as Stewart announced his arrival in a big way.

Stewart's debut was strong, but his next two albums, *Gasoline Alley* (1970) and *Every Picture Tells a Story* (1971), became classics, chock-full of great songs, inspired playing, and his signature vocals. Faces guitarist Wood was a fixture on the albums, and he and Stewart had developed a fruitful songwriting partnership. Stewart left the city behind for *Gasoline Alley*, adding mandolin, violin, and Wood's bottleneck guitar to create a bucolic country blues that was by no means laidback, and sounded equal parts English and American while mixing the rural feel with pulverizing blues rockers. *Every Picture Tells a Story* rocks harder and contains some of his best-known solo material. The smash single "Maggie May" employs a mid-tempo beat and tells an ambivalent tale of a young man in a relationship with an older woman, while "(I Know) I'm Losing You" is intensely heavy guitar rock. Stewart maintains the previous album's pastoral feel with the soothing "Mandolin Wind" and turns soulful on the emotional "Reason to Believe."

The album's success made Stewart a star. His outstanding follow-up, *Never a Dull Moment* (1972), with its witty single "You Wear It Well," maintained the momentum. Stewart had achieved such dazzling artistic heights in such a short time that it was easy to imagine no limits for the gifted vocalist. Unfortunately his next album, *Smiler* (1974), represented his first stumble. One reason was the absence of

Wood, who after the breakup of Faces had begun the career moves that led to membership in the Rolling Stones. Stewart missed working with his partner, and *Smiler* contained few original songs beyond a couple leftover collaborations with Wood. A cover of Chuck Berry's "Sweet Little Rock 'n' Roller" and a duet with Elton John on the John/Bernie Taupin composition "Let Me Be Your Car" were suitably rocking, but overall the album's sound was uninspired hard rock, lacking the distinctive touches that distinguished his first four solo albums.

After *Smiler*, Stewart fled the United Kingdom's punitive tax system and moved to the United States. Settling in Los Angeles, Stewart regained his footing. *Atlantic Crossing* (1975) was good enough to convince listeners that *Smiler* had merely been a slip and not a fall. The roadhouse rocker "Three Time Loser" was a cheerful ode to venereal disease, "Stone Cold Sober" was a sturdy Stones-style stomper, and the lovely "Sailing" showed Stewart still had a way with a ballad. Stewart kept up the pace with *A Night on the Town* (1976), which featured a glistening hit single cover of Cat Stevens's "The First Cut Is the Deepest" and the daring narrative of the murder of a gay man, "The Killing of Georgie." The naked intimacy of the hit single "Tonight's the Night (Gonna Be Alright)" was a sour note in an otherwise solid album.

The move to Los Angeles initially seemed to stimulate Stewart, but over time living among the stars proved to be detrimental to his artistic development. He reveled in playing the part of the decadent rock star, partying and womanizing to excess as he became ever more detached from the everyday life of his fans. The woeful *Foot Loose & Fancy Free* (1977) saw Stewart descend to a new low with the saccharine hit single "You're in My Heart' and the ludicrous macho strutting of "Hot Legs." While the material suffered artistically, it still sold well and Stewart remained as big a star as ever. Worse was yet to come, as Stewart bottomed out with the dismal disco hit "Do Ya Think I'm Sexy" from *Blondes Have More Fun* (1978).

Now the epitome of rock royalty, Stewart became the bane of punk rockers, who derided him as a sellout and found his fall from grace all the worse given the previous heights he had attained. Stewart's foppish appearance became roundly mocked, and his high-flying lifestyle was considered out of touch with the economically difficult times. Stewart responded by releasing a new wave–influenced album, *Foolish Behavior* (1980), that yielded the hit single "Passion," but it sold less well than previous albums. His fortunes began to wane in the 1980s, although he updated his sound sufficiently well to land two Top 20 hits in 1984 with "Infatuation" and "Some Guys Have All the Luck." While popular, the songs were hardly on a par with his greatest solo work. A 1991 cover of Van Morrison's "Have I Told You Lately" was another hit, and it established Stewart as an adult contemporary artist.

The new millennium saw Stewart finally regain his commercial footing with a series of albums featuring pop standards from the Great American Songbook. With his voice still in fine form, Stewart competently interpreted much-loved songs and found a receptive audience with fans eager for a touch of class in an increasingly ribald popular culture. Stewart's career had many highs and almost as many lows,

STILLS, STEPHEN

but ultimately one must wonder what he could have accomplished had he maintained his high early standards. Stewart has been inducted into the Rock and Roll Hall of Fame.

Suggested Albums: An Old Raincoat Won't Ever Let You Down (1969); *Gasoline Alley* (1970); *Every Picture Tells a Story* (1971); *Never a Dull Moment* (1972); *Atlantic Crossing* (1975); *A Night on the Town* (1976); *Vagabond Heart* (1991)

See also: Beck, Jeff; Faces

STILLS, STEPHEN (1945–)

Stephen Stills played an integral part in two of the most famous groups in rock history, so in some ways it's not surprising that his solo career has been a bit overlooked. One of the creative leaders in the groundbreaking 1960s band Buffalo Springfield, Stills was integral to the progress of rock in the 1960s and wrote a song that became emblematic of the era, "For What It's Worth." He then moved on to one of rock's great supergroups, the legendary Crosby, Stills, Nash & Young. Even as he was rising to superstardom with CSN&Y, Stills found time to begin a solo career that yielded a hit single and demonstrated his versatility as a guitarist and singer.

Stills spent his earliest years in the semi-nomadic course common to military families. He took up guitar, and while living in Florida played in a series of bands, crossing musical paths with future Eagles guitarist Don Felder. Like so many young musicians of the time, Stills gravitated to the folk-blues revival of Greenwich Village and hit the road with various folk groups, eventually meeting Richie Furay and Neil Young and forming Buffalo Springfield. Several albums and a hit single later, Buffalo Springfield broke up and Stills joined forces with David Crosby and Graham Nash to form Crosby, Stills, and Nash, with Neil Young completing the supergroup in time for their 1970 album, *Deja vu.*

It seemed that none of the members of CSN&Y were willing to fully commit to the group, and Stills was no different. His eponymous debut solo album (1970) was a star-studded event whose guest luminaries included Jimi Hendrix, Eric Clapton, Booker T. Jones, Ringo Starr, and John Sebastian as well as Crosby and Nash. While the prominent guest musicians added a sense of drama to the release, Stills was more than capable of carrying the record. A skilled guitarist, Stills was grounded in blues and rock styles, and used restraint and timing to fit tasteful licks and phrasing within the song's groove without becoming overpowering. His slightly hoarse vocal style had the depth for the blues, but was emotive enough for folk. The diverse collection of songs shifted from rousing rock, wistful folk, and country blues without ever seeming confused or incoherent. The hit single "Love the One You're With" epitomized Stills's approach, as a calypso guitar and rhythm guide an irresistibly building melody. Stills's soulful organ lifts the song to the point where one can overlook the lyric's celebration of infidelity.

Stills displayed the same musical variety on his next solo album, *Stephen Stills 2* (1971), although the songwriting was not as strong and some lyrics were burdened with overbearing messages. A saving grace was the lovely waltz tempo of the album's best-known song, "Change Partners," which seemed to rue the freedom of "Love the One You're With."

In 1971 Stills joined former Byrd and Flying Burrito Brother Chris Hillman to form the band Manassas. The group's self-titled first album (1972) ranks as some of Stills's finest work, carried by his guitar playing, dripping with the feel of Southern blues, and sliding effortlessly into breezy folk strumming and fingerpicking. Musically, *Manassas* runs the gamut of styles, with blues-rock and authentic country sitting side by side with folk to gospel–influenced songs. Sadly, the album was the group's high-water mark, as their next album, *Down the Road* (1973), was a less distinctive and somewhat burned-out sounding effort.

He was back on his own for *Stills* (1975), a rather mundane collection of undistinguished songs notable only for strong guitar work. Stills closed out the 1970s with two unremarkable albums, *Illegal Stills* (1976) and *Thoroughfare Gap* (1978), and spent the next decades touring as a solo act, recording and performing in various permutations with Crosby, Nash, and Young, and releasing an occasional solo album. A later career highlight was the beautiful acoustic blues of "Treetop Flyer" from *Stills Alone* (1991).

Suggested Albums: Stephen Stills (1970); *Stephen Stills 2* (1971); *Manassas* (1972)

STOOGES

See Pop, Iggy

STORIES

The Stories made a splash in the summer of 1973 with their chart-topping single "Brother Louie," a funky tale of interracial romance that proved to be their only real hit. But the band had deeper roots, and "Brother Louie" was actually an aberration from their sound and ambitions.

The New York–based band was founded in the early 1970s by keyboardist Michael Brown and singer Ian Lloyd, who set their sights on creating a Beatlesque sound for the group. Brown had enjoyed success as a member of Left Banke, whose baroque rock "Walk Away, Renee" hit the top 10 (1966). On the Stories' self-titled debut (1972), Lloyd's energetic singing stood out amidst the album's rather ordinary piano-based Beatles-influenced rock. *About Us* (1973) boasted better and more varied songwriting; after it became a hit, "Brother Louie" was added to a revised edition of the album. With an insinuatingly slinky bass line and menacing keyboard riff, "Brother Louie" told of a love story between a black woman and white man in the face of parental intolerance. The song was a bit daring for 1973, but changing racial attitudes and the catchy soul groove drove it to number one.

The song's success did push the band in a more rhythm and blues direction for the follow-up, *Traveling Underground* (1973). The album's best song was the energetic boogie single "If It Feels Good Do It," but Lloyd disliked the drift away from

360 STRAWBS

pop rock and left the band after the album's release. The Stories broke up shortly after his departure.

Suggested Album: About Us (1973)

STRAWBS

The Strawbs began in the early 1960s as the Strawberry Hill Boys, their name acknowledging their London neighborhood as well as their bluegrass repertoire. Many acts from the folk end of the folk-blues revival appended "Boys" to their moniker. Clipping their name to the enigmatic Strawbs in 1967, they recorded an album with British folksinger Sandy Denny released several years later after she left to join Fairport Convention. Their eponymous album debut (1969) found them stretching out into their own version of folk-rock. Keyboardist Rick Wakeman joined in time for a live LP, *Just a Collection of Antiques and Curios* (1970), and departed after the studio album *From the Witchwood* (1971). Wakeman's presence was a token of the band's step toward progressive rock with one foot remaining in folk-rock. Finding Strawbs insufficiently pretentious, Wakeman left for Yes.

Bursting at the Seams (1973) featured their biggest U.K. hits, the tuneful rock song "Lay Down" and the folky "Part of the Union," which expressed Britain's growing dismay over the irresponsibility of trade unions. Enduring many personnel changes, the Strawbs' continuity and distinction was maintained by the poetic vision and pleading warble of principal songwriter and vocalist Dave Cousins. After *Ghosts* (1975), which received a measure of airplay in the United States, the Strawbs sound teetered between folk, progressive, and indistinct hard rock influences. In recent years they have partially returned to their roots, touring as an acoustic act.

Suggested Albums: Strawbs (1969); *Dragonfly* (1970); *From the Witchwood* (1971); *Grave New World* (1972); *All Our Own Work* (aka *Sandy Denny and the Strawbs*) (1973); *Bursting at the Seams* (1973); *Hero and Heroine* (1974); *Ghosts* (1975)

STRING DRIVEN THING

String Driven Thing began in the late 1960s as a Scottish folk trio with married couple Chris and Pauline Adams joined by guitarist John Mannion. When their debut album (1970) disappeared with little trace, the group's rock inclinations surfaced. Their second album, *String Driven Thing* (1972), boasted staccato rhythms set by electric guitar, electric bass, and tambourine with newcomer Graham Smith from the Scottish National Orchestra playing violin as lead instrument. The results were tagged as progressive rock for lack of any ready category, but many songs betrayed a melancholy Celtic folk origin or even an inclination toward country rock. Smith was comfortable in the mode of sweet sadness or supercharged Dervish fury. Pauline Adams's vocals suggested resilience under a retiring demeanor.

For their second album, *The Machine That Cried* (1973), String Driven Thing employed a drummer, adding punch to a bleaker set of songs about nightmares, decadence, and loneliness. Smith's playing brought to mind the mad fiddler desperately keeping the unfathomable at bay in H. P. Lovecraft's story "The Music of Erich Zahn."

Afterward, the Adamses left but Smith kept String Driven Thing going with a new lineup through 1976. Smith went on to join Van der Graaf Generator. Later, he became a solo recording artist and a member of the Icelandic Symphony Orchestra. In the 1990s Chris Adams re-formed String Driven Thing with a lineup that included his son Robin on guitar with guest appearances by Pauline and Smith.

Suggested Albums: String Driven Thing (1972); *The Machine That Cried* (1973)

SURF MUSIC

The Beach Boys sang about surfing but did not play surf music. Properly defined, surf music was an instrumental genre whose preeminent figure, Dick Dale, recreated the physical, even spiritual rush of riding the ocean on electric guitar. Dale's signature hit, "Miserlou" (1963), was characteristic. A Near Eastern folk melody revved up to a rock tempo, "Miserlou" brought non-Western modes and mind-bending guitar solos to the hit parade. Jimi Hendrix was a Dale fan; with its aural sketches of ecstasy, surf music became an unacknowledged influence on psychedelia.

TANGERINE DREAM

Tangerine Dream began as a rock band amidst the cultural tumult of 1967 Germany. Inspired by surrealism, the minimalism of Terry Riley, and the avant-garde experimentation of fellow German Karlheinz Stockhausen, Tangerine Dream soon traded anything resembling conventional rock for the unexplored sonic worlds opened by the development of synthesizers. After the release of their first album, *Electronic Meditation* (1970), produced with conventional as well as homemade electronic instruments along with tapes of found sounds, drummer Klaus Schulze left to pursue electronic music as a solo artist. Synthesizer player, multi-instrumentalist, and producer Edgar Froese eventually became the sole original member and primary guiding light.

Their largely instrumental music soon caught the ears of fans beyond Germany for its chilly aural landscapes, initially produced by Moog synthesizer and mellotron. Although they prized improvisation, Tangerine Dream found inspiration in the patterns of classical music, J. S. Bach and Maurice Ravel as well as modernists such as Gyorgy Ligeti. Tangerine Dream's music lent itself to film scores beginning with director William Friedkin's *Sorcerer* (1977). During the 1980s they became Hollywood's go-to group for electronic soundtracks and worked on films as diverse as *Thief* (1981), *Risky Business* (1983), *Flashpoint* (1984), and *Miracle Mile* (1989). They later provided the music for the Grand Theft Auto V video game (2013).

Tangerine Dream released more than 140 albums, plus solo efforts by Froese. Froese died in 2015 from a pulmonary embolism.

Suggested Albums: Electronic Meditation (1970); *Alpha Centauri* (1971); *Zeit* (1972); *Atem* (1973); *Phaedra* (1974); *Rubycon* (1975); *Stratosfear* (1976); *Sorcerer* (1977)

TASTE

Taste's leader Rory Gallagher has been called the Irish Jimi Hendrix for his prowess on guitar. Gallagher grew up in Ireland during the 1950s, aware of Elvis Presley and Buddy Holly but moved more deeply by the blues and jazz programs heard on the BBC and American Forces Radio. He commented that hearing Muddy Waters changed his life, and he related the conditions of African Americans to the status of Roman Catholics in Ulster.

Gallagher became a professional musician by age 15, touring Eire and the Irish circuit of Great Britain in "show bands," rock and roll cover acts whose identically suited teenage members entertained their generational peers with familiar hits. In 1966 Gallagher founded a power trio, the Taste, sporting long hair, black leather, and a fiery guitar style steeped in the melancholy determination of the blues. Opening in Ulster for Cream led to a Tuesday night residency at London's Marquee Club, home to the Who, the Rolling Stones, and Hendrix.

By the time of Taste's self-titled debut album (1969), Gallagher had earned a reputation as a guitar magician who, with the aid of a treble booster, could do anything on his Stratocaster, improvising with vibrato and feedback as well as chording. Bassist John McCracken and drummer John Wilson kept apace, anchoring solos that approached avant-garde jazz with heavy rhythms. The jazz influence became more pronounced with *On the Boards* (1970). Gallagher took up alto saxophone in addition to guitar, pushing the sound toward Ornette Coleman and Eric Dolphy.

Taste entertained the huge crowd that converged for the chaotic Isle of Wight Festival (1970), but were never able to build on their success due to management problems. After their breakup up in 1970, Gallagher went on to enjoy a prolific solo career.

Suggested Albums: Taste (1969); *On the Boards* (1970)

See also: Gallagher, Rory

TAYLOR, JAMES (1948–)

The troubled son of an affluent family Taylor knocked around the Greenwich Village scene in the late 1960s. Two of his songs were recorded by folksinger Tom Rush on *The Circle Game* (1968). Off to London for a season, Taylor busked on the romantic streets of Notting Hill and became the first non-Brit signed to the Beatles' Apple Records. He struck Paul McCartney with his softly romantic yet somehow edgy voice, the Julian Bream classical influence on his otherwise folky guitar playing, and the soul-searching introspection of his lyrics. Apple released his eponymous debut (1968) in an elaborate production by Peter Asher with fashionably baroque pop touches. George Harrison sang backup vocals on Taylor's "Something in the Way She Moves" and borrowed the title for the opening line of "Something." "Carolina in My Mind," an oddly bittersweet paean to Taylor's home state, received airplay, yet the album and his career were enmeshed in the deteriorating politics of Apple Records. Taylor left for Los Angeles to attend the birth of a movement oxymoronically dubbed "soft rock."

Los Angeles was the epicenter for soft rock both because it had recently become a center for the music industry and also because of a prominent club with roots in the folk-blues revival, the Troubadour, where a coterie of prominent musicians gathered. Taylor was drawn to the milieu along with Jackson Browne, escaping the decadence of New York's Andy Warhol crowd, and Carole King, renewing her life and music after divorcing Gerry Goffin. From his aerie in faraway Woodstock,

New York, Bob Dylan seemed to grant his imprimatur on soft rock with albums such as *New Morning*, which extolled the virtues of rural family life.

The emotional genesis of soft rock was in reaction to the turbulence of the decade just ended. Jackson Browne's "Take It Easy" was heard as a call to simmer down and take stock. Graham Nash's "Our House" was an advertisement for a quiet life after the upheaval. Taylor's first album for Warner Brothers, *Sweet Baby James* (1970), was in keeping yet distinct from the trend. The album's hit, "Fire and Rain," was a cryptic plea from a heroin addict whose friend had committed suicide and whose musical career was in pieces. Pop music fans had no way of interpreting the lyrics yet were drawn to its mournful self-pity buoyed by just enough resilience to keep it from being maudlin. The words fit the introspective mood of self-searching that emerged from the 1960s. Asher produced the music without a hint of bathos.

Tellingly, two-thirds of Mark Ribowski's biography of the artist, *Sweet Dreams and Flying Machines* (2016), is over by the time the author reaches 1975. By then, Taylor had run out of anything interesting to say. During the 1970s his marriage to (and divorce from) singer Carly Simon put him in the celebrity press and his increasingly chronic mellowness triggered an antithesis in the form of glam and then punk rock. His most endearing hits from the late 1970s were easy-going renditions of soul songs, Otis Blackwell's "Handyman" (1977) and Sam Cooke's "Wonderful World" (1978).

Although Taylor has long since receded into easy listening radio formats, he remains a bankable recording artist. His 1976 greatest hits collection, *Diamond*, continues to sell half a million copies each year. Although he was inducted into the Rock and Roll Hall of Fame, he is seldom thought of any longer as a rock artist and found new audiences elsewhere, including country star Garth Brooks, who calls him one of his favorite artists. Taylor remains active playing benefit concerts and working for social causes.

Suggested Albums: James Taylor (1968); *Sweet Baby James* (1970)

10CC

Multi-instrumentalists Graham Gouldman and Eric Stewart, two of 10cc's founders, came to the project with extensive resumes. Gouldman had written several remarkable British rock hits from the 1960s, including "For Your Love," "Heart Full of Soul," and "Evil Hearted You" for the Yardbirds and "Bus Stop" and "Look Through Any Window" for the Hollies. Stewart had played with Gouldman in a popular U.K. band, the Mindbenders. In 1972 Stewart along with Lol Crème and Kevin Godley from the moderately successful Hotlegs joined with Gouldman to form 10cc.

Their self-titled debut (1973) and *Sheet Music* (1974) contained British hits but attracted limited American FM airplay for their musically eccentric satires "Rubber Bullets" and "The Wall Street Shuffle." Some of that humor continued to be heard on their American breakout album, *The Original Soundtrack* (1975), a cinematic

366 TEN YEARS AFTER

soundscape with a strikingly unusual hit single, "I'm Not in Love." Depending on breathy electronics, the song was an early example of synthesizers stepping outside their accustomed place in avant-garde or futuristic settings and into the pop mainstream. The lyrics were also remarkable as the narrative of a man in denial over heartbreak.

10cc never recorded an album as consistently interesting again after the departure of Godley and Crème in 1976, but enjoyed chart success with the tuneful "The Things We Do for Love" from *Deceptive Bends* (1977) and the reggae-flavored travel nightmare of "Dreadlock Holiday" from *Bloody Tourists* (1978). Gouldman and Stewart retired the band in 1983 and worked in production and on solo projects. The four original members regrouped to record . . . *Meanwhile* (1992) but continued without Godley and Crème for *Mirror Mirror* (1995). Various iterations of 10cc have surfaced since.

Suggested Albums: Sheet Music (1974); *The Original Soundtrack* (1975); *How Dare You!* (1976); *Deceptive Bends* (1977)

TEN YEARS AFTER

Ten Years After is primarily known for the supersonic guitar playing of Alvin Lee, whose blisteringly fast lead lines set the pace for future guitarists whose motto was "faster is better." As a band, Ten Years After is often tagged as blues boogie, but in some ways the label is unfair. Their style was more varied, and some of their best-known songs had nothing in common with boogie. To be sure, Ten Years After did play some boogie, but the persistence of the label has more to do with laziness on the part of critics than with the band's music.

Lee and bassist Leo Lyons formed Ten Years After in their hometown of Nottingham, England in 1966. Their name was a tribute marking the 10th anniversary of Elvis Presley's rise to stardom in 1956. Fans of American blues and early rock and roll, the band's self-titled debut album (1967) paid faithful homage to its influences along with the sort of British blues being made famous by Cream, but without the supergroup's musical diversity and experimental spirit. Consisting mostly of covers, the album's most striking feature was Lee's guitar playing. He stayed faithful to the blues form, but his playing was crisper and faster than most, with a razor-sharp tone that cut through the mix and commanded the listener's attention.

More British blues followed on the live album *Undead* (1968), but the closing song, "I'm Going Home," was revelatory for Lee's unfathomably fast guitar playing. As the band revved up behind him, Lee unleashed a sonic explosion of fleet-fingered fretting and picking that is still a worthy challenge for aspiring guitar players. Lee's rendition of the song at Woodstock would provide a breakout moment for the band.

Ten Years After began to move beyond strict British blues with the more experimental *Stonedhenged* (1969). There was the almost obligatory flirtation with psychedelia, but more unexpected was the inclusion of jazz and boogie-woogie–influenced piano, scat vocals, and extended jams that occasionally tipped the hat to what would soon become progressive rock. Following their successful stint at Woodstock, the band entered the studio and emerged with *Ssssh* (1969). The opening track, "Bad Scene," nods to the Yardbirds, but features a double-time tempo that would not have sounded out of place in punk rock clubs a few years later. The album also included a soulful ballad, some acoustic folk, and a dollop of Lee's lightning-fast guitar playing.

Cricketwood Green (1970) represented a satisfying return to their blues and rock and roll roots in a stellar production by Andy Johns, an engineer who worked with the Rolling Stones and Led Zeppelin. The greatest change in direction for Ten Years After came with *A Space in Time* (1971), featuring a more sophisticated reverberated production and a number of pensive acoustic songs that show songwriting maturation. The album's biggest hit was also the group's best-known song, "I'd Love to Change the World." Based on a minor chord progression, the song seamlessly shifts from soft to loud and back again, as Lee sings of the difficulties of coming to terms with a rapidly changing world. From the high of *A Space in Time*, the band fell to the relative low of *Rock & Roll Music to the World* (1972), a bland collection of blues thumpers along the lines of the boogie with which they are often associated.

Ten Years After broke up after *Positive Vibrations* (1974), although they would reunite and record from time to time after 1980. Their most recent release, *Evolution* (2008), is notable for Lee's absence. Lee had a lengthy and moderately successful solo career prior to his death in 2013, is widely recognized as pioneer of speed guitar, and has been called "rock's first shredder."

Suggested Albums: Ten Years After (1967); *Stonedhenged* (1969); *Ssssh* (1969); *Cricketwood Green* (1970); *A Space in Time* (1971)

THEM

Van Morrison was introduced to the world beyond Belfast by his first recording act, Them. Drawn together by a shared love of rhythm and blues and blues, Them leaped from Belfast's Maritime Hotel to London's club scene in 1964. They were signed quickly, swept up in the post-Beatles frenzy.

Morrison was the constant factor throughout the recording sessions, which were populated by some of London's best studio musicians. Among them were drummer Alan White (later with Plastic Ono Band and Yes) and organists Arthur Greenslade (arranger for Shirley Bassey's "Goldfinger") and Peter Bardens (who went on to form Camel). Some of the band's repertoire of hyperkinetic R&B covers made their way onto their debut album, *The Angry Young Them* (1965). The most distinctive of those numbers, "Baby Please Don't Go," which Morrison learned from a John Lee Hooker record, made the Top 10 on the British charts. The propulsive rendition was fueled by Jimmy Page's guitar, tuned down to sound like a bass.

Morrison was already writing songs inspired by the testifying style of American R&B or the grittier cadences of urban blues. However, his memorable early songs were the ones furthest removed from those roots. "Gloria" (1964) paved the way to the garage rock of the 1960s and became a touchstone for many young American bands. Built on a pounding beat, "Gloria" vividly evoked a youthful sexual encounter. The letter-by-letter recitation of the song's title in the refrain was a countdown to ecstasy.

"Gloria" was a U.K. hit but in the United States a cover by the Shadows of Knight rose higher in the charts. Later, with the rise of FM rock radio and the ascent of Morrison's solo career, Them's "Gloria" became the familiar stateside version.

Another original Morrison song from *Angry Young Them* became an unlikely hit single. "Mystic Eyes" was a wailing blues number but unlike any blues that had been heard before. With "Mystic Eyes," Morrison transliterated his American influences into something distinct. As the rhythm slipped into a hypnotic groove, the brief enigmatic lyric faded into the mist without resolution. Them's American producer Bert Berns, who had co-written the Isley Brothers' hit "Twist and Shout," penned their other major hit, "Here Comes the Night" (1965), a pop song whose jealously fretting lyrics were invested with pain by Morrison and elevated by Page's shimmering guitar.

In 1966 Them toured the American West Coast with the Doors as opening act. Jim Morrison listened intently; his vocals sometimes echoed Van Morrison's youthful yelp and "Gloria" became part of the Doors' stage show. By this time, some of the songs released on *Them Again* (1966) already began showing the jazz vocal inclinations that Morrison would explore through his solo years.

Them was clearly Morrison's show and for him, the pretense of being a band member made no sense. By 1967 Morrison embarked on his own path in music. Afterward, bassist Alan Henderson released a pair of competent but forgettable albums as Them.

Suggested Albums: The Angry Young Them (1965); *Them Again* (1966)

See also: Morrison, Van

THIN LIZZY

On the surface, Thin Lizzy appears to be nothing more than a successful 1970s hard rock band with a few notable hits to their name and a legion of loyal fans. A closer look reveals a more interesting and complex reality. Any band that hails from Ireland during its most turbulent time, with members from both Eire and Ulster and fronted by a black Irish singer, defies easy categorization. Similarly, it is a mistake to cover Thin Lizzy's music with the broad-brush label of hard rock, as they drew from many influences to fashion a unique and varied sound. With perhaps the most impressive lineage of guitar players since the Yardbirds, the popularity of the band's dual guitar sound would influence the course of both hard rock and heavy metal.

The band's origins date back to 1969 when singer Phil Lynott and drummer Brian Downey ran into two veterans of the legendary Irish rock band Them, Eric

Bell and Eric Wrixon. The four musicians decided to form a band, taking the name Thin Lizzy either from the nickname for the Ford Model T or a robot comic book character. On the band's self-titled debut album (1971), Lynott did double duty on vocals and bass. All the elements of the band's future success were there, with punchy hard rock with ample guitar solos, a suggestion of Irish folk and mysticism, and Lynott's distinctive vocal style that was part Van Morrison, part Jimi Hendrix, and entirely his own. The album was a respectable debut, but few songs were fully realized and the band was clearly searching for its voice. The search continued over the next album, *Shades of a Blue Orphanage* (1972), as the band tried their hand at hard rock boogie, Irish folk, blues, *Saint Dominic's Preview*–era Van Morrison, and some straight-ahead rock.

Ireland's Thin Lizzy gained the ear of rock fans in Europe and America through a hard rock sound riding on a rhythm and blues groove. Vocalist and founding member Phil Lynott died in 1986. (David Fowler/Dreamstime.com)

Thin Lizzy truly came together for the standout version of an Irish murder ballad, "Whiskey in a Jar," released as a single (1972). The band's sound began to emerge in full with their third album, *Vagabonds of the Western World* (1973), which was heavy but not overbearing, boogie but with a rhythm and blues groove. Lynott's storytelling became more personal and finely honed. "The Rocker" and "The Hero and the Madman" were involved narratives with well-defined characters. To boost lagging sales, the group adopted a radio-friendly sound for their next album, *Nightlife* (1974), but widespread success was yet to come.

Hoping to beef up their sound, the band decided to hire two lead guitarists, settling on a young Britisher named Brian Robertson and American Scott Gorham. The newcomers' impact on the band was immediate. Thin Lizzy's next album, *Fighting* (1975), packed a punch that was lacking on earlier efforts. The dual guitars exploded from speakers as Lynott sang hard-earned tales of working-class life, creating the perfect soundtrack for a rowdy Friday night on the town. Despite being from Ireland, the band's affinity for rhythm and blues was apparent, and they often sounded as if they would be as much at home in New York or Philadelphia as in Dublin.

The stage was set for Thin Lizzy's big break with the release of *Jailbreak* (1976), an epic powerhouse of massive power chording, intricate dual guitar lines, and

370 13TH FLOOR ELEVATORS

anthemic everyman tales of rage, frustration, and triumph. The album's center-pieces were the two-fisted title track and the international hit single "The Boys Are Back in Town," a working-class anthem loaded with big city attitude and a chorus featuring an unforgettable dual guitar pattern. Critics derided the song as a Springsteen knockoff, and while its release was fortuitously timed to capitalize on the Boss's *Born to Run* popularity, the comparisons are overblown. Lynott's writing style had been developing along similar lines prior to Springsteen's emergence, and similarities probably owe more to a shared love of American rhythm and blues and Van Morrison than anything else. Regardless of critical complaints, the album was a huge success and Thin Lizzy had arrived as stars.

The band would never quite replicate the runaway success of *Jailbreak*, although they remained popular and recorded strong albums such as the much darker *Johnny the Fox* (1976) and *Black Rose: A Rock Legend* (1979). *Black Rose* saw Robertson depart, only to be replaced by the scorching blues guitarist Gary Moore, who had briefly toured with the band in its early days. Moore would leave prior to *Chinatown* (1980). The band began to drift in the 1980s with Lynott's work suffering due an increasingly serious heroin addiction. *Thunder and Lightning* (1983) saw the addition of another notable guitarist, John Sykes, but it was to be the band's last studio album. Lynott left in 1983, and the years of drug abuse finally took their toll. He died of multiple organ failure in 1986.

In the ensuing years, Thin Lizzy has re-formed in various guises, sometimes as a serious touring group and other times as a tribute band. Lynott is remembered today as a pioneering black rock singer, and Gorham, Robertson, and especially Moore are highly regarded guitarists.

Suggested Albums: Thin Lizzy (1971); *Shades of a Blue Orphanage* (1972); *Vagabonds of the Western World* (1973); *Fighting* (1975); *Jailbreak* (1976); *Johnny the Fox* (1976); *Bad Reputation* (1977); *Black Rose: A Rock Legend* (1979); *Chinatown* (1980)

13TH FLOOR ELEVATORS

Tommy Hall, a philosophy major at the University of Texas in Austin and barely-out-of-high-school Roky Erikson, already a musical veteran with local recording act the Spades, formed the 13th Floor Elevators in 1965. Hall had emerged from the folk-blues revival and brought with him an instrument that lent the Elevators a note of distinction, the warbling sound of an amplified jug.

Hall and Erikson co-wrote much of their material, although Erikson had already recorded what became their most popular song, "You're Gonna Miss Me," with the Spades. Their debut, *The Psychedelic Sounds of the 13th Floor Elevators* (1966), was folk-rock dissolved to a primal essence of jangled reverb, a driving beat, and melancholy harmonies, yet the band's attack and Erikson's sneering vocals owed more to Them's "Gloria" than anything the Byrds ever recorded. The album's psychedelic reference reflected the origins of the group's distorted guitars and surreal lyrics. By some accounts, Hall was one of Austin's leading proselytizers for LSD as a key to the doors of perception.

Easter Everywhere (1967) displayed growing sophistication in songwriting but was unrelenting in the expressive primitivism of the band's performance. Bob Dylan's influence was honored through "Baby Blue," a cover of his "It's All Over Now, Baby Blue." Erikson's 1967 arrest for marijuana possession effectively ended the band's creative period. To avoid a tough Texas prison sentence, he pleaded insanity resulting from LSD use and was sent to a state hospital. Subjected to electroshock, he left the facility three years later as a broken man.

Two more Elevators albums were issued. *Live* (1968) was not a concert album, despite the overdubbed applause, but a collection of studio outtakes. *Bull of the Woods* (1969) included a few vocals recorded by Erikson before he was sentenced to the hospital and was as close as the Elevators came to a polished performance.

The 13th Floor Elevators were largely forgotten until "You're Gonna Miss Me" was included on Lenny Kaye's anthology of 1960s garage rock, *Nuggets* (1972). Through *Nuggets*, the Elevators became an influence on the nascent punk rock scene. Television included "Fire Engine," a song from *Psychedelic Sounds*, in their repertoire. Erikson has become a cult hero, an acid-damaged figure of aesthetic integrity. He recorded with fellow Texan Doug Sahm (1975), released an album produced by Creedence Clearwater Revival's Stu Cook (1980), and continues to sporadically release demon-haunted recordings. He was honored with *Where the Pyramid Meets the Eye: A Tribute to Roky Erikson* (1990), an album of his songs performed by ZZ Top, R.E.M., Julian Cope, and other fans in high places.

Suggested Albums: The Psychedelic Sounds of the 13th Floor Elevators (1966); *Easter Everywhere* (1967); *Bull of the Woods* (1969)

THOMPSON, RICHARD (1949–)

Richard Thompson is among the few rock musicians from the 1960s with his edge still intact and maybe sharp as ever. His highly developed yet intuitive playing combines the fluidity of jazz with the propulsive hardness of rock and echoes more ancient influences. He began his solo recording career as an already well-respected songwriter and guitarist. His work with Fairport Convention earned him plaudits and helped put the group in the vanguard of late 1960s British folk-rock. He left Fairport in 1971 without any clear direction or career plans and seems to have drifted a bit, doing sessions work before launching a solo career. That career would be long, creatively impressive, highly honored, and showing no signs of slowing down.

Thompson's love of music came at an early age. He fell under the spell of rock and roll while a teenager, and an interest in jazz dates back to watching his father play Django Reinhardt compositions on guitar. Thompson took up guitar himself and began soaking up myriad styles, absorbing and assimilating those influences rather than copying them. He developed a unique style of hybrid picking with alternate tunings, multiple string bends, and borrowing from a deep well of inspiration including early rock, jazz, country, and Anglo-Celtic folk.

His first solo album, *Henry the Human Fly* (1972), featured lovely melodies and inventive guitar playing, but it was panned by critics and ignored by the public.

Thompson married one of the album's background vocalists, singer Linda Peters, and the newlyweds began a fruitful musical partnership. Richard and Linda Thompson's first album, *I Want to See the Bright Lights Tonight* (1974), was a triumph. Thompson melded British folk and rock convincingly and without diluting or confusing the authenticity of either. The subject matter was largely downcast as Richard's poetic sense had evolved to a new level. He used religious imagery and a sense of cynicism to craft lyrics of pain and despair leavened with unexpected moments of hope. The couple's chemistry was apparent with Linda's beautiful soprano a stunning accompaniment to Richard's stellar guitar work. Somber songs like "Withered and Died" and "The Calvary Cross" coexisted nicely with more upbeat-sounding material.

Their next album, *Hokey Pokey* (1975), was a bleak look at the human condition littered with failed lives and relationships. Richard converted to Sufi Islam after *Hokey Pokey* was recorded but prior to its release. The impact of his newfound mystical faith was not felt until the couple's next album, *Pour Down Like Silver* (1975). The album had a stripped-down feel, and Thompson's guitar playing seems a bit restrained, perhaps as a result of conflicted feelings over balancing music with the dictates of religion. Nevertheless, *Pour Down* was a strong collection of songs with the cheerful Celtic lilt of "Streets of Paradise" and the chunky guitars of the repentant "For Shame of Doing Wrong" among the standouts.

The couple disappeared from the public eye after the album's release, as Richard put their career on hold as he continued to explore the mystic edges of Islam. They reemerged with the soulful *First Light* (1978). With folk-rock out of fashion, they were briefly without a recording contract in the early 1980s but returned with the harrowing, more rock-oriented *Shoot Out the Lights* (1982), a misanthropic masterpiece worthy of Elvis Costello. Some of the album's tension was due to the deteriorating state of the couple's marriage, leading to the dissolution of their musical partnership, and eventually their marriage itself by the mid-1980s. Linda continued to release albums under her own name but Richard proved more prolific. Highlights of his postdivorce output include the upbeat *Hand of Kindness* (1983), in which he rocks like Chuck Berry as interpreted by the Pogues, and the radio-friendly hard rock of *Across a Crowded Room* (1985).

Thompson continued to record and tour throughout the 1990s and into the 21st century. Sales have not been strong and Thompson turned his back on the record industry in favor of indie record labels. Thompson has developed a side career working with alternative music artists. His live show "1000 Years of Music" was an ambitious tour of music history from old England to Britney Spears. Thompson is widely recognized both for his exceptional songwriting as well as for being one of rock's greatest guitar players, noted for his individualistic style that reflects and reinterprets his influences in his own peerless voice.

Suggested Albums: Henry the Human Fly (1972); *I Want to See the Bright Lights Tonight* (1974) (with Linda Thompson); *Hokey Pokey* (1975) (with Linda Thompson); *Pour Down Like Silver* (1975) (with Linda Thompson); *First Light* (1978) (with Linda Thompson); *Sunnyvista* (1979) (with Linda Thompson); *Shoot Out the Lights* (1982) (with Linda Thompson); *Hand of Kindness* (1983); *Across a Crowded Room* (1985); *Amnesia* (1988); *Rumor and Sigh* (1991); *You? Me? Us?* (1996); *Mock Tudor* (1999); *The Old Kit Bag* (2003); *Front Parlour Ballads* (2005); *Sweet Warrior* (2007)

TOMORROW

Tomorrow was a psychedelic pop group that emerged from Britain's mid-1960s rock scene. Their best-known song was inspired by the plethora of white bicycles left on the streets for all to use in Amsterdam, Europe's countercultural capital. A merry romp, "My White Bicycle" was later covered by Nazareth and Neil the Hippy from the 1980s British television series *The Young Ones*. Guitarist Steve Howe left the short-lived group to join the progressive rock band Yes while their drummer, Twink, joined the Pretty Things before forming the Pink Fairies.

Suggested Album: Tomorrow (1968)

TOWNSHEND, PETE

See Who

TRAFFIC

Having already made a name for himself fronting the Spencer Davis Group, keyboardist and vocalist Steve Winwood was ready for a new challenge. In 1967 he found himself in a jam session with three veterans of the British music scene: guitarist Dave Mason, drummer Jim Capaldi, and flutist and sax player Chris Wood. Following the session, the four musicians decided to form a new band, which they promptly named Traffic. With four strong personalities from diverse backgrounds, Traffic could have become an unnamable hodgepodge of styles, but the band came together with an open-minded approach and created music that helped push the boundaries of rock. They still sound fresh and intriguing.

Most of the band's creative work took place at a secluded country cottage, and it was there that a communal spirit was born that would prove crucial to Traffic's chemistry. Their debut album, *Mr. Fantasy* (1967), was an exercise in psychedelia that reflected the album's rural origins and the band's experimental ethic. Sitar is featured prominently, and a cornucopia of instruments provided color and texture, including harpsichord, mellotron, tambura, and maracas. The band made use of a variety of styles, ranging from rock, rhythm and blues, psychedelia, jazz, to Eastern music, usually weaving multiple influences together in songs such as "Dear Mr. Fantasy." The happy-go-lucky "Hole in My Shoe" and the sitar-dominated "Paper Sun" were exceptions, being dependably psychedelic enough to serve as singles.

A turbulent season followed the release of *Mr. Fantasy*, with Mason leaving the band, only to return after a brief hiatus, cutting a few tracks for the next album before quitting for good to pursue a solo career. Mason's bluesy "Feelin' Alright" was featured on the album *Traffic* (1968) and would become a hit when covered by Joe Cocker. A bit more straightforward and less experimental than the first album, *Traffic* put Wood's talent to good use with his flute adding an ethereal touch to several tracks. As always, Winwood's powerful voice stood out, but the rest of the band had the chops to match, and his vocals were less of a focal point than they had been in the Spencer Davis Group.

Traffic took a year off in 1969, seemingly disbanding after Winwood left to join supergroup Blind Faith. He returned to work on a new Traffic album, *John Barleycorn Must Die* (1970), heavy on rhythm and blues with Wood's sax upfront and the band proving itself adept at extended jams. Far more diverse, their next album, *The Low Spark of High Heeled Boys* (1971), would prove their bestselling record, partly thanks to the heavy FM airplay of the jazzy 11-minute title cut. Capaldi took over vocal duties on the heavy rock single "Rock & Roll Stew" while the rest of the album takes in rock, jazz, folk, and rhythm and blues in a somewhat low-key but challenging blend.

The band hit a rough stretch after the commercial high of *Low Spark* with Winwood sidelined after a bout with peritonitis. Wood began to suffer the effects of alcoholism and drug addiction. Despite the problems, they managed to tour and recorded *Shootout at the Fantasy Factory* (1973). The album sold well, but it was surprisingly ordinary sounding, with a consistent rhythm and blues style that came off as monotonous when compared to the band's previous work.

Traffic's troubles continued as Wood's problems with drink and drugs grew worse and Winwood's recurring peritonitis sapped his energy. Not surprisingly, *When the Eagle Flies* (1974) was an undistinguished effort, highlighted only by some inspired flute playing by Wood. A tumultuous tour was brought to a dramatic end when Winwood walked offstage in the middle of a show and promptly quit the band. With the irreplaceable Winwood gone, Traffic broke up in 1975. Winwood went on to a distinguished solo career with hit albums such as *Arc of a Diver* (1980), *Talking Back to the Night* (1982), and *Back in the High Life* (1986). Capaldi recorded a series of solo albums and gained international chart success with a 1975 cover of the Everly Brothers' "Love Hurts." Wood's tale is one of tragedy, as his drinking became more and more debilitating and his health worsened. Work on a solo album was never finished. Wood died in 1982 of complications from alcoholism. Winwood and Capaldi reunited as Traffic for *Far from Home* (1994), and the surviving members of the band re-formed for a tour that same year. Capaldi died of cancer in 2005. Traffic was inducted into the Rock and Roll Hall of Fame.

Suggested Albums: Mr. Fantasy (1967); *Traffic* (1968); *John Barleycorn Must Die* (1970); *The Low Spark of High Heeled Boys* (1971); *Shoot Out at the Fantasy Factory* (1973)

T. REX

For a time in the early 1970s, T. Rex was the biggest thing in Britain since the Beatles hit a decade before. One of the leading glam rock bands, T. Rex made a splash across the Atlantic as well, racking up chart success with a hit single and album.

Led by its charismatic frontman Marc Bolan, the band had a strong pop sense, creating simple, catchy songs with easily singable choruses and sometimes silly lyrics. The band's impact was such that their name would be dropped in other artists' songs, and while never as big in the States as at home, their influence would be felt for decades to come.

Bolan founded the folk duo Tyrannosaurus Rex with percussionist Steve Peregin Took in 1967. They recorded four rather interesting if offbeat albums, multi-instrumental with Bolan's oddball, scat-influenced vocal style setting a good-natured psychedelic mood. Bolan already knew his way around songwriting, crafting beguiling melodies for his mythology-laden lyrics. The duo went their separate ways, with Took helping found the underground band Pink Fairies. Bolan also embraced rock, keeping the duo's name but shortening it to the sharper T. Rex.

The band's eponymous debut album sounded a bit like a plugged-in Tyrannosaurus Rex with Bolan writing fantasy-based lyrics and somewhat dreamlike songs. What was different was the chugging rock and roll beat of some of the songs powered by driving bass and overdriven guitar. With the Turtles' Howard Kaylan and Mark Volman (later Flo & Eddie) providing background vocals, the album caught on with the British underground and cracked the U.K. Top 10. The finger-snapping sing-along ditty "Ride a White Swan" was a hit, and Bolan's teen idol looks helped cement his longed-for success.

Around this time Bolan renewed his friendship with another rising star, David Bowie. Bowie was in the process of developing his glam image, and Bolan was sufficiently impressed to go about remaking his own appearance, sporting flamboyant clothing with feather boas to go with a full mane of curly hair. Bolan introduced his new look in a memorable performance by the band on the BBC's *Top of the Pops*. Bolan had glitter makeup applied under his eyes, and T. Rex was now officially a glam rock band. The band's next album, *Electric Warrior* (1971), is a classic of the genre. Stripped down and driven by distorted guitars, the album hearkens back to the roots of rock, with 12-bar songs rooted in blues and Chuck Berry. Bolan admitted that the smash hit "Bang a Gong (Get It On)" was his tribute to Berry's "Little Queenie." The album rocked with a lighthearted energy that was sorely lacking in the era's serious bands. Already a hit in the United Kingdom, "Bang a Gong" would also enjoy chart success in the United States, although the band's popularity there was nothing like it was at home where Bolan and band achieved "T.Rextasy," a wave of popularity similar to that of Beatlemania.

Entrenched as glam rock superstars, the band released their bestselling U.S. album, *The Slider* (1972). The pop-oriented sound, good-time guitar, and catchy melodies alienated some British journalists, who derided Bolan as a sellout and ripped his pretty boy image. The criticism didn't dent the band's popularity, as the album contained two number one U.K. hits. T. Rex was sufficiently notorious to have their name dropped by Mott the Hoople in their Bowie-written hit "All the Young Dudes."

A more polished and less energetic approach typified the band's next album, *Tanx* (1973). Bolan brought in female background vocalists and added strings and saxophones to create a less driving but richer, more rhythmic sound. The guitars were turned way up for the band's next single, "20th Century Boy" (1973), a massive sounding piece of pop metal that would have a profound influence on 1980s hard rock superstars Def Leppard. The band tried to broaden its sound to include funk and rhythm and blues on *Zinc Alloy and the Hidden Riders of Tomorrow* (1974). Unfortunately, Bolan's appeal was beginning to wear thin from overexposure. The album's popularity didn't replicate the band's previous success.

With sales plummeting and critics slamming him, Bolan became a tax exile and went to seed, gaining weight and drinking heavily. The disjointed *Future Dragon* (1976) threatened to sink the band for good, but Bolan rebounded by losing weight and rediscovering the band's classic sound for *Dandy in the Underworld* (1977). T. Rex was poised for a comeback just as punk was about to make their musical approach relevant again, but it was not to be, as Bolan was killed in an automobile accident a few months after the album's release.

T. Rex is now recognized as one of the most influential glam rock acts, second only in the minds of some to David Bowie. Punk rockers were inspired by the band's no-nonsense sound and driving rock beats. Bands influenced by T. Rex include the Smiths, the Replacements, R.E.M, and Oasis, and American underground minimalists Violent Femmes had a minor hit with a cover of the band's "Children of the Revolution." The Who's "You Better You Bet" and the Ramones' "Do You Remember Rock 'n' Roll Radio" make mention of T. Rex, and the band's music has appeared in numerous films. The surviving members have made occasional attempts to re-form the band since Bolan's death, with the most recent appearing in 2014.

Suggested Albums: Tyrannosaurus Rex: *My People Were Fair and Had Sky in Their Hair . . . But Now They're Content to Wear Stars on Their Brows* (1968); *Prophets, Seers & Sages: The Angels of the Ages* (1968); *Unicorn* (1969); *A Beard of Stars* (1970); T. Rex: *T. Rex* (1970); *Electric Warrior* (1971); *The Slider* (1972); *Tanx* (1973); *Dandy in the Underworld* (1977)

TROGGS

The raw sound of Britain's the Troggs is sometimes referred to as garage rock, even though that term is commonly associated with American bands of the 1960s. But the raw power of their simple and unpretentious music certainly occupies common ground with their American counterparts. Led by their dynamic frontman Reg Presley, the Troggs' primal energy and barebones songs influenced proto-punk legend Iggy Pop, and the notorious rock critic Lester Bangs called them "the progenitors of punk."

The Troggs are best known for their cover of a song by American garage band the Wild Ones, "Wild Thing," from their debut album *From Nowhere* (1966). The song shares the same chord progression as the Kingsmen's hit "Louie, Louie" and shows just how much a band can accomplish with just three chords and a world of attitude. The primitive force of the guitars and caveman drums are as subtle as a punch to the solar plexus, and Presley's leering vocals adds a sinister sexuality worthy of his more famous American namesake. The rest of the album is a throwaway set of covers, setting the pattern for the Troggs, who were the essence of a singles band. Fortunately, the Troggs excelled at singles, from the distorted guitars of "I Can't Control Myself" to the cheerful pop of "With a Girl Like You" and the soft ballad "Anyway You Want Me." A true highlight was the savage 1966 single "I Can't Control Myself," which kicks off with a feral-sounding Presley scream before giving way to a pounding beat and openly lecherous lyrics. One would have thought the Troggs would be the last band to go psychedelic, but their 1968 single "Love Is All Around" is as cheerful a slice of flower power as anybody would care to hear. It was to be the band's last hit before splitting up in 1969.

They reunited in the 1970s to little notice but were embraced by punk rockers who heard kindred spirits in the fierce energy and unpretentious simplicity of Presley and his bandmates. Years later, the Troggs collaborated with American alternative rock stars R.E.M. for the excellent album *Athens Andover* (1992). A revitalized Presley sounded 20 years younger, and the album successfully updated the band's sound, bringing it into the age of grunge. It was to be their last significant work. Presley died of lung cancer in 2013.

Suggested Albums: Best of the Troggs (1967); *Athens Andover* (1992)

TROWER, ROBIN (1945–)

Guitarist Robin Trower was already exploring the path opened by Jimi Hendrix before leaving progressive rock pioneers Procol Harum in 1971 for his solo career. Trower and Hendrix mined a heavy rock vein with explosive distorted guitar and an expansive blues vocabulary, and there is little doubt that Hendrix influenced Trower's playing. However, labeling Trower a Hendrix imitator is an oversimplification, as Trower was well grounded in the blues and cited blues great Albert King as an influence. Trower developed his own brand of Hendrix-styled hard rock and became influential in his own right, inspiring rock guitarists who came of age in the 1970s, some of them introduced to Hendrix by listening to Trower.

Trower's first solo album, *Twice Removed from Yesterday* (1973), already drew Hendrix comparisons. Vocalist James Dewar's phrasing was reminiscent of Hendrix, and Trower's riffing on "I Can't Stand It" owed a clear debt to the American guitar innovator. But other songs were simply based on the blues and showed Trower's command of the idiom. Trower's next album, *Bridge of Sighs* (1974), made him a bona fide guitar hero. Trower served up an impressive helping of neo-Hendrix hard rock with "Two Rolling Stoned," "Day of the Eagle," and the title cut becoming FM staples. Like Hendrix, Trower played a Fender Stratocaster switched to the neck pickup position, and he achieved his tone through use of fuzz, octave, and phase shifter pedals. However, Trower's firmly controlled vibrato and masterful extended bends were distinctive.

His follow-up album, *For Earth Below* (1975), sold well, but by then Trower could be accused of copying himself as well as Hendrix as the album differed little in style from its predecessor. Such would be the case with subsequent releases,

378 TURKISH PSYCHEDELIA

uniformly solid and uniformly similar. Over time Trower expanded his musical palette somewhat, adding bits of funk, soul, and Texas blues boogie, but his overall sound remained basically unchanged. He worked with Cream bassist Jack Bruce on two albums, *B.L.T.* (1981) and *Truce* (1982). Bruce's distinctive bass playing and vocal style provided a badly needed change of pace. Trower continues to tour and record, and is well respected for his expressive blues guitar style. His "Bridge of Sighs" tone is often studied.

Suggested Albums: Twice Removed from Yesterday (1973); *Bridge of Sighs* (1974); *For Earth Below* (1975); *B.L.T.* (1981)

TURKISH PSYCHEDELIA

With its Oriental modes, hand-slapped percussion, and array of exotic stringed instruments, the traditional music of the Near East lent itself to psychedelic rock just as well as the classical traditions of India. As the lynchpin of Europe and Asia, Turkey took a lead role in melding rock with Near Eastern influences. Cem Karaca was the key figure in the emergence of a distinctly Turkish rock sound.

Interestingly, Karaca was the child of parents from two distinct minority groups, Azerbaijani and Armenian, in a nation whose regime had little tolerance for ethnic minorities. Karaca began by playing in an Elvis Presley cover band; by 1967 he was performing original rock songs sung in Turkish in bands such as Apaslar (the Rowdies), Kardaslar (the Brothers), and Mogollar (the Mongols), and inspired other Turkish musicians. The political turmoil of Turkey during the 1970s prompted Karaca to leave for West Germany, where he remained until granted amnesty in 1987. He recorded prolifically. Some of his rock tracks were built from the music of his region; others used Turkish folk decoratively; others were Turkish-language versions of Western pop. Karaca died in 2004.

More accessible than Karaca's oeuvre were a pair of LPs by German multi-instrumentalist Alex Wiska, released under the name Alex. Sung in English, rock's international language, Alex achieved a unique fusion of rock with Turkish folk music. Employing a host of stringed instruments, including the plucked long-necked lute called the saz, Alex worked with Can's Holger Czukay and Jaki Liebezeit on his first album and produced and recorded all instruments on his follow-up.

Suggested Albums: Cem Karaca: *Kardaslar* (1973); Alex: *Alex* (1973); *That's the Deal* (1975)

TURTLES

Unlike the vast majority of aspiring musicians who found their way to Los Angeles in the mid-1960s, the Turtles were actually a product of Southern California. Beginning as a group of high school friends playing surf rock, the Turtles were caught up in the folk-rock explosion and switched styles to accommodate the trend. Although their folk-rock sound was not unique, what set the Turtles apart was their ability to capture the feel of Southern California youth culture at the precise moment it changed from the sunny optimism and relative conformity of the early 1960s to a movement that would question authority and challenge virtually all societal norms.

In the early 1960s, teenage musicians Howard Kaylan and Mark Volman enlisted a group of high school friends to play with them in a surf group called the Crossfires. Local radio personalities noticed the band and helped them get a record deal. By the mid-1960s with folk-rock all the rage in Los Angeles, the Crossfires packed up their surfboards and began to ride a new musical wave. Now called the Turtles, they recorded *It Ain't Me Babe* (1965). Following in the Byrds' footsteps, they turned to Bob Dylan for material; their Dylan cover, "It Ain't Me Babe," landed in the Top 10. Covering Dylan was not the only similarity between the Turtles and the Byrds as both bands favored ringing 12-string guitars and multiple-part harmonies. An exception was their second single, "Let Me Be," a P. F. Sloan–penned anthem of youthful defiance with a rousing chorus that gave voice to a generation coming of age and no longer willing to automatically follow the rules.

A recut version of the song was on their next album, *You Baby* (1966), another folk-rock effort but with several original songs, including Kaylan's startling tale of depravity, "House of Pain." The other originals were competent but not terribly distinctive, and the band turned again to Sloan for the album's title cut and hit single.

The Turtles tapped a young songwriter named Warren Zevon for their next two singles, the droning "Grim Reaper of Love" and the up-tempo "Outside Chance." Neither sold well and the Turtles' momentum stalled.

In need of a comeback and surrounded by the new musical landscape created by *Pet Sounds* and *Sgt. Pepper's Lonely Heart's Club Band*, the Turtles released the more ambitious *Happy Together* (1967). Strings and horns replaced 12-string guitar as the focal point of a number of tracks, and the band turned to outside songwriters in search of more musically and lyrically sophisticated material. After hearing a demo of an enchantingly hummable number with a memorable chorus, the band cut a brassy version of the title track, which returned the Turtles to the top of the charts. Even better was the ebullient "She'd Rather Be with Me," an energetic pop tour de force that became an international hit.

The chart success emboldened the band to take its music more seriously, and the result was the underrated concept album *The Turtles Present the Battle of the Bands* (1968). Based on the idea of the Turtles playing the role of a different band on each track, the result was a musical potpourri that showcased the band's irreverent sense of humor. The album's hit single "Elenore" parodied their own hit "Happy Together." The band adopted a hippie look for the cover of their next album, *Turtle Soup* (1969), a Ray Davies–produced effort that was a solid return to a more folk-rock sound. The quality of the material wasn't enough to ensure sales, and the record charted poorly. Frustrated by pressure to produce hit records, Kaylan and Volman resisted efforts to write more commercial material. The band split up in 1970.

After leaving the Turtles, Kaylan and Volman took the stage names Flo & Eddie and joined Frank Zappa's Mothers of Invention. As Flo & Eddie, they developed a

380 TURTLES

quirky career as session vocalists and counterculture cutup radio personalities. Their moderately successful show *Flo & Eddie by the Fireside* was syndicated on a number of radio stations, and they made it back to the charts singing background vocals on Bruce Springsteen's 1980 single "Hungry Heart." The duo rejoined the Turtles in 2010, and the band continues to tour on the oldies circuit.

Suggested Albums: It Ain't Me Babe (1965); *You Baby* (1966); *Happy Together* (1967); *The Turtles Present the Battle of the Bands* (1968); *Turtle Soup* (1969)

URIAH HEEP

Lifting their name from the obsequious character in *David Copperfield*, Uriah Heep began in 1969 and quickly became one of the top-selling hard rock acts of the early 1970s. The band's organ-guitar–driven sound, along with their proclivity toward progressive rock and orchestral arrangements, was comparable to the early work of Deep Purple. Considered heavy metal as the genre coalesced by 1970, Uriah Heep dabbled in dark imagery but was never as associated with the occult as Black Sabbath. While they similarly drew from eclectic sources, they never achieved Led Zeppelin's consistent high level of artistry. Uriah Heep's bestselling album, *Demons and Wizards* (1972), included a hard-driving rock song that received airplay in the United States, "Easy Livin'." "Stealin'" from *Sweet Freedom* (1973) was also heard often on American FM.

Personnel changes, disputes with management, and drug problems sapped the band's momentum. Changing fashions kept them out of the spotlight, especially after the departure of quasi-operatic vocalist David Byron in 1976. However, Uriah Heep soldiers on with one original member, guitarist Mick Box, and continues to tour and record in the 21st century. Their 23rd studio album, *Into the Wild*, was released in 2011.

Suggested Albums: Very 'Eavy . . . Very 'Umble (aka Uriah Heep) (1970); Salisbury (1971); Look at Yourself (1971); Demons and Wizards (1972)

VAN DER GRAAF GENERATOR

Unlike many of their progressive rock contemporaries, Britain's Van der Graaf Generator distanced itself from the pop music industry and evolved with integrity intact. After releasing nearly 50 albums under their name or that of their guiding force, Peter Hammill, they became the ultimate cult band. Throughout their estimable body of work are lyrics rich in possible meanings, wrapped in uncompromising music.

Hammill cofounded the band in 1967 with other students from Manchester University. *The Aerosol Grey Machine* (1969), recorded as a Hammill solo album but released as by Van der Graaf Generator, set the trajectory for his long journey. It was the sound of progressive rock emerging from the mists of psychedelia. Electric guitar was nowhere heard; the lead instrumentation was carried by Hugh Banton's classically informed organ. Banton and drum virtuoso Guy Evans would become Hammill's most consistent collaborators through shifting lineups. The distinction between albums credited to Hammill or Van der Graaf was largely a matter of record label politics or personal idiosyncrasy. Hammill has written most of the band's material and band members often played on his solo albums.

Simple in its complexity, Hammill's music largely dispenses with the conventions of pop-rock songwriting. His lyrics often dealt poetically with mystical, philosophical, or science-fiction themes. On early recordings, Hammill's fey yet acerbic vocals forecast the tone of David Bowie in the early 1970s. Although he could be thrillingly dynamic on electric guitar, Hammill usually deferred to Banton's keyboards and, during some periods, Graham Smith's electric violin or David Jackson's alto and tenor saxophone, played simultaneously under the spell of jazz avant-gardist Rahsaan Roland Kirk. One of Hammill's admirers, King Crimson's Robert Fripp, played guitar on *H to He, Who Am the Only One* (1970) and *Pawn Hearts* (1971).

Hammill's most influential project, the solo concept album *Nadir's Big Chance* (1975), was *A Clockwork Orange* fantasy of three-chord, punk rock bash. Devouring the recording was a young unknown who, under the name Johnny Rotten, emerged a year later at the head of British punk rock with the Sex Pistols. An aura of mystery clung to Van der Graaf Generator, captivating a tiny fandom that worked hard to find their albums in the pre-Amazon era and harder to understand them. Prominent fans include Marillion, Rush, and Julian Cope, though none have been able to match Hammill's idiosyncratic vision.

Van der Graaf Generator continues to record and tour in the 21st century. Hammill has undertaken several interesting projects, composing an opera based on Edgar Allan Poe's "The Fall of the House of Usher" and reciting H.P. Lovecraft's "The Music of Erich Zann" accompanied by the music of the Kronos Quartet.

Suggested Albums: Van der Graaf Generator: *The Aerosol Grey Machine* (1969); *The Least We Can Do Is Wave to Each Other* (1970); *H to He, Who Am the Only One* (1970); *Pawn Hearts* (1971); *Godbluff* (1975); *Still Life* (1976); *World Record* (1976); *The Quiet Zone/The Pleasure Dome* (1977); *Vital* (1978); Peter Hammill: *Fool's Mate* (1971); *Chameleon in the Shadow of the Night* (1973); *The Silent Corner and the Empty Stage* (1974); *In Camera* (1974); *Nadir's Big Chance* (1975); *Over* (1977); *The Future Now* (1978); *A Black Box* (1980); *Patience* (1983); *The Noise* (1993)

VANGELIS (1943–)

Born Evangelos Papathanassiou in the Greek village of Agria, Vangelis was among his country's first generation of rock musicians. He played keyboards and wrote songs for the recording act the Formynx in the early 1960s and moved on to the psychedelic Aphrodite's Child, which enjoyed European success from their Paris and London exile. Even before the group disbanded in 1972, Vangelis began a prolific solo career, focused on electronic soundtracks for film and television but occasionally recording music that accompanied nothing but his own imaginative flights. Among his best nonfilm albums, *The Dragon* (1971) was a progressive rock suite infused with Greek folk music influences and touching on space rock. *Hypothesis* (1978) was a spacey jazz jam occasionally reminiscent of Sun Ra.

Vangelis became internationally recognized when his music was used in Carl Sagan's *Cosmos* series (1980), but is best known for his theme from *Chariots of Fire* (1981), which earned an Oscar for Best Score. The lulling instrumental became a hit single and was influential for breaking with the use of orchestral scores for period films. Vangelis's success as a soundtrack artist was based on his ability to capture the appropriate mood of each project, whether the sunny nostalgia of *Chariots of Fire* or the bleak future vision of Ridley Scott's 1982 film *Blade Runner* (Vangelis's music was not released until 1994).

Although Vangelis declined when asked to join Yes, he went on to collaborate with the band's vocalist, Jon Anderson, recording a handful of albums together as Jon & Vangelis. The keyboardist continued to work with the singer from Aphrodite's Child, Demis Roussos, and has produced several Greek recording acts. With *Cosmos* as well as music composed for NASA and the European Space Agency on his resume, Vangelis became the only rock musician with a minor planet named in his honor, 6354 Vangelis.

Suggested Albums: The Dragon (1971); *Hypothesis* (1978); *Blade Runner* (1994)

See also: Aphrodite's Child

VELVET UNDERGROUND

The Velvet Underground sold few records but as Brian Eno later commented, it seemed as if every purchaser of their first album went on to form a band. The Velvets' enduring influence never registered in album sales or chart ranking. Truly underground, even relative to the cultural upheavals of the 1960s, they were exemplary of how fringe artists can change the world. The Velvet Underground inspired not only musicians in North America and Europe but dissidents everywhere, including Vaclav Havel, Czechoslovakia's first post-Communist president.

The Velvet Underground was an organic compound of rock, avant-garde music, and modernist literary influences. Primary songwriter Lou Reed began in garage bands during the 1950s and, like many musicians of his generation, gravitated to the folk-blues revival. While attending Syracuse University he met his literary mentor, Delmore Schwartz, a writer admired by T. S. Eliot and other modernists. While exploring the post-bebop jazz of John Coltrane at Greenwich Village clubs, Reed worked as a songwriter for New York's Pickwick International, a low-budget record label producing knock-offs of contemporary hits.

In 1964, Reed met John Cale, an accomplished violist from the National Youth Symphony of Wales whose American sojourn began with a letter of recommendation from composer Aaron Copland. Cale performed with John Cage and La Monte Young's Theatre of Eternal Music, whose experiments with sustained drones and amplification influenced the minimalist direction of composers such as Philip Glass as well as the Velvet Underground's early work.

With guitarist Sterling Morrison, Reed and Cale performed as the Warlocks, the Primitives, and the Falling Spikes at Manhattan art openings and poetry readings. Maureen Tucker joined the band, playing drums on a homemade kit. By the end of 1965 they debuted as the Velvet Underground and soon gained the ear of Andy Warhol, the prominent pop artist and avant-garde filmmaker. Warhol's studio, the Factory, was the center of New York's cutting-edge art scene, a place where socialites mingled with drag queens and fashion models with drug addicts. The Velvet Underground became the stars of Warhol's multimedia show, the Exploding Plastic Inevitable, performing with psychedelic lights, dancers, and screenings of his films. Adding glamor to the lineup, Warhol recruited a female vocalist from the Factory milieu, the German expatriate Nico.

Credited with producing their debut album, *The Velvet Underground and Nico* (1967), Warhol's contribution was much like his role as a film director. He simply watched as something interesting occurred. The album was contrary to everything contemporaneous in music. Although Morrison's fuzz tone linked them to garage psychedelia, the dangerous combustion captured the social decay rather than the optimism of the 1960s. Blues was virtually expunged as an influence, yet folk-rock echoes could be discerned alongside minimalist drones and the chaos theory of avant-garde jazz on "Black Angel's Death Song" and "European Son." The mood on ballads such as "Sunday Morning" and "Femme Fatale" was of melancholy resignation. "Heroin" and "Venus in Furs" were thematically closer to short stories from Paris's daring Olympia Press than anything conceivable in popular music. "Waiting for the Man," a matter-of-fact account of a heroin deal, edged toward metal under Tucker's staccato martial beat. Nico sang several songs, infusing them with jaded emotional detachment. "All Tomorrow's Parties" was probably the least joyous party song ever recorded. Warhol, a commercial artist by training who designed jackets for jazz LPs upon arriving in New York in the 1950s, was responsible for the album's front cover, a suggestive-looking banana capable of being peeled.

After Nico's departure, the Velvets recorded *White Light, White Heat* (1968). Not quite heavy but definitely metal, the dark and sometimes sardonic album brought rock across the threshold of noise and offered a foretaste of the industrial rock bands that grew out of the late 1970s punk movement. Cale left after *White Light, White Heat*. His replacement, bassist Doug Yule, is heard on *The Velvet Underground* (1969), an album startling for its hushed intimacy. Reed's ballad "Pale Blue Eyes" would enter the repertoire of Patti Smith, R.E.M., and others.

With each album selling less than its predecessor, MGM Records dropped the Velvet Underground. Remarkably, Atlantic Records gave them a final chance. Reed intended *Loaded* (1970) as an overture to both AM and FM radio. "Who Loves the Sun" was a winsome British Invasion–style pop tune sung by Yule in an innocent voice beyond Reed's range. The anthemic "Rock and Roll," which addressed the music's power to save its acolytes from lives of suburban boredom, would become a rock standard. "Sweet Jane," later well known from Reed's solo career and Mott the Hoople's cover, rebuked nihilism and endorsed life's potential. When the original lineup collapsed in the wake of *Loaded*'s commercial failure, Yule kept the band's name for a final album, the forgettable *Squeeze* (1972).

However, history soon caught up with the Velvet Underground. With David Bowie proselytizing on their behalf, the glitter rock scene of the early 1970s embraced them posthumously. The punk rock movement of the late 1970s followed suit. The Velvet Underground's blend of primal and artful was crucial to the ethos of Patti Smith, Television, Talking Heads, and other New York bands that emerged during the 1970s from the seminal rock club CBGB's. The spirit of the Velvet Underground, especially their willingness to swim against the mainstream, licensed new generations of cultural rebels.

While continuing to pursue solo careers, Reed, Cale, and Tucker briefly regrouped with Morrison for a 1993 European tour, documented on the album *Live MCMXCIII* (1993). The Velvet Underground has been inducted into the Rock and Roll Hall of Fame.

Suggested Albums: The Velvet Underground and Nico (1967); *White Light, White Heat* (1968); *The Velvet Underground* (1969); *Loaded* (1970); *Live at Max's Kansas City* (1972)

See also: Cale, John; Reed, Lou

WALSH, JOE (1947–)

Evidently weary of shouldering the creative load for his 1960s band the James Gang, Joe Walsh jettisoned his bandmates and embarked on a long and largely successful solo career that emphasized his assertive guitar playing and his eccentric personality. Walsh grew up in Ohio, where he learned guitar and eventually landed a gig as guitarist for the Cleveland-based James Gang, leading them to a series of successful albums and attracting considerable attention as an up-and-coming guitar player. A number of his contemporaries, including Jimmy Page, Eric Clapton, and Pete Townshend, openly admired his playing, and he went solo when he evidently realized the James Gang needed him more than he needed them.

Walsh's first solo album, *Barnstorm* (1972), was more laid-back than his work with the James Gang, but subsequent albums established a trademark Walsh sound featuring mid-tempo rockers based around often melodic power chord riffs, best heard in the FM rock staple "Rocky Mountain Way." The wackier elements of Walsh's personality became more prominent, as humorous album titles such as *So What* (1975), *You Can't Argue with a Sick Mind* (1976), and *There Goes the Neighborhood* (1981) became the norm. Walsh's sound and humor reached a synthesis in his 1978 hit "Life's Been Good," a sly look at the rock star excesses in which he famously indulged. By this time, Walsh had joined the Eagles and the entire band guested on the album featuring "Life's Been Good," *But Seriously Folks . . .* (1978), giving the effort a decidedly more Southern California feel.

Walsh's solo career took a backseat to his work with the Eagles, but resumed following the band's breakup in 1981. However, the frequency and quality of Walsh's creative output was hindered by his growing substance abuse, and he produced little of note until he got clean and took part in the Eagles' historic 1994 reunion tour. Once again, the Eagles became his primary focus as he toured and recorded with the group until the death of bandleader Glenn Frey in 2016.

He did make a spirited return to solo recording in 2012, releasing *Analog Man*, the title cut of which finds Walsh casting himself as a champion of old-school recording techniques in a new digital age. In promotional interviews Walsh mused about possibly running for Congress; however, he has yet to act on any political ambitions.

Suggested Albums: So What (1975); *But, Seriously Folks . . .* (1978); *Analog Man* (2012)

WAR

War grew out of several bands on Los Angeles's club circuit, starting with the Compton rhythm and blues act the Creators, which debuted in 1962. As the lineup grew, they began to incorporate Latin influences overheard from neighboring communities. By 1968 they were called Nightshift and boasted a full horn section. While backing LA Rams defensive end and aspiring singer Deacon Jones at a nightclub, manager Jerry Goldstein discovered Nightshift. Goldstein suggested they become the backup band for expatriate Englishman Eric Burdon, formerly vocalist for the Animals, and Burdon's accompanist, Danish harmonica player Lee Oskar. They became known as Eric Burdon and War.

Their lone hit under that name, "Spill the Wine" from *Eric Burdon Declares War* (1970), was a mostly spoken word recollection of a boozy libidinous fever dream set to a funky backdrop. Burdon recorded a second LP with them, *The Black-Man's Burdon* (1970), before he left in the midst of a European tour. With his uniquely melodic harmonica playing, Oskar remained in the band, which became simply War.

Establishing an identity apart from Burdon didn't take long. *War* (1971) solidified their rock fan base while making inroads in black radio. Singles from *All Day Music* (1971), including the serene title track and the despairing "Slippin' into Darkness," brought them FM airplay and AM chart success.

War's definitive album, *The World Is a Ghetto* (1972), isn't quite as bleak as the title portends, but acts as a kind of multicultural state of the union address a year after the dire *There's a Riot Goin' On* by the similarly genre- and race-spanning Sly and the Family Stone. Even in *Ghetto's* pessimistic yet soaring title song, there's a sense of hopefulness Sly Stone lacked after the 1960s ended. *Ghetto's* biggest hit, "Cisco Kid," was a curiously downbeat novelty song about the Mexican movie-radio drama-television hero. The nearly quarter-hour "City, Country City" became a dance floor favorite in New York City's nascent disco scene and continues to resonate in dance clubs. *Ghetto* topped *Billboard's* pop and rhythm and blues album charts, becoming the trade magazine's best seller for 1973.

War maintained their cachet on rhythm and blues radio for the rest of the decade while intermittently gaining the ears of rock programming directors. The charmingly clunky reggae of the title track of *Why Can't We Be Friends* (1975) received much play, as did the funky "Low Rider." The apotheosis of War's penchant for good-time music, "Summer," was their biggest hit and lone new track from their 1976 greatest hits compilation. They also tried their hands at jazz with *Platinum Jazz* (1976). As the decade closed, War moved into more aggressive funk comparable to Cameo and the Bar-Kays. During the 1980s their new music was heard primarily on black radio.

By the dawn of the 1990s, recordings from War's classic period in the 1970s became a trove for hip-hop producers and DJs seeking samples to rap over. Legal and personal disputes caused a rift, leading to a lineup of War that continued under Goldstein's management with other members breaking away to form Lowrider. At their best, War produced music that spoke of a unity that reflected their diverse influences. In the current commercial musical environment of narrowcasting, it's doubtful that such barrier-breaking generosity could achieve similar success.

Suggested Albums: War (1971); *All Day Music* (1971); *The World Is a Ghetto* (1972); *Why Can't We Be Friends* (1975)

WHO

One of the last British Invasion bands to achieve stardom in the United States, the Who became one of the most significant and influential groups to emerge from the era. From their debut in 1966 to their last album as a full band in 1982, the Who set standards for excellence and creativity, leaving behind a legacy of classic albums and songs. Few bands of any era can match the Who in terms of scope and ambition. Never a group to do things in half measures, the Who aimed high and did everything in a big way. Each album was intended to push music forward and seemed like a cultural landmark. One of rock's greatest live acts, their concerts were pure spectacle, among rock's loudest with almost unmatched showmanship. Things were no different offstage, as the band's members fought epic battles with each other and lived the rock star life to the hilt. The Who are simply one of the most admired, emulated, talked about, and quoted bands in the history of rock music.

Undoubtedly some of this is due to the fact that the band consisted of four strong, exceptionally talented individuals. It can be argued that the Who had the greatest collection of talent of any rock band, as each member ranked at the top of some aspect of their profession, whether as singers, songwriters, or musicians. The band was led by the creative genius of guitarist Pete Townshend, a songwriter of immense vision and intense focus. As a primarily rhythm guitar player he was often the band's actual timekeeper. Singer Roger Daltrey had one of rock's greatest set of pipes, a voice of majestic power capable of exhibiting raw intensity and tender sensitivity, street credibility and spiritual epiphany. Bassist John Entwistle filled the role usually occupied by lead guitarists in rock bands; his bass lines provided melodic riffing over Townshend's slashing rhythm guitar. Keith Moon was one of the most powerful and inventive rock drummers, a larger than life figure who has been called a one-man orchestra who used the drums as a lead instrument. Unique among drummers, Moon tracked the vocals and often punctuated each line with an accented beat. This collection of alpha talent should have resulted in chaos, but the band managed to come together to form a powerful whole.

Townshend, Daltrey, and Entwistle met in the early 1960s while attending grammar school in a London suburb. Seeking to escape the grind of working-class life, Daltrey set his sights on a career in music and enlisted Entwistle and Townshend to join him in the Detours, a band based around Daltrey's passion for rhythm and blues. With the street-tough Daltrey in charge, the band began playing gigs. They changed their name to the Who when they discovered another band called the Detours. Moon was signed on as drummer after he broke a bass drum pedal during an audition. Their lineup was set. After changing their name to the Who, the band switched again to become the High Numbers, flopping with their first single, "I'm

The Who rose from Britain's mod youth subculture to become one of the world's most recognized and respected rock bands. Guitarist Pete Townshend, vocalist Roger Daltrey, and drummer Keith Moon are seen here in a 1964 performance at London's famed Marquee Club. (Pictorial Press Ltd/Alamy Stock Photo)

the Face." With a steady following as regulars playing up-tempo rhythm and blues at London's Marquee Club, the band's manager Kit Lambert hustled a record deal for them under the name the Who. Their debut single released under that name, "I Can't Explain" (1965), was written by Townshend as a Kinks knock-off and attracted attention for an almost angry energy that captured the pent-up frustrations of British youth.

By now Townshend had emerged as the band's principal songwriter, and with a few notable exceptions would provide the band's original material. If "I Can't Explain" spoke to adolescent rage, the band's next single, "My Generation" (1965), is almost certainly rock's greatest youth anthem. A noisy, aggressive speeded-up blues, Townshend's song skewers his elders, proclaiming the generation gap and rejecting their refusal to get out of the way. Daltrey's stuttering vocal bespoke almost incoherent rage, and he all but spit out the line that would define and haunt Townshend for the rest of his career: "hope I die before I get old." Entwistle's memorable bass solo was countered with some bluesy fills by Townshend before the song explodes in a chaotic conclusion that could provide a soundtrack for the collapse of civilization. "My Generation" was a cultural milestone, a statement of youthful rebellion that remains relevant today.

As one might expect, the band chose the single as the focal point of their debut album, *My Generation* (1965), but it was hardly the only epochal moment on the record. At Lambert's suggestion, the band had become immersed in the mod sub-culture, adopting the smart dress and trendy haircuts popular in mod circles. While not mods themselves, the band became the voice of the movement, as Townshend wrote of the fears, frustrations, and joys of youth with empathy and insight. "The Kids Are Alright" is a true mod anthem whose chiming guitars and bright melody celebrated the peer spirit of the mods. The album stands with the Violent Femmes' 1983 debut as a poignant portrayal of adolescent experiences and impulses, as Townshend wrote perceptively of what it meant to be young in a time and place of rapid change.

The Who followed with a string of singles, including the exuberant "Anyway, Anyhow, Anywhere," the steamrolling identity crisis of "Substitute," and the gender-bending "I'm a Boy." As much as anything, this period reflected Townshend's fascination with pop art, developed during his days as an art school student. The band's look included cultural symbols such as Townshend's Union Jack sports jacket and Moon's gunnery target T-shirt; their music's sharp cultural awareness elevated the band's work to that of performance pop art. The Who's live shows became almost anarchic with a frenzied energy few bands could match, and were viewed by Townshend as an extension of the music's youthful fury. While in art school, Townshend had become intrigued with auto-destructive art, and at his urging the band climaxed their live sets by destroying their gear onstage. They introduced the concept to America on *The Smothers Brothers Comedy Hour* television show and at the band's breakout performance at the Monterey Pop Festival (1967).

Their concert finales almost rivaled the group's offstage conduct, as their interpersonal dynamic was always turbulent. The street tough Daltrey was almost sacked from the band for his violent behavior, and Moon and Entwistle actually quit for a short time after Townshend used his guitar to assault Moon. The Who would always patch things up, though, and amazingly the band's musical chemistry was never affected.

After a classic set of singles, the band's next album was a major step forward. *A Quick One* (1966) showed Townshend's increasing prowess as a songwriter, contributing the teen breakup classic "So Sad About Us" and a nine-minute mini rock opera, "A Quick One, While He's Away." This time Entwistle got in on the act, contributing the macabre humor of "Boris the Spider." The album's fine pop sensibility was abundant throughout. On its heels came their most ambitious work to date, the concept album *The Who Sell Out* (1967). Based around the idea that the album was a radio show replete with spoof commercials, *The Who Sell Out* was pop art genius featuring a new level of songwriting sophistication, especially on the powerfully transcendent single "I Can See for Miles." *The Magic Bus* (1968) was a collection of previously released songs and featured the clever depiction of adolescent lust, "Pictures of Lily."

Townshend's vision was expanding with each album as he imagined greater possibilities for rock as an art form. His most ambitious work was the rock opera *Tommy* (1969). The double album, which may have been based on parts of

Townshend's troubled childhood, loosely tells the story of a deaf, dumb, and blind boy who achieves a mystical ability to play championship pinball and eventually attains guru status, only to suffer rejection at the hands of his followers. *Tommy* was not the first rock opera, but it was the most important, as it came from a hugely popular group with the accessibility to bring the idea to the mainstream. It didn't hurt that the songs worked well apart from the album's concept. "Pinball Wizard," "I'm Free," "Amazing Journey" and "We're Not Gonna Take It/See Me Feel Me" attained classic status even among those who were unaware of the record's storyline. A slew of bands followed in the Who's footsteps to release ambitious concept albums of their own.

Townshend continued to ramp up expectations, and his ambition began to approach delusions of grandeur for his next project, *Lifehouse*. The projected rock opera featured a convoluted plot based around a futuristic world where rock music had the kinetic power to unify and enlighten the human race. The concept proved mystifying to all but Townshend, and his plans for a multimedia live show and film based on the opera collapsed.

Townshend salvaged pieces of the concept and began working obsessively on a new Who album. He spoke often of sensing the ideal Platonic form of his music. Working with producer Glyn Johns, Townshend became a studio perfectionist in search of that sound, spending countless hours working on synthesizer tape loops in an effort to reach the ideal. Townshend incorporated elements of *Lifehouse* along with the teachings of the Indian spiritual leader Meher Baba in the new material. The final result was the monumental album *Who's Next* (1971), one of the great albums of the 1970s. Framing the sprawling grandeur of "Baba O'Riley" and the defiant disillusionment of "Won't Get Fooled Again" are Townshend's complex keyboard loops. The antisocial sentiments of "Behind Blue Eyes" are a thumb in the eye of the peace and love hippies, and the lament of "The Song Is Over" says goodbye to that movement's dreams. *Who's Next* is littered with fallout from the 1960s. The album's influence went beyond mere music, as lines like "it's only teenage wasteland" and "meet the new boss, same as the old boss" became cultural catchphrases. Portions of *Lifehouse* also found their way onto Townshend's fine solo album *Who Came First* (1972).

The Who now stood astride the pinnacle of the rock world. Their live shows had become the stuff of legend and they were the epitome of rock star royalty. Offstage life told a different story, as Daltrey and Townshend clashed over the band's direction. Moon's behavior was becoming increasingly unpredictable. He became "Moon the Loon," an over-the-top madcap whose alcohol-fueled antics included smashing up hotel rooms and driving sports cars into swimming pools. Amidst these tensions, the band released what Townshend hoped would be his grandest achievement, the double album rock opera *Quadrophenia* (1973). Set against the backdrop of the mod versus rockers conflict of mid-1960s London, the album sought to tell the story of a troubled young man with multiple personalities based on each member of the Who. While the album contains some great songs, such as the angry rocker "The Real Me" and the redemptive finale "Love Reign O'er Me," overall *Quadrophenia* fell far short of expectations. Unlike *Tommy*, few of the songs stood on their own apart from the hard-to-follow story. The band's playing and Daltrey's singing overreached operatic grandeur and crossed the line into bombast. Townshend was becoming lost in the maze of his own ambition and was never able to translate his concept for the album into a live setting.

Another misstep was the unruly mess that was the film version of *Tommy* (1975). Directed by Ken Russell and starring Daltrey in the title role, the film was preposterous and pretentious, highlighted only by stellar cameos by Eric Clapton and Tina Turner. Also disappointing, at least by the Who's standards, was their next album, *The Who by Numbers* (1975). While it was refreshing to hear the band kick up its heels and have fun with the bluegrass polka of "Squeeze Box," for the most part the album seemed uncertain and dispirited, and Daltrey seemed to struggle with interpreting Townshend's increasingly personal musical statements.

By *Who Are You* (1978) punk had arrived and challenged the continuing relevance of superstar bands from the 1960s. Townshend's ambivalent response was reflected in the keyboard-dominated title track and the aspirational "Music Must Change." He seemed both thrilled and threatened by the rebelliousness of punk, as well as the movement's simultaneous embrace and rejection of the Who. Moon's personal excesses were spinning out of control, and disaster struck when Moon died of a drug overdose in September 1978. Faced with the crisis of replacing an irreplaceable component, the band chose to carry on, reaching back to its mod days to hire former Small Faces drummer Kenney Jones. Many fans felt it was wrong to continue without Moon, but others took some consolation in the fact that his successor at least was historically compatible with the band.

In retrospect, it would have been better had the Who done as Led Zeppelin would do when their famous drummer died and simply called it a day. Instead, they soldiered on, touring, producing an interesting film version of *Quadrophenia* (1979), and releasing two uninspired albums, *Face Dances* (1981) and *It's Hard* (1982). By continuing past their prime, the Who made it acceptable for other rock groups to ride the nostalgia bandwagon and tour endlessly, regardless of relevance or even if any of the original members remained.

The Who broke up in 1982, and Townshend continued an already established and often excellent solo career, while Daltrey and Entwistle enjoyed mixed success in varied solo projects. The band reunited as a touring entity in 1989. Daltrey and Townshend continued as the Who after Entwistle's death in 2002. As a duo, the Who released a strong concept album, *Endless Wire* (2006), and performed to mixed reviews at the 2010 Super Bowl. One of the most acclaimed groups in rock history, the Who have been inducted into the Rock and Roll Hall of Fame.

Suggested Albums: My Generation (1965); *A Quick One* (1966); *The Who Sell Out* (1967); *The Magic Bus* (1968); *Tommy* (1969); *Who's Next* (1971); *Quadrophenia* (1973); *The Who By Numbers* (1975); *Who Are You* (1978); *Endless Wire* (2006)

See also: Entwistle, John; Rock Opera

WINTER, JOHNNY (1944–2014)

The Texas-born guitarist braved the color barrier as a teenager by visiting black blues clubs and learning the music from close up in a time and place where segregation remained the rule. An albino, his presence at first startled the musicians whose mentoring he sought, but all came to value his sincerity and musicianship. Winter came from a musical family; his brother Edgar, also born with albinism, played in Johnny's band early on but achieved success with his own rock band, the Edgar Winter Group. Despite a detour into rock in the early 1970s, Johnny Winter was firmly invested in the blues.

Winter gained attention during a performance with Mike Bloomfield and Al Kooper at New York City's Fillmore East Ballroom (1968). His self-titled debut album (1969) included brother Edgar on keyboards along with blues legends Willie Dixon on bass and Big Walter Horton on harmonica. Winter played at Woodstock (1969) and formed a rock band called Johnny Winter And with guitarist Rick Derringer. Derringer's hard rock song "Rock and Roll, Hoochie Koo" from *Johnny Winter And* (1970) received much airplay. He returned to his roots in the late 1970s by producing a series of albums for blues guitarist Muddy Waters, *Hard Again* (1977), *I'm Ready* (1978), *Muddy "Mississippi" Waters Live* (1979), and *King Bee* (1981). During that period Winter also recorded his own album, *Nothin' But the Blues* (1977), backed by Waters's band.

In his later years, Winter toured the blues circuit, achieved respectable sales with live albums, and recorded instructional guitar DVDs. He was found dead in his hotel room while on tour in 2014. The cause of death was said to be complications of emphysema and pneumonia.

Suggested Albums: Johnny Winter (1969); *Nothin' But the Blues* (1977)

WOOD, ROY (1946–)

Roy Wood was the primary creative force behind the Move and the co-founder of Electric Light Orchestra. In 1969 he withdrew to Abbey Road Studio to record an entirely solo album, performing all instruments and singing all vocal parts. The result, *Boulders*, went unreleased until 1973. It was a superbly eccentric offering, opening with "Songs of Praise," which caught the joyful brotherhood of gospel music and was entered by the New Seekers in the 1972 Eurovision Song Contest. "Wake Up" could have been one of Paul McCartney's best ballads. On "Rock Down Low," he indulged his interest in reinventing early rock and roll with a heavier sound for the 1970s. One of the greatest truly solo albums ever recorded, Wood played guitars, drums, and bass and made imaginative use of cello, saxophone, sitar, recorder, and "watersplash bucket."

Wood's band Wizzard continued his reinvention of early rock and roll with cellists and a horn section, emulating Phil Spector's "Wall of Sound" production values on *Wizzard Brew* (1973) and *Introducing Eddy and the Falcons* (1974). With his penchant for face makeup and costumes, Wizzard became associated with the glitter rock movement and sold well in the United Kingdom but never found a U.S.

audience. Under his own name, Wood released *Mustard* (1975), featuring vocals by Phil Everly and Renaissance's Annie Haslam, but never regained the success he had known with the Move and Wizzard. He enjoyed a sporadic career as a producer and continues to perform.

Suggested Albums: Boulders (1973); Wizzard: *Wizzard Brew* (1973); *Introducing Eddy and the Falcons* (1974)

YAMASH'TA, STOMU (1947–)

Born Tsutomu Yamashita, Stomu Yamash'ta studied music at Kyoto University and the Juilliard and Berklee music schools. The virtuoso percussionist performed with symphony orchestras and could have concentrated on a career in classical music, but had a restless creative imagination in addition to talent. Yamash'ta organized and composed music for his Red Buddha Theatre company, which performed to good notices in France and Great Britain (1972–1973). He composed film scores, notably for Nicolas Roeg's *The Man Who Fell to Earth* (1976).

He solidified the interest of progressive rock fans with his band Stomu Yamash'ta's East Wind (1973–1974). The international ensemble included his classically trained wife, Hisako, on violin; Soft Machine's Hugh Hopper on bass; guitarist Gary Boye, formerly of Brian Auger's Trinity; and Brian Gascoigne, a friend from Berklee, on keyboards. Yamash'ta played percussion with an agile hand but never allowed pyrotechnics to outshine the compositions. The keyboard-driven music eschewed the classical rock clichés of Keith Emerson without emulating the jazz-fusion of Soft Machine or East of Eden. The softer guitar-violin passages exuded Zen-like calm.

East Wind set the stage for his supergroup, Stomu Yamash'ta's Go, featuring himself on synthesizer and percussion, Traffic's Steve Winwood on keyboards, Santana's Michael Shrieve on drums, German electronics wizard Klaus Schulze, fusion guitarist Al Di Meola, and Traffic's Rosko Gee on bass. After a trio of Go albums (1976, 1977), Yamash'ta returned home from his long American-European sojourn and checked in briefly at a Buddhist monastery. In the 1980s he experimented with blending synthesizers with orchestras. He remains active in the 21st century.

Suggested Albums: Stomu Yamash'ta: *Red Buddha* (1971); *Raindogs* (1975); Stomu Yamash'ta's Red Buddha Theatre: *The Soundtrack from The Man from the East* (1973); Stomu Yamash'ta Come to the Edge: *Floating Music* (1972); Stomu Yamash'ta's East Wind: *Freedom Is Frightening* (1973); *One by One* (1974); Stomu Yamash'ta's Go: *Go* (1976); *Go Live from Paris* (1976); *Go Too* (1977)

YARDBIRDS

The Yardbirds were extraordinary for including Britain's three most significant rock guitarists of the 1960s in their lineup: Eric Clapton, Jeff Beck, and Jimmy Page. A forum for many of the era's innovations, including the use of feedback and fuzz tone, the Yardbirds also spearheaded the progress of rock music and inspired garage bands in faraway America to push toward ecstasy. In the end, the Yardbirds gave birth to one of the most important bands of the 1970s, Led Zeppelin.

The Yardbirds were a product of London's burgeoning early 1960s blues subculture. Originally called the Metropolis Blues Quartet, they became the Yardbirds in 1963 after Charlie Parker's nickname, Yardbird. By the middle of that year the band's lineup stabilized around Clapton on lead guitar, Chris Dreja on rhythm guitar, Paul Samwell-Smith on bass, Jim McCarty on drums, and Keith Relf on vocals and harmonica. With the addition of Clapton, they began to put their signature on a repertoire of Howlin' Wolf, John Lee Hooker, and Bo Diddley through extended guitar solos. Calling their jams "rave ups," they broke tempo and started slowly, rising toward supersonic climaxes, only to fall away and repeat the ascent to ecstasy. The three-minute songs they learned from American blues records could be stretched toward infinity.

The band's manager, Giorgio Gomelsky, arranged for the Yardbirds to become the backup band for Sonny Boy Williamson, an African American bluesman on tour in the United Kingdom. It proved a chastening experience, as Williamson was openly disdainful of white British lads playing the blues. Clapton and company were forced to sharpen their sensibility and skills. Indeed, the band still sounded tentative on the live album they recorded at London's Crawdaddy Club, released after they achieved stardom as *Sonny Boy Williamson and the Yardbirds* (1965).

They played with greater authority on their first release, *Five Live Yardbirds* (1964), a set of blues and rhythm and blues covers recorded at London's Marquee Club. With Gomelsky encouraging the band to record singles that could capitalize on the popularity of British bands in the wake of the Beatles, Clapton grew impatient, feeling his credibility as a blues player would be compromised. The last straw was "For Your Love," the hit written by a young professional songwriter who later co-founded 10cc, Graham Gouldman. With bongos and an eerie harpsichord played by session keyboardist Brian Auger backing Relf's mournful vocals, "For Your Love" had nothing to do with the blues. Clapton left for John Mayall's Bluesbreakers and was replaced by the more open-minded Beck.

The U.S.-only album *For Your Love* (1965) included a mix of singles from Clapton's tenure as well as three new tracks recorded with Beck. Although also cobbled together from odds and ends, bits of Clapton and pieces of Beck, *Having a Rave Up with the Yardbirds* (1965) was a superb album that achieved a powerful totality. Gouldman contributed two more songs, the raga-influenced "Heart Full of Soul" and the minor-key Middle Eastern–inspired "Evil Hearted You." Recorded before the Beatles' sitar-filled "Norwegian Wood," "Heart Full of Soul" featured Beck bending the higher notes on his guitar and using a distortion device to achieve an Indian-like tone. "You're a Better Man Than I" was folk-rock but delivered with Beck's distinctive hard edge. The brooding "Still I'm Sad" was built on a droning Gregorian chant. Unlike many progressive rock bands to come, the Yardbirds' sonic adventures remained firmly grounded in hard rock with a pop sensibility. Clapton's contribution to *Having a Rave Up* included an eerie version of

"Smokestack Lightning" praised by its originator, Howlin' Wolf, and an energetic cover of Johnny Burnette's rockabilly number, "The Train Kept A-Rollin'," which introduced the song to the canon of classic rock.

The only Yardbirds album with all original material, *Over Under Sideways Down* (1966), was co-produced by Samwell-Smith and pushed deeper into psychedelic rock. Samwell-Smith left shortly afterward to pursue a career as a producer and was replaced on bass by Jimmy Page. Before long he shared lead guitar duties with Beck. The short-lived lineup was captured in the nightclub scene of Michelangelo Antonioni's film *Blow Up* (1966) performing "Stroll On," a slight reworking of "The Train Kept A-Rollin'." At Antonioni's instruction, Beck emulated the Who's Pete Townshend by smashing his guitar at the performance's climax.

By the end of 1966 Beck left the group, leaving Page as unchallenged lead guitarist. Their final album, *Little Games* (1967), was a hotchpotch of badly conceived pop tunes recorded under producer Mickie Most and a few songs containing elements that would blossom in Page's next venture. With the band disintegrating, Page was given permission to fulfill contractual obligations by touring Scandinavia under the name the New Yardbirds. For the tour, Page recruited vocalist Robert Plant, bassist John Paul Jones, and drummer John Bonham. They soon reinvented themselves as Led Zeppelin.

Relf and McCarty formed the progressive rock band Renaissance but left the group in other hands after two albums (1969, 1971). Relf continued as a producer and formed a hard rock recording act, Armageddon, before dying in an electrical accident in 1976. McCarty, Dreja, and Samwell-Smith recorded two albums together under the name Box of Frogs (1984, 1986). In the 21st century Dreja and McCarty began using the Yardbirds' name for recording and touring. The Yardbirds have been inducted into the Rock and Roll Hall of Fame.

Suggested Albums: Five Live Yardbirds (1964); *For Your Love* (1965); *Sonny Boy Williamson and the Yardbirds* (1965); *Having a Rave Up with the Yardbirds* (1965); *Over Under Sideways Down* (aka *Yardbirds*, aka *Roger the Engineer*) (1966)

See also: Beck, Jeff; Clapton, Eric; Led Zeppelin; Renaissance

YES

Yes was formed in 1968 by veteran British musicians with a desire to scale the heights of progressive rock. The fragile, high-voiced Jon Anderson and the wiry kineticism of bassist Chris Squire have been the most consistent features in the band's continually morphing membership. Despite several digressions, Yes is remembered for suite-like compositions and busy displays of instrumental virtuosity.

Their ascent on American FM radio began with *The Yes Album* (1971), whose songwriting was fortified by the arrival of guitarist Steve Howe, formerly of Tomorrow. Receiving much airplay was "Your Move/I've Seen All Good People," written by Anderson and Squire but given aural interest through Howe's employment of an oud-like Portuguese guitar and a restrained organ part by the band's other new member, ex-Strawbs keyboardist Rick Wakeman. *Fragile* (1971) saw their popularity increase with "Roundabout," which made the U.S. Top 20 singles chart in an edited version. They followed with the ambitious eclecticism and lengthy tracks of *Close to the Edge* (1972) and *Tales from Topographic Oceans* (1973). The Roger Dean fantasy art on the album covers was integral to their aesthetic. Wakeman left the band for a solo career, but the course continued with his replacement, Patrick Moraz, on *Relayer* (1974).

As if responding to the punk rock's assertion of brevity's virtue, *Going for the One* (1977) and *Tormato* (1978) featured short songs, alienating many old fans without gaining many new ones. Anderson briefly left the band, leaving it in the hands of Trevor Horn from the new wave act the Buggles on *Drama* (1980). Anderson returned for *90125* (1983), which introduced them to a younger audience of mainstream rock fans. Yes continued to tour and record with shifting lineups anchored by Squire into the 21st century. Their most recent release, *Heaven & Earth* (2014), featured Squire, Howe, vocalist Jon Davison, and an album cover by Dean.

Suggested Albums: The Yes Album (1971); *Fragile* (1971)

YOUNG, NEIL (1945–)

Neil Young has been a cantankerous individualist throughout his lifelong vocation as a songwriter and musician. Determined to break every mold, including those he fashioned for himself, Young has always pushed back against expectations from fans as well as record labels. In 1982 Geffen Records sued him for making music "unrepresentative" of himself after releasing an electronic pop album, *Trans* (1982). He responded by handing the label another "unrepresentative" album, a collection of rockabilly covers, *Everybody's Rockin'* (1983). Young would not be cowed.

During a peripatetic childhood in Canada, Young was weaned on radio stations happily innocent of formats and was exposed to country, early rock and roll, and rhythm and blues. In the early 1960s he led an instrumental band, the Squires, modeled after Britain's the Shadows. He came into his own during the mid-1960s in Toronto's folk-blues revival scene but joined rhythm and blues singer Rick James's group, the Mynah Birds. When James was arrested for being AWOL from the U.S. Army Reserves, Young left with bassist Bruce Palmer for Los Angeles, where he found fame with the seminal band Buffalo Springfield. After Buffalo Springfield's demise in 1968, he began his long odyssey as a soloist as well as his sporadic collaboration with Crosby, Stills & Nash, where he was always an outlier.

Licensed by Bob Dylan's roughly sanded vocals, Young sang in a voice of personal credibility so emotionally exposed as to be off-putting to many hearers. While in Buffalo Springfield, his record label insisted on handing lead vocals on several of his songs to other band members. Shaky, plaintive, even whiny at times, Young's fragile voice is a fascinating contrast to the aggression of his guitar playing. Working with a limited palette from the blues pentatonic scale, although seldom emulating blues styles of playing, Young has been called the world's best bad guitarist. Although his notes often crash together, his playing carries an emotional force often lacked by studied musicians. Distinct from Eric Clapton or Jimi Hendrix, his guitar never wept but cried angrily. When playing electric, he achieved an instantly recognizable thin tone sharpened by distortion pedals to a serrated edge.

Unlike most recording artists with a catalog spread across years and decades, Young displayed neither the evolution characteristic of the Beatles nor the distinct phases of David Bowie. He cannot be accused of the stasis that afflicts many performers after reaching popularity. Young followed three major tracks that wound in and out of his music over time like motifs in a symphony around occasional digressions. The major motifs are acoustic folk, scorching ragged rock, and heartfelt country. The digressions include rhythm and blues, industrial noise, techno-pop, and rockabilly.

The peculiar course of Young's artistry makes it difficult to discuss his albums in chronological order. Album releases were delayed because of record label intransigence or because Young lost interest, resulting in a catalog whose release dates do not always follow the order in which the recordings were completed. Complicating matters are individually recorded songs that finally turned up years later outside of their originally intended context. With a few notable exceptions, Young's albums bear little musical coherence with the date of their recording. *Trans* is a time capsule of early 1980s technology; likewise *Landing on Water* (1986) suffers from the oppressive mainstream rock production values of its era. Now and then a lyric pegged a song to a historical moment, such the raging civil rights message of "Southern Man" from *After the Gold Rush* (1970). His music from the 20th century was largely timeless. However, in the aftermath of his response to 9/11, "Let's Roll" (2001), Young has become a more topical songwriter.

Young's formative experience in the folk-blues revival left him forever suspicious of popularity and wary of stardom. After his only number one hit single, the rueful ballad "Heart of Gold" from *Harvest* (1972), Young seemed determined never to visit the pop singles charts again. He followed the bestselling *Harvest* with a career-documentary film and soundtrack album, *Journey Through the Past* (1972), featuring one new song recorded on guitar in a sawmill accompanied by the sound of the mill, and the deliberately rough-hewn concert album *Time Fades Away* (1973). However, Young would periodically reprise the relatively easy-going acoustic music of *Harvest*, notably with *Comes a Time* (1978). Young's protégé on that album, singer Nicolette Larson, enjoyed a Top 10 hit with her recording of a song from *Comes a Time*, the lulling "Lotta Love."

Young's hard rock albums have usually been recorded with his highly proficient garage band, Crazy Horse, initially featuring guitarist Danny Whitten, bassist Billy Talbot, and drummer Ralph Molina. Their first album together, *Everybody Knows This Is Nowhere* (1969), included the fiery rock songs "Cinnamon Girl" and "Down by the River," the former a love song and the latter a song of love ending in murder. Although "Down by the River" can be connected to a centuries-long tradition of murder ballads, the frank admission of homicide, heard regularly on FM radio, was startling to many listeners in the early 1970s and confirmed a suspicion that Young was a creature of darkness.

Whitten was troubled by heroin and other drug addictions and died from an overdose in 1972. Heroin was a theme Young returned to periodically, notably on the stark ballad "The Needle and the Damage Done" from *Harvest* and the album *Tonight's the Night* (1975), a downbeat song cycle steeped in bad drugs and remorse over the ebbing of 1960s idealism. Frank Sampedro replaced Whitten as Crazy Horse's rhythm guitarist.

Country influences can be heard throughout Young's journey, including the sad pedal steel guitar on "Old Man" and "Heart of Gold" from *Harvest*. *Hawks and Doves* (1980) included many original songs written in the country and western mode. During the mid-1980s he formed a country backup band called the International Harvesters and made an album with them, *Old Ways* (1985). The largely acoustic *Prairie Wind* (2005) was recorded in Nashville.

Almost alone among his North American generational music cohort, Young welcomed punk rock in the late 1970s. Characteristic of his penchant for abrupt directional turns, he followed his mellowest album in years, *Comes a Time*, with *Rust Never Sleeps* (1979) and *Live Rust* (1979), which contrasted the rise of punk with the decline of Elvis Presley in a pair of notable songs, the acoustic "My My, Hey Hey (Out of the Blue)" and the electric "Hey Hey, My My (Into the Black)." Young's failed comedy film *Human Highway* (eventually released in 1982) included an appearance by Devo.

No one should have been surprised when he followed the distortion-edged hard rock of *Freedom* (1989), featuring the anthemic "Rockin' in the Free World," and *Ragged Glory* (1990), recorded with Crazy Horse in a barn, with the mellow country of *Harvest Moon* (1992). Young will probably be the only musician to have the pleasure of recording with both James Taylor, whose backing vocals are heard on *Harvest Moon*, and Pearl Jam, his band on the live-in-the-studio *Mirror Ball* (1995). The sloppy grandeur of Young and Crazy Horse, along with the depression of his lyrics and his suspicion of the music industry, were inspirational to a generation of grunge bands, including Nirvana. Influenced by touring with Sonic Youth as his opening act, Young released an album of feedback distortion noise, *Arc* (1991). He also digressed into mellow soul on *Are You Passionate* (2002), backed by Booker T. & the MG's. Young finally found time for a full-blown concept album in *Greendale* (2003), whose story of the murder of a police officer in a small town was a metaphor of social problems.

Young always had an interest in social causes. With Willie Nelson and John Mellencamp, he co-founded the Farm Aid benefits to help keep farms in the hands of families. Occasionally he responded to events, notably his Crosby, Stills, Nash & Young single "Ohio" (1970) in the aftermath of the Kent State shootings. In the 21st century Young focused more than ever on topical issues. *Living with War* (2006) included "Let's Impeach the President," deriding George W. Bush for leading the United States into Iraq. Environmental activism was a theme on *Chrome Dreams II* (2007). *Fork in the Road* (2009) included attacks on the Wall Street bailout at the start of the Great Recession. On *The Monsanto Years* (2015), Young took on agribusiness. He found time to pen a much-admired memoir, *Waging Heavy Peace: A Hippie Dream* (2012). Despite the highly personal nature of his performances, bands as diverse as Oasis, Johnny Cash, Nick Cave, Willie Nelson, Roxy Music, the Pixies, Norah Jones, Matthew Sweet, Radiohead, and Cowboy Junkies have covered his songs. Young has been inducted into the Rock and Roll Hall of Fame.

Suggested Albums: Neil Young (1968); *Everybody Knows This Is Nowhere* (1969); *After the Gold Rush* (1970); *Harvest* (1972); *Time Fades Away* (1973); *On the Beach* (1974); *Tonight's the Night* (1975); *Zuma* (1975); *Long May You Run* (1976); *American Stars 'n Bars* (1977); *Decade* (1977); *Comes a Time* (1978); *Rust Never Sleeps* (1979); *Live Rust* (1979); *Old Ways* (1985); *This Note's for You* (1988); *Freedom* (1989); *Ragged Glory* (1990); *Weld* (1991); *Harvest Moon* (1992); *Unplugged* (1993); *Sleeps with Angels* (1994); *Mirror Ball* (1995); *Year of the Horse* (1996); *Are You Passionate* (2002); *Greendale* (2003); *The Archives Vol. 1 1963–1972* (2008); *Americana* (2012)

See also: Buffalo Springfield; Crosby, Stills, Nash & Young

YOUNGBLOODS

In 1965 Boston folksinger Jesse Colin Young recorded a solo album called *Young Blood*, but the age of folk-rock had dawned, a band was required, and a group called the Youngbloods soon coalesced around him. Young shared the band's lead vocals, guitar, and songwriting with another Massachusetts folksinger, Jerry Corbitt. Many listeners found the warm tones of their voices almost indistinguishable.

The Youngbloods recorded their self-titled debut (1967) under Cream's producer, Felix Pappalardi. Although Corbitt's "Grizzly Bear" recalled the band's roots in the folk-blues revival with its old-time melody and antique references, much of *The Youngbloods* was a gentle pas de deux between folk-rock and psychedelia, best represented on a song written by Quicksilver Messenger Service's Dino Valenti, "Get Together," which distilled the hippie love message into a chorus with lines suitable for a bumper sticker. The song languished until the National Council of Christians and Jews chose it for a 1969 public service television ad in a timely coincidence with the good-time vibrations of Woodstock.

Earth Music (1967) emphasized country rock more than its predecessor, including an austere reading of Tim Hardin's "Reason to Believe," a song later popularized in more dramatic fashion by Rod Stewart. *Elephant Mountain* (1969) contained a remarkable yin and yang in the form of two of their best-known songs, both written by Young, "Darkness, Darkness" and "Sunlight." The former was a cry of depression driven by ominous Appalachian fiddling and needling psychedelic guitar; the latter a gentle bossa nova evoking a relaxed mood of contented love. "Darkness, Darkness" has been given diverse interpretations over the decades by Mott the Hoople, Robert Plant, and the Irish American folk group Solas.

The Youngbloods recorded two live albums (1970, 1971) and a pair of studio albums (1971, 1972) before quitting. All of the Youngbloods' alumni went on to solo performances but only Young was successful, carrying on the lighter side of the band's music as a 1970s singer-songwriter. In recent years he has toured as Jesse Colin Young & Sons, backed by son Cheyenne and godson Ethan Turner.

Suggested Albums: The Youngbloods (1967); *Earth Music* (1967); *Elephant Mountain* (1969)

Z

ZAPPA, FRANK (1940–1993)

Frank Zappa was among the most distinctive, innovative and prolific artists to emerge from rock music. Inspired by blues, early rock and roll, and rhythm and blues as well as 20th-century modernism and jazz from the bebop era and beyond, Zappa distilled his influences into eclectic, complex rock music whose breadth and depth was seldom matched.

Although a superb guitarist who tackled the instrument with the improvisational spark of jazz, Zappa's popularity on the rock circuit was built less on his musicianship than his satirical, often smarmy lyrics spoken-sung in a droll baritone. Like the A student as class clown, Zappa wrapped his piercing intellect in a sheath of street smarts. He loved rock and roll but liked to make fun of it. Zappa refused to take himself too seriously, but was a serious composer. He was a contradiction in terms.

As a high school student during the late 1950s, Zappa played drums in rock and roll bands and arranged avant-garde performances with his school orchestra in Lancaster, California. Largely self-taught, he dropped out of the music program at Chaffey College in Alta Loma after one semester. Zappa's extravagant talent was already apparent in the early 1960s when he wrote songs for doo-wop groups and scores for B movies and produced records for other performers. His first brush with national attention was an appearance on the *Steve Allen Show*, where he played a bicycle with a violin bow and drum sticks for the amusement of a television audience. A record label rejected the demos he recorded during this period with his friend Captain Beefheart, declaring they had "no commercial potential." Having worked briefly in the advertising industry, Zappa was acutely aware of the demands of commercialism; America's increasingly market-driven society would be the butt of his fierce satire.

By 1966 the world was almost ready for a rock artist who drew equally from Howlin' Wolf and Edgar Varèse. Zappa's band the Mothers was signed to Verve, a prestigious jazz label transitioning to rock. The company insisted on changing the band's name to the Mothers of Invention to avoid any profane connotations. Zappa accepted the demand with good humor. After all, Verve allowed him to release his debut, *Freak Out!* (1966) in a format normally reserved for classical music, a two-LP set. The only previous double-LP by a rock artist was Bob Dylan's *Blonde on Blonde*.

The multitude of Zappa's ideas could not be contained on a single 12-inch disc. *Freak Out!* was psychedelically tinged and obviously marketed toward the nascent hippie movement, yet Zappa was a surly fellow traveler with the 1960s counterculture. He despised the drug culture, was a relentless disciplinarian, and fired any band member caught using illicit drugs.

With a beachhead in the recording industry, Zappa gained access to the rock touring circuit and FM rock radio. His music stood out for the smirking comedy of songs such as "Dirty Love" and "Don't Eat the Yellow Snow" and for quirky chord changes that sometimes suggested a thoroughly updated rendition of Carl Stalling's scores for 1940s Warner Brothers cartoons. With *Freak Out!* Zappa commenced a voluminous recording career spanning the remaining three decades of his life. But although several of his songs became staples on FM radio in the 1970s, much of his music mystified a rock audience unaccustomed to orchestral themes and electronic noise indebted to Igor Stravinsky and John Cage, not Chuck Berry or Elvis Presley. He was openly disdainful of many of the era's countercultural shibboleths. His album with the Mothers of Invention, *We're Only in It for the Money* (1968), spoofed the Beatles' *Sgt. Pepper's Lonely Hearts Club Band*. His FM hit "Cosmic Debris" poked fun at phony Aquarian mysticism while "Montana" satirized the counterculture's back to the land romanticism.

Like George Martin, Brian Wilson, and other leading producers of the 1960s, Zappa was fascinated by the burgeoning technology of sound recording and the potential to use the recording studio itself as a set of instruments. Tape editing became a compositional tool. He was among the era's rock stars to set up his own boutique labels. Distributed by Warner Brothers, Bizarre Records and Straight Records nurtured the careers of Captain Beefheart and Alice Cooper.

Zappa recorded under his own name as well as the Mothers of Invention moniker. The roster of talent to emerge from the Mothers' many lineups was impressive and included jazz keyboardists George Duke and Ian Underwood, jazz violinist Jean-Luc Ponty, rock drummer Aynsley Dunbar, Flo & Eddie from the Turtles, and guitarist Lowell George who went on to form Little Feat. Some of his orchestras numbered as many as 20 players. He found time to collaborate with Zubin Mehta; some of the resulting music was used in Zappa's notorious film about a touring rock band run amok, *200 Motels* (1971).

After being embroiled in lawsuits with his record labels, he established Zappa Records in 1979. He debuted with the bestselling album of his career, *Sheik Yerbouti*, a double-LP that included a modestly successful antidisco single, "Dancin' Fool," and "Jewish Princess," which drew complaints from the Anti-Defamation League. The year 1979 also saw the release of a rock opera, *Joe's Garage*, about a dystopian society where music was outlawed. In 1981 Zappa launched a new label, Barking Pumpkin Records, and released *Tinsel Town Rebellion* and a host of guitar instrumental albums, works composed for the electronic Synclavier, and an album of orchestral music conducted by one of his heroes, French atonal composer Pierre Boulez. One of his several albums from 1982, *Ship Arriving Too Late to Save a Drowning Witch*, included his bestselling single, "Valley Girl," a spoof of contemporary teenage culture featuring the pointedly vapid voice of his daughter,

Moon Unit. In 1987 his album *Jazz from Hell* won the Grammy Award for Best Instrumental Rock Album.

After being diagnosed with inoperable prostate cancer in 1990, Zappa continued recording. He was one of four composers chosen in 1992 for the prestigious Frankfurt Festival and was pleased to be honored alongside John Cage, Karlheinz Stockhausen, and Alexander Knaifel. It was his final performance. Zappa died at home in 1993, surrounded by his wife of many years, Adelaide Gail Sloatman, and their four children.

Suggested Albums: Freak Out! (1966); *We're Only in It for the Money* (1968); *Cruising with Ruben & the Jets* (1968); *Hot Rats* (1969); *Weasels Ripped My Flesh* (1970); *Burnt Weeny Sandwich* (1970); *Chunga's Revenge* (1970); *Over-Nite Sensation* (1973); *Apostrophe* (1974); *One Size Fits All* (1975); *Bongo Fury* (1975); *Zoot Allures* (1976); *Studio Tan* (1978); *Sheik Yerbouti* (1979); *Joe's Garage Act 1* (1979); *Boulez Conducts Zappa: The Perfect Stranger* (1984)

ZEVON, WARREN (1947–2003)

Warren Zevon emerged as one of rock's most distinctive songwriters after the end of the classic rock era, but his roots were firmly in the period. Leaving Los Angeles as a teenager for New York's folk music scene, Zevon found work as a session musician and songwriter, penning tunes for the Turtles and contributing "He Quit Me" to the soundtrack of *Midnight Cowboy* (1969). When his debut album, *Wanted Dead or Alive* (1969), failed to find an audience, Zevon went to work as keyboardist for the Everly Brothers. Afterward he became an expatriate, playing piano for his keep in a Madrid bar.

The experience inspired many of his best songs. Zevon often sounded like the witty piano man entertaining from the corner of a bar but holding the center of attention; one can easily imagine a tipsy crowd howling along with "Werewolves of London." In later years he embraced a similar format, touring smaller halls as a solo pianist.

In 1975 Zevon came home to Los Angeles and fell in with the Southern California rock crowd. Although Jackson Browne produced his signature albums, *Warren Zevon* (1976) and *Excitable Boy* (1978), he sounded like none of his Los Angeles contemporaries. Lacking their maudlin self-absorption, Zevon was too rollicking and sharp-witted to be confused with the laid-back ethos of Browne and his ilk. Already a fully developed artist, his more worldly sensibility was reflected in songs about mercenaries ("Roland the Headless Thompson Gunner"), criminal expatriates ("Lawyers, Guns and Money"), and heroin addiction ("Carmelita"). Linda Ronstadt helped introduce him to a wide audience through her recordings of Zevon songs such as "Poor Poor Pitiful Me" and "Mohammed's Radio."

Zevon was a distinct presence throughout the 1980s, operating somewhere between mainstream rock and the nascent alternative scene. He co-wrote "Jeannie Needs a Shooter" with Bruce Springsteen, recorded with members of R.E.M. as the Hindu Love Gods, and employed George Clinton, Flea, and Bob Dylan in the studio. Zevon wrestled with alcoholism and other addictions throughout his career. He died of cancer in 2003.

Suggested Albums: Warren Zevon (1976); *Excitable Boy* (1978); *Bad Luck Streak in Dancing School* (1980); *The Envoy* (1982); *Sentimental Hygiene* (1987)

ZOMBIES

The Zombies held a unique place among British Invasion groups. Unlike the Beatles or the Rolling Stones, their characteristic recordings owed relatively little to early rock and roll, blues, or R&B, but were indebted instead to the cool jazz and soul jazz of the 1950s and early 1960s. The Zombies achieved an organic marriage of rock with jazz that played out in some of the most unique popular recordings of the 1960s.

Their debut single, "She's Not There" (1964), was unlike anything on radio and set a high standard for the band commercially (it reached number two in the United States) and aesthetically. Written by keyboardist Rod Argent, "She's Not There" was a haunting two-and-a-half minutes of minor chords whose obsessive lyric of lost love was delivered by Colin Bluntstone with the voice of a frightened ghost. Argent's short solo on electric piano suggested Dave Brubeck on amphetamines, and Bluntstone's gulps for air signified the terror of loss. They followed up with "Tell Her No," a strangely ethereal song of romantic unease. The unusual chord progressions mirrored the contemporary songwriting of Burt Bacharach, but in a rock vein. The Zombies' first album included a lovely rendition of George Gershwin's "Summertime" that would not have embarrassed an accomplished jazz combo.

Frustrated by their dealings with the music industry, the Zombies opted to break up in 1967 after recording a song cycle that would be regarded as one of the great albums of the classic rock era, *Odyssey and Oracle*. When posthumously released a year later, the album yielded a number one hit single, "Time of the Season," whose moody melody and syncopation worked in counterpoint to the sunny lyric. The Zombies could not be induced to regroup and capitalize on the record's success, but *Odyssey and Oracle* remained a touchstone for musical intelligence and a successful realization of rock's high art ambition. Unlike many concept albums, pretense was kept in check by the band's command of succinct songwriting, which invoked emotional states of being, not grand narratives. *Odyssey and Oracle* painted aural watercolors in autumnal baroque and psychedelic hues, and featured vocal arrangements inspired by the Beach Boys' masterpiece, *Pet Sounds*.

After the Zombies, the group's keyboardist enjoyed a measure of success with his eponymous band, Argent. Bluntstone's early solo career was backed by Argent and continued the arc of the Zombies' creative development, notably on his debut album, *One Year* (1971). Bassist Chris White worked with Argent as a songwriter and producer and remained in the music business, helping discover Dire Straits in the late 1970s. Guitarist Paul Atkinson and drummer Hugh Grundy also worked for record labels searching for new talent. In the 21st century Argent and Bluntstone led a credible lineup under the Zombies' name.

Suggested Albums: Begin Here (1965): *Odyssey and Oracle* (1968)

See also: Argent

ZZ TOP

ZZ Top was one of rock music's Horatio Alger stories. They were the band that pulled themselves up the hard way, their straps fastened to cowboy boots complete with jangling spurs, through touring and building a fan base until they reached the summit of popularity. ZZ Top waved their Texas identity like a flag flying from the mast of a battleship. They were the Lone Star State's signal contribution to rock music during their platinum-selling years in the 1980s.

The hardworking blues-rock trio formed in Houston in 1969 from two previous groups active in Texas's prolific garage band scene. Drummer Frank Beard and bassist Dusty Hill had played together in American Blues and maintained ZZ Top's rollicking shuffle beat. Rock critics in the 1970s sometimes called the band primitive or crude, but guitarist Billy Gibbons belied the impression. He emerged from the psychedelic garage band the Moving Sidewalks, whose regional hit "99th Floor" earned them an opening spot on Jimi Hendrix's concert tour. Hendrix was impressed enough to name Gibbons one of America's best young guitarists.

Although faint echoes of the original blues-rock trio, Cream, can be discerned in *ZZ Top's First Album* (1971), boogie was already the band's hallmark. The word *boogie* has been applied elastically across several genres, including blues, swing, and rock, but probably first described the pounding, eight-to-the-bar rhythms of African American barrelhouse piano players from Texas and western Louisiana as the 20th century began. Texas blues had a different flavor than the Mississippi Delta blues that migrated and mutated in Chicago. White Texans such as Doug Sahm, Stevie Ray Vaughan, and Gibbons drew directly from this well of influence. Blues boogie became more downbeat in the hands of post–World War II guitarists; the persistent beat inspired more head-bobbing than dancing and emerged as an influence on scores of blues-based rock bands found everywhere in the United States by the early 1970s. ZZ Top was outstanding in the crowded field, tapping the rough emotions behind the deceptively simple musical format and infusing their songs with distinct personality. Their music had a punch lacked by their competitors; the lyrics were more vivid.

And then there was Gibbons, who overcame guitar-playing conventions by drawing big thick tones from very thin strings. His rhythm playing was never less than full and powerful, and his solos were sharp, not flashy, firmly rooted in the blues. His playing was restrained, his notes carefully selected for emotional impact rather than a desire to dazzle.

ZZ Top broke into FM rock radio with "La Grange" (1973), a salaciously amped-up reworking of John Lee Hooker's "Boogie Chillun," followed by the lusty "Tush" (1975), the hard rocking "Cheap Sunglasses" (1979), and a cover of Sam and Dave's soul classic "I Thank You" (1979). When punk rock and new wave threatened to retire boogie bands to the county fair circuit, ZZ Top responded by building a modern sonic superstructure over their rough-hewn sound, incorporating synthesizers and polished production without losing touch with their roots. The band rose from heartland auditoriums to the global arena in one of the most successfully calculated transformations in rock history, commercially as well as musically.

Keenly aware of the impending music video revolution, ZZ Top refashioned themselves visually as well as sonically, transmuting their bearded everyman look into an over-the-top personification of Texas complete with two-foot beards, ankle-brushing dusters, and sky-high cowboy hats. Videos for ZZ Top's "Legs," "Gimme All Your Lovin,'" and "Sharp Dressed Man" from their bestselling album, *Eliminator* (1983), were MTV staples in the music channel's early years and featured the visually unmistakable trio in congress with beautiful women of supermodel stature. With seven platinum albums and a string of sold-out concert tours, ZZ Top became one of the most successful rock acts of the 1980s.

In the 1990s they returned to their less polished roots, sold fewer records, but remained a draw on the concert circuit. The best way to own their early albums on CDs is *The Complete Studio Albums 1970–1990*, a 10-disc box set containing the original mixes of *ZZ Top's First Album*, *Rio Grande Mud* (1972), and *Tejas* for the first time in a digital format.

Suggested Albums: ZZ Top's First Album (1971); *Rio Grande Mud* (1972); *Tres Hombres* (1973); *Fandango!* (1975); *Deguello* (1979); *Eliminator* (1983)

Recommended Reading

During the time period covered by the *Encyclopedia of Classic Rock*, 1965–1975, scarcely a handful of serious books on rock music were published. Since then, that small shelf has grown into an entire library, albeit with many dubious titles. The bibliography that follows is not a comprehensive roster of literature on the subject, but includes all books that influenced our way of thinking about rock music or provided us with valid ideas and useful information.

Early Rock and Roll and the Roots of Post-1965 Rock

Several of these authors cleared up misconceptions about the birth of rock and roll music, especially Nick Tosches, Charlie Gillett, and Glen Jeansonne et al. Peter Guralnick and Robert Palmer brought to life the vernacular culture of an earlier America, while Greil Marcus identified rock and its antecedents as manifestations of American culture. Arnold Shaw was interesting as a music industry insider in the midst of the cultural and musical changes of the 1950s. Roy Carr et al. provided insights into the post–World War II birth of cool and hipness and the literary-jazz influences on many 1960s rock performers.

Carr, Roy, Case, Brian, and Dellar, Fred, *The Hip: Hipsters, Jazz and the Beat Generation* (London: Faber and Faber, 1986).

Gillett, Charlie, *The Sound of the City: The Rise of Rock and Roll* (Cambridge, Mass.: Da Capo Press, 1996, 3rd ed.).

Guralnick, Peter, *Feel Like Going Home: Portraits in Blues, Country and Rock'n'Roll* (Boston: Back Bay Books, 1971).

Guralnick, Peter, *Searching for Robert Johnson: The Life and Legend of the "King of the Delta Blues Singers"* (New York: Plume, 1989).

Jeansonne, Glen, Luhrssen, David, and Sokolovic, Dan, *Elvis Presley, Reluctant Rebel: His Life and Our Times* (Santa Barbara, Calif., 2011).

Marcus, Greil, *Mystery Train: Images of America in Rock'n'Roll Music* (New York: E. P. Dutton, 1975).

Palmer, Robert, *Deep Blues: A Musical and Cultural History of the Mississippi Delta* (London: Macmillan, 1981).

Shaw, Arnold, *Honkers and Shouters: The Golden Years of Rhythm and Blues* (New York: Macmillan, 1978).

Shaw, Arnold, *The Rockin' '50s* (New York: Hawthorne, 1974).

Tosches, Nick, *Country: The Twisted Roots of Rock'n'Roll* (Cambridge, Mass.: Da Capo Press, 1977).

412   RECOMMENDED READING

Tosches, Nick, *Unsung Heroes of Rock'n'Roll: The Birth of Rock in the Wild Years Before Elvis* (Cambridge, Mass.: Da Capo Press, 1984).

Rock History

New York Times critic Mike Jahn wrote the first important history on the subject. *Rolling Stone's* Jim Miller edited a collection of articles on important trends and artists from the roots of rock through the 1970s. Palmer and Rosenblum et al. provided engaging overviews of the music's development through the end of the 20th century. David Hajdu illuminated the rise of a particularly important artist, Bob Dylan, within the context of the historically important scene that nurtured him, the Greenwich Village folk-blues revival.

Hajdu, David, *Positively 4th Street: The Lives and Times of Joan Baez, Bob Dylan, Mimi Baez Farina and Richard Farina* (New York: Farrar, Straus and Giroux, 2001).

Jahn, Mike, *Rock: The Story of Rock from Elvis Presley to the Rolling Stones* (New York: Quadrangle/New York Times Book Co., 1973).

Miller, Jim, ed., *The Rolling Stone Illustrated History of Rock & Roll* (New York: Rolling Stone Press/Random House, 1976).

Palmer, Robert, *Rock & Roll: An Unruly History* (New York: Harmony Books, 1995).

Rosenblum, Martin Jack, and Luhrssen, David, *Searching for Rock and Roll* (Mason, Ohio: Cengage Learning, 2010, 4th ed.).

Artist Biographies

The vast majority of artist biographies are the ravings of fans or collections of salacious gossip. What follows are a selection of biographies that not only tried to get the facts straight but examined their subjects in the context of how their culture influenced them and how they in turn influenced their culture. Especially good are Heylin and MacDonald for their close readings of the songs of Bob Dylan and the Beatles.

Blake, Mark, *Pretend You're in a War: The Who & The Sixties* (London: Aurum Press, 2015).

Carr, Roy, and Murray, Charles Shaar, *Bowie: An Illustrated Record* (New York: Avon, 1981).

Chapman, Rob, *A Very Irregular Head: The Life of Syd Barrett* (Cambridge, Mass.: Da Capo Press, 2010).

Coleman, Ray, *Lennon* (New York: McGraw-Hill, 1984).

Fong-Torres, Ben, *Hickory Wind: The Life of Gram Parsons* (New York: Pocket Books, 1991).

Heylin, Clinton, *E Street Shuffle: The Glory Days of Bruce Springsteen & the E Street Band* (New York: Viking, 2013).

Heylin, Clinton, *Revolution in the Air: The Songs of Bob Dylan, 1957–1973* (Chicago: Chicago Review Press, 2009).

Heylin, Clinton, *Still on the Road: The Songs of Bob Dylan, 1974–2006* (Chicago: Chicago Review Press, 2010).

Hopkins, Jerry, and Sugarman, Danny, *No One Here Gets Out Alive* (Medford, N.J.: Plexus, 1980).

RECOMMENDED READING 413

Leibovitz, Liel, *A Broken Hallelujah: Rock and Roll, Redemption and the Life of Leonard Cohen* (New York: W. W. Norton, 2014).

Levy, Aidan, *Dirty Blvd.: The Life and Music of Lou Reed* (Chicago: Chicago Review Press, 2015).

MacDonald, Ian, *Revolution in the Head: The Beatles' Records and the Sixties* (Chicago: Chicago Review Press, 2007, 3rd ed.).

Marcus, Greil, *Invisible Republic: Bob Dylan's Basement Tapes* (New York: Henry Holt, 1997).

Marsh, Dave, *Before I Get Old: The Story of the Who* (New York: St. Martin's Press, 1983).

Marsh, Dave, *Born to Run: The Bruce Springsteen Story* (Garden City, N.Y.: Delilah Books/ Dolphin Books/Doubleday, 1979).

Nelson, Paul, and Bangs, Lester, *Rod Stewart* (New York: Delilah Books, 1981).

Norman, Philip, *Symphony for the Devil: The Rolling Stones Story* (New York: Linden Press/ Simon & Schuster, 1984).

Reynolds, Anthony, *Leonard Cohen: A Remarkable Life* (London: Omnibus Press, 2010).

Ribowski, Mark, *Sweet Dreams and Flying Machines: The Life and Music of James Taylor* (Chicago: Chicago Review Press, 2016).

Richards, Keith, *Life* (New York: Little, Brown, 2010).

Schumacher, Michael, *Crossroads: The Life and Music of Eric Clapton* (New York: Hyperion, 1985).

Stark, Steven D., *Meet the Beatles: A Cultural History of the Band That Shook Youth, Gender, and the World* (New York: HarperCollins, 2005).

Stump, Paul, *Unknown Pleasures: A Cultural Biography of Roxy Music* (New York: Thunder's Mouth Press, 1998).

Essay Collections

The first significant and serious essays on rock music were published in the rock press by publications such as *Crawdaddy*, *Creem*, and *Rolling Stone*. These are several examples of thoughtful and, especially in the case of Bangs, provocative music criticism collected in book form.

Bangs, Lester, *Psychotic Reactions and Carburetor Dung: The Work of a Legendary Critic*, Greil Marcus, ed. (New York: Anchor Press, 2003).

Gilmore, Mikal, *Night Beats: A Shadow History of Rock & Roll* (New York: Doubleday, 1998).

Palmer, Robert, *Blues & Chaos: The Music Writings of Robert Palmer*, Anthony De Curtis, ed. (New York: Scribner, 2009).

Santoro, Gene, *Dancing in Your Head: Jazz, Blues, Rock, and Beyond* (New York: Oxford University Press, 1994).

Index

Note: **Boldfaced** page numbers in the index refer to main entries in the encyclopedia.

Abba, 274
Ace, 285
Ackles, David, **1**, 9
Acuff, Roy, 6
Adams, John, 302
Adderley, Cannonball, 54
Aerosmith, **1–2**, 140, 303
Albion Country Band, 352
Allen, Daevid, 146–147, 338
Allison, Mose, 16, 37, 322
Allman, Duane, 3, 92, 258, 323, 341
Allman, Gregg, 3–4, 225
Allman Brothers Band, **2–4**, 216, 341
Altamont, 149, 306, 320
America, **4–5**
Amon Duul II, **5**, 200
Anderson, Ian, 36, 178–180, 352
Anderson, Jon, 384, 399–400
Anderson, Laurie, 295
Anderson, Lynn, 152
Ange, **5–6**
Animals, **6–7**, 9, 40, 163, 192, 276, 318, 388
Ant, Adam, 145
Aphrodite's Child, **7–8**, 384. *See also* Vangelis
Archies, 50, 240
Argent, Rod, 8, 9, 408
Argent, **8**, 408. *See also* Zombies
Arlen, Harold, 102
Armageddon, 399
Arnold, Eddie, 104
Ash Ra Tempel, **8–9**, 255, 323. *See also* Schulze, Klaus
Atkins, Chet, 157
Atomic Rooster, 116
Auger, Brian, **9–10**, 99, 220, 397, 398. *See also* Driscoll, Julie

Avalon, Frankie, 50
Average White Band, 9
Ayers, Kevin, **10**, 63, 118, 261, 338–339. *See also* Soft Machine

B-52s, 210, 273
Babe Ruth, **11**
Bach, J.S., 32, 116, 179, 187, 278, 282, 297, 329, 363
Bach, P.D.Q., 15
Bacharach, Burt, 212, 408
Bachman, Randy, 11, 151
Bachman-Turner Overdrive, **11**, 151. *See also* Guess Who
Back Street Crawler, 139
Bad Brains, 33
Bad Company, **11–12**, 139, 246
Bad Religion, 314
Badfinger, **12–14**, 158, 209, 255, 274. *See also* Beatles
Baez, Joan, **14–15**, 101, 105, 135, 136. *See also* Dylan, Bob
Baker, Ginger, **15–16**, 35, 41, 48, 68, 74, 80–81, 160, 161, 199. *See also* Bond, Graham; Bruce, Jack; Clapton, Eric; Cream
Baldry, Long John, 9, 183, 356
Balin, Marty, 176–178
Bambaata, Afrika, 201
Band, 15, **16–19**, 68, 76, 92, 99, 103, 104, 125, 148, 183, 184, 212, 226, 237, 244, 285, 344, 346, 350. *See also* Dylan, Bob
Bangles, 137
Bangs, Lester, 62, 286, 300, 376
Bar-Kays, 388
Barrett, Syd, 10, **19–20**, 268–271. *See also* Pink Floyd

416   INDEX

Bartok, Bela, 43, 193
Bauhaus, 255
Beach Boys, 5, **20–22**, 26, 58, 66, 75, 107, 213, 265, 281, 408
Beatles, 5, 7, 12, 13, 20, 21, **23–28**, 30, 31, 32, 33, 46, 47, 50, 53, 54, 59, 67, 71, 75, 79, 94, 102, 104, 110, 111, 114, 125, 130, 136, 137, 144, 147, 157, 158, 163, 166, 171, 181, 184, 190, 192, 193, 207, 209, 229, 230, 239, 240, 241, 247, 249, 256, 257, 258, 262, 263, 265, 274, 275, 276, 278, 279–281, 282, 284, 299, 303, 304, 305, 306, 311, 313, 324, 325, 332, 333, 335, 337, 349–350, 359, 364, 367, 374, 375, 398, 400, 406, 408. *See also* Harrison, George; Lennon, John; McCartney, Paul; Starr, Ringo
Beau Brummels, **28**, 55, 79, 136, 190, 215, 335
Bebop Deluxe, **28**
Beck, Jeff, 3, **28–30**, 42–43, 94, 121, 162, 167, 204, 337, 351, 356, 361, 397–399. *See also* Yardbirds
BeeGees, **30–31**, 43, 114
Bedford, David, 10
Beethoven, Ludwig van, 34
Belle & Sebastian, 208
Benitez, Jellybean, 11
Bennett, Tony, 43
Benson, George, 317
Berlioz, Hector, 283
Bernstein, Leonard, 1
Berry, Chuck, 67, 101, 114, 125, 148, 157, 175, 195, 207, 210, 225, 232, 282, 285, 299, 357, 372, 375, 406
Betts, Dickey, 3, 4
Bieber, Justin, 50
Big Brother and the Holding Company, **31–32**, 186–187. *See also* Joplin, Janis
Big Star, **32**, 274
Bishop, Elvin, 53, 342
Bjork, 255
Black, Cila, 281
Black Keys, 63
Black Merda, 33
Black Rock, **32–33**. *See also* Chambers Brothers; Hendrix, Jimi; Miles, Buddy; Otis, Shuggie; Rotary Connection

Black Sabbath, **33–35**, 52, 162, 231, 381
Blackmore, Ritchie, 34, **35**, 90, 289, 334. *See also* Deep Purple
Bley, Carla, 49, 99
Blind Faith, 15, 16, **35**, 69, 89, 123, 141, 374. *See also* Clapton, Eric; Traffic
Blondie, 195, 201
Blood, Sweat & Tears, **36**, 41, 112, 175, 192, 199, 216, 258. *See also* Kooper, Al
Bloodwyn Pig, **36**, 178, 322
Bloomfield, Mike, **37**, 53, 54, 102, 103, 112, 199, 394. *See also* Butterfield, Paul; Electric Flag
Blue Cheer, **37**, 161
Blue Oyster Cult, **38**, 338
Blues, **39–40**. *See also* Allman Brothers Band; Animals; Bloomfield, Mike; Butterfield, Paul; Canned Heat; Clapton, Eric; Cream; Derek and the Dominos; Gallagher, Rory; Joplin, Janis; Korner, Alexis; Mayall, John; Pretty Things; Rolling Stones; Ten Years After; Trower, Robin; Winter, Johnny; Yardbirds
Blues Magoos, **40**
Blues Project, 36, **40–41**, 199
Bluntstone, Colin, 8, 408
Blur, 198
Bobo, Willie, 320
BoDeans, 19
Bolan, Marc, 114, 142, 145, 373–374
Bond, Graham, 15, 16, **41–42**, 48, 74, 80, 199, 220, 223. *See also* Baker, Ginger; Bruce, Jack
Boney M, 82
Bono, 73, 118
Bono, Sonny, 245, 324
Booker T. and the MGs, 213, 318, 358, 402
Boomtown Rats, 244
Boone, Pat, 50, 105, 268
Boulez, Pierre, 406
Bowie, David, 28, **42–46**, 110, 117, 118, 138, 142, 145, 169, 183, 194, 195, 201, 207, 245, 250, 255, 271, 273, 291, 294, 295, 303, 307, 308, 311, 342, 352, 376, 383, 386, 400. *See also* Eno, Brian; Glitter Rock; Pop, Iggy; Reed, Lou; Ronson, Mick

INDEX   417

Box Tops, 71
Bradshaw, Tiny, 303
Bread, 62
Brecht, Bertolt, 1
Brenston, Jackie, 298
Brewer and Shipley, **46**
Brinsley Schwarz, 215, 285
British Invasion, **46–47**. *See also* Animals;
    Beatles; Hollies; Kinks; Mann,
    Manfred; Rolling Stones; Them; Who;
    Yardbirds; Zombies
Brooks, Garth, 365
Brothers Johnson, 263
Brown, Arthur, **47**, 78, 90, 116, 160
Brown, James, 16, 43, 140, 318
Brown, Roy, 298
Browne, Jackson, **48**, 50–51, 107, 190,
    255, 364, 365, 407
Brubeck, Dave, 16, 43, 179, 254, 408
Bruce, Jack, 16, 41, **48–49**, 68, 74,
    80–81, 111, 161, 199, 246, 378. *See
    also* Baker, Ginger; Bond, Graham;
    Clapton, Eric; Cream
Bubblegum, **49–50**
Buchanan, Roy, **50**
Buckinghams, 36
Buckley, Jeff, 51, 72
Buckley, Tim, 48, **50–51**
Budgie, **51–52**
Buffalo Springfield, **52–53**, 55, 85,190,
    271, 340, 358, 400. *See also* Crosby,
    Stills, Nash & Young; Stills, Stephen;
    Young, Neil
Burdon, Eric, 6, 7, 9, 276, 318, 388
Burnett, Johnny, 303, 399
Burnett, T Bone, 15
Burrell, Kenny, 243
Butterfield, Paul, 37, **53–54**, 103, 112.
    See also Bloomfield, Mike
Butts Band, 97
Byrds, 26, 32, **54–56**, 79, 94, 102, 109,
    125, 129, 136, 137, 157, 175, 177,
    213, 215, 233, 251, 266, 282, 286,
    292, 324, 331, 340, 359, 379. *See also*
    Dylan, Bob; Folk-Rock
Byrne, David, 118, 119, 262

Cage, John, 208, 385, 406, 407
Cale, J.J., **57**, 68, 190, 217, 317

Cale, John, 10, **57–59**, 69, 118, 124,
    255, 272, 295, 385–386. *See also*
    Eno, Brian; Nico; Reed, Lou; Velvet
    Underground
California, Randy, 343–344
Calloway, Cab, 190
Cambodian Rock, **59–60**
Camel, 367
Cameo, 388
Campbell, Glen, 20, 317
Camper van Beethoven, 190
Can, **60–61**, 118, 200
Canned Heat, **61**
Capaldi, Jim, 373–374
Captain Beefheart, **61–63**, 75, 76, 150,
    211, 405, 406. *See also* Zappa, Frank
Caravan, **63–64**
Carey, Mariah, 13, 256
Carmichael, Hoagy, 253
Carpenter, Mary Chapin, 15
Carroll, Jim, 323
Cars, 314
Cash, Johnny, 94, 104, 217, 326, 402
Cassidy, David, 307
Cat Power, 211
Cave, Nick, 58, 73, 402
Chambers Brothers, **64**
Chapin, Harry, 99
Charlatans, **64–65**, 319
Charles, Ray, 322, 333
Chase, 175
Cheap Trick, 248, 249, 314
Cher, 3–4
Chic, 44
Chicago, 36, **65–67**, 112, 128, 175
Chieftains, 244
Chiffons, 158
Chilton, Alex, 32
Chopin, Frederic, 297
Christgau, Robert, 300
Chrysalis, **67**
Clapton, Eric, 3, 16, 18, 27, 29, 30, 35,
    41, 48, 57, **67–70**, 80, 81, 90, 91, 92,
    102, 125, 141, 157, 158, 161, 163,
    167, 204, 206, 208, 214, 226, 228,
    229, 263, 296, 321, 329, 358, 387,
    393, 397–398, 400. *See also* Baker,
    Ginger; Bruce, Jack; Delaney and
    Bonnie, Derek and the Dominos

418 INDEX

Clark, Dave, 46
Clark, Gene, 54, 55, 136,
Clark, Petula, 46, 253,
Clash, 233, 246, 273
Clemens, Clarence, 48, 346, 347, 349, 350
Clinton, George, 33, 140, 407
Cluster, **70**, 118, 200. *See also* Eno, Brian
Cobain, Kurt, 27, 73
Cobham, Billy, 49, 220, 221
Cochran, Eddie, 37, 161, 247, 257
Cocker, Joe, 3, **70–71**, 317, 374
Cohen, Leonard, 51, 59, 71, **71–73**, 238, 319, 327
Cole, Nat King, 177
Coleman, Ornette, 175, 193, 295, 364
Collins, Judy, 14, **73–74**, 92, 156, 236
Collins, Phil, 44, 68, 142–144, 226, 324
Colosseum, **74**
Coltrane, Alice, 259, 321
Coltrane, John, 41, 55, 115, 175, 193, 219, 220, 231, 385
Como, Perry, 234
Concept Album, **74–75**. *See also* Beatles; Genesis; Who
Cooder, Ry, 62, **75–76**, 152, 212, 253, 319
Cooke, Sam, 163, 339, 346, 365
Cookies, 192
Coolidge, Rita, 71
Cooper, Alice, 22, 47, **76–78**, 145, 406. *See also* Glitter Rock
Cope, Julian, 371, 383
Copland, Aaron, 1, 57, 117, 253, 385
Corea, Chick, 175
Costello, Elvis, 1, 15, 198, 211, 259, 267, 281, 285, 296, 372
Country Joe & the Fish, **78–79**
Country Rock, **79–80**. *See also* Byrds; Eagles; Flying Burrito Brothers; Harris, Emmylou; New Riders of the Purple Sage; Parsons, Gram; Poco; Pure Prairie League
Covay, Don, 163
Cowboy Junkies, 402
Crazy Horse, 401–402
Cream, 3, 15, 39, 41, 48–49, 68, 74, **80–81**, 137, 141, 161, 174, 178, 214, 228, 236, 246, 249, 313, 322, 364, 366, 378, 403, 409. *See also* Baker, Ginger; Bruce, Jack; Clapton, Eric

Creation, **81–82**, 239. *See also* Mods
Creedence Clearwater Revival, 80, **82–85**, 125, 131–133, 148, 212, 303, 371. *See also* Fogerty, John
Crosby, Bing, 42, 279
Crosby, David, 53, 54, 55, 56, 85, 86, 177, 236, 266, 358
Crosby, Stills, Nash/Crosby, Stills, Nash & Young, 56, **85–87**, 166, 238, 358–359, 400, 402. *See also* Buffalo Springfield; Stills, Stephen; Young, Neil
Cross, Christopher, 340
Crow, Sheryl, 69, 267
Crowell, Rodney, 327–328
Crudup, Arthur, 39
Crusaders, 71, 237
Crystals, 98
Cult, 255
Culture Club, 145
Cummings, Burton, 151
Cure, 99
Curved Air, **87**
Cyrus, Miley, 50

Dale, Dick, 20, 107, 361
Daltrey, Roger, 307, 389–393
Damned, 214
Damone, Vic, 151
Daniels, Charlie, 341
Danko, Rick, 18, 19
Davies, Dave, 160, 195–198, 227
Davies, Ray, 25, 47, 195–198, 379
Davis, Miles, 54, 68, 115, 163, 175, 214, 220, 307, 320
Davis, Rev. Gary, 14, 62
Davis, Spencer, 65, **89–90**, 247, 373
Dead Can Dance, 324
Death Cab for Cutie, 241
Debussy, Claude, 219
Dee, Kiki, 184
Deep Purple, 33, 35, 42, **90**, 174, 179, 381. *See also* Blackmore, Ritchie
Def Leppard, 162, 376
Delaney and Bonnie, 3, 68, **90–91**, 92, 226–227, 317. *See also* Clapton, Eric
Dengue Fever, 60
Denny, Sandy, **91–92**, 122, 206, 360. *See also* Fairport Convention; Strawbs

Depeche Mode, 201
Derek and the Dominos, 3, 68, 71, 81, **92–93**. *See also* Clapton, Eric
Derringer, Rick, 394
Desert Rose Band, 56
DeShannon, Jackie, 324
Deviants, 268
Devo, 63, 78, 118, 402
Dexy's Midnight Runners, 244
Diamond, Neil, 19, 105, 240
Dictators, 233
Diddley, Bo, 17, 43, 68, 275, 398
Di Meola, Al, 220, 397
Dio, Ronnie James, 34, 35
Dire Straits, 57, 223, 408
Dissidenten, 115
Dixon, Willie, 69, 96, 126, 150, 207, 394
Dolby, Thomas, 237
Dolphy, Eric, 115, 243, 364
Domino, Fats, 125, 346
Dominoes, 298
Donegan, Lonnie, 334
Donovan, **93–94**, 99, 161, 162, 204, 319
Doobie Brothers, **94–95**, 353
Doors, **95–98**, 165, 190, 224, 255, 258, 272, 273, 286, 368. *See also* Manzarek, Ray
Doo-wop, **98**
Dr. Feelgood, 285
Dr. John, 37, 244, 350
Drake, Nick, **98–99**, 278
Dream Syndicate, 56
Dream Theater, 283
Drifters, 16, 192
Driscoll, Julie, 9, **99**. *See also* Auger, Brian
Drive By Truckers, 218
Ducks Deluxe, 215, 285
Duke, George, 406
Duran Duran, 312
Dury, Ian, 285
Dylan, Bob, 9, 14, 15, 17, 18, 20, 25, 36, 53, 54, 64, 68, 71, 72, 73, 80, **99–106**, 112, 121, 122, 130, 134, 136, 147, 155, 157, 158, 159, 163, 164, 169, 181, 197, 199, 207, 221, 223, 245, 248, 258, 265, 277, 281, 282, 292, 299, 305, 307, 310, 311, 317, 324, 331, 333, 335, 338, 345, 346,
365, 371, 379, 400, 405, 407. *See also* Baez, Joan; Band; Byrds; Folk-Blues Revival; Folk-Rock

Eagles, 48, 79, 80, **107–110**, 174, 251, 253, 271, 309, 326, 327, 340, 358, 387. *See also* Country-Rock
Earle, Steve, 15, 334
East of Eden, 175, 397
Easton, Sheena, 327
Eastern Bloc Rock, **110–111**
Echo and the Bunnymen, 271
Edmunds, Dave, 114, 125, 214–215, 223, 257, 285, 327, 350
Eire Apparent, **111–112**
Electric Flag, 32, 37, 46, 54, **112–113**, 128, 164, 175, 234. *See also* Jazz-Rock
Electric Light Orchestra, **113–115**, 247–248, 297, 394. *See also* Move; Progressive Rock; Wood, Roy
Electric Prunes, 258, 284
Elgar, Edgar, 113
Ellimen, Yvonne, 31
Ellington, Duke, 6, 353
Embryo, **115**
Emerson, Keith, 115–117, 254, 397
Emerson, Lake & Palmer, 82, **115–117**, 190, 194, 203, 254, 282. *See also* Progressive Rock
Eno, Brian, 10, 44, 58, 59, 70, **117–119**, 159, 173, 194, 250, 311–312, 324, 330, 385. *See also* Bowie, David; Cale, John; Cluster; Roxy Music
Entwistle, John, **119**, 350, 389–393. *See also* Who
Epstein, Brian, 23, 27, 209
Eurythmics, 312
Everly, Phil, 395
Everly Brothers, 407
Excellents, 295

Fabulous Thunderbirds, 215, 321
Faces, 29, 107, **121**, 306, 337, 356–357. *See also* Stewart, Rod
Fairport Convention, 92, 98, 99, **122–123**, 137, 177, 351, 360, 371. *See also* Denny, Sandy; Folk-Rock; Steeleye Span; Thompson, Richard
Faithfull, Marianne, 224

420 INDEX

Fame, Georgie, 220, 276
Family, 35, **123**, 194
Farina, Mimi, 14
Faust, 118, **123–124**
Feliciano, Jose, 57, 237
Fender, Freddie, 333
Ferguson, Jay, 343–344
Ferguson, Maynard, 36
Ferry, Bryan, 118, 311–312
Fier, Anton, 49
Fischer, Wild Man, **124**, 211. *See also*
    Zappa, Frank
Fishbone, 33
Flack, Roberta, 211
Flamin' Groovies, 56, 65, **124–125**, 325
Flamin' Lips, 211
Fleetwood Mac, **125–128**, 228, 320, 322
Flo & Eddy, 379–380, 406
Flock, **128**, 175. *See also* Jazz-Rock
Flying Burrito Brothers, 55, 80, 107,
    128–130, 156, 251, 266–267, 340,
    359. *See also* Country Rock
FM Radio, **130–131**
Focus, **131**, 145
Fogelberg, Dan, 340
Fogerty, John, 82–83, 84, **131–133**, 166,
    351. *See also* Creedence Clearwater
    Revival
Foghat, 322
Folk-Blues Revival, **133–136**. *See also*
    Baez, Joan; Collins, Judy; Dylan, Bob;
    Sainte-Marie, Buffy
Folk-Rock, **136–137**. *See also* Beau
    Brummels; Byrds, Denny, Sandy;
    Dylan, Bob; Fairport Convention;
    Guthrie, Arlo; Lovin' Spoonful; Mamas
    & the Papas; Simon & Garfunkel;
    Steeleye Span; Thompson, Richard
Foo Fighters, 98
Fool, 41, **137**, 145
Foreigner, 12, 193
Foster, Stephen, 253
Fotheringay, 92, 122
Four Freshmen, 20
Frampton, Peter, **137–138**, 168, 350. *See*
    also Humble Pie
Franklin, Aretha, 3, 192, 339
Free, 12, **138–139**, 168, 236

Freed, Allan, 32–33, 299, 302
Frey, Glenn, 48, 107, 108, 109, 110, 253,
    309, 326, 387
Fripp, Robert, 118, 193–195, 383
Frisell, Bill, 16
Frith, Fred, 173
Funk, **139–140**. *See also* Sly & the
    Family Stone
Funkadelic, 33, 140, 335
Furay, Richie, 52, 53, 340, 358
Fuse, 249

Gabriel, Peter, 142–144, 194, 237, 283,
    355
Gallagher, Rory, **141–142**, 363–364. *See*
    also Taste
Gamble, Kenny, 43
Garcia, Jerry, 136, 147–150, 251
Garfunkel, Art, 329, 330–333
Gaye, Marvin, 84, 114, 335
Geldorf, Bob, 271
Genesis, 75, **142–144**, 194, 203, 282,
    283, 302. *See also* Concept Album;
    Progressive Rock
Gentle Giant, **144–145**, 203, 250. *See*
    also Progressive Rock
George, Lowell, 211–212, 406
Gerry and the Pacemakers, 46, 281
Gershwin, George, 32, 102, 265, 297,
    408
Gil, Gilberto, 262
Gilbert and Sullivan, 10, 34, 247, 309,
    313
Gill, Vince, 287
Glass, Philip, 70, 124, 224, 248, 261,
    302, 385
Glitter, Gary, 145
Glitter Rock, **145**. *See also* Bowie, David;
    Cooper, Alice; John, Elton; New York
    Dolls; Queen; Reed, Lou; Roxy Music;
    T. Rex
Goffin, Gerry, 191–192, 240, 364
Golden Earring, **145–146**
Gong, 10, **146–147**, 173, 338
Goodman, Steve, 152, 277
Gore, Leslie, 311
Graham, Bill, 168, 320
Graham, Larry, 335–336

INDEX   **421**

Grand Funk Railroad, 314

Grass Roots, 213

Grateful Dead, 86, 106, **147–150**, 175, 178, 223, 251, 257, 284, 285, 292, 301, 306. *See also* Psychedelia; Rock Festivals

Great Society, 176, 335

Green, Peter, 125–126, 228, 229

Green Day, 75, 302

Groundhogs, **150**

Guess Who, 11, **150–151**. *See also* Bachman-Turner Overdrive

Guns N' Roses, 78, 107

Guru Guru, **151–152**

Guthrie, Arlo, 130, 134, **152–153**

Guthrie, Woody, 6, 74, 101, 134, 152, 345

Guy, Buddy, 126, 235

Hackett, Steve, 142, 143

Haden, Charlie, 16

Haggard, Merle, 80, 217, 266

Haley, Bill, 298

Hall, Daryl, 194

Hall & Oates, 43

Ham, Peter, 12–13

Hammill, Peter, 203, 383–384

Hammond, John, 101, 346

Hammond Jr., John, 37

Hardin, Tim, 403

Harmonia, 250,

Harmonicats, 280

Harper, Roy, **155–156**, 355

Harpers Bizarre, 253

Harpo, Slim, 147

Harris, Emmylou, 14, 18, 152, **156–157**, 267, 309. *See also* Country Rock; Parsons, Gram

Harrison, George, 5, 13, 15, 23, 25, 26, 27, 54, 69, 81, 91, 93, 94, 105, 114, **157–159**, 209, 230, 275, 280, 317, 329, 350, 364. *See also* Beatles; Lennon, John; McCartney, Paul; Starr, Ringo

Havens, Richie, 302

Hawkins, Dale, 83

Hawkins, Ronnie, 17, 18, 47

Hawkins, Screamin' Jay, 47, 77, 83, 276

Hawkwind, 16, 118, **159–160**, 268, 342. *See also* Space Rock

Hayes, Isaac, 91

Heavy Metal, **160–161**. *See also* Black Sabbath; Blackmore, Ritchie; Blue Cheer; Deep Purple; Led Zeppelin; Rush; Troggs

Hell, Richard, 252, 295

Helm Levon, 17, 19, 54, 103, 226, 350

Hendrix, Jimi, 7, 29, 33, 37, 39, 50, 81, 97, 112, 152, 161, **162–165**, 187, 196, 214, 220, 221, 226, 234, 240, 249, 263, 278, 284, 300, 313, 322, 358, 361, 364, 369, 377, 400, 409. *See also* Black Rock

Henley, Don, 107, 108, 109, 253, 309

Henry, Pierre, 345

Henry Cow, 173

Herman's Hermits, 192

Herrmann, Bernard, 281

Hicks, Dan, 65

High Llamas, 22

Hill, Lauryn, 321

Hillage, Steve, 146

Hillman, Chris, 52, 54, 55, 56, 109, 129, 156, 266, 340, 359

Hines, Earl "Fatha," 76

Hitchcock, Robyn, 19, 271, 284

Holiday, Billie, 101

Hollies, 85, 137, **165–166**, 256, 365. *See also* British Invasion; Crosby, Stills, Nash & Young

Holly, Buddy, 23, 79, 165–166, 218, 233, 236, 309, 363

Holst, Gustav, 42

Honeydrippers, 207

Hooker, John Lee, 68, 150, 231, 278, 367, 398,

Hot Tuna, **167**, 177. *See also* Jefferson Airplane

House, Son, 135, 207

Howe, Steve, 373, 399–400

H.P. Lovecraft, **167**. *See also* Psychedelia

Huff, Leon, 43

Human League, 44, 201

Humble Pie, 49, 121, 137, 138, **168**, 218, 337. *See also* Frampton, Peter

422 INDEX

Hunter, Ian, **169**, 245–246, 307. *See also* Mott the Hoople
Hynde, Chrissie, 290

Ian & Sylvia, 74
Ides of March, **171**
Idol, Billy, 237
Incredible String Band, **171–172**
Indigo Girls, 15
Insane Clown Posse, 78
Iron Maiden, 52, 162
Isley Brothers, 163, 339, 368
It's a Beautiful Day, **172**
Ives, Burl, 134

Jackson, Michael, 230, 321
Jade Warrior, **173**
Jagger, Mick, 1, 199, 251, 275, 303–307, 312, 328, 334
Jam, 82, 197–198, 239
James, Rick, 400
James, Skip, 135
James, Tommy, 50
James Gang, 109, **173–174**, 387. *See* Walsh, Joe
Jan and Dean, 20
Jane's Addiction, 301
Jansch, Burt, 355
Japan, 195
Jarrett, Keith, 354
Jay and the Americans, 352
Jazz Crusaders. *See* Crusaders
Jazz-Rock, **174–175**. *See also* Blood, Sweat & Tears; Chicago; Driscoll, Julie; Electric Flag, Flock; Mahavishnu Orchestra; Soft Machine; Steely Dan
Jefferson Airplane/Jefferson Starship, 86, 122, 167, **175–178**, 223, 238, 257, 258, 286, 292. *See also* Hot Tuna; Psychedelia
Jefferson, Blind Lemon, 176
Jennings, Waylon, 57, 267
Jesus and Mary Chain, 214
Jet, 254
Jethro Tull, 36, 131, 171, 173, **178–180**, 352
Jett, Joan, 290
Jo Jo Gunne, 344
Joel, Billy, 98, **180–183**

Johansen, David, 251–252
John, Elton, 1, 9, 43, 145, 180, 181, 182, **183–186**, 210, 317, 350, 357. *See also* Glitter Rock
Johnson, Lonnie, 228
Johnson, Robert, 39, 67, 68, 69, 76, 77, 81, 82, 93, 102, 105, 162, 207, 236, 306, 346
Jones, Brian, 213, 254, 282, 303–307
Jones, John Paul, 29, 94, 161, 199, 204–207, 399
Jones, Norah, 238, 402
Jones, Rickie Lee, 244, 259
Jones, Spike, 265
Jones, Tom, 151, 204
Joplin, Janis, 31–32, 97, 165, **186–188**. *See also* Big Brother and the Holding Company
Journey, 321
Joy Division, 44

Kaleidoscope, **189**
Kansas, 57, **190–191**, 313. *See also* Progressive Rock
Kaye, Lenny, 249, 257–258, 286, 300, 338, 371
Kenton, Stan, 65, 115
Kershaw, Doug, 84
Khatchaturian, Aram, 214, 297
King, Albert, 377
King, B.B., 69, 162
King, Ben E., 210
King, Carole, **191–192**, 240, 258, 313, 364
King, Curtis, 209
King Crimson, 5, 12, 41, 116, 118, 173, 175, **192–195**, 219, 283, 383. *See also* Progressive Rock
Kings X, 283
Kingsmen, 196, 376
Kingston Trio, 14, 21, 135, 136
Kinks, 8, 46, 75, 97, 128, 160, **195–198**, 204, 213, 227, 245, 276, 303
Kirk, Roland, 178, 383
Kiss, 8
Knickerbockers, 258
Knight, Curtis, 163
Knopfler, Mark, 57, 69

INDEX 423

Kooper, Al, 36, 37, 40, 41, 102, 103, **198–199**, 216, 263, 394. *See also* Blood, Sweat & Tears; Electric Flag
Korner, Alexis, 41, 48, **199–200**, 228, 303. *See also* Rolling Stones
Kraftwerk, 5, 44, **200–202**, 250
Kramer, Billy J., 281
Krauss, Alison, 207
Kristofferson, Kris, 187, 277
Kronos Quartet, 384
Kuti, Fela, 16

Labelle, 259
Lady Gaga, 44
LaFlamme, David, 172
Lake, Greg, 116, 193–194
Landau, Jon, 232, 300, 346
Larson, Nicolette, 401
Le Orme, **203**
Lead Belly, 6, 134, 135, 228, 334
League of Gentlemen, 193, 195
Led Zeppelin, 33, 52, 70, 82, 92, 94, 155, 156, 161–162, 168, 179, **204–207**, 216, 267, 276, 290, 296, 297, 315, 343, 344, 367, 381, 393, 398, 399. *See also* Yardbirds
Lee, Arthur, 213–214
Lee, Peggy, 253
Left Banke, **207–208**, 282, 359
Lennon, John, 13, 23, 25, 26, 27, 32, 43, 46, 101, 114, 137, 157, 163, 184, 192, 197, **208–211**, 229, 230, 256, 280, 334, 350. *See also* Beatles; Harrison, George; McCartney, Paul; Starr, Ringo
Lennon, Sean, 210
Les Variations, **211**
Levant, Oscar, 252
Lewis, Fury, 135
Lewis, Gary, 199, 317
Lewis, Jerry Lee, 48, 79, 180, 183
Lewis, Smiley, 215
Liberace, 145
Ligeti, Gyorgy, 363
Lightfoot, Gordon, 74
Lindley, David, 190
Little Eva, 192
Little Feat, **211–212**, 406
Little Richard, 25, 50, 84, 125, 164, 180, 183, 299, 318

Locomotiv GT, 111
Lofgren, Nils, 199, 350
Loggins and Messina, 53, 271
Lomax, Alan, 6, 134
Lomax, John, 134
Love, Courtney, 319
Love, 55, **212–214**. *See also* Folk-Rock; Psychedelia
Love Sculpture, **214–215**
Lovich, Lene, 160, 210
Lovin' Spoonful, 40, **215–216**. *See also* Folk-Rock
Lowe, Nick, 198, 281, 285
Lydon, John, 16, 60, 63, 160, 273, 383
Lynne, Jeff, 105, 113, 114, 115, 159, 247–248
Lynyrd Skynyrd, 57, 199, **216–218**, 225, 341, 342. *See also* Southern Rock

Madness, 198
Madonna, 273, 302
Magma, **219**. *See also* Progressive Rock
Mahavishnu Orchestra, 128, 175, **219–221**, 321. *See also* Jazz-Rock
Mahler, Gustav, 285
Mahogany Rush, **221**
Malmstein, Yngwie, 35, 214
Mamas & the Papas, 215, **221–222**. *See also* Folk-Rock
Man, **222–223**, 292, 319
Manassas, 359
Mancini, Henry, 311
Mann, Manfred, 48,199, **223–224**. *See also* British Invasion; Springsteen, Bruce
Manzanera, Phil, 49, 58, 311–312
Manzarek, Ray, 95–98, **224**
Marcus, Greil, 299
Marilion, 384
Mark-Almond, **224–225**
Marley, Bob, 68, 296
Marsh, Dave, 285–286
Marshall Tucker Band, **225**, 341, 342. *See also* Southern Rock
Martha and the Vandellas, 309
Martin, George, 5, 10, 23–24, 25, 26, 29, 58, 230, 275, 280–281, 282, 406
Martyn, John, **225–226**

424   INDEX

Mason, Dave, 91, 173, **226–227**, 373–374
Master Musicians of Jajouka, 307
Masters Apprentices, **227**. *See also* Mods
Matchbox Twenty, 321
Matching Mole, 64
Matthews, Dave, 321
Mayall, John, 48, 68, 80, 125, **227–229**, 398. *See also* Bruce, Jack; Clapton, Eric; Fleetwood Mac
McCartney, Linda, 229–230
McCartney, Paul, 12, 23, 25, 26, 27, 32, 101, 114, 121, 157, 172, 181, 192, 197, 208–210, **229–231**, 235, 241, 334, 350, 364, 394. *See also* Beatles; Harrison, George; Lennon, John; Starr, Ringo
McClinton, Delbert, 334
MC5, 161, **231–233**, 272, 317, 326, 338, 346. *See also* Punk Rock
McGhee, Brownie, 136
McGuinn, Roger, 54, 55, 56, 85, 105, 136, 282
McGuire, Barry, 55
McLaughlin, John, 41, 48, 49, 175, 219–221, 234, 321
McLean, Don, **233–234**
McTell, Blind Willie, 62
Meat Loaf, 314
Mellencamp, John, 15, 244, 318, 402
Meltzer, Richard, 38, 286, 299
Mercury, Freddie, 290–291, 342
Metallica, 38, 52, 180, 295
Metheny, Pat, 237
Midler, Bette, 187
Miles, Buddy, 112, 164, **234–235**. *See also* Hendrix, Jimi
Miller, Steve, **235–236**, 322–323. *See also* Scaggs, Boz
Mindbenders, 365
Mingus, Charles, 115, 193, 237, 243
Minnie, Memphis, 186, 206
Minutemen, 63
Mitchell, Joni, 14, 48, 73, 74, 85, 86, 105, **236–238**
Moby Grape, 176, **238–239**
Modern Jazz Quartet, 243
Mods, **239**. *See also* Creation; Masters Apprentices; Small Faces; Who

Molly Hatchet, 342
Monkees, 50, 192, **239–241**, 308
Montgomery, Wes, 65, 151
Moody Blues, 41, 193, 229, **241–242**, 247, 283. *See also* Progressive Rock
Moon, Keith, 29, 121, 337, 389–393
Moorcock, Michael, 38, 159, 160, 342
Moraz, Patrick, 400
Moroder, Giorgio, 343
Morrison, Jim, 95–98, 165, 187, 224, 272, 368
Morrison, Van, 112, **242–244**, 346, 357, 367–368, 369, 370. *See also* Them
Morrissey, 252
Morse, Steve, 220
Mothers of Invention, 405–406
Motorhead, 38, 160
Mott the Hoople, 12, 169, **244–246**, 273, 307, 345, 375, 386, 403. *See also* Hunter, Ian
Mountain, 49, 128, **246–247**. *See also* Cream
Move, 113, 114, 137, 239, **247–248**, 342, 394. *See also* Electric Light Orchestra; Wood, Roy
Moving Sidewalks, 409
Mozart, Wolfgang Amadeus, 254
Murphy, Elliott, **248**
Music Machine, 78
Musselwhite, Charlie, 37
Mussorgsky, Modest, 116

Nash, Graham, 53, 85, 86, 137, 166, 358, 365
Nash, Johnny, 296
Nazareth, 373
Nazz, **249**, 312–313. *See also* Rundgren, Todd
Nektar, **250**. *See also* Progressive Rock
Nelson, Bill, 28
Nelson, Rick, 80, 107
Nelson, Willie, 3, 152, 237, 267, 321, 402
Neu!, 44, **250**
Neville, Aaron, 310
New Christy Minstrels, 54
New Lost City Ramblers, 14
New Order, 201

New Riders of the Purple Sage, 80, 177, **251**. *See also* Country Rock; Grateful Dead
New Seekers, 394
New York Dolls, 145, **251–252**, 286. *See also* Glitter Rock; Punk Rock
Newman, Randy, 28, 74, **252–254**, 256, 276
Newton-John, Olivia, 104
Nice, 116, **254**. *See also* Emerson, Lake & Palmer
Nickelback, 322
Nico, 10, 48, 58, 96, 118, **254–255**, 385–386. *See also* Cale, John; Velvet Underground
Nilsson, Harry, 13, **255–257**, 350
Nine Inch Nails, 44
Nirvana, 27, 205, 281, 402
Nite City, 224
Nitzsche, Jack, 53, 319, 324
NRBQ, **257**
Nugent, Ted, 317
Nuggets, **257–258**. *See also* Punk Rock
Numan, Gary, 44, 201
Nyro, Laura, 3, **258–259**, 313

Oasis, 198, 250, 376, 402
Oberst, Connor, 73
Ochs, Phil, 73
Ohio Express, 50
O'Jays, 253
Olatunji, Babatunde, 320
Oldfield, Mike, 10, **261**
Oldham, Andrew Loog, 281, 303
One Direction, 27
Ono, Yoko, 26–27, 208–211, 229
Orbison, Roy, 79, 105, 114, 159, 234, 309, 346
Orchestral Manoeuvres in the Dark, 201
Orff, Carl, 219, 224
Osbourne, Ozzy, 34, 35, 162
Os Mutantes, **261–262**
Otis, Johnny, 262–263
Otis, Shuggie, **262–263**
Outsiders, 174
Owens, Buck, 80, 84, 190

Page, Jimmy, 3, 29, 30, 70, 82, 90, 94, 161, 162, 196, 204–207, 254, 297,

315, 334, 344, 355, 367, 368, 387, 397–399
Palmer, Carl, 116
Parker, Charlie, 68, 193, 220, 353, 398
Parker, Graham, 244, 285
Parks, Van Dyke, 21, 22, 28, **265**. *See also* Beach Boys
Parsons, Alan, 46, 269
Parsons, Gram, 55, 79–80, 128–130, 145, 156–157, 251, **266–267**, 341. *See also* Byrds; Country Rock; Flying Burrito Brothers; Harris, Emmylou
Parton, Dolly, 31, 309
Partridge Family, 50
Patton, Charlie, 105
Paul, Les, 29, 139, 235, 265, 279–280
Pearl Jam, 98, 402
Peel, David, 210
Pentangle, **267**
Pere Ubu, 63
Perkins, Carl, 257
Perry, Joe, 1, 2
Peter and Gordon, 46
Peter, Paul and Mary, 14, 101, 103, 136
Petty, Tom, 6, 56, 69, 105, 114, 137, 159, 181, 244, 267, 277, 317, 325
Phillips, Sam, 277, 280, 303, 341
Phish, 149
Pickett, Wilson, 3, 83, 112, 163
Pine, Courtney, 49
Pink Fairies, **268**, 373, 375
Pink Floyd, 10, 19, 75, 115, 131,155–156, **268–271**, 279, 282, 284, 285, 338, 342. *See also* Barrett, Syd; Progressive Rock; Space Rock
Pitney, Gene, 252
Pixies, 73, 402
Plant, Robert, 34, 156, 162, 204–207, 315, 344, 399, 403
Plastic People of the Universe, 111
Plasticland, 82, 284
Platters, 350
Poco, 53, 80, 109, 251, **271–272**. *See also* Country Rock
Pogues, 372
Poindexter, Buster, 252
Pointer Sisters, 347
Police, 87, 239, 296

426 INDEX

Ponty, Jean-Luc, 406
Pop, Iggy, 44, 97, **272–274**, 376. *See also* Punk Rock
Popol Vuh, **274**
Porcupine Tree, 211, 219, 283
Posies, 32
Power Pop, **274**. *See also* Beatles; Big Star; Who
Presley, Elvis, 23, 32, 39, 50, 58, 67, 77, 79, 217, 237, 266, 272, 277, 278–280, 299, 303, 319, 341, 345, 363, 366, 402, 406
Preston, Billy, 71, 158, 350
Pretenders, 56, 198
Pretty Things, 8, 75, 150, 159, 227, 268, **275–276**, 301, 303, 373. *See also* Rock Opera; Rolling Stones
Price, Alan, 6, 7, 9, 224, 253, **276–277**. *See also* Animals
Price, Ray, 182
Primal Scream, 250
Prince, 33, 205, 263, 284, 318
Prine, John, 152, **277**
Procol Harum, 7, 58, 70, 137, **278**, 282, 377. *See also* Progressive Rock; Trower, Robin
Producers, **278–281**. *See also* Bowie, David; Cale, John; Eno, Brian; Parks, Van Dyke; Rundgren, Todd
Progressive Rock, **281–283**. *See also* Beatles; Electric Light Orchestra; Emerson, Lake & Palmer; Gentle Giant; Kansas; King Crimson; Le Orme; Magma; Moody Blues; Nektar; Pink Floyd; Procol Harum; Quatermass; Renaissance; Van der Graaf Generator; Yes
Psychedelia, **283–284**. *See also* Barrett, Syd; Charlatans; Doors; Grateful Dead; H.P. Lovecraft; Jefferson Airplane; Love; Pink Floyd; Quicksilver Messenger Service; Seeds; 13th Floor Elevators; Zombies
Pub Rock, **284–285**
Public Image Ltd., 16, 60
Puente, Tito, 320
Pulsar, **285**
Punk Rock, **285–286**. *See also* MC5; New York Dolls; *Nuggets*; Pop, Iggy;

Reed, Lou; Seeds; Smith, Patti; Velvet Underground
Pure Prairie League, 80, **286–287**, 307. *See also* Country Rock

Quatermass, **289**. *See also* Progressive Rock
Quatro, Suzi, **289–290**
Queen, **290–291**, 343
Queens of the Stone Age, 274
Question Mark and the Mysterians, 285–286
Quicksilver Messenger Service, 223, **292**, 319, 403. *See also* Psychedelia
Quiet Riot, 335
Quiet Son, 311

Radiohead, 402
Rage Against the Machine, 35, 233, 349
Rain Parade, 284
Raitt, Bonnie, 14, 257
Ramones, 22, 47, 64, 274, 286, 376
Rascals, **293–294**
Raspberries, 32
Ravel, Maurice, 116, 363
Redding, Otis, 70, 142
Reed, Jimmy, 322
Reed, Lou, 49, 58, 59, 145, 273, **294–296**, 307, 385–386. *See also* Cale, John; Glitter Rock; Nico; Punk Rock; Velvet Underground
Reggae, **296**
Reich, Steve, 70, 274
Reinhardt, Django, 371
R.E.M., 32, 56, 73, 137, 371, 376, 377, 386
Renaissance, **297**, 395, 399. *See also* Yardbirds
Renbourn, John, 92, 267
REO Speedwagon, **297–298**
Replacements, 32, 376
Reznor, Trent, 44
Richard, Cliff, 244
Richards, Keith, 1, 39, 102, 129, 199, 252, 266, 275, 303–307
Richman, Jonathan, 59
Rifkin, Joshua, 73
Righteous Brothers, 280, 339
Riley, Terry, 58, 87, 194, 274, 363

INDEX 427

Riperton, Minnie, 310
Robertson, Robbie, 17–19, 103
Robeson, Paul, 14, 134
Robinson, Tom, 314
Roches, 194
Rock and Roll, **298–299**
Rock Criticism, **299–300**
Rock Festivals, **300–301**
Rock Opera, **301–302**. *See also* Concept
  Album; Kinks; Pretty Things; Who
Rockabilly, **302–303**. *See also* Creedence
  Clearwater Revival
Rodgers, Nile, 44
Rodgers and Hammerstein, 191
Rodgers and Hart, 81, 255, 307–308
Rogers, Kenny, 31, 327
Rolling Stones, 1, 23, 33, 37, 39, 43, 46,
  47, 49, 59, 70, 75, 79, 110, 121, 125,
  129, 145, 161, 199, 204, 207, 212,
  213, 218, 223, 225, 226, 227, 228,
  254, 258, 266, 267, 275, 276, 281,
  282, 300, **303–307**, 310, 322, 324,
  325, 333, 338, 341, 342, 356, 357,
  364, 367. *See also* British Invasion;
  Korner, Alexis; Pretty Things
Romantics, 166
Ronettes, 98, 280
Ronson, Mick, 42–43, 105, 169, 294,
  307–308. *See also* Bowie, David;
  Hunter, Ian; Reed, Lou
Ronstadt, Linda, 107, 190, **308–310**,
  340
Ross, Diana, 31
Rotary Connection, **310**. *See also* Black
  Rock
Rotten, Johnny. *See* Lydon, John
Roth, David Lee, 22
Roxy Music, 49, 58, 82, 117, 118, 145,
  254, **310–312**, 353, 402. *See also* Eno,
  Brian; Glitter Rock
Royal Teens, 198
Rubin, Rick, 35, 94
Run-DMC, 2, 140
Rundgren, Todd, 13, 76, 249, 252, 259,
  312–314, 342. *See also* Nazz
Rush, Tom, 48, 364
Rush, **314–317**, 384
Russell, Leon, 20, 71, 91, 158, **317**
Ryder, Mitch, **317–318**

Sadistic Mika Band, **319**
Sahm, Doug, 245, 333–334, 371, 409.
  See also Sir Douglas Quintet
Sainte-Marie, Buffy, 64, **319–320**
Santana, 126, **320–322**, 397
Satie, Eric, 57
Satriani, Joe, 35
Savoy Brown, **322**
Scaggs, Boz, 3, 235, **322–323**. *See also*
  Miller, Steve
Schoenberg, Arnold, 265
Schulze, Klaus, 8–9, **323–324**, 363, 397.
  See also Ash Ra Tempel; Tangerine
  Dream
Scott, Little Jimmy, 295
Scruggs, Earl, 14, 135
Seal, 322
Searchers, 136, **324–325**
Seatrain, 41
Sebastian, John, 215–216, 358
Sedaka, Neil, 184
Seeds, 258, **325–326**. *See also*
  Psychedelia; Punk Rock
Seeger, Pete, 55, 64, 134–135, 136
Seger, Bob, 107, **326–328**
Sex Pistols, 16, 44, 60, 252, 273, 383
Shadows, 261, 400
Shadows of Knight, 258, 368
Shags, 284
Shakira, 322
Shangri-Las, 252
Shankar, Ravi, 158
Shaw, Greg, 227, 274, 286
Sheridan, Tony, 23
Shirelles, 192
Shocking Blue, 145
Silver, Horace, 353
Silverchair, 265
Simon, Carly, **328**, 350, 365. *See also*
  Taylor, James
Simon, Paul, **328–330**, 355. *See also*
  Simon & Garfunkel
Simon & Garfunkel, 91, 101, 104, 281,
  330–333. *See also* Simon, Paul
Simone, Nina, 6, 253
Sinatra, Frank, 23, 58, 75,182, 236
Siouxsie and the Banshees, 255
Sir Douglas Quintet, **333–334**. *See also*
  Sahm, Doug

428 INDEX

Skiffle, **334**. *See also* Beatles
Slade, 133, 274, 289, **334–335**
Sledge, Percy, 3
Slick, Grace, 176–178
Sly & the Family Stone, **335–336**. *See also* Funk
Small Faces, 121, 137, 168, **336–338**, 393. *See also* Faces; Mods
Smith, Harry, 135, 257
Smith, Patti, 38, 59, 224, 257, 286, 314, **338**. 347, 386. *See also* Punk Rock
Smiths, 252, 376
Soft Cell, 201
Soft Machine, 10, 19, 49, 63, 146, 175, 289, **338–339**, 397. *See also* Ayers, Kevin; Jazz-Rock
Solas, 403
Sondheim, Stephen, 74
Sonic Youth, 402
Sonics, 272
Sonny and Cher, 20
Soul Music, **339–340**. *See also* Rascals; War
South, Joe, 90
Souther-Hillman-Furay Band, 271, **340**
Southern Rock, **340–342**. *See also* Allman Brothers Band; Lynyrd Skynyrd; Marshall Tucker Band
Southside Johnny and the Asbury Jukes, 347
Space Rock, **342**. *See also* Hawkwind; Pink Floyd
Spann, Otis, 126
Sparks, **342–343**
Spears, Britney, 372
Spector, Phil, 20, 27, 53, 72, 158, 182, 184, 185, 198, 209, 210, 280, 319, 346, 350, 394
Spence, Joseph, 75
Spirit, 207, **343–344**
Spock's Beard, 219, 283
Spooky Tooth, **344–345**
Springfield, Dusty, 253
Springsteen, Bruce, 6, 48, 49, 56, 75, 105, 169, 223, 224, 244, 248, 318, 325, 338, **345–349**, 370, 380, 407
Stalling, Carl, 406
Standells, 286
Stardust, Alvin, 145

Starr, Edwin, 33
Starr, Ringo, 13, 23, 49, 114, 119, 138, 158, 209, 215, 230, 256, **349–350**, 358. *See also* Beatles; Harrison, George; Lennon, John; McCartney, Paul
Status Quo, **351**
Stealers Wheel, 343
Steeleye Span, 122, **351–352**. *See also* Fairport Convention; Folk-Rock
Steely Dan, 94, 323, **352–354**. *See also* Jazz-Rock
Steppenwolf, 38, 161, **354**
Stevens, Cat, 204, **355**, 357
Stewart, Al, **355**
Stewart, Rod, 9, 29, 34, 99, 121, 302, 337, **356–358**, 403. *See also* Faces
Stills, Stephen, 37, 52, 53, 74, 85, 86, 171, 177, 199, 240, **358–359**. *See also* Buffalo Springfield; Crosby, Stills, Nash & Young; Young, Neil
Stockhausen, Karlheinz, 60, 200, 363, 407
Stone, Sly, 28, 33, 263, 335–336, 388
Stooges, 59, 272–274, 286, 317, 326
Stories, 208, **359–360**
Stravinsky, Igor, 60, 406
Strawbs, **360**
Stray Cats, 215
Streetwalker, 123
Streisand, Barbra, 258
String Cheese Incident, 149
String Driven Thing, **360–361**
Sullivan, Ed, 24, 47, 181
Summer, Donna, 343
Sun Ra, 231, 257, 384
Supertramp, 194
Surf Music, **361**
Survivor, 171
Sweet, Matthew, 402
Sweet, 289

Taj Mahal, 75
Talking Heads, 117, 118, 195, 286, 386
Tangerine Dream, 118, 323, **363**
Taste, 141, **363–364**. *See also* Gallagher, Rory
Taupin, Bernie, 1, 183–186, 357
Taylor, James, 99, 192, 328, **364–365**, 402. *See also* Beatles; Simon, Carly

INDEX **429**

Taylor, Mick, 49, 228, 229, 306
Teenage Fan Club, 214
Television, 286, 386
Television Personalities, 214
Tempest, 74
Temptations, 306
10cc, 166, 296, **365–366**, 398
Ten Years After, **366–367**
Terry, Sonny, 136
Texas Tornados, 334
Them, 43, 147, 204, 242, 325, 338,
    367–368, 370. *See also* Morrison, Van
Thin Lizzy, 74, 244, 327, **368–370**
13th Floor Elevators, 60, 258, **370–371**.
    See also Psychedelia
38 Special, 342
Thompson, Linda, 372
Thompson, Richard, 56, 92, 99, 122,
    355, **371–373**. *See also* Fairport
    Convention; Folk-Rock
Thornton, Big Mama, 32, 263
Three Dog Night, 253, 258
Throbbing Gristle, 124
Thunders, Johnny, 252
Tin Machine, 44
Tippett, Keith, 99
Tom & Jerry, 331
Tomorrow, **373**, 399. *See also* Yes
Toto, 12
Toussaint, Allen, 82
Townshend, Pete, 25, 46, 81, 119, 123,
    192, 197, 247, 275, 301–302, 315,
    337, 387, 389–393, 399
Traffic, 35, 60, 63, 71, 89, 226, 227, 351,
    373–374, 397
Traveling Wilburys, 105, 114, 159
T. Rex, 114, 145, **374–376**. *See also*
    Glitter Rock
TriBeCaStan, 190
Troggs, 161, 272, **376–377**. *See also*
    Heavy Metal
Trower, Robin, 49, 278, 312, **377–378**.
    See also Procol Harum
Tubes, 63
Tucker, Maureen, 385–386
Turner, Tina, 238, 280, 393
Turkish Psychedelia, **378**
Turtles, 199, 375, **378–379**, 406, 407
Twisted Sister, 78, 162

Tyler, Steve, 1–2
Tyner, McCoy, 43

UFO, 322
Ultravox, 201
Uriah Heep, **381**
Utopia, 313–314
U2, 105, 117, 119, 142, 244

Vagrants, 246
Vai, Steve, 35, 7
Valens, Ritchie, 207, 218, 321
Valli, Frankie, 31, 98
Van der Graaf Generator, 361,
    383–384
Van Halen, 52, 109, 198
Van Zandt, Steve, 293, 346
Vandross, Luther, 43
Vangelis, 7–8, **384**. *See also* Aphrodite's
    Child
Vanilla Fudge, 29
Vanilla Ice, 44
Varese, Edgar, 405
Vaughan, Jimmie, 334
Vaughan, Stevie Ray, 346, 409
Vedder, Eddie, 98
Veloso, Caetano, 262
Velvet Underground, 48, 57, 58, 60, 70,
    87, 111, 124, 175, 245, 254–255,
    272, 281, 286, 294–296, 318, 338,
    385–386. *See also* Cale, John; Nico;
    Punk Rock; Reed, Lou
Ventures, 20
Vincent, Gene, 210
Violent Femmes, 376

Wagner, Richard, 34, 43, 81, 116, 161,
    162, 205
Wainwright, Rufus, 72, 151
Waits, Tom, 15, 63
Wakeman, Rick, 360, 399–400
Waldron, Mel, 115
Walker, T-Bone, 322
Walsh, Joe, 109, 114, 174, 350, **387**. *See
    also* James Gang
Walter, Little, 228
War, 7, **388–389**
Warnes, Jennifer, 71
Warwick, Dionne, 31

430 INDEX

Waters, Muddy, 18, 39, 41, 54, 69,103, 161, 162, 164, 225, 235, 280, 325, 363, 394
Waters, Roger, 19, 268–271
Watson, Johnny, 235
Weather Report, 143
Weavers, 14, 135
Webber, Andrew Lloyd, 302
Weezer, 241
Weill, Kurt, 1, 43, 83, 95, 219, 253
Welch, Bob, 126
Wet Willie, 341
White, Josh, 6
White Stripes, 63
White Zombie, 78
Who, 8, 25, 37, 46, 75, 81, 107, 119, 121, 145, 146, 192, 204, 223, 239, 247, 249, 274, 276, 301–302, 325, 336, 337, 342, 364, 376, **389–393**, 399. *See also* Concept Album; Entwistle, John; Mods; Rock Opera
Widespread Panic, 149
Williams, Dar, 15
Williams, Don, 277
Williams, Hank, 133, 217
Williams, Maurice, 48
Williams, Paul, 299
Williams, Ralph Vaughn, 142, 282
Williams, Tony, 16, 49
Williams, Vaughn, 280
Williamson, Sonny Boy, 228, 398
Willis, Ellen, 299
Wills, Bob, 302
Wilson, Brian, 20–21, 58, 108, 114, 197, 247, 281, 313, 406
Wilson, Jackie, 163
Wilson, Tom, 199, 281, 331, 338
Wings, 229–230, 241
Winter, Edgar, 394
Winter, Johnny, **394**
Winwood, Stevie, 16, 35, 69, 89, 173, 351, 373–374, 397

Wizzard, 394–395
Wolf, Howlin', 53, 68, 84, 162, 280, 398–399, 405
Womack, Bobby, 187
Wonder, Stevie, 29, 206, 230, 335
Wood, Ron, 29, 121, 306, 334, 337, 356–357
Wood, Roy, 113, 114, 247–248, 297, **394–395**. *See also* Electric Light Orchestra; Move
Woodstock, 54. 164. 300, 320
Wray, Link, 160
Wright, Gary, 344–345
Wyatt, Robert, 10, 63, 64, 338–339

X, 98, 224
XTC, 22, 166, 198, 241, 271, 314

Yamashta, Stomu, 321, 323, **397**
Yardbirds, 9, 29, 62, 68, 166, 204, 227, 228, 297, 303, 351, 365, 367, 368, **397–399**. *See also* Beck, Jeff; Clapton, Eric; Led Zeppelin
Yes, 111, 115, 208, 282–283, 360, 367, 373, **399–400**
Young, Jesse Colin, 403
Young, La Monte, 26, 57, 295
Young, Neil, 18, 52, 53, 75, 85, 86, 217, 302, 319, **400–403**. *See also* Buffalo Springfield; Crosby, Stills, Nash & Young; Stills, Stephen
Youngbloods, 246, **403**

Zappa, Frank, 49, 61, 62, 63, 76, 98, 111, 124, 152, 175, 195, 211, 379, **405–407**. *See also* Captain Beefheart
Zevon, Warren, 48, 309, 379, **407–408**
Zombies, 8, 9, 321, **408–409**
ZZ Top, 334, 371, **409–410**

About the Authors

David Luhrssen is arts and entertainment editor of the *Shepherd Express* newspaper in Milwaukee, WI. He holds degrees in history from the University of Wisconsin–Milwaukee. He is coauthor of ABC-CLIO's *Elvis Presley, Reluctant Rebel: His Life and Our Times* and a contributor to *Ideas and Movements That Shaped America: From the Bill of Rights to "Occupy Wall Street"* and *100 People Who Changed 20th-Century America.*

Michael Larson is a guitar instructor, songwriter, recording artist, and attorney. He has written about music for the *Shepherd Express* newspaper in Milwaukee, WI. Larson holds a law degree from Case Western Reserve University.

Printed in the USA
CPSIA information can be obtained
at www.ICGtesting.com
LVHW080537120524
779928LV00007B/660